The United Nations Human Rights Treaty System: Law and Procedure

To Malachy

The United Nations Human Rights Treaty System: Law and Procedure

by
Suzanne Egan
B.C.L. (NUI), B.L., LL.M. (Osgoode Hall, York University)

Bloomsbury Professional

Published by
Bloomsbury Professional
Maxwelton House
41–43 Boltro Road
Haywards Heath
West Sussex
RH16 1BJ

Bloomsbury Professional
The Fitzwilliam Business Centre
26 Upper Pembroke Street
Dublin 2

ISBN: 9781847661098

© Bloomsbury Professional Limited 2011
Bloomsbury Professional, an imprint of Bloomsbury Publishing Plc

All rights reserved. No part of this publication may be reproduced in any material form (including photocopying or storing it in any medium by electronic means and whether or not transiently or incidentally to some other use of this publication) without the written permission of the copyright owner except in accordance with the provisions of the Copyright, Designs and Patents Act 1988 or under the terms of a licence issued by the Copyright Licensing Agency Ltd., Saffron House, 6–10 Kirby Street, London, EC1N 8TS, England. Applications for the copyright owner's written permission to reproduce any part of this publication should be addressed to the publisher.

Warning: The doing of an unauthorised act in relation to a copyright work may result in both a civil claim for damages and criminal prosecution.

British Library Cataloguing-in-Publication Data
A catalogue record for this book is available from the British Library

Typeset by Marlex Editorial Services Ltd, Dublin, Ireland
Printed and bound in Great Britain by
CPI Antony Rowe, Chippenham, Wiltshire

Acknowledgments

Part of the research for this book was conducted at the UN library in Geneva. I am very grateful to Cristina Giordano of the library staff there who assisted me greatly during my visit and in the months afterwards in locating many of the more obscure UN documents cited in this work. I also wish to acknowledge with thanks the assistance of Mark Tynan, Liaison Librarian for the School of Law, UCD, for his help in locating other research materials. My thanks also to Gerard Quinn and Maria Walls at the Centre for Disability Law and Policy at NUI Galway for helping me to track down documents relating to the drafting of the UN Disability Convention.

During my visit to the UN, a number of key actors in the treaty system were very generous in making space in their busy schedules to meet with me to clarify a number of issues and in some cases, to give their views on the operation of particular aspects of the system. My sincere thanks in this respect are due to Jane Connors, Paulo David, Kate Fox, Gabriella Habtom, João Nataf and Ibrahim Salana. While no one is quoted in this work, their comments helped to shape my own thinking on particular aspects of the system.

I wish to acknowledge, with gratitude, the research funding awarded to me by the School of Law at UCD for the book which enabled me to engage the services of one of my former students, Emma Keane BL. Emma provided excellent research assistance throughout the project for which I am very grateful. My thanks also to my colleagues in the School for their advice and friendship during the writing process, especially Blanaid Clarke, Caroline Fine, John Jackson, Imelda Maher, John O'Dowd and Colin Scott.

I am extremely grateful to a number of people for giving up their valuable time to read through individual parts of the book and for contributing incredibly helpful insights and suggestions. My sincere thanks in this respect to Philip Alston (New York University), Brice Dickson (Queen's University), Michael Farrell (Irish Human Rights Commission and FLAC), Kate Fox (Secretary of the Human Rights Committee), Ursula Kilkelly and Siobhan Mullally (University College Cork), Rachel Murray (University of Bristol), James Kingston (Legal Adviser, Department of Foreign Affairs, Ireland) and my colleagues at the School of Law, UCD, John O'Dowd and Fiona de Londras. Of course, all errors and omissions are my own.

My sincere thanks to Sandra Mulvey, Publishing Manager at Bloomsbury Professional, who first approached me to write this book for her absolute professionalism in preparing the book for publication. Many thanks also to Tessa Robinson for her careful editing of the final text and to Marian Sullivan who typeset the book. To the best of my ability, the law is stated until the 1 May 2011, with a few exceptions, including an update in relation to the drafting of the optional protocol for a complaint procedure for the Convention on the Rights of the Child which was approved by the Human Rights Council on 17 June 2011.

My final and greatest debt of gratitude is owed to my husband, Niallo, for his constant support and encouragement and to our children Seamus and Breffni, for their patience and abiding sense of fun which sustained me throughout.

Suzanne Egan

July 2011

Contents

Acknowledgments v
Contents vii
Table of Abbreviations xiii
Table of Cases xv
Table of Legislation xxv

Part I:
The Foundations of the UN Human Rights Treaty System

Chapter 1 Introduction

Treaties as a Source of International Law 4
Other Sources of International Law 5
    Customary International Law 6
    General principles of law 8
    Other sources 8
The Domestic Effect of International Treaties 10
The Principle of State Sovereignty 13
Development of International Human Rights Law 14

Chapter 2 The United Nations and Human Rights: Institutions and Structure

Introduction 21
The General Assembly 21
The Economic and Social Council (ECOSOC) 24
The Commission on Human Rights 27
The Sub-Commission on the Promotion and Protection
    of Human Rights 36
The Human Rights Council 41
    Membership 43
    Functions 45
Office of the United Nations High Commissioner
    for Human Rights 47

Chapter 3 United Nations Human Rights Treaties

Introduction 51
The International Bill of Rights 54
    The Universal Declaration of Human Rights 54
    The International Covenant on Civil and Political Rights 67

Nature and scope of the obligations 69
The International Covenant on Economic Social and Cultural Rights 74
Additional Human Rights Treaties 85
International Convention on the Elimination of All Forms of Racial
Discrimination (1965) 85
Convention on the Elimination of All Forms of Discrimination
against Women (1979) 90
United Nations Convention Against Torture and Other Cruel,
Inhuman or Degrading Treatment or Punishment (1984) 95
United Nations Convention on the Rights of the Child (1989) 101
International Convention on the Protection of the Rights of All
Migrant Workers and Members of Their Families (1990) 108
United Nations Convention on the Rights of Persons with
Disabilities (2006) and its Optional Protocol 113
International Convention for the Protection of All Persons
from Enforced Disappearance (2006) 122

Part II:
Reporting and Investigative Procedures

Chapter 4   Periodic Reporting Procedures

Introduction 131
Reporting Procedures Under United Nations Human Rights Treaties 134
International Covenant on Civil and Political Rights 134
International Covenant on Economic, Social and Cultural Rights 141
International Convention on the Elimination of all Forms of Racial
Discrimination 145
United Nations Convention on the Prevention of Torture and Other Cruel,
Inhuman or Degrading Treatment or Punishment 151
United Nations Convention on the Rights of the Child 155
United Nations Convention on the Elimination of All Forms
of Discrimination Against Women 159
International Convention on the Protection of Migrant Workers
and Members of Their Families 164
Convention on the Rights of Persons with Disabilities 166
International Convention on the Protection of All Persons from Enforced
Disappearance 169
Analysis of the Current Procedures 170

Chapter 5   Inquiry Procedures

Introduction 179
United Nations Convention against Torture and Other Forms
of Cruel, Inhuman and Degrading Treatment or Punishment 1984 179

Optional Protocol to the Convention on the Elimination of
Discrimination Against Women 193
Optional Protocol to the Convention on the Rights of Persons
with Disabilities... 205
International Convention for the Protection of All Persons from Enforced
Disappearance 209
Optional Protocol to the International Covenant on Economic,
Social and Cultural Rights... 212
Optional Protocol to the United Nations Convention on the
Rights of the Child 215

Chapter 6   Preventive Mechanisms

Introduction 221
Optional Protocol to the Convention Against Torture, and
    Other Forms of Cruel, Inhuman and Degrading Treatment
    or Punishment 2002 221
        The Protocol: Machinery, Scope and Obligations.. 226
        The SPT.. 228
        Visits... 232
        National Preventive Mechanisms (NPMs)... 238
        Prospects... 244
United Nations Convention on the Rights of Persons
    with Disabilities (2006) 247

Part III:
Individual Complaint Procedures

**Chapter 7   Optional Protocol to the International Covenant on Civil and
                Political Rights**

Introduction 253
Optional Protocol to the International Covenant on Civil
    and Political Rights 254
Procedure 257
Admissibility Criteria... 264
        Anonymous, abusive or incompatible communications.................................. 265
        Incompatible communications 266
        Unsubstantiated claims... 274
        Competing international procedures 275
        Exhaustion of domestic remedies... 277
Substantive Views 279
        Burden of proof 279
        Right to life... 281
        Freedom from torture or ill-treatment 282

Right to liberty and security 284
Fair trial 287
Privacy, family, home and correspondence 290
Freedom of thought, conscience and religion 292
Freedom of expression 296
Equality and non-discrimination 298
Right to an effective remedy 303
Minority rights 304
Appraisal 306

Chapter 8 Article 14 of the International Convention on the Elimination of All Forms of Racial Discrimination

Introduction 309
Procedure 313
Admissibility 316
    Incompatible communications 317
    Exhaustion of domestic remedies 320
Opinions 321
Appraisal 329

Chapter 9 Article 22 of the United Nations Convention against Torture and Other Cruel, Inhuman or Degrading Treatment or Punishment

Introduction 331
Procedure 333
    Interim measures 334
    Consideration of Admissibility and the Merits 336
Admissibility 339
    Incompatible communications 340
    Abusive and manifestly unfounded communications 347
    Competing International Procedures 348
    Exhaustion of Domestic Remedies 350
Views 353
    Interpretation of the Concepts of 'Torture' and 'Cruel, Inhuman
    and Degrading Treatment or Punishment' 361
    Duty of Investigation 366
    Appraisal 368

Chapter 10 Optional Protocol to the Convention on the Elimination of All Forms of Discrimination Against Women

Introduction 371
Procedure 376
Admissibility 379
Views 385
Appraisal 388

Chapter 11 Optional Protocol to the Convention on the Rights of Persons with Disabilities

Introduction 391
Admissibility 393
Procedure 394

Chapter 12 International Convention on the Protection of the Rights of All Migrant Workers and their Families

Complaint procedure 399

Chapter 13 Optional Protocol to the International Covenant on Economic, Social and Cultural Rights

Introduction 403
The Framework of the OP-ICESCR 406
    The Scope of Potential Complaints (art 2) 408
    Assessment on the Merits (art 8(4)) 412
    Admissibility Criteria (arts 2,3 and 4) 416
    International Cooperation and Assistance (art 14) 422
    Appraisal 423

Chapter 14 International Convention for the Protection of all Persons from Enforced Disappearances

Introduction 427
The Urgent Procedure 427
Individual complaint procedure 430

Chapter 15 Draft Optional Protocol to the Convention on the Rights of the Child

Introduction 433
The Framework of the Draft Protocol 436
    General provisions 436
    Complainants 438
    Scope of the complaints mechanism 441
    Admissibility 442
    Interim measures 443
Procedure 444
    Transmission of the communication 444
    Friendly settlement 445
    Consideration of the communication 446
    Follow-up 448
International Cooperation and Assistance 449
    Appraisal 449

Part IV:
Proposals for Reform

Chapter 16   Reform of the UN Human Rights Treaty System

Introduction 453
Reports of the Independent Expert 1989–1997 453
The United Nations: An Agenda for Change 456
    A unified standing treaty body 459
    Strengthening the treaty body system 465
The Way Forward 475

Index 479

Table of Abbreviations

Treaties

UDHR	Universal Declaration of Human Rights
ICCPR	International Covenant on Civil and Political Rights
ICESCR	International Covenant on Economic, Social and Cultural Rights
ICERD	International Convention on the Elimination of All Forms of Racial Discrimination
CEDAW	Convention on the Elimination of All Forms of Discrimination Against Women
CRC	Convention on the Rights of the Child
UNCAT	United Nations Convention against Torture and Other Cruel, Inhuman and Degrading Treatment or Punishment
ICRMW	International Convention on the Protection of the Rights of Migrant Workers and Their Families
CRPD	Convention on the Rights of Persons with Disabilities
ICPED	Convention for the Protection of All Persons from Enforced Disappearance
OP-ICCPR	First Optional Protocol to the ICCPR
OP-CEDAW	Optional Protocol to the CEDAW
OP-CRPD	Optional Protocol to the CRPD
OP-ICESCR	Optional Protocol to the ICESCR

Treaty Bodies

CCPR	Human Rights Committee
CESCR	Committee on Economic, Social and Cultural Rights
CERD	Committee on the Elimination of Racial Discrimination
CEDAW Committee	Committee on the Elimination of Discrimination Against Women
CAT	Committee Against Torture

SPT	Subcommittee on Prevention of Torture
CRC Committee	Committee on the Rights of the Child
CMW	Committee on the Protection of the Rights of All Migrant Workers and Members of Their Families
CRPD Committee	Committee on the Rights of Persons with Disabilities
CED	Committee on Enforced Disappearances

Other Treaties

ECHR	European Convention on Human Rights
ACHR	American Convention on Human Rights
CRSR	Convention Relating to the Status of Refugees
ECPT	European Convention for the Prevention of Torture and Inhuman or Degrading Treatment or Punishment

Other Bodies

UN	United Nations
GA	General Assembly
ECOSOC	Economic and Social Council
CHR	Commission on Human Rights
HRC	Human Rights Council
OHCHR	Office of the High Commissioner for Human Rights
NGOs	Non-Governmental Organisations
NHRIs'	National Human Rights Institutions
NPM	National Preventive Mechanism
CPT	European Committee for the Prevention of Torture and Inhuman or Degrading Treatment or Punishment

Table of Cases

A

A v Australia, Communication No 560/1993 .... 7.45, 7.46
A v New Zealand, Communication No 754/1997 .... 7.46
A v UK (1999) 27 EHRR 611 .... 7.23
AA v Azerbaijan, Communication No 247/2004 .... 9.21, 9.27
Äärelä Näkkäläjärvi v Finland, Communication No 779/97 .... 7.74
Abdelli v Tunisia, Communication No 188/2001 .... 9.25, 9.32
ACC v Sweden, Communication No 227/2003 .... 9.38
Adan v Denmark, Communication No 43/2008 .... 8.30, 8.33
Adel Tebourski v France, Communication No 300/2006 .... 9.06
Aduayom Diasso and Dobou v Togo, Communication Nos 422/1990,
    423/1990 and 424/1990 .... 7.63
Afuson v Cameroon, Communication No 1353/2005 .... 7.64
AG v Sweden, Communication No 140/1999 .... 9.27
Agiza v Sweden, Communication No 233/2003 .... 9.36, 9.39, 9.41
AH v Sweden, Communication No 250/2004 .... 9.33
Ahmad and Abdol-Hamid v Denmark, Communication No 1487/2006 .... 7.41
Ahmad Dar v Norway, Communication No 249/2004 .... 9.32
Ahmad Najaati Sadic v Denmark, Communication No 25/2002 .... 8.22
Ahmad v Denmark, Communication No 16/1999 .... 8.30
Ahmed Farah Jama v Denmark, Communication No 41/2008 .... 8.31
Ahmed v Austria (1997) 24 EHRR 278 .... 9.40, 9.45
Akdivar v Turkey (1997) 23 EHRR 143 .... 7.38
Akkoc v Turkey (2002) EHRR 1173 .... 7.44
Aliboeva v Tajikistan, Communication No 985/2001 .... 7.51
Althammer v Austria, Communication No 998/2001 .... 7.67
Alzery v Sweden, Communication No 1416/2005 .... 7.29, 7.44
AM v Finland, Communication No 398/1990 .... 3.32
AM v France, Communication No 302/2006 .... 9.25, 9.38
Anna Koptova v Slovak Republic, Communication No 013/1998 .... 8.22
APA v Spain, Communication No 433/1990 .... 7.40
AR v Sweden, Communication No 170/2001 .... 9.30
AR v The Netherlands, Communication No 203/2002 .... 9.36
ARA v Switzerland, Communication No 305/2006 .... 9.27
ARJ v Australia, Communication No 692/1996 .... 7.44
AS v Hungary, Communication No 4/2004 .... 10.19, 10.28
AS v Jamaica, Communication No 231/1987 .... 7.41
Ashurov v Tajikistan, Communication No 1348/2005 .... 7.48
Asylum Case (Colombia v Peru) (1950) ICJ Rep 1.07

Asylum Case (1950) ICJ Rep 266 ....1.11
AT v Hungary, Communication No 2/2003 .... 10.18, 10.25, 10.26
Attia v Sweden, Communication No 1999/2002 ....9.39
Aumeeruddy-Cziffra v Mauritius, Communication No 35/1978 ....7.27
Avedes Hamayak Korban v Sweden, Communication No 88/1997 ....9.39
AWRAP v Denmark, Communication No 37/2006 ....8.17

B

Babkin v Russian Federation, Communication No 1310/2004 ....7.53
Baboeram et al v Suriname, Communication No 146/1983 and 148 ....7.35, 7.43
Ballantyne et al v Canada, Communications Nos 359/1989 and 385/1989 ....7.73
Ballantyne v Canada, Communication Nos 359/1989 and 385/1989 ....7.63
Barakat and Family v Tunisia, Communication No 14/1994 ....9.04
Barbaro v Australia, Communication No 7/1995 ....8.22
Bayatyan v Armenia, Application 23459/03, 27 October 2009 ....7.60
Bazarov v Uzbekistan, Communication No 985/2001 ....7.44
Benaziza v Algeria, Communication No 1588/2007 ....7.44
Bertelli Gálvez v Spain, Communication No 1389/2005 ....7.37
Besim Osmani v Republic of Serbia, Communication No 261/2005
 ....9.10, 9.32, 9.43, 9.44, 9.45, 9.47
Bibaud v Canada, Communication No 1747/2008 ....7.40
BJ v Denmark, Communication No 17/1999 ....8.29, 8.31
B-J v Germany, Communication No 1/2003 ....10.25
Bleir v Uruguay, Communication No 30/1978 ....7.42
BM'B v Tunisia, Communication No 14/1994 ....9.16
BMS v Australia, Communication No 8/1996 ....8.26
Bodroži v Serbia and Montenegro, Communication No 1180/2003 ....7.63, 7.64
Boimurodov v Tajikistan, Communication No 1042/2001 ....7.46
Bolaos v Ecuador, Communication No 238/87 ....7.46
Borisenko v Hungary, Communication No 852/1999 ....7.49
Broeks v The Netherlands, Communication No 172/1984 ....7.66, 7.67
Brychta v Czech Republic, Communication No 1618/2007 ....7.19
BSS v Canada, Communication No 183/2001 .... 9.26, 9.39, 9.44

C

C v Australia, Communication No 900/99 ....7.40
Calcerrada Fornieles and Cabeza Mato v Spain (Application 17512/90) 7.37
Carlos Acua Inostroza et al v Chile 7.22
Carranza Alegre v Peru, Communication No 1126/2002 ....7.49
Cecilia Rosana Núñez Chipana v Venezuela, Communication
 No 110/1998 ....9.36
Chedi Ben Ahmed Karoui v Sweden, Communication No 185/2001 ....9.36, 9.38
Chisanga v Zambia, Communication No 1132/2002 ....7.43
Chongwe v Zambia, Communication No 821/198 ....7.43, 7.45
Chorlango v Sweden, Communication No 218/2002 ....9.26

Coeriel and Aurik v The Netherlands, Communication No 453/91 .... 7.37, 7.54
Coleman v Australia, Communication No 1157/2003 .... 7.64
Conteris v Uruguay Communication No 139/1983 .... 7.42
Costello-Roberts v United Kingdom (1994) 19 EHRR 112 .... 7.23
CP and his son MP v Denmark, Communication No 5/1994 .... 8.15, 8.22
Croes v The Netherlands, Communication No 164/84 .... 7.25
CT and KM v Sweden, Communication No 279/2005 .... 9.42

D

D v United Kingdom (1997) 24 EHRR 423 .... 9.44
Danilo Dimitrijevic v Serbia and Montenegro, Communication
  No 172/2000 .... 9.30, 9.32, 9.42, 9.47
Dayras et al v France, Communication No 13/2007 .... 10.21
Delgado-Páez v Colombia, Communication No 195/1985 .... 7.45
DF v Australia, Communication No 39/2006 .... 8.18, 8.26
Díaz v France, Communication No 194/2001 .... 9.32
DIII Mouvement de protestation civique v France 7.24
Dimitrijevic v Serbia and Montenegro, Communication
  No 207/2002 .... 9.09, 9.32, 9.42, 9.47
Documentation and Advisory Centre on Racial Discrimination
  v Denmark, Communication No 28/2003 .... 8.19, 8.20
DR v Australia, Communication No 42/2008 .... 8.26
DS v Sweden, Communication No 9/1997 .... 8.22
Dumont v Canada, Communication No 1467/2006 .... 7.52
Dung Thi Thuy Nguyen v The Netherlands, Communication No 3/2004 .... 10.27
Durmic v Serbia and Montenegro, Communication No 29/2003 .... 8.16, 8.29, 8.30
Dzemajl v Yugoslavia, Communication No 161/000 .... 3.74, 9.45

E

EA v Switzerland, Communication No 28/1995 .... 9.17
EJVM v Sweden, Communication No 213/2002 .... 9.07
El Alwani v Libyan Arab Jamahiriya, Communication No 1295/2004 .... 7.43
El Hassy v Libyan Arab Jamahiriya, Communication No 1422/2005 .... 7.45
Elif Pelit v Azerbaijan, Communication No 281/2005 .... 9.06, 9.39
Encarnación Blanco Abad v Spain, Communication No 59/1996 .... 9.46, 9.47
Enkelaar v France, Communication No 2/1989 .... 8.26, 8.29
Errol Simms v Jamaica, Communication No 541/1993 .... 7.34
Eshonov v Uzbekistan, Communication No 1225/2003 .... 7.43
Estrella v Uruguay, Communication No 74/1980 .... 7.28
Evans v United Kingdom (2008) 46 EHRR 34 .... 7.56
EW v The Netherlands, Communication No 429/1990 .... 7.24, 7.27

F

FA v Norway, Communication No 18/2000 .... 8.15
Faurisson v France, Communication No 550/1993 .... 3.32, 7.64
Fernandes et al v The Netherlands, Communication No 1513/2006 .... 7.34

Filartiga v Pena Irala 630F 2d 876 (1980), 19 ILM 966 .... 1.15
Fillastre and Bizouarn v Bolivia, Communication No 336/88 .... 7.39, 7.46

G

Gamal El Rgeig v Switzerland, Communication No 280/2005 .... 9.38
Gauthier v Canada, Communication No 633/1995 .... 7.64
GD and SF v France, Communication No 12/2007 .... 10.20, 10.21
Gobin v Mauritius, Application No 787/97 .... 7.19
Goeckce v Austria, Communication No 5/2005 .... 10.17, 10.26, 10.31
Goodwin (Christine) v United Kingdom (2002) 35 EHRR 447 .... 7.56
Gorki Ernesto Tapia Paez v Sweden, Communication No 39/1996 .... 9.35
Government of the Republic of South Africav Grootboom
    2000 (11) BCLR 1169 (CC) 13.08
GRB v Sweden, Communication No 83/1997 .... 9.40, 9.44, 9.45
GT v Australia, Communication No 706/1996 .... 7.44
Guesdon v France, Communication No 219/86 .... 7.49

H

Habassi v Denmark, Communication No 10/1997 .... 8.30
Hagan (Stephen) v Australia, Communication No 26/2002 .... 8.25
Hajrizi Dzemajl v Yugoslavia, Communication No 161/2000 .... 9.43, 9.44
Hak-Chul Sin v Republic of Korea, Communication No 926/2000 .... 7.63
Halil Haydin v Sweden, Communication No 101/1997 .... 9.38
Hartikainen v Finland, Communication No 40/1978 .... 7.61
Henri Unai Parot v Spain, Communication No 6/1990 .... 9.08, 9.46
Hermansen v Denmark, Communication No 44/2009 .... 8.18, 8.33
Hertzberg v Finland, Communication No 61/1979 .... 7.64
Hill and Hill v Spain, Communication No 526/93 .... 7.46
HLR v France (1998) 26 EHRR 29 .... 9.40, 9.45
HMHI v Australia, Communication No 177/2001 .... 9.39, 9.40
HS v France, Communication No 184/84 .... 7.39
Hugo Dermit Barbato v Uruguay, Communication No 84/81 .... 7.43
HWA v Switzerland, Communication No 48/1996 .... 9.17

I

Ionescu v Romania (App No 36659/04), (June 2010) 13.18
IP v Finland, Communication No 450/91 .... 7.54
Ismail Alan v Switzerland, Communication No 21/1995 .... 9.38, 9.39

J

JAG v Sweden, Communication No 215/2002 .... 9.28
Jenny v Austria, Communication No 1437/2005 .... 7.47
Jensen v Denmark, Communication No 202/2002 .... 9.32
Jewish Community of Oslo v Norway, Communication
    No 30/2003 .... 8.02, 8.19, 8.20, 8.21, 8.22, 8.28
Joseph v Sri Lanka, Communication No 18/11/2005 .... 7.67

Table of Cases

Josu Arkauz Arana v France, Communication No 63/1997 .... 9.32, 9.39, 9.41
Jovica Dimitrov v Serbia and Montenegro, Communication
  No 171/2000 .... 9.32, 9.42, 9.47
JP v Canada, Communication 446/91 .... 7.60
JRT and the WG Party of Canada v Canada, ... 7.24
Judge v Canada, Communication No 829/1998 .... 7.29, 7.43
Jung v Republic of Korea, Communication Nos 1593–1603/2007 .... 7.14, 7.60

K

Kaba v Canada, Communication No 1465/2000 .... 7.44
Kamal Quereshi v Denmark, Communication No 27/2002 .... 8.32
Kamal Quereshi v Denmark, Communication No 33/2003 .... 8.25
Karimov and Nursatov v Tajikistan, Communication No 1108/2002
  and 1121/2002 .... 7.48
Karnel Singh Bhinder v Canada, Communication No 208/1986 .... 7.59
Kashif Ahmad v Denmark, Communication No 16/1999 .... 8.30
Kavanagh v Ireland, Communication No 1114/2002 .... 7.71
Kavanagh v Ireland, Communication No 819/1998 .... 7.39, 7.68
Kaveh Yaragh Tala v Sweden, Communication No 43/1996 .... 9.38
Kayhan v Turkey, Communication No 8/2005 .... 10.22, 10.24
Kelly v Jamaica, Communication No 253/1987 .... 7.14
Kennedy v Trinidad and Tobago, Communication No 845/1999 .... 7.33
Kepa Urra Guridi v Spain, Communication No 212/2002 .... 9.46
Keremedchiev v Bulgaria, Communication No 257/2004 .... 9.28
Kim v Republic of Korea, Communication No 574/1994 .... 7.64
Kirpo v Tajikistan, Communication No 1401/2005 .... 7.44
Kisoki v Sweden, Communication No 41/1996 .... 9.38
Kivenmaa v Finland, Communication No 412/1990 .... 7.63
KJL v Finland Communication No 544/1993 (1994) 1 IHRR 74 .... 7.32
KNLH v Peru, Communication No 1153/2003 .... 7.42
Kodirov v Uzbekistan, Communication No 1284/2004 .... 7.39
Komarovski v Turkmenistan, Communication No 1450/2006 .... 7.46
Korneenko et al v Belarus, Communication No 1274/2004 .... 7.25
KRC v Denmark, Communication No 23/2002 .... 8.15
Kulov v Kyrgyztan, Communication No 1369/2005 .... 7.44
Kwok v Australia, Communication No 1442/2005 .... 7.43

L

Lacko v Slovakia, Communication No 11/1998 .... 8.22
Länsman v Finland, Communication No 511/92 .... 7.74
Larrañaga v The Philippines, Communication No 1421/2005 .... 7.44
Laureano v Peru, Communication No 540/1993 .... 7.25
Lecraft v Spain, Communication No 1493/2006 .... 7.66
Leyla Sahin v Turkey (2007) 44 EHRR 5 .... 7.59
LJR v Australia, Communication No 316/2007 .... 9.23, 9.37

LK v The Netherlands, Communication No 4/1991 .... 8.27, 8.29, 8.32
LO v Canada, Communication No 95/1997 .... 9.32
López Burgos v Uruguay, Communication No 52/1979 .... 7.30
Lovelace v Canada, Communication No R 6/24 ....7.21, 7.73
LR v Slovak Republic, Communication No 31/2003 .... 8.22, 8.24, 8.27
Ltaief v Tunisia, Communication No 189/2001 .... 9.25, 9.32
LTK v Finland, Communication No 185/84 .... 7.60
Lubicon Lake Band v Canada, Communication No 167/1984 .... 7.72, 7.73, 13.06
Lumanog and Santos v The Philippines, Communication No 1466/2006 .... 7.49
Lyashkevich v Uzbekistan, Communication No 1552/2007 .... 7.49

M

MA v Canada, Communication No 22/1995 .... 9.32
Maclaine Watson v Department of Trade and Industry (Tin Council Litigation)
 [1989] 3 All ER 523 .... 1.03
Mafhoud Brada v France, Communication No 195/2002 .... 9.16
Mahuika v New Zealand, Communication No 547/1993 .... 7.73
MAK v Germany, Communication No 214/2002 ....9.30, 9.36
Marinich v Belarus, Communication No 1502/2006 .... 7.44
Massiotti and Baritussio v Uruguay, Communication No R 6/25 .... 7.28
Massiotti and Baritussio v Uruguay, Communication No 25/1978 .... 7.70
Mawamba v Zambia, Communication No 1520/2006 .... 7.44
MB v Denmark, Communication No 20/2000 .... 8.29
MBB v Sweden, Communication No 104/1998 .... 9.35
Mbenge v Zaire, Communication No 16/1977 .... 7.49
Medjnoune v Algeria, Communication No 1297/2004 .... 7.46
MG v Germany, Communication No 1482/2006 .... 7.54
Miroslav Lacko v Slovakia, Communication No 11/1998 .... 8.30
MO v Denmark, Communication No 209/2002 .... 9.38
Mohammed Hassan Gelle v Denmark, Communication No 34/2004 .... 8.31
Mosul Boundary Case, PCIJ Rep Ser B, No 12 (1925) 1.10
MPS v Australia, Communication No 138/1999 ....9.40, 9.45
MRP v Switzerland, Communication No 122/1998 ....9.36, 9.37
Muños-Vargas Y Sainz de Vicuña v Spain, Communication
 No 7/2005 .... 10.19, 10.22
Murat Er v Denmark, Communication No 40/2007 .... 8.20, 8.29
Mustafa Dadar v Canada, Communication No 258/2004 .... 9.36
Mutumbo v Switzerland, Communication No 13/1993 .... 9.36, 9.37, 9.39
MV v The Netherlands, Communication No 201/2002 .... 9.23, 9.40, 9.44
Mwamba v Zambia, Communication No 1520/2006 ....7.44, 7.48

N

Nadeeem Ahmed Dar v Norway, Communication No 249/2004 .... 9.06
Narrainen v Norway, Communication No 3/1991 .... 8.29
Ng v Canada, Communication No 469/1991 ....7.29, 7.32, 7.44

Table of Cases

Nikoli and Nikoli v Serbia and Montenegro, Communication No 174/2000 .... 9.47
North Sea Continental Shelf Cases (1969) ICJ Rep 1.07
NSF v United Kingdom, Communication No 10/2005 .... 10.22

O

Öcalan v Turkey (2005) 41 EHRR 985 .... 7.44
O'Neill and Quinn v Ireland, Communication No 1314/2004 .... 7.69
Oliveró Capellades v Spain, Communication No 1211/2003 .... 7.51
Ominayak et al v Canada, Communication No 167/84 .... 7.39, 7.40
OR, MM and MS v Argentina, Communication Nos 1/1988, 2/1988
    and 3/1988 .... 9.10, 9.20
Osmani v Republic of Serbia, Communication No 261/2005 .... 9.30

P

Parot v Spain, Communication No 6/1990 .... 9.16, 9.33
Patino v Panama, Communication No 437/90 .... 7.40
Persaud v Guyana, Communication No 812/1998 .... 7.14, 7.43
Piandiong v The Philippines, Communication No 869/1999 (2000) 7.06, 15.11
Pinkney v Canada, Communication No 27/1978 .... 7.54
PK v Spain, Communication No 323/2007 .... 9.16, 9.22
POEM and FASM v Denmark, Communication No 22/2002 .... 8.21
PQL v Canada, Communication No 57/1996 .... 9.35
PR v Spain, Communication No 160/2000 .... 9.25
Pretty v United Kingdom (2002) 35 EHRR 1 .... 7.56
Prince v South Africa, Communication No 1474/2006 .... 7.57
PS v Denmark, Communication No 397/90, ... 7.41

Q

Qani Halimi-Nedzibi v Austria, Communication No 8/1991 .... 9.31, 9.47
Quereshi v Denmark, Communication No 33/2003 .... 8.17

R

R v France, Communication No 52/1996 .... 9.33
Radivoje Ristic v Yugoslavia, Communication No 113/1998 .... 9.47
Raihon Hudoyberganova v Uzbekistan, Communication No 931/2000 .... 7.59
Ramirez v Uruguay, Communication No R 1/4 .... 7.36, 7.39
Regerat v France, Communication No 24/2002 .... 8.22
Rodríguez Domínguez v Spain, Communication No 1471/2006 .... 7.39
Rodriguez v Uruguay, Communication No 322/1988 .... 7.70
Roitman Rosenmann v Spain, Communication No 176/2000 .... 9.15, 9.24,
Ross v Canada, Communication No 736/1997 .... 7.64
RS v Austria, Communication No 111/1998 .... 9.47
RS v Denmark, Communication No 225/2003 .... 9.26
RSAN v Canada, Communication No 284/2006 .... 9.33
Ruben David v Sweden, Communication No 220/2002 .... 9.38
Ruzmetov v Uzbekistan, Communication No 915/2000 .... 7.44, 7.46, 7.49

xxi

S

SA v Sweden, Communication No 243/2004 .... 9.26
Saadi Ali v Tunisia, Communication No 291/2006 .... 9.10, 9.25, 9.32, 9.42, 9.47
Sadiq Shek Elmi v Australia, Communication No 120/1998 .... 9.38, 9.40
Sarwar Seliman Mostafa v Denmark, Communication No 19/2000 .... 8.22
Sathasivam et al v Sri Lanka, Communication No 1436/2005 .... 7.42
Schmidl v Germany, Communication No 1516/2006 .... 7.37
SE v Argentina, Communication No 275/1988 .... 7.22
SE v Argentina, Communication No 717/1996 .... 7.22
Sefic v Denmark, Communication No 32/2003 .... 8.24, 8.25
Sextus v Trinidad and Tobago, Communication No 818/1998 .... 7.49
Sharifova et al v Tajikistan, Communication Nos 1209/2003, 1231/2003
   and 1241/2004 .... 7.50
Shukurova v Tajikistan, Communication No 1044/2002 .... 7.44
Simunek v Czech Republic, Communication No 516/1992 .... 7.21, 7.67
SL v Sweden, Communication No 150/1999 .... 9.36, 9.37
SPA v Canada, Communication No 282/2005 .... 9.36
SS and SA v The Netherlands, Communication No 142/1999 .... 9.37
SS v The Netherlands, Communication No 191/2001 .... 9.39
SSH v Switzerland, Communication No 254/2004 .... 9.35
SSS v Canada, Communication No 245/2004 .... 9.39
State (Healy) v Donoghue [1976] IR 325 .... 1.16
Stephens v Jamaica, Communication No 373/89 .... 7.46
Stolyar v the Russian Federation, Communication No 996/2001......................... 7.34
Stow and Modou Gai v Portugal, Communication No 1496/2006 .... 7.34, 7.36
Suárez de Guerrero v Colombia, Communication No R 11/45 (1979) 7.43
Suleymane Guengueng v Senegal, Communication
   No 181/2001 .... 9.18, 9.22, 9.46
SV v Canada, Communication No 49/1996 .... 9.40, 9.45

T

TA v Sweden, Communication No 226/2003 .... 9.38
Tcholatch v Canada, Communication No 1052/2002 .... 7.54
Thabti v Tunisia, Communication No 187/2001 .... 9.25, 9.32
Tim Anderson v Australia, Communication No 1367/2005 .... 7.21
Titiahonjo v Cameroon, Communication No 1186/2003 .... 7.45
Tiyagarajah v Sri Lanka, Communication No 1523/2006 .... 7.67
TM v Sweden, Communication No 228/2003 .... 9.23, 9.40, 9.44
Tomasi v France (1993) 15 EHRR 1 .... 7.44
Toonen v Australia (1994) 1(3) IHRR 99 .... 7.55
Toonen v Australia, Communication No 488/1992 .... 7.14, 7.27
Torres v Finland, Communication No 291/1988 .... 7.46
TPS v Canada, Communication No 99/1997 .... 9.06, 9.36

U

US Diplomatic and Consular Staff in Tehran Case (US v Iran) (1980) ICJ Rep 3 . 1.10
Uteev v Uzbekistan, Communication No 1150/2003 .... 7.43

V

Van Alphen v The Netherlands, Communication No 305/88 .... 7.45
Vertido v The Philippines, Communication No 18/2008 .... 10.29
Vincent v France, Communication No 1505/2006 .... 7.37
VL v Switzerland, Communication No 262/2005 .... 9.03, 9.38, 9.42
VNIM v Canada, Communication No 119/1998 .... 9.31
VXN and HN v Sweden, Communication Nos 130/1999 and 131/1999 .... 9.27

W

WBE v The Netherlands, Communication No 423/90 .... 7.46
Wdowiak v Poland, Communication No 1446/2006 .... 7.37
Weerasinghe v Sri Lanka, Communication No 1031/2001 .... 7.34
Wright v Jamaica, Communication No 349/89 .... 7.36

X

X v Canada, Communication No 26/1995 .... 9.27, 9.28

Y

Yildirim v Austria, Communication No 6/2005 .... 10.17, 10.26, 10.31
Yilmaz-Dogan v The Netherlands, Communication No 1/1984 .... 8.26, 8.32
Yoon and Choi v The Republic of Korea, Communication
   No 1321–1322/2004 .... 7.60

Z

Zentralrat Deutscher Sinti und Roma v Germany, Communication
   No 38/2006 .... 8.19
Zheikov v Russian Federation, Communication No 889/1999 .... 7.44
Zhen Zhen Zheng v The Netherlands, Communication No 15/2007 .... 10.24,
ZK v Sweden, Communication No 301/2006 .... 9.38
ZT v Norway, Communication No 127/1999 .... 9.08, 9.33
ZUBS v Australia, Communication No 6/1995 .... 8.21
Zvozskov et al v Belarus, Communication No 1039/2001 .... 7.25
Zwaan de Vries v Netherlands, Communication No 182/1984 .... 7.66

Table of Legislation

Ireland

Belfast/Good Friday Agreement 7.69
Bunreacht na hÉireann
   art 15 ....1.16
      15.2.1° 1.16
      29 ....1.16
      29.6 ....1.16
Criminal Justice (Release of Prisoners) Act 1998 ....7.69
Criminal Justice (United Nations Convention against Torture) Act 2000 ..... 1.16
European Convention on Human Rights Act 2003 ....1.16

International Treaties

African Charter on Human and Peoples' Rights 1.26, 7.35, 13.17
American Convention on Human Rights 1.26, 7.35
   art 44 ....9.02
      46(1)(b) 13.16
      48(f) 13.03
Charter of Fundamental Rights of the European Union 1.25, 3.39
Charter of the United Nations
   art 2(7) 1.23, 2.04, 2.16, 3.01
      7 ....1.23, 2.06
      9 ....2.02
      10 ....2.03
      13(1)(b) 2.03
      14 ....2.03
      15 ....2.03
      17 ....2.03
      18 ....2.02
      22 ....2.04
      39 ....1.23
      41 ....1.23
      42 ....1.23
      55 ....1.22, 2.03
      56 ....1.22, 2.03
      62 ....2.06
      63(2) 2.06
      64 ....2.06

Charter of the United Nations (contd)
    66 .... 2.06
    68 .... 2.06
Convention Relating to the Status of Refugees 9.27
    art 1A(2) 9.35, 9.40
    33 .... 3.76, 9.02, 9.35
        (1) 9.35
        (2) 9.35
Convention on the Elimination of All Forms of Discrimination
    against Women 3.45, 3.63–3.65, 7.02
    art 1 .... 3.65–3.66
    2 .... 5.42, 10.03, 10.16, 10.20, 10.26
        (1) 3.67
    3 .... 3.68, 10.16
    4 .... 3.68, 10.16
    5 .... 3.65, 3.68, 10.20
        (a) 3.68, 5.42, 10.29
        (b) 3.68
    6 .... 3.68, 5.42, 10.04
    7 .... 3.69, 10.04
    8 .... 3.65, 3.69, 10.04
    9 .... 3.69
        (1) 10.04
        (2) 10.04
    10 .... 3.69
        (h) 10.28
    11 .... 3.69, 10.24
        (2)(b) 10.27
    12 .... 3.69, 10.04, 10.28
        (1) 10.28
    13 .... 3.65, 3.69
    14 .... 3.69
    15 .... 3.69, 5.42
        (1) 10.04
        (4) 10.04
    16 .... 3.69, 10.04
        (1) 10.04
            (e) 10.28
            (g) 10.20–10.21
        (2) 10.04
    17 .... 3.70
    18 .... 3.71, 4.51–4.53, 5.36
        (1) 4.51

Convention on the Elimination of All Forms of Discrimination against Women (contd

19	3.70
20(1)	3.70, 4.53
21	3.70–3.72, 5.37, 5.55, 10.15
(1)	4.55
22	4.57
27(1)	3.65
28	3.69
29	3.71
76	3.65
Pt III	3.69
Pt IV	3.69
Pt V	3.98
Pt VI	3.98
Convention on the Rights of Persons with Disabilities	3.102, 5.49–5.51, 7.02, 11.01
art 1	3.107–3.111
1–33	4.69
3	3.108
4(1)	3.109
(3)	3.109, 4.70
5–9	3.110
10–30	3.111
12	3.111, 5.55, 11.08
16	3.111, 6.40
(3)	6.40
32	3.104
33(1)	3.115, 6.38
(2)	3.115, 6.38, 6.40
(3)	3.115
34	3.112
35	3.114, 4.06, 4.68–4.70, 5.54, 6.40
36	3.114, 4.68, 6.40
(1)	4.71
(4)	4.70
(5)	4.72
38	3.114
39	3.114, 5.55
Preamble	3.107
Convention on the Rights of the Child	3.81, 3.93, 3.102, 7.02, 15.01
art 1	3.82
2	3.82
3	3.82

Convention on the Rights of the Child (contd)

4	3.83
5	3.83
6	3.82
7	3.85
8	3.85
9	3.86
10	3.86
11	3.86
12	3.82, 15.05
13	3.85
14	3.85
15	3.85
16	3.85
17	3.85
18(3)	3.87
19	3.86
20	3.86
21	3.86
22	3.88
23	3.87, 3.102
24	3.87
25	3.86
26	3.87
27	3.87
28	3.87
29	3.87
30	3.88
31	3.87
32	3.88
33	3.88
34	3.88
35	3.88
36	3.88
37	3.85–3.88
38	3.88
39	3.86
40	3.88
43	3.89
44	3.84, 4.45, 5.66, 15.20
(1)	4.46
45	4.49
(a)	3.91
(b)	3.91, 4.49
54(a)	4.47

Table of Legislation

European Convention for the Prevention of Torture and Inhuman
or Degrading Treatment or Punishment 6.04
- art 1 .... 6.04
- 2 .... 6.04
- 7(2) 6.04
- 8 .... 6.04
  - (1) 6.14
- 9 .... 6.04, 6.15
- 10 .... 6.04
  - (2) 6.23
- 11 .... 6.04
- 4-6 .... 6.04

Draft Optional Protocol Convention on the Rights of the Child
to provide a Communications Procedure
- art 1 .... 15.05
  - (2) 15.05, 15.09
- 2 .... 15.05, 15.14
  - (1) 15.21
- 3 .... 15.05
  - (1) 15.08
  - (2) 15.07
- 4 .... 15.06
- 5 .... 15.07, 15.09
- 6 .... 15.11
  - (1) 15.11
  - (2) 15.06
  - (3) 15.04, 15.13
- 7 .... 15.10
  - (2) 15.15
- 8 .... 15.13, 15.20
- 9 .... 15.14
  - (1) 15.04, 15.14, 15.20
  - (2) 15.15
- 10 .... 15.08
  - (1) 15.10
  - (2) 15.16
  - (3) 15.16
  - (4) 15.18
  - (5) 15.19
- 11 .... 15.08, 15.20
  - (1) 15.20
  - (2) 15.13–15.15, 15.20
- 12 .... 15.17
- 13(3) 15.16

Draft Optional Protocol Convention on the Rights of the Child
  to provide a Communications Procedure (contd)
   14 .... 15.08
     (1) 15.20
   15(1) 15.21
   17 .... 15.19
   Pt 11 .... 15.05
European Convention on Human Rights 1.16, 1.25, 6.04, 7.15
                                                       7.19, 7.24, 7.34–7.35, 7.48, 9.50, 13.18, 15.10
   art 3 .... 5.16, 7.44, 9.02, 9.23, 9.35, 9.40, 9.42, 9.44–9.45
     4(3)(b) 7.60
     6 .... 7.48
     8 .... 7.54–7.56
     9 .... 7.37, 7.60
     10 .... 7.64
     14 .... 7.37, 7.66
     34 .... 7.24, 13.18
     35 .... 7.17
       (1) 7.19, 13.16
         (b) 7.37
       (3) 7.34
         (b) 13.18
     37 .... 15.15
     39 .... 13.03, 15.15
     46 .... 7.15
     56(6) 13.16
   Protocol 7 .... 7.48
   Protocol 12 .... 7.37, 7.66
European Social Charter 3.39, 11.03, 13.16
Helsinki Final Act 1975 .... 3.12
International Covenant on Economic, Social and Cultural Rights
                                                       3.03–3.05, 3.37, 3.39, 3.48–3.49, 7.02
   art 1 .... 3.37
   2 .... 3.41, 3.111
     (1) 3.40–3.43, 3.48
     (2) 3.42, 3.45
     (3) 3.42, 3.46
   2–5 .... 3.40
   3 .... 3.45
   4 .... 3.47
     (2) 3.111
   5 .... 3.37, 3.48
   6 .... 3.37

International Covenant on Economic, Social and Cultural Rights (contd)

7	3.37
(a)(i)	3.42
8	3.37, 3.42
9	3.37
10	3.37
(3)	3.42, 3.81
11	3.37
12	3.37
13	3.37
(2)(a)	3.42
(3)	3.42
(4)	3.42
14	3.37
15	3.37
(3)	3.42
16	4.17, 4.21
17	4.17, 4.21
21	4.21
22	4.21
16–25	3.50

Inter-American Convention on Forced Disappearance of Persons 1994

art II	3.118

Inter-American Convention to Prevent and Punish Torture 1985

art 2	3.74

International Bill of Rights 3.04

International Convention for the Protection of All Persons from Enforced Disappearance 7.02, 14.01

art 1(1)	3.118
2	3.118
3	3.118
4	3.118
5	3.118
6	3.118
7	3.118
9	3.118
10	3.118
11	3.118
12	3.118
13	3.118
14	3.118
15	3.118
17(1)	3.118

International Convention for the Protection of All Persons from Enforced Disappearance (contd)

17–23	3.118
22	3.118
24	3.118
25	3.118
26(1)	3.119
(4)	3.119
(6)	3.119
(8)	3.120
(9)	3.120
27	3.121
29	3.122, 4.74
(1)	4.73
(3)	4.73
30	3.122, 14.01, 14.04–14.07
(1)	14.03, 14.05
(2)	14.04–14.05
(c)	14.04
(e)	14.04
(3)	14.05
(4)	14.05
31	3.122, 14.01, 14.06
(1)	14.06
(2)(c)	14.07
(3)	14.08
(4)	14.08
(5)	14.08
32	3.122
32–33	4.01
33	3.122, 5.60
(1)	5.58, 5.68
(2)	5.58
(4)	5.58–5.60
(5)	5.58
34	3.122
35(2)	3.122
38–42	3.118
39(1)	3.117, 14.09
43	3.118
Pt II	3.119

Table of Legislation

International Convention on the Elimination of All Forms of Racial
    Discrimination 2.15, 3.53, 3.68–3.69, 4.07, 4.24
    .... 7.02, 7.19, 8.01–8.02, 16.10
- art 1 .... 3.54, 8.25
  - (1) 8.24–8.26
  - (2) 8.26
  - (4) 3.55–3.56, 8.24
- 2 .... 3.56, 3.59, 8.27
  - (1) 3.56
    - (a) 3.56
    - (b) 3.56, 8.27
    - (c) 3.56, 8.27
    - (d) 3.56, 8.27, 8.29–8.30
    - (e) 3.56
  - (2) 3.55–3.56
- 3–7 .... 3.57
- 4 .... 3.58, 8.28, 8.28–8.31
  - (a) 8.28
  - (b) 8.28
  - (c) 8.28
- 5 .... 3.58, 8.28–8.29
  - (a) 8.29
  - (e) 8.26, 8.29
  - (f) 8.29
- 6 .... 3.59, 8.16, 8.28–8.32
- 7 .... 3.59
  - (2) 3.59
- 8 .... 3.61
- 9 .... 3.62
  - (1)(b) 4.31
  - (2) 3.63, 4.30
- 10 .... 3.61
- 11 .... 3.62
- 11–13 .... 4.01
- 12 .... 3.62
- 14 .... 3.62, 8.01, 8.04–8.11, 8.14–8.19, 8.23, 8.33, 9.21, 13.12
  - (1) 8.02, 8.16–8.17
  - (2) 8.03, 8.15
  - (4) 8.03
  - (5) 7.19, 8.03, 8.15, 13.16
  - (6) 8.14
    - (a) 8.04, 8.11
    - (b) 8.08, 15.13
  - (7) 8.14

International Convention on the Elimination of All Forms of Racial Discrimination (contd)
  (a) 8.11, 8.21
  (b) 8.05, 8.12
 (8) 8.13
 20 .... 3.60
 28(2)–(5) 3.61
International Convention on the Protection of the Rights of Migrant Workers and Members of Their Families 3.92–3.93
 .... 4.60–4.63, 7.02, 12.01
art 1 .... 3.94
 2 .... 3.96–3.98
  (2) 4.64
  (3) 4.65
 4 .... 3.95
  (4) 4.65
 5 .... 3.100
  (a) 3.95
  (b) 3.95
  (5) 4.64
  (6) 4.65
 7 .... 3.94
 9 .... 3.97
 10–20 .... 3.97
 25–27 .... 3.97
 28 .... 3.97
 30 .... 3.97
 31 .... 3.97
 32 .... 3.97
 34 .... 3.99
 35 .... 3.99
 36 .... 3.96
 38–45 .... 3.98
 46–48 .... 3.98
 52–67 .... 3.98–3.99
 68 .... 3.98–3.99
 69 .... 3.99
 72(1) 3.100
  (2) 3.100
  (8) 3.100
 73 .... 3.101, 4.60
  (4) 4.60
 74 .... 3.101, 4.60
  (1) 4.63
  (4) 4.66

International Convention on the Protection of the Rights of Migrant Workers and Members of Their Families (contd)

    (7) 3.101
  76 ....3.101, 4.01
  77 ....3.101, 12.02–12.03
    (2) 12.03
    (3)(a) 12.03
      (b) 12.03, 13.14
    (4)–(6) 12.03
    (8) 12.02
  79 ....3.99
  87(1) 3.93
  Pt III 3.96–3.97
  Pt IV 3.96
International Covenant on Civil and Political Rights 1.11, 3.03–3.05
                                                           3.26, 3.48, 7.02, 7.05, 7.33
  art 1 ....3.26, 7.28, 7.72
    2 ....3.59, 7.23, 7.30, 7.65–7.66, 7.72
      (1) 3.27–3.28, 3.40, 3.45, 7.26–7.30, 7.65
      (2) 3.29
      (3) 3.30, 7.15, 7.44, 7.51, 7.66, 7.70–7.71
        (a) 7.70
        (b) 3.30, 7.70
        (c) 7.70
    3 ....3.28, 7.65
    4 ....3.31, 7.65
      (1) 7.65
      (2) 3.31, 7.57
    5 ....3.48
      (1) 3.32
      (2) 3.32
        (a) 7.37
        (b) 7.37, 7.40
      (3) 7.46
    6 ....3.26, 3.31, 7.43
      (1) 7.43
      (2) 7.43
    7 ....3.26, 3.31, 3.73, 7.23, 7.29, 7.43–7.44, 7.70
                                        9.03, 9.18, 9.23, 9.35, 9.40–9.42, 9.45–9.46
    8 ....3.26, 3.31, 7.60
      (3) 7.60
    9 ....3.26, 7.43, 7.45
      (1) 7.45, 7.46
      (2) 7.46, 7.49

International Covenant on Civil and Political Rights (contd)

(3)	7.46
(4)	7.46, 7.54, 7.70
(5)	7.46
10	3.26, 7.44
(1)	7.44
11	3.26, 3.31
12	3.26
13	3.26
14	3.26, 7.44, 7.47–7.48, 7.65, 7.68, 7.71
(1)	7.47, 7.65
(2)	7.48–7.49
(3)	7.47–7.49
(4)	7.50
(5)	7.48, 7.51
(6)	7.52
(7)	7.48, 7.53
15	3.26, 3.31
16	3.26, 3.31, 7.22
17	3.26, 7.23, 7.37, 7.54–7.56
(1)	7.54
18	3.26, 3.31, 7.57–7.60
(1)	7.60
(2)	7.58–7.59
(3)	7.57–7.58, 7.60
(4)	7.61
19	3.26, 7.62–7.63
(1)	7.58, 7.63
(2)	7.63
(3)	3.32, 7.62–7.64
(a)	7.64
20	3.26, 7.37, 7.41, 7.63, 7.64
(2)	7.65
21	3.26
22	3.26
23	3.26, 7.54, 7.65
(4)	7.65
24	3.26, 7.54, 7.65
(1)	3.81, 7.65
25	3.26, 7.65
26	3.26–3.28, 3.45, 7.23, 7.37, 7.65–7.69, 7.71–7.72
27	3.26, 7.37, 7.72–7.74
28	3.33
29	3.34

International Covenant on Civil and Political Rights (contd)

30	3.34
31	3.34
32	3.34
35	3.34
38	3.33
40	3.35, 3.49, 4.07, 4.10, 4.18
(1)	4.07
(2)	4.07
(3)	4.14
(4)	3.36, 4.12
41(1)	3.35
41–43	3.35, 4.01
Minorities Treaties of 1919	1.20
Optional Protocol to the Convention on the Elimination of All Forms of Discrimination against Women	5.27, 10.05–10.08, 13.12, 15.10
art 1	10.04
2	10.03, 10.17, 10.20, 11.02, 13.12
(c)	10.29
3	10.18
4	11.04
(1)	10.24, 11.04, 13.14
(2)(a)	10.22, 11.04
(b)	10.18
(d)	10.18
(e)	10.18, 13.16
5	10.11
(1)	10.11, 13.03
(2)	10.11
6	10.09
7 (2)	10.14
(3)	10.13
(4)	10.15, 11.11
(5)	10.15
8	3.71, 5.30, 5.38, 5.46, 5.57, 5.62, 5.66
(1)	5.31
(2)	5.33, 5.39–5.40
(3)	5.36
(4)	5.36
(5)	5.60
9	3.71, 5.30, 5.36, 5.63
(1)	5.36, 5.44
(2)	5.36, 5.41
10	5.30, 5.45

Optional Protocol to the Convention on the Elimination of All Forms of Discrimination against Women (contd)
    (1) 5.58
    11 .... 5.35
    12 .... 5.37, 5.41, 5.55
    16(1)(g) 10.20
    17 .... 10.05
Optional Protocol to the Convention on the Rights of Persons with Disabilities
    .... 5.55, 11.01, 13.12
  art 1 .... 11.08
    (1) 11.02
    1–5 .... 3.114
    2 .... 11.08
      (d) 13.14
      (f) 13.16
    3 .... 11.07
    4(1) 11.06, 13.03
      (2) 11.06
    5 .... 11.10
    6 .... 5.49–5.50, 5.66
      (1) 5.51
      (2) 5.52
      (3) 5.54
      (4) 5.54
      (5) 5.52, 5.60
    6–8 .... 3.114, 5.49
    7 .... 5.49, 5.63
      (1) 5.54
      (2) 5.54
    8–10 .... 5.49
    8 .... 5.58
    33(3) 6.38
    35(1) 6.38
Optional Protocol to the Convention on the Rights of the Child on the Involvement of Children in Armed Conflict 3.81, 4.45, 15.07
  art 8(2) 4.46
Optional Protocol Convention on the Rights of the Child, Sale of Children, Child Prostitution and Child Pornography 3.81, 15.07
  art 12 .... 4.46, 15.20

Optional Protocol to the International Covenant on Economic, Social
and Cultural Rights
....5.61, 12.02, 13.01, 13.03, 13.06, 13.15
....13.20, 15.06, 15.10, 15.14, 15.18
art 1 ....13.03
2 ....13.03
(1) 13.08–13.09, 13.19, 13.22
3(1) 13.14
(2) 13.16
(b) 13.16
(e) 13.16–13.17
4 ....13.18, 15.10
5 ....13.03
(1) 15.12
6 (1) 13.03
(2) 13.03
7 ....13.03
(2) 15.15
8 (1) 13.03
(3) 13.03
(4) 13.08, 13.22
9 ....13.03
10 ....4.01, 5.63, 13.03
11(1) 5.62–5.63
11–12 ....13.03
14 ....13.19, 15.21
(2) 13.19
(3) 13.19, 15.21
15 ....5.63
16 ....13.03
17 ....13.03
22 ....13.19
23 ....13.19
Optional Protocol to the International Covenant on Civil and Political Rights
....3.03, 3.35, 7.05, 7.11, 7.17, 7.33–7.34, 7.37, 7.42
....7.68, 7.76, 8.02, 8.11–8.14, 8.33–9.02
....9.04, 9.11, 9.16, 9.26, 9.50, 10.05, 10.16, 10.30, 13.03, 13.12
art 1 ....7.06, 7.24, 7.26–7.27
2 ....7.34
3 ....7.18, 9.21
4(2) 7.42
5(1) 8.11, 12.03
(2) 7.10
(a) 7.35–7.37

xxxix

Optional Protocol to the International Covenant on Civil and Political Rights (contd)

    (b) 7.39, 14.07
    (3) 7.12
    (4) 7.13–7.16
    (2)(b) 7.38
  26 .... 8.24

Optional Protocol to the United Nations Convention against Torture and Other Cruel, Inhuman and Degrading Treatment or Punishment 6.06
  art 1 .... 6.15, 6.32, 6.40
  2 .... 6.09, 6.16
    (2) 6.12
    (3) 6.12
    (4) 6.23
  3 .... 6.25–6.28
  4 .... 6.08, 6.13
    (1) 6.07, 6.15, 6.25, 6.32
  5 .... 6.09–6.10
  6–8 .... 6.10
  7(1)(c) 6.10
  9 .... 6.10
  11 .... 6.11
    (b)(ii) 6.34
  12 .... 6.13, 6.23
    (a) 6.15
    (b) 6.19
    (c) 6.34
    (d) 6.20
  13(1) 6.16, 6.31
    (2) 6.14
    (3) 6.17
    (4) 6.16, 6.31
  14 .... 6.19, 6.23, 6.32
    (1) 6.15, 6.19
    (2) 6.15, 6.32
  15 .... 6.19, 6.23
  16 .... 6.09, 6.24, 6.33–6.34
    (1) 6.20
    (2) 6.21
    (3) 6.24
    (4) 6.09, 6.23
  17 .... 6.25, 6.28–6.29, 6.40
  18 .... 6.27
  19(a) 6.30
    (b) 6.30, 6.33

*Optional Protocol to the United Nations Convention against Torture
and Other Cruel, Inhuman and Degrading Treatment or Punishment (contd)*
    (c) 6.30
  20 ....6.30–6.32
    (f) 6.30, 6.34
  22 ....6.30, 6.33
  23 ....6.30, 6.33
  24 ....6.29–6.29
  25 ....6.37
  27(1) 6.06

Rome Statute of the International Criminal Court 1998
art 7 ....3.118

South African Bill of Rights
art 26 ....13.08

Statute of UNHCR ....

Statute of the International Court of Justice
art 38 ....1.06, 1.10–1.13
  59 ....1.11

United Nations Convention against Torture and Other Cruel, Inhuman
    and Degrading Treatment or Punishment 3.73, 4.37, 5.02, 5.09
....7.02, 9.01
art 1 ....3.73–3.75, 5.15, 9.40, 9.42, 9.45, 9.49
  2 ....3.76, 3.80, 9.34, 9.37
    (1) 9.22, 9.34
    (2) 3.76
  3 ....3.76, 3.80, 9.06, 9.17, 9.22–9.23, 9.26
....................................9.30, 9.34, 9.36, 9.39–9.41, 9.42–9.45, 9.49, 15.11
  4 ....3.76, 9.46
  5 ....3.77
    (1)(c) 9.24
    (2) 9.18, 9.46
      (a) 9.27
  5–9 ....9.22
  6 ....3.77
  7 ....3.77, 9.18
  8 ....3.77, 9.24
  9 ....3.76–3.77, 9.24
  10 ....3.73, 3.77, 9.44
  11 ....3.73, 3.77, 9.44
  12 ....3.77, 9.25, 9.46–9.47
  13 ....3.77, 9.20, 9.25, 9.44, 9.46–9.47
  14 ....3.76–3.77, 9.20, 9.44, 9.47

United Nations Convention against Torture and Other Cruel, Inhuman and Degrading Treatment or Punishment (contd)

15	3.76–3.77
16	9.23, 9.32–9.34, 9.42–9.45
(1)	3.75–3.77
17(1)	3.78
18	6.36
19	3.79, 4.40, 5.05
(1)	4.37
(3)	4.43
20	3.79, 5.02, 5.05, 5.07, 5.12–5.15, 5.19–5.26, 5.56
(1)	5.05, 5.09, 5.57
(2)	5.09
(3)	5.10–5.11
(4)	5.13
(5)	5.04–5.06, 5.10, 5.17, 5.60, 5.63
21	3.79, 4.01
22	3.76, 3.79, 5.05, 9.01–9.03, 9.06–9.13
	9.21, 9.25–9.26, 9.34, 9.36, 9.38, 9.39, 9.42–9.43
	9.44–9.46, 9.48, 12.01–12.03
(1)	9.02–9.04, 9.13–9.16, 9.18–9.22
(2)	9.04, 9.13–9.14, 9.25
(3)	9.07
(4)	9.11, 12.03
(5)(a)	9.27–9.28
(b)	9.08, 9.13, 9.30–9.31, 13.14
(6)	9.03
(7)	9.11
(8)	9.02
24	3.80
26(9)	5.59
27	3.73
28	3.79, 5.03, 5.58
(1)	5.05
30	5.57
(2)	3.80
(3)	3.80
(4)	5.56
31	5.57
33	5.56–5.59, 9.40
34	5.59
17(2)–(6)	3.78
19–22	6.09

Universal Declaration of Human Rights 3.07, 3.08, 3.10, 3.12
....3.37, 3.58, 8.28
  art 1 ....3.08
    2 ....3.07–3.08, 3.13
    3 ....3.07
    4 ....3.07, 3.13
    5 ....3.07, 3.13, 3.73
    6 ....3.07
    7 ....3.07, 3.13
    8 ....3.07, 3.59
    9 ....3.07
    10 ....3.07
    11 ....3.07
    12 ....3.07
    12–17 ....3.08
    13 ....3.07
    14 ....3.07, 3.26
    15 ....3.07
    16 ....3.07
    17 ....3.07, 3.26
    18 ....3.07
    18–21 ....3.07–3.08
    22 ....3.07
    22–27 ....3.08
    23 ....3.07
    24 ....3.07
    25 ....3.07
      (2) 3.81
    26 ....3.07
    27 ....3.07
    29 ....3.09
    30 ....3.09
    Preamble 3.07, 3.10
Vienna Convention on the Law of Treaties 3.74
  art 2(1) (a) 1.03
      (b) 1.03
      (d) 1.04
    5 ....1.09
    11–16 ....1.03
    19 ....1.04
    20 ....1.04
    53 ....1.09

Part I:
The Foundations of the UN Human Rights Treaty System

Chapter 1

Introduction

[1.01] This book is about the regime that has been constructed by the United Nations (UN) for the protection of human rights through the vehicle of the UN human rights treaty system. Spawned from the ideal expressed in the UN Charter in 1945 of establishing universal human rights standards, there are now nine 'core' treaties which collectively form a substantial body of international human rights law. These treaties elaborate standards of human rights which must be adhered to by the State parties, as well as procedures by which the implementation of those rights are monitored by various 'treaty bodies' established for that purpose. While by no means the only human rights treaties adopted by the UN since its inception, the ability of a wide range of actors to engage with the treaty monitoring bodies in an effort to influence domestic implementation of the rights makes them an important tool in the arsenal of human rights victims and their advocates.[1] Nonetheless, there is a multiplicity of challenges involved in ensuring meaningful implementation of the rights enumerated in the treaties. These include the challenges posed for rights-holders, non-governmental organisations and national human rights institutions in properly accessing and utilising the procedures provided for in the treaties; as well as the challenges posed for the treaty bodies themselves in developing the procedures and executing their functions in ways that are likely to remedy breaches and enhance domestic protection of the rights in question.

[1.02] The aims of this book are threefold. First, to set the treaties in their institutional context by outlining the nature and functions of the organs of the United Nations from which they have emerged, some of which still play a central role in their operation. Second, to describe the development of each of the treaties, the substantive rights enshrined in them and the nature and functions of each of the treaty bodies established to monitor their implementation. Third, to describe and analyse the operation of each of the various procedures through which implementation is monitored by the latter bodies, *namely,* periodic reporting procedures, investigative procedures and individual complaints procedures.[2] The final aspect of the book involves a consideration of

---

[1] For other works on the treaty system, see Alston and Crawford eds, *The Future of UN Human Rights Treaty Monitoring* (CUP, 2001); Bayefsky edn, *The UN Human Rights Treaty System in the 21st Century* (Kluwer Law, 2000); Bayefsky, *How to Complain to the UN Human Rights Treaty System* (Transnational, 2002); O'Flaherty, *Human Rights and the UN: Practice Before the Treaty Bodies* (2nd edn, Kluwer Law, 2002); and Vandenhole, *The Procedures Before the UN Human Rights Treaty Bodies: Divergence or Convergence* (Intersentia, 2004).

[2] Inter-State procedures are not considered on the basis that while such procedures have been incorporated into most of the United Nations treaties, they have never been used in practice. See generally, Leckie, 'The Inter-State Complaint Procedure in International Human Rights Law: Hopeful Prospects or Wishful Thinking' (1988) 10 HRQ 249.

proposals for reforming the operation of the treaty system. Before embarking on this comprehensive analysis, this introductory chapter aims to explain the nature of an international human rights treaty itself and to describe how human rights treaties 'fit' in the overall scheme of the sources of international law.

TREATIES AS A SOURCE OF INTERNATIONAL LAW

[1.03] A treaty is an agreement between States which imposes binding legal obligations in international law on the States which agree to be bound by its terms.[3] Treaties are also referred to as 'conventions' and occasionally as covenants or charters. They can be of two varieties: *bilateral* (between two States) or *multilateral* (between a number of States). The core international human rights treaties examined in this book are multilateral in character. A *protocol* to a treaty is itself a separate treaty which may be added to the original treaty and in which the parties undertake additional obligations or otherwise vary the original terms. It is easy to see why an analogy is often made between treaties and contracts under domestic law.[4] Once a State 'signs' a treaty, it indicates its *intention* to be bound by its terms.[5] Once it 'ratifies'[6] or 'accedes'[7] to the treaty, the State is unequivocally consenting to be bound by the terms of the treaty as regards all the other States parties thereto. The obvious corollary to this position is that if a State does not ratify or accede to a treaty, it is not bound by the treaty. However, as we shall see in the next section, in certain circumstances the norms enshrined in a treaty may in fact bind non-contracting States where the obligations in question are deemed to have the character of *customary international law*.

[1.04] It should also be noted that States are entitled under international law to opt out of certain obligations in a treaty on ratification under certain strict conditions. This occurs where a State enters a 'reservation' to a particular obligation at the time of signature or ratification. A 'reservation' is a unilateral statement made by the State which either modifies or excludes the terms of the obligation which would otherwise be legally

---

[3] Vienna Convention on the Law of Treaties, art 2(1)(a) itself defines a treaty as follows: 'An international agreement concluded between States in written form and governed by international law, whether embodied in *a single instrument or in two or more related instruments and whatever its particular designation*'. The convention, adopted by the General Assembly of the UN on 23 May 1969, sets forth established rules of law regarding the operation of treaties: http://untreaty.un.org/ilc/texts/instruments/english/conventions/1_1_1969.pdf (last accessed May 2011).
[4] In *Maclaine Watson v Department of Trade and Industry (Tin Council Litigation)* [1989] 3 All ER 523, Lord Templeman expressed the view that a 'treaty is a contract between the governments of two or more sovereign states'.
[5] See Vienna Convention 1969, art 12.
[6] See Vienna Convention 1969, arts 2(1)(b), 11, 14 and 16. For the UN human rights treaties, the process of ratification involves the execution of an instrument of ratification and the depositing of it with the Secretary General of the UN.
[7] 'Accession' is the formal term used when a State that has not first signed a treaty consents to become a party to the treaty. See Vienna Convention 1969, arts 2(1)(b), 15 and 16.

binding.[8] States may also enter 'interpretive declarations' at the time of signature or ratification, indicating their specific understanding of a particular obligation.[9] The latter have no legal effect, strictly speaking, but rather serve simply to give an indication of the view held by the State in regard to the nature of the obligation at issue. The distinction between a reservation and an interpretive declaration may cause difficulties of construction in some cases.[10] Very specific rules govern the effect of reservations and it is sufficient here to note that a reservation will never be effective if it is incompatible with the object and purpose of the treaty in question or if it is expressly prohibited by the treaty in question.[11] Despite these rules, it is a disconcerting fact that significant numbers of States continue to resile from obligations set forth in human rights treaties by means of reservations, especially in regard to children's and women's rights.[12]

[1.05] It is also important to note that the terms of a treaty may allow for States to derogate from its terms in particular circumstances. A 'derogation' involves a declaration by the State that it is no longer in a position to comply with certain stated obligations. Provision for derogation is quite common in human rights treaties in times of war or other national emergency. However, derogation is never permissible from certain core obligations, such as the prohibitions on torture and slavery. The latter, as is explained below, are generally considered to be peremptory norms of international law ('*jus cogens*').

OTHER SOURCES OF INTERNATIONAL LAW

[1.06] Treaties may now be considered the 'primary' source of international law,[13] but they are by no means the only source. The consent of States to the rules of international

---

[8] Vienna Convention 1969, art 2(1)(d), defines a reservation as a 'unilateral statement, however phrased, made by a State, when signing, ratifying, accepting, approving or acceding to a treaty, whereby it purports to exclude or to modify the legal effect of certain provisions of the treaty in their application to that State'.

[9] The International Law Commission (ILC) has defined an interpretive declaration as being '... a unilateral statement, however phrased or named, made by a State or by an international organization whereby that State or that organization purports to specify or clarify the meaning or scope attributed by the declarant to a treaty or to certain of its provisions'. Text of the set of draft guidelines constituting Guide to Practice on Reservations, provisionally adopted by the ILC: Annual Report of the ILC, 2010, UN Doc A/65/10, Chapter IV(C), para 1.2.

[10] As to the method of distinguishing between a reservation and an interpretive declaration, see paras 1.3.1 and 1.3.2 of the ILC draft Guide to Practice on Reservations.

[11] Vienna Convention 1969, arts 19 and 20. A State party to a treaty may object to a reservation being made by another contracting State, and while this will not usually affect the entry into force of the treaty for the reserving State, specific rules also govern this issue: see arts 20 and 21 of the Vienna Convention and see generally Shaw, *International Law* (6th edn, CUP, 2008), pp 913–925.

[12] 'The extensive usage of reservations and the less common deployment of vague expressions to restrict legal obligations are particularly evident with regard to conventions that relate to the rights of women and children': Rehman, *International Human Rights Law* (2nd edn, Pearson, 2010), p 21.

[13] Dixon, *Textbook on International Law* (6th edn, OUP, 2007), p 30.

law can be indicated in a variety of ways. Article 38 of the Statute of the International Court of Justice (ICJ)[14] is the principal point of reference when attempts are made to define the 'sources' of international law. In addition to specifying treaties as a source of international law, Article 38 articulates a number of other sources which that court may have regard to in seeking to settle disputes arising between States which submit to its jurisdiction. These include 'international custom', the general principles of law recognised by civilised nations and 'judicial decisions and the teachings of the most highly qualified publicists'.[15]

Customary International Law

[1.07] A considerable proportion of the rules of international law have been deduced from the second source referred to in art 38, namely, 'international custom', commonly referred to as *customary international law*.[16] Two elements must be established to indicate the existence of a rule of customary international law. First, that the practice[17] is consistent as between States; and second, that there is a belief on the part of States adhering to the practice that the practice is in some sense obligatory (*opinio juris*).[18] The consistency of the practice must be evidenced by 'extensive and virtually uniform'[19] actions or omissions or practice that is in some sense substantial on the part of a significant number of States.[20] The second, more subjective element of *opinio juris* is

---

[14] The Statute of the ICJ, establishing the court, is annexed to the Charter of the United Nations (discussed further below). The statute sets forth the composition and functions of the court: See generally: http://www.icj-cij.org/documents/index.php?p1=4&p2=2&p3=0 (last accessed May 2011).

[15] Article 38 provides as follows: 'The Court, whose function is to decide in accordance with international law such disputes as are submitted to it, shall apply:

(a) international conventions, whether general or particular, establishing rules expressly recognised by the contesting States;

(b) international custom, as evidence of a general practice accepted as law;

(c) the general principles of law recognised by civilised nations;

(d) judicial decisions and the teachings of the most highly qualified publicists of the various nations, as subsidiary means for the determination of rules of law.'

[16] See generally, Cassese, *International Law* (2nd edn, OUP, 2005) pp 156–169 and Villiger, *Customary International Law and Treaties: A Manual on the Theory and Practice of the Interrelation of Sources* (2nd edn, Kluwer Law, 1997).

[17] Villiger, *Customary International Law and Treaties: A Manual on the Theory and Practice of the Interrelation of Sources* (2nd edn, Kluwer Law, 1997) defines State practice at p 16 as '…any act, articulation or other behaviour of a State, as long as the behaviour in question discloses the State's conscious attitude with respect to its recognition of a customary rule'.

[18] *North Sea Continental Shelf Cases* (1969) ICJ Rep, para 74.

[19] *North Sea Continental Shelf Cases* (1969) ICJ Rep, para 74. The phrase 'constant and uniform' was used by the ICJ in the *Asylum Case (Colombia v Peru)* (1950) ICJ Rep 266.

[20] On the difficulties in identifying 'State practice', see Kammerhofer, 'Uncertainty in the Formal Sources of International Law: Customary International Law and Some of its Problems' (2004) EJIL 523.

notoriously difficult to identify in practice.[21] It is generally assumed to exist where there is evidence of sufficient State practice, consensus in academic literature or in decisions of international tribunals.[22] It has been aptly described as a necessary requirement because without it 'it would be impossible to determine where habit stopped and law began'.[23]

[1.8] As mentioned above, obligations enshrined in treaties may be embodied in or crystallise into rules of customary international law.[24] In this respect, the view is often expressed in contemporary academic commentary that the prohibitions on torture, slavery, genocide and racial discrimination as expressed in international treaties, for example, have achieved the status of customary international law.[25] However, the question of whether particular treaty-based human rights norms can also be characterised as norms of customary international law has not been entirely free from controversy.[26] Some commentators have queried whether such assertions can validly be made in the face of clear evidence of 'State practice' to the contrary.[27] While such divergent opinion is symptomatic of a wider debate on the sources of customary international law itself[28] – the very existence of such a dialogue emphasises the importance of international treaties as playing the 'most obvious role'[29] in the field of human rights.

Jus cogens

[1.09] Certain rules of treaty law and customary international law are considered to be so fundamental as to be deemed 'peremptory rules of international law', and are otherwise referred to by the use of the Latin phrase, '*jus cogens*'. Article 53 of the

---

[21] See generally, Mendelson, 'The Subjective Element in Customary International Law' (1995) 66 BYIL 177 and Elias, 'The Nature of the Subjective Element in Customary International Law' (1995) 44 ICLQ 501.
[22] Brownlie, *The Rule of Law in International Affairs* (Martinus Nijhoff, 1998), p 21.
[23] Dixon, *Textbook on International Law* (6th edn, OUP, 2007), p 35.
[24] Report of the ILC to the General Assembly of the UN (1950): UN Doc A/1316, para 29: YBILC (1950) vol II, 364 at p 368.
[25] See the range of views set out in Simma and Alston, 'The Sources of Human Rights Law: Custom, Jus Cogens, and General Principles' (1988–1989) 12 Australian Year Book of International Law 82, pp 90–94.
[26] See generally, Simma and Alston, 'The Sources of Human Rights Law: Custom, Jus Cogens, and General Principles' (1988–1989) 12 Australian Year Book of International Law 82.
[27] For an early exponent of this view, see Watson, 'Legal Theory, Efficacy and Validity in the Development of Human Rights Norms in International Law' (1979) Univ Ill L Rev 609. More recently, see Hathaway, The Rights of Refugees under International Law (CUP: 2005) pp 15–39. See, for example, Hathaway, *The Rights of Refugees under International Law* (CUP: 2005), pp 15–39.
[28] For an analysis of recent challenges to the traditional view of the sources of customary international law, see Baker, 'Customary International Law and the 21st Century: Old Challenges and New Debates' (2010) EJIL 173.
[29] Simma and Alston, 'The Sources of Human Rights Law: Custom, Jus Cogens, and General Principles', p 107.

Vienna Convention on the Law of Treaties defines a peremptory rule of international law, or *jus cogens*, as:

> '... a norm accepted and recognised by the international community of States as a whole as a norm from which no derogation is permitted and which can be modified only by a subsequent norm of general international law having the same character'.

Thus, any treaty provision which conflicts with a rule of *jus cogens* is void.[30] Again, the question of whether a rule of international law has attained the status of *jus cogens* is sometimes contentious, but definitive examples that are routinely cited in the field of human rights include the prohibitions on genocide, torture, slavery and racial discrimination.[31]

General principles of law

[1.10] Treaties and customary international law are considered to be the main sources of international law, though over time other sources have been considered to be helpful means of determining rules of international law. One such source is the 'general principles of law' mentioned in art 38 of the Statute of the ICJ. While the exact meaning of the phrase 'general principles of law' is debateable,[32] the 'better' view appears to be that it was intended to include the rules and principles of law common to all legal systems.[33] The reference in the statute was probably included to provide procedural and substantive solutions for the ICJ in seeking to resolve disputes between States where custom or treaty was unable to supply the deficiency.[34] Principles identified by the court and other international tribunals to date have frequently emanated from domestic administrative law, such as the right to be heard by a court before judgment is pronounced[35] and the principle that no one should be a judge in his or her own cause.[36] Such principles are of obvious relevance to human rights protection, and as we shall see, have found expression in later years in international human rights treaties.

Other sources

[1.11] The final sources of international law mentioned in art 38 of the Statute of the ICJ include judicial decisions and 'the teachings of the most highly qualified publicists of the various nations'. As regards 'judicial decisions', these may include decisions of the ICJ itself, other international tribunals, regional tribunals and domestic courts. In regard

---

[30] Vienna Convention 1969, art 53, specifically provides that: 'A treaty is void if, at the time of its conclusion, it conflicts with a peremptory norm of general international law'.
[31] See, for example, the views of Brownlie, *Principles of Public International Law* (Clarendon Press, 1990) p 513; and Cassese, *International Law* (2nd edn, OUP, 2005), pp 202–203 and 394.
[32] Waldock, *General Course on Public International Law* (1962–II) 106 Hague Recueil des Cours.
[33] Dixon, *Textbook on International Law* (6th edn, OUP, 2007), p 41. The reference to 'civilised nations' is anachronistic and is disregarded in contemporary international law.
[34] Wallace, *International Law* (2nd edn, Sweet & Maxwell), pp 21–22.
[35] *US Diplomatic and Consular Staff in Tehran Case (US v Iran)* (1980) ICJ Rep 3.
[36] *Mosul Boundary Case*, PCIJ Rep Ser B, No 12 (1925), p 32.

to the ICJ, it should be remembered that decisions of that Court have no force except between the parties and in respect of the particular case before it.[37] In this respect, therefore, the Court bears no resemblance to a constitutional court and its decisions are not, strictly, to be regarded as 'binding precedent'. Nonetheless, the Court does, in practice, refer to its previous decisions and its judgments have been described as having 'quasi-legislative value'.[38] Certain judgments of the ICJ have been important in determining particular aspects of international human rights law.[39] Likewise, while the International Criminal Court (ICC)[40] is at an embryonic stage, it is likely to produce judgments that will have implications for the development of international human rights law, particularly in the criminal justice field.[41]

[1.12] As regards the 'teachings of the most highly qualified publicists of the various nations', the influence of prominent academics has substantially waned in modern day international law. In its early formation, traditional international law was largely shaped by the writings of jurists like Hugo Grotius.[42] In the present day, the proliferation of scholars in the field has meant that the views of leading academics can often be cited on both sides of a dispute and therefore must be regarded as being of evidential value as opposed to formative sources of international law.[43]

[1.13] Though not specifically mentioned in art 38 of the Statute of the ICJ, the question is often raised whether the actions of international bodies can be regarded as sources of international law. These would include, for example, resolutions of the General

---

[37] Statute of the ICJ, art 59.
[38] See judgment of Judge Azevedo in the *Asylum Case* (1950) ICJ Rep 266.
[39] See, for example, 'Advisory Opinion on Legal Consequences on the Construction of a Wall in the Occupied Palestinian Territory', 9 July 2004, 43 International Legal Materials 1009 (2004) in which the Court held that the International Covenant on Civil and Political Rights (the principal instrument of the United Nations dealing with civil and political rights, discussed in Ch 3, paras **3.25–3.36**) and Ch 7 applied to the conduct of Israel in the Occupied Territories.
[40] The International Criminal Court (ICC) is an independent, permanent court, established by a treaty entitled the Rome Statute of the International Criminal Court: UN General Assembly, *Rome Statute of the International Criminal Court (last amended January 2002)*, 17 July 1998, UN Doc A/CONF 183/9. The Court was set up for the purposes of trying persons accused of the most serious crimes of international concern, namely genocide, crimes against humanity and war crimes. See generally, Schabas, *The International Criminal Court: A Commentary on the Rome Statute* (OUP, 2010); Schabas, *An Introduction to the International Criminal Court* (CUP, 2011); Broomhall, *International Justice and the International Criminal Court: Between Sovereignty and the Rule of Law* (OUP, 2004); and Schiff, *Building the International Criminal Court* (CUP, 2008).
[41] For an analysis of the ICC's judicial practice to date in the realm of fair trial rights, see Croquet, 'The International Criminal Court and the Treatment of Defence Rights: A Mirror of the European Court of Human Rights' Jurisprudence?' (2011) Hum Rts L Rev 91–131.
[42] See generally, Bull, Kingsbury and Roberts, *Hugo Grotius and International Relations* (Oxford Scholarship Online, 2003): http://www.oxfordscholarship.com/oso/public/content/politicalscience/9780198277712/toc.html (last accessed May 2011).
[43] Dixon, *Textbook on International Law* (6th edn, OUP, 2007), p 47.

Assembly of the United Nations, which, as we shall see, is the main political, deliberative organ of that organisation. Resolutions of that body may include 'declarations' on particular aspects of international law. A declaration is not considered binding on States, but its content may often be the forerunner of a treaty in later years. As we shall see, a great number of declarations on human rights matters have been promulgated by the General Assembly, including its most famous instrument, the Universal Declaration of Human Rights.[44] Other international organisations, such as the Council of Europe (COE), the Organization for Security and Cooperation in Europe (OSCE) and the International Labour Organization (ILO) have also promulgated similar non-binding instruments, which frequently deal directly or tangentially with human rights matters. The established view is that while many of these instruments are useful means of determining customary international law, they are not properly regarded as independent sources of law.[45]

THE DOMESTIC EFFECT OF INTERNATIONAL TREATIES

[1.14] Before embarking on an examination of the development of the UN treaty system, it is important to consider first the extent to which the treaties themselves may be relied on in the national legal system for the purposes of human rights litigation. In this respect, it must first be remembered that when a State ratifies or accedes to an international treaty, it is automatically obliged to meet the obligations in the treaty. In the case of human rights treaties, this will require the State to ensure that the rights in question are implemented in its domestic legal system. The treaties are not prescriptive as regards the *method* by which States must implement the rights: States are responsible only for the *results* of that implementation. The focus of this book is on the procedures in the treaties comprising the UN treaty system which impose additional obligations on States to engage with the treaty bodies established therein to monitor domestic implementation of the rights. These procedures are designed to exert external pressure on States to ensure adequate implementation of the rights in the domestic legal system. In this respect, the scheme of the UN human rights treaty system is implicitly based on the principle of subsidiarity,[46] whereby the primary responsibility for implementing the rights rests with the national authorities of the States parties to each treaty. International supervision, as such, is subsidiary to domestic implementation mechanisms.

[1.15] An optimum means of guaranteeing true penetration of the rights in the national legal system is by ensuring that they are enforceable in domestic law.[47] Whether or not

---

[44] See Ch 3, paras **3.06–3.24**.
[45] Dixon, *Textbook on International Law* (6th edn, OUP, 2007), pp 47–49.
[46] The principle of subsidiarity is most typically associated with the framework for the protection of human rights established in the European Convention on Human Rights. See generally, Petzhold, 'The Convention and the Principle of Subsidiarity' in Macdonald et al (eds), *The European System for the Protection of Human Rights* (Martinus Nijhoff, 1993).
[47] A notorious example of the usefulness of calling upon international legal principles to establish a human rights claim in the domestic context is the landmark decision of the US Court of Appeals in the case of *Filartiga v Pena Irala* (630F 2d 876 (1980); 19 ILM 966) (contd.../)

the terms of a treaty are automatically applicable and enforceable in the domestic legal system, however, is a matter which is governed by the particular theoretical approach taken by each State on the matter and ultimately by its domestic law. In this respect, there are two basic approaches: *monism* and *dualism*. Monism posits a unitary concept of law whereby all law, both domestic and international law, is perceived to be part of an integrated system. In States which adopt a monistic approach, international law is often regarded as being automatically 'incorporated' into national law without the need for any domestic enabling act or constitutional referendum.[48] The theory of *dualism*, on the other hand, conceives of international law and domestic law as regulating totally separate spheres. According to the dualist approach, national law regulates the rights and duties of individuals within the State, whereas international law regulates issues on the international plane. Accordingly, in States which operate the dualist system, national courts will not apply a rule of international law directly unless it has first been 'transformed' into national law, ie, integrated into the national legal system by an appropriate legal method such as a constitutional amendment or legislative enactment.[49]

[1.16] In Ireland, the issue of the domestic effect of international law is governed by the Constitution and specifically Articles 15 and 29 thereof. Article 15.2.1° provides that:

'The sole and exclusive power of making laws for the State is hereby vested in the Oireachtas; no other legislative authority has power to make laws for the State'.

Article 29.6 of the Irish Constitution takes a pronounced dualist stance:

'No international agreement shall be part of the domestic law of the State save as may be determined by the Oireachtas'.

It is clear from the terms of Article 29.6 that for an international treaty to be a source of law in the domestic legal context,[50] it must have been specifically transformed into

---

[47] (\...contd) in which the plaintiffs sought to establish liability of a non-US citizen who was living in the US for acts of torture against a family member while he had been a member of the police force in Paraguay. The US Court of Appeals (Second Circuit) held that torture was a recognised crime under international law and in the absence of a congressional enactment, the US courts were bound to apply international law as part of the law of the land. The family was awarded substantial compensation.

[48] Examples of States which adopt a monist approach where treaties are regarded as automatically forming part of national law include Brazil, Colombia, the Czech Republic, Egypt, Estonia, Iran, Japan, the Philippines, Romania, Russia, Senegal and Spain. See Heyns and Viljoen in *The Impact of the United Nations Human Rights Treaties on the Domestic Level* (Kluwer Law International, 2002), p 7.

[49] Dixon, *Textbook on International Law* (6th edn, OUP, 2007), p 95. Domestic courts may still refer to provisions of international law as a *guide* to interpreting domestic standards – giving rise to a process by which international human rights standards can be viewed as '... building blocks in the construction of domestic rights regimes': Lord and Stein, 'The Domestic Incorporation of Human Rights Law and the United Nations Convention on the Rights of Persons with Disabilities' (2008) 83 U Wash L Rev 449 at 474.

[50] It should be noted that matters are somewhat different in respect of the incorporation of customary international law into Irish domestic law. See Symmons, 'The Incorporation of Customary International Law into Irish Law' in Biehler, *International Law in Practice: An Irish Perspective* (Thomson Round Hall, 2005), pp 111–152.

domestic law by legislative enactment or by a constitutional amendment.[51] This means that, as a rule, judges will not entertain arguments based on the provisions of an international treaty unless it is part of domestic law.[52] While the rights enshrined in the European Convention on Human Rights have been enacted into domestic law and given limited effect by the terms of the European Convention on Human Rights Act 2003,[53] successive Irish governments have been notoriously reluctant to countenance blanket incorporation of the core United Nations human rights treaties.[54] This reluctance is based on the argument that the substantive rights in the treaties are already implemented adequately in national law through the fundamental rights guarantees in the Constitution as well through legislation and administrative action.[55] Such a blanket position necessarily lessens the impact of the treaties on the national legal system, leaving room

---

[51] Other countries which adopt a dualist approach to international treaties include Australia, Canada, Finland, India, South Africa and Zambia: Heyns and Viljoen in *The Impact of the United Nations Human Rights Treaties on the Domestic Level* (Kluwer Law International, 2002), p 8. The same is true as regards the United Kingdom: See Dixon, *Textbook on International Law* (6th edn, OUP, 2007) pp 97–104. Although Article 6 of the US Constitution provides that all treaties made or which shall be made under the authority of the US shall be the supreme law of the land, the US in fact takes a dualistic approach in respect of treaties whereby a distinction (regarded as controversial, particularly in its application to human rights treaties) is made between self-executing treaties and non-self executing treaties: See: Louis Henkin, 'US Ratification of Human Rights Conventions: The Ghost of Senator Bricker' (1995) 89 AJIL 341; CM Vazquez, 'The Four Doctrines of Self-Executing Treaties' (1995) 89 AJIL 965 and CA Bradley, 'The United States and Human Rights Treaties: Race Relations, the Cold War, and Constitutionalism' (2010) 9 Chinese Journal of International Law 321.

[52] Nonetheless, it is possible to cite an unincorporated international treaty provision in an Irish court in limited circumstances, for instance, as evidence of the existence of a claimed unenumerated right in the Irish Constitution. For example, in the case of *The State (Healy) v Donoghue* [1976] IR 325 (decided prior to the enactment of the ECHR Act 2003), the fact that the ECHR guaranteed the right to free legal assistance appears to have been taken as evidence that a similar right is protected by the Irish Constitution.

[53] See generally, Egan, 'The European Convention on Human Rights Act 2003: A Missed Opportunity for Domestic Human Rights Litigation' (2004) DULJ 248; O'Connell, 'Watched Kettles Boil (Slowly): The Impact of the ECHR Act 2003' in Kilkelly (ed), *ECHR & Irish Law* (2nd edn, Jordans, 2009), pp 1–20; 'The Added Value of Sub-Constitutional Incorporation: ECHR Act 2003' in Carolan and Doyle (eds), *The Irish Constitution: Governance & Values*, (Thomson Round Hall, 2008), pp 490–506; and de Londras and Kelly, *The European Convention on Human Rights Act: Operation, Impact and Analysis* (Round Hall/Thomson Reuters, 2010).

[54] The only UN human rights treaty to have been specifically transformed into domestic law is the Convention Against Torture and other Cruel, Inhuman or Degrading Treatment or Punishment (see Ch 3, paras **3.73–3.80**) by means of the Criminal Justice (United Nations Convention Against Torture) Act 2000.

[55] See, for example, Written Replies by the Government of Ireland concerning the List of Issues (CCPR/C/IRL/Q/3) to be taken up in connection with the consideration of the Third Periodic Report of Ireland under the International Covenant on Civil and Political Rights: UN Doc CCPR/C/IRL/3/Add 1, Issue 1, p 2.

for lacunae in rights' protection in a number of instances. At the same time, it shifts attention to the international stage and emphasises the importance of a muscular international system of supervision and implementation.

THE PRINCIPLE OF STATE SOVEREIGNTY

[1.17] Before embarking on a critical analysis of the procedures by which human rights are implemented at the international level, it is important to set these in context by recalling the unexpected 'birth' of human rights concepts into the domain of international law. Traditional international law had no interest in the area of human rights. While concepts of individual liberty and rights were being articulated by seventeenth and eighteenth century European philosophers,[56] and finding expression in the constitutional documents that emerged from the English, French and American revolutions,[57] human rights at that time were not regarded as a subject of international concern. Individuals were regarded as 'objects' of international law, in the same manner as 'beasts, fish and fowl'.[58] They did not have any locus standi under international law because they were considered to be incapable of holding rights and duties under it. They were beneficiaries of international law only because of their membership in the State.[59]

[1.18] A key principle underpinning the corpus of international law precluded the very notion of human rights being the subject of international concern, namely, the principle of State sovereignty. Sieghart succinctly summarises the principle as one '... which reserves to each sovereign State the exclusive right to take any action it thinks fit, provided only that the action does not interfere with the rights of other States and is not prohibited by international law on that or any other ground'. The net effect of this principle, at its most extreme, means that each State has total freedom in dealing with its own nationals ('personal sovereignty') as well as in dealing with its own territory ('territorial sovereignty').[60]

[1.19] A 'necessary corollary' to the principle of State sovereignty is the *rule of non-intervention*.[61] Simply stated, this rule provides that in all matters falling within the

---

[56] See further Ch 3, paras **3.16**.
[57] Davidson, *Human Rights* (Open University Press, 1993), pp 2–6.
[58] 'Lack of international personality is the common characteristic of all objects of international law. In all other respects they may be of the most disparate character: individuals, tribes, nations, cars, trains, ships, aircraft, land, lakes, rivers, seas, beasts, fish and fowl': Schwarzenberger, *A Manual of International Law* (5th edn, Stevens and Sons, 1967), p 120.
[59] Writing in 1934, Fenwick, *International Law* (2nd edn, Appleton-Century, 1934), at p 87 explained the position of individuals in international law in the following terms: '... [I]ndividuals ... are not 'subjects', but merely 'objects' of international law. Their apparent international rights and duties are merely the rights and duties of their respective governments to assert claims on their behalf or to address wrongs arising indirectly from their conduct. Strictly speaking, international law as it exists today, knows only the state of which such individuals are nationals and will protect through their rights or punish their acts only through the interposition of their state'.
[60] Sieghart, *The International Law of Human Rights* (OUP, 1983), p 11.
[61] Davidson, *Human Rights* (OUP, 1993), p 48.

domestic jurisdiction of any State, traditional international law did not permit *any* intervention by another State.[62] As long as a matter fell within the domestic jurisdiction of a State '... a State's own citizens were almost completely at its mercy, and international law had little to say about mistreatment of persons by their own government'.[63] Indeed, the ability of a State to control jurisdiction over its own citizens and its own territory without intervention from other States is one that has been jealously guarded by States for centuries. It was (and still is to a large extent) a major obstacle in the development of an effective body of international human rights law.

DEVELOPMENT OF INTERNATIONAL HUMAN RIGHTS LAW[64]

[1.20] Historically, there were a number of discrete exceptions to the doctrine of State sovereignty which perhaps presaged an enhanced status for individuals in the realm of international law. For example, citizens of a foreign State (formerly referred to as 'aliens') were always entitled to the protection of their nation State when travelling abroad. Hence, if a foreign national was injured on the territory of another State, her State of nationality would have a right to intervene to find out why.[65] Treaties banning the slave trade and slavery, concluded in the nineteenth and twentieth centuries,[66] are often mentioned as examples of exceptions to the harshness of the doctrine of sovereignty. Another example is the response of the international community to certain linguistic and ethnic minorities who, as a result of the territorial settlements concluded in the wake of the First World War, found themselves marginalised in the territory of a foreign State. The Minorities Treaties of 1919 allowed members of the Council of the League of Nations to intervene if the foreign State mistreated those minorities and to bring violations of the treaty to the attention of the Council.[67] The establishment of the International Labour Organization (ILO) in 1919 also evinced an indication of the shifting concern in international law towards the rights of individuals. It came into effect at the end of First World War with the intention of formulating human rights standards in the field of labour. Many conventions relating to conditions of work and health and safety have been elaborated since then under the auspices of this organisation.[68]

---

[62] Sieghart, *The International Law of Human Rights* (OUP, 1983), p 11.
[63] Sohn, 'The New International Law: Protection of the Rights of Individuals Rather Than States' (1983) 32 Am UL Rev 1 at 9.
[64] See generally, Buergenthal, 'The Evolving International Human Rights System' (2007) 100 Am J Int'l L 783.
[65] See Sieghart, *The International Law of Human Rights* (OUP, 1983), pp 11–12.
[66] See Smith, *Textbook on International Human Rights Law* (3rd edn, OUP, 2007), p 14.
[67] See generally, Brownlie, *Principles of Public International Law* (Clarendon Press, 1990), pp 569–571.
[68] The ILO was founded in 1919 as part of the Treaty of Versailles to reflect the belief that universal and lasting peace can only be accomplished if it is based on social justice and the decent treatment of working people. It became the first specialised agency of the United Nations in 1946: www.ilo.org (last accessed May 2011).)

[1.21] While these exceptions existed, it remained the case until the middle of the twentieth century that international law did not concern itself with the problems of citizens *within* particular States. Rather, it was more concerned instead with regulating affairs *between* States. It was only after the full nature of the atrocities committed during the Second World War came to light that the full implications of an unfettered application of the principle of State sovereignty become apparent.[69] In the aftermath of the war, there was mounting pressure on the international community of States to establish recognition and protection of the fundamental and inalienable rights of all human beings at the international level.[70]

[1.22] The first step towards a coherent body of international human rights law was taken at a conference in San Francisco in 1945 when governments gathered together to draft the United Nations Charter.[71] Signed in 1945, the Charter establishes the United Nations (UN) as an inter-governmental organisation whose primary *raison d'être* was to provide a structure for collective security among States in the event of potential conflict. The value of human rights protection as an integral aspect of that objective is reflected in the text of the Preamble which states the aim of the signatories 'to save succeeding generations from the scourge of war ... and to reaffirm faith in fundamental human rights'. Further concessions to the notion of human rights are peppered throughout the document. Article 1(3) lists the promotion and encouragement of respect for human rights and for fundamental freedoms for all among the main purposes of the organisation. Article 56 provides that all members *pledge* to cooperate with the organisation for the achievement of the purposes set forth in art 55. Article 55, in turn, lists a number of purposes, including that of promoting 'universal respect for, and observance of human rights and fundamental freedoms for all without distinction as to race, sex, language, or religion' as mentioned in art 1.[72]

---

[69] 'Many of those atrocities were committed with complete legality under National Socialist legislation: the domestic law authorized, and paralleled, the pernicious injustice of the acts ... According to the strict doctrine of national sovereignty, any foreign criticism of those laws was therefore formally illegitimate; according to the strict positivist position, it was also meaningless': Sieghart, *The International Law of Human Rights* (OUP, 1983), p 14.

[70] At that time it was also formally recognised by States that individuals could in certain circumstances be subject to duties under international law. At the Nuremberg war crimes trial, 22 defendants were indicted before the International Military Tribunal and charged with crimes against humanity. They were held accountable as individuals under international law for committing acts in violation of the laws of war. The Tribunal held that crimes against international law could be committed by individuals: Sohn, 'The New International Law: Protection of the Rights of Individuals Rather Than States' (1982) 32 Am UL Rev 1 at pp 9–11.

[71] Charter of the United Nations, 26 June 1945, 59 Stat. 1031, TS No 993.

[72] See generally, Humphrey, 'The United Nations Charter and the Universal Declaration of Human Rights' in Luard, *The International Protection of Human Rights* (Praeger, 1967), p 39. Acute differences of view emerged in academic discourse on the Charter soon after it was drafted on the precise nature of the legal obligations assumed by States in regard to human rights, having regard to the use of the word 'pledge' in art 56 of the Charter. (contd.../)

[1.23] However, the Charter made little mention about the implementation of human rights, nor did it identify the rights which the international community deemed worthy of protection. Indeed, art 2(7) preserves the principle of State sovereignty and the rule of non-intervention by providing explicitly that the UN is not entitled to intervene in the domestic affairs of any State unless the Security Council[73] determines an interference to be necessary due to a threatened breach of the peace.[74] Nonetheless, the Charter was a crucial step in the development of a body of international human rights law.[75] As Lauren has observed, since its inception, the world has experienced an 'explosion of instruments, procedures, declarations and decisions designed to confront the global issue of basic human rights'.[76] The bulwark of this continuously evolving scheme resides in the United Nations treaty system which through the elaboration of substantive rights and procedures provides a set of standards and benchmarks through which State conduct on human rights can be measured. While this book focuses on the procedures established by these treaties to monitor implementation, it is important to bear in mind that the treaty system thus rests alongside a plethora of other 'extra-conventional' mechanisms established by the United Nations since 1945 aimed at promoting and protecting human rights. These include a broad range of procedures operated under the auspices of the newly established Human Rights Council, referred to in Ch 2.

---

[72] (\...contd) See, for example, Hudson, 'Integrity of International Instruments' (1948) 42 AJIL 105. Compare: Lauterpacht, *International Law of Human Rights* (Archon Books, 1968), pp 147–148 who argues that there is a distinct level of legal duty in the language of arts 55 and 56.

[73] The Security Council is one of the principal organs of the United Nations established by art 7 of the Charter. It is composed of 15 members of the United Nations, five of whom are permanent Members (China, France, Russia, the United Kingdom and the United States of America). Article 24 sets out, in broad terms, the primary responsibility of this institution as being '... the maintenance of international peace and security'. The Security Council's most robust powers are provided for in Chapter VII of the Charter, art 39 of which provides that whenever the Security Council determines the existence of any 'threat to the peace, breach of the peace, or act of aggression', it shall make recommendations or decide what measures shall be taken in accordance with arts 41 and 42 of the Charter, to maintain or restore international peace and security. Under art 41, the Council may decide that measures *not* involving the use of force should be employed by the Member States, including the partial or complete imposition of economic sanctions and the severance of diplomatic relations. At the most extreme end of the scale, art 42 provides that where the latter measures are considered to be inadequate or have proved to be inadequate, the Security Council may decide to take such armed action as may be necessary to maintain or restore international peace and security.

[74] Article 2(7) provides that: 'Nothing in the present Charter shall authorize the United Nations to intervene in matters which are essentially within the domestic jurisdiction of any State or shall require the Members to submit such matters to settlement under the present Charter; but this principle shall not prejudice the application of enforcement measures under Chapter VII'.

[75] Though conscious of the many compromises incorporated in the document, Cassese rightly regards the UN Charter as the 'turning point' in the development of an international law of human rights: Casses, *International Law* (2nd edn, OUP, 2005), pp 377–379.

[76] Lauren, 'First Principles of Racial Equality: History and the Politics and Diplomacy of Human Rights Provisions in the United Nations Charter' (1983) HRQ 1 at 25.

[1.24] Of course, it must also be remembered that the universal system is further supplemented by regional systems of human rights protection which have evolved principally in Europe, Africa and the Americas.[77] The UN Charter expressly provided in art 52 that nothing in the Charter precludes the creation of regional arrangements as long as they are consistent with the purposes and principles of the UN. The development of an autonomous response to human rights issues within each of these regions was prompted by particular historical and political factors[78] which in turn contributed to more cohesive normative and procedural frameworks. While political, socio-economic or cultural values and goals may not exactly be uniform in a given region, there was at least more of a basis for agreement on the substance of the rights to be protected and the manner in which they should be given protection, than might be said to exist at the global level.[79]

[1.25] The Council of Europe was the first organisation to attempt to tackle the issue of human rights at the regional level.[80] The Council is an organisation of some 47 Member States which seeks to promote human rights, pluralist democracy and the rule of law through inter-governmental and parliamentary cooperation.[81] Its most important contribution to the protection of human rights has been the European Convention on Human Rights (ECHR) which came into force in 1951.[82] Aptly termed as the 'jewel in the crown' of the Council of Europe,[83] the ECHR provides a template of basic civil and

---

[77] See generally, Shelton, *Regional Protection of Human Rights* (OUP, 2007), p 16; and Rehman, *International Human Rights Law* (Pearson, 2010), pp 181–397

[78] Shelton, 'The Promise of Regional Human Rights Systems' in Weston and Marks (eds), *The Future of International Human Rights* (Transnational Press, 2000) cited in Shelton, *Regional Protection of Human Rights* (OUP, 2007), p 16.

[79] See generally, Weston, Lukes and Hnatt, 'Regional Human Rights Regimes: A Comparison and Appraisal' (1987) Va J of Transnatl L 585.

[80] See generally Weston, Lukes and Hnatt, 'Regional Human Rights Regimes: A Comparison and Appraisal' (1987) Va J of Transnatl L 585 and the Council of Europe website: http://www.coe.int/lportal/web/coe-portal (last accessed May 2011).

[81] The Statute of the Council of Europe which created the organisation, signed in 1949, provides that the maintenance and realisation of human rights and fundamental freedoms were to be among the aims of the Council in achieving greater unity among its members (art 1(b)): ETS 1/6/7/8/11 http://conventions.coe.int/Treaty/en/Treaties/Word/001.doc (last accessed May 2011). See generally, Huber, *A Decade which Made History: The Council of Europe 1989–1999* (COE Publishing, 1999).

[82] The ECHR is complemented by a range of other human rights treaties promulgated by the Council of Europe: see generally: http://www.coe.int/lportal/web/coe-portal/home (last accessed May 2011). These include the *The European Social Charter (Revised)* which guarantees a range of social and economic rights, albeit with less muscular implementation machinery: Council of Europe, *European Social Charter (Revised)*, 3 May 1996, ETS 163, available at: http://conventions.coe.int/Treaty/Commun/QueVoulezVous.asp?NT=163&CM=1&DF=&CL=ENG (last accessed May 2011). See generally, Harris and Darcy, *The European Social Charter* (Transnational Publishers, 2001).

[83] Lalumière, 'Human Rights in Europe: Challenges for the Next Millennium' in Macdonald, Matscher and Petzold (eds), *The European System for the Protection of Human Rights* (Martinus Nijhoff, 1993), p xv.

political rights as well as finely-tuned institutional machinery designed to ensure their enforcement by the contracting States.[84] The powerhouse of that machinery is the European Court of Human Rights which has jurisdiction under the Convention to interpret and apply the substantive rights set forth therein in contentious cases coming before it.[85] The Council of Europe human rights machinery is further supplemented by human rights initiatives adopted by the Organization for Security and Cooperation in Europe (OSCE)[86] and the European Union (EU).[87]

[1.26] Another comparable regional mechanism for the protection of human rights is the one established in the Americas under the auspices of the Organization of American States (OAS).[88] Composed of some 35 Member States, the aims of the OAS include that of strengthening democracy, promoting human rights, and confronting shared problems such as poverty, terrorism, illegal drugs and corruption.[89] It has moved to protect human rights principally through the American Convention on Human Rights 1969 and the OAS Charter System.[90] Of more recent vintage is the scheme adopted by the African

---

[84] For a detailed analysis of the ECHR and the jurisprudence of the Court, see Harris, O'Boyle, Warbrick, Bates and Buckley, *Law of the European Convention on Human Rights* (2nd edn, OUP, 2009); and Jacobs, White and Ovey, *The European Convention on Human Rights* (5th edn, OUP, 2010). See generally the website of the Council of Europe dedicated to the ECHR: http://human-rights-convention.org/ (last accessed May 2011).

[85] On the development of the Court since its establishment, see Bates, *The Evolution of the European Court of Human Rights: From its Inception to the Creation of a Permanent Court of Human Rights* (OUP, 2010). See generally the website of the European Court of Human Rights: http://www.echr.coe.int/echr/homepage_EN (last accessed May 2011).

[86] The OSCE is the successor of the CSCE which was formally established in 1975 following the signing by 35 nations of the Helsinki Final Act. Intended to serve as a multilateral forum for dialogue and negotiation between East and West, the organisation has since grown to 56 States. Respect for human rights forms a key component of the activities of the organisation. See generally: http://www.osce.org/what/human-rights (last accessed May 2011).

[87] The EU's evolving competence in the field of human rights has culminated recently in the entry into force of the Treaty of Lisbon in 2009 which gave legal effect to the Charter of Fundamental Rights of the European Union: 7 December 2000, ([2000 OJ C364/01), available at: http://www.unhcr.org/refworld/docid/3ae6b3b70.html (last accessed May 2011). See generally http://www.europarl.europa.eu/charter/default_en.htm (last accessed May 2011). The Charter obliges the institutions of the EU (the EU Commission, the European Council and the Parliament) to legislate consistently with the catalogue of civil, political, economic and social rights enshrined therein. It also allows the European Court of Justice to strike down EU legislation which contravenes the provisions of the Charter. See generally, Rehman, *International Human Rights Law* (2nd edn, Pearson, 2010), p 256–261.

[88] See generally Harris and Livingstone (eds), *The Inter-American System of Human Rights* (CUP, 1998); and Buergenthal and Shelton, *Protecting Human Rights in the Americas: Cases and Materials* (4th edn, Engel, 1995).

[89] The purposes and principles of the OAS are set forth in Chapters 1 and II of the Charter of the OAS, signed in Bogotá in 1948 and amended by the Protocol of Buenos Aires in 1967, by the Protocol of Cartagena de Indias in 1985, by the Protocol of Washington in 1992, and by the Protocol of Managua in 1993. See generally: http://www.oas.org/ (last accessed May 2011).

[90] See Shelton, *Regional Protection of Human Rights* (OUP, 2010), pp 70–85; and Rehman, *International Human Rights Law* (Pearson, 2010), pp 271–304.

Union for protecting human rights through the vehicle of the African Charter on Human and Peoples' Rights 1981;[91] and that which has been adopted in the revised Arab Charter on Human Rights adopted by the Council of the League of Arab States in 2004.[92]

[1.27] The positive note to strike as regards the huge developments in the field of international human rights protection over the decades since the UN Charter was drafted is that the treaties, procedures and monitoring bodies generated in its wake all provide a means of holding governments accountable at the international level for the treatment of anyone under their jurisdiction.[93] Though undoubtedly imperfect, as we shall see, at the very least they have provided a means for exerting pressure on governments 'in a way that was unthinkable before 1945'.[94] At the same time, it is important at the outset to grasp the inherent limitations of this body of law. In the first place, attempts to forge a universal body of substantive law have been plagued by divergent conceptions of human rights as between nation States as well as amongst different cultural communities. The increasing 'privatisation' of human rights abuses, whereby the actors are not necessarily governments, but private parties or groups of individuals, has simultaneously posed new challenges to the reach of substantive law, as well as threatening the traditional foundations on which it rests.[95]

[1.28] Perhaps the most powerful exposition of the limitations of the international human rights regime to affect change in the lives of oppressed individuals is that made by Watson over 30 years ago. He essentially argues that international law is necessarily

---

[91] See Evans and Murray (eds), *The African Charter on Human and Peoples' Rights: The System in Practice, 1986–2006* (CUP, 2008); Shelton, *Regional Protection of Human Rights* (OUP, USA) pp 85–90; Rehman, *International Human Rights Law* (Pearson, 2010), pp 305351and see generally: http://www.africa-union.org/ (last accessed May 2011).

[92] Reprinted in (2005) 12 Int'l Hum Rts Reports 893. See generally Rishmawi, 'The Revised Arab Charter on Human Rights: a Step Forward?' (2005) Hum Rts L Rev 361–376 and 'The Arab Charter on Human Rights and the League of Arab States: An Update' (2010) Hum Rts L Rev 169–178. See also, Rehman, *International Human Rights Law* (Pearson, 2010), pp 377–384.

[93] 'The concept of accountability provides the overarching rationale for the establishment of an international human rights regime': Alston, 'Richard Lillich Memorial Lecture: Promoting the Accountability of Members of the New UN Human Rights Council' (2005) 15 J Transnat'l L & Pol'y 49 at 50.

[94] Dorr, 'An Introduction to Developments in Human Rights Since 1945' in Heffernan (ed), *Human Rights: A European Perspective* (1994) at 15. Cassese has commented in even stronger terms that 'Today the human rights doctrine forces States to give account of how they treat their nationals, administer justice, run prisons, and so on. Potentially, therefore, it can subvert their domestic order and, consequently, the traditional configuration of the international community as well': *International Law* (OUP, 2005) at 375.

[95] See generally, Clapham, *Human Rights Obligations of Non-State Actors* (OUP, 2007); and Weissbrodt, 'Non-State Entities and Human Rights within the Context of the Nation-State in the 21st Century' in Castermans-Holleman, Smith, van Hoof and Baehr, (eds), *The Role of the Nation State in the 21st Century: Essays in Honour of Peter Baehr* (Martinus Nijhoff, 1998) 163 at pp 174–195.

limited in regard to human rights for the reason that the States which compose it simply have no appetite or incentive to implement an effective regime of rights protection.[96] Indeed, there is no escaping the reality that of its very nature, international human rights law is limited by the reluctance of States to cede their sovereign prerogative to regulate and protect human rights in their own territory. This reluctance is amply reflected in the weakness of the implementation mechanisms that are examined throughout the remainder of this book. The challenge for any student, practitioner, advocate or interested observer of these procedures is to reach a critical understanding of their capacity to affect meaningful change in the lives of oppressed individuals, having due regard to their intrinsic limitations.

---

[96] Watson, 'Legal Theory, Efficacy and Validity in the Development of Human Rights Norms in International Law' (1979) Univ Ill L Rev 609 at 619.

Chapter 2

The United Nations and Human Rights: Institutions and Structure

INTRODUCTION

[2.01] As noted in the previous chapter, international human rights law has evolved, principally since the end of the Second World War, as a challenge to the principle of State sovereignty. In addition to the substantive references to human rights in the UN Charter, that document also provided the foundations for the development of several institutions through which human rights would be promoted and protected. In many ways, it is the emergence of these *institutions* through which the human rights standards in the treaties have been developed and promoted that has posed the most radical threat to State sovereignty. Their evolution within the structure of the United Nations (UN) was completely new; nation States had simply no comparators for their construction. While in some cases, as we shall see, the results were disappointing, in the context within which they emerged initially, they are nothing short of impressive. As we shall see, the institutional structure for the protection of human rights has been significantly altered recently, with the establishment of a new organ, the Human Rights Council by the UN in 2006. To this extent, the UN is thus embarking on a new phase in terms of the operation of its human rights agenda. This chapter seeks to set the UN treaty system in context by tracing the history, growth and development of each of the UN organs that has thus far contributed to its development.

THE GENERAL ASSEMBLY

[2.02] The General Assembly (GA) is the main plenary organ of the United Nations. It is also the most representative body of the organisation, consisting as it does of all the Member States[1] (currently 193), each of which has an equal vote.[2] Its functions, powers, voting and procedures are enumerated in Chapter IV of the UN Charter.

[2.03] Technically, the Assembly is the most powerful body in the UN in regard to human rights for three distinct reasons. First, the UN Charter vests it with original jurisdiction in regard to human rights. Article 10 empowers it to discuss any questions or any matters within the scope of the Charter and to make recommendations to the Member States or to the Security Council,[3] while art 13(1)(b) sets out its specific

---

[1] Charter of the United Nations, art 9, 26 June 1945, 59 Stat 1031, TS No 993: http://www.un.org/aboutun/charter/ (last accessed May 2011).
[2] UN Charter, art 18.
[3] See Ch 1, para **1.23**.

functions in relation to human rights. These are to initiate studies and make recommendations for the purposes of promoting international co-operation in the economic, social and cultural, educational, and health fields and assisting in the realisation of human rights and fundamental freedoms for all without distinction as to race, sex, language, or religion. As has been previously noted, these responsibilities are further augmented by the terms of arts 55 and 56 of the Charter which enjoin the UN to promote, *inter alia*, universal respect for, and observance of, human rights and fundamental freedoms for all without distinction. Member States must pledge themselves to take joint and separate action for the achievement of this purpose, and responsibility for discharging this function is vested in the General Assembly.[4] Article 14 of the Charter is also of relevance here insofar as it authorises the GA to 'recommend measures for the peaceful adjustment of any situation, regardless of origin, which it deems likely to impair the general welfare or friendly relations among nations', including situations resulting from a violation of the provisions of the Charter which set forth the purposes and principles of the UN. Since the latter provisions specifically mention 'human rights', this article clearly covers the making of recommendations in cases where a failure to protect human rights leads to the potential impairment of the general welfare or friendly relations between States.[5] The second reason for the General Assembly's technical prominence in regard to human rights is because all of the other UN organs report directly to the General Assembly.[6] Thirdly, by virtue of its overall budgetary control of the organisation, the Assembly can veto decisions or programmes agreed to by the other bodies,[7] including those dealing specifically with human rights.

[2.04] The GA also has authority to create subsidiary bodies for any purpose enumerated or implied in the UN Charter,[8] which has included the recently established Human Rights Council.[9] Most of the actions taken by the GA plenary begin with a discussion by a committee of initiatives taken by one of the subsidiary bodies. The GA currently has six 'main' committees.[10] The Third Committee (Social, Humanitarian and Cultural) is normally the starting place for discussion of human rights matters.[11] Since each of the six main committees consists of all members of the UN, all members of the

---

[4] Ch 1, see text accompanying para **1.22**.
[5] Humphrey, *No Distant Millennium: The International Law of Human Rights* (UNESCO, 1989), p 74.
[6] UN Charter, art 15.
[7] UN Charter, art 17.
[8] UN Charter, art 22.
[9] See further para **2.26–2.35** below.
[10] The First Committee: Disarmament and International Security (DISEC); The Second Committee: Economic and Finance (ECOFIN); the Third Committee: Social, Humanitarian and Cultural (SOCHUM); the Fourth Committee: Special Political and Decolonization (SPECPOL); the Fifth Committee: Administrative and Budgetary; and the Sixth Committee: Legal.
[11] See Quinn, 'The General Assembly into the 1990s' in Alston (ed), *The United Nations and Human Rights: A Critical Appraisal* (OUP, 1992), pp 60–65.

organisation have an opportunity to contribute to such discussions at an early stage.[12] Initially, art 2(7) of the Charter presented a potential impediment to the General Assembly's work. As noted in Ch 1, the latter provided that the UN should not 'intervene' in the domestic affairs of any State, save in situations where the Security Council has determined the existence of a threat to international peace and security.[13] Analysis of the *travaux preparatoires* to the Charter has revealed the intention of the framers that art 2(7) should prohibit the General Assembly from discussing matters falling within the domestic affairs of any State.[14] However, as Cassese points out, no bright lines or 'measuring rods' were supplied to delineate when a discussion might actually constitute intervention in the domestic affairs of a State.[15] In the result, the position of the Assembly in regard to art 2(7) has gradually evolved over time from the early days in which it only regarded itself as free to pass judgment on the human rights situation in a particular State where there was a danger that friendly relations between States might be impaired; to the present day, when the General Assembly no longer regards 'discussion' of a State's human rights record to constitute 'intervention' in domestic affairs in cases of violations of recognised human rights standards.[16] The shift in attitude took place mainly as a result of the increased influence of developing countries from the mid-1960s which had begun to fashion a particular agenda of their own, which included placing emphasis on problems such as apartheid and economic development.[17] Against this backdrop, the Assembly not only involved itself in drafting and approving international human rights declarations and treaties, but also began to pass resolutions regarding violations of human rights in specific States without any

---

[12] Alleged violations of human rights have also been routed to one of the Assembly's special committees. The latter are ad hoc committees which are established by the GA pursuant to its powers under art 7 of the Charter to set up subordinate organs. Examples of such committees include the Special Committee to Investigate Israeli Practices affecting the Human Rights of the Population of the Occupied Territories which was set up in 1968 (http://www.un.org/ga/committees.shtml) (last accessed May 2011); and the Special Committee on the Situation with Regard to the Implementation of the Declaration on the Granting of Independence to Colonial Countries and Peoples which is still in operation since 1961: (http://www.un.org/Depts/dpi/decolonization/index.html) (last accessed May 2011).

[13] Ch 1, para, **1.23**.

[14] Cassese, 'The General Assembly: Historical Perspective 1945–1989' in Alston (ed), *The United Nations and Human Rights: A Critical Appraisal* (OUP, 1992), p 27. According to Cassese, the use of the word 'essentially' as opposed to 'exclusively' in art 2(7) was apparently deliberately chosen so as to increase the discretion of States as regards what lay within their domestic affairs.

[15] Cassese, 'The General Assembly: Historical Perspective 1945–1989' in Alston (ed), *The United Nations and Human Rights: A Critical Appraisal* (OUP, 1992), p 28.

[16] Cassese traces the political evolution of the General Assembly's position in regard to Article 2(7) in-depth: Cassese, 'The General Assembly: Historical Perspective 1945–1989' in Alston (ed), *The United Nations and Human Rights: A Critical Appraisal* (OUP, 1992), pp 32–46.

[17] Cassese, 'The General Assembly: Historical Perspective 1945–1989' in Alston (ed), *The United Nations and Human Rights: A Critical Appraisal* (OUP, 1992), pp 40–46.

requirement that such situations would be likely to impair friendly relations between States.[18]

[2.05] In terms of the content of this book, the important role of the GA in elaborating international treaties must be acknowledged. While much of the preparatory work for these may be done by one of the subsidiary organs or by one of the Assembly's committees, the Assembly acts as the 'final arbiter' in approving (and occasionally re-drafting) the texts which are opened for signature, ratification and accession by the Member States.[19] The main substantive human rights treaties opened for signature by the General Assembly are examined in Ch 3. The chapters in Parts 2 and 3 of the book go on to examine the methods by which State implementation of the rights is monitored by the various treaty bodies established for that purpose, all of which report ultimately to the General Assembly.[20] While the GA's level of direct engagement with the work of the treaty bodies has been limited, it exercises significant budgetary control over their work and has begun, in recent years, to play a more prominent role in facilitating initiatives for reform of their operation.[21]

THE ECONOMIC AND SOCIAL COUNCIL (ECOSOC)

[2.06] This body used to serve as the principal organ of the UN in the field of human rights, subject to the ultimate authority of the General Assembly. A glance at the text of the Charter indicates that the drafters certainly envisaged a central role for ECOSOC in the functioning of the United Nations, having established it as one of the principal organs of the organisation.[22] Initially composed of 18 State representatives,[23] its number of seats was augmented in 1963 to 27,[24] and again in 1971 to the current number of 54.[25] ECOSOC's functions and powers are set forth in arts 62 to 66 of the Charter. Article 62 empowers it to 'make or initiate studies and reports with respect to international economic, social, cultural, educational, health and related matters and to make recommendations with respect to such matters to the General Assembly, to the Member States and to the specialized agencies'. Specifically in relation to human rights, art 62(2) provides for ECOSOC '… to make recommendations for the purpose of promoting respect for and observance of human rights and fundamental freedoms for all'. Further,

---

[18] Cassese, 'The General Assembly: Historical Perspective 1945–1989' in Alston (ed), *The United Nations and Human Rights: A Critical Appraisal* (OUP, 1992), pp 44–46.

[19] Quinn, 'The General Assembly into the 1990s' in Alston (ed), *The United Nations and Human Rights: A Critical Appraisal* (OUP, 1992), p 65 and see generally pp 65–68.

[20] Quinn, 'The General Assembly into the 1990s' in Alston (ed), *The United Nations and Human Rights: A Critical Appraisal* (OUP, 1992), pp 68–71.

[21] Quinn, 'The General Assembly into the 1990s' in Alston (ed), *The United Nations and Human Rights: A Critical Appraisal* (OUP, 1992), pp 68–71.

[22] UN Charter, art 7.

[23] The composition of ECOSOC is dealt with in art 61 of the Charter.

[24] GA Res 1991B (XVIII) (1963).

[25] GA Res 2847 (XXVI) (1971). These are elected on an equitable, geographical basis by the General Assembly for a term of three years.

ECOSOC is mandated to prepare draft conventions for submission to the General Assembly,[26] and to call international conferences on matters falling within its competence, which, of course, includes human rights.[27] Articles 63 to 66 provide, *inter alia,* for ECOSOC to coordinate the activities of the specialised agencies;[28] to obtain reports from those agencies and from States on the steps taken to give effect to its own recommendations and relevant ones made by the General Assembly[29] and to report its observations to the General Assembly;[30] and to perform such other functions conferred on it by the General Assembly.[31] Under art 68, ECOSOC was further empowered to set up commissions in the economic and social fields for the protection of human rights. One of the first actions taken by ECOSOC was to establish immediately two subsidiary bodies, namely, the Commission on Human Rights[32] and the Commission on the Status of Women.[33] Over the years, it also appointed various ad hoc Committees and special rapporteurs to help it by preparing reports on technical subjects.

[2.07] The original premise on which ECOSOC was created was that it should be a driving force for decision-making in the economic and social field. The earlier success of the League of Nations in regard to activities of an economic and social nature, as distinct from its political failures, was the catalyst for creating a strong institution in this field within the rubric of the new United Nations organisation.[34] However, this optimistic plan never quite panned out, and as a number of analysts have recorded,[35] ECOSOC is an institution whose influence has substantially diminished over the years, particularly in regard to human rights. While initially active in the early years in taking actions to deal with general human rights problems (most notably, slavery and forced labour),[36] from the mid-1960s onwards, the institution has been effectively sidelined

---

[26] UN Charter, art 62(3).
[27] UN Charter, art 62(4).
[28] UN Charter, art 63(2).
[29] UN Charter, art 64(1).
[30] UN Charter, art 64(2).
[31] UN Charter, art 66.
[32] See further paras **2.10–2.20** below.
[33] The Commission was established by ECOSOC Resolution 11(II) of 21 June 1946 with the a mandate to prepare recommendations and reports for the Council on the promotion of women's rights in the political, economic, civil, social and educational fields. See generally, Reanda, 'The Commission on the Status of Women' in Alston (ed), *The United Nations and Human Rights: A Critical Appraisal* (OUP, 1992), pp. 265–303 and the website of the CSW: http://www.un.org/womenwatch/daw/csw/ (last accessed May 2011).
[34] O'Donovan, 'The Economic and Social Council' in Alston (ed), *The United Nations and Human Rights: A Critical Appraisal* (OUP, 1992), pp 107–108.
[35] O'Donovan, 'The Economic and Social Council' in Alston [(ed)], *The United Nations and Human Rights: A Critical Appraisal* (OUP, 1992), pp 107–108.
[36] O'Donovan, 'The Economic and Social Council' in Alston [(ed)], *The United Nations and Human Rights: A Critical Appraisal* (OUP, 1992), pp 113–114, citing Green, *The United Nations and Human Rights* (Brookings Institution, 1956) p 137, who recounts ECOSOC's success in establishing, with the ILO, a Fact-Finding and (contd.../)

almost completely in regard to its human rights mandate. A number of factors account for this decline. These include, first, the Council's reluctance from the outset to interpret its mandate proactively so as to allow itself and indeed its subsidiary body, the Commission on Human Rights, to take action on individual complaints of human rights abuse. By the time that this policy was reversed in 1967,[37] the Commission had already begun to supersede the Council as the main hub in which issues of human rights were discussed, examined and elaborated.[38] Second, developing countries, which by that stage were in the ascendancy in terms of representation in the UN, had largely turned their attention to the Commission and, indeed, the General Assembly as vehicles for the articulation of concrete policies in the human rights field. The Council was perceived to be a bureaucratic structure which, in the words of one commentator, '... delegated its powers, transferred its functions, and got lost in its own sprawl of activities'.[39] Its diminishing influence in regard to human rights was soon mirrored in regard to its broader mandate in the economic and social field in a similar way, when those activities began to become increasingly devolved to other UN bodies reporting directly to the General Assembly.[40] Structurally, the organ's declining fortunes are evidenced by two further factors: first, the streamlining of its meeting time in 1991 from two regular sessions of four weeks duration to just one four-week session in July of each year; and second, the fact that governments have long since ceased to send high-ranking politicians to represent them at those sessions, opting instead most typically for their permanent representatives in New York or Geneva.[41]

[2.08] There have been several attempts to rescue the fate of ECOSOC over the years by way of reform proposals. At the 2005 World Summit,[42] where representatives of all of the Member States of the UN met to discuss past and future challenges facing the UN, agreement was reached on a way forward for strengthening ECOSOC's existing functions and entrusting it with important new functions. It was agreed that the Council should promote global dialogue, *inter alia*, through the hosting of 'annual ministerial

---

[36] (\...contd) Conciliation Commission on Freedom of Association which was the '... first standing international agency (outside the special fields of minorities, mandates and the trustee system) ever empowered to examine allegations concerning violations of human rights'.

[37] See para **2.16** below, Commission on Human Rights.

[38] See para **2.16–2.18** below. Humphrey describes the role of the Council in relation to the Commission as little more than a 'post-office – that did not always forward the mail' for much of the standard-setting activities of the latter body: Humphrey, *No Distant Millennium: The International Law of Human Rights* (UNESCO, 1989), p 100.

[39] O'Donovan, 'The Economic and Social Council' in Alston (ed), *The United Nations and Human Rights: A Critical Appraisal* (OUP, 1992), p 121.

[40] These include, for example, the United Nations Conference on Trade and Development (UNCTAD): www.UNCTAD.org; and the United Nations Development Fund (UNDP): www.UNDP.org.

[41] O'Donovan, 'The Economic and Social Council' in Alston (ed), *The United Nations and Human Rights: A Critical Appraisal* (OUP, 1992), p 109.

[42] For further details, see http://www.un.org/summit2005 (last accessed May 2011).

substantive reviews' to assess the progress made in the implementation of the outcomes of the major conferences and summits convened by the UN over the past 15 years; and by holding a biennial Development Cooperation Forum to review trends in international development cooperation.[43] In 2006, these outcomes were fortified by the adoption of a Resolution by the General Assembly on the 'Strengthening of the Economic and Social Council', mapping out the manner and means by which these new functions undertaken by ECOSOC should be implemented.[44] The first annual ministerial review (AMR) took place at ECOSOC's annual substantive session, at which the biennial Development Cooperation Forum was also held.[45] It remains to be seen whether this renewed focus for ECOSOC will result in the regeneration of the institution.

[2.09] As far as human rights are concerned, ECOSOC still retains a qualified significance. In particular, it is still the body responsible for accreditation of NGOs who wish to participate in sessions of the Human Rights Council.[46] It still coordinates various different United Nations programmes, including the United Nations Development Programme. It receives annual reports from specialised agencies whose work is of importance to the protection of human rights, such as the United Nations Educational, Scientific and Cultural Organization (UNESCO), the International Labour Organization (ILO) and the World Health Organization (WHO).

THE COMMISSION ON HUMAN RIGHTS

[2.10] The Commission on Human Rights was, for many years, the most dominant, productive[47] and influential institution in the United Nations system in regard to human rights.[48] Though now defunct, having been effectively replaced by the Human Rights Council in 2006, the contribution made by the Commission to standard setting and implementation in the human rights field over the 60 years of its existence cannot be gainsaid. Analysis of the evolution of the Commission over the years, from an institutional point of view, is also of considerable interest. As will be shown, it demonstrates how rapidly a human rights organ can transform itself from a technical institution to a highly politicised body, by means of a determined and gradual reinterpretation of its mandate.

[2.11] The genesis of the Commission on Human Rights can be traced back to the negotiations that took place between Member States of the UN during the drafting of the

---

[43] See, in particular, paragraphs 155 and 156 of the 2005 World Summit Outcome Document, GA Res 60/1, UN Doc A/Res/60/1.
[44] GA Res 61/16, Strengthening the Economic and Social Council: UN Doc A/RES/61/16.
[45] See the official website of ECOSOC: http://www.un.org/ecosoc/(last accessed May 2011).
[46] See paragraph 11 of UN GA Resolution 60/251 establishing the Human Rights Council, UN Doc A/RES/60/251.
[47] Humphrey, *No Distant Millennium: The International Law of Human Rights* (UNESCO, 1989), p 93.
[48] Writing in 1992, Alston described the Commission as the 'single most important United Nations organ in the human rights field': Alston, 'The Commission on Human Rights' in Alston (ed), *The United Nations and Human Rights: A Critical Appraisal* (OUP, 1992), p 126.

UN Charter. One of the clear expectations of the conference which drafted the Charter was that such a Commission would be established and given a mandate immediately to draft an international Bill of Rights.[49] A preparatory commission was convened straight after the conference by the signatory States to make provisional arrangements for the first sessions of the primary organs of the UN.[50] In its report in December 1945,[51] it recommended that ECOSOC should establish a Commission on Human Rights,[52] and that, in general, the functions of the Commission should be to assist the Council in carrying out its responsibility under the Charter to promote human rights.[53] The studies and recommendations of the Commission 'would encourage the acceptance of higher standards ... and help to check and eliminate discrimination and other abuses'.[54] Specifically, the preparatory commission recommended that that the work of the Commission should be directed towards the following objects:

(a) formulation of an international bill of rights;
(b) formulation of recommendations for an international declaration or convention on such matters as civil liberties, status of women, freedom of information;
(c) protection of minorities;
(d) prevention of discrimination on grounds of race, sex, language, or religion; and
(e) any matters falling within the field of human rights considered likely to impair the general welfare or friendly relations among nations.[55]

Two months later, at its very first session in February 1946, ECOSOC established the Commission on Human Rights.[56] Interestingly, in its initial Resolution establishing the Commission, ECOSOC substantially adopted the recommendations of the preparatory commission as regards the mandate of the Commission, save for the matters mentioned in (e) above.[57] Provision was nonetheless made for the Commission in turn to propose to the Council any changes to its terms of reference.[58] The same Resolution provided that

---

[49] For this reason, art 68 was specifically inserted in the Charter, giving ECOSOC authority to set up commissions in the economic and social fields and for the promotion of human rights. See Humphrey, *Human Rights and the United Nations: A Great Adventure* (Transnational Publishers, 1984) p 13. The expectation is also clear from the address of President Harry S Truman of the United States of America, at the closing session of the San Francisco Conference which drafted the UN Charter. See http://www.presidency.ucsb.edu/ws/index.php?pid=12188 (last accessed May 2011).

[50] For the administrative history of the Preparatory Commission of the UN, see http://archives.un.org/unarms/doc/archivalcollections/ag_009.pdf (last accessed May 2011).

[51] Report of the Preparatory Commission of the United Nations, 23 December 1945: UN Doc PC/20.

[52] Report of the Preparatory Commission of the United Nations, para 14.

[53] Report of the Preparatory Commission of the United Nations, para 15.

[54] Report of the Preparatory Commission of the United Nations, para 15.

[55] Report of the Preparatory Commission of the United Nations, para 16.

[56] ECOSOC Res 5(1), 16 February 1946. See http://daccess-dds-ny.un.org/doc/RESOLUTION/GEN/NR0/041/47/IMG/NR004147.pdf?OpenElement (last accessed May 2011).

[57] ECOSOC Res 5(1), s 2.

[58] ECOSOC Res 5(1), para 4.

the Commission should initially meet for a short period as a 'nucleus' of nine members to make recommendations to the Council 'on the definitive composition of the Commission'.[59]

[2.12] This 'nuclear' commission[60] met soon afterwards[61] and issued its report to the second session of ECOSOC in May 1946.[62] In its report, it agreed with the Council's proposed terms of reference for the Commission, but requested that the Council consider adding a clause substantially similar to clause (e), as recommended by the preparatory commission. The nuclear commission explained that this would enable the Commission to deal with any matter not covered by items (a) to (d), such as the 'eventual punishment of certain crimes which must be considered as international, as they constitute an offence against mankind'.[63] As regards the membership of the Commission, the nuclear commission recommended that as ECOSOC was itself elected by the governments in the General Assembly, the Commission on Human Rights, appointed by the Council, should not also consist of governmental representatives. Rather, all members of the definitive Commission on Human Rights should be highly qualified persons who would serve as non-governmental representatives, appointed by the Council from a list of nominees submitted by the Member States.[64]

[2.13] The advice on both fronts was not followed by ECOSOC. Having considered the nuclear commission's report at its second session, ECOSOC decided to approve the original terms of reference, save for the addition of a new sub-paragraph (e).[65] Thus, the functions of the Commission henceforth would be directed towards the:

(a) formulation of an international bill of rights;
(b) formulation of recommendations for an international declaration or convention on such matters as civil liberties, status of women, freedom of information;
(c) protection of minorities;
(d) prevention of discrimination on grounds of race, sex, language, or religion; and
(e) any other matter concerning human rights not covered by items (a), (b), (c) and (d).

---

[59] ECOSOC Res 5(1), para 6.
[60] The nuclear commission consisted of nine individuals who served in a personal capacity, chaired by Eleanor Roosevelt: see Glendon, *A World Made New: Eleanor Roosevelt and the Universal Declaration of Human Rights* (Random House, 2001), pp 30–32.
[61] The meetings of the nuclear commission took place in Hunter College New York from 29 April to 20 May 1946.
[62] Report of the Commission on Human Rights to the Second Session of the Economic and Social Council: UN Doc E/38/Rev 1, 21 May 1946.
[63] Report of the Commission on Human Rights to the Second Session of the Economic and Social Council: UN Doc E/38/Rev 1, s 1.
[64] Report of the Commission on Human Rights to the Second Session of the Economic and Social Council: UN Doc E/38/Rev 1, s 3.
[65] ECOSOC Res 9(II), adopted on 21 June 1946: UN Doc E/56/Rev 1.

As regards the composition of the Commission, ECOSOC decided that it should consist of 18 members of the United Nations, selected by the Council.[66] In other words, ECOSOC opted firmly in favour of governmental representatives rather than individuals acting in a personal capacity.

[2.14] This chronology of events is of interest for two reasons: first, it demonstrates how ECOSOC clearly viewed the Commission as having a low-key role in terms of the promotion and protection of human rights; a mandate that was obviously envisaged to be more oriented towards standard-setting and providing advice to its more powerful parent body on human rights issues. This fact is evidenced by its refusal to endorse a mandate that would give the Commission specific power to deal with breaches of international peace. In fact, as Alston points out, the eventual mandate which it did approve was of a very general character,[67] and as we shall see, ultimately led to an interpretation by the Commission stretching, no doubt, far beyond the original intention of its architects in ECOSOC. Second, the fact that ECOSOC refused to conceive of the Commission as an independent body completely changed the character of the body from the independent version conceived of by the nuclear commission, to a body with an overtly political dimension. There is no doubt but that had it been structured along the lines envisaged by the nuclear commission, there would have been much more chance of it being able to function objectively and without obvious political bias.

[2.15] As matters turned out, the status of the Commissioners as governmental representatives was not a hugely significant issue in the first 20 years of the Commission's life. The Commission's contribution to the promotion and protection of human rights during this phase was largely confined to standard-setting. As is documented in Ch 3, it was the Commission which was at the forefront of drafting the International Bill of Rights, the Convention on the Elimination of All Forms of Racial Discrimination, as well as Declarations on the rights of the child and territorial asylum.[68] Humphrey has noted that, in this context, it was probably a wise move for the Commissioners to be governmental representatives when the primary task was drafting international instruments, since 'there would have been no point in preparing drafts that would not have been acceptable to governments'.[69] Moreover, it seems that the Commission deliberately eschewed taking a more prominent role at this time, perceiving itself to be largely a technical, drafting body, rather than a political one capable of acting

---

[66] ECOSOC Res 9(II), para 2(a).
[67] Alston, 'The Commission on Human Rights' in Alston (ed), *The United Nations and Human Rights: A Critical Appraisal* (OUP, 1992), p 128.
[68] Alston comments that this phase of the Commission's life was not as productive as it might have been. Its preoccupation with the covenants resulted in it being deflected from involvement in the drafting of other important conventions of direct concern to its mandate: Alston, 'The Commission on Human Rights' in Alston (ed), *The United Nations and Human Rights: A Critical Appraisal* (OUP, 1992), pp 131–134.
[69] Humphrey, *No Distant Millennium: The International Law of Human Rights* (UNESCO, 1989), p 94.

on individual complaints.[70] Indeed, at its very first session in 1947, it decided that it had 'no power to take any action in regard to any complaints regarding human rights',[71] a decision that was subsequently endorsed by ECOSOC.[72]

[2.16] It may, of course, be true that the Commission's failure in its initial phase of development to respond to complaints of human rights violations was partly motivated by political reasons. Alston and Gutter each note that western States at that time were keen to avoid scrutiny on issues such as racial discrimination, while socialist States were generally opposed to complaint procedures on the basis that they would constitute interference in domestic affairs contrary to art 2(7) of the Charter.[73] However, the huge shift in the geo-political structure of the United Nations during the mid-1960s had a major effect on the functioning of the Commission. In 1961, ECOSOC increased the membership of the Commission from 18 to 21 Member States; and again in 1966, from 21 to 32 Member States, the majority of whom were representatives of Third World States.[74] Those States were understandably pre-occupied with racism and colonial policies, particularly in Southern Africa at that time. With the support of the Eastern European bloc, they pressed for the initiation of procedures by the Commission which would help to bring an end to the policies of apartheid and racial segregation being practised in colonial countries and dependent territories. These various developments led to the adoption of two ground-breaking Resolutions by ECOSOC (Resolutions 1503 and 1235) which substantially involved the Commission on Human Rights in identifying and acting on situations of gross violations of human rights in particular countries in the world. Resolution 1503 allowed for the Commission to examine complaints in private session which appeared to reveal 'a consistent pattern of gross and reliably attested violations of human rights';[75] while Resolution 1235 provided an opportunity for the Commission to engage in public debate on such situations, having made a thorough study of the situation.[76] Moreover, a discussion under the 1503 *confidential* procedure could and did result in the situation being discussed publicly under the 1235 *public* procedure.[77] Following on from these 'country-specific' procedures, the Commission

---

[70] Alston describes this period of the Commission's life as one of 'apolitical functionalism': 'The Commission on Human Rights' in Alston (ed), *The United Nations and Human Rights: A Critical Appraisal* (OUP, 1992), p 130.

[71] Report to the ECOSOC on the First Session of the Commission (27 January–18 February 1947): UN Doc E/259, para 22.

[72] ECOSOC Res 75(V) of 5 August 1947, UN Doc E/573, (1947).

[73] Alston, 'The Commission on Human Rights' in Alston (ed), *The United Nations and Human Rights: A Critical Appraisal* (OUP, 1992), p 142; and Gutter, 'Special Procedures and the Human Rights Council: Achievements and Challenges Ahead' (2007) 71 HRL Rev 93 at 96.

[74] Alston, 'The Commission on Human Rights' in Alston (ed), *The United Nations and Human Rights: A Critical Appraisal* (OUP, 1992), p 143.

[75] ECOSOC Res 1503 (XLVIII), 48 UN ESCOR (No 1A) at 8, UN Doc E/4832/Add1 (1970).

[76] ECOSOC Res 1235 (XLII), 42 UN ESCOR Supp (No 1) at 17, UN Doc E/4393 (1967).

[77] On the operation of these procedures generally, see Bossuyt, 'The Development of Special Procedures of the United Nations Commission on Human Rights' (1985) 6 HRLJ 179; and Alston, 'The Commission on Human Rights' in Alston (ed), *The United Nations and Human Rights: A Critical Appraisal* (OUP, 1992), pp 144–173.

went on to develop broader 'thematic' procedures. The latter involved the appointment by the Commission of individual 'special rapporteurs' or 'working groups' to examine a particular theme of human rights abuse as it occurred anywhere in the world.[78] Over the years, for example, special rapporteurs have been appointed to examine particular issues such as torture, summary or arbitrary executions, freedom of religion and belief, and racism; while working groups have been appointed to investigate arbitrary detention, and enforced and involuntary disappearances. While the terms of reference of each of the rapporteurs and working groups are context specific, in general terms the common goal of the thematic procedures appears to be that of investigating the phenomenon in question, in a non-adversarial way, and seeking to 'respond effectively' to information that comes to light in the course of their investigations.[79]

[2.17] All of these matters, therefore, were capable of winding up on the Commission's agenda at its annual meeting in Geneva in March and April over a six-week period. Only members of the Commission had a right to vote on any given matter within its competence. By 1992, membership of the Commission had been enlarged to 53 States.[80] It was also entitled to invite any other State to participate, but not vote, in deliberations of direct concern to them. Crucially, non-governmental organisations with consultative status at the UN, as well as national human rights institutions and representatives of other international organisations were also entitled to sit in on its meetings as observers and to contribute to its discussions, thus giving them vital lobbying and awareness-raising opportunities. A typical session of the Commission might result in thousands of statements being made on various human rights issues, including the operation of the thematic procedures, with the Commission ultimately voting to take action or not on particular situations.[81]

---

[78] See generally, Rodley, 'United Nations Non-Treaty Procedures for Dealing with Human Rights Violations' in Hannum, *Guide to International Human Rights Practice* (2nd edn, University of Pennsylvania Press, 1992), p 60; and Bossuyt, 'The Development of Special Procedures of the United Nations Commission on Human Rights' (1985) 6 HRLJ 179.

[79] See Weissbrodt, 'The Three-Theme Special Rapporteurs of the United Nations Commission on Human Rights' (1986) 80 AJIL 685 and Alston, 'The Commission on Human Rights' in Alston (ed), *The United Nations and Human Rights: A Critical Appraisal* (OUP, 1992), pp 173–181.

[80] Seats were apportioned by ECOSOC on the basis of equitable geographical distribution and representatives were appointed for three-year terms. At the time of its extinction in 2005, the largest voting bloc was that of Africa with 15 seats, followed by Asia with 12 seats, 11 from Latin American and Caribbean states, 10 from Western European and others and 5 from Eastern Europe.

[81] At the 61st and last working session of the Commission in 2005, for example, over one thousand statements were made by States, NGOs, NHRIs and representatives of international organisations: International Service for Human Rights, *A New Chapter for Human Rights: A Handbook on Issues of Transition from the Commission on Human Rights to the Human Rights Council* (June 2006): http://www.ishr.ch/guides-to-the-un-system/handbook (last accessed May 2011).

[2.18] The adoption of both the 'country' and 'thematic' procedures (known collectively as the 'special procedures') firmly changed the course of the Commission's work in two key respects. First, henceforth, the Commission's focus shifted from standard-setting to that of implementation,[82] whereby crucial decisions were being made to investigate and discuss (often publicly) human rights abuses occurring throughout the world. Second, the operation of the procedures inevitably resulted in the political character of the body itself emerging to the forefront. Because the potential upshot of all of them was the 'naming and shaming' of individual governments for human rights abuses, the operation of these procedures within the Commission gradually became the subject of considerable political jockeying as countries formed strategic alliances with each other within the Commission in an effort to avoid public censure for their human rights practices.[83] In recent years, the election of States such as Libya as chair of the Commission in 2003,[84] and Sudan as a member in 2004 (at the height of the crisis in Darfur),[85] further weakened the overall credibility of the institution.[86] These developments highlighted the reality that States with poor human rights records were

---

[82] While the focus clearly shifted, the Commission still performed an important and influential role in the realm of standard-setting in the latter decades of its existence: Alston, 'The Commission on Human Rights' in Alston (ed), *The United Nations and Human Rights: A Critical Appraisal* (OUP, 1992), pp 135–137.

[83] As Gutter notes: 'Accusations of the use of double standards and selectivity in the treatment of country situations led to the much criticized institutional culture of excessive politicization and regional alliances, where membership was sought not to advance the cause of human rights, but to avoid criticism and criticize others': Gutter, 'Special Procedures and the Human Rights Council: Achievements and Challenges Ahead' (2007) 71 HRL Rev 93, p 104.

[84] There was a widespread negative reaction to this development on the part of many human rights groups, as well as other States which opposed the motion. The US Ambassador to the UN apparently stated afterwards that: 'This is not a defeat for the United States, this is a defeat for the Human Rights Commission', http://news.bbc.co.uk/2/hi/africa/2672029.stm(last accessed May 2011).

[85] The submission of Sudan's candidacy for membership of the Commission resulted in a walk-out on the part of the US delegation to ECOSOC. Prior to leaving the meeting, the US delegation called on ECOSOC to consider the consequences of allowing the Commission to become a safe haven for the world's worst human rights violators, especially one engaged in ethnic cleansing. Sudan was subsequently elected to the Commission and remained a member of it until the Commission's demise in 2006: http://www.un.org/News/Press/docs/2004/ecosoc6110.doc.htm (last accessed May 2011).

[86] In his closing statement to the Commission at its 59th annual session on 24 April 2003, the High Commissioner for Human Rights, Mr Sergio Vieira de Mello stated: 'There really is nothing more serious than the protection of human rights. Yet at times I have felt that, in the course of competitive debate, delegates were losing sight of the noble goal of protecting human rights, in the very body whose duty is to promote them'. See http://www.unhchr.ch/huricane/huricane.nsf/0/997CB87D98CAB294C1256D16002B1276?opendocument (last accessed May 2011). The Secretary General voiced his concerns in even stronger terms in a speech to the Commission at the same session on 23 April 2003: 'Divisions and disputes in recent months have made your voice not stronger, but weaker; your voice in the great debates about human rights more muffled, not clearer'. (contd.../)

lining up to join the Commission in order to put a stop to discussion of their egregious human rights records.[87]

[2.19] These various developments ultimately led to a searing critique of the Commission in 2005 by the Secretary General of the United Nations, Kofi Annan in his 'In Larger Freedom' report to the General Assembly.[88] In advocating a package of reform measures for the UN generally, Annan stated that the Commission's capacity to perform its tasks had '… been increasingly undermined by its declining credibility and professionalism'.[89] In particular, he noted that States had sought membership of the Commission 'not to strengthen human rights but to protect themselves against criticism or to criticize others'.[90] As a result, he concluded '… a credibility deficit has developed,

---

[86] (\...contd) 'This must change' he asserted, 'if the cause of human rights is to be advanced in the broad and universal manner'. See http://www.un.org/News/Press/docs/2003/sgt2372.doc.htm (last accessed May 2011). See also Buhrer, 'UN Commission on Human Rights Loses All Credibility: Wheeling and Dealing, Incompetence and 'Non-Action' (Reporters without Borders, 2003), http://www.rsf.org/IMG/pdf/Report_ONU_gb.pdf (last accessed May 2011).

[87] As Alston points out, however, the question of the appropriate composition and criteria for membership of a body like the UN Commission on Human Rights or the new Human Rights Council is complex, raising questions 'to which there are far fewer easier answers than most of the debate to date has implied': Alston, 'Reconceiving the UN Human Rights Regime: Challenges Confronting the New UN Human Rights Council' (2006) 7 Melb J Int'l L 185 at 188.

[88] Report of the Secretary-General to the General Assembly, 'In Larger Freedom: Towards Development, Security and Human Rights for All' 23 May 2005: UN Doc A/59/2005. The Secretary General was here echoing advice he had earlier received from a High Level Panel on Threats, Challenges and Change which he had convened in 2004. In its report to the Secretary General, it had expressed the view that in recent years, the Commission's capacity to perform its tasks '…has been undermined by eroding credibility and professionalism. Standard-setting to reinforce human rights cannot be performed by States that lack a demonstrated commitment to their promotion and protection. We are concerned that in recent years States have sought membership of the Commission not to strengthen human rights but to protect themselves against criticism or to criticize others. The Commission cannot be credible if it is seen to be maintaining double standards in addressing human rights concerns': 'A More Secure World: Our Shared Responsibility' (United Nations, 2004) UN Doc A/59/565, para 283, available at: http://www.un.org/secureworld/ (last accessed May 2011).

[89] Report of the Secretary-General to the General Assembly, 'In Larger Freedom: Towards Development, Security and Human Rights for All' 23 May 2005: UN Doc A/59/2005, para 182.

[90] Report of the Secretary-General to the General Assembly, 'In Larger Freedom: Towards Development, Security and Human Rights for All' 23 May 2005: UN Doc A/59/2005, para 182.
Report of the Secretary-General to the General Assembly, 'In Larger Freedom: Towards Development, Security and Human Rights for All' 23 May 2005: UN Doc A/59/2005, para 182.

which casts a shadow on the reputation of the United Nations as a whole'.[91] His conclusions in this regard ultimately prompted him to recommend the replacement of the Commission with a new body to be known as the Human Rights Council.[92] This eventually happened on 16 June 2006, when the Commission was abolished and replaced three days later by a completely new organ, the Human Rights Council.[93]

[2.20] It is certainly paradoxical that the development by the Commission of concrete implementation procedures for the protection of human rights ultimately led to its undoing. Had the Commission not moved forward in the direction of implementation, it might have remained frozen in a standard-setting mode, which though vital in its own right, provides a limited means of international human rights implementation. It was inevitable that a Commission composed of political representatives, once it moved in the direction of 'hands-on' implementation, ran the gauntlet of compromising its integrity to political considerations.[94] Nonetheless, the fact that the Commission ultimately ended its days as a discredited institution should not completely obliterate the fact that in its 60 years of existence, it was responsible for some of the most enduring initiatives in the standard-setting field, including the elaboration of many of the core human rights treaties examined in detail in the next chapter. Moreover, the evolution and operation of the special procedures had many positive aspects and have gone on to serve as an important blueprint for the procedures currently operated under the auspices of the Human Rights Council.

---

[91] Report of the Secretary-General to the General Assembly, 'In Larger Freedom: Towards Development, Security and Human Rights for All' 23 May 2005: UN Doc A/59/2005, para 182. These criticisms were echoed in many other quarters, particularly in NGO circles: See *Joint NGO Statement on UN Reform* – presented to the 61st Session of the UN Commission on Human Rights (12 April, 2005), http://www.hrw.org/english/docs/2005/04/12/global10463.htm (last accessed May 2011). See also, Shelton, 'International Human Rights Law: Principled, Double, or Absent Standards?' (2007) 25 Law & Inequality 467 at 469–470; and Ghanea, 'From UN Commission on Human Rights to UN Human Rights Council: One Step Forwards or Two Steps Sideways' 55 ICLQ 695 at 697–698: 'All in all, the CHR lost its integrity and direction over time; with much of its membership decisions, powers and focus coming to be fuelled by disreputable goals rather than motivated by the aim of promoting, protecting and advancing human rights'.

[92] Report of the Secretary-General to the General Assembly, 'In Larger Freedom: Towards Development, Security and Human Rights for All' 23 May 2005: UN Doc A/59/2005, para 183.

[93] GA Res 60/251, UN Doc A/RES/60/251 3 April 2006, available at: http://www2.ohchr.org/english/bodies/hrcouncil/docs/A.RES.60.251_En.pdf (last accessed May 2011).

[94] Writing in 1992, Alston correctly asserted that '... a politically composed commission dealing with human rights must, if it is to be effective, work in an inherently political milieu': 'The Commission on Human Rights' in Alston (ed), *The United Nations and Human Rights: A Critical Appraisal* (OUP, 1992) p 130.

THE SUB-COMMISSION ON THE PROMOTION AND PROTECTION OF HUMAN RIGHTS

[2.21] To assist it in its work, the Commission itself established a Sub-Commission in 1947, originally called the Sub-Commission on the Prevention of Discrimination and the Protection of Minorities.[95] The establishment of this Sub-Commission, with a particular focus on discrimination and minorities, was the product of an initiative by the Soviet Union. Apparently irked by the nuclear commission's[96] recommendation to ECOSOC that a Sub-Commission on Freedom of Information be immediately established on the motion of the United States, the Soviet Union insisted that it was just as important to prevent discrimination and to protect minorities as it was to promote freedom of information.[97] In the result, the Commission established two Sub-Commissions, one on freedom of information and the press, and the other concerned with the prevention of discrimination and the protection of minorities.[98] While the former was abolished some four years later in 1951, the latter ended up becoming, in the view of many commentators, one of the most important United Nations bodies concerned with human rights.[99] In 1999, the Sub-Commission was renamed the Sub-Commission on the Promotion and Protection of Human Rights in order to reflect the wider brief which its work had grown to encompass over the years.

[2.22] The Sub-Commission was intended to be a panel of non-political, independent experts, subordinate in the UN institutional hierarchy to the Commission and ECOSOC. Originally, it was mandated to provide advice and analysis to the Commission in the areas of discrimination and the protection of minorities and to perform any other functions entrusted to it by ECOSOC.[100] However, as matters evolved, initial attempts by

---

[95] See generally, Haver, 'The United Nations Sub-Commission on the Prevention of Discrimination and the Protection of Minorities' (1982) 21 Colom J Transnat'l L 103; Eide, 'The Sub-Commission on Prevention of Discrimination and Protection of Minorities' in Alston (ed), *The United Nations and Human Rights: A Critical Appraisal* (OUP, 1992), p 211; Humphrey, 'The United Nations Sub-Commission on the Prevention of Discrimination and the Protection of Minorities' (1968) 62 Am J Int'l L 869; and Humphrey, *No Distant Millennium: The International Law of Human Rights* (UNESCO, 1989), pp 112–117.

[96] See para **2.12** above.

[97] Humphrey, 'The United Nations Sub-Commission on the Prevention of Discrimination and the Protection of Minorities' (1968) 62 Am J Int'l L 869.

[98] Humphrey has commented that it was a mistake to fuse the two areas into the terms of reference of a single sub-commission. ECOSOC had clearly intended that there should be two separate commissions on discrimination and protection of minorities: Humphrey, 'The United Nations Sub-Commission on the Prevention of Discrimination and the Protection of Minorities' (1968) 62 Am J Int'l L 869, p 870.

[99] Humphrey, 'The United Nations Sub-Commission on the Prevention of Discrimination and the Protection of Minorities' (1968) 62 Am J Int'l L 869, p 112.

[100] The mandate originally given to it by the Commission in 1947 was as follows: (a) In the first instance, to examine what provisions should be adopted in defining the principles to be applied in the field of the prevention of discrimination on grounds of race, sex, language or religion, and in the field of the protection of minorities, and to make recommendations to the Commission on urgent problems in these fields; (contd.../)

the Sub-Commission to give equal weight to the protection of minorities and the prevention of discrimination were not supported by the parent bodies, as a result of which the main focus for the Sub-Commission's work in the first few decades was on the prevention of discrimination.[101] Much of its work in this regard took the form of a series of studies of discrimination in various fields, including education, religious rights and practices, and political rights.[102] The Sub-Commission also contributed to standard-setting during this time. Most notably, it contributed to the drafting of the International Bill of Rights,[103] as well as the drafting of the Declaration and International Convention on the Elimination of All Forms of Racial Discrimination. In the late 1960s and early 1970s, the functions of the Sub-Commission were augmented quite substantially by the terms of ECOSOC Resolutions 8 (XXIII), 1235 and 1503, each of which gave the Sub-Commission a role in responding to situations that revealed a consistent pattern of gross violations of human rights. Later still, the Sub-Commission's work expanded to include not only a renewed focus on minorities,[104] but also a number of other areas quite distinct from minority rights and discrimination. For example, it established working groups to examine such issues as contemporary forms of slavery, the administration of justice, and transnational corporations.[105] Over the years, it also addressed issues as diverse as the

---

[100] (\...contd) (b) To perform any other functions which may be entrusted to it by the Economic and Social Council or the Commission on Human Rights' (*Report of the First Session of the Commission on Human Rights in 1947* E/259 (1947) para 19). In 1949, paragraph (a) was amended by the Commission to read: 'to undertake studies, particularly in the light of the Universal Declaration of Human Rights concerning the prevention of discrimination of any kind relating to human rights and fundamental freedoms and the protection of racial, national, religious and linguistic minorities'. Paragraph (b) of the original mandate was not altered: *Report of the Fifth Session of the Commission on Human Rights* E/1371 (1949), para 13, s A.

[101] See generally, Humphrey, 'The United Nations Sub-Commission on the Prevention of Discrimination and the Protection of Minorities' (1968) 62 Am J Int'l L 869, pp 869–876; Haver, 'The United Nations Sub-Commission on the Prevention of Discrimination and the Protection of Minorities' (1982) 21 Colom J Transnat'l L 103, pp 105–108; and Eide, 'The Sub-Commission on Prevention of Discrimination and Protection of Minorities' in Alston (ed), *The United Nations and Human Rights: A Critical Appraisal* (OUP, 1992), pp 219–222.

[102] See generally, Humphrey, 'The United Nations Sub-Commission on the Prevention of Discrimination and the Protection of Minorities' (1968) 62 Am J Int'l L 869, pp 876–882.

[103] See Ch 3, para **3.01–3.04**.

[104] The Sub-Commission established a working group on the rights of Indigenous Populations (see generally Eide, 'The Sub-Commission on Prevention of Discrimination and Protection of Minorities' in Alston (ed), *The United Nations and Human Rights: A Critical Appraisal* (OUP, 1992), pp 235–239) and a Working Group on Minorities in 1995.

[105] As regards the Working Group on Contemporary Forms of Slavery, see generally Eide, 'The Sub-Commission on Prevention of Discrimination and Protection of Minorities' in Alston (ed), *The United Nations and Human Rights: A Critical Appraisal* (OUP, 1992), pp 232–235. By its Resolution 1998/8 of 20 August 1998, the Sub-Commission established, for a three-year period, a sessional working group of the Sub-Commission, composed of five of its members, to examine the working methods and activities of transnational corporations. The Sub-Commission established the Working Group on the Administration of Justice by its Decision 2006/103.

prevention of conflicts,[106] adequate food, the rights of disabled person, mental health, as well as human rights issues affecting women and children.[107] A particularly innovative move was the establishment in 2001 of a Social Forum, to consider ways of improving economic, social and cultural rights in the era of globalisation.[108]

[2.23] Apart from its output, the most significant aspect of the Sub-Commission which distinguished it from all of the other Charter-based human rights bodies, was the fact that it was ostensibly composed of independent persons as opposed to governmental representatives. Originally, there were 12 such members; though this figure was soon augmented to 14 in 1959, 18 in 1965, and then to 26 in 1968.[109] Members were elected by the Commission on the basis of equitable geographical distribution for four-year terms. In 1985, the Commission stressed in a Resolution that members of the Sub-Commission should be 'independent experts not subject to government instructions in the performance of their functions'.[110] In 1988, an Irish delegate on the Commission on Human Rights expressed the view that prospective candidates for election to the Sub-Commission should have the qualities of '… independence, including independence of their own Governments; personal commitment to the cause of human rights; and, lastly, expertise'.[111] However, while this view of the ideal qualities of a member of the Sub-Commission may well have been shared in many quarters,[112] it was neither explicitly formalised by the adoption of specific criteria,[113] nor routinely honoured in practice. Many members of the Sub-Commission did indeed act independently of their

---

[106] Eide, 'The Role of the Sub-Commission on Promotion and Protection of Human Rights and its Working Groups in the Prevention of Conflict' (2001) 8 Int'l J on Minority Rights 25.

[107] Eide, 'The Sub-Commission on Prevention of Discrimination and Protection of Minorities' in Alston (ed), *The United Nations and Human Rights: A Critical Appraisal* (OUP, 1992), pp 225–226.

[108] UN Doc E/CN4/Sub 2/RES/1999/10 (1999). See generally: Sub-Commission Resolution 2001/24: http://www2.ohchr.org/english/issues/poverty/sforum.htm (last accessed May 2011).

[109] ECOSOC Res 728F (XXVII) (1959); ECOSOC Res 1974 G (XXIX) (1965); and ECOSOC Res 1334 (XLIV) (1968).

[110] CHR Res 1985/28, para 4.

[111] Statement of Mr Lillis (Representative of Ireland): E/CN4/1988/SR36/Add1, para 14. Since the election of members to the Sub-Commission was the most significant opportunity for the Commission to influence the work of its advisory body in the years to come, he suggested that in so doing, the Commission should be guided by the eighteenth century maxim: 'Man, not measures'.

[112] Similar qualities were espoused by the representative of the Philippines at the same session in 1988 (Mr Ingles) who commented that the election would give the Commission the opportunity 'to choose men and women of independence, integrity and proven experience in the protection and promotion of human rights': UN Doc E/CN4/1988/SR37.

[113] The decision of the Commission in 1947 which established the Sub-Commission simply provided that the Sub-Commission be composed of 'twelve persons selected by the Commission in consultation with the Secretary General and subject to the consent of the country of which person are nationals; and (b) that not more than one person be selected from any single country'. Report to ECOSOC of the First Session of the Commission on Human Rights (January 1947): UN Doc E/259, para 20.

governments while simultaneously having expertise in the field;[114] others unfortunately did not satisfy either standard. As one authority has noted, some persons with 'little or no expertise' in the field of human rights did serve on the Sub-Commission, while others with expertise nonetheless acted as governmental representatives.[115] This reality was exacerbated by the ability of governments to avoid the *de facto* independence requirement, by designating persons who emphatically did not have sufficient expertise as alternates where the expert in question was unable to attend. This could be done until 1983 for either the whole or part of a session of the Sub-Commission without seeking UN approval.[116] Many governments availed of this possibility to appoint as designates persons who clearly were acting as governmental representatives.[117] In any case, the very fact that members of the Sub-Commission were elected by the Commission, which itself was a politically composed body, meant that there would always be an inevitable political nexus between the two bodies.[118]

[2.24] Regrettably, the fact that the composition of the Sub-Commission was in some cases compromised did lead to accusations over its lifetime that its workings had become politicised.[119] The fact that governmental representatives were entitled to sit in

---

[114] In this respect, it is shocking to read the accusation made by the Irish representative of the Commission on Human Rights at its 44th session in 1988 regarding the situation of the representative of Romania (Mr Mazilu) at that time. According to the Irish representative, '... the Permanent Mission of Romania had informed the Secretariat, by a letter dated 11 August 1987, that Mr. Mazilu was unable to attend the Sub-Commission's 1987 session because of the state of his health. However, the Irish delegation had definite and unimpeachable evidence that Mr. Mazilu had applied for permission to the Romanian authorities to visit Geneva but had failed to secure such permission; and that, since May 1986, Mr. Mazilu had been unable to perform his duties as a member of the Sub-Commission, because of the attitude of his country's authorities'. This, in the view of the Irish representative, was '... in several ways, the single most disturbing development to have occurred within the Sub-Commission for a number of years and one which had major implications as far as the credibility of that institution was concerned': UN Doc E/CN4/1988/SR36/Add1, p 5.

[115] Eide, 'The Sub-Commission on Prevention of Discrimination and Protection of Minorities' in Alston (ed), *The United Nations and Human Rights: A Critical Appraisal* (OUP, 1992), p 254.

[116] Eide, 'The Sub-Commission on Prevention of Discrimination and Protection of Minorities', p 254.

[117] In making this point, Eide gives as an example the appointment by the Argentinean government of a series of government officials as replacements for the elected expert in the 1980s, 'thus making a nonsense of the procedures': 'The Sub-Commission on Prevention of Discrimination and Protection of Minorities' in Alston (ed), *The United Nations and Human Rights: A Critical Appraisal* (OUP, 1992), p 254.

[118] Haver notes that the governments represented on the commission were always 'firmly in control over membership on the Sub-Commission': 'The United Nations Sub-Commission on the Prevention of Discrimination and the Protection of Minorities' (1982) 21 Colom J Transnat'l L 103, note 2.

[119] International Service for Human Rights, *A New Chapter for Human Rights: A Handbook on Issues of Transition from the Commission on Human Rights to the Human Rights Council* (June 2006), p 54. (contd)

on Sub-Commission meetings can only have contributed to this perception.[120] At the other end of the spectrum, however, the Sub-Commission was also accused on occasion of not acting independently by giving too much credence to the concerns of NGOs.[121] In this regard, it is important to note that of all the Charter-based bodies, the Sub-Commission was the one which forged the strongest connection with the NGO community. NGOs with consultative status at the United Nations were entitled to sit in as observers at the public meetings of the Sub-Commission and its working groups, and the Sub-Commission was entitled to consult with them either directly or indirectly through its committees. Consultation could take place either at the request of the Sub-Commission or the organisation concerned.[122] This level of access to the Sub-Commission meant that human rights activists in NGOs from all corners of the world would regularly come to Geneva to address the Sub-Commission with their concerns.[123] There can be little doubt but that the close interaction between NGOs and the Sub-Commission, while occasionally tense, significantly shaped its work and provided its members with a constant reservoir of practical experience and information on a wide range of issues pertinent to its work.[124]

---

[119] (\...contd) See the comments of the representative of Cyprus (Mr Yiango): 'Much criticism of the Sub-Commission's work had arisen from the widely held view that politicization of its activities had taken on unacceptable proportions. Such politicization was clearly not in keeping with the independence, impartiality, objectivity and integrity expected of an independent body of experts participating in their personal capacity, but some degree of politicization was inevitable, given the nature of some of the subjects dealt with, the more so since Government observers participated freely in the discussion on practically every item on the Sub-Commission's agenda': UN Doc E/CN4/1988/SR36/Add1, p 3.

[120] International Service for Human Rights, *A New Chapter for Human Rights: A Handbook on Issues of Transition from the Commission on Human Rights to the Human Rights Council* (June 2006), p 54.

[121] Eide, 'The Sub-Commission on Prevention of Discrimination and Protection of Minorities' in Alston (ed), *The United Nations and Human Rights: A Critical Appraisal* (OUP, 1992), p 255.

[122] See Rules 75 and 76 of the Sub-Commission's Rules of Procedure: Un Doc HRI/NONE/2001/126 http://www.unhchr.ch/huridocda/huridoca.nsf/(Symbol)/ (last accessed May 2011). HRI.NONE.2001.126.En?Opendocument (last accessed May 2011).

[123] See Weissbrodt, 'An Analysis of the Fifty-First Session of the United Nations Sub-Commission on the Promotion and Protection of Human Rights' (2000) 22 HRQ 788 at 789. Weissbrodt gives as an example the fact that at the 51st session of the Sub-Commission in 1999, over one thousand participants attended, representing 116 governments, 19 UN agencies, 10 specialised agencies and 124 NGOs. A unique example of this level of cooperation was reflected in the establishment of on-going dialogue with NGOs and other stakeholders on ways of improving economic, social and cultural rights in this era of globalisation.

[124] Eide, 'The Sub-Commission on Prevention of Discrimination and Protection of Minorities' in Alston (ed), *The United Nations and Human Rights: A Critical Appraisal* (OUP, 1992), pp 259–260. He notes, for example, that as well as being instrumental to the operation of the special procedures, NGOs also played a vital role in the establishment of a number of the Sub-Commission's working groups, including the Working Group on Contemporary Forms of Slavery and Indigenous Populations.

[2.25] The Sub-Commission played an extremely valuable role throughout its lifetime in the implementation of human rights. Its work helped to highlight emerging issues and situations of abuse, and in the formulation and interpretation of human rights standards. However, it was subject to criticism on the grounds of politicisation, and also in regard to certain of its working methods.[125] When it was established in 2006, the Human Rights Council inherited responsibility for the Sub-Commission from the Commission on Human Rights. While the Council extended the Sub-Commission's mandate on an exceptional one-year basis, the Sub-Commission held its last session in August 2006.[126] The Council subsequently established an Advisory Committee of eighteen independent experts to function as a 'think-tank' for the Council and 'work at its direction'.[127]

THE HUMAN RIGHTS COUNCIL[128]

[2.26] As noted above, Kofi Annan's 'In Larger Freedom' report acted as a catalyst for intense discussion about the appropriate institution to replace the now discredited Commission on Human Rights.[129] His report, together with an explanatory note issued a week later, indicated his view that the Member States should agree to replace the Commission on Human Rights with a smaller, standing Human Rights Council, either as a principal organ of the United Nations or a subsidiary organ of the General Assembly.[130] In either case, its members should be directly elected by the General Assembly by a two-thirds majority of members, present and voting.[131] The creation of

---

[125] See the numerous statements made to this effect by delegates at the 44th session of the Commission on Human Rights in 1988: UN Doc E/CN4/1988/SR36/Add1. See also Eide, 'The Sub-Commission on Prevention of Discrimination and Protection of Minorities' in Alston (ed), *The United Nations and Human Rights: A Critical Appraisal* (OUP, 1992), pp 263–264.

[126] Just a year previously, the Sub-Commission had itself noted the need for a 'representative independent expert body that is able to think collectively, free from specialized mandate constraints and political considerations, in order to initiate and pursue new and innovative thinking in human rights and implementation': Report of the Sub-Commission on the Promotion and Protection of Human Rights on its 57th Session (25 July – 12 August 2005), Decision 2005/114, Annex (para 6): UN Doc E/CN.4/2006/2 or E/CN.4/Sub2/2005/44 (17 October 2005).

[127] Human Rights Council, Resolution 5/1 (18 June 2007): U.N. Doc. A/HRC/5/21, paras 65–84.

[128] See generally, Boyle, 'The United Nations Human Rights Council: Origins, Antecedents, and Prospects' in Boyle (ed), *New Institutions for Human Rights Protection* (OUP, 2009), pp 11–47.

[129] Report of the Secretary-General to the General Assembly, 'In Larger Freedom: Towards Development, Security and Human Rights for All' 23 May 2005: UN Doc A/59/2005.

[130] Report of the Secretary-General to the General Assembly, 'In Larger Freedom: Towards Development, Security and Human Rights for All' 23 May 2005: UN Doc A/59/2005, para 166 and paras 181–183; and see explanatory note by the Secretary General, Human Rights Council, Addendum 1 to 'In Larger Freedom': UN Doc A/59/2005/Add1 (23 May 2005).

[131] Report of the Secretary-General to the General Assembly, 'In Larger Freedom: Towards Development, Security and Human Rights for All' 23 May 2005: UN Doc A/59/2005, para 183.

such a Council would, in his view, 'accord human rights a more authoritative position, corresponding to the primacy of human rights in the Charter',[132] on a par with other main purposes of the organisation – security and development – for which dedicated Councils already exist.[133] He emphasised the advantages of a standing body, in that it would be able to meet regularly and at any time in order to deal with imminent crises, while at the same time allowing for detailed and in-depth consideration of human rights issues.[134] Election by the entire membership of the General Assembly would, in his view, make the Council more representative, more accountable and ultimately more authoritative than the Commission, which was simply a subsidiary body of ECOSOC. In the explanatory memo, the Secretary General elaborated on an idea which he had previously put to the Commission on Human Rights, that the new Human Rights Council should have as one of its functions the task of 'peer review', whereby it would evaluate the fulfilment by all States of their human rights obligations.[135] This concept of 'universal periodic review' would later form a central plank of the functions of the Human Rights Council.

[2.27] The proposal to abolish the Commission and replace it with a Human Rights Council was endorsed by the Member States at the World Summit in September 2005,[136] and following negotiations on the mandate, functions, composition, size, working methods and procedures,[137] the new Human Rights Council (HRC) was finally created by General Assembly Resolution 60/251 on the 15 March 2006.[138] The model which emerged from the negotiations was broadly similar to that originally proposed by the

---

[132] Report of the Secretary-General to the General Assembly, 'In Larger Freedom: Towards Development, Security and Human Rights for All' 23 May 2005: UN Doc A/59/2005, para 183.

[133] Explanatory note by the Secretary General, Human Rights Council, Addendum 1 to 'In Larger Freedom': UN Doc A/59/2005/Add1 (23 May 2005), para 1.

[134] Explanatory note by the Secretary General, para 4.

[135] Speech of Kofi Annan to the Commission on Human Rights, 7 April 2005: http://www.un.org/News/Press/docs/2005/sgsm9808.doc.htm (last accessed May 2011); and see explanatory note paras 6–8.

[136] See 2005 World Summit Outcome Document: UN Doc A/Res/60/1 (24 October 2005), paras 157–160. For more on the outcome of the summit, including the proposal for a Human Rights Council, see generally, Prove, 'Reform at the UN: Waiting for Godot?' (2005) 24 U Queensland LJ 293.

[137] The Member States had requested the President of the General Assembly (ultimately Ambassador Jan Eliasson of Sweden) to conduct open, transparent and inclusive negotiations along these lines in the Outcome Document: See 2005 World Summit Outcome Document, para 160.

[138] UN Doc/Res/60/251. 170 States voted in favour of the Resolution; four voted against (United States of America, Israel, Marshall Islands and Palau); while three abstained (Belarus, Venezuela and Iran).

Secretary General, though certain important compromises were obviously made along the way. The following analysis sets out the main features of the resolution.[139]

[2.28] Resolution 60/251 establishes the HRC as a subsidiary body of the General Assembly. As such, it will report directly to the General Assembly as opposed to ECOSOC.[140] Thus, the Council has an enhanced status to that of the former Commission on Human Rights, but an inferior one to the other option mooted by Kofi Annan, namely, that of a principal body of the United Nations with the same status as, for example, the Security Council, the General Assembly and ECOSOC. Annan clearly envisaged the possibility of the Council being elevated to a similar status so as to give further effect to the prominence which human rights had been given in the Charter. However, despite the efforts of a number of delegations and NGOs, the Member States opted, for the moment, to make it a subsidiary organ of the General Assembly. Nonetheless, a window of opportunity remains for this decision to be reviewed in that paragraph 1 of the Resolution specifically calls upon the General Assembly to review the status of the Council within five years, which review is ongoing at the time of writing.[141]

[2.29] The Council's meeting time is significantly longer than the former Commission's, in that it will meet regularly throughout the year and schedule no fewer than three sessions *per* year, including a main session, for a total duration of no less than 10 weeks. Moreover, it shall be able to hold special sessions, when needed, at the request of any member of the Council with the support of one-third of the entire membership of the Council.[142] This latter provision will enable the Council, if a third of its members are so minded, to respond to emergency situations outside its regular sessions.

Membership

[2.30] Under the terms of the Resolution, the Council is composed of 47 Member States of the UN, based on equitable geographical distribution,[143] and 'elected directly and individually by secret ballot by the *majority* of the members of the General Assembly'. When electing members of the Council, Member States 'shall take into account the contribution of candidates to the promotion and protection of human rights and their

---

[139] See further, Scannella and Splinter, 'The United Nations Human Rights Council: A Promise to be Fulfilled' (2007) 7 HRL Rev 41; Upton, 'The Human Rights Council: First Impressions and Future Challenges' (2007) 7 HRL Rev 29; Alston, 'Reconceiving the UN Human Rights Regime: Challenges Confronting the New UN Human Rights Council' (2006) 7 Melb J Int'l L 185; Ghanea, 'From UN Commission on Human Rights to UN Human Rights Council: One Step Forwards or Two Steps Sideways' 55 ICLQ 695; and International Service for Human Rights, *A New Chapter for Human Rights: A Handbook on Issues of Transition from the Commission on Human Rights to the Human Rights Council* (June 2006).

[140] UN Doc/Res/60/251, para 1.
[141] UN Doc/Res/60/251, para 1.
[142] UN Doc/Res/60/251, para 10.
[143] Thus, election to the Council is as follows: 13 States from Africa; 13 from Asia; six from the Eastern Europe; eight from the Latin American and Caribbean States; and seven from Western Europe and other states.

voluntary pledges and commitments thereto'.[144] Members of the Council shall serve for a period of three years and shall not be eligible for re-election after two consecutive terms. Finally, the rights of membership of any member elected to the Council that commits 'gross and systematic violations of human rights' may be suspended by a two-thirds majority vote of the members of the General Assembly.[145]

[2.31] A few points may be made about the above provisions. First, it can be observed that the HRC is thus a larger body than the 15 to 20 member versions suggested by Annan and the US respectively, but smaller than the former Commission on Human Rights which some had come to regard as unmanageable. This compromise is probably appropriate as it would have been difficult for less influential States to become members of a smaller body which would inevitably be open to potential domination by more powerful States.[146] The Member States also opted not to introduce formal criteria for membership, as had been advocated by many States (including the US and the European Union) and NGOs,[147] preferring instead to adopt a more flexible approach whereby candidate States are effectively encouraged to put forward a platform for their election which includes voluntary pledges and commitments. As Alston notes, formal criteria for membership probably would have proved to be unworkable in the long run.[148] Opinion is divided on the worth of the compromise formula. Upton, for example, concludes that it is 'a step in the right direction' and has in fact resulted, in the first phase of election, in all of the candidate States making pledges which 'included some substantive, serious and forward looking measures that can be monitored post-election by non-governmental organizations (NGOs) and civil society.'[149] Alston, on the other hand, points out that despite attempts by Amnesty International and the Office of the United Nations High Commissioner for Human Rights (OHCHR) to inveigle candidate States into making firm commitments by way of pledges, many States have 'confined themselves to only

---

[144] UN Doc/Res/60/251, para 7.
[145] UN Doc/Res/60/251, para 8.
[146] This point is made by Alston in 'Reconceiving the UN Human Rights Regime: Challenges Confronting the New UN Human Rights Council' (2006) 7 Melb J Int'l L 185, p 198.
[147] See the Joint Statement made by 160 NGOs for Foreign Ministers and Permanent Representatives on criteria perceived to be essential to the establishment of the Human Rights Council: http://www.hrw.org/en/news/2006/01/18/160-ngos-identify-essential-elements-un-human-rights-council (last accessed May 2011).
[148] Alston, 'Reconceiving the UN Human Rights Regime: Challenges Confronting the New UN Human Rights Council' (2006) 7 Melb J Int'l L 185, p 196. See, however, his interesting suggestions for the compilation of a Human Rights Accountability Index for aspiring members of the Human Rights Council in: 'Richard Lillich Memorial Lecture: Promoting the Accountability of Members of the New UN Human Rights Council' (2005-06) 15 J Transnat'l L & Pol'y 49.
[149] Upton, 'The Human Rights Council: First Impressions and Future Challenges' (2007) 7 HRL Rev 29, p 32.

the most general expressions of good intentions, while some have altogether ignored the request to submit'.[150]

[2.32] Finally, it is certainly regrettable that States can be elected to the HRC by a majority of votes, as opposed to the two-thirds requirement suggested by Annan. The latter would clearly have been preferable in that it would have made it more difficult for States with poor human rights records to be elected. Indeed, as Ghanea notes, it is somewhat ironic that the provisions for suspension of membership from the Council are more demanding than those for membership itself.[151]

Functions

[2.33] Under the terms of Resolution 60/251, the HRC shall be responsible for promoting universal respect for the protection of all human rights and fundamental freedoms for all, without distinction of any kind and in a fair and equal manner.[152] The Council should also 'address situations of violations of human rights, including gross and systematic violations, and make recommendations thereon. It should also promote the effective coordination and the mainstreaming of human rights within the United Nations system'.[153] Detailed functions are set out in paragraph 5 of the Resolutions to the effect that the Council shall:

(a) Promote human rights education and learning as well as advisory services, technical assistance and capacity-building, to be provided in consultation with and with the consent of Member States concerned;

(b) Serve as a forum for dialogue on thematic issues on all human rights;

(c) Make recommendations to the General Assembly for the further development of international law in the field of human rights;

(d) Promote the full implementation of human rights obligations undertaken by States and follow-up to the goals related to the promotion and protection of human rights emanating from United Nations conferences and summits;

(e) Undertake a universal periodic review, based on objective and reliable information, of the fulfilment of each State of its human rights obligations and commitments in a manner which ensures universality of coverage and equal treatment with respect to all States;[154] members of the Council, in particular, shall be reviewed under this mechanism during their term of membership;[155]

---

[150] Alston, 'Reconceiving the UN Human Rights Regime: Challenges Confronting the New UN Human Rights Council' (2006) 7 Melb J Int'l L 185, p 201.

[151] Ghanea, 'From UN Commission on Human Rights to UN Human Rights Council: One Step Forwards or Two Steps Sideways' 55 ICLQ 695, p 701.

[152] UN Doc/Res/60/251, para 2.

[153] UN Doc/Res/60/251, para 5.

[154] UN Doc/Res/60/251, para 5(e) continues by stating that the 'review shall be a cooperative mechanism, based on an interactive dialogue, with the full involvement of the country concerned and with consideration given to its capacity-building needs; such a mechanism shall complement and not duplicate the work of treaty bodies; the Council shall develop the modalities and necessary time allocation for the universal periodic review mechanism within one year after the holding of its first session'.

[155] UN Doc/Res/60/251, para 9.

(f) Contribute, through dialogue and cooperation, towards the prevention of human rights violations and respond promptly to emergencies;

(g) Assume the role and responsibilities of the Commission on Human Rights relating to the work of the Office of the United Nations High Commissioner for Human Rights;

(h) Work in close cooperation in the field of human rights with governments, regional organisations, national human rights institutions and civil society;

(i) Make recommendations with regard to the promotion and protection of human rights;

(j) Submit an annual report to the General Assembly.

[2.34] In June 2007, the Council adopted Resolution 5/1, otherwise known as its 'Institution-building package', which sets forth the elements which it considered necessary for conducting its future work.[156] The package delineated the principles and objectives on which the universal periodic review (UPR) mechanism is based, as well as the process and modalities of its operation.[157] It also established a new Advisory Committee, comprised of 18 independent experts, intended to serve as the Council's 'think tank' on thematic human rights issues;[158] and set forth the framework for a complaints procedure, which allows individuals and NGOs to make complaints to the Council about 'consistent patters of gross and reliably attested violations of all human rights'. Finally, Resolution 5/1 included provisions regarding a review of all special procedures mandates formerly established by the Commission on Human Rights and criteria for the selection of mandate holders.[159]

[2.35] Thus, the HRC has assumed the standard-setting role previously performed by the former Commission on Human Rights. Likewise, the Council now maintains a system of special procedures,[160] a complaint procedure[161] as well as operating the system of UPR. The latter mechanism essentially involves the Council in conducting a review of the human rights record of each of the UN member States every four years, based on information contained in reports supplied to it by the State in question, the OHCHR and other stakeholders, including NGOs and NHRIs. The conduct of the review involves an inter-active dialogue between the State under review and other UN member States, culminating in an 'outcome report' of recommendations to the State. An opportunity is given in the process for the State under review to accept or reject recommendations

---

[156] Human Rights Council, Resolution 5/1, Institution-Building of the United Nations Human Rights Council UN Doc A/HRC/5/21 (18 June 2007): http://www2.ohchr.org/english/bodies/hrcouncil/ (last accessed May 2011).
[157] Resolution 5/1, paras 1–38.
[158] Resolution 5/1, paras 65–84.
[159] Resolution 5/1, paras 39–64.
[160] For the full list of Special Procedures mandate holders of the Human Rights Council, see the website of the HRC: http://www2.ohchr.org/english/bodies/chr/special/index.htm (last accessed May 2011).
[161] For information on the Human Rights Council's Complaints Procedure, see: http://www2.ohchr.org/english/bodies/complaints.htm (last accessed May 2011).

made to it, but ultimately it has responsibility to implement the recommendations made in the final outcome report.[162] While the UPR mechanism is clearly the most innovative function of the Human Rights Council, initial expectations as to its potential benefits to effect meaningful change in domestic human rights implementation have ranged from positive rhetorical flourishes[163] to concerns that it could '... do great harm to the idea of genuine accountability'.[164] One specific issue raised is whether UPR might duplicate the work being done by the UN treaty bodies (examined in detail in Parts 2 and 3 of this book) or worse still undermine the monitoring function of those bodies being carried out, in particular, through the vehicle of the periodic reporting procedures.[165] This is because the opportunity presented by UPR to re-formulate, condense and attract explicit rejection of recommendations already made by the independent experts appointed to the treaty bodies has the potential to weaken the authority of those bodies and the substance of their work. While this issue is beyond the scope of this work, it is one which undoubtedly merits closer scrutiny if complementarity between the respective systems is to be achieved.[166]

OFFICE OF THE UNITED NATIONS HIGH COMMISSIONER FOR HUMAN RIGHTS

[2.36] A survey of UN institutions involved in the promotion and protection of human rights would be incomplete without reference to the centrally important role played by the Office of the United Nations High Commissioner for Human Rights (OHCHR). Although mooted at intervals since as far back as 1947,[167] this office was formally

---

[162] For details on the operation of the UPR, see http://www.ohchr.org/EN/HRBodies/UPR/Pages/UPRmain.aspx (last accessed May 2011).

[163] The universal periodic review 'has great potential to promote and protect human rights in the darkest corners of the world': Ban Ki-moon, UN Secretary-General. See http://www.ohchr.org/en/hrbodies/upr/pages/uprmain.aspx(last accessed May 2011).

[164] Hampson, 'An Overview of the Reform of the UN Human Rights Machinery' (2007) HRL Rev 7 at 9.

[165] See Ch 4. See generally, Bernaz, 'Reforming the UN Human Rights Protection Procedures: A Legal Perspective on the Establishment of the Universal Periodic Review Mechanism' in Boyle (ed), *New Institutions for Human Rights Protection* (OUP, 2009), 75 at p 77. See generally Rodley, 'The United Nations Human Rights Council, Its Special Procedures and Its Relationship with the Treaty Bodies: Complimentarity or Competition?' in Boyle (ed) *New Institutions for Human Rights Protection* (OUP, 2009), pp 49–73.

[166] In this respect, it should be noted that Resolution 60/251, which establishes the UPR as a core function of the Human Rights Council, specifically provides that UPR '... shall complement and not duplicate the work of the treaties bodies': para 5(e).

[167] For details on the evolution of the OHCHR, see: Van Boven, 'The United Nations High Commissioner for Human Rights: The History of a Contested Project' in Skouteris and Vermeer-Künzli, *The Protection of the Individual in International Law: Essays in Honour of Jon Dugard* (CUP, 2007) pp 39–56; Hobbins, 'Humphrey and the High Commissioner: The Genesis of the Office of the UN High Commissioner for Human Rights' (2001) 3 J Hist Int'l L 38; Clapham, 'Creating the High Commissioner for Human Rights: The Outside Story' (1994) 5 EJIL 556–558; and Alston, 'Neither Fish Nor Fowl: The Quest to Define the Role of the UN High Commissioner for Human Rights' (1997) 2 EJIL 321.

established by the General Assembly of the United Nations in the aftermath of the World Conference on Human Rights which took place in Vienna in 1993. At the World Conference, NGOs had lobbied hard for the creation of such an office. They envisaged the post as 'a high level independent authority within the United Nations system, with the capacity to act rapidly in emergency situations of human rights violations and to ensure the coordination of human rights activities within the United Nations system and the integration of human rights into all United Nations programmes and activities'.[168] Down through the years, however, this initiative had been hotly 'contested' on a broad spectrum of political, procedural and legalistic grounds.[169] Though the matter was the subject of lengthy negotiation at the conference, States could not agree to a final proposal, as a result of which a compromise was reached to refer the matter to the General Assembly.[170] As Alston notes, it came as a surprise that the matter was brought to a swift conclusion in December 1993 when the General Assembly managed to arrive at a consensus on the establishment and mandate of the new Office of the High Commissioner for Human Rights.[171]

[2.37] Under the terms of the General Assembly resolution creating the post of High Commissioner for Human Rights,[172] persons appointed must be of 'high moral standing and personal integrity', possess expertise in the field of human rights, as well as a general knowledge and understanding of diverse cultures necessary for 'impartial, objective, non-selective and effective performance of the duties of the High Commissioner'.[173] He or she is appointed by the Secretary General and approved by the General Assembly, with due regard to equitable geographical rotation, for a fixed term of four years with a possibility of renewal for one further term.[174]

[2.38] The Commissioner's mandate is a broad one; he or she is the UN official with principal responsibility for the UN's human rights activities under the direction and authority of the UN Secretary General. The role is, to all intents and purposes, principally that of providing leadership in the human rights field.[175] Specifically,

---

[168] NGO-Forum final report to the Conference: UN Doc A/CONF157/7 at 4.

[169] Van Boven, 'The United Nations High Commissioner for Human Rights: The History of a Contested Project' in Skouteris and Vermeer-Künzli, *The Protection of the Individual in International Law: Essays in Honour of Jon Dugard* (CUP, 2007), pp 49–52.

[170] Accordingly, para 18 of the Vienna Declaration and Programme of Action provided that: 'The World Conference on Human Rights recommends to the General Assembly that, when examining the report of the Conference at its forty-eighth session, it begin, as a matter of priority, consideration of the question of the establishment of a High Commissioner for Human Rights for the promotion and protection of all human rights': UN Doc A/CONF/157/23 (12 July 1993).

[171] Alston, 'Neither Fish Nor Fowl: The Quest to Define the Role of the UN High Commissioner for Human Rights'(1997) 2 EJIL 321, p 323.

[172] UN Doc A/RES/48/141 (20 December 1993).

[173] UN Doc A/RES/48/141 (20 December 1993), para 2(a).

[174] UN Doc A/RES/48/141 (20 December 1993), para 2(b).

[175] Robertson and Merrills, *Human Rights in the World* (4th edn, Manchester University Press, 1996), p 113.

Resolution 48/141 mandates the High Commissioner to promote and protect the effective enjoyment by all of all human rights;[176] to coordinate human rights activities throughout the UN system (including education and public information programmes); to engage in dialogue with governments; to assist other UN human rights organs by performing delegated tasks; to provide advisory services and technical assistance to States to support actions and programmes in the human rights field; and to play a role in rationalising, adapting, strengthening and streamlining the United Nations human rights machinery. While this mandate originally provided that the High Commissioner should carry out overall supervision of the former Centre for Human Rights (which served as the UN's administrative headquarters for human rights activities), both the OHCHR and the Centre for Human Rights were consolidated into a single Office of the High Commissioner for Human Rights in September 1997.[177] In practice, the key activities of the OHCHR have been in regard to the provision of technical assistance;[178] increasing its presence 'in the field';[179] assisting in the operation of the universal periodic review operated by the Human Rights Council; as well as supporting and facilitating reform of the UN human rights treaty system. The activities of the office in respect of the latter function form a substantial part of the analysis presented in Ch 16.

[2.39] Persistent calls for increased funding for the OHCHR's activities were given a major boost in 2005 when the Secretary General of the UN made this issue a central plank of his suggestions for reform of the UN human rights system. In his 'In Larger Freedom' speech, Kofi Annan stressed that the office was 'woefully ill-equipped to respond to the broad range of human rights challenges facing the international community' and further that the 'proclaimed commitment to human rights' of the member States must now be matched by resources to strengthen the ability of the OHCHR to perform its mandate.[180] He also called upon the High Commissioner to

---

[176] Note that the right to development is given special mention in this regard in para 4(c) of Resolution 48/141: UN Doc A/RES/48/141 (20 December 1993).

[177] See, Report of the UN Secretary General, 'Renewing the United Nations: A Programme for Reform': UN Doc A/51/950, para 79.

[178] The provision of 'technical assistance' takes the form of offering practical help on the ground to states, NGOs and even UN bodies to enable them in implementing human rights standards. At the national level, this can include, for example, assistance in the training of law enforcement personnel, revision of national legislation, advice on reform of the administration of justice, as well as advice and assistance in establishing national human rights institutions: see generally, Mertus, *The United Nations and Human Rights: A Guide for a New Era* (Global Institutions Series, 2005), pp 8–43.

[179] In countries in which a more dedicated long-term presence is required, the OHCHR has moved to establish 'country offices' to provide sustained assistance in the promotion and protection of human rights. This can range from 'human rights monitoring, public reporting, provision of technical assistance, and the development of long-term national capacities to address human rights issues': http://www.ohchr.org/EN/Countries/Pages/WorkInField.aspx (last accessed May 2011).

[180] See Report of the Secretary-General to the General Assembly, 'In Larger Freedom: Towards Development, Security and Human Rights for All' 23 May 2005: UN Doc A/59/2005, para 145.

[2.40] submit a comprehensive plan of action within 60 days, which plan was later presented to the General Assembly.[181] The plan sets forth action points in five areas: greater country engagement through the expansion of country offices and regional support; enhancing the leadership role of the office through, amongst other things, increased interaction with relevant UN bodies and actors; making closer partnerships with civil society and UN agencies; creating greater synergy between OHCHR and the various UN human rights bodies, including consideration of a unified standing treaty body;[182] and lastly, strengthening the management and planning for the office itself. Echoing the call of the Secretary General, the High Commissioner stressed the need for considerably more resources from the Member States to implement the plan. Having taken account of the action plan, the Member States gave a commitment at the World Summit to strengthen the OHCHR by doubling its regular budget resources over the following five years.[183]

[2.40] There have been six High Commissioners for Human Rights since the post was first occupied in 1994.[184] It would appear that each has emphasised different aspects of the role:[185] from diplomacy,[186] to advocacy and accountability,[187] through to intensive organisational reform.[188] As Mertus has observed, there is no doubt but that 'the OHCHR's efforts have helped the UN move beyond human rights standard-setting' and that the process of 'mainstreaming, monitoring and implementing human rights norms through its programs, funding and field presences has contributed significantly towards the growth of a strong international system of human rights'.[189]

---

[181] UN Doc A/59/2005/Add.3 (26 May 2005).

[182] This action point is considered in detail in Ch 16.

[183] World Summit Outcome Document, para 124. The OHCHR is funded from the United Nations regular budget and from voluntary contributions from Member States, intergovernmental organisations, foundations and individuals. Following the summit outcome, the regular budget funding for the 2006–2007 biennium was set at $85.9m, or 2.26 per cent of the United Nations' global budget of $3.8b. This represented an increase of $18.3m, or 28 per cent, over the previous biennium: http://www.ohchr.org/EN/AboutUs/Pages/FundingBudget.aspx(last accessed May 2011).

[184] José Ayala-Lasso, Ecuador (1994–1997); Mary Robinson, Ireland (1997–2002); Sergio Vieira de Mello, Brazil (2002–2003); Louise Arbour, Canada (2004–2008); Navanethem Pillay (2008–present).

[185] See Mertus, *The United Nations and Human Rights: A Guide for a New Era* (Global Institutions Series, 2005), pp 38–41. Sergio de Mello's tenure was cut short by his tragic death as a result of a bombing in Iraq in 2003. Although he did not have much time to make an impact on this office, he had stressed in his initial speech that strengthening the rule of law would be a key goal of his office.

[186] Ayala-Lasso: Mertus, *The United Nations and Human Rights: A Guide for a New Era* (Global Institutions Series, 2005), pp 38–39.

[187] Robinson: Mertus, *The United Nations and Human Rights: A Guide for a New Era* (Global Institutions Series, 2005), pp 39–40.

[188] Arbour: Mertus, *The United Nations and Human Rights: A Guide for a New Era* (Global Institutions Series, 2005), p 41.

[189] Mertus, *The United Nations and Human Rights: A Guide for a New Era* (Global Institutions Series, 2005), p 43.

Chapter 3

United Nations Human Rights Treaties

INTRODUCTION

[3.01] As noted in Ch 1, there was a general reluctance on the part of States during the drafting of the United Nations Charter to elaborate or define the rights and freedoms which were to be the subject of international protection. While willing to make concessions to the growing clamour amongst smaller nations[1] that assurances be given at the international level in regard to human rights, most States, and in particular the great powers of the day, were by no means committed to a comprehensive extrapolation of the nature of those rights.[2] Indeed, as one commentator notes, '... they did not expect these assurances to interfere with their national sovereignty'.[3] Certainly, the preservation of the principle of State sovereignty in art 2(7) of the UN Charter bears witness to that reality.[4]

[3.02] Accordingly, it was decided that the first task of the newly established Commission on Human Rights would be to draw up a detailed International Bill of Rights.[5] This Bill would be intended to serve as a complement to the Charter. It would

---

[1] The impetus for an international bill of rights to be inserted into the text of the Charter itself came mainly from the representatives of Latin American and Caribbean States: Glendon, 'The Forgotten Crucible: The Latin American Influence on the Universal Human Rights Idea' (2003) 27 Harv Hum Rts J 27 at 27.

[2] While some of the smaller countries represented at the San Francisco Conference which drafted the Charter proposed the inclusion of a bill of rights in the body of the Charter, a great majority of countries refused to agree to such a radical limitation of their sovereignty: Humphrey, 'The UN Charter and the Universal Declaration of Human Rights' in Luard (ed), *The International Protection of Human Rights* (Praeger, 1967), p 46. See also, Henkin, 'The International Bill of Rights: The Universal Declaration and the Covenants' in Bernhardt and Jolowicz, *Reports Submitted to the Colloquium of the International Association of Legal Science* (Max-Planck-Institut, 1985), p 2.

[3] Glendon, *A World Made New: Eleanor Roosevelt and the Universal Declaration of Human Rights* (Random House, 2001), p xvi.

[4] See Ch 1, paras **1.18–1.19** and **1.23**.

[5] President Truman stated in his speech at the closing of the San Francisco Conference that '... under this document we have good reason to expect the framing of an international bill of rights acceptable to all nations involved': Humphrey, 'The UN Charter and the Universal Declaration of Human Rights' in Luard (ed), *The International Protection of Human Rights* (Praeger, 1967), p 47.Dennis and Stewart, 'Justiciability of Economic, Social, and Cultural Rights: Should There be an International Complaints Mechanism to Adjudicate the Rights to Food, Water, Housing, and Health?' (2004) 98 Am J INt'l L 450, pp 476–489.

delineate the precise human rights which would be worthy of international protection. At an early stage in the Commission's deliberations, it was decided that the Bill of Rights would consist of three distinct parts: a declaration of rights which itself would not be legally binding; a convention that would legally bind States parties to protect those rights; and implementation procedures for their enforcement.[6] Work on these three elements of the Bill initially proceeded simultaneously in independent working groups drawn up for this purpose. However, the attempt to draft the convention and implementation procedures stalled at an early stage when States, predominantly from the Soviet bloc, simply refused to accept binding obligations let alone implementation procedures without first agreeing to a satisfactory definition of human rights.[7] By way of compromise, it was agreed to proceed first with the drafting of a non-binding declaration of rights, and then to proceed to draft a binding convention with implementation procedures. The declaration which would eventually emerge from this process is the Universal Declaration of Human Rights (UDHR), finally adopted by the General Assembly of the United Nations on the 10 December 1948.[8]

[3.03] Following the adoption of the Universal Declaration, the Commission subsequently decided that the best strategy for drafting the convention containing implementation procedures would be to split it into two separate instruments, one dealing with civil and political rights; and the other dealing with economic, social and cultural rights.[9] This division, as we shall see, was considered necessary because of the fundamentally different theoretical conceptions which emerged on the part of particular States as regards the rights which should be protected in an international convention and the measures required for their implementation.[10] The dramatic political tensions that

---

[6] Humphrey, 'The UN Charter and the Universal Declaration of Human Rights' in Luard (ed), *The International Protection of Human Rights* (Praeger, 1967), p 47.

[7] Glendon, *A World Made New: Eleanor Roosevelt and the Universal Declaration of Human Rights* (Random House, 2001), pp 94–98.

[8] GA res 217A (III), UN Doc A/810 at 71 (1948). See generally, Glendon, *A World Made New: Eleanor Roosevelt and the Universal Declaration of Human Rights* (Random House, 2001); Alfredsson and Eide, *The Universal Declaration of Human Rights: A Common Standard of Achievement* (Martinus Nijhoff, 1999); Morsink, *The Universal Declaration of Human Rights: Origins, Drafting and Intent* (Pennsylvania Press, 1999); Humphrey, 'The Universal Declaration of Human Rights: Its History, Impact and Juridical Character' in Ramcharan, (ed) *Human Rights: Thirty Years After the Universal Declaration* (Martinus Nijhoff, 1979), p 21; Johnson and Symonides, *The Universal Declaration of Human Rights: A History of its Creation and Implementation, 1948–1998* (UNESCO, 1998); Steiner, Alston and Goodman, *International Human Rights in Context: Law, Politics and Morals* (3rd edn, OUP, 2008), pp 151–160; Rehman, *International Human Rights Law* (2nd edn, Pearson, 2010), pp 75–83.

[9] See *Annotations on the Text of the Draft International Covenants on Human Rights* (1 July 1955) UN Doc A/2929, Ch I, paras 13 and 14.

[10] UN Doc A/2929 (1 July 1955), Ch II, paras 9 and 10. Dennis and Stewart make a convincing argument that 'ideological cleavage' was not the only factor at play in the decision to divide the two covenants. Rather, they argue that both sides of the ideological divide had reservations about the justiciability of economic, social and cultural rights. States also recognised that the UN specialised agencies were already responsible for implementing those rights: (contd.../)

ensued during the Cold War took their toll on the drafting of these two instruments and it would take no less than 18 years before the members States of the United Nations finally agreed to adopt them. The resulting two instruments are known as the International Covenant on Civil and Political Rights (ICCPR) and the International Covenant on Economic, Social and Cultural Rights (ICESCR), each adopted by the General Assembly of the UN on 16 December 1966. The ICCPR is supplemented by the First Optional Protocol (OP-ICCPR), also adopted in 1966, by which contracting States may agree to a complaints procedure allowing individuals within their respective jurisdictions to complain to an independent monitoring body about alleged breaches of their rights protected by that Covenant; [11] and the Second Optional Protocol, adopted in 1989, by which contracting States agree to abolish the death penalty in their jurisdictions.[12] Collectively, these instruments are referred to as the International Bill of Rights.

[3.04] The International Bill of Rights is commonly regarded as the nucleus of international human rights law promulgated by the United Nations. It is without doubt the most comprehensive statement by the international community of the human rights which are subject to protection on the international plane. It also sets up a variety of procedural mechanisms which are designed to ensure that these rights are implemented and enforced. The first section of this chapter outlines the nature of the substantive rights enshrined in the Bill of Rights and elaborates on some of the issues that have emerged since it was drafted in terms of the framework for implementation chosen by the drafters.

[3.05] In addition to the ICCPR and the ICESCR, the United Nations has adopted numerous other international treaties in the field of human rights, many of which elaborate in much greater detail on the substantive rights provided for in the latter instruments. Like the two International Covenants, these seven 'core' treaties contain specific procedures which are intended to ensure the implementation of the guaranteed rights by those States which have ratified them. Together with the ICCPR and the ICESCR, these instruments collectively comprise what is commonly referred to as the UN human rights treaty system. The origins and provisions of each of these treaties and the various 'treaty bodies' which have been established to monitor their implementation, are outlined in the second section of this Chapter. The chapters in Parts 2 and 3 focus on the procedural mechanisms contained in all of these various treaties with the aim of assessing their efficacy in practice.

---

[10] (\...contd) Dennis and Stewart, 'Justiciability of Economic, Social, and Cultural Rights: Should There be an International Complaints Mechanism to Adjudicate the Rights to Food, Water, Housing, and Health?' (2004) 98 Am J INt'l L 450, pp 476–489. See also, Langford, 'Closing the Gap? An Introduction to the International Covenant on Economic, Social and Cultural Rights' (2009) 27 Nordic Journal of Human Rights 1, pp 3–5.

[11] The genesis, procedure and operation of the First Optional Protocol to the ICCPR are dealt with extensively below in Ch 7, para **7.03–7.41**.

[12] Second Optional Protocol to the International Covenant on Civil and Political Rights, Aiming at the Abolition of the Death Penalty (15 December 1989) UN Doc A/RES/44/128.

THE INTERNATIONAL BILL OF RIGHTS

The Universal Declaration of Human Rights

[3.06] Writing on the 50th anniversary of the adoption of the Declaration, Alston comments that its adoption was 'the greatest ethical and normative achievement of the United Nations, and perhaps even of the international community as a whole in the course of the past fifty years'.[13] The apparent coherence[14] of the document belies the fact that it was drafted in an atmosphere of increasing ideological tension, particularly between East and West, and it is often remarked that had the final text not been agreed to as it was in December 1948,[15] the Declaration might never have seen the light of day.[16]

[3.07] As it stands, the Declaration appears as a list of some 30 short articles. Drafted in a civil law style,[17] the Preamble and 1;arts 1 and 2 are regarded as the 'general part' of the instrument, and as such they set forth the principles and premises guiding the interpretation of the substantive norms of the document. Referring to the pledge, which member States had already undertaken in the Charter to achieve, in cooperation with the organisation, the promotion of respect for and observance of fundamental rights, the final paragraph of the Preamble proclaims the Declaration as:

> '... a common standard of achievement for all peoples and all nations, to the end that every individual and every organ of society keeping this Declaration constantly in mind, shall strive by teaching and education to promote respect for these rights and freedoms and by progressive measures, national and international, to secure their universal and effective recognition and observance, both among the peoples of the member states themselves and among the peoples of territories under their control'.

---

[13] Alston, 'The Universal Declaration in an Era of Globalisation' in Van Der Heijden and Tahzib-Lie (eds), *Reflections on the Universal Declaration of Human Rights* (Martinus Nijhoff, 1998), p 28.

[14] There are many commentators who have argued to the contrary that the Declaration is by no means a coherent one: see paras **3.15–3.24** below.

[15] The Declaration was adopted without dissent by the General Assembly of the UN on 10 December 1948. Forty-eight States voted in favour of the Declaration, while some eight States abstained in the vote (Saudi Arabia, South Africa, the USSR, Byelorussian Soviet Socialist Republic, Czechoslovakia, Poland, Ukrainian Soviet Socialist Republic, and Yugoslavia).

[16] 'It is doubtful whether the feat could be repeated today, notwithstanding the marked improvement in relations between the principal protagonists of the Cold War': Humphrey, 'The UN Charter and the Universal Declaration of Human Rights' in Luard (ed), *The International Protection of Human Rights* (Praeger, 1967), p 49.

[17] The civil law style is largely attributed to the influence of the distinguished French jurist, René Cassin, who was appointed by the eight-person drafting committee of the Commission to fine-tune the text of the Declaration to be debated by the Commission. It should be noted however that the first 'outline' of the Declaration was initially submitted to the drafting committee by the Canadian Director of the United Nations' Division of Human Rights, Humphrey on the 9 June 1947. A somewhat unfortunate controversy emerged in later years as regards who could properly be credited as the author of the original text of the Declaration: see Glendon, *A World Made New: Eleanor Roosevelt and the Universal Declaration of Human Rights* (Random House, 2001), pp 65–66.

Article 1 provides that: 'All human beings are born free and equal in dignity and rights. They are endowed with reason and conscience and should act towards one another in a spirit of brotherhood'.[18] Article 2 builds on the tone set for the document as a truly universal one by stating that: 'Everyone is entitled to all the rights and freedoms set forth in this Declaration, without distinction of any kind, such as race, colour, sex, language, religion, political or other opinion, national or social origin, property, birth or other status'.[19] Articles 2–27 set forth the substantive rights and freedoms as follows.[20]

Article 3:	The right to life, liberty and security of the person
Article 4:	Right to freedom from slavery or servitude
Article 5:	Right to freedom from torture or cruel, inhuman or degrading treatment or punishment
Article 6:	Right to recognition everywhere as a person before the law
Article 7:	Right to equality before the law and to protection from discrimination
Article 8:	Right to an effective remedy by competent national tribunals
Article 9:	Right to freedom from arbitrary arrest, detention or exile
Article 10:	Right to a fair trial
Article 11:	Right to be presumed innocent before being proven guilty and guarantees against retroactive penal legislation
Article 12:	Freedom from arbitrary interference with one's privacy, family life, or correspondence
Article 13:	Right to freedom of movement
Article 14:	Right to seek and be granted asylum
Article 15:	Right to a nationality
Article 16:	Right to marry and found a family
Article 17:	Right to own property
Article 18:	Right to freedom of thought, conscience and religion
Article 19:	Right to freedom of expression and opinion
Article 20:	Right to freedom of peaceful assembly and association

---

[18] The gender neutral language of the text, with its reference to 'human beings' as opposed to the original draft text 'men' can be largely credited to the contributions of the Indian delegate to the Commission on Human Rights, Mrs Mehta, who warned her colleagues repeatedly that the use of the words 'all men' could be construed in some societies as excluding women. Glendon, *A World Made New: Eleanor Roosevelt and the Universal Declaration of Human Rights* (Random House, 2001), pp 90 and 92.

[19] In a second paragraph, it goes on to state that 'Furthermore, no distinction shall be made on the basis of the political, jurisdictional or international status of the country or territory to which a person belongs, whether it be independent, trust, non-self governing or under any other limitation of sovereignty'.

[20] Glendon, 'Knowing the Universal Declaration of Human Rights' (1997–98) 73 Notre Dame L Rev 1153, p 1158.

Article 21: Right to participate in the governance of the State, and the right to democracy
Article 22: Right to social security
Article 23: Right to work
Article 24: Right to rest and leisure
Article 25: Right to an adequate standard of living
Article 26: Right to education
Article 27: Right to participate in the cultural life of the community

[3.08] According to Glendon, René Cassin, one of the main drafters of the Declaration, drew an analogy between the Declaration and the portico of a temple. The Preamble corresponded to the 'courtyard steps' towards the entrance of the temple, arts 1 and 2 constituted the portico's main foundation blocks, with the main body of the instrument, consisting of rights arranged in four columns.[21] The first set of rights in arts 3–11 is easily recognisable in many national bills of rights and constitutions as rights pertaining to individuals. By contrast, the second set of rights in arts 12–17 was aimed at protecting people in their relations with others and within civil society.[22] The third set, arts 18–21, contains rights by now in long-practised usage in western democracies to freedom of thought, conscience and religion, expression and assembly and association. The fourth set, arts 22–27 of the Declaration, contains the 'economic, social and cultural' rights provisions. While agreement on the substance of these latter rights was not particularly difficult to achieve at the time that the Declaration was drafted,[23] the controversy which did ensue during the drafting as regards their relationship with the other rights provided for in the Declaration still endures to this day.[24]

[3.09] The final three articles of the Declaration constituted the over-arching 'pediment' to Cassin's temple analogy. These speak to the conditions which were regarded as being necessary for the realisation of the rights as a whole.[25] Article 28 is thus addressed to the international order in general and provides that: 'Everyone is entitled to a social and international order in which the rights and freedoms set forth in this Declaration can be fully realized'. It was intended to serve as a pre-cursor to the final two articles of the

---

[21] Glendon, *A World Made New: Eleanor Roosevelt and the Universal Declaration of Human Rights* (Random House, 2001), pp 173–191.

[22] Glendon, 'Knowing the Universal Declaration of Human Rights' (1997–98) 73 Notre Dame L Rev 1153, p 1165.

[23] The inclusion of economic, social and cultural rights in the text of the Declaration was supported by the US, the Latin American countries, the Soviet Union and countries of Eastern Europe. Australia, the United Kingdom and South Africa opposed their inclusion: Steiner and Alston, *International Human Rights in Context: Law, Politics and Morals* (2nd edn, OUP, 2000), p 271.

[24] Glendon, 'Knowing the Universal Declaration of Human Rights' (1997–98) 73 Notre Dame L Rev 1153, p 1167.

[25] Glendon, 'Knowing the Universal Declaration of Human Rights' (1997–98) 73 Notre Dame L Rev 1153, pp 1168–1169.

Declaration which illuminate the conditions which are in turn required for such an order to be realised.[26] First is the consideration set forth in art 29(1) that: 'Everyone has *duties* to the community in which alone the free and full development of his personality is possible'. Second is the stricture that the exercise of the rights in the Declaration may be subject to *limitations*, but only those, 'as are determined by law' and 'solely for the purpose of securing due recognition and respect for the rights and freedoms of others and of meeting the just requirements of morality, public order and the general welfare in a democratic society'.[27] Further limitations on the exercise of the rights are set forth in art 29(3) ('These rights and freedoms may in no case be exercised contrary to the purposes and principles of the United Nations); and in art 30 ('Nothing in this Declaration may be interpreted as implying for any State, group or person any right to engage in any activity or to perform any act aimed at the destruction of any of the rights and freedoms set forth herein').

As Glendon argues, the Declaration should thus not be read as a pick and choose 'catalogue' of rights, but rather as an 'organic document ... a set of principles that are related to one another and to certain over-arching ideas'.[28] The full import of the Declaration, therefore, can only be appreciated when it is read as a whole.

Juridical status

[3.10] During the final debate of the General Assembly that led to the adoption of the UDHR on the 10 December 1948, the view was expressed that: 'The best way of deciding whether the Declaration was incomplete or unsatisfactory might be to allow it time and then judge from the results obtained'.[29] In this regard, the original intent of the drafters of the Declaration was that the document should not be considered a legally binding instrument.[30] To begin with, it was adopted by the General Assembly as a resolution of that body, and, as we have seen in Ch 1, resolutions of the latter body are not binding in international law, but rather only have the status of a recommendation. The Preamble to the document fortifies this intent, by emphasising the proclamation of the Declaration as a 'common standard of achievement' for all peoples and all nations. In her closing address to the General Assembly on the eve of the adoption of the Declaration, the chair of the Commission on Human Rights which had drafted the original text of the document made sure to clarify the point:

---

[26] Glendon, 'Knowing the Universal Declaration of Human Rights' (1997–98) 73 Notre Dame L Rev 1153, p 1169.
[27] UDHR, art 29(2).
[28] Glendon, 'Knowing the Universal Declaration of Human Rights' (1997–98) 73 Notre Dame L Rev 1153, p 1163.
[29] Statement of Mr Carrera Andrade (Ecuador): 183rd Plenary Meeting, UN Doc A/PV.183, p 920.
[30] Immediately following the vote of the General Assembly adopting the Declaration, its President, Mr HV Evatt (Australia) put the matter succinctly: '... the Declaration only marked a first step since it was not a convention by which States would be bound to carry out and give effect to the fundamental human rights; nor would it provide for enforcement; yet it was a step forward in a great evolutionary process': UN Doc A/PV.183, p 934.

'In giving our approval to the Declaration today it is of primary importance that we keep clearly in mind the basic character of the document. It is not a treaty; it is not an international agreement. It is not and does not purport to be a statement of law or of legal obligation. It is a Declaration of basic principles of human rights and freedoms, to be stamped with the approval of the General Assembly by formal vote of its members, and to serve as a common standard of achievement for all people of all nations'.[31]

While stressing the absence of legal obligation, the drafters emphasised instead the moral authority of the instrument in serving as a 'guide to the Governments in their efforts to guarantee human rights by legislation and through their administrative and legal practice'.[32]

[3.11] Notwithstanding this clarity of intent in 1948, the question of the juridical status of the Declaration has occupied the minds of many academics and diplomats alike over the years since the document was first adopted. Even before the ink was dry on the Declaration, the assertion was being made that a degree of legal obligation attached to the Declaration as an 'authoritative interpretation' of the human rights clauses of the Charter.[33] While this view was by no means accepted at the time,[34] the meteoric rise in fame of the Declaration in the public mind and in diplomatic practice on human rights[35] emboldened others to argue in later years that the instrument as a whole now forms part

---

[31] Statement of Mrs Roosevelt, 9 December 1948, to the General Assembly of the United Nations: http://www.udhr.org/history/ergeas48.htm (last accessed May 2011).

[32] Statement of the British Representative, Mr Mayhew, 93rd Meeting, 3rd Committee, General Assembly, UN Doc AC 3/SR 93.

[33] This view was held by René Cassin, amongst others: Humphrey, 'The UN Charter and the Universal Declaration of Human Rights' in Luard (ed), *The International Protection of Human Rights* (Praeger, 1967), p 50. It is interesting to note that 40 odd years after that argument was made, Humphrey, who had participated in the original drafting exercise, regarded it as the 'beginning of a now developed practice of regarding the Declaration as an authoritative and therefore binding interpretation of the Charter': Humphrey, *No Distant Millennium: The International Law of Human Rights* (UNESCO, 1989), pp 159–160. See also Sohn, 'The New International Law: Protection of the Rights of Individuals Rather Than States' (1982) 32 Am UL Rev 1, p 16: 'The Declaration thus is now considered to be an authoritative interpretation of the UN Charter, spelling out in considerable detail the meaning of the phrase 'human rights and fundamental freedoms,' which Member States agreed in the Charter to promote and observe'.

[34] See, for example, the response of Sir Hersch Lauterpacht to this view, 'The Universal Declaration of Human Rights' (1949) BYIL 354, pp 365–367.

[35] A certain annoyance has been expressed by some scholars and even judges as regards the notoriety of the Declaration as compared with legally binding human rights instruments like the two Covenants discussed further below. See, for example, the comments of Judge Rosalyn Higgins, 'I have sometimes been quite puzzled by the hold that the Universal Declaration of Human Rights continues to have on the minds not only of ordinary people but of government officials ... As a former member of the Human Rights Committee, I remained perplexed (and, if I am honest, sometimes irritated) by the constant reference by governments during examination of their reports to the Universal Declaration, when the instrument under examination was a later instrument by which they were legally bound – the ICCPR': (contd.../)

of customary international law. According to this view, the consistent practice of States and international institutions in invoking its provisions as evidence of the content of international law are sufficient to infuse it with the status of customary international law, thus making its provisions legally binding on all States.[36]

[3.12] The fact that references to the Declaration are made in several subsequent human rights instruments adopted by the United Nations is typical of the evidence cited in this regard. For example, in 1968, the First World Conference on Human Rights was convened by the United Nations to discuss progress made on human rights in the intervening years since the Declaration was adopted. In the document which emerged from the discussions by State representatives, known as the *Declaration of Tehran*, the International Conference on Human Rights proclaimed that the UDHR 'states a common understanding of the peoples of the world concerning the inalienable and inviolable rights of all members of the human family and constitutes an obligation for the members of the international community'.[37] Likewise, attention is paid to the Helsinki Final Act in 1975 in which the participating States agreed that in the field of human rights they would 'act in conformity with the purposes and principles of the Charter of the United Nations and with the Universal Declaration of Human Rights'.[38]

---

[35] (\...contd) Higgins, 'From a Legal Point of View' in Van Der Heijden and Tahzib-Lie, *Reflections on the Universal Declaration of Human Rights* (Martinus Nijhoff, 1998), 161, p 163. See also in the same volume, Van Dijk, 'The Universal Declaration is Legally Non-binding; So What?' p 108 at p 110: 'The Universal Declaration is frequently cited as the epitomization of human rights standards and obligations in public debates on human rights and in the media, in cases where it would have been more appropriate, legally speaking, to refer to a specific human rights treaty'.

[36] Robertson and Merrills, for example, argue that the Declaration '... has inspired more than forty State constitutions, together with the regional human rights treaties of Europe, Africa and the Americas, and examples quoting or reproducing provisions of the Declaration can be found in all continents. Thus the impact of the Universal Declaration has probably exceeded its authors' most sanguine expectations, while its constant and widespread recognition means that the principles it contains can now be regarded as customary international law': Robertson and Merrills, *Human Rights in the World* (4th edn, Manchester University Press, 1996), p 29. See also, Voitto Saario and Higgins Cass, 'The United Nations and the International Protection of Human Rights: A Legal Analysis and Interpretation' (1977) 7 Ca W Int'l LJ 591, p 596: 'From an international law perspective, one is justified in maintaining that the Declaration, which technically has only the force of moral persuasion, has now become part of customary international law and, thus, legally binding on all states'. See also Humphrey, *No Distant Millennium: The International Law of Human Rights* (UNESCO, 1989), pp 154–166; and Sohn, 'The New International Law: Protection of the Rights of Individuals Rather Than States' (1982) 32 Am UL Rev 1, p 17.

[37] 23 UN GAOR Supp (N 41) at 1, UN Doc A /Conf32/41 (1968), para 2.

[38] The Helsinki Final Act is a non-binding agreement between participating States of Western Europe, North America and Eastern Europe which significantly eased the political tensions of the Cold War and served as the foundation for the CSCE (now OSCE): Final Act of the Conference on Security and Cooperation in Europe, 1 August 1974, para 1(a)(VII). See http://www.osce.org/documents/mcs/1975/08/4044_en.pdf (last accessed May 2011). See also Ch 1, para **1.25**.

Also of obvious relevance in this context would be the numerous references to the UDHR in the Vienna Declaration and Programme of Action agreed between 171 participating States at the Second World Conference on Human Rights in 1993.[39] Moreover, the fact that the Declaration has influenced the drafting of many national bills of rights and constitutions, and has been relied upon in national courts in interpreting domestic human rights law, has also been cited as evidence of the enhanced status of the Declaration as customary international law.[40]

[3.13] Certain commentators have gone on to express the more extreme position that the Declaration now forms part of *jus cogens*,[41] while others maintain that the Declaration is still just a Declaration and as such possesses at best 'a quasi-legal significance'.[42] Perhaps the most measured approach is that while the entire Declaration may not be considered to be customary international law, certain of its precepts and principles have acquired that status over time.[43] According to this view, a failure to respect certain of the principles enshrined in the Declaration would constitute a violation of international law.[44] Thus, freedom from slavery and servitude (art 4), freedom from torture and cruel, inhuman or degrading treatment or punishment (art 5), freedom from racial discrimination (arts 2 and 7) may be viewed as principles of customary international law and also *jus cogens*.[45]

[3.14] In conclusion, it must be borne in mind that most of the principles in the Declaration have been subsequently incorporated into international human rights treaties, such as the two covenants examined later below. These instruments, by their very nature, are automatically binding as a matter of international law on the States which have ratified them. As we shall see, the core international human rights treaties generally enjoy high participation ratios. Therefore, in practical terms, academic wrangling about whether the Declaration has attained the status of customary

---

[39] UN GAOR A/CONF 157/23, 12 July 1993: http://www.unhchr.ch/huridocda/huridoca.nsf/(Symbol)/A.CONF.157.23.En (last accessed May 2011).

[40] Hannum, 'The Status of the Universal Declaration of Human Rights in National and International Law' (1995–1996) 25 Ga J Int'l & Comp L 287, p 322.

[41] Humphrey, *No Distant Millennium: The International Law of Human Rights* (UNESCO, 1989), p 164. See also McDougal, Lasswell and Chen, *Human Rights and World Public Order* (Yale University Press, 1980), p 274.

[42] Daes, *Freedom of the Individual Under Law: A Study On the Individual's Duties to the Community and the Limitations on Human Rights and Freedoms Under Article 29 of the Universal Declaration of Human Rights* (United Nations, 1990), p 50.

[43] Kamminga, *Inter-State Accountability for Violations of Human Rights* (University of Pennsylvania Press, 1992), p 133.

[44] See Henkin, 'The International Bill of Rights: The Universal Declaration and the Covenants' in Bernhardt and Jolowicz (eds), *International Enforcement of Human Rights* (Max-Planck Institut, 1985), p 6.

[45] Rehman, *International Human Rights Law* (2nd edn, Pearson, 2010), p 82. 'While endorsing the customary value of many of the rights contained in the Declaration, at the same time some caution is recommended ... not all the rights contained in the Universal Declaration have generated a sufficient degree of consensus to be recognised as binding in customary law'; Cassese, *International Law* (2nd edn, OUP, 2005), p 394.

international law is only of relevance in the rare circumstance in which a State has not ratified a treaty, or has qualified its acceptance of particular obligations by a reservation.[46]

Appraisal of the UDHR: universal or unrealistic?

[3.15] The drafters of the Declaration intended it to be a comprehensive description of the rights and freedoms which nations of the world considered to be vital for human emancipation and human dignity. Buergenthal notes that while the UN Charter '... internationalized human rights as a legal concept, the Universal Declaration gave the concept the moral force that captured the imagination of mankind and transformed it into a powerful political manifesto'.[47] Notwithstanding its subsequent claim to fame in the public domain, a number of critiques of the Declaration have surfaced over the years since it was drafted, many of which still persist today.

[3.16] Perhaps the chief criticism levelled at the Declaration, in one form or another, has been that the rights enshrined in it predominantly reflect a notion of human rights prevalent in western liberal democracies, at the expense of non-western conceptions of human rights.[48] To understand this critique, it is necessary to review briefly the various theoretical conceptions of human rights which did in fact influence the drafting of the Declaration.[49] In this regard, the meaning that has historically been attributed to 'human rights' in the Anglo-American tradition is essentially an individualistic one. Most closely identified with the development of natural rights theory by John Locke,[50] this

---

[46] Sieghart, *The International Law of Human Rights* (OUP, 1983), p 55; and Van Dijk, 'The Universal Declaration is Legally Non-binding; So What?' Van Der Heijden and Tahzib-Lie, *Reflections on the Universal Declaration of Human Rights* (Martinus Nijhoff, 1998), 108, p 109.

[47] Buergenthal, 'Centrepiece of the Human Rights Revolution' in Van Der Heijden and Tahzib-Lie (eds), *Reflections on the Universal Declaration of Human Rights* (Martinus Nijhoff, 1998), p 91.

[48] For a thorough examination of the arguments initially raised regarding the validity of the Declaration, see Alston, 'The Universal Declaration of Human Rights at 35: Western and Passé or Alive and Universal' (1983) 31 ICJ Review 60.

[49] See generally, Tomuschat, *Human Rights: Between Idealism and Realism* (OUP, 2003), ch 2, pp 6–23; and Shestack, 'The Jurisprudence of Human Rights' in Meron (ed), *Human Rights in International Law* (Clarendon Press, 1986), p 70.

[50] In his famous work *Two Treatises of Civil Government* Locke developed the idea that humans were 'by nature all free, equal and independent' and possess human rights as a gift of nature: Locke, *Two Treatises of Civil Government* (1690), Book II, Ch VII, para 95. An online version is accessible at http://etext.lib.virginia.edu/toc/modeng/public/LocTre2.html (last accessed May 2011). Locke's views may be contrasted with those of Thomas Hobbes, an earlier exponent of the social contract theory, who believed that if humans wish to live peacefully they must relinquish most of their natural rights to a sovereign authority in order to avoid the condition of war that would otherwise ensue: Hobbes, *The Leviathan* (1660) Online version accessible at http://oregonstate.edu/instruct/phl302/texts/hobbes/leviathan-contents.html (last accessed May 2011). In contrast, Locke believed that human beings could not divest themselves of their natural rights to the arbitrary power of another or to the 'legislative power': Locke, *Two Treaties of Civil Government* (1690), Book II, Ch XI, para 135.

conception of human rights is based on the premise that 'rights' are naturally inherent in human beings by virtue of their being human and not simply because they are conferred by law.[51] Reflecting the emergence of capitalism and industrialisation, this liberal philosophy broadly defined rights as being inherent in the individual *per se*.[52] They are not *granted* by the State, but rather are superior to the State and take precedence over it.[53] According to this model, States are viewed as the facilitators of individual rights, but also as 'the greatest potential violators of those rights'.[54]

[3.17] In contrast to this emphasis on the rights of individuals, non-western conceptions of human rights tended to place more emphasis on the *duties* which individuals owed to society as providing the path for realising human dignity.[55] Traditional socialist theory, for example, which was a dominant ideology for many of the States which drafted the Universal Declaration, envisaged a society in which the *unity* of rights and duties can be achieved.[56] Socialist States place much more importance on the *combination* of rights and duties which individuals owe to society. Societal goals are to be achieved by mutual cooperation, and ultimately through the agency of the State,[57] rather than through individual self-fulfilment.[58] As Selbourne has explained, 'social-ism' was perceived to be the 'ethical antithesis to individual-ism'.[59] This emphasis on the group or society was, and still is, manifest in Asian and African conceptions of human rights.[60] Somewhere between these two extremes lay a middle-ground approach reflected in the continental

---

[51] See generally, Donnelly, 'Human Rights as Natural Rights' (1982) HRQ 390.
[52] Pollis and Schwab, *Human Rights: New Perspectives, New Realities* (Boulder, 2000), p 2.
[53] See generally, Donnelly, 'Human Rights and Human Dignity: An Analytic Critique of Non-Western Conceptions of Human Rights' (1982) 76 Am Pol Sci Rev 303.
[54] Donnelly, 'Human Rights and Human Dignity: An Analytic Critique of Non-Western Conceptions of Human Rights', (1982) 76 Am Pol Sci Rev 303, p 306.
[55] Donnelly, 'Human Rights and Human Dignity: An Analytic Critique of Non-Western Conceptions of Human Rights', (1982) 76 Am Pol Sci Rev 303, pp 306–311.
[56] See generally, Hodgson, *Individual Duty Within a Human Rights Discourse* (Ashgate, 2003), pp 193–206.
[57] In outlining the ideological precepts of the former Soviet system, Donnelly explains that its emphasis was '... on objective and concrete rights, which the individual enjoys only through state agency, rather than subjective, abstract or formal rights inhering in the individual per se': Donnelly, 'Human Rights and Human Dignity: An Analytic Critique of Non-Western Conceptions of Human Rights', (1982) 76 Am Pol Sci Rev 303, p 310.
[58] As Hodgson explains: 'The socialist ideal is that of a society in which individuals are fulfilled primarily through co-operative efforts rather than through individual pursuit of self-fulfilment. A further condition precedent to the enjoyment of human rights by socialist citizens is the discharge of their individual duties owed to the socialist community'. Hodgson, *Individual Duty Within a Human Rights Discourse* (Ashgate, 2003), p 194.
[59] Selbourne, *The Principle of Duty: An Essay on the Foundations of the Civic Order* (Sinclair Stephenson, 1994), pp 38–39.
[60] Donnelly, 'Human Rights and Human Dignity: An Analytic Critique of Non-Western Conceptions of Human Rights', (1982) 76 Am Pol Sci Rev 303 at 307–309. See also Hodgson, *Individual Duty Within a Human Rights Discourse*, (Ashgate, 2003) on Islam (pp 48–52), Confucianism (pp 53–60) and Africa (pp 125–137).

European tradition of rights which tended to place emphasis on the concepts of equality and fraternity, as well as on the importance of balancing rights with restrictions, and placing duties on rights-holders.[61] This emphasis on duties was also central to the development of Latin-American conceptions of rights.[62]

[3.18] These competing conceptions of human rights inevitably led to differences in the character of the rights which were preferred by their adherents. Thus, western liberal democracies traditionally placed more emphasis on rights of a 'civil and political' character, such as the right to liberty and freedom of expression, as being the principal means by which human dignity can be attained. These rights were considered to be '... the core of the defence strategy against arbitrary use of power by governments'.[63] Socialist States, on the other hand, placed more emphasis on rights of an 'economic, social and cultural' nature, such as the rights to food and housing, which are largely dependent on State structures for their fulfilment.[64] In what has proved to be an enduring, though somewhat controversial, taxonomy, Vasak has classified these rights in terms of 'generations'.[65] According to his scheme, 'civil and political rights' can be classified as 'first generation rights'. They are 'attributive rights' of the human person, which can only be invoked *against* a State. 'Economic, social and cultural rights', on the other hand, can be designated as 'second generation rights' or 'rights of credit' against the State and organised national and international bodies as a whole, in other words, rights which can only be achieved through the vehicle of the State.

[3.19] The rapid wave of decolonisation which took place in the 1950s and 1960s led to the emergence of what Vasak has termed a 'third generation' of rights. These 'new' rights or 'solidarity rights' include, for example, the right to development, the right to a

---

[61] This tradition can be traced to the political philosopher, Rousseau, who believed that civil society is based on a contractual arrangement of natural rights and duties, applicable to all persons in that society: Rousseau, *The Social Contract, or Principles of Political Right* (1762), Book 1, Ch 8. Online version accessible at http://www.constitution.org/jjr/socon.htm (last accessed May 2011).

[62] See generally Glendon, 'The Forgotten Crucible: The Latin American Influence on the Universal Human Rights Idea' (2003) 27 Harv Hum Rts J 27.

[63] Tomuschat, *Human Rights: Between Idealism and Realism* (OUP, 2003), p 27.

[64] Cassese, *International Law in a Divided World* (OUP, 1986), p 301.

[65] Vasak, 'For the Third Generation of Human Rights': Inaugural Lecture Delivered to the Tenth Study Session of the International Institute of Human Rights (July 1979). While Vasak's scheme of rights is at this stage in very common usage in the literature on international human rights law, some authors deliberately eschew it on the basis that it is simplistic or unhelpful. 'The history of the evolution of human rights at the national level does not make it possible to place the emergence of different rights into clear-cut stages': Eide and Rosas, 'Economic, Social and Cultural Rights: A Universal Challenge' in Eide, Krause and Rosas (eds), *Economic, Social and Cultural Rights: A Textbook* (2nd edn, Martinus Nijhoff, 2001), p 4. See also, Tomuschat, *Human Rights: Between Idealism and Realism* (OUP, 2003), pp 24–25. Eschewing the language of 'generations', Cassese refers to the development of these various strands of rights in terms of 'stages': Cassese, *International Law in a Divided World* (OUP, 1986), pp 297–311.

clean environment and the right to peace.[66] They were most obviously relevant to less developed nations, then in the process of freeing themselves from the shackles of colonial domination. The difference between this category and the previous two is that these rights are also dependent on international cooperation for their fulfilment, as opposed to being solely dependent on domestic legal measures or resources. At the same time, less developed nations also place huge emphasis on economic, social and cultural rights for economic reasons; as well as for political reasons.[67] Civil and political rights are regarded as being less relevant to the more pressing societal goal of economic development. In fledgling states, or ones emerging from factional fighting, restriction of civil and political rights is often deemed necessary so as to strengthen the authority of the State in order to build strong central government.[68]

[3.20] Returning now to the text of the Declaration, one major critique that has been mounted of its terms is that the primary emphasis in the Declaration is on civil and political rights, as opposed to economic, social and cultural rights; and that the terminology used in the instrument is unremittingly individualistic. This critique forced Pollis and Schwab to conclude in 1978 that the instrument was meaningless in its application to the non-western world.[69] Taking a different, though equally critical tack, Szabo argued that the Declaration does not possess a 'sound political character' and that in its attempt to achieve universality, the instrument does not achieve a defined position on the scale of political values.[70] This perceived imbalance was often attributed to the fact that when the Declaration was being drafted, the vast majority of Asian and African countries that have since assumed independence, were still under colonial domination and hence were simply not at the drafting table.[71]

---

[66] On the development of these particular rights, see Tomuschat, *Human Rights: Between Idealism and Realism* (OUP, 2003), pp 48–50. See also proceedings from the UNESCO 'Symposium on the Study of New Human Rights: The Rights of Solidarity' held in Mexico from 12 to 15 August 1980: http://unesdoc.unesco.org/images/0004/000407/040770eo.pdf (last accessed May 2011). On solidarity rights generally, see Alston (ed), *Solidarity Rights* (OUP, 2001).

[67] Cassese, *International Law in a Divided World* (OUP, 1986), pp 307–308.

[68] Cassese, *International Law in a Divided World* (OUP, 1986), pp 307–308.

[69] Pollis and Schwab, 'Human Rights: A Western Construct with Limited Application' in Pollis and Schwab (eds), *Human Rights: Cultural and Ideological Perspectives* (Praeger, 1978).

[70] Szabo, 'Historical Foundations of Human Rights' in Vasak (ed), *The International Dimensions of Human Rights* (UNESCO, 1982), pp 23–27.

[71] An-Na'im, 'Human Rights in the Muslim World: Socio-Political Conditions and Scriptural Imperatives' (1990) 3 Harv Hum Rts J 13, p 15. While acknowledging this imbalance to be true in numerical terms, Glendon has argued convincingly that their participation was by no means insignificant and that the effort to include every conceivable perspective on human rights was painstaking on the part of the drafters. Moreover, she argues that the text of the Declaration was far more influenced by the rights traditions of continental Europe and Latin America, than by the Anglo-American emphasis on individualism: Glendon, *A World Made New: Eleanor Roosevelt and the Universal Declaration of Human Rights* (Random House, 2001), pp 224–227.

[3.21] The latter critique was reflective of a time when cold war politics and ideologies were still dominating the international agenda. It was subsequently overtaken by a broader criticism of the Declaration (and indeed of the entire corpus of international human rights law) that by carrying such a distinctly western imprint, it fails to take account of the many and varied cultural[72] contexts in which human rights are upheld and applied.[73] According to this cultural relativist view, beliefs about rights are dependent on the cultural context in which they are conceived.[74] Cultural relativism, therefore, in its strongest form[75] contradicts the basic premise of universality so integral to the Declaration. This critique of the Declaration has opened up an ongoing debate between advocates of universality and those who argue that human rights are culturally dependent.[76]

[3.22] In the midst of these challenges, the United Nations as an organisation has continued to promote vigorously the 'universal' nature of the instrument [77] and the 'interdependence' of the rights which it proclaims. In this respect, the statements made at the World Conference on Human Rights in 1993 as regards the status of the Declaration are of obvious significance.[78] In para 1 of the Vienna Declaration and Programme for Action, which emerged from that Conference, States reaffirmed their

---

[72] The term 'culture' here may refer to various indigenous populations who practice particular customary practices, or it may refer to various religious ideologies and institutions in particular States.

[73] See Matua, 'Savages, Victims and Saviours: The Metaphor of Human Rights' (2001) 42 Harvard Int'l LJ 201; and Pannikar, 'Is the Notion of Human Rights a Western Concept?' (1982) Diogenes 120: 75–102.

[74] The cultural relativist challenge to international human rights law generally is explained by Binder in 'Cultural Relativism and Cultural Imperialism in Human Rights Law' (1999) 5 Buff Hum Rts L Rev 211.

[75] Donnelly posits a spectrum of cultural relativist and universalist views according to which 'radical cultural relativism' is defined as the belief that culture is the sole source of a moral right or rule: Donnelly, 'Cultural Relativism and Human Rights' (1984) 6 HRQ 400.

[76] See further Cerna, 'Universality of Human Rights and Cultural Diversity: Implementation of Human Rights in Different Socio-Cultural Contexts' (1994) 16 HRQ 740; Perry, 'Are Human Rights Universal? The Relativist Challenge and Related Matters' (1997) 19 HRQ 461; Harris-Short, 'International Human Rights Law: Imperialist, Inept and Ineffective? Cultural Relativism and the UN Convention on the Rights of the Child' (2003) 25 HRQ 130; and Twining (ed), *Human Rights, Southern Voices* (CUP, 2009).

[77] See very recently, for example, the emphasis placed on the universality of the Declaration by UN Secretary General, Ban Ki-moon, on Human Rights Day 2007:
  'The extraordinary vision and determination of the drafters produced a document that for the first time set out universal human rights for all people in an individual context. Now available in more than 360 languages, the Declaration is the most translated document in the world – a testament to its universal nature and reach. It has inspired the constitutions of many newly independent States and many new democracies. It has become a yardstick by which we measure respect for what we know, or should know, as right and wrong.'
  http://www.un.org/events/humanrights/2007/statements.shtml (last accessed May 2011)

[78] Vienna Declaration and Programme for Action, Preamble.

solemn commitment 'to fulfil their obligations to promote universal respect for and observance of all human rights', the universal nature of which was deemed to be 'beyond question'. Much of the document focuses on third generation rights and on development issues.[79]

[3.23] At a formal level, this ringing endorsement of the Declaration has done much to reaffirm its legitimacy as a touchstone for the evolving international human rights agenda. In the face of such apparently overwhelming support from some 172 different States, arguments to the effect that its precepts continue to be foisted on the non-western world are difficult to sustain. Its enduring constancy is indeed a tribute to its drafters who created an instrument which in Glendon's words is '… flexible enough to allow for differences in emphasis and means of implementation, but not so malleable as to permit any basic human rights to be completely eclipsed or unnecessarily subordinated for the sake of other rights'.[80]

[3.24] The gap between form and substance is equally enduring, however, and while the debate concerning the Declaration itself may have dissipated in recent years, many challenges still exist in implementing its precepts. For one thing, as Harris-Short notes, the consensus on the principle of universality reached by governmental representatives at the Vienna Conference is profoundly lacking at the 'grassroots' or local level *within* many States where the language of 'rights' is a completely alien construct.[81] Thus, while governments may be less inclined to contest the validity of human rights norms on the basis of cultural relativism, there is often a difficulty in commanding respect for such norms within the local populace.[82] For another, the Declaration and the normative framework that it has generated now operates in the context of the phenomenon of globalisation, in which new actors have emerged, such as multinational corporations, whose activities have major implications in the human rights field.[83] Operating outside the traditional paradigm of reciprocal State obligations on which the structure of international human rights law is based, such actors remain largely unaccountable under

---

[79] Vienna Declaration and Programme for Action, art 10.
[80] Glendon, *A World Made New: Eleanor Roosevelt and the Universal Declaration of Human Rights* (Random House, 2001), p 232.
[81] Harris-Short, 'International Human Rights Law: Imperialist, Inept and Ineffective? Cultural Relativism and the UN Convention on the Rights of the Child' (2003) 25 HRQ 130, p 134. A similar point is made by Katarina Tomaševski in relation to public awareness of human rights treaties in 'Has the Right to Education a Future Within the United Nations? A Behind-the-Scenes Account by the Special Rapporteur on the Right to Education 1998–2004' (2005) 5 Human Rights Law Review 205 at 225.
[82] Harris-Short, 'International Human Rights Law: Imperialist, Inept and Ineffective? Cultural Relativism and the UN Convention on the Rights of the Child' (2003) 25 HRQ 130, p 134.
[83] See generally, Schwab and Pollis in Schwab and Pollis (eds), 'Globalization's Impact on Human Rights' in *Human Rights: New Perspectives and New Realities* (Rienner, 2000), pp 209–221; Coicaud, Doyle and Gardner, *The Globalization of Human Rights* (United Nations University Press, 2003); and Steiner, Alston and Goodman, *International Human Rights in Context: Law, Politics and Morals* (3rd edn, OUP, 2008), pp 1385–1432.

this system for activities which breach human rights standards.[84] Against this backdrop, the debate has largely moved on from the *content* of the rights enshrined in the Declaration to the challenge of *implementing* and *developing* international human rights law in such a way as to hold States and other such actors accountable for the multiplicity of human rights violations arising.[85]

The International Covenant on Civil and Political Rights

[3.25] As noted above, following the adoption of the Declaration, negotiations began on the text of a legally binding convention on human rights which would also contain measures of implementation.[86] However, the political tensions which by that stage began to dominate the discussion resulted in entrenched positions being taken by East and West on the character of the rights to be protected in the covenant and the methods by which they should be enforced.[87] In the result, a decision was eventually taken by the General Assembly to draw up two distinct and separate covenants, one dealing with civil and political rights and the other dealing with economic, social and cultural rights.[88]

[3.26] The first of these to be examined here is the International Covenant on Civil and Political Rights (ICCPR), which was adopted by the General Assembly of the United Nations on 16 December 1966, and which entered into force some 10 years later in 1976, once the requisite number of 35 States had ratified it.[89] While we shall see that other treaties subsequently elaborated by the United Nations deal with particular rights of a civil and political character, the ICCPR is the most 'comprehensive and well-

---

[84] Smith, Bolyard and Ippolito, 'Human Rights and the Global Economy: A Response to Meyer' (1999) 21(1) HRQ 207, p 211. On the difficulties that obtain in regulating the activities of multinational corporations, see Clapham, *Human Rights Obligations of Non-State Actors* (OUP, 2006), pp 195–270; and Picciotto, 'Rights, Responsibility and Regulation of International Business', Paper delivered at the First Appel Conference, Columbia Law School, New York, 26th-27th March 2003, http://www.lancs.ac.uk/staff/lwasp/appel03.pdf (last accessed May 2011).

[85] Robinson 'Making Human Rights Matter: Eleanor Roosevelt's Time Has Come': (2003) 16 Harv Hum Rts J 1.

[86] McGoldrick, *The Human Rights Committee* (OUP, 1994), para 1.6.

[87] Humphrey, *No Distant Millennium: The International Law of Human Rights* (UNESCO, 1989), p 171.

[88] GA Res 543 (VI) (1952), GAOR 6th session, Supp 20, UN Doc A/2199, p 36. McGoldrick, *The Human Rights Committee* (OUP, 1994), para 1.8.

[89] GA Res 2200A (XXI), 21 UN GAOR Supp (No 16) at 52, UN Doc A/6316 (1966); 999 UNTS 171; 6 ILM 368 (1967). See generally, McGoldrick, *The Human Rights Committee* (OUP, 1994); Joseph, Schultz and Castan, *The International Covenant on Civil and Political Rights: Cases, Materials and Commentary* (OUP, 2003); Conte and Burchill, *Defining Civil and Political Rights: The Jurisprudence of the Human Rights Committee* (2nd edn, Ashgate, 2009). Bair, *The International Covenant on Civil and Political Rights and its (First) Optional Protocol* (Lang, 2005); Nowak, *UN Covenant on Civil and Political Rights: CCPR Commentary* (NP Engel, 2005); Steiner, Alston and Goodman, *International Human Rights in Context: Law, Politics and Morals* (3rd edn, OUP, 2008), pp 151–262; Rehman, *International Human Rights Law* (2nd edn, Pearson, 2010), pp 84–139.

established' UN convention to deal with this category of rights.[90] As of May 2011, there are 167 States parties to the Covenant.[91]

The ICCPR contains in total 23 articles which elaborate in much greater detail the civil and political rights set out in the Declaration. They are as follows:

Article 1:	The right to self-determination
Article 6:	The right to life
Article 7:	Freedom from torture, cruel, inhuman or degrading treatment or punishment
Article 8:	Freedom from slavery and the slave trade
Article 9:	The right to liberty and security
Article 10:	The right of detained persons to be treated with dignity and humanity
Article 11:	Freedom from imprisonment for debt
Article 12:	Freedom of movement and choice of residence
Article 13:	Freedom of aliens from arbitrary expulsion
Article 14:	Right to a fair trial
Article 15:	Prohibition on retrospective criminal legislation
Article 16:	Right to recognition as a person before the law
Article 17:	Freedom from interference with privacy, family, home and correspondence
Article 18:	Freedom of thought, conscience and religion
Article 19:	Freedom of expression and opinion
Article 20:	Prohibition on propaganda for war and of incitement to national, racial or religious hatred
Article 21:	Right of peaceful assembly
Article 22:	Freedom of association
Article 23:	Protection of the family and the right to marry and found a family
Article 24:	Rights of the child
Article 25:	Right to political participation, to vote and to access to the public service
Article 26:	Right to equality before the law and non-discrimination on any ground
Article 27:	Rights of persons belonging to ethnic, religious and linguistic minorities

---

[90] Joseph, Schultz and Castan, *The International Covenant on Civil and Political Rights: Cases, Materials and Commentary* (2nd edn, OUP, 2004), p 8.

[91] UN General Assembly, *International Covenant on Civil and Political Rights*, 16 December 1966, United Nations, Treaty Series, vol. 999, p. 171, available at: http://www2.ohchr.org/english/law/ccpr.htm (last accessed May 2011). Ireland ratified the ICCPR on 8 December 1989. The Covenant is supplemented by two further Protocols, the first of which establishes an individual complaint procedure which is referred to below in para **3.35** and examined in detail in Ch 7, paras **7.03–7.41**. The Second Optional Protocol provided for the elimination of the death penalty: UN General Assembly, *Second Optional Protocol to the International Covenant on Civil and Political Rights, Aiming at the Abolition of the Death Penalty*, 15 December 1989, A/RES/44/128, at: http://www2.ohchr.org/english/law/ccpr-death.htm (last accessed May 2011). Ireland ratified the Second Optional Protocol on 18 June 1993.

It is interesting to note that certain new rights appear in this list which did not appear in the Declaration and that others which were present in the latter instrument, are much more heavily emphasised in the legally binding document. In particular, the special emphasis on the rights of the child in art 24 and of minorities in art 27 is noteworthy. On the other hand, it is equally noteworthy that rights which were included in the Declaration were subsequently dropped from the Covenant. In particular, the contentious right to property in art 17 of the Declaration is absent,[92] as well as the right to seek and enjoy asylum in art 14.[93]

Nature and scope of the obligations

[3.27] Articles 2–5 in Part II of the Covenant set forth the nature of States' obligations in regard to the rights and guarantees set forth therein. By virtue of art 2(1), each contracting State undertakes '*to respect and to ensure*' the rights enshrined in the Covenant 'to all individuals within its territory and subject to its jurisdiction ... without distinction of any kind'. Thus, the obligations being assumed here by States are necessarily immediate. First, there is an automatic obligation 'to *respect*' the rights. The use of the word 'respect' reflects the negative character of civil and political rights referred to earlier whereby States are required to *refrain* from interfering with the exercise of the rights, subject to such restrictions as are expressly provided for in the text. The requirement to '*ensure*' the rights, on the other hand, indicates that certain positive measures are necessarily called for to guarantee properly civil and political rights, including, in certain circumstances, 'positive obligations' to protect individuals from acts committed by private parties or entities which impair the enjoyment of the rights. In this respect, the terms of the Covenant do have a certain 'horizontal' effect insofar as States parties can be held indirectly responsible for breaches of the Covenant where they fail to take appropriate measures to 'prevent, punish, investigate or redress' harm caused to individuals by private persons.[94]

---

[92] The views expressed on the content, if any, of property rights in the UDHR were so many and varied that the actual formulation chosen was extremely vague and general. See Glendon, *A World Made New: Eleanor Roosevelt and the Universal Declaration of Human Rights* (Random House, 2001), pp 182–183; and Henkin, 'The International Bill of Rights: The Universal Declaration and the Covenants' in Bernhardt and Jolowicz, *Reports Submitted to the Colloquium of the International Association of Legal Science* (Max-Planck-Institut, Heidelberg, 1985) 1, p 8: 'That omission doubtless was not a rejection of the essential right but was the result of sharp disagreement as to the scope and definition of the right, and perhaps a spill-over of the controversy, particularly intense during those years, over the protection of properties of foreign nationals'.

[93] The wording of art 14 of the UDHR, which provides that everyone has the right to 'seek and to enjoy' asylum (thus stopping short of a right 'to be granted asylum') had provoked considerable controversy. It has been described, for example, as a formulation that is artificial to the point of flippancy': Lauterpacht, 'The Universal Declaration of Human Rights' (1948) 25 BYIL 354, p 374.

[94] General Comment No 31 of the Human Rights Committee, Nature of the General Legal Obligation Imposed by States Parties to the Covenant (26/05/04), para 8: UN Doc CCPR/C/21/Rev1/Add13.
http://www.unhchr.ch/tbs/doc.nsf/(Symbol)/CCPR.C.21.Rev.1.Add.13.En?Opendocument (last accessed May 2011).

[3.28] The phrase 'to all individuals within its territory and subject to its jurisdiction' in art 2(1) indicates the territorial and jurisdictional reach of the Covenant.[95] As regards territorial jurisdiction, in general terms, States parties are obliged to implement the rights in the Covenant within their sovereign territory and within territory over which they have effective control.[96] As regards the personal jurisdiction of the Covenant, there is no distinction as to nationality or citizenship; once individuals are subject to the jurisdiction of a contracting State, whether as a citizen, asylum-seeker, refugee, stateless person, migrant worker, illegal immigrant or tourist, they are entitled to the protection by that State of the rights guaranteed in the Covenant.[97] The obligation not to discriminate on any ground is fortified by the obligation in art 3 to ensure the equal rights of men and women to the enjoyment of the rights in the Covenant. The emphasis on non-discrimination is further reflected in the open-textured guarantee to non-discrimination and equal protection of the law in art 26 of the Covenant.

[3.29] Article 2(2) of the ICCPR provides the 'overarching framework within which the rights specified in the Covenant are to be promoted and protected'.[98] By its terms, each State party is obliged to 'undertake the necessary steps' to adopt such legislative or other measures as may be necessary to give effect to the rights recognised in the Covenant. While the obligation 'to take steps' is clearly a progressive one, it is nonetheless an unqualified obligation and applies immediately upon ratification. Accordingly, States may not justify a failure to take steps immediately by reference to political, social or economic considerations.[99] The article makes clear that States are required on ratification to 'make such changes to their domestic laws and practices as are necessary to ensure conformity with the Covenant'. Incorporation of the Covenant into domestic law[100] is not required as the terms of para 2 specifically provide that States may pursue these changes in accordance with their own domestic constitutional structures. The Human Rights Committee (CCPR), which was set up under the terms of the Covenant to interpret its terms and monitor their implementation, has nonetheless routinely encouraged contracting States in which the Covenant is not incorporated into domestic law to consider incorporation in order to facilitate full realisation of the rights in the domestic legal order.[101]

---

[95] See further Ch 7, para **7.23–7.31**.
[96] See further Ch 7, para **7.28–7.31**.
[97] See Ch 7, para **7.26**.
[98] General Comment No 31 of the Human Rights Committee, Nature of the General Legal Obligation Imposed by States Parties to the Covenant (26/05/04): UN Doc CCPR/C/21/Rev1/Add13, para 5.
[99] General Comment No 31 of the Human Rights Committee, Nature of the General Legal Obligation Imposed by States Parties to the Covenant (26/05/04): UN Doc CCPR/C/21/Rev1/Add13, para 14.
[100] See Ch 1, para **1.14–1.16**.
[101] General Comment No 31 of the Human Rights Committee, Nature of the General Legal Obligation Imposed by States Parties to the Covenant (26/05/04): UN Doc CCPR/C/21/Rev1/Add13, para 13.

[3.30] Article 2(3) next imposes an obligation on States parties to ensure an effective remedy to any person whose rights or freedoms under the Covenant are violated. Article 2(3)(b) specifies that individuals who claim such a remedy should have access to a competent judicial, administrative or legislative authority, and that States should develop, in particular, the possibilities for access to a judicial remedy. The provision of effective remedies includes a duty to investigate allegations of a violation of any of the guaranteed rights, and a failure to investigate can give rise to an independent breach of the Covenant.[102]

[3.31] Certain of the substantive rights in Part III of the Covenant provide that States may legitimately restrict the enjoyment of the rights for the protection of specific public interests. Article 4 goes further by allowing States to derogate from the rights, or suspend their protection, in times of 'public emergency which threatens the life of the nation'. The conditions for derogation in such extreme circumstances are exacting. States may only take measures derogating from their obligations in such circumstances 'to the extent strictly required by the exigencies of the situation', and provided that they are not inconsistent with their other obligations under international law or discriminatory on the ground of race, colour, sex, language, religion or social origin. Furthermore, by the terms of art 4(2), no derogation is ever permissible from art 6 (right to life), art 7 (freedom from torture, cruel, inhuman or degrading treatment or punishment), art 8 (freedom from slavery and servitude), art 11 (prohibition on imprisonment for failure to fulfil a contractual obligation), art 15 (prohibition on retrospective application of the criminal law), art 16 (right to recognition as a person before the law) and art 18 (freedom of thought, conscience and religion).[103]

[3.32] Finally, art 5(1) of the Covenant provides that the rights provided for in the Covenant may not be drawn upon by any State, group or person in order to destroy or undermine the enjoyment of the rights enshrined in it by others.[104] Article 5(2) is a

---

[102] General Comment No 31 of the Human Rights Committee, Nature of the General Legal Obligation Imposed by States Parties to the Covenant (26/05/04): UN Doc CCPR/C/21/Rev1/Add13, para 13.

[103] See generally General Comment No 29 of the Human Rights Committee (States of Emergency): UN Doc CCPR/C/21/Rev1/Add11 (31 August 2001); and Joseph, Schultz and Castan, *The International Covenant on Civil and Political Rights: Cases, Materials and Commentary* (2nd edn, OUP, 2004), pp 823–836.

[104] According to the Human Rights Committee, this provision is intended to be a general undertaking by *States* and cannot be invoked by individuals without reference to other specific articles of the Covenant: *AM v Finland*, Communication No 398/1990, UN Doc CCPR/C/45/D/398/1990, para 4.2. In *Faurisson v France*, the government sought to rely on art 5(1) in proceedings taken against the State for breach of the right to freedom of expression by an individual who had been convicted under French law for denying the existence of gas chambers in Nazi concentration camps. The Human Rights Committee did not, however, decide the case by reference to art 5(1), holding instead that the restriction of the applicant's freedom of expression was necessary in accordance with the provisions of art 19(3) to protect the rights of others: *Faurisson v France*, Communication No 550/1993, UN Doc CCPR/C/58/D/550/1993, 8 November 1996.

'savings provision' which forbids contracting States from cutting back on more extensive obligations assumed in other conventions, regulations, custom or domestic law on the pretext that a lower level of protection is required by the terms of the Covenant.

The Human Rights Committee

[3.33] Article 28 of the ICCPR establishes a committee, to be known as the Human Rights Committee (CCPR), to interpret the terms of the Covenant and to monitor compliance with it by the contracting States.[105] The CCPR is composed of 18 experts[106] on human rights, drawn from nationals of the States parties to the Covenant.[107] Members of the CCPR are elected by the States parties and shall serve in their personal capacity.[108] They should be of 'high moral character' and 'recognised competence in the field of human rights' with 'consideration being given to the usefulness of the participation of some persons having legal experience'.[109] To date, most of the members have been legal experts of one kind or another. While they are to serve in their personal capacity, the Covenant does not stipulate that the members must be personally independent of their governments. As a result, membership of the Committee has included politicians, former government ministers, former ambassadors, as well as judges.[110] In his in-depth study of the work of the CCPR in 1991, McGoldrick commented that with one or two exceptions, members of the Committee appear over the years to have insulated themselves from any political pressure being brought to bear on their decision making, and further, that members have often stressed their independence from government.[111] While subsequent commentary on the CCPR reflects the view that the Committee is largely composed of human rights experts,[112] there is much force in the opinion expressed by Bayefsky that a linkage to government inevitably compromises the work of any such monitoring body.[113]

---

[105] The acronym CCPR used here is that which is used by the OHCHR. It is a helpful means of avoiding confusion between the Human Rights Committee (which essentially is the 'Committee on Civil and Political Rights' from the Human Rights Council which is more commonly referred to by the acronym HRC.

[106] ICCPR, art 28(1).

[107] ICCPR, art 28(2).

[108] ICCPR, art 28(3). Article 38 also provides that members of the Committee, before taking up their duties, must make a solemn declaration to perform their duties impartially and conscientiously.

[109] ICCPR, art 28(2).

[110] A number of these professional categories is reflected in the current membership of the Committee. For further details see http://www2.ohchr.org/english/bodies/hrc/members.htm (last accessed May 2011).

[111] McGoldrick, *The Human Rights Committee* (OUP, 1994), p 45.

[112] Joseph, Schultz and Castan, *The International Covenant on Civil and Political Rights: Cases, Materials and Commentary* (2nd edn, OUP, 2004), p 17.

[113] In her report on the work of all of the treaty monitoring bodies, she recommended that that individuals who are employed in any way or unprepared to terminate such employment upon their election, should not be nominated or elected for membership of any treaty body: Bayefsky, *The UN Treaty System: Universality at the Crossroads* (Transnational Publishers, 2003), p 99–103.

[3.34] The method of election and terms of office of Committee members is dealt with in further detail in Part IV of the Covenant. Members are elected by States parties by secret ballot[114] from a list of nominees supplied by each State party.[115] Not more than one national *per* contracting State may be elected, with consideration being given to equitable geographical distribution.[116] Membership of the Committee is part-time[117] and members are elected for four-year terms, with the possibility of re-election.[118] The Committee meets for three, three-week sessions each year at the UN headquarters in Geneva or New York.

[3.35] The functions of the CCPR with regard to the Covenant are essentially four-fold. First, the Committee has competence under art 40 of the Covenant to receive, study and evaluate reports which the States parties are required to send to it as regards the measures they have taken and the progress made in implementing the terms of the Covenant in their respective jurisdictions. Second, the ICCPR assigns competence to the Committee to mediate between States in the event of one contracting State making a complaint to it that another State party has breached the terms of the Covenant. This possibility is provided for in the 'inter-State' complaint procedure provided for in arts 41–42 of the Covenant. Unlike the mandatory provision in art 40, the inter-State complaint procedure is optional insofar as both the complainant and respondent States must have accepted the jurisdiction of the Committee to consider the complaint.[119] The CCPR has not been exercised by this procedure as it has never once been invoked by a contracting State to the Covenant. The third area of competence of the Committee relates to the First Optional Protocol to the ICCPR (OP-ICCPR).[120] This instrument provides for the possibility of *individuals* making complaints to the CCPR about alleged breaches of their rights under the Covenant by a State party to both instruments. The Committee is given jurisdiction under the Protocol to receive and consider such communications. The periodic reporting mechanisms and the individual complaint mechanisms provided for in the OP-ICCPR are examined in Chs 4 and 7 of this book respectively.

[3.36] Finally, it should be noted that the Committee also regularly publishes its interpretation of particular provisions of the Covenant and the First Optional Protocol in the form of 'general comments'.[121] The basis for formulating these comments is to be

---

[114] ICCPR, art 29.
[115] ICCPR, art 30.
[116] ICCPR, art 31.
[117] ICCPR, art 35. While art 35 makes provision for members of the CCPR to be paid, in fact the annual payment made to them since 2002 has been no more than $1. On this issue, see Tyagi, *The UN Human Rights Committee* (CUP, 2011), pp 118–120.
[118] ICCPR, art 32.
[119] ICCPR, art 41(1).
[120] Optional Protocol to the International Covenant on Civil and Political Rights, G.A. res. 2200A (XXI), 21 UN GAOR Supp (No 16) at 59, UN Doc. A/6316 (1966), 999 UNTS 302, available at: http://www2.ohchr.org/english/law/ccpr-one.htm (last accessed May 2011).
[121] The general comments of the Human Rights Committee may be accessed at: http://www2.ohchr.org/english/bodies/hrc/comments.htm (last accessed May 2011).

found in the text of art 40(4).[122] Over time, these comments have become an important source of guidance for States as well as non-governmental organisations and litigants in relation to the legal obligations enshrined in the Covenant.[123]

The International Covenant on Economic Social and Cultural Rights

[3.37] The ICCPR's sister covenant, the International Covenant on Economic, Social and Cultural Rights (ICESCR) was adopted on the same date, 16 December 1966.[124] It entered into force in 1976 following the requisite number of 35 ratifications. There are currently 160 States parties to this Covenant.[125] The fact that a similar number of States have ratified the ICESCR as the ICCPR, to some extent, breathes continued life into the notion expressed in the UDHR and reiterated in the Preambles of both instruments that civil and political rights, and economic, social and cultural rights are indivisible and inter-dependent.[126]

---

[122] See generally, Alston, 'The Historical Origins of the Concept of 'General Comments' in Human Rights Law' in Boisson de Chaournes and Gowland Debbas (eds), *The International Legal System in Quest of Equity and Universality* (2001), p 763; extract reproduced in Steiner, Alston and Goodman, *International Human Rights in Context: Law, Politics and Morals* (3rd edn, OUP, 2008), pp 873–876.

[123] Alston describes the General Comments as '... a tool of fundamental importance in the armoury of those seeking to promote international human rights law ...': Alston, 'The Historical Origins of the Concept of 'General Comments' in Human Rights Law' in Boisson de Chazournes and Gowland Debbas (eds) *The International Legal System in Quest of Equity and Universality: Liber Amicorum Georges Abi-Saab* (2001) reproduced in Steiner, Alston and Goodman, *International Human Rights in Context: Law, Politics and Morals* (3rd edn, OUP, 2008), p 876 and Schultz and Castan as '... a valuable jurisprudential resource', *The International Covenant on Civil and Political Rights: Cases, Materials and Commentary* (2nd edn, OUP, 2004), p 21.

[124] International Covenant on Economic, Social and Cultural Rights: GA Res 2200A (XXI), 21 UN GAOR Supp (No 16) at 49, UN Doc A/6316 (1966); 993 UNTS 3; 6 ILM 368 (1967), available at: http://www2.ohchr.org/english/law/cescr.htm (last accessed May 2011). See generally, Craven, *The International Covenant on Economic, Social and Cultural Rights: A Perspective on its Development* (Clarendon Press, 1995); Eide, Krause and Rosas, *Economic, Social and Cultural Rights: A Textbook* (Martinus Nijhoff, 2001); Steiner, Alston and Goodman, *International Human Rights in Context: Law, Politics and Morals* (3rd edn, OUP, 2008), pp 263–374; Ssenyonjo, *Economic, Social and Cultural Rights in International Law* (Hart, 2009); and Rehman, *International Human Rights Law* (2nd edn, Pearson, 2010), pp 140–180.

[125] Source: http://treaties.un.org (last accessed May 2011). Ireland ratified the ICESCR on 8 December 1989.

[126] The Preamble of the ICESCR recognises specifically that '... in accordance with the Universal Declaration of Human Rights, the ideal of free human beings enjoying freedom from fear and want can only be achieved if conditions are created whereby everyone may enjoy his economic, social and cultural rights, as well as his civil and political rights'; while the Preamble to the ICCPR recognises that '... in accordance with the Universal Declaration of Human Rights, (contd.../)

With the exception of the right to property,[127] the ICESCR elaborates in detail and augments the list of economic, social and cultural rights previously outlined in the UDHR. These are set forth in Parts I and III of the instrument as follows:

Article 1:	Right to self-determination
Article 6:	Right to work
Article 7:	Right to just and favourable conditions of work
Article 8:	Right to form trade unions and right to strike
Article 9:	Right to social security, including social insurance
Article 10:	Right to protection and assistance to the family, including special assistance for mothers and children
Article 11:	Right to an adequate standard of living, including adequate food, clothing and housing and continuous improvement of living conditions
Article 12:	Right to enjoyment of the highest attainable standard of physical and mental health
Articles 13 & 14:	Right to education
Article 15:	Right to take part in the cultural life, to enjoy the benefits of scientific progress, and to benefit from the moral and material protection of any scientific, literary or artistic work of which he or she is author

Eide has described the economic, social and cultural rights set forth in the Covenant as constituting 'three interrelated components of a more comprehensive package' with the different components also being linked to civil and political rights.[128] As he explains, the 'social rights' dimension finds expression in the right to an adequate standard of living (art 11); the right to protection and assistance to the family (art 10); the right to health (art 12); the right to work (art 6); and the right to social security (art 9). These social rights may only be enjoyed where economic rights are also protected. The latter include the right to work (again), which when backed up by just and favourable conditions of work (art 7) and the support of a trade union (art 8) can also be described as economic rights, as can the rights to social security and an adequate standard of living. The interlocking nature of the three sets of rights is further demonstrated when one considers the

---

[126] (\...contd) the ideal of free human beings enjoying civil and political freedom and freedom from fear and want can only be achieved if conditions are created whereby everyone may enjoy his civil and political rights, as well as his economic, social and cultural rights'.

[127] While a draft article on the right to property was apparently considered, it was ultimately abandoned due to disagreement on issues such as expropriation and compensation. Proposals regarding the inclusion of the rights to water and transport apparently also foundered: Craven, 'The Covenant on Economic, Social and Cultural Rights' in Hanski and Suksi (eds), *An Introduction to the International Protection of Human Rights: A Textbook* (Institute for Human Rights: Abo Akademi University, 1999) 101, p 106.

[128] Eide, 'Economic, Social and Cultural Rights as Human Rights' in Eide, Kraus and Rosas (eds), *Economic, Social and Cultural Rights: A Textbook* (2nd edn, Martinus Nijhoff, 2001) 9, p 17.

cultural rights dimension of the Covenant which includes art 15 (incorporating the right to enjoy the benefits of scientific progress)[129] and the right to education (arts 13 & 14). The enjoyment of these latter rights, particularly the right to education, is increasingly important if individuals are to have meaningful enjoyment of their social and economic rights.[130]

[3.38] It has been argued that while the scope of the economic, social and cultural rights contained in the Covenant is impressive, the phraseology used in regard to the individual articles is overly broad. In this respect, Craven points out that the decision to adopt very generally worded provisions was a deliberate one on the part of the drafters in order to preclude overly restrictive interpretations of the rights.[131] As he points out, this decision may well increase the possibilities for dynamic interpretation of the rights, while simultaneously placing a heavy onus on the monitoring body to define and extrapolate their content.[132]

[3.39] It is important to note that many other treaties contain similar rights and elaborate further on the rights contained in the ICESCR. At a regional level, the Council of Europe has promulgated the European Social Charter 1961 (Revised).[133] While the latter instrument is in many respects more extensive in the scope and detail of the rights protected than the Covenant, it does adopt an 'á la carte' approach to State participation in that States parties are afforded a certain degree of discretion in accepting obligations under its terms.[134] The Charter of Fundamental Rights of the European Union also includes a catalogue of economic and social rights which bind the institutions of the

---

[129] It might be noted, however, that despite their promise, cultural rights have been somewhat neglected in the lifetime of the Covenant and very few benchmarks as to their content have been established. See generally, Yupsansis, 'The Concept and Categories of Cultural Rights in International Law – Their Broad Sense and the Relevant Clauses of the International Human Rights Treaties' (2010) 37 Syracuse Journal of International Law and Commerce 207–266.

[130] Eide, 'Economic, Social and Cultural Rights as Human Rights' in Eide, Kraus and Rosas (eds), *Economic, Social and Cultural Rights: A Textbook* (2nd edn, Martinus Nijhoff, 2001) 9, p 19.

[131] Craven, 'The Covenant on Economic, Social and Cultural Rights' in Hanski and Suksi (eds), *An Introduction to the International Protection of Human Rights: A Textbook* (Institute for Human Rights: Abo Akademi University, 1999) 101, p 105.

[132] Craven, 'The Covenant on Economic, Social and Cultural Rights' in Hanski and Suksi (eds), *An Introduction to the International Protection of Human Rights: A Textbook* (Institute for Human Rights: Abo Akademi University, 1999) 101, pp 105–106.

[133] Council of Europe, *European Social Charter (Revised)*, 3 May 1996, ETS 163, available at: http://conventions.coe.int/Treaty/Commun/QueVoulezVous.asp?NT=163&CM=1&DF=&CL=ENG (last accessed May 2011).

[134] See Part III (Article A) of the revised Charter and see generally, Rehman, *International Human Rights Law* (2nd edn, Pearson, 2010), pp 233–243; and Brillat, 'The European Social Charter' in Alfredsson et al, *International Human Rights Monitoring Mechanisms* (2nd edn, Martinus Nijhoff, 2009), pp 503–513.

European Union in implementing EU Law.[135] However, as the only instrument of universal application, the ICESCR is still unparalleled as the most important reference point for economic, social and cultural rights in existence in the field.[136] At the same time, the extent of its reach also means that more difficulties obtain in reaching consensus on the scope of the rights, but also, as we shall see, on the appropriate methods for their implementation.

Nature and scope of States' obligations

[3.40] Articles 2–5 in Part II of the ICESCR outline the basic obligations undertaken by the contracting States in relation to the rights outlined in Parts I and III. In this regard, the critical provision is that contained in art 2(1), which provides as follows:

> 'Each State Party to the present Covenant undertakes to take steps, individually and through international assistance and co-operation, especially economic and technical, to the maximum of its available resources, with a view to achieving progressively the realization of the rights recognized in the present Covenant by all appropriate measures particularly the adoption of legislative measures'.

At first blush, it is apparent that the language of obligation being expressed here is qualitatively different than the general undertaking expressed in art 2(1) of the ICCPR on States parties 'to respect' and 'to ensure' the rights contained therein. The wording employed in art 2(1) of the ICESCR was deliberately intended to reflect the assumption made by the majority of the drafters of the Covenant that the implementation of economic, social and cultural rights required a progressive approach, while in contrast, civil and political rights were capable of immediate application. As will become clear, in examining the content of particular rights, the absolute character of that precise assumption as regards both categories of rights has been gradually eroded and it is now generally accepted that meaningful implementation of both categories requires both progressive and immediate elements.

[3.41] True to Craven's prediction mentioned above, the Committee on Economic, Social and Cultural Rights (CESCR), which is responsible for monitoring implementation of the ICESCR, has risen to the challenge of interpreting the Covenant in a dynamic fashion. It has issued guidelines to States in regard to the nature of the general obligations assumed by them pursuant to art 2.[137] In its view, art 2 generally contains obligations of 'conduct' and obligations of 'result'.[138] In respect of art 2(1), this

---

[135] European Union, *Charter of Fundamental Rights of the European Union*, 7 December 2000, Official Journal of the European Communities, 18 December 2000 (2000/C 364/01), available at: http://www.europarl.europa.eu/charter/pdf/text_en.pdf (last accessed May 2011). The Charter became legally binding when the Treaty of Lisbon entered into force on 1 December 2009. See Rehman, *International Human Rights Law* (2nd edn, Pearson, 2010), pp 256–262.

[136] Rehman, *International Human Rights Law* (2nd edn, Pearson, 2010), p 105.

[137] CESCR General Comment No 3, The Nature of States Parties' Obligations: UN Doc HRI/GEN/1/Rev.6 at 14 (14/12/1990).

[138] General Comment No 3, para 1. However, note the critique by Langford and King of this aspect of the CESCR's output: 'Committee on Economic, Social and Cultural Rights' in Langford (ed) Social Rights Jurisprudence: Emerging Trends in International and Comparative Law (Cambridge, 2008) 477, 482–483.

means that while the full realisation of the rights set forth in the Covenant may be achieved 'progressively', the taking of 'steps' towards that goal must be taken within a reasonably short time after the Covenant's entry into force.[139] Moreover, those steps should be 'deliberate, concrete and targeted as clearly as possible towards meeting the obligations recognized in the Covenant'.[140] Thus, the taking of steps discharges the 'obligations of conduct', while the ultimate realisation of the rights fulfils the 'obligations of result'.[141] As regards the *nature* and *extent* of the steps to be taken by each contracting State, art 2(1) asserts broadly that these should be 'by all appropriate means, including particularly the adoption of legislative measures'. In this regard, the CESCR has stated that while legislative measures may be highly desirable and in some cases indispensable, they are by no means exhaustive in terms of the obligations on States.[142] Moreover, the CESCR has applied the 'tripartite typology' of rights according to which the rights in the Covenant impose three 'types' or 'levels' of obligation, ie the obligations to respect, to protect and to fufil.[143] The use of this typology is aimed at highlighting the full spectrum of positive and negative elements involved in achieving full compliance with the obligations.[144] Each State party is free to decide upon the choice of means by which any particular right in the Covenant is best protected; though the ultimate arbiter of whether the choice exercised is appropriate is the CESCR.[145]

---

[139] CESCR General Comment No 3, The Nature of States Parties' Obligations (14/12/1990), para 2.

[140] CESCR General Comment No 3, The Nature of States Parties' Obligations (14/12/1990), para 2.

[141] On the distinction between obligations of conduct and obligations of result in the context of economic, social and cultural rights, see Eide, 'Realization of Social and Economic Rights and the Minimum Threshold Approach' (1989) 10 HRLJ 35, p 38: 'An obligation of *conduct* (active or passive) points to behaviour which the duty-holder should follow or abstain from. An obligation of *result* is less concerned with the choice of the line of action taken, but more concerned with the results which the duty-holder should achieve or avoid'.

[142] CESCR General Comment No 3, The Nature of States Parties' Obligations (14/12/1990), para 4.

[143] Asbjørn Eide developed the typology in this context: The Rights to Adequate Food as a Human Right: UN Doc E/CN4/Sub2/1987/23, paras 66–70. On the development and conceptual problems arising from the CESCR's deployment of this typology, see Koch 'Dichotomies, Trichotomies or Waves of Duties?' (2005) 5 Human Rights Law Review 81–103.

[144] See CESCR General Comment No 12 on the right to adequate food (art 11): UN Doc E/C 12/1999/5, para.15; CESCR General Comment No 13 on the right to education (art 13): UN Doc HRI/GEN/1/Rev 6 at 70, paras 46–47 and 50; CESCR General Comment No 14 on the right to the highest attainable standard of health (art 12): UN Doc E/C 12/2000/4, paras 33–37; CESCR General Comment No 15 on the right to water: UN Doc E/C 12/2002/11, paras 20–29; and CESCR General Comment 19 on the right to social security (art 9), paras 43–51.

[145] CESCR General Comment No 3, The Nature of States Parties' Obligations (14/12/1990), para 4.

[3.42] In this respect, the CESCR has maintained from an early stage of its deliberations that States may be obliged in certain circumstances to provide judicial remedies for the breach of certain rights in the Covenant which may, in accordance with the national legal system, be considered justiciable.[146] This viewpoint represents a clear progression in thinking from the original premise on which the Covenants were divided, namely, that economic, social and cultural rights could not be immediately guaranteed in the same way as civil and political rights. On the contrary, the view has long since been taken[147] and endorsed by the CESCR that there are a number of rights in the ICESCR which are certainly of immediate application, including the right not to be discriminated against in the enjoyment of the rights (arts 2(2) and (3); the right to fair wages and equal remuneration without distinction of any kind (art 7(a)(i)); the right to form and join a trade union (art 8); children's rights (art 10(3)); the right to free primary education (art 13(2)(a)); the rights of parents to choose the appropriate school for their children (art 13(3)); the right to establish educational institutions in conformity with minimum standards (art 13(4)); and freedom to engage in scientific research and creative activity (art 15(3)).[148] Other measures besides legislative or judicial measures may also be appropriate, including administrative, financial, educational and social measures.[149]

[3.43] As regards the ultimate obligation stated in art 2(1) to take steps 'with a view to achieving progressively[150] the full realization of the rights recognized in the Covenant', the CESCR has stated that this phrase imposes a clear obligation on States to move as expeditiously as possible towards that goal.[151] Furthermore, it embodies '... a minimum core obligation on each State party to ensure the satisfaction of, at the very least, minimum essential levels of each of the rights'.[152] While identification of the minimum

---

[146] CESCR General Comment No 3, The Nature of States Parties' Obligations (14/12/1990), para 5.

[147] See generally Van Boven, 'Distinguishing Criteria of Human Rights' in Vasak (ed), *The International Dimensions of Human Rights* (UNESCO, 1982) p 49.

[148] CESCR General Comment No 3, The Nature of States Parties' Obligations (14/12/1990), para 5.

[149] CESCR General Comment No 3, The Nature of States Parties' Obligations (14/12/1990), para 7.

[150] Felner has warned that the standard of 'progressive achievement' has been sidelined by human rights advocates and that the focus instead has been on whether States have violated their 'immediate obligations' which are much more easily established. To redress this imbalance, she advocates a methodological 'toolkit' for monitoring the obligation of progressive realisation: Felner, 'Closing the 'Escape Hatch': A Toolkit to Monitor the Progressive Realization of Economic, Social and Cultural Rights' (2009) 1 Journal of Human Rights Practice 402.

[151] CESCR General Comment No 3, The Nature of States Parties' Obligations (14/12/1990), para 9.

[152] CESCR General Comment No 3, The Nature of States Parties' Obligations (14/12/1990), para 10. See generally the seminal article by Alston and Quinn, 'The Nature and Scope of States Parties' Obligations under the International Covenant on Economic, Social and Cultural Rights' (1987) 9 HRQ 16.

core content of each particular right is an enduring problem,[153] the Committee has recognised that the setting of national benchmarks can provide an extremely valuable indication of progress and has indicated that the setting of quantitative and qualitative data by States is required in order to accurately assess whether progressive realisation has been achieved.[154] In this respect, the CESCR acknowledges that any assessment as to whether a State has discharged its minimum obligations in regard to each of the rights must take account of the particular resource constraints operating in the country concerned.[155] This qualification is reflected in the text of art 2(1) which specifically obligates each State party to take steps 'to the maximum of its available resources'. If a country fails to meet its minimum obligations in relation to any of the rights on the basis of inadequate resources, it will need to demonstrate to the satisfaction of the Committee that every effort has still been made to use all the resources which it does have at its disposal (both domestic and international)[156] to satisfy those minimum obligations.[157] Moreover, resource constraints will never excuse a State from failing to take *some* operational measures to promote the rights in the Covenant.[158]

[3.44] Before leaving the issue of core obligations, it may be noted that the ICESCR does not discriminate between any particular form of government or economic system. As the CESCR has emphasised, the Covenant is decidedly neutral on this point; its principles are not predicated on '... the desirability of a socialist or a capitalist system, or a mixed, or centrally planned, or *laisser-faire* economy, or upon any particular

---

[153] It should be acknowledged that the conceptual and practical problems arising from the notion of a 'minimum core obligation' has led to its rejection in many quarters: See generally, Young, 'The Minimum Core of Economic and Social Rights: A Concept in Search of Content' (2008) 33 Yale Journal of International Law 113-175 (Available at SSRN: http://ssrn.com/abstract=1136547) (last accessed May 2011).

[154] See CESCR General Comment No 1, Reporting by States Parties: UN Doc HRI/GEN/1/Rev.6 at 8 (24/02/1989), paras 6 and 7. On further possible methods of establishing compliance, see Anderson and Foresti, 'Assessing Compliance: The Challenges for Economic and Social Rights' (2009) 1 Journal of Human Rights Practice 469; and Welling, 'International Indicators and Economic, Social and Cultural Rights' (2008) 30(4) HRQ 933.

[155] CESCR General Comment No 3, *The Nature of the States Parties' Obligations* (14/12/1990), para 10.

[156] In this respect, the CESCR has noted that the phrase 'to the maximum of its available resources' was intended by the drafters of the Covenant to refer both to the resources existing *within* the State and those available from the international community through international cooperation and assistance: General Comment No 3, *The Nature of the States Parties' Obligations* (14/12/1990), para 13.

[157] CESCR General Comment No 3, *The Nature of the States Parties' Obligations* (14/12/1990), para 13.

[158] CESCR General Comment No 3, *The Nature of the States Parties' Obligations* (14/12/1990), paras 11 and 12. The duty of progressive realisation also implicitly includes a prohibition on taking deliberately retrogressive measures: para 9. On the budget-related obligations in terms of 'resources' which stem from art 2(1), see Nolan and Dutschke, 'Article 2(1) ICESCR and States Parties' Obligations: Whither the Budget?' (2010) EHRLR 280.

approach'.[159] By the same token, States in which public goods or services are privatised cannot escape liability under the Covenant where problems of access arise.[160] To this extent, States parties have positive obligations to promote and protect the rights where their direct implementation is either wholly or partly in the hands of private parties.

[3.45] Article 2(2) provides for a general, open-ended non-discrimination provision which prohibits States parties from discriminating between persons as regards the enjoyment of rights on any grounds. Grounds specifically enumerated are those of race, colour, language, religion or political or other opinion, national or social origin, property or birth, though these should not be regarded as taking any particular order nor are they exhaustive.[161] This provision is buttressed by the terms of art 3 which enjoins the States parties to guarantee equal access by men and women to the enjoyment of the economic, social and cultural rights enshrined in the Covenant. Unlike art 26 of the ICCPR, art 2(2) is not a free-standing equality provision;[162] rather its range is limited to the rights guaranteed by the Covenant.[163] Klerk argues that States must interpret the implications of art 2(2) in conjunction with obligations undertaken by them in other anti-discrimination conventions, such as the Convention on the Elimination of Racial Discrimination and the Convention on the Elimination of All Forms of Discrimination against Women.[164] Moreover, arts 2(2) and 3 in combination have been interpreted as implying general obligations on States parties to take affirmative action for the benefit

---

[159] CESCR General Comment No 3, *The Nature of the States Parties' Obligations* (14/12/1990), para 8.

[160] As Craven notes: 'This means that even if housing or education are to be delivered by the private sector, the State must ensure that the operation of the market is fair and equitable and that marginalized and disadvantaged sectors of the population are guaranteed at least minimum levels of employment'. Craven, 'The Covenant on Economic, Social and Cultural Rights' in Hanski and Suksi (eds), *An Introduction to the International Protection of Human Rights: A Textbook* (Institute for Human Rights: Abo Akademi University, 1999), p 110.

[161] Klerk, 'Working Paper on Article 2(2) and Article 3 of the International Covenant and Economic, Social and Cultural Rights' (1987) 9 HRQ 250, p 259.

[162] The difference in the use of the word 'discrimination' in art 2(2), as opposed to 'distinction' in art 2(1) of the ICCPR is of no significance, as the drafters apparently intended the same meaning to apply to both terms: Klerk, 'Working Paper on Article 2(3) and Article 3 of the International Covenant on Economic, Social and Cultural Rights' (1987) 9 HRQ 250, p 252.

[163] As to the equality provision in art 26 ICCPR, see Ch 7, paras **7.65–7.69**.

[164] Klerk, "Working Paper on Article 2(2) and Article 3 of the international Covenant and Economic, Social and Cultural Rights" (1987) 9 HRQ 250, p 259. This point is reinforced by Principle 41 of the Limburg Principles on the Implementation of the International Covenant on Economic, Social and Cultural Rights, UN Doc E/CN 4/1987/17Annex (1987); reprinted in (1987) 9 HRQ 122. These principles were agreed by some 29 experts in international law at a symposium held in The Netherlands in 1986 and provide helpful guidance in interpreting the obligations in the ICESCR. The principles were later published as an official UN document, following their formal transmission to the Commission on Human Rights by the Dutch government. They were endorsed by the Commission on Human Rights subsequently in 1993 at its 49th session: see CHR Res, 1993/14. UN DOC E/CN4/1993/122 at 87.

of disadvantaged groups[165] and to prohibit private parties from discriminating against individuals in regard to essentially public activities.[166]

[3.46] As regards limitations on the rights in the ICESCR, three features should be noted. First, art 2(3) provides somewhat obscurely that: 'Developing countries, with due regard to human rights and their national economy, may determine to what extent they would guarantee the economic rights recognized in the present covenant to non-nationals'. This provision was apparently inserted in the Covenant to assuage the concerns of those countries then emerging from colonial domination about control of their countries' resources remaining in the hands of economically more powerful non-national elites.[167] Article 2(3) was thus intended to allow developing countries[168] some leverage in ensuring that economic rights could be exercised and enjoyed by most of the people in their countries. Thus, '... gross inequality between non-nationals and nationals, which is a colonial heritage, can be redressed through resort to Article 2(3)'.[169] While of considerable historical interest, the article has attracted little practical attention as no State has ever sought to rely on its terms in order to restrict the economic rights of its non-nationals.[170] The terms of the Covenant thus apply, as a general rule, equally to nationals and non-nationals.[171]

[3.47] Second, art 4 sets forth the circumstances in which States may impose limitations on the guaranteed rights. Specifically, it provides that the States may subject the rights '... only to such limitations as are determined by law only in so far as this may be compatible with the nature of these rights and solely for the purpose of promoting the

---

[165] Principle 39 of the Limburg Principles. This principle includes a caveat that such measures do not lead to the maintenance of separate rights for different groups and should be discontinued after their intended objectives have been achieved.

[166] Principle 40 of the Limburg Principles: UN Doc E/CN 4/1987/17Annex; and Klerk, 'Working Paper on Article 2(2) and Article 3 of the International Covenant on Economic, Social and Cultural Rights' (1987) 9 HRQ 250, pp 266–267.

[167] See generally, Dankwa, 'Working Paper on Article 2(3) of the International Covenant on Economic, Social and Cultural Rights' (1987) 9 HRQ 230. See also Principle 43 of the Limburg Principles: 'The purpose of Article 2(3) was to end the domination of certain economic groups of non-nationals during colonial times. In the light of this, the exception in art 2(3) should be interpreted narrowly'.

[168] This term was never defined by the drafters but was generally understood to refer to 'economically weak countries': Dankwa, 'Working Paper on Article 2(3) of the International Covenant on Economic, Social and Cultural Rights' (1987) 9 HRQ 230 at 238. Principle 44 of the Limburg Principles states that the terms refers to those countries which have 'gained independence and which fall within the appropriate United Nations classifications of Developing countries'.

[169] Dankwa, 'Working Paper on Article 2(3) of the International Covenant on Economic, Social and Cultural Rights' (1987) 9 HRQ 230, pp 248-249.

[170] Craven, 'The Covenant on Economic, Social and Cultural Rights' in Hanski and Suksi (eds), *An Introduction to the International Protection of Human Rights: A Textbook* (Institute for Human Rights: Abo Akademi University, 1999), p 111.

[171] Limburg Principle 42.

general welfare in a democratic society'. Unlike the ICCPR, which sets forth permissible limitations on specific rights, art 4 sweeps with a broader brush, allowing for potential limitations on any of the guaranteed rights, provided they conform to the requirements of art 4. In essence, this means that no limitation can be made on the exercise of a right unless it is already provided for in national law,[172] the terms of which are clear and accessible to everyone,[173] and not arbitrary or unreasonable.[174] Limitations must only be imposed to promote the general welfare in a democratic society,[175] ie, to 'further the well-being of the people as a whole'.[176] Any State which imposes limitations on rights has the burden of demonstrating that the limitations in question do not impair the functioning of the society.[177] Lastly, the terms of art 4 can never be raised to defend or promote discriminatory practices.[178]

[3.48] Third, unlike the ICCPR, and indeed most subsequent human rights conventions, the ICESCR does not include a derogation clause. Apparently, the drafters considered the terms of art 2(1) broad enough to allow States to cut back on their obligations in circumstances which would otherwise qualify for formal derogation under other instruments.[179]

Finally, it should be noted that art 5 of the ICESCR contains a prohibition on destruction of the rights and a 'savings provision' in exactly the same terms as those provided for in art 5 of the ICCPR.

The Committee on Economic, Social and Cultural Rights

[3.49] The ICESCR provides that international supervision of the obligations undertaken should take place exclusively by means of a periodic reporting requirement, similar to that contained in art 40 of the ICCPR. However, unlike the latter instrument, the ICESCR does not establish an independent monitoring body to which reports may be submitted and evaluated. Rather, the drafters agreed that State reports should be submitted to and considered by ECOSOC.[180] This was a potentially very unsatisfactory arrangement, given that ECOSOC is not an independent body, composed as it is of State representatives and not individuals acting in their personal capacity. Moreover, as soon

---

[172] Limburg Principle 48.
[173] Limburg Principle 50.
[174] Limburg Principle 49.
[175] A 'democratic society' may be understood as referring to a society which recognises and respects the human rights set forth in the UN Charter and the UDHR: Limburg Principle 55.
[176] Limburg Principle 52.
[177] Limburg Principle 54.
[178] Klerk, 'Working Paper on Article 2(3) and Article 3 of the International Covenant on Economic, Social and Cultural Rights' (1987) 9 HRQ 250, p 264. Likewise, see Limburg Principle 49 which provides that laws imposing limitations cannot be discriminatory.
[179] Craven, 'The Covenant on Economic, Social and Cultural Rights' in Hanski and Suksi (eds), *An Introduction to the International Protection of Human Rights: A Textbook* (Institute for Human Rights: Abo Akademi University, 1999), p 111. Higgins, 'Derogations under Human Rights Treaties' (1976–77) 48 BYIL 281–320, pp 281–286.
[180] See Ch 2, para **2.06–2.09**.

as the Covenant entered into force in 1976, it had become clear that an already overburdened ECOSOC would be unable to administer the reporting requirement competently. Instead, it experimented with a sessional working group of 15 of its members, but this proved to be totally unsuccessful.[181] In 1985, ECOSOC agreed to delegate its functions under the Covenant to a separate committee, to be called the Committee on Economic, Social and Cultural Rights (CESCR).[182] The CESCR is clearly styled along similar lines to the CCPR, being composed as it is of 18 independent experts with recognised competence in the field of human rights.[183] They are elected by ECOSOC and are to serve in their personal capacity. It is important to note that the status of this committee is thus quite different from the CCPR in that it serves entirely at the pleasure of ECOSOC, rather than being anchored to the terms of the Covenant like the CCPR.

[3.50] The method of election and terms of office of the CESCR are dealt with in detail in the resolution by which the Committee was originally established.[184] Like the CCPR, members are elected by secret ballot, from a list of nominees supplied by each State Party. Not more than one national *per* State may be elected with due consideration being given to equitable geographical distribution and to representation of different forms of social and legal systems. Membership is also part-time, with travel and subsistence expenses being paid by the UN.[185] Members serve for four-year terms with the possibility of re-election. The Committee meets for three, three-week sessions each year at the UN headquarters in Geneva or New York.

As a result of the establishment of the CESCR, the operation of the periodic reporting requirement envisaged by the drafters is quite different in practice to the procedure provided for in the text of arts 16–25 of the Covenant. This will be examined in more detail in Ch 4.

[3.51] Originally, provision was not made for an inter-State complaint mechanism or an individual complaint procedure in the ICESCR, again on the now discredited basis that economic, social and cultural rights were in essence not justiciable. However, following protracted efforts on the part of the CESCR to stimulate progress on this issue, an Optional Protocol to the ICESCR (OP-ICESCR) was adopted by the General Assembly in December 2008.[186] As Melish notes, the Protocol '... rectified a three-decades old

---

[181] See generally, Robertson and Merrills, *Human Rights in the World* (4th edn, Manchester University Press, 1996), p 274*ff*.

[182] ECOSOC Res 1985/17 of 28 May 1985: http://www2.ohchr.org/english/bodies/cescr/index.htm, (last accessed May 2011) and see 'mandate'.

[183] ECOSOC Res 1985/17 of 28 May 1985, para (b). The current composition of the CESCR appears to be evenly balanced between academics and legal professionals on the one hand and persons with a diplomatic background on the other: http://www2.ohchr.org/english/bodies/cescr/members.htm (last accessed May 2011).

[184] ECOSOC Res 1985/17 of 28 May 1985, para (c).

[185] ECOSOC Res 1985/17 of 28 May 1985, para (e).

[186] Optional Protocol to the International Covenant on Economic, Social and Cultural Rights: UN Doc A/RES/63/117 (10th December 2008), available at: http://www2.ohchr.org/english/bodies/cescr/docs/A-RES-63-117.pdf (last accessed May 2011).

asymmetry in international human rights law'[187] by providing most significantly for an individual complaints procedure, which will enable individuals in States parties to the Protocol to make complaints to the CESCR about a breach by that State of their rights under the Protocol. It also provides for an inter-State complaint procedure (allowing one State party to the Protocol to complain to the CESCR about a breach of the Covenant's provisions by another State party to the Protocol); and an inquiry procedure (which authorises the CESCR to instigate an inquiry where it receives reliable information concerning 'grave or systematic violations' of the Covenant in one of the States parties to the Protocol). The Optional Protocol opened for signature on 24 September 2009 and will enter into force three months after it has been ratified by 10 States.[188] The inquiry and individual complaint procedures provided for in the Protocol are examined further below in Chs 5 and 13 respectively.

[3.52] Finally, it should be noted that since 1988, the CESCR has been active in issuing general comments to States, indicating its views on the implementation and interpretation of particular aspects of the Covenant.[189] It also holds 'general discussion days' at each of its sessions at which it discusses specific issues relating to the Covenant. To facilitate these discussions, the Committee has drawn on the expertise of a wide range of actors including UN special rapporteurs, representatives of the specialised agencies, national human rights institutions and non-governmental organisations.[190]

ADDITIONAL HUMAN RIGHTS TREATIES[191]

International Convention on the Elimination of All Forms of Racial Discrimination (1965)

[3.53] The origins of the International Convention on the Elimination of All Forms of Racial Discrimination (ICERD)[192] can be traced to an 'epidemic of swastika painting'

---

[187] Melish, 'Introductory Note to the Optional Protocol to the International Covenant on Economic, Social and Cultural Rights' (2009) International Legal Materials, vol 48. Available at SSRN: http://ssrn.com/abstract=1393568 (last accessed May 2011).

[188] http://treaties.un.org. (last accessed May 2011). As of May 2011, 3 States have ratified the OP-ICESCR while 36 States are signatories to it.

[189] See the full range of General Comments adopted by the CESCR to date: http://www2.ohchr.org/english/bodies/cescr/comments.htm (last accessed May 2011).

[190] The CESCR publishes information on its days of general discussion on its official website, see: http://www2.ohchr.org/english/bodies/cescr/index.htm (last accessed May 2011).

[191] It should be reiterated that the choice of human rights treaties selected here is based on those treaties which establish international monitoring mechanisms and which are commonly regarded as the 'core' UN human rights treaties, comprising the UN human rights treaty system. For the full range of human rights treaties promulgated by the UN, see: http://www2.ohchr.org/english/law/index.htm#instruments (last accessed May 2011).

[192] UN General Assembly, *International Convention on the Elimination of All Forms of Racial Discrimination*, 21 December 1965, United Nations, Treaty Series, vol. 660, p 195, available at: http://www2.ohchr.org/english/law/cerd.htm (last accessed May 2011).

and other manifestations of anti-Semitism and racial and religious hatred that occurred in many countries in the winter of 1959–1960.[193] In addition, the subject of racial discrimination was an understandable priority for newly independent African States, who placed pressure on the various organs of the United Nations to take action in regard to colonialism and racial discrimination.[194] As a result, the General Assembly of the United Nations first adopted a Declaration on the Elimination of All Forms of Racial Discrimination on 20 November 1963.[195] This was quickly followed by a binding treaty on the subject, which was adopted by the General Assembly by 106 votes with only one abstention[196] on 21 December 1965. The Convention entered into force on 4 January 1969.[197] In general terms, the Convention sets out far-reaching obligations on States to prohibit and eliminate racial discrimination in all its forms; and provides for specific mechanisms to ensure that these obligations are in turn implemented by the contracting States. Implementation of the Convention is monitored by the Committee on the Elimination of Racial Discrimination (CERD). There are currently 174 States parties to the Convention.[198]

State obligations

[3.54] Article 1[199] of the Convention defines the term 'racial discrimination' as meaning:

'... any distinction, exclusion, restriction or preference based on race, colour, descent, or national or ethnic origin which has the purpose or effect of nullifying or impairing the

---

[193] Schwelb, 'The International Convention on the Elimination of all Forms of Racial Discrimination' (1966) 15 ICLQ 996, p 997. On the Convention generally, see also Meron, 'The Meaning and Reach of the International Convention on the Elimination of Racial Discrimination' (1985) 79 AJIL 283; and Rehman, *International Human Rights Law* (2nd edn, Pearson, 2010), pp 416–431.

[194] Schwelb, 'The International Convention on the Elimination of all Forms of Racial Discrimination' (1966) 15 ICLQ 996, p 997. This included at that time the ongoing policy of apartheid in South Africa.

[195] GA Res 1904 (XVIII), November 20, 1963, UN Doc A/RES/18/1904.

[196] Mexico, which later joined the majority and ratified the treaty on 20 February 1975.

[197] This occurred 30 days after the deposit of the 27th instrument of ratification deposited in accordance with art 19 of the Convention. It is interesting to note that of 27 States that ratified the convention by that date, 19 were from the third world, 5 from Eastern Europe and only three from Western Europe: Partsch, 'The Committee on the Elimination of Racial Discrimination' in Alston (ed), *The United Nations and Human Rights* (OUP, 1992), p 399.

[198] Source: http://treaties.un.org/Pages/Treaties.aspx?id=4&subid=A&lang=en (last accessed May 2011). While Ireland signed the Convention on 21 March 1968, it did not ratify it until 29 December 2000. The reason for the delay in ratification was stated to be on account of the need for the State to put in place legislative measures to implement the Convention. This was eventually done by means of the Employment Equality Act 1998 and the Equal Status Act 2000, thus enabling the State to ratify the Convention which eventually entered into force for Ireland on 28 January 2001. Ireland's First National Report to the Committee on the Elimination of Racial Discrimination (Government Publications, 2004), para 4: http://www.integration.ie/website/omi/omiwebv6.nsf/page/managingdiversity-UNCERD-en (last accessed May 2011).

[199] See CERD General Recommendation No 14 on the Definition of Discrimination (Art 1, para 1) (contd.../)

recognition, enjoyment or exercise, on an equal footing, of human rights and fundamental freedoms in the political, economic, social, cultural or any other field of public life'.[200]

[3.55] Article 1(4) does allow for affirmative action programmes 'taken for the sole purpose of securing advancement of certain racial or ethnic groups or individuals' where these are deemed necessary to ensure their equal enjoyment of human rights. Thus, any such measures taken by a State will not be deemed to be discrimination provided they do not lead to separate rights for different racial groups and are not continued for any longer than necessary.[201]

[3.56] Article 2 of the ICERD sets out the general obligations of States parties in regard to racial discrimination. Article 2(1) requires contracting States to 'condemn racial discrimination and undertake to pursue by all appropriate means and without delay a policy of eliminating racial discrimination in all its forms and promoting understanding among all races'. Specifically, art 2(1) goes on to spell out both negative and positive obligations on States in regard to this overall obligation. Thus, it obliges States not to engage in racial discrimination, and to ensure that all public authorities and institutions do not do so.[202] States are also obliged not to sponsor, defend or support racial discrimination by any persons or organisations.[203] In terms of positive obligations, States are required to prohibit and bring to an end such practices, if necessary by legislation,[204] and to amend, rescind or nullify any laws or regulations that have discriminatory effect.[205] Lastly, they are obliged to encourage, where appropriate, 'integrationist multi-racial organizations and movements', as well as other ways of breaking down barriers between races.[206] Echoing the terms of art 1(4), art 2(2) further obliges States, when the

---

[199] (\...contd) and CERD General Recommendation No 24 on Reporting of Persons Belonging to Different Races, National/Ethnic Groups, or Indigenous Peoples (Article 1) http://www2.ohchr.org/english/bodies/cerd/comments.htm (last accessed May 2011).

[200] Note that art 1(2) of the ICERD specifically provides that the Convention shall not apply to distinctions, exclusions, restrictions or preferences made by a State Party as between citizens and non-citizens. This was intended to allow for States to legitimately distinguish between citizens and non-citizens for the purposes of general immigration law and citizenship law. However, it does not permit States to discriminate against non-citizens on grounds of their race, colour, descent, or national or ethnic origin: Schwelb, 'The International Convention on the Elimination of all Forms of Racial Discrimination' (1966) 15 ICLQ 996, p 1007. Likewise, note the provisions of art 1(3) in regard to provisions of States parties in regard to nationality, citizenship or naturalization. CERD has clarified the parameters of these provisions in its General Recommendation No 30 on Discrimination Against Non-Citizens: http://www2.ohchr.org/english/bodies/cerd/comments.htm (last accessed May 2011).

[201] Provision for affirmative action is also required, where the circumstances warrant, by the terms of art 2(2), ICERD.

[202] ICERD, art 2(1)(a).

[203] ICERD, art 2(1)(b).

[204] ICERD, art 2(1)(d).

[205] ICERD, art 2(1)(c).

[206] ICERD, art 2(1)(e). Rehman argues that the terms of art 2(1)(e) 'perhaps reveal the essence of the whole section': Rehman, *International Human Rights Law* (2nd edn, Pearson, 2010), p 419.

circumstances warrant, to take 'special and concrete measures' in the social, economic, cultural fields, to ensure the adequate development and protection of certain racial groups, for the purposes of guaranteeing them equality in the enjoyment of their human rights. As with the terms of art 1(4), such measures, however, must necessarily only be of a temporary nature.[207] This attempt in the Convention to oblige States to pursue not only *de jure* but also *de facto* equality for various racial, ethnic and national groups is one of its distinctive features[208] and perhaps just one of the reasons why it has been described as a 'pioneering experience'.[209]

[3.57] Articles 3 to 7 of the ICERD proceed to clarify in greater detail the substantive obligations on States parties to the Convention. Article 3 enjoins States to prevent, prohibit and eradicate all practices of racial segregation and apartheid. While this article was originally directed primarily at the regime of apartheid then in operation in South Africa, CERD has ensured its continuing relevance by clarifying that its terms can also apply to practices and policies of ghettoisation or *de facto* segregation of ethnic minorities.[210]

[3.58] Article 4 requires States parties to adopt immediate and positive measures to eradicate incitement to racial hatred. This includes the duty to declare punishable by law certain offences concerning incitement to racial hatred (eg, racist propaganda, acts of violence or incitement to racial violence, or assisting racist activities, including financing thereof); to declare illegal and prohibit racist organisations; and not to permit public authorities or institutions to promote or incite racial discrimination. While the terms of art 4 specifically provide that these duties should be exercised 'with due regard to the principles embodied in the Universal Declaration of Human Rights' as well as to the rights expressly set forth in art 5 of the Convention itself (which deals with the right to freedom of expression), clearly this provision has the capacity to lead to a conflict between the rights to freedom of expression and association on the one hand, and that of non-discrimination on the other.[211]

[3.59] Article 5 requires States, in accordance with art 2, to prohibit and eliminate racial discrimination and to guarantee the right of everyone, regardless of race, colour, or national or ethnic origin, to equality before the law, particularly as regards a range of specific rights enumerated in the text. Article 6 requires States parties to provide effective protection and remedies for persons in respect of any acts of racial

---

[207] ICERD, art 2(2) thus provides specifically that: 'These measures shall in no case entail as a consequence the maintenance of unequal or separate rights for different racial groups after the objectives for which they were undertaken have been achieved'.

[208] Rehman, *International Human Rights Law* (2nd edn, Pearson, 2010), p 420.

[209] Flinterman and Henderson, 'Special Human Rights Treaties' in Hanski and Suksi (eds), *An Introduction to the International Protection of Human Rights: A Textbook* (Institute for Human Rights: Abo Akademi University, 1999)125–129, p 126.

[210] CERD General Recommendation 19 on Racial Segregation and Apartheid, para 3: http://www2.ohchr.org/english/bodies/cerd/comments.htm (last accessed May 2011).

[211] Rehman, *International Human Rights Law* (2nd edn, Pearson, 2010), p 421. The views of the CERD on this point are set forth below in Ch 8, paras **8.28**.

discrimination, including the right to seek just and adequate compensation for any damage suffered in that regard.[212] Finally, art 7 requires States parties to adopt immediate and effective measures, particularly in the fields of teaching, education, culture and information, designed to combat racial prejudices which lead to racial discrimination. States parties are also enjoined by the terms of art 7 to promote understanding, tolerance and friendship among nations and racial or ethnic groups.

[3.60] Finally, while there is no provision for derogation from the obligations in the Convention, art 20 does envisage the possibility of States making reservations to certain of its terms, provided that these are not incompatible with the object and purpose of the Convention. In accordance with the general principles of international law, States are also entitled to enter 'interpretative declarations' as regards how they intend to interpret particular provisions of the Convention.[213]

The Committee on the Elimination of Racial Discrimination

[3.61] Implementation by the States parties of the obligations in the ICERD is monitored by the Committee on the Elimination of Racial Discrimination, otherwise known as CERD.[214] Article 8 provides for the establishment of CERD. It is to be composed of 18 independent experts of 'high moral standing and acknowledged impartiality' who shall serve in their personal capacity.[215] The members of CERD are elected[216] by States parties from among their nationals, with due regard being given to the principle of equitable geographical distribution.[217] Members of the Committee serve

---

[212] According to Lerner, this provision arguably goes further than the terms of art 8 of the UDHR, art 2 of the ICCPR and art 7(2) of the Declaration on the Elimination of all Forms of Racial Discrimination: Lerner, *Group Rights and Discrimination in International Law* (Martinus Nijhoff, 2003), pp 60-61, cited in Rehman, *International Human Rights Law* (2nd edn, Pearson, 2010), p 421.

[213] Many States have availed of the right to enter reservations and interpretations: http://www2.ohchr.org/english/bodies/ratification/2.htm#reservations (last accessed May 2011).

[214] See generally Partsch, 'The Committee on the Elimination of Racial Discrimination' in Alston (ed), *The United Nations and Human Rights* (OUP, 1992), p 339 and Banton, 'Decision-Taking in the Committee on the Elimination of Racial Discrimination' in Alston and Crawford, *The Future of UN Human Rights Treaty Monitoring* (CUP, 2000), 55.

[215] ICERD, art 8(1). In contrast to the Human Rights Committee, a significant number of the current members of the Committee have a diplomatic background: http://www2.ohchr.org/english/bodies/cerd/members.htm (last accessed May 2011). The failure of the Convention to make explicit provision for conflicts of interest in this respect has resulted in the Committee having to defend its character as an 'independent' treaty body on a number of occasions: Partsch, 'The Committee on the Elimination of Racial Discrimination' in Alston (ed), *The United Nations and Human Rights* (OUP, 1992), p 341. In this respect, Bayefsky's recommendations in regard to the independence of treaty body members generally would appear to be particularly germane to CERD: see Bayefsky, *The UN Treaty System: Universality at the Crossroads* (Transnational Publishers, 2003).

[216] Detailed provisions for election to the Committee are set forth in art 8(2)–(5), ICERD.

[217] ICERD, art 8(2)–(5).

for four-year terms.[218] The Committee adopts its own rules of procedure.[219] It meets at the UN headquarters in Geneva, normally for two, four-week sessions *per* year.

[3.62] The ICERD makes provision for CERD to exercise its monitoring functions through three principal mechanisms. First, through the operation of a periodic reporting procedure, provided for in art 9 of the Convention. Second, through an optional, 'inter-State' complaint procedure, provided for in arts 11 - 13 of the Convention; and third, through an optional 'individual complaints' procedure provided for in art 14. The Committee also operates an 'early warning procedure', aimed at preventing the escalation of a situation of racial discrimination into conflict. The periodic reporting mechanism (together with the early warning procedure) and the individual complaint mechanism are examined in greater detail in Chs 4 and 8 respectively.

[3.63] Finally, like the CCPR and the CESCR, the CERD also regularly publishes its interpretation of particular provisions of the Covenant or thematic issues relating to its operation. The latter are referred to as 'general recommendations' in the practice of this particular committee (but otherwise know as 'general comments' in the practices of the other treaty bodies). The basis for adopting these recommendations is located in art 9(2) of the Convention. To date, CERD has adopted 33 such recommendations.[220]

Convention on the Elimination of All Forms of Discrimination against Women (1979)

[3.64] The relationship between women's rights and international human rights law and practice has been a subject of intense legal and political analysis over the past few decades.[221] Questions raised about the legitimacy and value of rights discourse generally in regard to women[222] have been buttressed by the manner in which legal norms and

---

[218] ICERD, art 8(5)(a).
[219] ICERD, art 10.
[220] The General Recommendations of CERD are available at: http://www2.ohchr.org/english/bodies/cerd/comments.htm (last accessed May 2011).
[221] See generally, Cook (ed), *Human Rights of Women: National and International Perspectives* (University of Pennsylvania Press, 1994), in particular Charlesworth, 'What Are Women's International Human Rights?', p 58; Mullally, *Gender, Culture and Women's Rights: Reclaiming Universalism* (Hart, 2006); Bunch, 'Women's Rights as Human Rights: Toward a Re-Vision of Human Rights' (1990) 12 HRQ 486; Cook, 'Women's International Human Rights Law: The Way Forward' (1993) 15 HRQ 230; Galey, 'International Enforcement of Women's Rights' (1984) 6 HRQ 463; Charlesworth and Chinkin, *The Boundaries of International Law: A Feminist Analysis* (Manchester University Press, 2000); Engle, 'International Human Rights and Feminism' (1992) 13 Michigan Journal of International Law 517–610; MacKinnon, *Are Women Human? And Other International Dialogues* (Harvard University Press, 2006); Bell, 'Women's Rights as Human Rights: Old Agendas in New Guises' in Hegarty and Leonard (eds), *Human Rights: An Agenda for the 21st Century* (Cavendish, 1999), p 139 and Rehman, *International Human Rights Law* (2nd edn, Pearson, 2010), pp 511–554.
[222] See Coomaraswamy, 'To Bellow Like a Cow: Women, Ethnicity, and the Discourse of Rights' Cook (ed), *Human Rights of Women: National and International Perspectives* (University of Pennsylvania Press: 1994), p 39.

mechanisms for the protection of women's rights were developed through the United Nations framework. While the normative development of women's rights looked at least promising from the outset, as we shall see, the establishment of mechanisms for the enforcement of those rights has been less impressive.

[3.65] The UN's early focus on the issue of sex discrimination manifested itself in the pioneering provisions included in that respect in the UN Charter[223] and also in the establishment of a nuclear Commission on the Status of Women.[224] The latter body, established in 1946,[225] was intended to be the main policy-making organ of the UN dealing with all issues relating to women.[226] Within a relatively short time, the Commission recognised the need to develop human rights standards at the international level dealing exclusively with discrimination against women. Its efforts in this regard culminated in the elaboration of a Declaration on the Elimination of Discrimination against Women in 1967,[227] followed by the adoption on 18 December 1979 of a binding convention on the subject, known as the Convention for the Elimination of All Forms of Discrimination against Women (CEDAW).[228] Undoubtedly the 'definitive international instrument requiring respect for and observance of the human rights of women',[229] it entered into force on 3 September 1981, once the requisite number of 20 ratifications had been obtained.[230] There are currently 186 States parties to the Convention, making it

---

[223] Provisions relating to sex discrimination and equality are located in the Preamble to that instrument, as well as in United Nations Convention on the Elimination of All Forms of Discrimination against Women, arts 1, 8, 13, 55 and 76.

[224] The Commission is a functional Commission of ECOSOC. It is serviced by the Division for the Advancement of Women (formerly the Section on the Status of Women) of the UN Department of Economic and Social Affairs: http://www.un.org/womenwatch/daw/daw/index.html (last accessed May 2011).

[225] ECOSOC Resolutions 2/II (1946) of 21 June 1946; and 48(IV) of 29 March 1947.

[226] The Commission's mandate was to 'prepare recommendations and reports to the Economic and Social Council on promoting women's rights in political, economic, civil, social and educational fields' and to make recommendations 'on urgent problems requiring immediate attention in the field of women's rights': ECOSOC Res 48 (1V) quoted in Galey, 'Promoting Non-Discrimination Against Women: The United Nations Commission on the Status of Women' (1979) 23 International Studies Quarterly 273, p 275. See also Reanda, 'The Commission on the Status of Women' in Alston (ed), *The United Nations and Human Rights*, (OUP, 1992), pp 265–303.

[227] UN General Assembly, *Declaration on the Elimination of Discrimination against Women*, 7 November 1967, Un Doc A/RES/2263.

[228] UN General Assembly, *Convention on the Elimination of All Forms of Discrimination Against Women*, 18 December 1979, United Nations, Treaty Series, vol. 1249, p. 13, available at: http://www2.ohchr.org/english/law/cedaw.htm (last accessed May 2011). For a detailed exposition of the path taken by the Commission in regard to standard-setting, culminating in the adoption of the Convention, see Reanda, 'The Commission on the Status of Women' in Alston, *The United Nations and Human Rights* (OUP, 1992), pp 281–289.

[229] Cook, 'Reservations to the Convention on the Elimination of All Forms of Discrimination Against Women' (1990) 30 Va J Int'l L 643, p 643.

[230] *Convention on the Elimination of Discrimination against Women*, art 27(1).

one of the most widely ratified of all of the United Nations human rights treaties.[231] The Convention sets forth a detailed definition of discrimination on the basis of sex, as well as a catalogue of rights and obligations on States in regard to the issue of discrimination against women. It is supplemented by a range of implementation mechanisms, monitored again by a committee of independent experts, known as the Committee on the Elimination of Discrimination against Women (CEDAW Committee).

State obligations

[3.66] Article 1 of the Convention defines 'discrimination against women' as: '… any distinction, exclusion or restriction made on the basis of sex which has the effect or purpose of impairing or nullifying the recognition, enjoyment or exercise by women, irrespective of their marital status, on a basis of equality of men and women, of human rights and fundamental freedoms in the political, economic, social, cultural, civil or any other field'.[232]

[3.67] By the terms of art 2, States parties are required to 'pursue by all appropriate means and without delay a policy of eliminating discrimination against women'. Specifically, they undertake to (a) embody the principle of equality of men and women in their national constitutions or other legislation, and to ensure, through law or otherwise, the practical realisation of this principle; (b) adopt appropriate legislative and other measures prohibiting discrimination against women; and (c) establish legal protection for women's rights on an equal basis with men and ensure, through competent national tribunals and other public institutions, effective protection for women against discrimination. Article 2(d) to (g) enjoin States further to refrain from and prevent any act or practice of discrimination against women, including by public authorities and institutions,[233] as well as private persons, organisations or enterprises;[234] and to guarantee the modification or repeal of existing laws, regulations, customs, practices[235] or penal provisions[236] that discriminate against women.

---

[231] Source: http://treaties.un.org/Pages/Treaties.aspx?id=4&subid=A&lang=en (last accessed May 2011). Ireland acceded to the Convention on 23 December 1985.

[232] Rehman has noted that this definition of sex discrimination appears to have a 'wider field of influence' than the definition of racial discrimination provided for in art 1 of the ICERD, insofar as the former applies to the 'political, economic, social, cultural, civil or any other field', whereas the latter is circumscribed to the 'political, economic, social, cultural *or any other field of public life*' (emphasis added): Rehman, *International Human Rights Law* (2nd edn, Pearson, 2010), p 520. Article 1 of the Convention on the Elimination of Discrimination against Women, therefore, clearly includes an obligation on States parties to eliminate discrimination (including gender-based violence) in private life – the sphere in which women are particularly vulnerable to abuse. This obligation is specifically referred to by the CEDAW Committee in its General Recommendation No 19 on violence against women, U.N. Doc. A/47/38 at 1, available at: http://www2.ohchr.org/english/bodies/cedaw/comments.htm (last accessed May 2011).

[233] CEDAW art 2(1)(d).

[234] CEDAW, art 2(1)(e).

[235] CEDAW, art 2(1)(f).

[236] CEDAW, art 2(1)(g).

[3.68] Article 3 of the Convention provides for a broad obligation on the contracting States to take all appropriate measures, particularly in the political, social, economic and cultural fields, 'to ensure the full development and advancement of women'. As with the ICERD, the drafters of the CEDAW also anticipated and allowed for the adoption by States of temporary measures of affirmative action for the benefit of women by States for the purposes of accelerating *de facto* equality between the sexes. By the terms of art 4, such measures shall not be deemed to constitute discrimination, provided they are of a temporary nature. Article 5 further obliges States to take all appropriate measures 'to modify the social and cultural patterns of conduct of men and women, with a view to achieving the elimination of prejudices and customary and all other practices which are based on the idea of the interiority or the superiority of either of the sexes or on stereotyped roles for men and women'.[237] There is a slight elaboration of this provision in art 5(b) which stipulates that family education must include a proper understanding of maternity as a 'social function' and the recognition of the common responsibility of men and women in regard to the rearing of children. Otherwise, the article is silent on the type of measures envisaged as being necessary to fulfil the obligations in art 5.[238] Finally, in terms of general obligations, art 6 obliges States to take all appropriate measures, including legislative ones, to suppress all forms of traffic in women and exploitation of the prostitution of women.[239]

[3.69] Further obligations on the contracting States in regard to the elimination of discrimination are set forth in the Convention in terms of the classic dichotomy of 'civil and political rights' on the one hand, and 'economic, social and cultural rights' on the other. Thus, Part II of the Convention provides for specific obligations on States in regard to the elimination of discrimination against women in political and public life,[240] as well as with respect to ensuring equal status in the determination of nationality, following marriage or in regard to children.[241] Part III of the Convention contains specific obligations on States to take all appropriate measures to eliminate discrimination against women in the fields of education,[242] employment,[243] health care,[244] and in other areas of economic and social life.[245] States are required to take account of the particular problems faced by women in rural areas and to take specific measures to

---

[237] CEDAW, art 5(a).
[238] The CEDAW Committee has attempted to clarify the ambit of this article, both in its general recommendations to States as well as in its concluding observations on States' reports. See, in particular, General Recommendation No 19 (1992), paras 11 and 12.
[239] See CEDAW Committee General Recommendation No 19 (1992), paras 13–16.
[240] CEDAW, arts 7 and 8.
[241] CEDAW, art 9.
[242] CEDAW, art 10.
[243] CEDAW, art 11.
[244] CEDAW, art 12.
[245] CEDAW, art 13. Particular measures are mentioned here including the right to family benefits; the right to bank loans, mortgages and other forms of financial credit; and the right to participate in recreational activities, sports and all aspects of cultural life.

eliminate discrimination against them.[246] Part IV of the Convention requires States, both broadly and in specific detailed terms, to ensure equality of men and women before the law;[247] and to eliminate discrimination against women in matters relating to marriage and family relations.[248]

Finally, as with the ICERD, specific provision is made in art 28 of the CEDAW for States to make reservations to any term(s) of the Convention at the time of ratification. The decision by many States to exercise their prerogative in this regard has been a notorious difficulty in regard to the operation of this Convention.[249]

The Committee on the Elimination of Discrimination against Women

[3.70] Implementation of the Convention is monitored by the Committee on the Elimination of Discrimination against Women (CEDAW Committee).[250] Article 17 of the Convention provides for the establishment of the CEDAW Committee as the largest of the United Nations treaty bodies, composed as it is of 23 experts of 'high moral standing and competence in the field covered by the Convention'.[251] Members are elected by States parties to the Convention from among their nationals on the basis of equitable geographical distribution and with consideration being given to 'the different forms of civilization as well as principal legal systems'.[252] They are also required to serve in their 'personal capacity'.[253] Members are elected to serve on the Committee for four-year terms.[254] The Committee adopts its own rules of procedure[255] and reports annually to the General Assembly through ECOSOC.[256] To cope with its workload, the

---

[246] CEDAW, art 14.
[247] CEDAW, art 15.
[248] CEDAW, art 16.
[249] See the numerous reservations and declarations entered by the States parties to the CEDAW, available at: http://treaties.un.org/Pages/ViewDetails.aspx?src=TREATY&mtdsg_no=IV-8&chapter=4&lang=en (last accessed May 2011). See generally, Cook, 'Reservations to the Convention on the Elimination of All Forms of Discrimination Against Women' (1990) Va J Int'l L 643 and Clark, 'The Vienna Convention Reservations Regime and the Convention on Discrimination Against Women' (1991) 85 AJIL 281.
[250] See generally, Jacobson, 'The Committee on the Elimination of Discrimination Against Women' in Alston (ed), *The United Nations and Human Rights* (OUP, 1992) p 444; Bustelo, 'The Committee on the Elimination of Discrimination Against Women at the Crossroads' in Alston and Crawford, *The Future of UN Human Rights Treaty Monitoring* (CUP, 2000), p 79; and Schopp-Schilling, 'Treaty Body Reform: the Case of the Committee on the Elimination of Discrimination Against Women' (2007) 7 HRLR 201.
[251] CEDAW, art 17(1).
[252] CEDAW, art 17(1).
[253] CEDAW, art 17(1). The current composition of the CEDAW Committee includes a significant number of academics, lawyers as well as persons with a diplomatic background: http://www2.ohchr.org/english/bodies/cedaw/membership.htm (last accessed May 2011).
[254] CEDAW, art 17(5). Article 17(2)–(7) provide in detail for the procedure in regard to election of Committee members.
[255] CEDAW, art 19.
[256] CEDAW, art 21.

Committee normally meets for three, three-week sessions annually.[257] Recently, the servicing of the Convention has been transferred from the Division for the Advancement of Women (based in New York) to the OHCHR (based in Geneva), as a result of which the Committee's sessions have been transferred accordingly from New York to Geneva.[258]

[3.71] The CEDAW Committee monitors implementation of the Convention through three principal mechanisms. First, a mandatory periodic reporting mechanism provided for in art 18 of the Convention. Second, an optional 'inquiry' procedure provided for in a Protocol to the Convention known as the Optional Protocol to the Convention on the Elimination of All Forms of Discrimination against Women, adopted by the General Assembly on 6 October 1999.[259] Pursuant to art 8 of the Optional Protocol, contracting States to the Protocol can accept the competence of the CEDAW Committee to conduct an inquiry where it receives reliable information indicating 'grave or systematic violations' by that State of the rights set forth in the Convention.[260] Third, an optional, individual complaint mechanism, also provided for in the Protocol. These various mechanisms are examined in detail below in Chs 4, 5 and 10 of this book respectively.

[3.72] Finally, the CEDAW Committee also regularly publishes its interpretation of particular provisions of the Convention or issues relating to its implementation in the form of general recommendations. The basis for adopting these recommendations is located in art 21 of the Convention. To date, CEDAW has adopted 28 such general recommendations.[261]

United Nations Convention Against Torture and Other Cruel, Inhuman or Degrading Treatment or Punishment (1984)

[3.73] Next to slavery, torture is aptly described as one of the most extreme forms of dehumanization[262] and a horrific form of human rights violation. While it has been practised throughout the world in different cultures and societies since the beginning of time, its resurgence and usage in the twentieth century, in particular, by totalitarian

---

[257] In this respect, the GA has in recent years extended the normal meeting time of the CEDAW Committee from the limited two-week period stipulated in art 20(1) of the Convention.

[258] For an interesting historical overview of the servicing and location of the CEDAW Committee's meetings, see Schopp-Schilling, 'Treaty Body Reform: the Case of the Committee on the Elimination of Discrimination Against Women' (2007) 7 HRLR 201, pp 218–223.

[259] UN General Assembly, *Optional Protocol to the Convention on the Elimination of All Forms of Discrimination against Women: resolution / adopted by the General Assembly*, 15 October 1999, UN Doc A/RES/54/4, available at: http://www2.ohchr.org/english/law/cedaw-one.htm (last accessed May 2011).

[260] In addition, it should be noted that art 29 of the CEDAW establishes a procedure whereby States parties to the Convention can refer disputes over the interpretation or application of the Convention to the International Court of Justice, though this procedure has never been used.

[261] The general recommendations adopted by CEDAW are available at: http://www2.ohchr.org/english/bodies/cedaw/comments.htm (last accessed May 2011).

[262] Nowak and McArthur, *The United Nations Convention Against Torture: A Commentary* (OUP, 2008), p 1.

regimes[263] made it an urgent point of focus for the United Nations human rights regime from an early juncture. In this respect, the United Nations Convention against Torture and Other Cruel, Inhuman or Degrading Treatment or Punishment (UNCAT) is but one of a wide range of measures taken by the UN to combat it.[264] Torture, inhuman and degrading treatment or punishment was, for example, already prohibited in the UDHR[265] and the ICCPR,[266] as well as in a number of other international instruments adopted by the United Nations.[267] The widespread and documented reports of torture and enforced disappearances taking place in Chile under the Pinochet regime during the 1970s acted as a catalyst for many important initiatives. In 1975, the General Assembly adopted the Declaration on the Protection of all Persons from Being Subjected to Torture and Other Cruel, Inhuman or Degrading Treatment or Punishment.[268] As well as positing a definition of torture,[269] the Declaration set forth a framework by which States should seek to prevent and investigate acts of torture and inhuman or degrading treatment,[270] criminalise the activities in question, as well as prosecute and punish those responsible[271] and provide redress and compensation for victims of torture.[272] The

---

[263] For a historical perspective on the practice of torture, see generally Evans and Morgan, *Preventing Torture* (OUP, 1998), pp 1–25.

[264] UN General Assembly, *Convention Against Torture and Other Cruel, Inhuman or Degrading Treatment or Punishment*, 10 December 1984, United Nations, Treaty Series, vol. 1465, p. 85, available at: http://www2.ohchr.org/english/law/cat.htm (last accessed May 2011). See generally Nowak and McArthur, *The United Nations Convention Against Torture: A Commentary* (OUP, 2008), p 1; Ingelse, *The UN Committee Against Torture: An Assessment* (Kluwer Law International, 2001); Levinson (ed) *Torture: A Collection* (OUP, 2006); Boulesbaa, *The UN Convention on Torture and Prospects for the Enforcement* (Brill, 1999); Burgers and Danelius, *The United Nations Convention Against Torture: A Handbook on the Convention Against Torture and Other Cruel, Inhuman or Degrading Treatment or Punishment* (Kluwer, 1988); and Rehman, *International Human Rights Law* (2nd edn, Pearson, 2010), pp 808–850.

[265] UDHR, art 5.

[266] ICCPR, art 7.

[267] See, for example, the Convention on the Prevention and Punishment of the Crime of Genocide 1948, UN Doc E/CN.4/RES/1999/67, art II; the International Convention on the Elimination of All Forms of Racial Discrimination 1966, art 5(b); the International Convention on the Suppression and Punishment of the Crime of Apartheid 1973, G.A. Res. 3068 (XXVIII)), 28 U.N. GAOR Supp. (No. 30) at 75, U.N. Doc. A/9030 (1974), 1015 UNTS 243, Article II(ii).

[268] UN General Assembly, *Declaration on the Protection of All Persons from Being Subjected to Torture and Other Cruel, Inhuman or Degrading Treatment or Punishment*, 9 December 1975, UN Doc A/RES/3452, available at: http://www2.ohchr.org/english/law/declarationcat.htm (last accessed May 2011).

[269] Declaration against Torture and Other Cruel, Inhuman or Degrading Treatment or Punishment, art 1.

[270] Declaration against Torture and Other Cruel, Inhuman or Degrading Treatment or Punishment, arts 4, 5, 6, 8 and 9.

[271] Declaration against Torture and Other Cruel, Inhuman or Degrading Treatment or Punishment, arts 7 and 10.

[272] Declaration against Torture and Other Cruel, Inhuman or Degrading Treatment or Punishment, art 11.

Declaration, in effect, proved to be a blue-print for the Convention, which the Commission on Human Rights was subsequently asked to draft by the General Assembly in 1977.[273] Negotiations on a draft text of the Convention proceeded between 1977 and 1984, with agreement being particularly difficult to reach in regard to international monitoring measures as well as the principle of universal jurisdiction.[274] A compromise text was eventually arrived at in the form of the Convention which was adopted by the General Assembly on 10 December 1984 and opened for signature on 5 February 1985.[275] It entered into force on 26 June 1987, after 20 States had ratified it, in accordance with art 27 of the text. There are currently 146 States parties to the Convention.[276] The Convention is supplemented by an Optional Protocol, adopted in 2002, which provides for a system of preventive and unexpected visits to places of detention in States parties by an international monitoring body as well as by an independent national mechanism.[277]

State obligations

[3.74] Article 1 of the Convention sets forth, for the first time in a binding international instrument, a definition of torture as meaning:

> '... any act by which severe pain or suffering, whether physical or mental, is intentionally inflicted on a person for such purposes as obtaining from him or a third person information or a confession, punishing him for an act he or a third person has committed or is suspected of having committed, or intimidating or coercing him or a third person, or for any reason based on discrimination of any kind, when such pain or suffering is inflicted by or at the instigation of or with the consent or acquiescence of a public official or other person acting in an official capacity. It does not include pain or suffering arising only from, inherent in or incidental to lawful sanctions'.

The definition has proved controversial, not least because of its complexity, but more particularly because it appears to be confined to acts which are 'intentionally inflicted'

---

[273] Draft Convention against Torture and Other Cruel, Inhuman or Degrading Treatment or Punishment: GA Res 32/62, 8 December 1977, UN Doc A/RES/32/62.

[274] On the principle of universal jurisdiction, see below re art 5, para 3.77. For the drafting history of the Convention, see Nowak and McArthur, *The United Nations Convention Against Torture: A Commentary* (OUP, 2008), pp 3–7.

[275] UN General Assembly, *Convention Against Torture and Other Cruel, Inhuman or Degrading Treatment or Punishment*, 10 December 1984, United Nations, Treaty Series, vol. 1465, p. 85, available at: http://www2.ohchr.org/english/law/cat.htm (last accessed May 2011).

[276] Source: http://treaties.un.org/Pages/Treaties.aspx?id=4&subid=A&lang=en (last accessed May 2011). Ireland ratified the Convention on 11 April 2002.

[277] UN General Assembly, *Optional Protocol to the Convention Against Torture and other Cruel, Inhuman and Degrading Treatment or Punishment*, 18 December 2002, A/RES/57/199, available at: http://www2.ohchr.org/english/law/cat-one.htm (last accessed May 2011). The terms of the Protocol are examined in detail below in Ch 6, para **6.03–6.37**. The work of the UN Special Rapporteur on Torture and Other Cruel, Inhuman or Degrading Treatment or Punishment, a 'thematic procedure' established by the former Commission on Human Rights in 1985, also forms part of the UN's efforts to punish and prevent torture. See generally: http://www2.ohchr.org/english/issues/torture/rapporteur/(last accessed May 2011).

for particular specified purposes, thus potentially excluding, for example, acts inflicted simply for the sadistic pleasure of causing intense pain or suffering, or for medical or scientific experimentation.[278] Secondly, the stipulation that such acts must be inflicted by or at the instigation of public authorities, or with their consent or acquiescence, has also been a source of criticism on the basis that this potentially excludes the horizontal effect of the Convention from acts committed by private parties which are not adequately prevented or punished by the State.[279] Lastly, criticism has been levelled at the stipulation in the final clause that torture 'does not include pain or suffering arising only from, inherent in or incidental to lawful sanctions'.[280]

[3.75] Article 16(1) of the Convention provides that each State party shall undertake to prevent in any territory under its jurisdiction other acts of 'cruel, inhuman or degrading treatment or punishment' which do not amount to torture as defined in art 1. While the terms 'cruel', 'inhuman', 'degrading' and 'treatment or punishment' are not defined, there is no specificity as to the 'purpose' for which such acts are perpetrated, as is the case with torture under art 1. The only stipulation made in art 16(1) is that acts of cruel, inhuman or degrading treatment must be 'committed by or at the instigation of or with

---

[278] Each of these 'purposes' were apparently proposed by the British and Swiss representatives during the drafting of the Convention, but ultimately rejected: Nowak and McArthur, *The United Nations Convention Against Torture: A Commentary* (OUP, 2008), p 75. Convention against Torture and Other Cruel, Inhuman or Degrading Treatment or Punishment, art 1 can be contrasted with the definition of torture set forth in art 2 of the Inter-American Convention to Prevent and Punish Torture 1985 which includes the words 'or any other purpose': OAS Treaty Series, No 67, available at http://www.unhcr.org/refworld/docid/3ae6b3620.html (last accessed May 2011).

[279] See Flinkerman and Henderson, 'Special Human Rights Treaties' in Hanski and Suksi, (eds), *An Introduction to the International Protection of Human Rights: A Textbook* (Abo Akademi University, 1999) 125, p 137. However, note that the Committee Against Torture (CAT), which has jurisdiction to interpret the Convention, has interpreted the same clause as it appears in art 16 of the Convention widely so as to hold States responsible for 'turning a blind eye' to cruel, inhuman or degrading treatment or punishment meted out by private parties. See *Dzemajl et al v Yugoslavia* (CAT/C/29/1/161/2000, 2 December 2002). The views of Committee against Torture (CAT) which monitors implementation of UNCAT on the parameters of the definition are considered in detail below in Ch 9, para **9.42–9.45**.

[280] See, for example, the critique made by Ingelse, *The UN Committee Against Torture: An Assessment* (Kluwer Law International, 2001), pp 211–217, who concludes that this sentence is a 'monstrosity' because, *inter alia*, it is capable of being interpreted in such a way as to allow for certain forms of corporal punishment. Likewise, see Burgers and Danelius, *The United Nations Convention Against Torture: A Handbook on the Convention Against Torture and Other Cruel, Inhuman or Degrading Treatment or Punishment* (Kluwer, 1988), p 122. Nowak and McArthur argue that critiques of the clause generally fail to find any meaningful scope or application for it, and that an interpretation of art 1, in accordance with the general rules of interpretation laid down in the Vienna Convention on the Law of Treaties leads to the inevitable conclusion that the 'lawful sanctions' clause has 'no scope or application and must be simply ignored': Nowak and McArthur, *The United Nations Convention Against Torture: A Commentary* (OUP, 2008), p 84.

the consent or acquiescence of a public official or other person acting in an official capacity'.[281]

[3.76] Articles 2 to 16 set forth the substantive obligations on contracting States. It is important, however, to note that most of the obligations provided for in UNCAT are expressed as specifically relating to acts of torture as defined in art 1, as opposed to acts of 'cruel, inhuman or degrading treatment or punishment'. Thus, in respect of torture only, arts 2 to 9, and 14 and 15 oblige States:

- To take effective legislative, administrative, judicial or other measures to prevent acts of torture in any territory under its jurisdiction (art 2).[282]
- Not to expel, return or extradite a person to another State where there are substantial grounds for believing that he would be subjected to torture (art 3).[283]
- To make torture a criminal offence under domestic criminal law, including an attempt to commit torture or an act by any person which constitutes complicity or participation in torture. Such offences should attract appropriate penalties, taking into account the grave nature of the crime (art 4).

[3.77] Articles 5 to 7 of the Convention subject the offences provided for in art 4 to a system of 'universal jurisdiction'. The principle of 'universal jurisdiction' is aimed at preventing the perpetrators of torture or their accomplices from evading prosecution in a 'safe haven'. Accordingly, art 5 obliges States to establish their jurisdiction over the offence of torture comprehensively, not only in any territory under its jurisdiction, but also on board a ship or aircraft registered in the State, when the offender is a national of that State, or where the victim is a national, if appropriate. Article 6 obliges States parties to take alleged torturers into custody, while art 7 obliges States to prosecute any offender present on its territory whom it does not extradite (*aut dedere aut iudicare*). Article 8, in turn, authorises States to consider the Convention to be a legal basis for extradition. Article 9 requires States to afford each other the greatest measure of mutual judicial assistance in connection with criminal proceedings brought in respect of the offences mentioned in art 4.

- Article 14 obliges States to ensure that victims of torture obtain a fair and adequate form of compensation in the national legal system;

---

[281] As to the meaning of 'cruel, inhuman or degrading treatment or punishment', see the views of CAT in Ch 9, see paras **9.42–9.45**.

[282] UNCAT, art 2(2) provides that no exceptional circumstances whatsoever, whether a state of war or a threat of war, internal political in stability or any other public emergency, may be invoked as a justification of torture. Likewise, according to art 2(3), an order from a superior officer or a public authority may not be invoked as a justification of torture.

[283] Article 3 thus enshrines in the Convention the principle of *non-refoulement*, already well established in international law through its articulation in art 33 of the Convention Relating to the Status of Refugees 1951. This principle has generated most of the cases communicated to the Committee Against Torture under the optional individual communications procedure provided for in art 22 of the Convention and examined further in paras **9.34–9.41**.

- Article 15 obliges them to ensure that any statement established as a result of torture shall not be invoked as evidence in any proceedings.

Articles 10 to 13 contain a further list of obligations aimed at preventing acts of torture. They include specific obligations on each State party:

- To train relevant personnel in regard to the prohibition against torture (art 10);
- To keep under systematic review its interrogation and prison rules (art 11);
- To conduct *ex officio* investigations where there are reasonable grounds for believing that an act of torture has been committed in any of its territories (art 12);
- To ensure that any individual who alleges that he or she has been tortured in the State's territory shall have the right to complain to and have his or her case promptly and impartially investigated by the competent authorities (art 13).

In obliging States to prevent acts of ill-treatment not amounting to 'torture', art 16(1) provides that, in particular, the obligations in arts 10 to 13 also apply in relation to acts of cruel, inhuman or degrading treatment or punishment.[284]

The Committee against Torture

[3.78] Implementation of the UNCAT is monitored by the Committee against Torture (CAT). Currently one of the smallest of the treaty bodies,[285] CAT is composed of 10 independent experts 'of high moral standing and recognized competence in the field of human rights', who shall be elected by the States parties, with consideration being given to equitable geographical distribution.[286] In regard to expertise, the Convention also requires that in the election of members, consideration should be given to the usefulness of participation of some persons having legal experience. As Byrnes notes, this is a rather surprising provision in many respects, given the subject matter of the Convention, when one would have thought that expertise in the areas of medicine, health and law enforcement would have taken centre-stage.[287] Indeed, it is striking that the current cohort of Committee members is dominated by lawyers and civil servants, with only one member having a background in psychology and practical experience specifically in the field of torture.[288] The Convention further stipulates that in nominating its own nationals, States parties should bear in mind the usefulness of nominating persons who are also members of the Human Rights Committee (CCPR). However, it appears that

---

[284] See the views of CAT on whether further obligations on States in respect of 'cruel, inhuman or degrading treatment' can be derived from art 16: Ch 9, para **9.44**.

[285] The Committee on the Protection of the Rights of All Migrant Workers and Members of their Families is also currently composed of 10 experts, with a possibility, however, for expansion: see para **3.100**.

[286] UNCAT, art 17(1). Detailed provisions governing the election of members are set forth in art 17(2)–(6).

[287] Byrnes, 'The Committee Against Torture' in Alston, *The United Nations and Human Rights* (OUP, 1992) 509, p 512.

[288] The CVs of all committee members are accessible at: http://www2.ohchr.org/english/bodies/cat/members.htm (last accessed May 2011).

this provision has had a very limited bearing to date on the composition of the CAT.[289] Members are elected for four-year terms, with a possibility for re-election, if re-nominated. The Committee normally holds sessions, twice *per* year, each of three weeks' duration, normally in May and November at the United Nations headquarters in Geneva.

[3.79] The Committee has competence to monitor the implementation by the States parties of the Convention by virtue of four discrete mechanisms. First, a periodic reporting mechanism provided for in art 19 of the Convention. Second, an optional[290] 'inquiry' procedure, provided for in art 20 of the Convention. Third, an optional, inter-State complaint mechanism, provided for in art 21; and fourth, an optional, individual complaints procedure, provided for in art 22. The activities of CAT in relation to the periodic reporting procedure, the inquiry procedure and the optional individual complaint procedure are considered further below in Chs 4, 5 and 9 respectively.

[3.80] Under art 24, the Committee shall submit an annual report on its activities under the Convention to the General Assembly of the United Nations. Although the Convention does not give the Committee an explicit power to issue 'general recommendations' or 'comments', as is the case with other treaty bodies, the Committee has fortunately taken the view that such a power is implicit in the Convention, in view of the monitoring functions conferred on it, as well as the need for guidance on the part of States as regards the implementation of certain of the Convention's provisions. Accordingly, it has issued two general comments to date, on the implementation of arts 2 and 3 of the Convention.[291]

Finally, it should be noted that while provision is made in the Convention for the States to enter reservations in regard to particular terms of the Convention,[292] given the subject-matter involved, it is hardly surprising that there is no provision whatsoever for the possibility of derogation.

United Nations Convention on the Rights of the Child (1989)

[3.81] The Convention on the Rights of the Child 1989 (CRC) sets forth in a comprehensive manner the human rights of children and the obligations on States parties to uphold them.[293] Variously described as a 'landmark' for children and their

---

[289] None of the present members have previously served on the Human Rights Committee. See also Byrnes, 'The Committee Against Torture' in Alston, *The United Nations and Human Rights* (OUP, 1992), p 511.

[290] See UNCAT, art 28.

[291] The general comments of the Committee against Torture are available at: http://www2.ohchr.org/english/bodies/cat/comments.htm (last accessed May 2011).

[292] UNCAT, art 30(2) and 28(1). As for the possibility of other reservervations, see Nowak and McArthur, *The UN Convention Against Torture: A Commentary*, pp 13-14.

[293] UN General Assembly, *Convention on the Rights of the Child*, 20 November 1989, United Nations, Treaty Series, vol. 1577, p 3, available at: http://www2.ohchr.org/english/law/crc.htm (last accessed May 2011). See generally Van Beuren, *The International Law on the Rights of the Child* (Martinus Nijhoff, 1998); Detreck, *A Commentary on the United Nations Convention on the Rights of the Child* (Kluwer, 1999); (contd.../)

rights,[294] and a 'world constitution' for children,[295] the unique aspect of the Convention is the manner in which it places children centre-stage as 'rights holders' in a legally binding instrument. Previous international instruments in regard to children did not fully recognise children as subjects of rights, but rather as objects deserving of international protection.[296] Despite its title, the Geneva Declaration of the Rights of the Child 1924 promulgated by the League of Nations, for example, emphasises the duties owed to children, rather than expressing the needs of children in terms of 'rights'.[297] Although the language of the UN Declaration of the Rights of the Child 1959[298] was a significant improvement in that respect, like its predecessor, it was non-binding, having only the status of a recommendation in international law. While children, as persons, were obviously covered by the terms of the International Bill of Rights,[299] and by other international instruments, it was not until the late 1970s[300] that the international community was galvanized into developing a legally binding instrument that would articulate the rights of children entirely from their perspective. In 1978, the General

---

[293] (\...contd) Fotrell (ed), *Revisiting Children's Rights: Ten Years of the UN Convention on the Rights of the Child* (Kluwer, 2000); Freeman, *Children's Rights: A Comparative Perspective* (Dartmouth, 1996); Alen et al (eds), *A Commentary on the United Nations Convention on the Rights of the Child* (Martinus Nijhoff, 2010); Goonesekere et al, *Protecting the World's Children: Impact of the Convention on the Rights of the Child in Diverse Legal Systems* (CUP, 2007); McGoldrick, 'The United Nations Convention on the Rights of the Child' (1991) Int'l J of Law, Policy and Family 132–169; Rehman, *International Human Rights Law* (2nd edn, Pearson, 2010), pp 555–599; Fortin, *Children's Rights and the Developing Law* (2nd edn, CUP, 2005), pp 31–51; Hammarberg, 'The United Nations Convention on the Rights of the Child – and How to Make it Work' (2000) 14 Children and Society 277; Kilkelly, 'UN Committee on the Rights of the Child – An Evaluation in the Light of Recent UK experience' (1996) 8(2) Child and Family Law Quarterly pp 105–120; and Smith, 'Monitoring the CRC' in Alfredsson et al (eds), *International Human Rights Monitoring Mechanisms* (2nd edn, Martinus Nijhoff, 2009), pp 109–116.

[294] OHCHR Fact Sheet No 10 (Rev 1), *The Rights of the Child*: http://www.unhchr.ch/html/menu6/2/fs10.htm (last accessed May 2011).

[295] Lopatka, 'An Introduction to the United Nations Convention on the Rights of the Child' (1996) 6 Transnat'l & Contemp Probs 251, p 252.

[296] For a brief review of the history of the rights of the child, see Shackel, 'The UN Convention on the Rights of the Child: A Review of its Successes and Future Directions' (2003) Aust Int'l L J 21, pp 24–27.

[297] Geneva Declaration of the Rights of the Child, League of Nations OJ Spec Supp 21, p 43, adopted 26 September 1924: http://www.un-documents.net/gdrc1924.htm (last accessed May 2011).

[298] UN General Assembly, *Declaration of the Rights of the Child*, proclaimed by General Assembly Res 1386 (XIV) 20 November 1959, available at: http://www.unhcr.org/refworld/docid/3ae6b38e3.html (last accessed May 2011).

[299] See also specific references to children in the UDHR, art 25(2); ICCPR, art 24; and ICESCR, art 10(3).

[300] Focus on the needs and corresponding rights of children was heightened by the UN General Assembly's action in declaring 1979 as the International Year of the Child in GA Res 31/169 of 21 December 1976.

Assembly requested the Commission on Human Rights to draft a binding convention on the subject.[301] In 1979, the Commission established an open-ended Working Group on the Question of the Rights of the Child.[302] After a very lengthy process of negotiation,[303] the text of the Convention was eventually adopted by the General Assembly on 20 November 1989. The Convention rapidly entered into force a year later in 1990 after the requisite number of 20 States had ratified it in accordance with the terms of art 49. To this day, it is the most widely subscribed to international human rights convention, having a record number of 193 States parties to its terms.[304] The obligations in the Convention in respect of children are augmented by two Optional Protocols: the Optional Protocol to the Convention on the Rights of the Child on the involvement of children in armed conflict [305] (OPAC) and the Optional Protocol to the Convention on the Rights of the Child on the sale of children, child prostitution and child pornography[306] (OPSC).

State obligations

[3.82] For the purposes of the CRC, a 'child' is defined as 'every human being below the age of eighteen years unless, under the law applicable to the child, majority is attained earlier'.[307]

There are four general principles which lie at the heart of the Convention and which are intended to underpin all of its other provisions.[308] These principles may be drawn on

---

[301] GA Res 33/166, 20 December 1966.

[302] Commission on Human Rights, Report on the 35th session: UN Doc E/1979/36, para 42.

[303] On the drafting history of the Convention, see Detrick (ed), *The United Nations Convention on the Rights of the Child: A Guide to the 'Travaux Préparatoires'* (Kluwer, 1992); *Legislative History of the Convention on the Rights of the Child* (OHCHR, 2007); and Smith, 'The Rights of the Child' in Castermans-Holleman et al (eds), *The Role of the Nation State in the 21st Century: Essays in Honour of Peter Baehr* (Martinus Nijhoff, 1998) 163, pp 166–169.

[304] Source: http://treaties.un.org/Pages/Treaties.aspx?id=4&subid=A&lang=en (last accessed May 2011). The only States which have not ratified the Convention are Somalia and the United States of America. Ireland ratified the Convention on 28 September 1992.

[305] UN General Assembly, *Optional Protocol to the Convention on the Rights of the Child on the Involvement of Children in Armed Conflict*, UN Doc A/RES/54/263, Annex I. OPAC entered into force on 12 February 2002 and has been ratified by 132 States parties. Ireland ratified the Protocol on 18 November 2002.

[306] UN General Assembly, *Optional Protocol to the Convention on the Rights of the Child on the Sale of Children, Child Prostitution and Child Pornography*, UN Doc A/RES/54/263 Annex II. OPSC entered into force on 18 January 2002 and has been ratified by 137 States parties. Ireland signed the Protocol on 7 September 2000 but it has not yet ratified the instrument.

[307] CRC, art 1.

[308] In General Comment 5 on general measures of implementation of the Convention on the rights of the child, the CRC Committee states that 'The development of a children's rights perspective throughout Government, parliament and the judiciary is required for effective implementation of the whole Convention and, in particular, in the light of the following articles identified by the Committee as general principles', ie arts 2, 3(1), 6 and 12: UN Doc CRC/GC/2003/5, para 12.

in the interpretation of the Convention and as a guide for States in implementing their obligations under it. They include the principle of non-discrimination in art 2; the principle of the 'best interests of the child' in art 3, which crucially provides that in all decisions taken by the authorities affecting children, the 'best interests of the child shall be a primary consideration'; the right to life, survival and development of the child (art 6); and the principle, articulated in art 12 of the Convention, that every child capable of forming his or her own views, be assured the right to express their views in all matters them and that the views of the child be given due weight in accordance with the age and maturity of the child.[309]

[3.83] In terms of general obligations, art 4 of the CRC provides that the States parties shall undertake all appropriate legislative, administrative, and other measures for the implementation of the rights recognised in the present Convention.[310] Where economic, social and cultural rights are concerned, such measures shall be undertaken to the maximum extent of each State's available resources and, where needed, within the framework of international co-operation.[311] Other general implementation obligations are specified in art 2 (non-discrimination) and art 3(2) which requires that States parties must '... undertake to ensure the child such protection and care as is necessary for his or her well-being, taking into account the rights and duties of his or her parents, legal guardians, or other individuals legally responsible for him or her, and, to this end, shall take all appropriate legislative and administrative measures'.[312]

[3.84] The Convention then sets forth an extensive catalogue of children's rights, some of which expand and develop on rights enshrined in other instruments from a child's perspective, while others articulate additional rights of particular relevance to children. The specific rights in the Convention can be grouped in various ways. The template chosen here is based on one set forth by the Committee on the Rights of the Child, which

---

[309] See generally, CRC Committee General Comment 12 on the right of the child to be heard: UN Doc CRC/C/GC/12.

[310] See generally CRC Committee General Comment 5 on general measures of implementation of the Convention on the rights of the child: UN Doc CRC/GC/2003/5.

[311] In this respect, the CRC Committee has stated its view that the second sentence of art 4 '... reflects a realistic acceptance that lack of resources – financial and other resources – can hamper the full implementation of economic, social and cultural rights in some States; this introduces the concept of 'progressive realisation' of such rights: States need to be able to demonstrate that they have implemented 'to the maximum of their available resources' and, where necessary, have sought international cooperation': CRC Committee General Comment 5, para 7.

[312] CRC Committee General Comment No 5, paras. 3 and 4. The Convention also obliges States to respect 'the responsibilities, rights and duties of parents' or other appropriate persons to provide appropriate direction and guidance to the child, in a manner consistent with his or her evolving capacities, in the exercise by the child of the rights recognised in the Convention; as well as the role of parents in the upbringing and development of their children (art 5).

monitors implementation by the States parties of their obligations under the Convention.[313]

[3.85] As regards civil and political rights, the CRC provides for the following specific, additional rights of the child: to a name and nationality (art 7); the right to preservation of identity (art 8); freedom of expression (art 13); access to appropriate information (art 17); freedom of thought, conscience and religion (art 14); freedom of association and of peaceful assembly (art 15); protection of privacy (art 16); the right not to be subjected to torture or other cruel, inhuman or degrading treatment or punishment and the right to liberty (art 37).

[3.86] As regards family, environment and alternative care, the CRC provides for the right of children not to be separated from their parents (art 9); family reunification (art 10); special protection and assistance in circumstances where they are deprived of a family environment (art 20); safeguards in regard to adoption (art 21); obligations on States to combat the illicit transfer and non-return of children (art 11); protection against abuse and neglect (art 19), including physical and psychological recovery and social reintegration (art 39);[314] and the right to periodic review of placement in circumstances where the child has been taken into care (art 25).

[3.87] In terms of economic, social and cultural rights, and specifically the field of health and welfare, the Convention provides for particular rights in regard to disabled children (art 23);[315] health and health services (art 24);[316] social security and child-care services and facilities (arts 26 and 18(3));[317] as well as an adequate standard of living (art 27). The right to education is catered for in arts 28 and 29,[318] while leisure, recreation and cultural activities are provided for in art 31.

[3.88] Finally, it should be noted that the Convention provides for special measures of protection to be taken in the case of a number of categories of children, including:

(i) Children in situations of emergency, such as refugee children (art 22); and children in armed conflicts (art 38),[319]

---

[313] General guidelines regarding the form and contents of initial reports to be submitted by States parties under the CRC, art 44, para 1(a), adopted by the Committee on the Rights of the Child at its first session, in October 1991 (see Official Records of the General Assembly, 47th Session, Supplement No 41 (A/47/41), annex III).

[314] CRC Committee General Comment No 8 on the right of the child to protection from corporal punishment and other cruel or degrading forms of punishment: UN Doc CRC/C/GC/8); and General Comment No 13 on the right of the child to be free from all forms of violence: UN Doc CRC/C/GC/13.

[315] CRC Committee General Comment No 9 on the rights of children with disabilities: UN Doc CRC/C/GC/9.

[316] CRC Committee General Comment No 4 on adolescent health and development in the context of the CRC: UN Doc CRC/GC/2003/4.

[317] CRC Committee General Comment No 7 on implementing child rights in early childhood: UN doc CRC/C/GC/7.

[318] CRC Committee General Comment No 1 on the aims of education: UN Doc CRC/GC/2001/1.

[319] CRC Committee General Comment No 6 on treatment of unaccompanied and separated children outside their country of origin: UN Doc CRC/GC/2005/6.

(ii) Children in conflict with the law (arts 37 and 40);[320]
(iii) Children in situations of exploitation, such as economic exploitation (art 32), child victims of any form of neglect, exploitation or abuse (art 39); drug abuse (art 33); sexual exploitation and sexual abuse (art 34); sale, trafficking and abduction (art 35) and all other forms of exploitation (art 36); and
(iv) Children belonging to a minority or indigenous group (art 30).[321]

The Committee on the Rights of the Child

[3.89] The treaty body established to monitor States parties' implementation of the Convention is known as the Committee on the Rights of the Child (CRC Committee). While the original text of the Convention provided that the CRC Committee should be composed of 10 independent experts in the field covered by the Convention,[322] the Committee's burgeoning workload since its inception necessitated an amendment to art 43(2) of the CRC which took effect in 2002,[323] providing for an increase in the membership to 18 persons. In line with all of the other treaties, membership of the Committee is based on the principle of equitable geographical distribution, with the Convention stipulating also that regard be had in the election[324] to the principal legal systems.[325] Members are elected for four-year terms with an open-ended possibility of re-election, if re-nominated.[326] The Convention also initially provided that the CRC Committee would normally meet annually.[327] However, again in view of the rapid rate of ratification of the Convention and the corresponding expansion of the Committee's workload, the Committee has been holding three sessions annually, each of three weeks' duration, since 1995.[328]

[3.90] The Committee currently has competence to monitor implementation of the CRC and its Protocols by means only of a periodic reporting mechanism, explored further below in Ch 4. In recent years, a concerted campaign on the part of non-governmental organisations has been underway to persuade the United Nations to adopt an optional

---

[320] CRC Committee General Comment No 10 on children's rights in juvenile justice: UN Doc CRC/C/GC/10
[321] CRC Committee General Comment No 11 on indigenous children and their rights under the Convention: UN Doc CRC/C/GC/11.
[322] There are very few serving or retired diplomats on the CRC Committee. Rather, the current membership would appear to be dominated by consultants and persons with an academic background: http://www2.ohchr.org/english/bodies/crc/members.htm (last accessed May 2011).
[323] The amendment was approved by the General Assembly in 1995 by the terms of Resolution 50.155 of 21 December 1995. It entered into force on 18 November 2002 as soon as it was accepted by two-thirds of the States parties to the Convention.
[324] The detailed provisions in the Convention regarding the procedure for election to the CRC Committee are set forth in CRC, art 43(3)–(7).
[325] CRC, art 43(2).
[326] CRC, art 43(6).
[327] CRC, art 43(10).
[328] An extra week is also scheduled at the beginning of each session for a pre-sessional working group. See below Ch 4. Report of the 5th Session of the CRC: UN Doc A/49/41.

individual complaint mechanism[329] and, in 2009, the Human Rights Council established an open-ended working group to explore the possibility.[330] In its first report on the possibility of establishing a complaint mechanism, the working group noted that part of the motivation for assembling the group was the fact that the CRC is now the only core human rights treaty with respect to which there is no individual complaint mechanism.[331] The text of a draft Protocol has since been drawn up by the working group over several sessions and has recently been adopted by the Human Rights Council.[332] It provides for an individual complaint mechanism and an inquiry procedure.[333] The drafting of the text of the draft Protocol and the resulting provisions in respect of each of these procedures is examined further in Chs 5 and 15 respectively.

[3.91] Finally, the CRC Committee is empowered by art 45(d) to make suggestions and general recommendations based on the information it receives under the CRC, which it does in the form of 'general comments' on the interpretation and operation of the Convention.[334] The CRC Committee also holds a 'day of general discussion' each year in which representatives of governments, United Nations human rights mechanisms, United Nations bodies and specialised agencies,[335] non-governmental organisations, national human rights institutions as well as individual experts and children are welcome to take part. The days of discussion are aimed at fostering '… a deeper understanding of the contents and implications of the Convention as they relate to specific articles or topics'.[336]

---

[329] 'Campaign for a CRC Complaints Mechanism' (Child Rights Information Network): http://www.crin.org/law/crc_complaints/ (last accessed May 2011).

[330] Resolution 11/1 of the Human Rights Council (17 June 2009): http://ap.ohchr.org/documents/E/HRC/resolutions/A_HRC_RES_11_1.pdf (last accessed May 2011).

[331] 'Report of the Open-Ended Working Group to Explore the Possibility of Elaborating an Optional Protocol to the Convention on the Rights of the Child' (21 January 2010) UN Doc A/HRC/13/43.

[332] See the resolution adopted by the HRC: UN Doc A/HRC/17/L.8 (9 June 2011). It is anticipated that the draft Protocol will be adopted by the General Assembly in December 2011:http://www.crin.org/NGOGroup/childrightsissues/ComplaintsMechanism/(last accessed May 2011).

[333] A procedure for inter-State complaints is also included in art 12 of the draft Protocol the text of which is annexed to the HRC resolution in U.N. Doc. A/HRC/17/L.8 (9 June 2011).

[334] The CRC Committee has issued 13 such general comments to date: http://www2.ohchr.org/english/bodies/crc/comments.htm (last accessed May 2011).

[335] Particular provision is made in the CRC for interaction between the CRC Committee and the specialised agencies in art 45(a) and (b).

[336] For more information on the themes that have been explored by the CRC Committee in its days of general discussion, see: http://www2.ohchr.org/english/bodies/crc/discussion2008.htm (last accessed May 2011).

International Convention on the Protection of the Rights of All Migrant Workers and Members of Their Families (1990)[337]

[3.92] It has been estimated that there are now more than 190 million migrants in the world; that migrants make up 3% of the global population; and that the numbers involved, if brought together, would constitute the fifth most populous country in the world.[338] It is little wonder, therefore, that the International Organisation for Migration (the leading inter-governmental organisation on migration in the world) has described migration as 'one of the defining issues of the 21st century' and 'now an essential, inevitable and potentially beneficial component of the economic and social life of every country and region'.[339] International action regarding the vulnerable position of migrants can be traced back to the early 1970s. A noticeable rise in the levels of illegal trafficking of labour into Europe, as well as concern regarding discrimination being faced by foreign workers at that time,[340] ultimately acted as twin catalysts for the adoption of a number of actions being taken by the United Nations on the theme of migration.[341] In

---

[337] See generally, Cholewinski, *Migrant Workers in International Human Rights Law: Their Protection in Countries of Employment* (OUP, 1997); Aleinikoff and Chetail (eds), *Migration and International Legal Norms* (Asser, 2003); Berg, 'At the Border and Between the Cracks: The Precarious Position of Irregular Migrant Workers under International Human Rights Law' (2007) 8 Melb J Int'l L1; Rehman, *International Human Rights Law* (2nd edn, Pearson, 2010), pp 680–711; Robinson Diakité, 'A Brief Look at the International Convention on the Protection of the Rights of All Migrant Workers and Members of Their Families' in Alfredsson et al (eds), *International Human Rights Monitoring Mechanisms* (2nd edn, Martinus Nijhoff, 2009), pp 117–131; Pécoud and de Guchteneire, 'Migration, Human Rights and the United Nations: An Investigation into the Obstacles to the UN Convention on Migrant Workers' Rights' (2006) 24 Windsor YB Access Just 24; Hasenau, 'ILO Standards on Migrant Workers: The Fundamentals of the UN Convention and Their Genesis' (1991) 25 IMR 687; Hune, 'Drafting an International Convention on the Protection of the Rights of all Migrant Workers and Their Families' (1987) 3 IMR 570–615 and (1987) 21 IMR 123; Niessen, 'Using the New Migrant Workers' Rights Convention' (1991) 25 IMR 859; Nafziger and Bartel, 'The Migrant Workers Convention: Its Place in Human Rights Law' (1991) 25 IMR 771; Böhning, 'The ILO and the New UN Convention on Migrant Workers: The Past and the Future' (1991) 25 IMR 698; and Lönnroth, 'The International Convention on the Rights of All Migrant Workers and Members of their Families in the Context of International Migration Policies: An Analysis of Ten Years of Negotiation' (1991) 25 IMR 710.

[338] International Organization for Migration: http://www.iom.int/jahia/Jahia/pid/254(last accessed May 2011).

[339] International Organization for Migration: http://www.iom.int/jahia/Jahia/about-migration/lang/en (last accessed May 2011).

[340] UN Fact Sheet No 24 (Rev 1), p 2: http://www.ohchr.org/Documents/Publications/FactSheet24rev.1en.pdf. (last accessed May 2011).

[341] These included ECOSOC Resolutions 1706 (LIII); ECOSOC Res 6 (XXXVI) of 19 September 1973; two major studies undertaken by the Sub-Commission on Prevention of Discrimination and Protection of Minorities (one by Mrs Halimi Warzazi in 1976 on the *Exploitation of Labour Through Illicit and Clandestine Trafficking*, UN Publications, Sales No E86 XIV.1; and one in 1979 by Baroness Elles on *International Provisions Protecting the Human Rights of Non-Citizens*, UN Publications, Sales No E.80.XIV.2); (contd.../)

1979, the General Assembly adopted a resolution in which it decided to establish a working group, open to all member states of the UN 'to elaborate an international convention on the protection of the rights of all migrant workers and their families'.[342] After 10 years of negotiations, the Convention on the Protection of the Rights of All Migrant Workers and Members of Their Families (ICRMW) was adopted by the General Assembly and opened for signature on the 18 December 1990.[343]

[3.93] The ICRMW constitutes the most comprehensive statement of the rights of migrant workers and their families and the obligations and duties owed to them by States in a legally binding international instrument. Complementing numerous specific international conventions and measures promulgated by the International Labour Organization in regard to migrants,[344] it articulates a much wider spectrum of the human rights standards applicable to migrants and their families at all stages of the migration process.[345] It has been described as 'ambitious and broad-ranging',[346] but these epithets also provide clues as to the ultimately unsuccessful nature of this Convention compared to many of its counterparts.[347] Its lack of impact is verified by the fact that it took 13 years before it entered into force on 1 July 2003;[348] and currently, only 44 States have

---

[341] (contd.../) and General Assembly Resolutions 33/163 in 1978 and 2920 (XXVII). See generally OHCHR Fact Sheet No 24, The Rights of Migrant Workers: http://www.unhchr.ch/html/menu6/2/fs24.htm; (last accessed May 2011) and in more detail in Bohning, 'The ILO and the New UN Convention on Migrant Workers: The Past and the Future' (1991) 25 Int'l Migration Review 698.

[342] GA Res 34/172, 17 December 1979 on *Measures to Improve the Situation and Ensure the Human Rights and Dignity of All Migrant Workers*: http://www.un.org/documents/ga/res/34/a34res172.pdf. (last accessed May 2011).

[343] UN General Assembly, *International Convention on the Protection of the Rights of All Migrant Workers and Members of their Families*, 18 December 1990, UN Doc A/RES/45/158 available at: http://www2.ohchr.org/english/law/cmw.htm (last accessed May 2011). Ireland has not signed the Convention.

[344] The ILO has promulgated two major conventions concerning migrant workers: (i) the Migration for Employment Convention (Revised) (No 97) of 1949 and the Migrant Workers (Supplementary Provisions) Convention (No 143) of 1975. For a general overview of the work of the ILO in regard to migrants, see OHCHR Fact Sheet No 24 (Rev 1), The International Convention on Migrant Workers and its Committee: http://www.ohchr.org/Documents/Publications/FactSheet24rev.1en.pdf (last accessed May 2011).

[345] This comprises preparation for migration, departure, transit and the entire period of stay and remunerated activity in the State of employment as well as return to the state of origin or habitual residence: see ICMW, art 1(2).

[346] Bosniak, 'State Sovereignty, Human Rights and the New UN Migrant Workers Convention' (1992) 86 Am Soc Int'l L Proc 634, p 635.

[347] Bosniak's perhaps overly pessimistic prediction in 1992 was that the Convention's '... very breadth and ambitiousness are almost certain to leave it without sufficient international support to enter into force': Bosniak, 'State Sovereignty, Human Rights and the New UN Migrant Workers Convention' (1992) 86 Am Soc Int'l L Proc 634.

[348] The ICRMW entered into force following ratification by 20 States in accordance with the provisions of art 87(1).

ratified it,[349] a meagre number in comparison, for example, with the almost universal ratification of the Convention on the Rights of the Child. Numerous theories abound as to why the Convention enjoys such a low participation ratio.[350] While structural and financial obstacles in implementing the obligations in the Convention facing, in particular, receiving States,[351] are obviously a factor,[352] political impediments are clearly the most challenging.[353] In this respect, as we shall see, the fact that the scope of the Convention covers not only the rights of regular and documented migrants, but also those of irregular migrants, raises dramatic tensions in regard to State sovereignty.[354] Moreover, the increasingly more hostile public attitude towards migration in many States than was the case when the Convention was being drafted has also acted as a disincentive for governments in regard to ratification.[355]

State obligations

[3.94] The 'overarching principle'[356] underpinning the rights in the ICRMW is that of non-discrimination. This is reflected in art 1 which provides that the Convention is applicable to all migrant workers and members of their families without distinction of any kind 'such as sex, race, colour, language, religion or conviction, political or other opinion, national, ethnic or social origin, nationality, age, economic position, property, marital status, birth or other status'. Article 7 in Part II of the Convention complements this basic principle by obliging States to respect and ensure the rights contained in the Convention without distinction of any kind, including those enumerated already in art 1.

[3.95] Perhaps the most contentious issue to confront the working group which drafted the ICRMW, and one which still persists today, was how the term 'migrant worker' should be defined for the purposes of the Convention;[357] and, in effect, whether the

---

[349] Source: http://treaties.un.org/Pages/Treaties.aspx?id=4&subid=A&lang=en:(last accessed May 2011).

[350] See generally, Pecoud and de Guchtenerie, 'Migration, Human Rights and the United Nations: An Investigation into the Obstacles to the UN Convention on Migrant Worker's Rights' (2006) 24 Windsor YB Access Just 241.

[351] Indeed, it is striking that of the 44 States which have ratified the Convention to date, the vast majority are States of origin in Africa, Latin America and the Caribbean as well as Asia. Not one western European State, for example, has yet either signed or ratified the Convention.

[352] See Edelenbos, 'The International Convention on the Protection of the Rights of all Migrant Workers and Members of Their Families' (2005) 24(4) Refugee Survey Quarterly 93, p 97.

[353] As to these, see the many factors cited by Pecoud and de Guchtenerie, 'Migration, Human Rights and the United Nations: An Investigation into the Obstacles to the UN Convention on Migrant Worker's Rights' (2006) 24 Windsor YB Access Just 241, pp 257–263.

[354] Bosniak, 'State Sovereignty, Human Rights and the New UN Migrant Workers Convention' (1992) 86 Am Soc Int'l L Proc 634, p 637.

[355] Pecoud and de Guchtenerie, 'Migration, Human Rights and the United Nations: An Investigation into the Obstacles to the UN Convention on Migrant Worker's Rights' (2006) 24(4) Windsor YB Access Just 241, pp 253–254.

[356] Edelenbos, 'The International Convention on the Protection of the Rights of all Migrant Workers and Members of Their Families' (2005) 24(4) Refugee Survey Quarterly 93, p 94.

[357] Bosniak, 'State Sovereignty, Human Rights and the New UN Migrant Workers Convention' (1992) 86 Am Soc Int'l L Proc 634, p 636.

guarantees in the Convention should cover documented or regular migrants or, also, non-documented or irregular migrants.[358] The definition of 'members of the family' was not contentious; it is defined in art 4 as generally including married persons, or persons in an equivalent situation, dependent children and other dependent persons recognised as such by domestic law or international agreement.

[3.96] In the finish, art 2(1) defines 'migrant worker' as 'a person who is to be engaged, or is engaged or has been engaged in a remunerated activity in a State of which he or she is not a national'. This definition clearly covers both regular and irregular migrants. However, the Convention then goes on to distinguish between the two categories by providing in Part III for a range of rights that apply to all migrant workers and members of their families, whether they are regular or irregular; while Part IV sets forth a further range of rights which only apply to migrant workers and their families who are regular migrants, ie, those who 'are documented or in a regular situation in the State of employment'.[359]

[3.97] The rights provided for in Part III are comprehensive. They range across the entire spectrum of civil and political rights, to rights of an economic, social and cultural nature, in many cases re-stating and re-framing previously recognised rights from the perspective of migrant workers.[360] They include basic rights to life (art 9); freedom from torture, cruel, inhuman or degrading treatment or punishment (art 10); freedom from slavery, servitude or forced labour (art 11); freedom of thought, conscience, religion and expression (arts 12 and 13); privacy (art 14); property rights (arts 15 and 32); liberty and due process rights (arts 16–20); employment related rights and social security (arts 25–27); medical care (art 28); the right to education (art 30); and the right to cultural identity (art 31).

[3.98] The range of rights provided for in Part IV, which is limited to regular migrants and their families, includes rights to freedom of movement within the State and choice of residence (art 38); the right to participate in the public affairs of the State (art 41); more specific employment and work related rights (arts 43, 52, 54 and 55); family unity (art 44); equality of treatment with nationals in a range of areas including education, social and health services and cultural life (art 45); and rights in regard to financial and taxation matters (arts 46 to 48).

---

[358] ICRMW, art 5(a) clarifies that migrant workers and their families, for the purposes of the Convention, are considered as 'documented or in a regular situation if they are authorized to enter, to stay and to engage in a remunerated activity in the State of employment' pursuant to domestic law or to international agreements to which the State is party. Article 5(b) provides that migrant workers and members of their families are considered as 'non-documented or in an irregular situation' if they do not comply with the conditions provided for in sub-paragraph (a). The latter group would include asylum-seekers whose application for status has been refused, but who have remained in the territory of the receiving State and who are working there illegally.
[359] ICRMW, art 36.
[360] See generally, in this respect, Nafziger and Barterl, 'The Migrant Workers Convention: Its Place in Human Rights Law' (1991) 25 Int'l Mig Rev 771–799.

Part V of the Convention goes on to specify further rights for specific categories of regular or documented migrants, including frontier, seasonal, itinerant and project-tied workers.[361]

Part VI of the Convention provides for the 'promotion of sound, equitable, humane and lawful conditions' regarding the international migration of workers and members of their families. It includes obligations on States to consult and cooperate with each other with a view to promoting such conditions (art 64); to maintain appropriate services to deal with questions of international migration (art 65); to regulate the recruitment of workers (art 66); and in regard to the return of workers and members of their families to the State of origin (art 67). Particular obligations are imposed on transit States in regard to preventing and eliminating illegal or clandestine movements and employment of migrant workers and their families (art 68).

[3.99] As Edelenbos observes, the charge that the Convention sweeps with too broad a brush in the matter of migrants' rights or even that it implicitly encourages illegal migration is countered by the argument that it is balanced by a detailed enumeration of the sovereign rights of States in regard to the migration process.[362] For example, art 35 provides that nothing in the Convention shall be interpreted as implying the regularisation of the situation of irregular migrant workers or members of their families or any right to the regularisation of their situation; art 34 also emphasises that nothing in the Convention shall relieve migrant workers or members of their families from the obligation to comply with the laws and regulations of the State of transit or employment. Article 68, as we have seen, specifically contemplates the taking of measures by transit States to control illegal migration, while art 69 obliges States to take appropriate measures to ensure that a situation of irregular migration on their territory ceases to persist. Finally, art 79 makes it crystal clear that nothing in the Convention shall affect the right of each State party to lay down criteria for admission of migrant workers and their families to the State; while art 52 specifies the rights of States in regard to controlling access to particular categories of employment.

The Committee on the Protection of the Rights of All Migrant Workers and Members of their Families

[3.100] Part VII of the ICRMW provides for the establishment and mandate of the Committee on the Protection of the Rights of All Migrant Workers and Members of their Families (CMW).[363] Following the 41st ratification of the Convention, the membership of the Committee has increased from 10 to 14 members who are required to be of 'high moral standing, impartiality, and recognized competence in the field of migration'.[364] While members shall be elected[365] in their personal capacity, it is surely incongruous that a significant proportion of the current cohort are serving ministers, diplomats or senior

---

[361] These categories of workers are all defined in art 2(2), ICRMW.
[362] See Edelenbos, 'The International Convention on the Protection of the Rights of all Migrant Workers and Members of Their Families' (2005) 24(4) Refugee Survey Quarterly 93, p 94.
[363] ICRMW, art 72(1)(a).
[364] ICRMW, art 72(1)(b).
[365] Detailed provisions regarding the method of election are set forth in ICMW, art 72(2)–(6).

civil servants.[366] Members serve for four-year terms with an open-ended possibility of re-election if re-nominated.[367] The Convention stipulates, as usual, that in electing members, States parties should give due consideration to equitable geographical distribution, including in this case both States of origin and States of employment, and to representation of the principal legal systems.[368] Like the other treaty bodies, membership of the Committee is part-time and essentially voluntaryl.[369] Members meet in Geneva, normally for two sessions *per* year.[370]

[3.101] The ICRMW vests responsibility in the CMW to supervise States' implementation of the Convention in three principal ways: First, by means of a mandatory, periodic reporting procedure, provided for in arts 73 and 74 of the Convention (which is examined further below in Ch 4);[371] second, by means of an optional inter-state complaint procedure, provided for in art 76 of the Convention; and third, by means of an optional, individual complaint procedure, provided for in art 77, detailed below in Chapter 12. Neither of the latter procedures has, however, entered into force due to the limited number of States which have accepted the Committee's competence in either regard.[372] The Committee also has explicit authority to issue 'general comments' or recommendations in accordance with the provisions of art 74(7) of the Convention.[373]

United Nations Convention on the Rights of Persons with Disabilities (2006) and its Optional Protocol

[3.102] There can be little doubt but that disability has been a heretofore 'invisible element of international human rights law'.[374] Notwithstanding the fact that all of the

---

[366] For the CVs of the current members, see: http://www2.ohchr.org/english/bodies/cmw/members.htm (last accessed May 2011).

[367] ICRMW, art 5. Note that the Convention provides for a detailed scheme to ensure a roll-over of membership of the Committee, while simultaneously preserving the experience of some members.

[368] ICRMW, art 72(2).

[369] CRMW, art 72(8) provides: 'The members of the Committee shall receive emoluments from United Nations resources on such terms and conditions as the General Assembly may decide' The GA has indicated that such emoluments should be nominal only.

[370] Heretofore, the length of each session was one week. However, in 2007, due to its expanding workload, the Committee decided to increase its meeting times in 2008 to one session of two weeks duration, and one session of one week: CMW Annual Report 2007, UN Doc A/62/48, paras 4–5.

[371] The operation of the reporting procedure is examined in detail in Ch 4, para **4.60–4.67**.

[372] ICRMW, arts 76 and 77 will only enter into force when 10 States parties have entered positive declarations in respect of them. Thus far, only one State (Guatemala) has entered a declaration accepting the competence of the Committee in respect of inter-State complaints under art 76; and only two States have accepted the right of individual petition under art 77 (Guatemala and Mexico).

[373] Since its establishment, the CMW has issued one general comment, ie CMW General Comment No 1 on migrant domestic workers: UN Doc CMW/C/GC/1.

[374] Kayess and French, 'Out of the Darkness into Light? Introducing the Convention on the Rights of Persons with Disabilities' (2008) HRLR 1, p 12. (contd.../)

human rights instruments so far examined undoubtedly apply to all persons,[375] persons with disability are not explicitly mentioned in any of them, [376] save for one limited exception in the Convention on the Rights of the Child.[377] Accordingly, the UN Convention on the Rights of Persons with Disabilities (CRPD)[378] is a landmark in international human rights law, aimed as it is at addressing directly for the first time in a binding international human rights instrument,[379] '... the long history of discrimination, exclusion and dehumanization of persons with disabilities'.[380] While official UN pronouncements on the Convention proclaim that it does not recognise any new rights of persons with disability, but rather merely 'clarifies the obligations and legal duties of States to respect and ensure the full and equal enjoyment of human rights by persons

[374] (\...contd) See generally, Quinn, 'The United Nations Convention on the Rights of Persons with Disabilities: Toward a New International Politics of Disability' (2009–2010) 15 Tex J on CL & CR 33; Degener and Quinn, *Human Rights and Disability: The Current Use and Future Potential of United Nations Human Rights Instruments in the Context of Disability* (United Nations, 2002); Lawson, 'The United Nations Convention on the Rights of Persons with Disabilities: New Era or False Dawn?' (2006–2007) 34 Syracuse J Int'l L and Commerce 563; Stein, 'Disability Human Rights' (2007) 95 Cal L Rev 75; Kanter, 'The Promise and Challenge of the UN Convention on the Rights of Persons with Disabilities' (2006–2007) Syracuse J Int'l L and Commerce 287; MacKay, 'The United Nations Convention on the Rights of Persons with Disabilities' (2006–2007) Syracuse J Int'l L and Commerce 323; Bruce, 'Negotiating the Monitoring Mechanism for the Convention on the Rights of Persons with Disabilities: Two Steps Forward, One Step Back' in Alfredsson et al (eds), *International Human Rights Monitoring Mechanisms* (Martinus Nijhoff, 2009), pp 133–148; Quinn and Arnardottir, *The United Nations Convention on the Rights of Persons with Disabilities: European and Scandinavian Perspectives* (Brill, 2008); and de Búrca, 'The EU in the Negotiation of the UN Disability Convention' (2010) ELR 174.

[375] CESCR General Comment No 5 on Persons with Disabilities specifically defines disability-based discrimination in the context of the ICESCR (9 December 1994): http://www2.ohchr.org/english/bodies/cescr/comments.htm (last accessed May 2011). See also the work done by the other treaty bodies in terms of integrating a disability perspective into their work: See Disability and Human Rights (Instruments) http://www2.ohchr.org/english/issues/ (last accessed May 2011).

[376] Indeed, it is striking that discrimination on the basis of a disability is not specifically mentioned in the equality clauses in the UDHR, the ICCPR or the ICESCR.

[377] UNCRC, art 23 does refer to 'mentally or physically disabled children'.

[378] UN General Assembly, *Convention on the Rights of Persons with Disabilities: Resolution / adopted by the General Assembly*, 24 January 2007, A/RES/61/106, available at: http://www2.ohchr.org/english/law/disabilities-convention.htm (last accessed May 2011).

[379] Previous efforts by the UN in regard to disability specifically included only non-binding measures, such as the Standard Rules on the Equalization of Opportunities for Persons with Disabilities 1993 (20 December 1993): UN Doc A/RES/48/96: http://www.un.org/documents/ga/res/48/a48r096.htm (last accessed May 2011).

[380] *Handbook for Parliamentarians on the Convention on the Rights of Persons with Disabilities and its Optional Protocol* (OHCHR, 2007), p III: http://www.un.org/disabilities/default.asp?id=212 (last accessed May 2011). The Handbook also provides an overview of historical developments leading to the adoption of the CRPD, pp 9–12.

with disabilities',[381] even the most casual glance at its terms reveals that it certainly goes further than this and has in fact 'modified, transformed and added to traditional human rights concepts in key respects'.[382]

[3.103] Before setting out in detail States' obligations as enshrined in the Convention, it is worth noting a number of significant features of the Convention generally. First, the text of the Convention embodies for the first time in an international instrument a 'rights-based' approach to disability, as opposed to perpetuating the social-welfare approach to disability.[383] In this regard, it is worth noting that the development of the CRPD was clearly heavily influenced by the social model of disability which conceptualises the experience of disability as being rooted in oppression by social structures and practices, with a resulting emphasis being placed on action to break down physical and social barriers in society so as to ensure the full participation and inclusion of persons with disability.[384] This contrasts with the traditional and now discredited 'medical' or 'impairment' model of disability which focuses on the 'affliction' caused by the particular impairment, with a resulting emphasis being placed on the provision of cure, care and protection so that the person can be assimilated to social norms.[385] The fact that the Convention largely incorporates this major attitudinal re-conceptualisation

---

[381] *Handbook for Parliamentarians on the Convention on the Rights of Persons with Disabilities and its Optional Protocol* (OHCHR, 2007), p 5. Indeed, this official attitude is reflected in the General Assembly Resolution which specifically established the open-ended Ad hoc Committee which drafted the Convention 'to consider proposals for a comprehensive and integral international convention to promote and protect the rights and dignity of persons with disabilities, based on the holistic approach in the work done in the fields of social development, human rights and non-discrimination', GA Res 56/168 of 19 December 2001: http://www.un.org/esa/socdev/enable/disA56168e1.htm (last accessed May 2011).

[382] Kayess and French, 'Out of the Darkness into Light? Introducing the Convention on the Rights of Persons with Disabilities' (2008) HRLR 1, pp 32–33. Quinn characterises the Convention as providing a '…moral compass for change as well as legal benchmarks against which to measure that change': Quinn, 'The United Nations Convention on the Rights of Persons with Disabilities: Toward a New International Politics of Disability' (2009–2010) 15 Tex. J on CL & CR 33 at 34. See also, Mégret, 'The Disabilities Convention: Human Rights of Persons with Disabilities or Disability Rights?' (2008) 30 HRQ: http://ssrn.com/abstract=1267723, (last accessed May 2011) who at p 23 concludes that the Convention is part of a process of reformulation of rights and that '… the superficial assessment that the Convention 'does not create new rights' is at least unhelpful, and probably misleading'. (last accessed May 2011)

[383] See *Handbook for Parliamentarians on the Convention on the Rights of Persons with Disabilities and its Optional Protocol* (OHCHR, 2007), pp III–IV.

[384] Kayess and French, 'Out of the Darkness into Light? Introducing the Convention on the Rights of Persons with Disabilities' (2008) HRLR 1, pp 5–7. The authors, however, observe at p 21 that in spite of its professed adherence to the social model of disability, certain provisions of the Convention actually incorporate and entrench elements of the medical or impairment model.

[385] Kayess and French, 'Out of the Darkness into Light? Introducing the Convention on the Rights of Persons with Disabilities' (2008) HRLR 1, pp 5–7.

of disability is in no small part due to the efforts of persons with disability and their representative organisations who played a very substantial part in its drafting.[386]

[3.104] Second, the Convention also uniquely places emphasis on international cooperation in supporting national efforts to implement the objectives of the Convention. In this respect, art 32 of the text obliges the States parties to undertake appropriate and effective measures to cooperate with each other, in partnership with other regional and international organisations, as well as civil society to promote the rights of persons with disability. It includes, amongst other things, obligations to cooperate in regard to international development programmes, research programmes and to facilitate access to scientific knowledge; capacity building; and technical and economic assistance.[387]

[3.105] Third, the process by which the Convention was drafted is also worthy of attention, involving as it did the most inclusive and transparent series of negotiations ever engaged in by the United Nations in the framing of a human rights instrument.[388] In this respect, the Ad Hoc Committee of member States which ultimately drafted the text decided at the outset to allow all accredited NGOs and NHRIs to participate in all public meetings, informal consultations and closed meetings conducted during the drafting process.[389] This included the capacity to make extensive formal presentations on the UN floor during the negotiations and to receive all official documentation.[390] Member States were also encouraged to include persons with disabilities as well as experts on disability

---

[386] Kayess and French, 'Out of the Darkness into Light? Introducing the Convention on the Rights of Persons with Disabilities' (2008) HRLR 1, pp 3–4.

[387] This article proved controversial during the drafting process, however, as developed countries became concerned that its inclusion would give rise to an expectation on the part of developing and transitional States that the former would provide increased aid to the latter in order to assist them in implementing the terms of the Convention, or that CRPD, art 32 would provide an excuse for States to delay implementation of the Convention: Kayess and French, 'Out of the Darkness into Light? Introducing the Convention on the Rights of Persons with Disabilities' (2008) HRLR 1, pp 31–32. See also, Stein and Lord, 'Monitoring the Convention on the Rights of Persons with Disabilities: Innovations, Lost Opportunities, and Future Potential' Human Rights Quarterly, Vol. 31, 2010. Available at SSRN: http://ssrn.com/abstract=1533482 at 21 (last accessed May 2011).

[388] See generally, Melish, 'The UN Disability Convention: Historic Process, Strong Prospects, and Why the US Should Ratify' (2007) 14(2) Human Rights Brief, available at SSRN: http://ssrn.com/abstract=997141 (last accessed May 2011). On the process of drafting the Convention, see also, Kanter, 'The Promise and Challenge of the UN Convention on the Rights of Persons with Disabilities' (2006–2007) Syracuse J Int'l L and Commerce, pp 287–306; and de Búrca, 'The EU in the Negotiation of the UN Disability Convention' (2010) ELR 174.

[389] See Melish, *The UN Disability Convention: Historic Process, Strong Perspectives and Why the US Should Ratify*, pp 4–6.

[390] Significant efforts were made to make such documents available in Braille as well as in other accessible ways. Melish pp 5–6.

into their official delegations by the Ad Hoc Committee. Finally, the Committee also established a Voluntary Fund on Disability to support the participation of NGO experts from less developed countries in the negotiation process. As Melish notes, the combination of all these initiatives greatly influenced the outcome of the negotiations in very positive ways, especially as regards its implementation and monitoring methodologies.[391]

[3.106] The Convention and its Optional Protocol (which provides for an optional complaint mechanism and inquiry mechanism) were adopted by the UN General Assembly on 13 December 2006.[392] Both instruments entered into force in May 2008 and there are now 101 States parties to the Convention, 61 of which are also party to the Protocol.[393]

State obligations

[3.107] Article 1 of the Convention states that the purpose of the Convention is 'to promote, protect and ensure the full and equal enjoyment of all human rights and fundamental freedoms by all persons with disabilities, and to promote respect for their inherent dignity'. The Convention deliberately eschews any attempt to rigidly define the terms 'disability' or 'persons with disabilities', but rather indicates that 'persons with disabilities' *includes* 'those who have long-term physical, mental, intellectual or sensory impairments which in interaction with various barriers may hinder their full and effective participation in society on an equal basis with others'. This conscious effort to avoid concrete definition is explicitly based on the view that 'disability' is an 'evolving concept',[394] thus deserving of 'a dynamic approach that allows for adaptations over time and within different socio-economic settings'.[395]

[3.108] Article 3 sets forth the eight general principles of the Convention, intended to guide the States parties and other actors in the implementation of the Convention. They are:

(a) Respect for the inherent dignity, individual autonomy including the freedom to make one's own choices, and independence of persons;

---

[391] Melish pp 5–6. When the instruments were opened for signature in March 2007, a record number of 81 States signed the Convention with 44 of those also signing the Protocol.

[392] UN General Assembly, *Optional Protocol to the Convention on the Rights of Persons with Disabilities*, 13 December 2006, A/RES/61/106, Annex II, available at: http://www2.ohchr.org/english/law/disabilities-op.htm (last accessed May 2011). Ireland signed the Convention, but not the Protocol, on 30 March 2007. It has still not signed the Protocol, nor ratified the Convention. The terms of the Protocol in respect of inquiries and the individual complaint procedure are considered further below in Chs 5 and 11 respectively.

[393] Source: http://www2.ohchr.org/english/issues/disability/index.htm (last accessed May 2011). The Convention and its Protocol entered into force on 3 May 2008 in accordance with the terms of arts 45 and 13 respectively.

[394] CRPD, Preamble, para (e).

[395] *Handbook for Parliamentarians on the Convention on the Rights of Persons with Disabilities and its Optional Protocol* (OHCHR, 2007), p 13.

(b) Non-discrimination;
(c) Full and effective participation and inclusion in society;
(d) Respect for difference and acceptance of persons with disabilities as part of human diversity and humanity;
(e) Equality of opportunity;
(f) Accessibility;
(g) Equality between men and women;
(h) Respect for the evolving capacities of children with disabilities and respect for the right of children with disabilities to preserve their identities.

[3.109] Articles 4 to 9 of the Convention set forth the general obligations assumed by States on ratification of the Convention. These include obligations to adopt legislation and administrative measures to promote the human rights of persons with disabilities[396] and to abolish discrimination;[397] to protect and promote the rights of persons with disabilities in all policies and programmes;[398] to ensure that the public sector respects the rights of persons with disabilities;[399] to take measures to eliminate discrimination by private parties;[400] to undertake research and development of accessible goods, services,[401] and technology for persons with disabilities;[402] to provide accessible information about assistive technology to persons with disabilities;[403] to promote training on the rights of the Convention to professionals and staff who work with persons with disabilities;[404] and to consult with and involve persons with disabilities in developing and implementing legislation and policies and in decision-making processes that concern them.[405]

[3.110] Article 5 contains the overarching non-discrimination and equality clauses of the Convention; arts 6 and 7 specifically address the particular situation of women and girls with disabilities, and children with disabilities respectively, obliging States to ensure that they are able to exercise their human rights and fundamental freedoms on an equal basis with others. Article 8 spells out very detailed obligations on States in regard to awareness-raising; likewise, art 9, with respect to ensuring accessibility for persons with disabilities to the physical environment on an equal basis with others.

[3.111] Articles 10 to 30 of the Convention enumerate specific obligations on States parties, certain of which elaborate, build-upon or indeed supplement rights already identifiable in the civil and political realm; while others focus on the particular rights of

---

[396] CRPD, art 4(1)(a).
[397] CRPD, art 4(1)(b).
[398] CRPD, art 4(1)(c).
[399] CRPD, art 4(1)(d).
[400] CRPD, art 4(1)(e).
[401] CRPD, art 4(1)(f).
[402] CRPD, art 4(1)(g).
[403] CRPD, art 4(1)(h).
[404] CRPD, art 4(1)(i).
[405] CRPD, art 4(3).

persons with disabilities in the economic, social and cultural realm. As regards the latter rights, art 4(2) reiterates the stipulation in art 2 of the ICESCR that States are obliged to achieve these rights progressively, to the maximum of their available resources. In regard to all of these provisions, the focus of the Convention is to oblige contracting States to take actions to ensure that persons with disabilities enjoy these rights on an equal basis with others.

The particular civil and political rights addressed include:

- The right to life (art 10);
- Protection of persons with disabilities in situations of risk and humanitarian emergencies (art 11);
- Equal recognition before the law (art 12);
- Access to justice (art 13);
- Liberty and security of the person (art 1);
- Freedom from torture or cruel, inhuman or degrading treatment or punishment (art 15);
- Freedom from exploitation, violence and abuse (art 16);
- Protection of physical and mental integrity (art 17);
- Liberty of movement and nationality (art 18);
- Right to live independently in the community (art 19);
- Right to personal mobility (art 20);
- Freedom of expression and opinion and access to information (art 21);
- Respect for privacy (art 22);
- Respect for home and family (art 23); and
- Right to participation in political and public life (art 29).

The particular economic, social and cultural rights specified in the Convention are:

- Right to education (art 24);
- Right to health (art 25);
- Right to habilitation and rehabilitation (art 26);
- Right to work and employment (art 27);
- Right to an adequate standard of living and to social protection (art 28); and
- Right to participation in cultural life, recreation, leisure and sport (art 30).

The Committee on the Rights of Persons with Disabilities

[3.112] Article 34 of the Convention provides for the establishment of a Committee on the Rights of Persons with Disabilities (CRPD Committee) which is comprised of 18 members.[406] Members are required to serve in their personal capacity, and be of high moral standing with recognised expertise in the field of disability.[407] Members are elected by the States parties, with due consideration being given to equitable geographical distribution, representation of different forms of civilisation and of the principal legal systems, balanced gender representation and, significantly, participation

---

[406] Initially, the CRPD Committee consisted of 12 individual experts, but this number was augmented to 18 in accordance with the provisions of art 34(2).

of experts with disabilities.[408] Members of the Committee shall be elected[409] for a term of four years, with the possibility of re-election once.[410] The Committee has established its own rules of procedure[411] and is entitled to the facilities, privileges and immunities of experts on mission for the United Nations.[412]

[3.113] The framing of the international monitoring mechanism for the UN Disability Convention proved to be contentious during the negotiations on that instrument.[413] Taking place at a time of on-going debate on UN treaty-body reform, some delegations involved in the negotiations strongly questioned the need to establish a new monitoring body in the first place, let alone a separate monitoring framework.[414] Support for the

---

[407] A perusal of the CVs of the current cohort of Committee members reveals that this stipulation has been respected. All of the experts appear to have been very active in the field and there is a notable absence of diplomats on the Committee, in contrast to many of the other treaty bodies. See: http://www.ohchr.org/EN/HRBodies/CRPD/Pages/Membership.aspx (last accessed May 2011)].

[408] CRPD, art 34(4).

[409] Detailed provisions regarding the procedure for election are set forth in CRPD, art 34(5)–(9).

[410] Note, however, that the term of six of the first 12 members elected to the Committee shall expire at the end of two years to allow for continuity of expertise between old members and the injection of fresh membership at each election: CRPD, art 34(7).

[411] CRPD, art 34(10). See Rules of Procedure of the Committee on the Rights of Persons with Disabilities (13 August 2010): UN Doc CRPD/C/4/2.

[412] CRPD, art 34(13).

[413] See generally, Bruce, 'Negotiating the Monitoring Mechanism for the Convention on the Rights of Persons with Disabilities: Two Steps Forward, One Step Back' in Alfredsson et al (eds), *International Human Rights Monitoring Mechanisms* (Martinus Nijhoff, 2009), pp 134–136; Quinn, 'Resisting the 'Temptation of Elegance': Can the Convention on the Rights of Persons with Disabilities Socialise States in Rights Behaviour?' in Arnardóttir and Quinn (eds), *The UN Convention on the Rights of Persons with Disabilities: European and Scandinvavian Perspectives* 215; and Stein and Lord, 'Monitoring the Convention on the Rights of Persons with Disabilities: Innovations, Lost Opportunities, and Future Potential' Human Rights Quarterly, Vol. 31, 2010. Available at SSRN: http://ssrn.com/abstract=1533482. (last accessed May 2011).

[414] See, for example, the contributions of Australia and the US at the 6th session of the working group of the Ad Hoc Committee which drafted the text of the UN Convention, Daily summary of discussion at the sixth session (11 August 2005): http://www.un.org/esa/socdev/enable/rights/ahc6sum11aug.htm (last accessed May 2011); and the remarks of the US during the 7th session, Daily summary of discussion at the seventh session (27 January 2006): http://www.un.org/esa/socdev/enable/rights/ahc7sum27jan.htm (last accessed May 2011);. These concerns were apparently raised again during negotiations at the 8th session by Sudan, China, the Russian Federation and Australia. See Ad Hoc Committee on a Comprehensive and Integral International Convention on the Protection and Promotion of the Rights and Dignity of Persons with Disabilities (8th session, New York, 14–25 August 2006), International Service for Human Rights: http://www.handicap-international.fr/kit-pedagogique/documents/ressourcesdocumentaires/redactionconv/ISHR/8thsession.pdf (last accessed May 2011), p 15. See also, DPI Disability Convention Daily Update (14 August 2006) (Day One): www.dpi.org/lang-en/resources/topics_detail.php?page=676 (last accessed May 2011).

establishment of an international body was firmly advocated, however, by NHRIs and NGOs involved in the drafting process, as well as the vast majority of States.[415] Their concern that the drafting of the Convention should not be 'held hostage' to reform efforts currently underway within the UN ultimately held sway, with agreement being reached that the monitoring provisions of the Convention should be '...at least as good, and preferably better, than those of other treaties'.[416] However, when negotiations began on the precise mechanisms for international monitoring, some delegations apparently voiced concern about the inclusion of an inquiry and individual complaint procedure.[417] In an effort to achieve consensus, the Mexican delegation, which acted as a facilitator for discussions on international monitoring, proposed the inclusion of such procedures in a separate Protocol.[418] Although this proposal met with disapproval from the NGOs, they were eventually persuaded to accept the compromise whereby the Protocol would be adopted simultaneously with the adoption of the parent Convention.[419]

[3.114] Accordingly, the CRPD has jurisdiction to monitor the States parties' implementation of the Convention through three principal mechanisms: first, a periodic-reporting mechanism provided for in arts 35 and 36 of the Convention; second, through an optional individual complaint procedure provided for in arts 1 to 5 of the Optional Protocol to the Convention (OP-CRPD); and third, through an optional 'inquiry' procedure, also provided for in arts 6 to 8 of the Protocol. Each State party is explicitly required to cooperate with the CRPD Committee in fulfilling its mandate. An enhanced role is also envisaged for the specialised agencies and other UN organs in assisting the

---

[415] Daily summary of discussion at the sixth session (11 August 2005): http://www.un.org/esa/socdev/enable/rights/ahc6sum11aug.htm (last accessed May 2011).

[416] Report of the Ad-Hoc Committee on a Comprehensive and Integral International Convention on the Protection and Promotion of the Rights and Dignity of Persons with Disabilities on its sixth session: UN Doc A/60/266, paras 157–158, http://www.un.org/esa/socdev/enable/rights/ahc6reporte.htm (last accessed May 2011).

[417] DPI Disability Convention Daily Update (14 August 2006) (Day One): www.dpi.org/lang-en/resources/topics_detail.php?page=676 (last accessed May 2011). The OHCHR had by that stage submitted an expert paper for the consideration of the Ad Hoc Committee which had advocated the inclusion of inquiry and individual complaint procedures. Expert Paper on existing monitoring mechanisms and possible innovations in monitoring mechanism for a comprehensive and integral international convention on the protection and promotion of the rights and dignity of person with disabilities: UN Doc A/AC265/2006/CRP4, paras 43–50.

[418] See Draft Optional Protocol to the International Convention on the Rights of Persons with Disabilities (Facilitator's Text): http://www.un.org/esa/socdev/enable/rights/ahc8contfacilitator.htm (last accessed May 2011). See also Kayess and French, 'Out of the Darkness into Light? Introducing the Convention on the Rights of Persons with Disabilities' (2008) HRLR 1, p 19.

[419] Melish has noted that the priority of drawing up innovative approaches to monitoring was thus '... largely scuttled in the final session by a group of States flexing muscle in a politicized showdown unrelated to either international monitoring or persons with disabilities': Melish, 'The UN Disability Convention: Historic Process, Strong Prospects, and Why the US Should Ratify' (2007) 14(2) Human Rights Brief, p 11, available at SSRN: http://ssrn.com/abstract=997141 (last accessed May 2011).

Committee to fulfil its mandate;[420] and the Committee is also required to consult, as appropriate, with other relevant treaty bodies with a view to avoiding inconsistency with their outputs or duplication with their respective functions.[421]

The Committee is also required to report every two years to the General Assembly and to ECOSOC on its activities and is empowered by the CRPD to make 'general recommendations', based on the examination of State reports and information received from the States parties.[422] it has also instituted a practice of holding days of 'general discussion' during its meeting time '... to foster a deeper understanding of the contents and implications of the Convention as they relate to specific articles or topics'.[423]

National implementation

[3.115] In addition to these standard provisions for international monitoring, the Convention also obliges States to put in place a structure at the national level to facilitate implementation of the Convention. This includes an obligation to designate one or more 'focal points' within government for matters relating to implementation; and to give 'due consideration' to the establishment or designation of a coordination mechanism within government to facilitate related action in different sectors and at different levels.[424] Article 33(2) of the Convention further obliges the States parties to '... maintain, strengthen, designate or establish within the State party, a framework, including one or more independent mechanisms, as appropriate, to promote, protect and monitor implementation' of the Convention. Civil society, and, in particular, persons with disabilities and their representative organisations shall be involved and participate fully in the monitoring process.[425] As we shall see further below in Ch 6, this emphasis on national implementation is part of a new trend in human rights treaties of equipping independent, national bodies to maintain oversight of governmental implementation of their human rights obligations.

International Convention for the Protection of All Persons from Enforced Disappearance (2006)[426]

[3.116] The egregious practice of enforced disappearance has been a long-standing issue of concern for the United Nations.[427] As far back as 1978, the General Assembly

---

[420] CRPD, art 38(a).
[421] CRPD, art 38(b).
[422] CRPD, art 39.
[423] See generally the website of the Committee: http://www.ohchr.org/EN/HRBodies/CRPD/Pages/DGD.aspx (last accessed May 2011).
[424] CRPD, art 33(1). 'This article lies at the very heart of the Convention, for it attempts to put in place an architecture for change at home – in Washington D.C., or Dublin – that can transform processes that if left undisturbed simply lead to even more bad laws and policies': Quinn, 'The United Nations Convention on the Rights of Persons with Disabilities: Toward a New International Politics of Disability' (2009-2010) 15 Tex. J. on C.L. & C.R. 33 at 48.
[425] CRPD, art 33(3).
[426] Hereinafter, referred to as the ICPED.
[427] See generally, Scovazzi and Citroni, *The Struggle against Enforced Disappearance and the 2007 United Nations Convention* (Martinus Nijhoff, 2007).

called upon governments to take action to prevent enforced or involuntary disappearances taking place on their territories, to investigate such practices and to ensure that those responsible were made accountable; and requested the Commission on Human Rights to consider the question of disappeared persons with a view to making appropriate recommendations.[428] The Commission in turn responded by first establishing the UN Working Group on Enforced and Involuntary Disappearances (WGEID) in 1980;[429] and by issuing a number of resolutions on the subject over the years. In 1992, the Commission transmitted a draft Declaration on the Protection of All Persons from Enforced Disappearances to the General Assembly where it was subsequently adopted.[430] While the latter was regarded as a 'milestone' in efforts to combat the practice of disappearances,[431] it nevertheless stopped short of imposing legally binding obligations on States in regard to the matter of disappearances. Such measures were contemplated later in a draft convention on the subject which was elaborated by a working group of the Sub-Commission on Human Rights and transmitted to the Commission in 1998.[432] Notwithstanding the disparate views expressed at that point by States on the question of developing a binding treaty on the subject,[433] the Commission on Human Rights appointed Professor Manfred Nowak as an independent expert to examine the 'existing international criminal and human rights framework for the protection of persons from enforced or involuntary disappearances'

---

[428] GA Res 33/173 on Disappeared Persons (20 December 1978), UN Doc A/RES/33/173.

[429] The Working Group is one of the 'thematic' special procedures established by the Commission on Human Rights to examine and make recommendations concerning particular human rights violations. It consists of five individual experts, and was originally appointed for a one-year term, with a mandate '… to examine questions relevant to enforced or involuntary disappearances of persons'. The mandate and terms of reference of the Working Group were continually renewed by the Commission on Human Rights, and approved by ECOSOC; and have most recently been renewed by the Human Rights Council for a three-year term on 12 April 2011: UN Doc A/HRC/RES/16/16. See the website of the WGEID: http://www.ohchr.org/EN/Issues/Disappearances/Pages/DisappearancesIndex.aspx (last accessed May 2011). See further, Rodley, 'United Nations Action Procedures Against 'Disappearances', Summary or Arbitrary Executions and Torture' (1986) 8 HRQ 700.

[430] Declaration on the Protection of All Persons from Enforced Disappearances, UN GA Res 47/133, 18 December 1992, UN Doc A/RES/47/133.

[431] Apparently, this was the view of the WGEID as recorded in the UN Fact Sheet No 6 (Rev 2), Enforced or Involuntary Disappearances: http://www.ohchr.org/Documents/Publications/FactSheet6rev.2en.pdf. (last accessed May 2011).

[432] Sub-Commission on Prevention of Discrimination and Protection of Minorities, Report of the Sessional Working Group of the Administration of Justice (19 August 1998): UN Doc E/CN4/Sub2/1998/19, paras 9–64 and see Annex 1.

[433] See the comments and information provided by States and NGOs on the draft convention in Commission on Human Rights, Civil and Political Rights, Including Questions of Disappearances and Summary Executions: UN Doc E/CN4/2001/69 and Annex 1. See also McCrory, 'The International Protection of All Persons from Enforced Disappearance' (2007) HRLR 545, pp 547–548.

and to identify gaps 'in order to ensure full protection from enforced or involuntary disappearance'. In the same resolution, it also moved to establish an open-ended inter-sessional working group to draft a legally binding instrument on the subject.[434]

[3.117] In his comprehensive report on the subject, the independent expert identified a number of gaps and deficiencies in the existing international framework as regards enforced disappearances, including, *inter alia,* in regard to the definition of what is an 'enforced disappearance', the concept of 'victims' and the human rights violated by such a disappearance.[435] He concluded that these clearly indicated the need for a 'legally binding normative instrument for the protection of all persons from enforced disappearance'.[436] In turn, the first meeting of the inter-sessional working group of the Commission on Human Rights was convened in January 2003. Within just three years, the group had agreed a draft text for a convention, which was ultimately presented to the Human Rights Council in June 2006 where it was adopted as the first resolution of the Council and referred to the General Assembly.[437] The draft Convention was subsequently adopted by the General Assembly on 20 December 2006 and opened for signature on 6 February 2007.[438] Despite the speed at which it was drafted and the initially impressive number of signatories,[439] the pace of ratification of this Convention has been slow and it has only recently entered into force.[440] There are currently only 27 States parties to the Convention, with a notable absence of ratifications from countries in which the occurrence of disappearances is high.[441]

State Obligations

[3.118] The Convention is divided into three parts. In Part I, the Convention clearly affirms for the first time in an international treaty that the right not to be subject to an

---

[434] CHR Res 2001/46, paras 11 and 12. UN Doc E/CN4/2001/L.11/Add. 5, p. 32.
[435] Report of the Independent Expert (8 January 2002): UN Doc E/CN4/2002/71, Section VIII, paras 72–94.
[436] Report of the Independent Expert (8 January 2002): UN Doc E/CN4/2002/71, Section VIII, para 96.
[437] Human Rights Council, Resolution 1/1, 29 June 2006.
[438] For the text of the Convention, see: http://www2.ohchr.org/english/law/disappearance-convention.htm. (last accessed May 2011). For landmarks along the way to the ultimate adoption of the Convention, see International Coalition against Enforced Disappearances: http://www.icaed.org/the-convention/history-and-background-of-the-convention/(last accessed May 2011).
[439] Fifty-seven States signed the Convention on the 6 February 2006 when it was first opened for signature.
[440] UN General Assembly, *International Convention for the Protection of All Persons from Enforced Disappearance*, 20 December 2006, available at: http://www2.ohchr.org/english/law/disappearance-convention.htm (last accessed May 2011). The Convention entered into force on 23 December 2010 after the 20th ratification, in accordance with the provisions of art 39(1). Ireland signed the Convention on 29 March 2007 but has not yet ratified it.
[441] Source: http://treaties.un.org/Pages/Treaties.aspx?id=4&subid=A&lang=en (last accessed May 2011). On the paucity of ratifications, see generally, Rehman, *International Human Rights Law* (2nd edn, Pearson, 2010), p 862.

enforced disappearance is an internationally recognised human right by providing in art 1(1) that 'No one shall be subjected to an enforced disappearance'.[442] Moreover, this is a non-derogable right insofar as no exceptional circumstances, including a state of war or any other public emergency, can be invoked as a justification for enforced disappearance.[443] Article 2 defines the meaning of 'enforced disappearance' for the purposes of the Convention as:

> '... the arrest, detention, abduction or any other form of deprivation of liberty by agents of the State or by persons or groups acting with the authorization, support or acquiescence of the State, followed by a refusal to acknowledge the deprivation of liberty or by concealment of fate or whereabouts of the disappeared person, which place such a person outside the protection of the law'.[444]

The remainder of Part I goes on to spell out the principal obligations on States in the matter of enforced disappearances. These include obligations:

- To investigate such acts (arts 3 and 12);[445]
- To make 'enforced disappearance' a crime under national law, punishable by appropriate penalties and to take the necessary measures to establish its competence to exercise jurisdiction over the offence in particular circumstances (arts 4, 7 and 9);
- To take the necessary measures to hold persons involved criminally responsible (arts 6 and 22);
- To cooperate with other States in ensuring that offenders are prosecuted or extradited, and with the assistance of victims (arts 10, 11, 13, 14 and 15);

---

[442] Note that art 17(1) also provides clearly that: 'No one shall be held in secret detention'.

[443] ICED, (2006), art 1(2).

[444] This definition is broadly similar to the definition in art II of the Inter-American Convention on Forced Disappearances of Persons 1994 Organization of American States, *Inter-American Convention on Forced Disappearance of Persons* (9 June 1994), available at: http://www.unhcr.org/refworld/docid/3ae6b38ef.html (last accessed May 2011). However, it is wider than the crime of 'enforced disappearance of persons' contained in art 7(1)(i) and 7(2)(i) of the Rome Statute of the International Criminal Court 1998 and may for that reason cause certain difficulties for States parties to the ICC Statute who have already adopted national laws allowing for the domestic prosecution of crimes under the ICC Statute. Article 5 of the Convention makes it clear that the systematic practice of enforced disappearance constitutes a crime against humanity which should attract consequences under applicable international law. This further underlines the wider definition in art 2 of the Convention and while, as McCrory notes, art 5 could be construed as a reference to the applicable provisions of the ICC Statute, there is nothing to stop the Convention itself being applied to 'systematic practices' of enforced disappearance: McCrory, 'The International Protection of All Persons from Enforced Disappearance' (2007) HRLR 545, pp 549–552.

[445] Note that the obligation to investigate arises in regard to disappearances '... committed by persons or groups of persons acting without the authorization, support or acquiescence of the State and to bring those responsible to justice'. As Rehman notes, this would appear to incorporate disappearances conducted by private actors: Rehman, *International Human Rights Law* (2nd edn, Pearson, 2010), p 864.

- Not to hold persons in 'secret detention' and to take preventive measures generally to guard against enforced disappearances, including the adoption of minimum legal standards in regard to the right to liberty, providing access to information, under clearly defined circumstances, to relatives of the person deprived of their liberty, as well as training and education to personnel who may be involved in the custody or treatment of persons deprived of their liberty (arts 17 to 23);
- To provide information to 'victims' and to ensure an enforceable right to compensation for an enforced disappearance in the national legal system (art 24); and
- To take particular measures in regard to enforced disappearance involving children (art 25).

Part III of the Convention provides, *inter alia*, for the formal requirements of ratification to the Convention and its entry into force.[446] It also explains the relationship between the Convention and international humanitarian law.[447]

The Committee on Enforced Disappearances

[3.119] One of the contentious issues arising during the drafting of the ICPED was whether it would be necessary to create a new monitoring mechanism.[448] In view of the proliferation of treaty bodies generally, some delegations believed that fresh obligations in regard to enforced disappearances should be enshrined in a Protocol to the ICCPR, with monitoring of those obligations entrusted to the Human Rights Committee (CCPR),[449] or a sub-committee thereof.[450] Others believed that entrusting the CCPR with the task would over-burden that Committee and would involve difficulties from a technical point of view.[451] During the final drafting session, a compromise solution was arrived at by consensus whereby a new monitoring body would be established under the terms of the new convention, but that a clause should be included allowing the contracting States to review the functioning of that body several years after entry into force of the convention.[452] Accordingly, as ultimately drafted, Part II of the ICPED provides for the establishment and mandate of a Committee on Enforced Disappearances (CED) which shall be responsible for monitoring compliance by the contracting States with their obligations under the Convention. The Committee shall consist of 10 independent experts of high moral character and recognised competence in

---

[446] ICPED, arts 38–42.
[447] ICPED, art 43.
[448] See the discussions of the Intersessional Open-ended Working Group to elaborate a draft legally binding normative instrument for the protection of all persons from enforced disappearances: UN Doc E/CN4/2003/71 (12 February 2003), para 23; UN Doc E/CN4/2004/59 (23 February 2004), paras 143–148; UN Doc E/CN4/2005/66 (10 March 2005), paras 147–168; and UN Doc E/CN4/2006/57 (2 February 2006), paras 69–84.
[449] UN Doc E/CN4/2004/59, para 144.
[450] UN Doc E/CN4/2004/59, para 155.
[451] UN Doc E/CN4/2004/59, para 145.
[452] UN Doc E/CN4/2006/57 (2 February 2006), paras 70–84.

the field of human rights.[453] Members are to be elected by the States parties according to equitable geographical distribution, with due account being taken of relevant legal expertise and of balanced gender representation.[454] Members are to be elected for four-year terms with the possibility of re-election for a further term.[455] The Committee, like the other treaty bodies, shall establish its own rules of procedure.[456]

Interestingly, the Convention makes it an explicit obligation on States to cooperate with the CED and to assist its members in the fulfilment of their mandate to the extent that they have accepted same.[457] Members of the Committee are also to be entitled to the facilities, privileges and immunities of experts on mission for the United Nations.[458] For its part, the Committee is itself required to cooperate with all the relevant organs of the United Nations, including all of the treaty bodies and the special procedures of the UN, the relevant regional inter-governmental organisations, as well as State institutions working towards the protection of persons against enforced disappearances.[459] Particular mention is made regarding consultation with the Human Rights Committee, which monitors the implementation of the ICCPR, 'with a view to ensuring consistency of their respective observations and recommendations'. The latter is a particularly appropriate stipulation given the increasing efforts of the treaty bodies to harmonise their working methods to ensure, *inter alia*, consistency in their respective observations and recommendations.[460]

[3.120] Article 27 requires States parties to the Convention to convene a conference between four and six years following the entry into force of the Convention 'to evaluate the functioning of the Committee' and to decide whether it is appropriate to transfer its functions to another body. Given that the Convention was eventually opened for signature at a time when proposals were afloat within the United Nations to establish a unified treaty body to monitor implementation by States of all their treaty obligations, this provision would certainly make any such transition easier in the unlikely event that it were to come about within the specified timeframe.[461] The provision also leaves room to revisit the option of assigning the monitoring role for enforced disappearances to the CCPR preferred by so many States during the drafting process. Finally, art 27 will focus

---

[453] ICPED, art 26(1). The first cohort of Committee members was elected by the States parties on 31 May 2011: http://www.ohchr.org/EN/HRBodies/CED/Pages/Elections2011.aspx (last accessed May 2011).

[454] ICPED, art 26(1).

[455] ICPED, art 26(4). Note that five of the first round of elected members shall only serve for a two-year term in order to allow for the Committee to be regularly renewed without losing all of its acquired expertise. Detailed provision is made in art 26 regarding the election of members.

[456] ICPED, art 26(6).

[457] ICPED, art 26(9).

[458] ICPED, art 26(8).

[459] ICPED, art 28 (1).

[460] ICPED, art 28(2). The issue of reform of the treaty system generally and the working methods of the treaty bodies is dealt with in Ch 16.

[461] Proposals for a unified treaty body are examined in detail in Ch 16, paras **16.06–16.20**.

minds on any potential clash that may emerge between the functioning of the CED and the operation of the Working Group on Enforced and Involuntary Disappearances (WGEID).

[3.121] Articles 29 to 36 of the Convention set forth the mandate of the CED. In this respect, the Committee is given jurisdiction to monitor the implementation of the Convention through five principal means:

(1) Article 29 provides for a truncated reporting mechanism, whereby States shall report to the Committee within two years on the measures taken to give effect to the obligations in the Convention. There is no requirement, however, of periodicity, as with the other Conventions examined above; [462]

(2) Article 30 provides for an 'urgent action procedure' whereby relatives of a disappeared person or other authorised representative can submit a request to the Committee that a 'person be sought and found'; [463]

(3) An optional individual petition procedure in art 31, whereby contracting States may accept the competence of the Committee to receive and consider communications from or on behalf of individuals claiming to be a 'victim' of a violation under the provisions of the Convention;[464]

(4) An optional inter-State complaint procedure in art 32;

(5) An on-site visiting procedure in art 33 in circumstances where the Committee receives 'reliable information' indicating that a State is seriously violating the provisions of the Convention. Article 34 also gives the Committee explicit power urgently to bring to the attention of the General Assembly information regarding the possibility of widespread or systematic disappearances in the territory of any State party to the Convention.[465]

The extensive mandate of the CED is to a certain extent circumscribed in that the Convention specifically provides that the obligations of States in regard to the Committee shall only apply prospectively with respect to disappearances commencing after entry into force of the Convention for that State.[466]

---

[462] Ch 4, paras **4.73–4.74**.
[463] Ch 14, paras **14.02–14.05**.
[464] Ch 14, paras **14.06–14.08**.
[465] Ch 5, paras **5.56–5.60**.
[466] ICPED, art 35(2).

Part II:
Reporting and Investigative Procedures

Chapter 4

Periodic Reporting Procedures

INTRODUCTION

[4.01] As noted in the last chapter, since its inception, the United Nations has sponsored many multilateral treaties in the field of human rights. While the ICCPR and ICESCR sweep with a comprehensively broad brush in terms of human rights obligations, the aim of all of the other treaties promulgated by the United Nations is to deal with specific dimensions of the broader scheme of human rights. In order for the standards in those treaties to become embedded in the national legal and administrative systems of the Contracting States, it is crucial that they contain effective implementation techniques at the international level. In relation to most of the treaties concerned, the primary method of international supervision is by means of a periodic reporting procedure. While further means of implementation are sometimes incorporated into the treaty by means of optional inquiry, inter-State or individual complaint mechanisms,[1] periodic reporting requirements are usually the only *mandatory* means of international supervision of adherence to the human rights standards established by the particular treaties in question.

[4.02] In a nutshell, a periodic reporting procedure generally requires each State party to the treaty to inform an international monitoring or 'treaty body', at regular intervals, about the measures it has taken to bring its domestic laws and administrative systems into line with the particular standards established by the treaty. This information is relayed to the treaty body by means of a written report, which is followed up later by a dialogue between the body in question and representatives of the State. The treaty body is generally given authority by the treaty at the end of the process to make non-binding suggestions and recommendations which are supposed to be designed to assist the State in meeting its obligations under the treaty.[2]

[4.03] At face value, this procedure appears to be an extremely weak form of international supervision of States' implementation of their treaty commitments. As Leckie has noted, an impartial lay observer might well ask:

---

[1] Inter-State complaint mechanisms are provided for in ICCPR, arts 41–42; OP-ICESCR, art 10; ICERD, arts 11–13; UNCAT, art 21; ICMW, art 76; and ICPED, art 32. The detail of these procedures is not examined in this book as no State has ever drawn upon an inter-State procedure within the framework of the UN treaties.

[2] On the process of periodic reporting generally under all of the UN human rights treaties, see Kjaerum, 'State Reports' in Alfredsson, Grimheden, Ramcharan and Zayas (eds), *International Human Rights Monitoring Mechanisms* (2nd edn, Martinus Nijhoff, 2009), p 17.

'How can it be...that the procedures for securing compliance with major human rights treaties hinge upon a system that makes governments entirely responsible for reporting on themselves,...subject to soft questioning for a few hours by cautious committees, elected by those very governments, and with almost no likelihood of serious censure or real sanctions?'[3]

However, the context in which these procedures were first devised must first be borne in mind in any exposition of the manner in which they operate or evaluation of their efficiency in practice. As Steiner and Alston have observed, the notion of a State reporting on its human rights obligations to an international monitoring body at the time when these procedures were first mooted some 60 years ago would have been quite simply inconceivable.[4] The fact that they were first successfully negotiated between States in the midst of the Cold War political tensions that dominated the negotiations of many of the principal human rights treaties is itself an impressive achievement.[5]

[4.04] Moreover, as we shall see, these procedures have evolved gradually over time to the extent that there is now significant input into the process from independent sources. While certain of the treaties specifically provide for input from other sources, all of the treaty bodies now actively encourage the participation of non-governmental organisations (NGOs) in the reporting process. This input takes the form of active participation at the national level in the preparation of the State's report, through to the direct provision by NGOs of their own reports to the treaty bodies on the State's performance in implementing the particular treaty in question.[6] As Connors has noted:

'Most who analyze the system conclude that its most critical dependency is on NGO participation during report preparation at the national level, during consideration by the committee and thereafter. NGOs are crucial players in ensuring that preparation is a

---

[3] Leckie, 'The Committee on Economic, Social and Cultural Rights: Catalyst for Change in a System Needing Reform' in Alston and Crawford, *The Future of UN Human Rights Treaty Monitoring* (CUP, 2000) 129, p 130.

[4] Steiner and Alston, *International Human Rights in Context: Law, Politics and Morals* (3rd edn, OUP, 2008), p 850.

[5] However, the 'watering down' of the control mechanisms in the treaties is itself directly attributable to the political tensions that dominated discussion of human rights machinery at that time: see Cassese, 'The General Assembly: Historical Perspective 1945–1989' in Alston, *The United Nations and Human Rights* (OUP, 1991) 25, pp 38–39.

[6] For a critical perspective of the experiences of NGOs with the UN treaty reporting procedures, see Clapham, 'UN Human Rights Reporting Procedures: An NGO Perspective' in Alston and Crawford, *The Future of UN Human Rights Treaty Monitoring* (CUP, 2000), p 175; and 'Defining the Role of Non-Governmental Organizations with Regard to the UN Human Rights treaty Bodies', in Bayefsky (ed) *The United Nations Human Rights Treaty System in the 21st Century* (Kluwer Law International, 2000) 183, pp 192–194. See also in the latter volume, Theytaz-Bergman, 'State Reporting and the Role of Non-Governmental Organisations', p 45; Brett, 'State Reporting: An NGO perspective', p 57; and Thomson, 'Defining the Role of Non-Governmental Organizations: Splendid Isolation or Better Use of NGO Expertise', p 219.

dynamic process, that consideration is a moment of critical monitoring, and that the results of that monitoring are an important part of civil society's interface with government.'[7]

[4.05] Similarly, the increasing priority that has been placed by the United Nations in recent years on the establishment and development of national human rights institutions[8] is also reflected in the enhanced role which these institutions have been given in the reporting processes of most of the UN treaties.[9] Over the past decade, treaty bodies generally have begun to engage to a significant degree with those institutions in the reporting process. As we shall see, certain of the treaty bodies have instituted a practice of allowing national human rights institutions (NHRIs) to address them orally while they are formally examining the State's report. In turn, NHRIs have themselves begun to forge a common approach for engagement with the work of the treaty bodies.[10]

[4.06] This Chapter examines the substance of each of the current UN treaty periodic reporting procedures. Paragraphs **4.07–4.74** examine the working methods and practices adopted by each of the individual treaty bodies, noting the individual nuances and variations that exist between them; while paras **4.75–4.84** critically evaluate the operation of reporting procedures generally in terms of their capacity to exert meaningful pressure on States parties to implement the rights set forth in the treaties.

---

[7] Connors, 'An Analysis and Evaluation of the System of State Reporting' in Bayefsky (ed) *The United Nations Human Rights Treaty System in the 21st Century* (Kluwer Law International, 2000), 3 at p 15.

[8] National human rights institutions are administrative bodies, established by government with the aim of promoting and protecting human rights. The General Assembly adopted guidelines in 1993 on the functions and status of such institutions known as the *Paris Principles relating to the status and functioning of national institutions for protection and promotion of human rights*. A formal means of accrediting NHRIs as being compliant with these Principles is operated by an International Coordinating Committee (ICC) which is considered crucial in establishing the credibility and authority of each institution with other NHRIs and within the UN system: See generally, UN FactSheet No 19, National Institutions for the Promotion and Protection of Human Rights, available: http://www.ohchr'org/Documents/Publications/ FactSheet19.en.pdf (last accessed May 2011); Kjaerum National Human Rights Institutions Implementing Human Rights (Danish Institute for Human Rights, 2003) and Murray, 'National Human Rights Institutions: Criteria and Factors for Assessing their Effectiveness' (2007) 25(2) Netherlands Quaterly of Human Rights, p 189.

[9] See generally, Gallagher, 'Making Human Rights Treaty Obligations a Reality: Working with New Actors and Partners' in Alston and Crawford, *The Future of UN Human Rights Treaty Monitoring* (CUP, 2000), p 201; and Müller and Seidensticker, *The Role of National Human Rights Institutions in the United Nations Treaty Body Process* (German Institute for Human Rights, 2007).

[10] See Conclusions of the International Roundtable on the Role of National Human Rights Institutions and Treaty Bodies (Berlin, 23–24 November 2006): http://www.nhri.net/pdf2006/ Conclusions_Int_RT_rev8dec.pdf (last accessed May 2011) and see Ch 16, paras **16.26– 16.27**.

REPORTING PROCEDURES UNDER UNITED NATIONS HUMAN RIGHTS TREATIES

International Covenant on Civil and Political Rights

[4.07] Article 40 of the International Covenant on Civil and Political Rights (ICCPR)[11] requires States to submit reports to the Human Rights Committee (CCPR)[12] on the measures they have adopted to give effect to the rights set forth in the Covenant; and on the progress made in enjoyment of those rights.[13] Reports should also indicate the 'factors' and 'difficulties', if any, affecting implementation of the Covenant.[14] Initial reports are to be presented within one year of ratification '… and thereafter whenever the CCPR so requests'.[15] While the Committee formerly applied a practice rule whereby periodic reports were to be submitted every five years, since 1997 it has adopted a working rule under which subsequent periodic reports now fall due at a time individually specified by the Committee for each State party.[16] This change of practice was due to the recognition by the Committee that a generic time-frame of five years for all State parties had become completely impractical, given the growth in the number of

---

[11] On the ICCPR, see Ch 3, paras **3.25**–**3.36**. On the reporting procedure, see generally, Tyagi, *The UN Human Rights Committee* (CUP, 2011), pp 151–324; O'Flaherty and Heffernan, *International Covenant on Civil and Political Rights: International Human Rights Law in Ireland* (Brehon Publishing, 1995), pp 64–85; McGoldrick, *The Human Rights Committee: Its Role in the Development of the International Covenant on Civil and Political Rights* (OUP, 1991), pp 62–119; Joseph, Schultz and Castan, *The International Covenant on Civil and Political Rights: Cases, Materials and Commentary* (OUP, 2004) pp 18–20; Steiner and Alston, *International Human Rights in Context: Law, Politics and Morals* (3rd edn, OUP, 2008), pp 850–873; and Rehman, *International Human Rights Law* (2nd edn, Pearson, 2008), pp 115–118.

[12] As to the composition and mandate of the Human Rights Committee, see Ch 3, para **3.33**–**3.36**.

[13] ICCPR, art 40(1). See also the CCPR's Rules of Procedure: UN Doc CCPR/C/3/Rev 9 (January 2011).

[14] ICCPR, art 40(2).

[15] Ireland has reported to the CCPR on the State's progress in implementing the ICCPR on three separate occasions. The State's initial report was examined by the Committee in 1993 the second periodic report in 2000; and the third periodic report in 2008. The State's reports as well as the Committee's concluding observations can be obtained at: http://tb.ohchr.org/default.aspx. See also commentaries by O'Flaherty and Heffernan, *International Covenant on Civil and Political Rights: International Human Rights Law in Ireland* (Brehon Publishing, 1995) and Fotrell, 'Reporting to the UN Human Rights Committee – A Ruse by Any Other Name? Lessons For International Human Rights Supervision From Recent Irish Experiences' (2001) 4 ILT 61.

[16] The time frame specified is normally within four years of the last report. However, the CCPR may call for a report after three years or five years, depending on the State's record of compliance with the Covenant, including the reporting requirements: Report on the Working Methods of the Human Rights Treaty Bodies Relating to the State Party Reporting Process 2010 (24 June 2009) UN Doc HRI/ICM/2010/2, para 30.

States parties to the Covenant and the limited meeting times of the Committee itself.[17] It is possible for the Committee to request reports on an ad hoc basis, for example, in an emergency situation.[18] While this did occur on a number of occasions in the 1990s, the Committee has rarely applied the procedure since then.[19]

Submission of Reports

[4.08] As regards the content of each State's report, all of the treaty bodies have recently approved new harmonised guidelines to guide States in the submission of their reports to the treaty bodies.[20] These guidelines include guidelines on a 'common core document' which should be used by States when submitting a report to any of the treaty bodies to which they are obliged to report. The 'common core document' should include general information on the reporting State, including statistical information, and the framework in place in that State for the promotion and protection of human rights. The recent revision included directions for States to provide general and factual information on non-discrimination, equality and effective remedies. The preparation of this now 'expanded' core document for submission to all the treaty bodies avoids the necessity of duplicating basic information on the State's geography, demography, constitutional, legal and political structures, as well as on non-discrimination, equality and remedies. In addition, each of the treaty bodies has produced treaty-specific guidelines for the guidance of States in producing a treaty-specific report which will include relevant information under the particular articles of the particular treaty in question. Thus, the 'core document' and the 'treaty-specific report' are submitted together as the State's initial/periodic report. The treaty bodies have recommended that States use these guidelines when submitting their reports under all of the reporting procedures.[21] As we

---

[17] See United Nations Fact Sheet No 15, Civil and Political Rights: The Human Rights Committee, p 15: http://www.ohchr.org/Documents/Publications/FactSheet15rev.1en.pdf (last accessed May 2011). As noted earlier in Ch 3, the CCPR is a part-time body which meets for three sessions of three weeks *per* year, during which time it must fulfill not just its reporting functions but also its other functions under the Covenant, including the consideration of individual communications submitted under the Optional Protocol to the International Covenant on Civil and Political Rights.

[18] The CCPR requested a number of States during the early 1990s (Bosnia and Herzegovina, Croatia, Federal Republic of Yugoslavia, Burundi, Angola, Haiti, Rwanda and Nigeria) either to present their overdue initial/periodic report without delay or prepare ad hoc reports on specific issues. Only Bosnia and Herzegovina, Croatia and the Federal Republic of Yugoslavia reacted to this initiative and submitted ad hoc reports: http://www2.ohchr.org/english/bodies/hrc/workingmethods.htm#a11 (last accessed May 2011).

[19] In March 2004, the Committee's secretariat discussed the possibilities of reviving the urgent procedure/ad hoc report procedure. In March 2005, the Committee did request one State party to produce an ad hoc report which was submitted in 2006: Report on the Working Methods of the Human Rights Treaty Bodies 2009 (24 June 2009) UN Doc HRI/MC/2009/4, para 88.

[20] Compilation of Guidelines on the Form and Content of Reports to be Submitted by States Parties to the International Human Rights Treaties (3 June 2009): UN Doc HRI/GEN/2/Rev6, ch 1.

[21] Report on the Implementation of Recommendations of the Seventh and Eighth Inter-Committee Meeting and the Twentieth Meeting of Chairpersons (24 June 2009): UN Doc HRI/MC/2009/2, para 30(e).

shall see, the CCPR, along with a number of the treaty bodies (CEDAW, CERD, CESCR, CRC and CMW), have recently revised their treaty specific guidelines so as to complement the new expanded guidelines for the common-core document. [22]

[4.09] The CCPR's new treaty-specific guidelines provide information on the appropriate format for submission of initial reports, as well as subsequent periodic reports.[23] Initial reports are generally supposed to be more detailed than subsequent periodic reports. They should focus on specific issues relating to the implementation of the ICCPR and should not duplicate information already submitted in the common core document.[24] In this respect, the initial report should deal specifically with and be structured so as to provide information on every article in Parts I–III of the Covenant.[25] After the report has been submitted to the Committee, the Committee will commence its examination of the report by assigning it to a Country Report Task Force (CRTF) which is comprised of country rapporteur(s) and between four and six other members of the Committee.[26] The CRTF is expected to produce a 'list of issues' arising from the State's report and from other information supplied to the Committee.[27] The list of issues is then sent to the relevant State in advance of the public session at which the plenary Committee will formally examine the State's report.

[4.10] As regards subsequent periodic reports, these are intended to focus more particularly on issues of compliance identified by the Committee as most pressing at the examination of a State's initial report or last periodic report and on developments since that report. While submission of these reports has followed a similar pattern to the submission of initial reports, the CCPR has recently introduced, on a trial basis, a pilot procedure for the submission of periodic reports.[28] Under this new procedure, instead of

---

[22] Report on the Working Methods of the Human Rights Treaty Bodies (2010), para 19.

[23] Guidelines for the treaty-specific document to be submitted by States parties under article 40 of the International Covenant on Civil and Political Rights (22 November 2010): UN Doc CCPR/C/2009/1 [hereinafter 'CCPR treaty specific guidelines'].

[24] CCPR treaty-specific guidelines: UN Doc CCPR/C/2009/1, para 5. If a State party has not already submitted its common core document, all relevant information should be submitted in the ICCPR-specific document.

[25] CCPR treaty-specific guidelines, UN Doc CCPR/C/2009/1, para 18 and see *ff* paras 28–104.

[26] The initiative of establishing Country Report Task Forces to examine each State's report was taken in 2002 in an effort to streamline the reporting process. One member of each CRTF should normally hail from the same region as the reporting State.

[27] See para **4.14** below re 'other relevant information'.

[28] CCPR treaty-specific guidelines, UN Doc CCPR/C/2009/1, para 14 and see further, Focused reports based on replies to lists of issues prior to reporting (LOIPR): Implementation of the new optional reporting procedure (LOIPR procedure) (29 September 2010): UN Doc CCPR/C/99/4. The new procedure will operate for a period of five years (from November 2010), after which the CCPR will appoint a working group to assess and review its functioning in terms of '... practicability, effectiveness and capacity to improve the examination of the human rights situation in the States parties': Focused reports based on replies to lists of issues prior to reporting (LOIPR): Implementation of the new optional reporting procedure (29 September 2010): UN Doc CCPR/C/99/4, para 7.

the State submitting a periodic report in the usual format, the CCPR itself will prepare and adopt a 'list of issues' to be transmitted to the State *prior* to the submission of its report.[29] The State party's *replies* to this list of issues will then constitute that State's periodic report for the purposes of art 40 of the Covenant.[30] Although States may 'opt-out' of this procedure and choose to submit a full report,[31] the CCPR believes that this new procedure will strengthen the effectiveness of the reporting procedure by allowing the Committee to receive more focused information, thus enabling it to improve its assessment of States' compliance with their obligations under the Covenant.[32] States parties should be given at least one year to reply to the 'list of issues', while the resulting reports based on that list should be examined by the CCPR no later than one year after their submission.[33]

Formal Examination of Reports

[4.11] As regards the formal examination of the State's report (whether 'initial' or periodic'), the stated aim of the Human Rights Committee in regard to the reporting process is to engage in a 'constructive dialogue' with States as regards compliance with the obligations set forth in the Covenant. To this end, the Committee invites State representatives to attend at a formal session of the Committee at which the Committee examines the State's report in public session.[34] Normally, one and a half days will be devoted to this process. The State party's delegation will formally present the report to the Committee. Committee members then question the delegation in regard to particular

---

[29] This procedure is now referred to by the acronym LOIPR. The substance and format of the LOIPR is set forth in *Focused reports based on replies to lists of issues prior to reporting (LOIPR): Implementation of the new optional reporting procedure* (29 September 2010) UN Doc CCPR/C/99/4, as well as the information to be relied on for their drafting, paras 11–12.

[30] CCPR treaty-specific guidelines, para 14. This procedure will not apply as regards periodic reports that have been submitted to the CCPR prior to November 2010.

[31] CCPR treaty-specific guidelines, UN Doc CCPR/C/2009/1, para 15.

[32] The Committee also believe that the new procedure will enable it to re-initiate a dialogue with States whose periodic reports are long overdue. Focused reports based on replies to lists of issues prior to reporting (LOIPR): Implementation of the new optional reporting procedure (29 September 2010): UN Doc CCPR/C/99/4, para 4.

[33] Focused reports based on replies to lists of issues prior to reporting (LOIPR): Implementation of the new optional reporting procedure (29 September 2010): UN Doc CCPR/C/99/4, paras 15–16.

[34] Rule 68 of the Rules of Procedure of the Human Rights Committee (13 January 2011): UN Doc CCPR/C/3/Rev9. While attendance by a State delegation at the formal examination of the report is not obligatory, it has become the norm for all of the treaty reporting procedures. If a delegation does not materialise, the treaty body is entitled to proceed in its absence. Where a State seeks to postpone examination of its report to a later session, practice differs amongst the treaty bodies. The CCPR, at its discretion, may notify the State party of the alternative date on which it intends to examine the report; or consider the report at the time originally scheduled, in the absence of the delegation, in which case it will adopt provisional 'concluding observations'. The latter will be submitted to the State party and the date when the report will be further considered or on which a new periodic report should be submitted, will be stipulated: Rule 68(2), CCPR Rules of Procedure.

aspects of the State's report. The aim of this part of the process is supposed to be non-contentious and non-adversarial. The Committee's questions are supposed to '… clarify or deepen understanding of issues arising concerning the implementation and enjoyment of Covenant rights in the State party'.[35] Once the oral dialogue is concluded, a short time will usually be set aside for the delegation to supply additional information to the Committee.

[4.12] As regards the Committee's ultimate jurisdiction in regard to the reporting process, art 40(4) of the ICCPR provides that the Committee shall '… [t]ransmit its reports and such general comments as it may consider appropriate to the States parties'. Since 1992, the Committee has adopted 'concluding observations' at the end of each State's report. These observations are public documents which set out clearly the results of the dialogue conducted on the State's report. These observations follow a general pattern, including an introductory section, positive factors, principal subjects of concern and recommendations.[36] The final paragraph of the observations identifies matters of particular priority and asks the State to provide information to the Committee within one year on measures taken to address those matters. The final paragraph also sets out the date on which the next report of that State should be submitted to the Committee.

Follow-up

[4.13] In 2002, the Committee decided to establish a new position from amongst its ranks, namely that of special rapporteur for follow-up on concluding observations.[37] The role of the special rapporteur is that of liaising with States as regards their implementation of the Committee's recommendations in its concluding observations on each State's report. The rapporteur will assess the follow-up information, if any, provided by the State to the Committee and makes recommendations regarding what steps may be appropriate in the circumstances. The Committee ultimately decides on further action, which may range from requesting further information, requesting that State representatives meet with the special rapporteur, or changing the date for submission of the next report. A failure to respond to this process may prompt the Committee to record this fact in its annual report to the General Assembly.[38]

Input from non-state actors

[4.14] As regards input from other actors into the reporting process, the ICCPR specifically anticipates the potential involvement of the specialised agencies of the United Nations in the reporting process by providing for relevant aspects of a State'sreport to be submitted to such agencies, thus giving them the opportunity to comment.[39] By contrast, no mention is made in the Covenant whatsoever as regards the

---

[35] See Human Rights: Fact Sheet No 15 (Rev 1), p 19: http://www.ohchr.org/Documents/Publications/FactSheet15rev.1en.pdf (last accessed May 2011).

[36] Concluding observations on all States' reports can be accessed on the website of the Office of the United Nations High Commissioner for Human Rights: http://www.unhchr.ch/tbs/doc.nsf.

[37] Annual Report of the Human Rights Committee (30 October 2002) UN Doc A/57/40 (vol 1), para 55 and Annex III.

[38] On the operation of the procedure, see the Paper of the Special Rapporteur for Follow-Up On Concluding Observations (Sir Nigel Rodley) (2 July 2009): UN Doc CCPR/C/95/3, paras 4–7.

[39] ICCPR, art 40(3).

involvement of other actors in the process. Nevertheless, from an early stage, non-governmental organisations (NGOs) have contributed to the process, albeit initially at a very informal level. From the outset, the practice of most Committee members was to receive information from NGOs in their independent capacity and to meet with representatives between sessions, thus allowing those bodies to exert an informal influence on the proceedings.[40] However, their lack of official standing with the Committee was an obvious limitation.[41] Lack of progress on this issue was directly attributable to the Cold War tensions that dogged the Committee's early development, whereby Eastern European members, in particular, frowned upon any overtly investigatory role on the part of the Committee. As those tensions eased, the involvement of NGOs in the process correspondingly increased.[42] In 1992, a breakthrough was achieved when the Committee formally recognised the role of NGOs in the reporting process.[43] For the purposes of streamlining the procedure, the Committee now encourages NGOs within States to join forces by producing a 'shadow report' on the State's performance in implementing the Covenant for the Committee's consideration.[44] These shadow reports typically mimic the formal State reports by setting out article-by-article the views of the various groups concerned as regards whether the rights in the ICCPR are being adequately implemented in the State under review. This has the effect of giving an enhanced and indeed more formalised role to NGOs in the process. More recently, National Human Rights Institutions (NHRIs) have also become increasingly involved in the reporting processes, through the production of their own shadow reports. The CCPR has further stepped up its practice by inviting NGOs and NHRIs to present oral information to them at each plenary session before the State presents its report.[45] At these meetings, NGOs and NHRIs are given an opportunity to conduct what are in effect briefing sessions with Committee members,

---

[40] See the account by McGoldrick of the use made by the majority of the members of the Committee of information from non-governmental organisations in the early years of the operation of the reporting procedure, *The Human Rights Committee: Its Role in the Development of the International Covenant on Civil and Political Rights* (OUP, 1991), para 3.17, pp 77–78. See also Opsahl, *The Human Rights Committee* in Alston (ed), *The United Nations and Human Rights: A Critical Appraisal* (OUP, 1992), p 369 at 406–407.

[41] McGoldrick, *The Human Rights Committee: Its Role in the Development of the International Covenant on Civil and Political Rights* (OUP, 1991), para 3.18, p 79.

[42] McGoldrick, *The Human Rights Committee: Its Role in the Development of the International Covenant on Civil and Political Rights* (OUP, 1991), para 3.18, p 79.

[43] Annual Report of the Human Rights Committee (2002) UN Doc A/57/40 (Vol I), ANNEX III, para 12.

[44] Overview of the Working Methods of the Human Rights Committee: http://www2.ohchr.org/english/bodies/hrc/workingmethods.htm#a2a (last accessed May 2011), Section VIII.

[45] These formal briefing sessions for NGOs and NHRIs take place on the first morning meeting of each plenary session. Lunch-time briefings are also organised to allow non-governmental organizations to provide further information to Committee members before the examination of the State report by the Committee. Overview of the Working Methods of the Human Rights Committee: http://www2.ohchr.org/english/bodies/hrc/workingmethods.htm#a2a, Section VIII (last accessed May 2011).

raising particular issues of concern vis-à-vis the State's implementation of the Covenant. The practice of the Committee has not yet evolved to a point where NGOs or NHRIs are entitled to make oral presentations to the Committee during the formal presentation by States of their reports, as is the practice of certain of the other treaty monitoring bodies in operating their respective reporting procedures.[46] Nonetheless, there can be no doubt but that the input of NGOs, and increasingly NHRIs, in the reporting process has gradually evolved to the point that their active participation is openly encouraged by the Committee and is clearly extremely influential in the monitoring process.[47]

[4.15] As discussed at paras **4.77–4.78**, most of the criticisms levelled at the effectiveness of periodic reporting requirements generally point to the low levels of State compliance, as regards both the submission of reports and the human rights obligations in the treaties. As regards compliance with the ICCPR procedure, the statistics are certainly discouraging, with more States failing to submit reports than those which do. In its most recent annual report in 2010, the Committee documents particularly egregious examples of non-compliance.[48] These include Gambia, whose second periodic report has been overdue for 25 years and Equatorial Guinea whose initial report has been overdue for 21 years. Indeed, 54 States parties were cited as having reports that were more than five years overdue, 22 of which are initial reports.[49] Since 2001, the Committee has adopted a review procedure for dealing with recalcitrant States which have persistently failed to submit reports. In such circumstances, the Committee will consider the measures taken by the State in question to implement the Covenant from the material currently available to it.[50]

---

[46] However, the Committee has stated that it has reserved the right to determine, at a later stage, whether other briefings by non-governmental organisations should also become part of the Committee's official proceedings which would require official interpretation: Second Annual Report of the Human Rights Committee (2002), Annex III, para 12, UN Doc A/57/40 (Vol I).
[47] In each of its Annual Reports in recent years, the Committee has specifically mentioned the material submitted by international and national human rights non-governmental organisations to the country report task forces, and has welcomed their interest and participation and thanked them for the information provided.
[48] Annual Report of the CCPR (2010) (Vol 1), UN Doc A/65/40.
[49] Annual Report of the CCPR (2010), para 51.
[50] Information will instead be received from the UN specialised agencies, NGOs and NHRIs. While the State will be invited to send a delegation to attend the Committee's examination of this information in a private session, the Committee will proceed with the process even if the State declines to accept the invitation. The Committee will then formulate provisional concluding observations, including recommendations, which will be forwarded to the State. The Committee will then take into account any comments made by the State party on its provisional observations, before adopting its final concluding observations, which are public documents. See rule 70 of the CCPR's rules of procedure. See also CCPR General Comment No 30, Reporting Obligations of States Parties under Article 40 of the Covenant (18/09/2002): UN Doc CCPR/C/21/Rev2/Add12. As to the application of this procedure since its inception, see Annual Report of the CCPR (2010), paras 55–63.

[4.16] A related concern contributing to long delays in the processing of State reports is the fact that the Human Rights Committee is a part-time body. It meets in formal session for up to 9 weeks *per* year. The fact that its workload has to be compressed into such a confined period means that there are inevitable delays in processing State reports and that those which are examined do not necessarily receive the scrutiny they deserve.

International Covenant on Economic, Social and Cultural Rights

[4.17] As with the ICCPR, the only mandatory implementation mechanism provided for in the International Covenant on Economic, Social and Cultural Rights (ICESCR) is the periodic reporting requirement provided for in arts 16 and 17 of the Covenant.[51] Article 16 provides that the States shall undertake to submit reports on the measures that they have adopted and the progress made in achieving observance of the rights recognised in the Covenant. Bearing in mind the nature of the rights provided for in the Covenant and the notion that their implementation should be progressively achieved, art 17 goes on the provide that the reports submitted may indicate the factors and difficulties 'affecting the *degree* of fulfillment' of the obligations in the Covenant. Responsibility for monitoring States' compliance with their obligations under the monitoring mechanism has been vested in the Committee on Economic, Social and Cultural Rights (CESCR), which comprises 18 persons elected by ECOSOC, acting in their personal capacity.[52]

[4.18] The procedure under the ICESCR is substantially similar to the one operated by the CCPR under art 40 of the ICCPR. The ICESCR is not specific as to the periodicity of States' reports, but the CESCR has traditionally required that States submit an initial report within one year of entry into force of the Covenant and thereafter every five years.[53] Since 2000, however, the Committee has decided to reduce that period in regard to some States, depending on a variety of factors, including the timeliness of the submission of the reports, the quality of information provided, the quality of the constructive dialogue between the Committee and the State party, the State's response to the Committee's concluding observations, and its record in practice in regard to the implementation of the obligations in the Covenant.[54] Unlike the CCPR, since 2004, the CESCR has accepted 'combined' reports on an informal basis, ie, where a periodic report is already due or due within the year following the consideration of an earlier

---

[51] On the ICESCR, see Ch 3, paras **3.37**–**3.52**. On the reporting procedure, see generally, Leckie, 'The Committee on Economic, Social and Cultural Rights: Catalyst for Change in a System Needing Reform' in Alston and Crawford (eds), *The Future of UN Human Rights Treaty Monitoring* (CUP, 2000), p 129; Craven, *The International Covenant on Economic, Social and Cultural Rights: A Perspective on Its Development* (OUP, 1995), pp 66–89; and Rehman, *International Human Rights Law* (2nd edn, Pearson, 2008), pp 166–174. This procedure has been applied to Ireland on two occasions to date. The relevant documents can be accessed at: http://tb.ohchr.org/default.aspx (last accessed May 2011).

[52] As to the composition and mandate of the CESCR, see Ch 3, paras **3.49**–**3.52**.

[53] Rule 58(2) of the CESCR rules of procedure (1 September 1993) UN Doc E/C12/1990/4/Rev1.

[54] Report of the CESCR on the 25th, 6th and 7th sessions to ECOSOC: UN Doc EC 12/2001/17, para 1024.

periodic report.[55] This practice is intended to assist the Committee in clearing the ever-present backlog of unconsidered reports. The CESCR has also adopted a new set of revised general guidelines[56] which take into account the new harmonised guidelines for the submission of the common-core document.[57]

[4.19] As regards the actual operation of the reporting procedure, a pre-sessional working group, composed of five members of the CESCR nominated by the chairperson, meets for one week prior to each of the Committee's sessions.[58] The purpose of the pre-sessional working group is to identify the questions that will form the basis of the 'constructive dialogue' to be held between the Committee and each of the States parties whose reports are due to be considered by the full Committee.[59] The working group in turn divides initial responsibility for particular reports between themselves by designating each member of the group as a 'country rapporteur' for a specific number of reports. Each rapporteur is thus responsible for compiling an initial list of issues on each country report which is then reviewed and adopted by the working group as a whole. The pre-sessional working group prepares these lists of issues up to 12 months prior to the consideration of each State's report. The list of issues is then given directly to a representative of the State concerned and the State in question is encouraged to reply in writing to the list of issues. Any written responses received from the State, if submitted in a timely fashion, will be posted on the CESCR's website.[60]

[4.20] The Committee welcomes submissions from NGOs and NHRIs[61] at any time prior to consideration of a given State party's report and has adopted specific guidelines

---

[55] See Report on the Working Methods of the Human Rights Treaty Bodies (2010), para 29.

[56] Guidelines on Treaty-Specific Documents to be submitted by states parties under Articles 16 and 17 of the International Covenant on Economic Social, and Cultural Rights (24 March 2009): EC 12/2008/2.

[57] Compilation of Guidelines on the Form and Content of Reports to be Submitted by States Parties to the International Human Rights Treaties (3 June 2009): UN Doc HRI/GEN/2/Rev6. As the harmonised guidelines, see para **4.08**.

[58] Regard is had to the desirability of equitable geographical distribution in the selection of the working group.

[59] It should be noted that the pre-sessional working group also undertakes a number of other tasks aimed at facilitating an efficient dialogue with the reporting States. These include considering the most appropriate allocation of time for the upcoming discussion with the State, how best to respond to supplementary reports containing additional information, examining draft general comments and other relevant matters: Report of the CESCR to ECOSOC (2006): E/2006/22, EC 12/2005/5, para 31.

[60] Source: http://www2.ohchr.org/english/bodies/cescr/workingmethods.htm (last accessed May 2011). Ireland has reported to the CESCR on two occasions in 1997 and 2002. The State's reports as well as the concluding observations of the Committee can also be accessed at: http://www.dfa.ie/home/index.aspx?id=319 (last accessed May 2011).

[61] In General Comment No 10, the CESCR specifically acknowledges the role of NHRIs in monitoring and promoting implementation of economic, social and cultural rights in the national legal system: (14 December 1998) UN Doc E/C 12/1998/25, available at: http://www2.ohchr.org/english/bodies/cescr/comments.htm (last accessed May 2011).

for this purpose.⁶² These may be made in writing or in person to the pre-sessional working group in advance of the Committee's formal session. The Committee sets aside part of the first afternoon at each of its sessions to enable representatives of NGOs and NHRIs to provide oral information to it.⁶³ This marks an advance on the procedure adopted by the CCPR which, thus far has not permitted either NGOs or NHRIs to address the plenary Committee orally at its formal sessions. It is important to note that the CESCR engages with the special procedures mandate holders of the current Human Rights Council in order to inform its own work.⁶⁴ The Committee has frequently invited the special procedures mandate holders to meet with it during its sessions, to address the Committee formally and to engage in discussions. Though these invitations take place, strictly speaking, outside the context of the periodic reporting process, the dialogue with the mandate holders (especially the special rapporteurs on the right to housing, the right to education and the rights of indigenous persons,) has obviously informed the work of the Committee within the reporting process.

[4.21] The 'constructive dialogue' that ensues between the CESCR and each contracting State under the reporting procedure follows a similar pattern and structure to that conducted by the CCPR under the ICCPR procedure.⁶⁵ The CESCR normally devotes three, three-hour meetings to the consideration of each State report, though it has on occasion considered a State's report in two such meetings.⁶⁶ The country rapporteur normally opens the dialogue with questions regarding implementation of the Committee's previous concluding observations (where a periodic report, as opposed to an initial report, is under consideration). Other members of the Committee then normally ask questions regarding the implementation of particular articles, or clusters of articles of the Covenant. The Committee will allow the State to submit supplementary written information to it in answer to its questions, where necessary, within several days of the conclusion of the dialogue which will be taken into account in formulating its concluding observations.⁶⁷ The Committee's concluding observations are made public

---

⁶² See generally, 'Non-governmental organization participation in the activities of the Committee on Economic, Social and Cultural Rights': (7 July 2006) UN Doc E/C12/2000/6. Representatives of the UN specialised agencies are also invited to meet with the Committee during its sessions to discuss the situation in those countries whose reports are being considered. They may also address the pre-sessional group of the Committee at the beginning of its session. See Report on the Working Methods of the Human Rights Treaty Bodies Relating to the State Party Reporting Process: UN Doc HRI/ICM/2010/2, para 97.
⁶³ Annual Report of the CESCR (2010): UN Doc E/2010/22-EC12/2009/3, para 59.
⁶⁴ See Ch 2, paras **2.34–2.35** and Report on the Working Methods of the Human Rights Treaty Bodies (2010), para 102.
⁶⁵ Where a State fails to send a delegation to a scheduled examination, or seeks postponement of the examination, the CESCR follows a strict practice rule whereby it will proceed to examine the report in the absence of the State's delegation: Rule 62(3) of the rules of procedure of the CESCR (1 September 1993): UN Doc E/C12/1990/4/Rev 1.
⁶⁶ Report on the Working Methods of the Human Rights Treaty Bodies (2010), para 55.
⁶⁷ There is no express reference to 'concluding observations' in the text of arts 16 or 17 of the ICESCR which simply provides that State reports shall be transmitted to ECOSOC for its 'consideration'. (contd.../)

on the last day of the Committee's session, when they are sent to the States parties concerned. The observations follow a similar structure to that of the CCPR.[68] States parties are entitled to submit written responses to the CESCR's observations and the Committee will in turn make these public for information purposes.[69]

[4.22] As regards follow-up procedures, the CESCR has not adopted a formal mechanism for this purpose, as is the case with the appointment by the CCPR of the special rapporteur for follow-up on concluding observations.[70] At its 21st session in 1999, however, the Committee decided that in its concluding observations, the Committee may specifically request that a State party provide it with more information or statistical data prior to the date on which its next periodic report falls due. Any such information provided by the State will be considered at the next pre-sessional working group of the Committee. The latter group may then decide variously either to recommend the Committee to take note of the information, recommend that a request be made for more information, recommend that the Committee adopt specific additional concluding observations based on the new information, or authorise the chairperson of the Committee to inform the State that the Committee will take up the issue at its next session, preferably in the presence of a representative of the State concerned.[71] If, on the other hand, the State in question fails to submit the requested information, or such information as is requested is considered to be unsatisfactory, the chairperson may pursue the matter with the State party.[72] This procedure apparently is rarely applied in practice.[73] In situations where the Committee has been unable to obtain the requisite information on the basis of the latter procedure, it may decide to adopt a different approach. It may request that the State Party accept a technical assistance mission to its territory, consisting of one or two Committee members, but again this has only been applied to two States.[74] If a State is not willing to accept such a mission, the Committee may make appropriate recommendations to ECOSOC. In all other cases, Committee members who have served as country rapporteurs for particular States are expected to follow up on those countries in the inter-sessional period until those countries appear to present their next periodic report to the Committee.[75]

---

[67] (\...contd) However, ECOSOC Resolution 1985/17 specifically provides that the CESCR 'Shall make suggestions and recommendations of a general nature on the basis of its consideration of those reports and of the reports submitted by the specialized agencies, in order to assist the Council to fulfill, in particular, its responsibilities under Articles 21 and 22 of the Covenant'.

[68] Indeed, it should be pointed out that the CESCR was the first Committee in fact to adopt 'concluding observations' and thus in reality, it is the other Committees which have followed its practice in this regard.

[69] CESCR Annual Report to ECOSOC, UN Doc E/2010/22, EC12/2009/3, para. 40.

[70] See above, para **4.13**.

[71] See Report on the Working Methods of the Human Rights Treaty Bodies (2010), para 79.

[72] The procedure is outlined in detail in the CESCR Annual Report (2000): UN Doc E/2000/22; E/C12/1999/11, paras 38 –40.

[73] See Report on the Working Methods of the Human Rights Treaty Bodies (2010), para 79.

[74] See Report on the Working Methods of the Human Rights Treaty Bodies (2010), para 79.

[4.23] As regards the situation of persistent non-reporting states, the CESCR adopts a similar approach to that of the CCPR, namely, having warned the State of its intentions, it will move to consider the implementation of economic, social and cultural rights in that State, in the absence of a report, on the basis of all available information.[76] Where such a State does indicate that it will provide a report to the Committee, the Committee may defer its consideration for one session. In 2006, the Committee indicated that as many as 26 States were overdue with their initial reports to the Committee, many of which were overdue since 1990; 14 States were overdue on their second periodic reports; while Romania was overdue by 12 years with its third periodic report.[77]

International Convention on the Elimination of all Forms of Racial Discrimination

[4.24] The periodic reporting procedure in the International Convention on the Elimination of all Forms of Racial Discrimination (ICERD) is set out in art 9 thereof.[78] It provides that States parties to that instrument should submit reports to the Committee on the Elimination of Racial Discrimination (CERD)[79] on the 'legislative, judicial, administrative or other measures' which they have adopted to give effect to the provisions of the Convention.[80] Article 9(1) specifically provides that initial reports should be submitted within one year after entry into force of the Convention and thereafter every *two* years and whenever the Committee so requests. Fortunately, the Committee has taken a much more flexible attitude to the submission of State reports. In 1988, it decided that States parties should submit a comprehensive report every four years and a brief updating report in the interim two year period.[81] Like the CESCR, it allows for the submission of combined reports in circumstances where a State is backlogged with its submission of reports to the Committee.[82] CERD has also adopted guidelines for the treaty-specific report, which take into account the new harmonised guidelines for the common-core document.[83]

---

[75] See Report on the Working Methods of the Human Rights Treaty Bodies (2010), para 79.
[76] CESCR, Annual Report (2009), E/2009/22, para 34.
[77] CESCR, Annual Report (2009), E/2009/22, pp. 106–107.
[78] On the ICERD, see Ch 3, paras **3.53**–**3.63**. On the reporting procedure, see generally, Banton, 'Decision-Taking in the Committee on the Elimination of Racial Discrimination' in Alston and Crawford, *The Future of UN Human Rights Treaty Monitoring* (CUP, 2000), p 55; and *A User's Guide to the International Convention on the Elimination of Racial Discrimination* (Joint Committee of the Irish Human Rights Commission and the Northern Ireland Human Rights Commission, 2003): http://www.ihrc.ie/publications/list/a-users-guide-to-the-international-convention-on-t/ (last accessed May 2011); and Rehman, *International Human Rights Law* (2nd edn, Pearson, 2008), pp 423–426. See also CERD's rules of procedure: UN Doc HRI/GEN/3/Rev 3, p 57, rules 63–68.
[79] CERD is composed of 18 independent experts of high moral standing and acknowledged impartiality (art 8). See Ch 3, para **[3.61]**.
[80] Ireland submitted its initial and second periodic report to CERD in 2005: UN Doc CERD/C/460/Add1. CERD's concluding observations are reproduced in UN Doc CERD/C/IRL/CO/2. Ireland's 'Follow-Up' Response: UN Doc CERD/C/IRL/CO/2/Add1 (16 June 2006). It submitted its third and fourth periodic reports in 2010: UN Doc CERD/C/IRL3-4. CERD's concluding observations on the latter reports are contained in UN Doc CERD/C/IRL/CO/3-4.
[81] Report on the Working Methods of the Human Rights Treaty Bodies (2010), para 31.

[4.25] Unlike the CESCR, CERD does not host pre-sessional meetings. Rather, the Committee designates individual members of the Committee to be 'country rapporteurs' for particular States which are due to report to the Committee. Since August 2010, each country rapporteur, at his or her discretion, draws up a 'list of main themes' for the State assigned to them based on the State's report and other information received, which is then transmitted to that State ten weeks in advance of the session at which the State's report will be examined by the Committee as a whole. The lists of main themes are generally formulated on an article-by-article basis. CERD does not request a written reply by the States parties to the list of main themes.[84]

[4.26] CERD was the first Committee to operate its reporting procedure and hence the first to adopt the practice of considering each State report in the presence of representatives of the reporting State – a practice which has since been imitated by all of the other treaty bodies. Typically, CERD will end up examining on average 12 reports *per* session.[85] It will usually put aside two, three-hour meetings (to take place on different days) at each session to the public examination of each State report.[86] The constructive dialogue generally follows the same pattern as that of the other Committees. Following the opening statement by the State party's delegation, its representatives are asked to give specific responses to the list of themes posed by the country rapporteur who leads the questioning. Other members of the Committee may then pose additional questions, (which may raise issues beyond the list of themes) to which the State representatives are then given an opportunity to respond.

[4.27] As regards participation in the reporting procedure by other actors, CERD has been to the forefront in acknowledging and supporting the potential involvement of NHRIs, in particular. In its general recommendation No XVII, which deals with the establishment of NHRIs to facilitate implementation of the Convention, the Committee recommends that where NHRIs have been established, they should be associated with

---

[82] Since 2001, the Committee has allowed States to adjust their reporting schedule in order to get back on track with the standard four year schedule: Annual Report of CERD (2001) UN Doc A/56/18, para 477.

[83] See Guidelines for the CERD-Specific Document to be Submitted by States parties under Article 9, Paragraph 1, of the Convention (13 June 2008): UN Doc CERD/C/2007/1.

[84] CERD discussed the possibility of adopting the LOIPR approach pioneered by the UNCAT (see para **4.40** below) and operated by the CCPR (see para **4.10** above) but declined to adopt it, opting instead in February 2010 to follow the 'lists of main themes' approach outlined above. See the Report on the Working Methods of the Human Rights Treaty Bodies (2010), paras 36 and 42.

[85] Report on the Working Methods of the Human Rights Treaty Bodies (2010), para 52.

[86] CERD has not adopted a rule of procedure to cover situations where a State may fail to appear at a scheduled examination or seek to postpone a scheduled examination. In principle, it may consider a report in the absence of a delegation when the State fails to provide compelling reasons for deferral of examination. Report on the Working Methods of the Human Rights Treaty Bodies Relating to the State Party Reporting Process: UN Doc HRI/ICM/2010/2, para 69.

the preparation of State reports.[87] CERD routinely informs NHRIs about its work, by sending to them its programme of work for each session and providing them with copies of the reports to be considered by the Committee.[88] Since 2005, like CESCR, it has instituted a practice of allowing national human rights institutions to address the Committee orally while it is formally examining the State's report.[89] In 2007, the Committee formally amended its Rules of Procedure to reflect this practice of allowing for the possibility of NHRIs, accredited to take part in deliberations of the Human Rights Council, to address the Committee, with the consent of the State concerned, in official meetings and on issues relating to the dialogue with that State.[90]

[4.28] NGOs are also invited to submit shadow reports containing country-specific information when the reports of their States are due for consideration by the Committee. The procedure before the Committee has not yet evolved to the point of allowing NGOs to intervene orally during the Committee's sessions, and since there is no pre-sessional meeting under this procedure, the Committee will allocate time to meet NGOs informally, for example, on the first day on which a State's report is due to be formally examined.[91]

[4.29] As regards input from the United Nations specialised agencies, CERD receives information routinely from the International Labour Organization (ILO), the United Nations Educational, Scientific and Cultural Organization (UNESCO)[92] and the United Nations High Commissioner for Refugees (UNHCR). It invites representatives of the specialised agencies to a designated meeting of the Committee in plenary at the beginning of each session.[93] CERD also cooperates with the special procedures mandate

---

[87] UN Doc A/48/18 (25 March 1993), p 116. The terminology chosen here should not be interpreted too widely because as Müller and Seidensticker point out, NHRIs should not become directly involved in the *drafting* of State reports since to do so would conflict with their independent status: Müller and Seidensticker, *The Role of National Human Rights Institutions in the United Nations Treaty Body Process* (German Institute for Human Rights, 2007), pp. 40–42.

[88] UN Doc A/58/18, Annex IV

[89] The Irish Human Rights Commission was the first Human Rights Commission to formally address the Committee in open session when the Committee examined Ireland's initial report under that Convention in March 2005.

[90] CERD Rules of Procedure, Rule 40(2). CERD Annual Report 2007, UN Doc A/62/18/2007/ Annex IX. Interestingly, at its most recent session in February 2011, the Committee held a public session at the beginning of the week during which all NGOs from the countries whose reports were due to be examined made brief oral presentations and answered questions from Committee members. This was additional to the individual briefing sessions for NGOs held prior to the examination of their State's particular report. While obviously a positive development, it remains to be seen whether this particular practice will be repeated at future sessions.

[91] Report on the Working Methods of the Human Rights Treaty Bodies (2010), para 112; and See Annual Report of CERD (2003) UN Doc A/58/18, Annex IV, Section B.

[92] See CERD Decision 2(VI) of 21 August 1972: UN Doc A/8718 (Chapter XI, section B).

[93] Report on the Working Methods of the Human Rights Treaty Bodies (2010), paras 97–98.

holders by inviting them to participate in its annual thematic debates as well as ad hoc debates. The Committee has also entered into wide-ranging dialogues with several of the mandate holders, including the special rapporteurs on racism, adequate housing, health and minority issues. The Committee also cooperates with the special adviser of the Secretary General on genocide.[94]

[4.30] Article 9(2) of the ICERD specifically provides that: 'The Committee shall report annually, through the Secretary-General, to the General Assembly of the United Nations on its activities and may make suggestions and recommendations based on the examination of the reports and information received from the States Parties'. Accordingly, like the other Committees, CERD adopts 'concluding observations' at the end of its examination of each State's report. These are made public at the end of each session and in accordance with art 9(2) are included in the Committee's annual report to the General Assembly.

[4.31] The follow-up procedure adopted by CERD in regard to its concluding observations is perhaps the most well-developed of all of the treaty bodies. First, as noted above, art 9(1)(b) of the Convention provides that the Committee may request a State to provide a report to the Committee 'whenever the Committee so requests'. Rule 65 of the Committee's Rules of Procedure elaborates on the modalities for making requests for additional reports from States. In 2004, the Committee decided to amend rule 65 of its Rules of Procedure in a way that would specifically make the request for additional reports relevant to its follow-up activities. It did so by adopting a second paragraph to rule 65 which provides for the appointment of a follow-up coordinator for a two-year period, who shall cooperate with the country rapporteurs in fulfilling their tasks.[95] In 2005, the Committee fleshed out the specific terms of the mandate of the follow-up coordinator,[96] as being principally that of monitoring the follow-up by States parties on the observations and recommendations of the Committee, in cooperation with the respective country rapporteur.[97] He or she is charged with setting appropriate deadlines for additional information, as well as analysing and assessing that information when received from the State.[98] The coordinator makes recommendations to the Committee for appropriate action on foot of the information or in cases where it is simply not received. The coordinator may, *inter alia,* recommend that the Committee take note of the information, request further information in the next periodic report, or remind the State party of recommendations included in the last set of concluding

---

[94] Report on the Working Methods of the Human Rights Treaty Bodies (2010), para 102.
[95] CERD Rules of procedure, Rule 65(2).
[96] Terms of Reference for the Work of the CERD Follow Up Coordinator (10 March 2005): UN Doc CERD/C/66/ Misc11/Rev2, http://www2.ohchr.org/english/bodies/cerd/docs/Terms_of_Reference.pdf (last accessed May 2011).
[97] Terms of Reference for the Work of the CERD Follow Up Coordinator (10 March 2005), para 1.
[98] Terms of Reference for the Work of the CERD Follow Up Coordinator (10 March 2005), paras 2 and 3.

observations of the Committee and their obligations under the Convention.[99] The coordinator is required to submit a report to the Committee at each of its sessions, and the Committee in turn is required to set aside sufficient time to discuss the coordinator's findings and to adopt formal recommendations, if necessary.[100]

[4.32] As regards the procedure to be adopted in the case of persistent non-reporting by States, CERD can be credited as the treaty body which pioneered the practice of examining a State's implementation of the Convention in cases where no report has been received. In its last annual report of 2010 the Committee gives details of 23 contracting States whose reports are seriously overdue by 10 years, with perhaps the most egregious examples being that of Sierra Leone whose fourth to twentieth periodic reports are overdue since 1976.[101] It is striking that the list of offenders is almost entirely composed of less developed States on the African continent, some of which have been in the throes of civil strife for many of those years.[102] Twenty-four further States are overdue in their reporting obligations by over five years.[103] The Committee scheduled the consideration of all of these States in its review procedure, thus prompting promises from a number of them that reports would be produced for the Committee within specified deadlines.[104]

Early warning and urgent procedure

[4.33] Since 1993, CERD has adopted a sophisticated 'early warning' and 'urgent action' procedure aimed at preventing serious violations of the ICERD. In 2007, it updated its guidelines for the application of this procedure from the initial working procedure adopted since 1993. The Committee's focus on early prevention is particularly important in that many of the situations which it has had to address concern massive or persistent patterns of racial discrimination which have sometimes had genocidal dimensions.[105]

[4.34] Under the revised guidelines, the Committee shall act under the early warning and urgent procedure when it deems it necessary to address serious violations of the Convention 'in an urgent manner'. Particular indicators which shall guide the Committee in its assessment are set out in the guidelines, including:

---

[99] Terms of Reference for the Work of the CERD Follow Up Coordinator (10 March 2005), para 4.
[100] Terms of Reference for the Work of the CERD Follow Up Coordinator (10 March 2005), para 5.
[101] CERD Annual Report (2010): UN Doc A/65/18, para 58.
[102] Somalia, Liberia, Sierra Leone, and Zimbabwe.
[103] CERD Annual Report (2010): UN Doc A/65/18, para 59.
[104] CERD Annual Report (2010): UN Doc A/65/18, paras 60–61.
[105] Guidelines for the Early Warning and Urgent Action Procedure, CERD Annual Report 2007, UN Doc A/62/18, Annex III, para 7. The Committee's decision to revise its guidelines in regard to early warning and urgent procedures was clearly prompted by the emphasis placed on the prevention of genocide by the former Secretary General, Kofi Annan in his key-note speech to the Stockholm International Forum on Preventing Genocide in 2004 and his references to this fundamental imperative in his 'In Larger Freedom' report in 2005 (UN Doc A/59/2005, para 125): see guidelines, paras 4–6.

(a) the presence of a significant and persistent pattern of racial discrimination, as evidenced in social and economic indicators;
(b) the presence of a pattern of escalating racial hatred and violence, or racist propaganda or appeals to racial intolerance by persons, groups, or organisations, notably by elected or other State officials;
(c) the adoption of new discriminatory legislation;
(d) segregation policies or *de facto* exclusion of members of a group from political, economic, social or cultural life;
(e) lack of an adequate legislative framework defining and criminalising all forms of racial discrimination or lack of effective mechanisms;
(f) policies or practices of impunity;
(g) significant flows of refugees or displaced persons, especially those belonging to specific ethnic groups;
(h) encroachment on the traditional lands of indigenous peoples or forced removal of those peoples from their lands; and
(i) polluting or hazardous activities that reflect a pattern of racial discrimination with substantial harm to specific groups.[106]

Since these indicators may be present in situations which do not necessarily require urgent intervention, the Committee assesses their significance in the light of the 'scale and gravity of the situation'.[107] In deciding whether to consider a specific State under this procedure, the Committee draws on information made available to it by, *inter alia*, the United Nations agencies, regional human rights mechanisms, NHRIs and NGOS.[108]

[4.35] A range of measures may be taken by the Committee under the early warning and urgent action procedure. These include: (a) requesting the State to submit urgently information on the situation being considered under the procedure; (b) requesting the secretariat to collect information from the field presences of the OHCHR, specialised agencies, NHRIs and NGOs on the situation under consideration; and (c) adopting a decision including the expression of specific concerns, along with recommendations for action to a range of parties including the State party, relevant special procedures mandate holders[109] or human rights bodies of the Human Rights Council, regional intergovernmental organisations and human rights mechanisms, the Human Rights Council, the special adviser of the Secretary General on the prevention of genocide, or the Secretary General or the High Commissioner for Human Rights together with a recommendation that the matter be brought to the attention of the Security Council.[110] The Committee can also offer to send one or more members of the Committee to the

---

[106] Guidelines for the Early Warning and Urgent Action Procedure, para 12.
[107] Guidelines for the Early Warning and Urgent Action Procedure, para 12.
[108] Guidelines for the Early Warning and Urgent Action Procedure, para 13.
[109] Specifically, the Special Rapporteur on contemporary forms of racism, racial discrimination and xenophobia and related intolerance, the Special Rapporteur on the situation of human rights and fundamental freedoms of indigenous persons, or the independent expert on minority issues.
[110] Guidelines for the Early Warning and Urgent Action Procedure, para 14.

State to assist in the implementation of international standards or technical assistance; or it can recommend that the State avail itself of the advisory services and technical assistance of the OHCHR.

[4.36] A five-member working group of the Committee (established since 2004) is mandated to analyse and assess in a preliminary way information received on situations that may require urgent action. The group makes its assessment in private meetings and makes recommendations to the Committee, based on the criteria outlined above. The Committee then, in turn, may adopt in a private meeting any decision or action to be taken under the procedure.[111] Decisions of the Committee under the procedure are subsequently made public in the Committee's annual report and on its website.[112]

United Nations Convention on the Prevention of Torture and Other Cruel, Inhuman or Degrading Treatment or Punishment

[4.37] The reporting procedure provided for in the United Nations Convention on the Prevention of Torture and Other Cruel, Inhuman or Degrading Treatment or Punishment (UNCAT) is set forth in art 19 of that instrument.[113] Under art 19(1), States parties are obliged to submit reports to the 10-member Committee against Torture (CAT) established by the Convention[114] on the measures they have taken to give effect to their undertakings in respect of the UNCAT.[115] Initial reports are to be submitted within one year of entry into force of the Convention, with subsequent reports required every four years.[116]

[4.38] CAT has recommended that States adopt the new harmonised guidelines on reporting to all of the treaty bodies, though it has not yet updated its own treaty-specific guidelines.[117] Its guidelines, therefore, provide separate guidance in regard to initial reports[118] and periodic reports.[119] Initial reports should be structured in two parts, the

---

[111] Guidelines for the Early Warning and Urgent Action Procedure, paras 15–23.
[112] http://www2.ohchr.org/english/bodies/cerd/early-warning.htm (last accessed May 2011).
[113] On UNCAT, see Ch 3, paras **3.73–3.80**. On the reporting procedure, see generally Bank, 'Country-Oriented Procedures under the Convention Against Torture: Towards a New Dynamism' in Alston and Crawford (eds), *The Future of UN Human Rights Treaty Monitoring* (CUP, 2000), p 145; Nowak and McArthur, *The United Nations Convention Against Torture: A Commentary* (OUP, 2008), pp 624–659; and Rehman, *International Human Rights Law* (2nd edn, Pearson, 2008), pp 830–834.
[114] On the composition and mandate of CAT, see paras **3.78–3.80**.
[115] See generally the CAT's rules of procedure: UN Doc CAT/C/3/Rev 5, Rules 65–73.
[116] Ireland submitted its initial report under the procedure (which was due in 2003) in 2009: UN Doc CAT/C/IRL/1 (26 January 2010). The State's report and the CAT's concluding observations thereon are available on the CAT's website: http://www2.ohchr.org/english/bodies/cat/cats46.htm (last accessed May 2011)
[117] The Committee asked the OHCHR secretariat to prepare a first draft of new treaty-specific guidelines at its session in April/May 2008. Report on the Implementation of Recommendations of the Sixth Inter-Committee Meeting and the Nineteenth Meeting of Chairpersons (22 May 2008): UN Doc HRI/MC/2008/2, para 10.
[118] UN Doc CAT/C/4/Rev 3 (18 July 2005).
[119] UN Doc CAT/C/14/Rev 1 (2 June 1998).

first of which should provide general information, while the second should address each substantive article of the Convention. Under the traditional procedure, periodic reports should be divided into three parts. The first part should set forth new measures and developments in regard to the implementation of the substantive articles since the previous report; the second part should cover any additional information requested by the Committee; and the third part should describe compliance by the State with the Committee's concluding observations on its previous report.[120]

[4.39] The Committee adopts a quasi-flexible approach in regard to submission of reports in that it is open to variation on the due dates for periodic reports. While it has shown itself to be willing to accept combined reports on an exceptional basis,[121] it has not adopted a formal position on this in its reporting guidelines. In its annual report of 2007, the Committee indicated that its *raison d'être* for allowing combined reports was the fact that there was a massive number of reports overdue under this reporting procedure.[122] In its annual report of 2010, the Committee revealed the staggering fact that as of May 2010, 229 reports were overdue under the procedure.[123] Since it only meets for two sessions *per* year, the Committee is only able to deal with an average of 14 reports *per* session. This state of affairs has induced the Committee on a number of occasions to request approval from the General Assembly of extra meeting time – a request which has only been granted for the first time recently as a temporary measure.[124] It is striking, however, and indeed peculiar that such requests had not thus far been granted to CAT, in contrast to the authorisation by the General Assembly to many of the other committees, including CESCR, CERD, CEDAW and the CRC.[125]

[4.40] Until recently, CAT adhered exclusively to the traditional reporting process whereby it would transmit a list of issues to States parties whose reports were already submitted and which were due for examination by the Committee. The States parties would then be encouraged to submit written replies to the lists of issues, which replies would be taken into consideration at the formal examination of the State's report. In 2007, the Committee initiated a new optional procedure, on a trial basis, for the processing of periodic reports.[126] Under the new procedure, the Committee will prepare

---

[120] See generally Guidelines On The Form And Content Of Initial Reports Under Article 19 To Be Submitted By States Parties To The Convention Against Torture (18 July 2005): UN Doc CAT/C/4/Rev3. Note the new optional procedure for periodic reports in para **4.40**.

[121] CAT Annual Report 2007: UN Doc A/62/44, para 22. Accordingly, combined reports will be accepted, provided that the information provided by the State party covers the entire period of the overdue reporting period. This measure will be reviewed by the Committee on a case-by-case basis.

[122] CAT Annual Report 2007: UN Doc A/62/44, para 22. At that stage, a total of 232 reports were overdue under this procedure: CAT Annual Report 2007, para 21.

[123] CAT Annual Report 2010: UN Doc A/65/44, para 31.

[124] GA Res. 65/204, UN Doc A/RES/65/204.

[125] Working Methods of the Treaty Bodies Relating to the State Party Reporting Process: UN Doc HRI/ICM/2010/2, para 52.

[126] CAT Annual Report 2007, UN Doc A/62/44, paras 23–24.

and adopt a list of issues *prior* to the submission of the State's report. The State party's written replies to the list of issues will then constitute the State's report under art 19 of the Convention.[127] The Committee discussed this new procedure with States parties in advance of its adoption and initiated it in December 2007 in regard to periodic reports falling due in 2009 and 2010.[128] It remains to be seen whether the new procedure will live up to the Committee's expectation that it will assist States in preparing more focused reports and in fulfilling their reporting obligations in a timely and effective manner.[129] While these objectives are undoubtedly worthy, the procedure has paradoxically placed an even greater strain on this already over-burdened Committee since the preparation of the 'list of issues prior to reporting' requires even more work than is required to compile a 'list of issues' under the traditional procedure.[130] Moreover, for it to work properly, it is imperative that the reports submitted on foot of the lists of issues are considered by the Committee itself in a timely manner.[131] All of these factors further underscore the need for extra meeting time to be granted to the Committee to enable it to efficiently fulfil its mandate under the reporting procedure.

[4.41] As regards the 'constructive dialogue' with States parties, the Committee normally devotes one and one and a half 'meetings' to the consideration of each State report.[132] The State representatives will present the report and update the Committee on any new information not contained in it. Committee members may then pose follow-up questions. Where State representatives fail to turn up for the examination of the report, CAT may, at its own discretion, either notify the State party of an alternative date at which the report will be examined or consider the report in the absence of the delegation.[133]

[4.42] As regards participation of in the reporting process by other actors, the Committee invites NGOs to provide it with shadow reports containing information on the State party due to report.[134] In 2005, the Committee began to meet with NGOs in private on the afternoon immediately before the consideration of each State party's report. This new practice replaced the previous one of scheduling lunchtime briefings

---

[127] CAT Annual Report 2007, UN Doc A/62/44, para 23. The procedure – known by the acronym LOIPR – and pioneered by CAT has since been adopted by the CCPR: see para **4.10**.

[128] CAT Annual Report 2007, UN Doc A/62/44, para 24. For reports due in 2009, 2010 and 2011, the Committee transmitted lists of issues to 11, 9 and 19 States parties respectively: CAT Annual Report (2010), paras 35–37.

[129] The CAT has received 'positive feedback' from States and has continued to operate the procedure. CAT Annual Report 2009: UN Doc A/64/44, para 27.

[130] CAT Annual Report (2010), para 39.

[131] Otherwise, as the CAT itself has observed '... the added value of the procedure will be defeated as new lists of issues would have to be adopted and transmitted to the States parties to update the information they provided'. CAT Annual Report (2010), para 33.

[132] Report on the Working Methods of the Human Rights Treaty Bodies (2010), para 55. A meeting is three hours in duration.

[133] CAT Rules of Procedure, r 68(2).

[134] CAT Rules of Procedure, r 63.

with Committee members which were not facilitated by interpretation services. NHRIs of any State party due to report (where such institutions exist), are informed about the submission of the State's report and are invited to submit written information to the Committee. While the Committee had also held private meetings with NHRIs on the day before the examination of the State party in question, it decided to discontinue this practice in 2010 due to a lack of meeting time.[135] Henceforth, the country rapporteurs assigned to the State in question, together with any other member wishing to attend, will meet with representatives of NHRIs before the consideration of the report of the State party concerned outside the plenary of the Committee.[136] The specialised agencies and other UN bodies are invited to submit information relevant to the Committee's activities under the Convention, including its reporting activities,[137] and the Committee has requested the United Nations High Commissioner for Refugees (UNHCR), whose mandate is close to that of CAT, to address it in private on a regular basis.[138] Finally, the Committee has a close working relationship with the special rapporteur on torture,[139] which includes the sharing of country-specific information relating to the States parties' reports, as well as a formal annual meeting between the Committee and the rapporteur.[140]

[4.43] Under art 19(3), the Committee is given the task of considering each State report and making such 'general comments' as it may consider appropriate. Following the practice of the other treaty bodies, the Committee issues concluding observations on each State report at the end of the session at which those reports have been examined. Since 2003, the concluding observations will contain a limited number of specific recommendations, known as 'follow-up' recommendations, for which the State is requested to provide additional information to the Committee within one year.[141] In 2005, the Committee established the position of 'rapporteur for follow-up to concluding observations',[142] whose mandate is to monitor the responses of States to the recommendations made by the Committee in its concluding observations and to make progress reports thereon to the Committee.[143] The Committee's annual report regularly contains statistics on the responses received by the rapporteur. The most recent results indicate that since the procedure was first initiated, approximately two-thirds of the States parties to which it has been applied have submitted follow-up reports, with the

---

[135] CAT Annual Report 2010, paras 17–19.
[136] CAT Annual Report 2010, para 19.
[137] CAT Rules of Procedure, rule 63.
[138] CAT Annual Report 2010, para 97.
[139] As to the special rapporteur, see: http://www2.ohchr.org/english/issues/torture/rapporteur/ (last accessed May 2011).
[140] Report on Working Methods of the Human Rights Treaty Bodies Relating to the State Reporting Process (2009): UN Doc HRI/MC/2009/4 (24 June 2009), para 97.
[141] CAT Rules of Procedure, r 71.
[142] CAT Rules of Procedure, r 68(2).
[143] The current rapporteur, Ms Felice de Gaer, has emphasized that the follow-up procedure aims 'to make more effective the struggle against torture and other cruel, inhuman or degrading treatment or punishment': CAT Annual Report 2009, UN Doc A/64/44, para 56.

remaining reports still outstanding.[144] Nonetheless, the rapporteur has indicated that the follow-up procedure has been '... remarkably successful in eliciting valuable additional information from States on protective measures taken during the immediate follow-up to the review of the periodic reports'.[145] While comparatively few States have submitted the requisite information precisely on time, the sending of reminder letters has helped, in the long run, to elicit the necessary responses.[146]

[4.44] Finally, in theory, CAT operates a review procedure similar to CERD to deal with cases of persistent non-reporting.[147] However, it has never applied this procedure to any State because notices of planned reviews have always provoked offending States to submit a report.[148] This factor should not be construed as indicating that CAT has a higher success rate than the other treaty bodies in terms of timely submission of reports. Recent statistics record a dismal participation ratio, with no less than 23 States overdue by over 10 years in the submission of their initial or second periodic reports to the Committee.[149]

United Nations Convention on the Rights of the Child

[4.45] Article 44 of the Convention on the Rights of the Child (CRC) sets forth the basis for the reporting procedure under that instrument.[150] Supervision of State reporting under the Convention is carried out by the 18-member Committee on the Rights of the Child (CRC Committee).[151] The CRC Committee also monitors implementation of the Optional Protocol to the Convention on the Rights of the Child on the involvement of

---

[144] Since May 2003, the CAT Committee has reviewed 95 reports for which it has identified follow-up recommendations. Of the 81 States parties that were due to have submitted their follow-up reports to the Committee by 15 May 2010, 57 had completed this requirement. As of 14 May 2010, 24 States had not yet supplied follow-up information that had fallen due: CAT Annual Report 2010, para 70.

[145] CAT Annual Report 2009, UN Doc A/64/44, para 59.

[146] As regards the quality of the follow-up information, the rapporteur was generally pleased overall, but noted some recurring concerns which are not fully addressed in the follow-up replies. These are itemised at CAT Annual Report 2010, para 79.

[147] CAT Rules of Procedure, rule 67.

[148] Report on the Working Methods of the Human Rights Treaty Bodies (2010), para 87.

[149] CAT Annual Report 2010, Annex XI.

[150] On the CRC generally, see Ch 3, paras [3.81]–[3.91]. On the reporting procedure under the CRC, see generally Lansdown, 'The Reporting Process under the Convention on the Rights of the Child' in Alston and Crawford (eds), *The Future of UN Human Rights Treaty Monitoring* (2000), p 113; Smith, 'Monitoring the CRC' in Alfredsson et al (eds), *International Human Rights Monitoring Mechanisms* (Martinus Nijhoff, 2009), p 109; O'Flaherty, *Human Rights and the UN: Practice Before the Treaty Bodies* (Martinus Nijhoff, 2002), pp 147–175; Kilkelly, 'UN Committee on the Rights of the Child – An Evaluation in the Light of Recent UK experience' (1996) 8(2) Child and Family Law Quarterly pp 105–120; and Rehman, *International Human Rights Law* (2nd edn, Pearson, 2008), pp 586–589. For the CRC Committee's rules of procedure as they pertain to the reporting process, see UN Doc CRC/C/4/Rev 2, Rules 70–76.

[151] For the composition and mandate of the CRC Committee, see paras **3.89–3.91**.

children in armed conflict[152] (OPAC) and the Optional Protocol to the Convention on the Rights of the Child on the sale of children, child prostitution and child pornography[153] (OPSC) by the States parties to those respective instruments. The States parties to OPAC and OPSC are also required under arts 8 and 12 respectively to report to the CRC Committee on the measures they have taken to implement the terms of the Protocols in their respective jurisdictions.[154]

[4.46] Pursuant to art 44(1), initial reports concerning implementation of the CRC must be submitted within two years of entry into force of the Convention and thereafter every five years. States parties to the CRC who are simultaneously parties to OPAC and/or OPSC must submit their initial reports under those Protocols within two years of entry into force, and thereafter, periodic reports may be submitted in tandem with periodic reports falling due under the Convention every five years. States parties to either of the Protocols which are not party to the Convention are required to submit periodic reports to the CRC Committee every five years.[155] The Committee has adopted a series of guidelines for States regarding the submission of initial and periodic reports under both the Convention and the two Optional Protocols. The most recent revised guidelines in relation to the Convention were adopted in 2010.[156] The guidelines are very detailed and specific, grouping the articles of the Convention CRC into eight clusters according to which the States parties should provide the requisite information. The partitioning of the

---

[152] OPAC entered into force on 12 February 2002 and has been ratified by 132 States parties.

[153] OPSC entered into force on 18 January 2002 and has been ratified by 137 States parties.

[154] Ireland has reported to the CRC Committee on two occasions in respect of the Convention on the Rights of the Child. For the State's reports, see UN Doc CRC/C/11/Add 12 (17 June 1996) and UN Doc CRC/C/IRL/2 (9 December 2005) and for the CRC's concluding observations on those reports, see UN Doc CRC/C/15/Add 85 (4 February 1998) and UN Doc CRC/C/IRL/CO/2 (29 September 2006) respectively. Ireland has reported once in respect of OPAC: See UN Doc CRC/C/OPAC/IRL/1 (5 February 2007). The CRC Committee's concluding observations in respect of that report are contained in UN Doc CRC/C/OPAC/IRL/CO/1 (14 February 2008).

[155] OPAC, art 8(2) and OPSC, art 12(2). It may be noted, however, that since 2005, initial reports under OPAC are only considered at a regular session of the CRC Committee where the State Party is facing or has faced serious difficulties in implementing the provisions of the Protocol. Otherwise, States parties not experiencing such difficulties may be offered a 'technical review' by the Committee whereby the it considers all available information in writing only (without a dialogue with the State) and adopts its concluding observations on that basis: CRC Committee Dec No 8 (2005), para 3(a). Pursuant to art 44(1), initial reports must be submitted within two years of entry into force of the Convention and thereafter every five years.

[156] These 'treaty specific' guidelines are to be read in conjunction with the harmonized guidelines on reporting to international human rights treaty bodies, referred to in para. 4.08. See *Treaty Specific Guidelines regarding the form and content of periodic reports to be submitted by States parties under article 44(1)(b) of the Convention on the Rights of the* Child: U.N. Doc. CRC/C/58/Rev. 2 [hereinafter, CRC Committee Guidelines]. The most recent revised guidelines in regard to the OPSC and OPAC were adopted in September 2006 and 2007 respectively. See: http://www2.ohchr.org/english/bodies/crc/index.htm (last accessed May 2011).

Convention rights into clusters is intended to facilitate a more focused discussion during the Committee's actual consideration of the report. The Committee has requested States parties to the Convention to submit periodic reports that are concise and analytical and which focus on implementation of the Convention.[157] In exceptional cases, the CRC Committee will permit States to submit combined reports.[158]

[4.47] The CRC Committee convenes pre-sessional working groups to prepare for consideration of State reports for one week, immediately after a formal session, but prior to the session at which the reports will be considered. The working group consists of all members of the Committee, though it has (with the authorisation of the GA) met in two parallel sessions in order to speed up the processing of reports.[159] Article 54(a) of the Convention itself envisages a role for NGOs in the work of the CRC Committee and their work is particularly important to the work of the Committee at the pre-sessional stage.[160] Likewise, the CRC Committee has emphasised the important contribution of independent NHRIs in the promotion and protection of the rights of the child from an early stage.[161] The Committee encourages both NGOs (including national coalitions or committees of NGOs)[162] and NHRIs to submit reports, documentation or other information to it. Based on the written information submitted to it, the Committee will issue a written invitation to selected NGOs and to accredited NHRIs to participate in the pre-sessional working group of the Committee.[163] In this way, both types of organisation play a fundamental role in framing the list of issues to be transmitted to the State party at the end of the session.[164] The list of issues will include requests for specific information on implementation of the Convention, new measures adopted since the submission of the report and data and statistics and other information, if available.[165] States are

---

[157] The length of these reports should not exceed 120 regular size pages. See Decision No 4 (2002), para 2.1: http://www2.ohchr.org/english/bodies/crc/decisions.htm#4 (last accessed May 2011).

[158] CRC Committee Dec No 3 (2002): http://www2.ohchr.org/english/bodies/crc/decisions.htm#3 (last accessed May 2011).

[159] CRC Committee Recommendation No 6 (2003): http://www2.ohchr.org/english/bodies/crc/decisions.htm#6 (last accessed May 2011). See GA Res 63/244, UN Doc A/RES/63/244.

[160] See 'Guidelines for the participation of partners (NGOs and individual experts) in the pre-sessional working group of the Committee on the Rights of the Child' (CRC/C/90 Annex VIII).

[161] See CRC Committee General Comment No 2 (2002): CRC/GC/2002/2 (15 November 2002).

[162] Report on the Working Methods of the Human Rights Treaty Bodies (2010), para 118.

[163] See Overview of the Working Methods of the Committee on the Rights of the Child: http://www2.ohchr.org/english/bodies/crc/workingmethods.htm (last accessed May 2011), para VIII.

[164] The pre-sessional meeting is held in private. NGOs and NHRIs are also entitled to request a private meeting with the Committee.

[165] This 'three-part' structure for lists of issues was adopted by the CRC Committee in February 2010. Report on the Working Methods of the Human Rights Treaty Bodies (2010), para 45. The list of issues produced by the CRC Committee in regard to OPAC and OPSC is normally much more concise. See Report on the Working Methods of the Human Rights Treaty Bodies (2009), para 44.

encouraged to respond in writing to the list of issues in no more than 40 pages and within six weeks.[166]

[4.48] The CRC Committee will typically devote one full day (ie, two, three-hour meetings) to the consideration of each State report, although extra time may be allocated in exceptional circumstances.[167] Authorisation given by the General Assembly for consideration of reports by the Committee in parallel chambers in 2010 has meant that it has been able to consider 17 to 19 reports per session in 2010, including reports pursuant to the two Optional Protocols.[168] The constructive dialogue between the Committee and the State party in respect of the Convention follows the same pattern as that of the other reporting procedures, with the State introducing the report, followed by the posing of issues and questions by members of the Committee. The Committee will have appointed two members of the Committee to act as country rapporteurs for each State report and these individuals will lead the questioning with the State representatives. Reports are considered by clusters of articles, in accordance with the framework outlined earlier for the submission of State reports.[169] The concluding observations, in turn, follow a similar pattern to that of the other treaty bodies, although given the volume of obligations in the Convention, normally the Committee's observations are nearly twice as long as that of their counterparts.[170] These are made public on the last day of the session of the Committee at which the State's report has been considered.

[4.49] The CRC Committee does not have a formal follow-up procedure in regard to State reports. Rather, it expects and determinedly strives to ensure that concerns expressed by it in its concluding observations will be addressed by the State in a detailed manner in its next report.[171] The reason why a more formalised follow-up procedure has not been implemented is because of the huge burden of State reports which the Committee has to consider under the Convention and the two Protocols, and because it relies in part on the special role played by UNICEF in monitoring implementation of the Convention.[172] This special role is derived from art 45 of the Convention which allows for UNICEF and other specialised agencies to be represented at the consideration of the State reports, as well as allowing them to provide expert advice to the Committee on areas falling within the scope of their respective mandates. The Committee in turn may transmit, as it considers appropriate, to UNICEF and the other specialised agencies or

---

[166] Report on the Working Methods of the Human Rights Treaty Bodies (2010), para 48.
[167] See Report on the Working Methods of the Human Rights Treaty Bodies (2010), para 55. When the CRC Committee is due to consider reports under the CRC and the two Protocols in respect of a State, it will normally consider the reports over three, two-hour meetings.
[168] See GA Res 63/244 and Report on the Working Methods of the Human Rights Treaty Bodies (2010), para 53.
[169] See Report on the Working Methods of the Human Rights Treaty Bodies (2010), para 59.
[170] See Report on the Working Methods of the Human Rights Treaty Bodies (2010), para 71.
[171] Convention on the Rights of the Child, Overview of the Reporting Procedure (24 October 1994): UN Doc CRC/C/33, para 23.
[172] Report on the Working Methods of the Human Rights Treaty Bodies (2010), para 81.

competent bodies, any reports that contain a request or indicate a need for technical advice or assistance, along with the Committee's recommendations, if any, thereon.[173] The CRC Committee, it should also be noted, regularly interacts with relevant special procedures mandate holders, as well as with the independent experts appointed by the Secretary General to lead an in-depth study on the question of violence against children.[174]

[4.50] Likewise, the Committee's practice in regard to non-reporting States appears to be more flexible than that of the other treaty bodies. Despite a considerable backlog of reports, the Committee's practice is to issue reminder letters to defaulting States and to make informal contacts with them, either through the chairperson, or through UNICEF or OHCHR field presences. While the Committee does have a review procedure in place to deal with persistent non-reporting which again would theoretically involve the consideration of a non-reporting State's implementation of the Convention,[175] like CAT, it has never actually resorted to applying the review procedure in practice.[176]

United Nations Convention on the Elimination of All Forms of Discrimination Against Women

[4.51] A skeletal provision for State reporting under the Convention on the Elimination of All Forms of Discrimination Against Women (CEDAW) is provided for in art 18 thereof.[177] It provides that States parties to the Convention undertake to report to the 23-member Committee on the Elimination of All Forms of Discrimination Against Women (CEDAW Committee).[178] Initial reports must be submitted within one year of entry into force and periodic reports 'at least every four years' and further whenever the CEDAW Committee so requests.[179]

[4.52] The CEDAW provides that State reports may indicate factors and difficulties affecting the degree of fulfilment of obligations under the Convention.[180] With a reputation for continually striving to improve its working methods in relation to the

---

[173] Convention on the Rights of the Child, art 45(b).
[174] Overview of the Working Methods of the Committee on the Rights of the Child, http://www2.ohchr.org/english/bodies/crc/workingmethods.htm (last accessed May 2011).
[175] CRC Committee's Rules of Procedure, rule 71 and see UN Doc CRC/C/33, paras 29–32.
[176] Report on the Working Methods of the Human Rights Treaty Bodies (2010), para 87.
[177] On the CEDAW generally, see Ch 3, paras **3.64–3.72**. On the reporting procedure under art 18, see generally Bustelo, 'The Committee on the Elimination of Discrimination Against Women at the Crossroads' in Alston and Crawford (eds), *The Future of UN Human Rights Treaty Monitoring* (Cambridge University Press, 2000), 79, at pp 84–96; and Rehman, *International Human Rights Law* (2nd edn, Pearson, 2008), pp 537–541.
[178] For the composition and mandate of the CEDAW Committee, see Ch 3, paras **3.70–3.72**.
[179] Convention on the Elimination of All Forms of Discrimination Against Women, art 18(1). Ireland has reported to the Committee on two occasions to date. For the State reports, see UN Doc CEDAW/C/IRL/2-3 (22 August 1997) and UN Doc CEDAW/C/IRL/4-5 (10 June 2003). For the concluding observations on those reports, see UN Doc A/54/38/Rev1, Part 2 Chapter IV, paras 161–201 and UN Doc A/60/38, Part 2, Chapter IV, paras 359–405.
[180] Convention on the Elimination of All Forms of Discrimination Against Women, art 18(2).

reporting process,[181] the CEDAW Committee has issued a number of guidelines over the years to States with regard to the submission of initial and periodic reports. Like CERD, the CEDAW Committee has reviewed its treaty-specific guidelines, so as to complement the harmonised guidelines[182] adopted by the chairpersons of the treaty bodies in 2006. Accordingly, States parties to the Convention are encouraged to submit a common-core document prepared for the Committee in accordance with the harmonised guidelines, as well as a treaty-specific document containing information particular to the implementation of the Convention.[183] This practice should apply in the case of both initial and periodic reports. The treaty- specific document should include data and statistics disaggregated by sex which are relevant to the implementation of each article of the Convention and the general recommendations of the Committee. This requirement is necessary in order to assist the Committee in assessing the State's progress in implementing the Convention.[184] While initial reports should deal with every article in the Convention, periodic reports should focus on the period between the consideration of the State party's previous report and the presentation of the current one. The CEDAW Committee also follows the practice of many of the other treaty bodies in allowing States with overdue reports to combine all outstanding reports in a single document.[185]

[4.53] Article 20(1) of the Convention provides that the CEDAW Committee shall not normally meet for more than one two-week session *per* year to deal with reports submitted under art 18. However, the Committee has long been struggling with a massive backlog of State reports,[186] as a result of which the General Assembly has for many years authorised the Committee to hold extra sessions in order to cope with its workload. In 2007, the GA authorised CEDAW to hold three annual sessions, each of three weeks duration, with an additional one-week pre-sessional working group for each session. This arrangement has been effective on an interim basis since January 2010, pending the entry into force of an amendment to art 20(1).[187] In the meantime, the GA approved the Committee's request to hold a total of five sessions in 2008 and 2009 to manage its workload, with three of these sessions being conducted in parallel chambers of the Committee.[188] The CEDAW Committee normally considers an average of eight

---

[181] See generally, Bustelo, 'The CEDAW Committee at the Crossroads' in Alston and Crawford (eds), *The Future of UN Human Rights Treaty Monitoring* (CUP, 2000), p 79.

[182] See UN Doc HRI/GEN/2/Rev 6, ch 1. On the harmonised guidelines, see para **4.08**.

[183] Reporting Guidelines of the Committee on the Elimination of Discrimination Against Women: http://www2.ohchr.org/english/bodies/cedaw/docs/AnnexI.pdf (last accessed May 2011).

[184] See UN Doc HRI/GEN/2/Rev 6, Ch V; and Reporting Guidelines of the Committee on the Elimination of Discrimination Against Women: http://www2.ohchr.org/english/bodies/cedaw/docs/AnnexI.pdf (last accessed May 2011).

[185] CEDAW Committee Decision 23/II (30/06/2000) UN Doc A/55/38.

[186] Bustelo, 'The CEDAW Committee at the Crossroads' in Alston and Crawford (eds), *The Future of UN Human Rights Treaty Monitoring* (CUP, 2000), pp 84–93.

[187] See UN Doc GA Res A/RES/62/218, 12 February 2008.

[188] Report on the Working Methods of the Human Rights Treaty Bodies (2010), para 52.

reports *per* session when operating as a full committee and 13 when working in parallel working groups.[189]

[4.54] The CEDAW Committee convenes a pre-sessional working group immediately after each formal session of the Committee at which reports due to be considered in two sessions time are reviewed.[190] The pre-sessional working group may consist of up to 10 members of the Committee, including designated country rapporteurs for each State report where possible.[191] The country rapporteur prepares a draft list of issues for the benefit of the working group, which in turn draws up the final list of issues and questions to be transmitted to the State party. In relation to initial reports, the list of issues is drawn up on an article-by-article basis,[192] whereas lists of issues for periodic reports are normally arranged in clusters.[193] The list is transmitted to the State concerned within a week of the pre-sessional meeting, and States are encouraged to submit written replies to the Committee (of no more than 25 to 30 pages) within six weeks of transmission.[194]

[4.55] The constructive dialogue between the CEDAW Committee and reporting States follows a similar pattern to that of the other reporting procedures. Like the CRC Committee, the CEDAW Committee devotes two half-day meetings to its consideration of State reports, on the same day.[195] The Committee considers initial reports on an article-by-article basis, while periodic reports focus on clusters of articles.[196] Questions are posed by Committee members to State representatives on this basis. Where a State requests that consideration of its report be postponed, the Committee will agree to reschedule consideration to another session. However, if the State's representatives fail to turn up at the subsequent session, the Committee has decided that it may proceed with the examination of the report in the absence of representatives, though only as a matter of last resort.[197] In the case of persistent non-reporting, the CEDAW Committee has put in place a procedure to deal with recalcitrant States and is prepared to consider such a State's compliance with the Convention in the absence of a report.[198] Article 21(1) of the

---

[189] Report on the Working Methods of the Human Rights Treaty Bodies (2010), para 53.
[190] Report on the Working Methods of the Human Rights Treaty Bodies (2010), para 38.
[191] Report on the Working Methods of the Human Rights Treaty Bodies (2010), para 39.
[192] Except in regard to arts 1 and 2, 7 and 8, and 15 and 16 which are considered together: Report on the Working Methods of the Human Rights Treaty Bodies (2010), para 43.
[193] Report on the Working Methods of the Human Rights Treaty Bodies (2010), para 43.
[194] Report on the Working Methods of the Human Rights Treaty Bodies (2010), para 47.
[195] Report on the Working Methods of the Human Rights Treaty Bodies (2010), para 55.
[196] With the exception of arts 1 and 2, 7 and 8, and 15 and 16, which are considered as three clusters: Report on the Working Methods of the Human Rights Treaty Bodies (2010), para 59.
[197] See r 51(5) of the CEDAW Committee's rules of procedure: UN Doc HRI/GEN/3/Rev 3, p 93.
[198] In 2007, the CEDAW Committee decided to send reminder letters to States whose reports were 10 years overdue and to request States whose reports were more than 20 years overdue to submit all their overdue reports as combined reports by a fixed date. Failing receipt of the latter reports, the CEDAW Committee considered for the first time a report of a State in the absence of its report (but in the presence of a delegation) in 2009: Report on the Working Methods of the Human Rights Treaty Bodies (2010), para 87.

Convention empowers the Committee to make 'suggestions and general recommendations' based on its examination of the reports to the General Assembly. Since 1994, the CEDAW Committee has interpreted this provision as authorising it to issue 'concluding observations' at the end of each State's report, in a similar manner to the other treaty bodies.[199] These are sent to the State as soon as possible after the session at which the report was considered and are made public several days later in advance unedited versions.

[4.56] As regards input from independent sources into the reporting process, the CEDAW Committee invites representatives of NGOs to provide country-specific information or documentation on States parties whose reports are before it to its pre-sessional working group, either in writing and/or by way of oral statements.[200] In addition, the full Committee sets aside time at each session, usually at the beginning of the first and second weeks, to allow NGOs to provide oral information to the Committee.[201] NHRIs are also encouraged to submit information on a similar basis. In 2008, the Committee specifically acknowledged the role played by NHRIs in the reporting process, and committed itself to enhancing the visibility of such institutions through the allocation of time for their contributions at the pre-sessional working group meetings and at sessions of the Committee.[202] In January 2005, at its 33rd session, the Irish Human Rights Commission was the first NHRI to make an oral presentation in its capacity as a national human rights institution to CEDAW during the examination of the State's 4th and 5th combined periodic reports to the Committee.[203] Like CERD, the Committee now routinely adopts this practice in respect of NHRIs.

[4.57] Pursuant to art 22 of the Convention,[204] the CEDAW Committee also actively encourages participation by the specialised agencies and bodies of the UN in the reporting process. They are invited to provide country-specific information to the pre-sessional working group and to address it orally.[205] Representatives are also invited to

---

[199] The CEDAW Committee has sought to enhance the quality of its concluding observations, especially in regard to their specificity and headings: see Decision 41/11, UN Doc A/63/38, Part II.

[200] Rule 47 of the CEDAW Committee's Rules of Procedure.

[201] Ways and Means of Expediting the work of the CEDAW Committee: UN Doc CEDAW/C/2009/II/4, para 30 available at http://www2.ohchr.org/english/bodies/cedaw/docs/working_methods_CEDAW_en.pdf (last accessed May 2011).

[202] Statement by the Committee on the Elimination of Discrimination Against Women on its relationship with national human rights institutions: UN Doc E/CN6/2008/CRP1.

[203] Submission of the Irish Human Rights Commission to the UN Committee on the Elimination of Discrimination Against Women in respect of Ireland's Combined 4th and 5th Periodic Reports under the Convention on the Elimination of all Forms of Discrimination Against Women (2005), available at www.ihrc.ie.

[204] See art 22 of the Convention on the Elimination of All Forms of Discrimination Against Women.

[205] The CEDAW Committee has adopted guidelines for the submission of reports by the specialised agencies and other bodies of the UN: UN Doc A/61/38, Part 1, Annex II. As to their participation at the pre-sessional working groups, see Report on the Working Methods of the Human Rights Treaty Bodies (2010), para 98.

participate in a closed meeting with the Committee at the beginning of each of its sessions.[206] The Committee has also built up a good working relationship with the special rapporteur on violence against women and the special rapporteur on the right to health.[207]

[4.58] The CEDAW Committee has only recently introduced a follow-up procedure in respect of Concluding Observations in 2008. Its failure to do so sooner was apparently directly related to its lack of resources.[208] Under the new procedure, States will be requested in the concluding observations to provide follow-up information on the implementation of a limited number of the recommendations made in the observations to the Committee within two years.[209] In 2009, the Committee appointed a rapporteur on follow-up and an alternate.[210] The rapporteur's mandate includes the identification of a maximum of two recommendations for follow-up. The criteria for selecting the latter recommendations is on the basis that their lack of implementation constitutes '… a major obstacle to the implementation of the Convention and implementation was feasible during the suggested time-frame'.[211] The follow-up report is public and the follow-up rapporteur, in collaboration with the country rapporteur, assesses each follow-up report and reports to the plenary Committee at each session.[212]

[4.59] Finally, the CEDAW Committee has adopted a review procedure in respect of persistent non-reporting States.[213] In May 2007, the Committee sent reminder letters to States parties whose reports were more than 10 years overdue and requested States whose initial reports were more than 20 years overdue, to submit all overdue reports in a combined report.[214] Where such reports were not received, the Committee decided to proceed with their evaluation in the absence of a report. In January 2009, it considered

---

[206] Report on the Working Methods of the Human Rights Treaty Bodies (2010), para 98.
[207] Report on the Working Methods of the Human Rights Treaty Bodies (2010), para 103.
[208] Report of the Chairpersons of the Human Rights Treaty Bodies on their 16th Meeting: UN Doc A/59/254 (11 August 2004), Annex (report of the Third Inter-Committee Meeting of Human Rights Treaty Bodies), para 16. Report on the Working Methods of the Human Rights Treaty Bodies (2009), para 80.
[209] Report of the Chairpersons of the Human Rights Treaty Bodies on Their 16th Meeting: UN Doc A/59/254 (11 August 2004), Annex. Follow-up reports submitted by the States parties are published on the Committee's website: see http://www2.ohchr.org/english/bodies/cedaw/followup.htm (last accessed May 2011).
[210] Annual Report of the CEDAW Committee (2010): UN Doc A/65/38, para 24.
[211] Annual Report of the CEDAW Committee (2010): UN Doc A/65/38, para 25.
[212] The report of the follow-up rapporteur is in turn included in the CEDAW Committee's annual report to the General Assembly: Annual Report of CEDAW (2010): UN Doc A/65/38, para 25.
[213] See the CEDAW Committee's rules of procedure, r 49 and see Report on the Working Methods of the Human Rights Treaty Bodies (2010), para 87.
[214] Report on the Working Methods of the Human Rights Treaty Bodies (2010), para 87. Reminder letters were sent in 2009 to all States whose reports were more than five years overdue: Annual Report of CEDAW (2010), para 26.

the implementation of the Convention for the first time in the absence of a report, but in the presence of a delegation.[215]

International Convention on the Protection of Migrant Workers and Members of Their Families

[4.60] Given that the International Convention on the Protection of Migrant Workers and Members of their Families (ICRMW) only entered into force in 2003, the Committee on Migrant Workers (CMW)[216] is only just beginning to operate the reporting procedure.[217] The framework for that procedure, as set forth in arts 73 and 74, is undoubtedly the most detailed of all of the treaties so far examined. It provides that States parties to the Convention undertake to submit reports for the consideration of the CMW on the legislative, judicial, administrative and other measures that they have taken to give effect to the provisions of the Convention, within one year of entry into force and thereafter every five years and whenever the Committee so requests. One feature of particular note is that the Convention requires States to make their reports 'widely available to the public in their own countries'.[218]

[4.61] As regards submission of the reports, the CMW has adopted treaty-specific guidelines to complement the harmonised guidelines for the common core document.[219] Separate guidelines apply as regards the submission of initial and periodic reports.[220] Once the report has been submitted, the Committee will formally adopt a list of issues which is initially drawn up by two country rapporteurs.[221] The list of issues is drawn up in a closed meeting during plenary sessions of the Committee.[222] States are required to respond to the list of issues in writing.[223]

[4.62] The Convention does not prescribe the amount of formal sessions to be held by the Committee. Initially, it met twice a year for one-week sessions. However, following

---

[215] Report on the Working Methods of the Human Rights Treaty Bodies (2010), para 103.
[216] As to the ICRMW and the mandate and composition of the CMW, see ch 3, paras **3.92–3.101**.
[217] See generally Rehman, *International Human Rights Law* (2nd edn, Pearson, 2008), pp 698–701 and Diakité, 'A Brief Look at the International Convention on the Protection of the Rights of All Migrant Workers and Members of Their Families' in Alfredsson et al (eds), *International Human Rights Monitoring Mechanisms* (2nd edn, Martinus Nijhoff, 2009), p 117.
[218] Convention on the Protection of Migrant Workers and Members of their Families, art 73(4).
[219] On the harmonised guidelines, see para **4.08**.
[220] The guidelines for the treaty-specific part of the initial report, which were adopted in April 2005, request States to provide information on the framework in the State for the implementation of the Convention, followed by information on implementation for each substantive article. These may be arranged in clusters to reflect the distinction in the Convention between all migrant workers and those that are documented: UN Doc HRI/GEN/2/Rev2/Add1. The Committee's guidelines for periodic reports were adopted in May 2008: UN Doc CMW/C/2008/1.
[221] Report on the working Methods of the Human Rights Treaty Bodies (2010), para 42.
[222] Report on the working Methods of the Human Rights Treaty Bodies (2010), para 38.
[223] Report on the working Methods of the Human Rights Treaty Bodies (2010), para 47.

the approval of the General Assembly, it has been meeting since 2008 for one, two-week session in April, and one, one-week session in November.[224] Obviously, due to the fact that the Committee is new to its various tasks and is still developing its working methods, the Committee's turnover of reports is much less than that of the other treaty bodies. Since this new arrangement has come in to play, it has only managed to consider three to four reports in total over its two sessions.[225]

[4.63] The constructive dialogue between the Committee and State representatives is similar to that conducted by all of the other treaty bodies. The Convention specifically provides that the Committee shall examine the reports and 'transmit such comments as it may consider appropriate to the State party concerned'.[226] These comments have been styled as concluding observations by the Committee to conform to the practice of the other treaty bodies. The CMW makes its concluding comments public at the end of each session. Interestingly, the Convention specifies that States parties may submit observations to the Committee on any comment made by it in regard to their reports.[227]

[4.64] The Convention requires that the Secretary General of the UN transmit copies of all State reports to the director general of the International Labour Organisation (ILO) and information relevant to the reports.[228] This process is aimed at enabling that organisation to assist the Committee with the expertise which it has on matters being dealt with by the Convention. The Committee must consider in its deliberations such comments and materials as the ILO may provide.[229] The ILO must also be invited to participate in a consultative capacity in the meetings of the Committee.[230]

[4.65] Similarly, the Secretary General may, after consultation with the CMW, transmit to the specialised agencies and other inter-governmental organisations, copies of such parts of the reports as may fall within their competence.[231] The Committee may in turn invite those agencies and organisations 'and other concerned bodies' to submit, for its consideration, written information on such matters that fall within the scope of their activities.[232] All of these bodies are routinely informed of the States that are due to be considered at sessions of the Committee. Pursuant to the Convention, the Committee also invites representatives of the specialised agencies to meet with it during its sessions to discuss the situations in countries whose reports are under consideration.[233] The

---

[224] Report on the working Methods of the Human Rights Treaty Bodies (2010), para 52. In its annual report of 2009, the CMW again welcomed the authorisation by the General Assembly that enables it to hold two sessions per year. CMW Annual Report 2009: UN Doc A/64/48 at para 7.

[225] Report on the Working Methods of the Human Rights Treaty Bodies (2010), para 53.

[226] ICRMW, art 74(1).

[227] ICRMW, art 74(1).

[228] ICRMW, art 74(2). On the ILO generally, see Ch 1, para **1.20**.

[229] ICRMW, art 74(2).

[230] ICRMW, art 74(5).

[231] ICRMW, art 74(3).

[232] ICRMW, art 74(4).

[233] ICRMW, art 74(6).

CMW also interacts in particular with the special rapporteur on the human rights of migrants.[234]

[4.66] The CMW's attitude to NHRIs is a progressive one insofar as it regularly informs them of the States parties whose reports are due to be considered and invites them to submit written information.[235] NHRIs are also invited to attend both the private meeting at which the list of issues is considered and also the meeting at which there is formal consideration of the report. Since its fifth session in 2006, the Committee affords representatives of NHRIs who are present at the consideration of the State's report an opportunity to make an oral presentation in public regarding its views.[236] As regards NGOs, the Committee has interpreted the phrase 'other concerned bodies' in art 74(4) of the Convention to include NGOs.[237] They are thus invited to submit written information to the Committee on the State's report[238] and to brief it publicly during the session at which the report of the State concerned is to be considered.[239]

[4.67] Finally, in view of the fact that the reporting procedure under the Convention is still in its infancy, it is not surprising that the CMW has so far not adopted a formal 'follow-up mechanism' or a 'review procedure' for persistent non-reporting States. On the other hand, it is perhaps also no surprise to note that as early as 2005, the Committee had already expressed concern in regard to the 'many initial reports' which had not been received by it. It decided to send reminders to those States parties whose reports were overdue.[240] It would seem that there is no reason why the CMW should not move immediately to adopt a similar policy to that which has been adopted by the other treaty monitoring bodies in regard to persistently defaulting States, but no formal decision has as yet been taken on this issue. In 2009, the Committee decided that it would not include specific requests for follow-up in its concluding observations. Where follow-up reports are proffered voluntarily by States, the country rapporteurs should examine the follow-up information and report back to the Committee.[241]

Convention on the Rights of Persons with Disabilities

[4.68] As with the CMW, the Committee on the Rights of Persons with Disabilities (CRPD Committee) is only just beginning to operate the reporting procedure under arts

---

[234] Report on the Working Methods of the Human Rights Treaty Bodies (2010), para 103.
[235] Report on the Working Methods of the Human Rights Treaty Bodies (2010), para 107.
[236] Report on the Working Methods of the Human Rights Treaty Bodies (2009), para 103.
[237] Article 74(4) provides as follows: 'The Committee may invite the specialized agencies and organs of the United Nations, as well as intergovernmental organizations and *other concerned bodies* to submit, for consideration by the Committee, written information on such matters dealt with in the present Convention as fall within the scope of their activities' (emphasis added).
[238] See rule 28 of the CMW's rules of procedure: UN Doc HRI/GEN/3/Rev.1/Add 1.
[239] Report on the Working Methods of the Human Rights Treaty Bodies (2010), para 116.
[240] CMW Annual Report 2007, UN Doc A/62/48, para 18. See, more recently, the CMW's Annual Report (2010) which indicates a total of no less than 31 States whose initial reports were overdue since 2004: UN Doc A/65/48, Annex III.
[241] Annual Report of the CMW (2009), UN Doc A/64/48, paras 18–19.

35 and 36 of the Convention on the Rights of Persons with Disabilities (CRPD).[242] While the CRPD Committee may well finesse its working methods in respect of the procedure over time, the broad parameters of how it intends to operate the procedure are contained in its Rules of Procedure.[243]

[4.69] In line with the other treaty bodies, the CRPD Committee has adopted treaty-specific guidelines,[244] which take account of the harmonised guidelines on reporting under international human rights treaties.[245] Accordingly, each State party is required to submit a common core document, containing general information about the reporting State, the general framework for the protection and promotion of human rights, disaggregated according to sex, age, population and disabilities, as well as information on non-discrimination and equality and effective remedies in accordance with the harmonised guidelines.[246] The treaty-specific document should not repeat that information, but rather include specific information regarding the implementation, in law and practice, of arts 1 to 33 of the Convention.[247] The initial treaty-specific document and the common core document will constitute the State party's 'initial report' which falls due within two years of ratification of the Convention.[248] The initial treaty-specific document should thus set out, *inter alia*, a detailed analysis of the impact of legal norms on the factual situation of persons with disabilities, as well as the implementation and effect of remedies for violations of the Convention.[249] Subsequent treaty–specific documents, together with the common-core document, will constitute subsequent 'periodic reports' which fall due at least every four years and whenever the Committee requests.[250] The latter should not repeat information previously provided.[251] Subsequent treaty-specific documents should also be structured so as to follow the articles of the Convention and should contain three 'starting points':

---

[242] As to the Convention generally and the composition and mandate of the CRPD, see Ch 3, paras **3.102–3.115**. Tunisia and Spain only have thus far reported under art 35(1).

[243] Rules of procedure of the CRPD Committee: UN Doc CRPD/C/4/2 (13 August 2010).

[244] Guidelines on treaty-specific document to be submitted by States parties under Article 35, paragraph 1 of the Convention on the Rights of Persons with Disabilities, UN Doc CRPD/C/2/3: http://www.ohchr.org/Documents/HRBodies/CRPD/CRPD-C-2-3.pdf (last accessed May 2011).

[245] Guidelines on treaty-specific document to be submitted by States parties under Article 35, paragraph 1 of the Convention on the Rights of Persons with Disabilities, UN Doc CRPD/C/2/3 (hereinafter CRPD treaty-specific guidelines): http://www.ohchr.org/Documents/HRBodies/CRPD/CRPD-C-2-3.pdf (last accessed May 2011). On the harmonised guidelines, see para **4.08**.

[246] CRPD Committee's treaty-specific guidelines, para A.2.1.

[247] CRPD Committee's treaty-specific guidelines, para A.3.1 and see generally A.3.1. to A.3.5

[248] CRPD, art 35(1).

[249] CRPD Committee's treaty-specific guidelines, para A.4.2. Particular attention should be paid to vulnerable groups like women and children. See also paras A.4.3 to A.4.4.

[250] CRPD, art 35(2).

[251] CRPD, art 35(3).

'(a) Information on the implementation of the concluding observations (particularly 'concerns' and 'recommendations') from the previous report, as well as explanations for instances of non-implementation or difficulties encountered;

(b) An analytical and result-oriented examination of additional and other appropriate steps taken towards the implementation of the Convention; and

(c) Information on any remaining or emerging obstacles to the exercise and enjoyment by persons with disabilities of their human rights…as well as information on measures envisaged to overcome these obstacles'.[252]

[4.70] When preparing any of the above reports for the CRPD Committee, the State parties are invited to consider doing so '… in an open and transparent process' and to give due consideration to art 4(3) of the Convention which requires States parties to consult and actively involve persons with disabilities in the development and implementation of legislation, policies and decision-making processes which affect them.[253] States parties are also required to make their reports widely available to the public in their own countries and to facilitate access to the suggestions and recommendations made relating to the reports.[254]

[4.71] As regards the procedure by which the reports will be examined, the CRPD Committee is poised to follow the traditional approach of the other Committees whereby following the submission of the State's report, a 'list of issues' which the Committee intends to take up in the formal examination of the report will be drawn up and forwarded to the State party.[255] The Committee will notify the State party in writing as early as possible of the date, duration and place of the session at which such formal examination will take place and invite it to send a delegation to attend the meetings at which the report will be examined. State representatives will be expected to answer questions which may be put by the CRPD Committee and will be entitled to submit further information.[256] Provision is also made in the CRPD Committee's Rules of Procedure for input from the specialised agencies and other UN bodies,[257] intergovernmental organisations and regional integration organisations,[258] NHRIs[259] and NGOs,[260] each of whom may be invited to make oral or written statements to the Committee.

[4.72] Following the formal examination of the report, the CRPD Committee will issue concluding observations which shall contain suggestions and recommendations on the

---

[252] CRPD Committee's treaty-specific guidelines, para A.5.3 and see further paras A.5.4. to A.5.6.
[253] CRPD, art 35(4).
[254] CRPD, art 36(4).
[255] The Committee is entitled to elicit further information from the State by the terms of CRPD, art 36(1). See also CRPD Committee's Rules of Procedure, r 44.
[256] CRPD Committee's Rules of Procedure, r 41.
[257] CRPD Committee's Rules of Procedure, r 49.
[258] CRPD Committee's Rules of Procedure, r 50.
[259] CRPD Committee's Rules of Procedure, r 51.
[260] CRPD Committee's Rules of Procedure, r 52.

State's implementation of the Convention as appropriate.[261] The Committee may make other general recommendations based on information received by it pursuant to the reporting process and include these in its reports to the General Assembly.[262] Interestingly, the Convention itself contains an innovative provision in regard to the reporting process whereby the Committee may transmit to the specialised agencies and other competent bodies (including NGOs), reports from the States parties in order to address a request or an indication of a need for technical advice of assistance contained therein, along with the Committee's own observations and recommendations if any on same.[263] The Committee may in turn request information on the technical advice or assistance provided and the progress achieved.[264] The CRPD Committee's has not yet fashioned a 'follow-up' procedure, though it may be expected to follow the practice of most of the other Committees in this matter. Anticipating the problem of non-submission of reports, it has adopted a 'review procedure' in its Rules of Procedure whereby it may examine the implementation of the Convention in a State party which has fallen behind significantly in the submission of a report, based on reliable information available to the Committee.[265]

International Convention on the Protection of All Persons from Enforced Disappearance

[4.73] For the sake of completeness, it should be recalled that a mechanism for reporting is also a mandatory feature of implementation under the Convention on the Protection of All Persons from Enforced Disappearance (ICPED).[266] It is important to note, however, that this mechanism differs from its predecessors insofar as the requirement to report on an on-going or 'periodic' basis to the Committee on Enforced Disappearances (CED) is absent.[267] Rather, art 29(1) of the Convention requires the States parties to the Convention to submit a report to the Committee on Enforced Disappearances within two years after the entry into force of the Convention for each State party. The report shall be considered by the CED, which shall issue such 'comments, observations or recommendations as it may deem appropriate'.[268] The latter shall be communicated to the State party which may respond to them on its own initiative or at the request of the Committee.[269] Article 29(4) further provides that the CED may request the States parties to provide additional information on the implementation of the Convention.

---

[261] CRPD, art 36(1). CRPD Committee's Rules of Procedure, r 42.
[262] CRPD Committee's Rules of Procedure, r 46.
[263] CRPD, art 36(5). CRPD Committee's Rules of Procedure, r 45(1) and (2).
[264] CRPD Committee's Rules of Procedure, r 45(3).
[265] The operation of the review procedure is set forth in CRPD Committee's Rules of Procedure, r 40.
[266] As to the content of the ICPED, see generally Ch 3, paras **3.116–3.122**.
[267] As to the composition and functions of the Committee on Enforced Disappearances (CED), see above Ch 3, paras **3.119–3.122**.
[268] ICPED, art 29(3). Article 29(2) provides that each State's report shall be made available to all the States parties to the Convention.
[269] ICPED, art 29(3).

[4.74] The reporting procedure in art 29 is not yet operative. Given that the Convention itself only entered into force in December 2010, the first reports under art 29 will not fall due until December 2012. [270] Furthermore, since the CED itself has only recently been established, it will take some time before the barebones procedure provided for in art 29 will be fleshed out in rules of procedure. It is yet to be determined, for example, whether the procedure will involve a 'constructive dialogue' similar to that provided for in the traditional periodic reporting mechanisms described in the foregoing sections of this chapter. Furthermore, the manner and extent to which the CED will deploy its powers in requesting additional information from the States parties remains to be seen. It seems that the reason why the instrument eschews the more traditional reporting method stems from a realisation at the earliest stages of the drafting process that more innovative monitoring methods would be called for in order to combat this most egregious form of human rights abuse.[271] Moreover, at the third session of the Working Group which drafted the Convention, many participants apparently indicated that they did not favour a system of periodic reports because they considered it to be 'too unwieldy'.[272] The need for procedures that were more suited to the form of abuse in question is thus reflected in the inclusion of a range of monitoring procedures in the Convention, such as the 'urgent' action procedure in art 30, considered in Ch 14[273] as well as an on-site visiting procedure in art 33, considered further in Ch 5.[274]

ANALYSIS OF THE CURRENT PROCEDURES

[4.75] It is important to consider the positive elements of the reporting procedures and the initiatives taken by the treaty bodies in recent years to streamline and energise their work. The UN position has always been that reporting procedures should be viewed more like 'a carrot than a stick'. As Alston has succinctly summarised, the purpose of

---

[270] The instrument entered into force following the deposit of the twentieth instrument of ratification or accession, pursuant to the terms of ICPED, art 29(1). This means that reports from those twenty States will fall due in December 2012.

[271] The Independent Expert charged with the task of examining the existing international criminal and human rights framework for the protection of persons from enforced disappearances, Professor Manfred Nowak first made this point in his seminal report to the Commission on Human Rights: 'A future binding instrument on enforced disappearance should ... go beyond these traditional monitoring procedures and also include, for instance, special mechanisms for the tracing of disappeared persons, an inquiry procedure with visits to the territory of States parties and possibly also preventive visits to, or at least monitoring of, places of detention': *Report submitted by Mr Manfred Nowak, independent expert charged with examining the existing international criminal and human rights framework for the protection of persons from enforced or involuntary disappearances, pursuant to paragraph 11 of Commission resolution 2001/46*: UN Doc E/CN.4/2002/71, para. 101.

[272] *Report of the Intersessional Open-ended Working Group to elaborate a draft legally binding normative instrument for the protection of all persons from enforced disappearance*: UN Doc E/CN.4/2005/66 at para. 123.

[273] Ch 14, paras **14.02–14.05**.

[274] See Ch 5, paras **5.56–5.60**.

preparing a State report for any of the treaty bodies is supposed to be an opportunity for a State to:

'(a) Conduct a comprehensive review of the measures it has taken to harmonise national law and policy with the provisions set forth in the relevant treaty;

(b) Monitor progress in promoting the enjoyment of rights;

(c) Identify problems and shortcomings in its approach to the implementation of the treaty;

(d) Assess future needs and goals for more effective implementation;

(e) Plan and develop appropriate policies to achieve those goals'.[275]

In other words, reporting procedures are supposed to make States 'more conscious' of their obligations under the particular treaty in question;[276] they exist as tools for the national authorities in the first place to scrutinise progress in implementing the particular treaty in question. In addition to the primary focus on facilitating individual States, reporting also generates an informal process of 'benchmarking' in so far as it allows the treaty bodies to assess the standards being applied in various parts of the world by the States parties, which, in turn, facilitates the development and interpretation of those standards.[277] The role of the treaty bodies, as groups of experts, is to advise the State on its performance and not to cast itself in a judicial role. The efforts made by the treaty bodies in recent years to inveigle contracting States into taking the procedures more seriously have generated incremental results. These include the closer involvement of NGOs and NHRIs; the initiation by some of the treaty bodies, at least, of more structured follow-up mechanisms; and the streamlining of reporting procedures generally. The recent initiation of the 'list of issues prior to reporting' procedure by CAT and the CCPR is also aimed at generating more focused and timely reports, though it remains to be seen whether this innovation will exert even greater pressures on the already over-stretched treaty bodies, especially if strict timelines are not observed in its operation.

[4.76] Nonetheless, as Connors has noted, opinions on the value and effectiveness of reporting procedures range along a spectrum from those who consider the exercise to be no more than 'an empty diplomatic ritual' to those who consider them to be a 'valuable

---

[275] See Alston, 'The Purpose of Reporting' in *Manual on Human Rights Reporting* (United Nations, 1991) and see updated version in 1997 available at: http://www.ohchr.org/Documents/Publications/Manualhrren/pdf (last accessed May 2011). See also the seven objectives identified by the CESCR in its first General Comment, adopted during its third session in 1989: UN Doc HRI/GEN/1/Rev 7; and those identified by the OHCHR in the Concept Paper on the High Commissioner's Proposal for a Unified Standing Treaty Body: UN Doc HRI/MC/2006/2 (22 March 2006), para 8.

[276] This was one of the rationales advanced for inclusion of a reporting procedure in the ICCPR: See Annotations on the Text of the Draft International Covenants on Human Rights: UN Doc A/2929 (1 July 1955), Ch 7, para 163.

[277] Again, this was one of the reasons advanced for including a system of reporting in the ICCPR, para 163.

tool' for implementing the standards and rights established in treaties.[278] Any analysis of the effectiveness of the procedures depends entirely on one's starting point. For those who regard these mechanisms as a potential weapon in censuring a government on its human rights record, the results are inevitably disappointing. For those who consider them to be a useful method of encouraging implementation, the picture is much more positive, particularly in the light of recent reforms and indeed others projected for the future.

[4.77] Among the 'institutional pathologies'[279] that have been identified as bedevilling the system, the quality of information produced by States in their reports is undoubtedly high on the list.[280] Many States appear to ignore totally the guidelines which the treaty bodies have produced to assist them in preparing their reports. The quality of the reports can range from being inadequate to blatantly derisory.[281] Formal presentation of the report in the public sessions can often serve to reinforce the impression that the process

---

[278] Connors, 'An Analysis and Evaluation of the System of State Reporting' in Bayefsky (ed), *The UN Human Rights Treaty System in the 21st Century* (Kluwer Law International, 2000), 3 at p 4.

[279] Lamer, 'Enforcing International Human Rights Law: The Treaty System in the 21st Century' in Bayefsky (ed), *The UN Human Rights Treaty System in the 2st Century* (Kluwer Law International, 2000), pp 306–307.

[280] Connors, 'An Analysis and Evaluation of the System of State Reporting' in Bayefsky (ed), *The UN Human Rights Treaty System in the 21st Century* (Kluwer Law International, 2000), pp 8–11.

[281] Writing ten years after the procedure under the ICCPR was first initiated, Moskowitz observed that, 'Not only have governments been unwilling and unable to escape the bias of their own perspectives, but the information that they have been furnishing can hardly be said to provide an expanding vision of reality. In the first place, there are fixed national habits of thought that assign different values to the same fact or set of facts. Secondly, the separate facts do not add up to make a whole; if for no other reason than that they are rarely representative samples of the total situation they attempt to describe. The irrelevancies contained in the reports are only exceeded by their omissions...Ten years of periodic reports have not given us a settled vision of the world scene of human rights': Moskowitz, *The Politics of Human Rights* (Oceana Publications, 1968), p 94. Over 40 years later, it is clear that matters have not changed radically as regards a significant proportion of States. As Connors comments, 'Many reports are self-serving and non-critical, descriptive of the formal legal and policy framework, rather than reflective of a *de facto* implementation of treaty obligations in states parties and the difficulties confronting such implementation. Only a minority of reports suggest that States parties have taken the views of civil society into account in their preparation or that the state is working to integrate the reporting process into domestic policy-making and seeking to align domestic and international objectives through that process': Connors, 'An Analysis and Evaluation of the System of State Reporting' in Bayefsky (ed), *The UN Human Rights Treaty System in the 21st Century* (Kluwer Law International, 2000), p 10.

is not taken seriously by many governments, or is at best regarded as an obligatory, but essentially shallow, diplomatic exercise.[282]

[4.78] As against this, even with the best will in the world, the proliferation of reporting systems and attendant costs involved in fulfilling their monitoring obligations have posed serious difficulties for many States. Many States are obliged to report under several of the reporting systems described above. The current lack of coordination between the treaty bodies in timetabling and scheduling of reports can mean that some States have to report to a number of treaty bodies in the same year. It is hardly surprising that even the most compliant of States can fall behind in their reporting obligations. For many of the worst offenders, the problems of compliance may not necessarily be linked to political apathy as much as to basic financial or indeed structural incapacity to fulfil their obligations.[283] As participation by States in the treaty system progresses towards the holy grail of universal ratification, this has in turn had obvious knock-on effects on the output of the treaty bodies themselves.[284] Given the contracted nature of their meeting

---

[282] One of the most vocal critics of the operation of the reporting process, Professor Anne Bayefsky, has stated that the States parties themselves must take primary responsibility for the failures of the system: 'In large numbers, they fail to produce timely reports, do not engage in reform activities in the course of producing reports, author inadequate reports, send uninformed representatives to the examination of reports by the treaty bodies, fail to respond to questions during the examination of reports, fail to disseminate reports and the results of the examinations within the state, elect government employees rather than independent persons to treaty body membership, make reservations that are incompatible with the object and purpose of the treaties, fail to object to reservations and fail to challenge reservations by additional means'. Bayefsky, 'Making the Treaty Bodies Work' in Henkin and Hargrove (eds), *Human Rights: An Agenda for the Next Century Human Rights: An Agenda for the Next Century* (ASIL: Studies in Transnational Legal Policy, 1994), p 239.

[283] Alston's refutation of Bayefsky's analysis in this regard is compelling: 'Beyond Them and 'Us': Putting Treaty Body Reform into Perspective' in Alston and Crawford, *The Future of UN Human Rights Treaty Monitoring* (Cambridge University Press, 2000), p 501.

[284] Universal ratification of the treaties has been a consistent priority for the United Nations. See, for example, Part II, para 4 of the Vienna Declaration and Programme of Action in which participating States strongly recommended that '… a concerted effort be made to encourage and facilitate the ratification of and succession to international human rights treaties and protocols adopted with the framework of the United Nations system with the aim of universal acceptance'. The goal of universal ratification is premised on the belief that it is essential '…to strengthen and consolidate the universalist foundations of the United Nations human rights regime': Report of the Independent Expert on 'Effective Functioning of Bodies Established Pursuant to United Nations Human Rights Instruments', UN Doc E/CN 4/1997/74 (27 March 1997). On the other hand, it has been argued that the deliberate emphasis on ratification has in part caused the 'implementation crisis' facing the UN treaties on the basis that, 'For a great many states ratification has become an end in itself, a means to easy accolades for empty gestures…ratification by human rights adversaries is purchased at a price, namely, diminished obligations, lax supervision and few adverse consequences from non-compliance': International Law Association Report on the Treaty System, *Report on the UN Human Rights Treaties: Facing the Implementation Crisis* (Helsinki Conference, 1996), http://www.bayefsky.com/reform/ila.php/pfriendly/1 (last accessed May 2011).

times, most of the treaty bodies are hopelessly behind schedule in the consideration of reports already submitted by States. It is now an almost clichéd observation that the current system actually *relies* on defaulting states, since if all States were to report on time, the treaty bodies themselves would be in a situation of complete crisis overload.[285] The inclusion of mandatory reporting procedures in the two newly adopted Conventions on Disability and Enforced Disappearances means that the stage is clearly set for these difficulties to intensify rather than diminish.

[4.79] Another criticism is the obvious lack of publicity which the entire process seems to generate. In contrast to the media attention focused on the output of other human rights institutions, the work of the treaty bodies receives very little media attention, especially as regards the reporting process. Opsahl once commented that the Human Rights Committee could not expect '… to obtain much publicity for its work and even less for itself'.[286] Unfortunately, that prediction has remained true nearly two decades later, despite valiant efforts on the part of the Committee itself to pursue a media and public information strategy. The deficit in terms of public knowledge of the mechanisms is true *a fortiori* in respect of all of the other Committees. While most of the treaty bodies have made some effort to encourage publicity, their work has rarely captured the public's attention in the States parties, despite the fact that their concluding observations can often contain newsworthy information by any standards.[287]

[4.80] A related problem is the perceived lack of independence and impartiality of at least some members of the treaty bodies. There can be no doubt but that appointment procedures to human rights treaty bodies in many States lack transparency and accountability, and while appointment is supposed to be based on recognised expertise and competence, there are certainly situations in which diplomatic considerations have superseded the requisite qualifications.[288] Indeed, a considerable number of treaty body members are career diplomats, including current and former ambassadors and cabinet ministers.[289] This inevitably detracts from the potential *gravitas* and credibility of their

---

[285] Crawford, 'The UN Human Rights Treaty System: A System in Crisis?' in Alston and Crawford, *The Future of UN Human Rights Treaty Monitoring* (CUP, 2000), p 5.

[286] Opsahl, 'The Human Rights Committee' in Alston (ed), *The United Nations and Human Rights: A Critical Appraisal* (OUP, 1992), p 395.

[287] In a working paper adopted in 2009, the CCPR acknowledged that its work '… in promoting respect for human rights is little known outside a small circle of academic and government lawyers who specialize in human rights law and the international human rights NGO community': A Strategic Approach to Public Relations including Relations with the Media, UN Doc CCPR/C/94/3, para 5.

[288] Banton's observations in this regard are amusing. He notes that while formally speaking, members of the various treaty bodies are not State representatives, they are '… restrained by little more than the solemn declaration made after election that they will perform their duties 'honourably, faithfully, impartially and conscientiously'. Yet they cannot, for six weeks of the year, slough their national identities as snakes slough their skins': Banton, 'Decision-Taking in the Committee on the Elimination of Racial Discrimination' in Alston and Crawford (eds), *The Future of UN Human Rights Treaty Monitoring* (CUP, 2000), p 57.

[289] Connors, 'An Analysis and Evaluation of the System of State Reporting' in Bayefsky (ed), *The UN Human Rights Treaty System in the 21st Century* (Kluwer Law International, 2000), 12.

pronouncements, as compared with other judicial human rights bodies like the European Court of Human Rights.

[4.81] As regards their actual pronouncements on States' reports, the 'concluding observations' produced by the treaty bodies at the conclusion of the reporting process have also proved to be contentious. As O'Flaherty observes, these observations are probably the most significant output of the treaty bodies in so far as they provide an 'opportunity for delivery of an authoritative overview of the state of human rights in a country and for the delivery of forms of advice which can stimulate systemic improvements'.[290] In this regard, they also serve as a tangible means of holding States accountable for any deficiencies in complying with the terms of the various treaties. It is at the very least unfortunate, therefore, that the quality of concluding observations has been a consistent source of concern on the part of States and observers of the system for years. Writing in 1997, the UN independent expert on enhancing the long-term effectiveness of the United Nations human rights treaty system, Philip Alston, noted that there was '…considerable room for improvement in the quality of concluding observations, especially in terms of their clarity, degree of detail, level of accuracy and specificity'.[291] Another problem frequently noted in regard to concluding observations is that of divergent interpretations being given by different treaty bodies to related provisions and the insufficiency of coordination and cross-referencing in that regard.[292] Flaws in the quality of concluding observations are inevitably linked to the pressures of the system generally and there can be little doubt that efforts have been made in recent years by the treaty bodies to improve their individual and collective performances in this regard.[293] Nonetheless, inaccuracy and inconsistency in such an important output of the process detracts from the credibility and even legitimacy of the process. Indeed, in

---

[290] O'Flaherty, 'The Concluding Observations of United Nations Human Rights Treaty Bodies' (2006) 6 HRL Rev 27.

[291] Effective Functioning of Bodies Established Pursuant to United Nations Human Rights Instruments: UN Doc E/CN4/1997/74 (27 March 1997), para 109. See further Ch 16, para **16.02–16.04**. See also the concerns expressed by O'Flaherty, 'The Concluding Observations of United Nations Human Rights Treaty Bodies' (2006) 6 Hum Rts L Rev 27; and Bayesfsky, *The United Nations Human Rights treaty System: Universality at the Crossroads* (Transnational, 2001), pp 61–66.

[292] See Tistounet, 'The Problem of Overlapping Among Treaty Bodies' in Alston and Crawford, *The Future of UN Human Rights Treaty Monitoring* (Cambridge University Press, 2000), p 389 *et seq*. Quite apart from the deficiencies in coordination between themselves, another critique of treaty bodies is that they are too aloof from the rest of the UN system: O'Flaherty and O'Brien, 'Reform of the UN Human Rights Treaty Monitoring Bodies: A Critique on the High Commissioner's Proposal for a Unified Standing Treaty Body' (2007) HRLR 141, p 143; and Clapham, who describes the treaty bodies as operating in 'splendid isolation' from the rest of the UN system: 'UN Human Rights Reporting Procedures: An NGO Perspective' in Alston and Crawford, *The Future of UN Human Rights Treaty Monitoring* (CUP, 2000), p 175.

[293] See Ch 16, para **16.08**.

situations where States feel unjustly criticised, it may possibly play a factor in their unwillingness to undergo further scrutiny.[294]

[4.82] As recently as 2006, the opinion has been voiced that 'a major weakness of the current system is the absence of effective, comprehensive follow-up mechanisms to ensure that the system has a sustained and systematic impact on the enjoyment of human rights at the national level'.[295] It is difficult to refute this criticism, even though a number of the treaty bodies have made concerted efforts to improve their follow-up procedures. These mechanisms are still inherently weak, being limited in general to the appointment of a special rapporteur to monitor and liaise with States as regards their implementation of the Committees' concluding observations. Where States simply fail to respond, the most extreme sanction available to the Committees is to record this lack of cooperation in their annual reports. Certainly, more imaginative and higher-profile methods might yield firmer results (such as regular visits by Committee members to the particular States to discuss follow-up and implementation); however, the Committees are far too over-extended and under-resourced to even contemplate such strategies. These factors make it all the more imperative for the Committees to focus in each reporting cycle on the extent to which their previous concluding observations have been implemented in a particular State.[296]

[4.83] Finally, an overarching problem affecting the entire functioning of the reporting process is the issue of resources.[297] The treaty bodies are increasingly under-financed and under-resourced. Lack of money and staff necessarily leads to inefficiencies. This

---

[294] Beate Schopp-Schilling, 'Treaty Body Reform: the Case of the Committee on the Elimination of Discrimination Against Women' (2007) 7 HRL Rev 201, p 203.

[295] Concept Paper on the High Commissioner's Proposal for a Unified Standing Treaty Body (22 March 2006): UN Doc HRI/MC/2006/2, para 26.

[296] See O'Flaherty, 'The Concluding Observations of United Nations Human Rights Treaty Bodies' (2006) 6 HRL Rev 27, p 40. In relation to the evaluation made by the Human Rights Committee of Ireland's performance under the ICCPR over the course of two reporting cycles, Deirdre Fotrell makes the cutting criticism that the fact that many of the concerns raised by the Committee in its first set of concluding observations are replicated in the second set not only indicates that very little attention was paid by the State to the Committee's initial observations, but also, and perhaps more importantly, that the Committee itself must be rebuked for not drawing particular attention to the high degree of overlap between the two sets of observations: 'Reporting to the UN Human Rights Committee-A Ruse by Any Other Name? Lessons For International Human Rights Supervision From Recent Irish Experiences' (2001) 4 ILT 61.

[297] The work of the treaty bodies is funded from resources made available to the OHCHR from the UN regular budget as well as from voluntary contributions which are received from the member States. The latter may be ear-marked or not earmarked for particular purposes. The OHCHR has persistently highlighted the paucity of the UN overall budget that is dedicated to human rights (most recently estimated at 2.8% of the overall budget). It has also reported a noticeable decline in voluntary contributions to its overall funding needs in 2010: http://www.ohchr.org/EN/ABOUTUS/Pages/FundingBudget.aspx [last accessed May 2011]. (contd.../)

issue has been identified almost from the outset of the work of the various treaty bodies and it is a problem that has gradually intensified rather than diminished.[298] Injection of more resources into the reporting procedures would undoubtedly help to improve the individual shortcomings identified above; however, there is little prospect of States ever showing the collective political will necessary to ensure that such further resources are forthcoming.[299]

[4.84] These various deficiencies have led Thynne to draw the nuclear conclusion that the current practice of the treaty bodies may in fact be threatening the rule of law and leading to fragmentation of the international human rights law system.[300] It is little wonder, therefore, in such an atmosphere of scepticism, that attention has turned in recent years to a radical reform of the treaty body system, with potentially far-reaching implications, in particular, for periodic reporting procedures. These reform proposals are considered in detail in Ch 16.

---

[297] (\...contd) In its most recent annual report, the OHCHR noted that '... achieving maximum harmonization of the treaty body system and streamlining treaty body working methods may further rationalize the use of resources'. Further, in the view of the OHCHR, the issue of resources '... needs to be addressed in the context of the regular budget, especially taking into account the self-expending nature of the treaty body system, with the development of new instruments, increased ratifications and reporting, new follow-up procedures and increased input from other stakeholders': OHCHR 2009 Report: Activities and Results (http://www.ohchr.org/Documents/Publications/I_OHCHR_Rep_2009_complete_final.pdf (last accessed May 2011) at p. 40.

[298] See generally, Evatt, 'Ensuring Effective Supervisory Procedures: The Need for Resources' in Alston and Crawford, *The Future of UN Human Rights Treaty Monitoring* (CUP, 2000), 461. The provision of greatly enhanced budgetary resources was recommended as a necessary *quid pro quo* for improving the effectiveness of the treaty bodies by Philip Alston, in his capacity as the special independent expert appointed by the UN Secretary General to examine functioning of the treaty monitoring bodies. See Ch 16, paras **16.02–16.04** and, in particular, Effective Functioning of Bodies Established Pursuant to United Nations Human Rights Instruments: UN Doc E/CN4/1997/74 (27 March 1997), para 120.

[299] Evatt, 'The Future of the Human Rights Treaty System: Forging Recommendations' in Bayefsky (ed), *The UN Human Rights Treaty System in the 21st Century* (Kluwer Law International, 2000), p 289.

[300] 'The treaty bodies should uphold the basic principles of the rule of law which they enforce. By contrast, the treaty bodies are failing to sufficiently monitor performance through overloaded schedules and the delays, inefficiencies and ineffectiveness mean the rule of law is lacking ... The lack of consistency in practice between the committees is the major concern with the treaty body system, leading to duplication of comments and interpretations of the law by Committees. This inconsistency also could mean greater fragmentation of human rights laws, with some obligations that are the same under each treaty applied in different ways depending on the focus of the Committee, creating even more difficulty for states to perform their human rights obligations': Thynne, 'Reform of the United Nations Human Rights Institutions: Current Developments – Enhancing the Rule of Law in International Human Rights Treaty Bodies' [2007] IHLRes 9 (28 June 2007), http://222.worldii.org/int/journals/IHLRes/2007/9.html at 3.

Chapter 5

Inquiry Procedures

INTRODUCTION

[5.01] One of the many difficulties associated with the mandatory periodic reporting procedure discussed in the previous chapter is its complete dependency on State participation. The success of the procedure fundamentally depends on States producing adequate and timely reports, engaging with the relevant treaty bodies in constructive dialogue and implementing their concluding observations. Further along the spectrum of United Nations treaty-based human rights procedures, however, there exist mechanisms which do not rely, at least for their initiation, on the contribution of the State. Rather, they are 'investigative' mechanisms by nature, involving as they do an international treaty body taking the lead in investigating the actual situation on the ground in a given State as regards particular human rights issues. These mechanisms can be divided into two varieties. First, 'inquiry procedures' which provide for the possibility of a treaty body responding to reliable information on systematic abuses in a particular country by conducting a dedicated inquiry into such allegations. An inquiry will often involve an on-site inspection of the territory in question, following which the treaty body will issue conclusions and recommendations which will usually reach the public domain in varying levels of detail. The second type of investigative mechanism developed in more recent years is *preventive* in nature. Preventive mechanisms may be distinguished from inquiry procedures in that they do not depend for their initiation on an allegation of systematic rights abuse. Rather, under the preventive model, international and, indeed, national bodies may be designated to pro-actively monitor the implementation of the obligations in the treaty generally, including by means of on-site inspections in the territories of the States parties. As we shall see, the genesis of *inquiry* procedures, as well as *preventive* mechanisms derives from the realm of torture prevention. The current chapter focuses on inquiry procedures while Chapter Six examines the preventive mechanisms.

United Nations Convention against Torture and Other Forms of Cruel, Inhuman and Degrading Treatment or Punishment 1984

[5.02] The original draft for the UN Torture Convention (UNCAT),[1] proposed by the Swedish government in 1978,[2] contained a ground-breaking proposal that the instrument should include an inquiry procedure. Specifically, the proposal suggested that if the

---

[1] As to the provisions of UNCAT generally and the mandate of the Committee Against Torture (CAT) which monitors its implementation, see Ch 3, paras **3.73**–**3.80**.

[2] The Commission on Human Rights was formally requested to draft the Convention by the General Assembly in December 1977: GA Res 32/62 of 8 December 1977. (contd.../)

supervisory body[3] charged with the task of monitoring compliance with the Convention received information that torture was being systematically practised in a certain State party, it could proceed to designate one or more of its members to carry out an inquiry and to report to the Committee urgently. Such an inquiry could include a visit to the State concerned, provided that the government of that State consented. This proposal was entirely unique insofar as treaties were concerned. An inquiry procedure had not, for example, even been mooted for either the ICCPR or the ICESCR, nor for the International Convention on the Elimination of All Forms of Racial Discrimination. However, the United Nations had initiated other forms of inquiry procedures through the auspices of the former Commission on Human Rights[4] and the International Labour Organization,[5] and the genesis of art 20 in UNCAT can be traced to these earlier precedents.[6] For those States which championed an inquiry procedure from the outset, such a power was considered to be 'a minimal step forward'[7] and one that was justified by the particular context of torture.[8]

[5.03] The adoption of an inquiry procedure proved to be the most contentious issue in the negotiations on the draft text. Taking place in the context of a Cold War that was still

---

[2] (\...contd) The Commission immediately entrusted the task to an informal, inter-session working group of its members: CHR Res 18 (XXXIV) of 7 March 1978. At that stage, both the International Association of Penal Law (IAPL) and the Swedish government had already prepared draft texts for a Convention. The working group apparently used the Swedish draft as the basis for its deliberations: See Nowak and McArthur, *The United Nations Convention Against Torture: A Commentary* (OUP, 2008), pp 3–4. The drafting history of the inquiry procedure in the Convention is thoroughly documented in that text: see pp 662–673. See also Ingelse, *The UN Committee Against Torture: An Assessment* (Kluwer Law, 2001), p 185; and Burgers and Danelius, *The United Nations Convention Against Torture and Other Cruel, Inhuman or Degrading Treatment or Punishment* (Martinus Nijhoff, 1988), pp 5–113.

[3] The Swedish draft itself proposed that the Human Rights Committee which monitors implementation of the ICCPR should be charged with the task. This suggestion was later overruled by the working group in favour of the establishment of the Committee Against Torture (CAT).

[4] ECOSOC Resolution 1503 allowed the Commission to examine privately complaints which appeared to reveal 'a consistent pattern of gross and reliably attested violations of human rights'. See Ch 2, paras **2.16–2.18**.

[5] Articles 26 to 34 of the ILO Constitution provides for a procedure of investigation which can be triggered where a complaint is filed against a member State for not complying with an ILO convention that it has ratified: http://www.ilo.org/global/standards/applying-and-promoting-international-labour-standards/complaints/lang--en/index.htm (last accessed, May 2011).

[6] Ingelse, *The UN Committee Against Torture: An Assessment* (Kluwer Law, 2001), p 157.

[7] Statement of Switzerland, Question of the Human Rights of All Persons Subjected to Any Form of Detention or Imprisonment, In Particular: Torture or Other Cruel, Inhuman or Degrading Treatment or Punishment, Commission on Human Rights, 35th Session, 19 December 1978: UN Doc E/CN4/1314, para 108. Indeed, the Swiss government took the view that the procedure should be strengthened by making it possible for an inquiry to include a visit to the State in question *unless* the State in question objected.

[8] Report of the Working Group on a Draft Convention against Torture and Other Cruel, Inhuman or Degrading Treatment or Punishment: UN Doc E/CN4/1982/L40, para 74.

firmly being waged, positions between East and West soon became polarised along predictable lines with the USSR and its allies arguing that the proposed procedure was unnecessary and should at best be optional.[9] Most of the other delegations considered the procedure to be essential to the effective implementation of the Convention and, hence, were strongly in favour of its proposed mandatory character.[10] As always, a political compromise was ultimately reached whereby the procedure was incorporated into the Convention, with the possibility of allowing countries to 'opt-out' of its application at the time of ratification or accession.[11] That the former Soviet countries were by no means alone in their objection to the inquiry procedure is amply evidenced by the fact that some 21 States did in fact make such reservations at the time of ratification or accession to the treaty.[12] However, with the melt-down of the Cold War, many of these States went on to withdraw their reservations subsequently.[13] Some countries have, however, maintained them, most notably Poland, China, Indonesia, Israel, Saudi Arabia and Syria.[14]

Article 20: The inquiry procedure

[5.04] Article 20 of the Convention sets forth in broad strokes the inquiry procedure, as well as the mandate of the Committee against Torture (CAT) in respect of it. Rules 75–90 of the Committee's Rules of Procedure fill in the details as regards its practical operation.[15] The Committee has so far completed inquiries on seven different occasions

---

[9] This position was supported by the German Democratic Republic, while the Ukrainian Soviet Socialist Republic proposed a compromise whereby the inquiry procedure would only be binding on States if they expressly accepted it at the time of ratification or accession: Report of the Working Group on a Draft Convention against Torture and Other Cruel, Inhuman or Degrading Treatment or Punishment: Commission on Human Rights, 40th session, 9 March 1984: UN Doc E/CN4/1984/72, para 52.

[10] Report of the Working Group on a Draft Convention against Torture and Other Cruel, Inhuman or Degrading Treatment or Punishment, para 34.

[11] See UNCAT, art 28. The proposal for an opt-out clause was suggested by the Byelorussian Soviet Socialist Republic during the negotiations on the draft text in the General Assembly: UN Doc A/39/708, para 8. Nowak and McArthur comment that while the proposal presented '... a victory for States seeking a form of optionality, it nevertheless raised the political cost of opting out by requiring a State party to reserve explicitly out of the procedure, unlike previous proposals, which would have allowed States to ratify the Convention fully without acceding to the inquiry competence': Nowak and McArthur, *The United Nations Convention Against Torture: A Commentary* (OUP, 2008), p 672.

[12] See the list of reservations made to the Torture Convention on the CAT website: http://treaties.un.org/Pages/ViewDetails.aspx?src=TREATY&mtdsg_no=IV-9&chapter=4&lang=en (last accessed May 2011).

[13] These countries include all the former Eastern bloc States (with the exception of Poland), as well as Chile, Guatemala, Morocco, Zambia and Bahrain.

[14] To these may be added Equatorial Guinea, Kuwait and Mauritania.

[15] CAT Rules of Procedure, UN Doc CAT/C/3/Rev 5 (21 February 2011).

in respect of Turkey (1990),[16] Egypt (1991),[17] Peru (1995),[18] Mexico (1998),[19] Sri Lanka (1999),[20] Serbia and Montenegro (2000),[21] and Brazil (2003).[22] A further compromise to the operation of the inquiry procedure is that all proceedings of the CAT in respect of it are to be conducted confidentially, until the final stage, when the Committee may, after consultation with the State party concerned, decide to include a summary account of the inquiry in its annual report.[23] These latter reports do assist in providing some further insight into the application of the procedure generally.

As Nowak and McArthur note, the procedure can be divided into four distinct stages[24] which are outlined here broadly as follows: (1) information gathering; (2) evaluation and decision; (3) conduct of the inquiry; and (4) conclusion and report.

Information gathering

[5.05] An inquiry under art 20 may only be initiated in circumstances where the Committee receives 'reliable information which appears to it to contain well-founded indications that torture is being systematically practised in the territory of a State party'.[25] The normal conduit for this information is the Secretary General who is obliged under the Committee's Rules of Procedure to bring to its attention information which is, or appears to be, submitted for the Committee's consideration under art 20(1).[26] Usually, information concerning the need for an inquiry will be sent to the Committee by a

---

[16] CAT Summary Account of Inquiry on Turkey, UN Doc A/49/44 (1994), Section V, paras 172–177 and UN Doc A/48/44/Add 1.
[17] CAT Summary Account of Inquiry on Egypt, UN Doc A/51/44 (1996), Section V, paras 180–222.
[18] CAT Summary Account of Inquiry on Peru, UN Doc A/56/44 (2001), Section V, paras 144–193.
[19] CAT Summary Account of Inquiry on Mexico, UN Doc A/58/44, Section V, paras 147–153 and see CAT Art 20 Report on Mexico, UN Doc CAT/C/75.
[20] CAT Summary Account of Inquiry on Sri Lanka, UN Doc A/57/44 (2002), paras 123–195.
[21] CAT Summary Account of Inquiry on Serbia and Montenegro, UN Doc A/59/44, paras 156–240.
[22] CAT Summary Account of Inquiry on Brazil, UN Doc A/63/44 (2008), paras 64–72 and see CAT Art 20 Report on Brazil UN Doc CAT/C/39/2. A recent statement by the chairperson of CAT indicates that a number of other countries are currently being considered under the art 20 procedure: Statement of Mr Claudio Grossman to the 64th Session of the General Assembly (20 October 2009), http://www.wcl.american.edu/dean/documents/20091015_UN_GeneralAssembly.pdf?rd=1 (last accessed May 2011). However, because of the confidential nature of the process, it is not possible to know the identity of those countries.
[23] UNCAT, art 20(5), and CAT Rules of Procedure, r 90(1).
[24] Nowak and Mc Arthur, *United Nations Convention Against Torture: A Commentary* (OUP, 2008), p. 674.
[25] UNCAT, art 20(1).
[26] Rules of Procedure, r 75(1). The Secretary General is obliged further to maintain a permanent register of such information and shall make it available to any committee member on request (r 76). Furthermore, the Committee is not to receive such information if the State in question has opted out of the procedure in accordance with art 28(1) of the Convention (r 75(2)).

local[27] and[28] / or international non-governmental organisation,[29] or even by NGOs in another country to which alleged victims may have fled.[30] Other possible sources of information could include a National Human Rights Institution (NHRI), though as far as is known, this has not happened yet. Likewise, there is nothing in the Convention which forbids the Committee from acting on its own initiative in regard to an inquiry, by, for example, basing a decision to undertake an art 20 inquiry on information gleaned from a State party itself in the course of the art 19 reporting exercise. Likewise, it is entirely possible that information concerning a systematic practice of torture may come to light through the vehicle of an individual complaint, submitted to the Committee via the art 22 individual complaint mechanism.[31]

Evaluation and decision

[5.06] Having obtained or gathered the necessary information, the Committee's next task is to decide whether the information concerned is 'reliable' and whether it contains 'well-founded' indications that torture is being systematically practised in the State in question such as to justify the initiation of an inquiry.[32] As regards the meaning of 'reliable' and 'well-founded', the Convention does not define these terms and the Committee does not specifically elaborate in any of its reports the factors it takes into account in considering whether information is reliable and well-founded for the purposes of *initiating* an inquiry. Since its discussions concerning the question of whether to embark on an inquiry are confidential,[33] the level of scrutiny applied to the information submitted is open to speculation. In many respects, the question of whether information is reliable depends on its likely veracity and the reputation of its source. To

---

[27] The inquiry in respect of Mexico was initiated following information submitted by an NGO based in Mexico City (the Human Rights Centre Miguel Agustin Pro-Juarez (PRODH)); in the case of Serbia and Montenegro, following information received from the Humanitarian Law Center (HLC), an NGO based in Belgrade.

[28] The inquiry into Peru was initiated on the basis of information received from Human Rights Watch and the Coordinadora Nacional de Derechos Humanos, a Peruvian non-governmental body comprising some 60 NGOs. The inquiry into Brazil began following information received from two NGOs: World Organisation against Torture and Action by Christians Against Torture (ACAT–Brazil).

[29] The inquiries into the situation in Turkey and Egypt were initiated following information submitted by Amnesty International. In the case of Egypt, that initial information was followed-up by reports from the special rapporteur on torture, the Egyptian Organization for Human Rights and the World Organization Against Torture.

[30] The inquiry into Sri Lanka was initiated following information received from five NGOs based in London, namely, the British Refugee Council, the Medical Foundation for the Care of Victims of Torture, the Refugee Legal Centre, the Immigration Law Practitioners Association and the Refugee Legal Group.

[31] The individual complaint procedure under Article 22 of the UNCAT is examined in Ch 9.

[32] UNCAT, art 20(1), Rule 81(2) provides that the Committee shall determine whether it appears to it that the information received contains well-founded indications that torture, as defined in art 1 of the Convention, is being systematically practised in the territory of the State party concerned: CAT Rules of Procedure.

[33] UNCAT, art 20(5). See also r 78 of the Rules of Procedure.

this extent, it is clear that the Committee will seek to test, if necessary, the probity of information submitted by seeking corroboration in accordance with rule 81(1) of its Rules of Procedure.[34]

[5.07] Some indication of the Committee's understanding of reliability and well-foundedness can be gleaned from its summary report on Egypt.[35] In that instance, information was initially submitted to the Committee by Amnesty International (AI) pursuant to art 20.[36] Drawing on its rules of procedure, the Committee decided to invite AI to submit additional relevant information substantiating the facts of the situation, including statistics.[37] When the Committee next came together to consider the situation, it had before it the additional information submitted by AI, as well as information submitted by other non-governmental organisations, the reports of the special rapporteur on torture, as well as preliminary observations made by the government of Egypt on the initial information submitted by AI.[38] The Committee was forced to *conclude* its inquiry without being able to verify the information by means of an on-site investigation because permission for such an investigation was not given by the Egyptian government.[39] It decided nonetheless that the information submitted was 'well-founded' on the basis of the existence of a great number of allegations from different sources which largely coincided and described in the same way '...the methods of torture, the places where torture is practised and the authorities who practice it'.[40] In addition, the Committee noted that the sources in question had proved to be reliable in connection with other activities of the Committee.[41] It must be remembered that this evaluation was being made at a different stage of the art 20 inquiry process, ie, at a point when the Committee was actually deciding whether a systematic practice of torture had taken place when presumably a higher standard of proof arises. Nonetheless, the conclusions adopted are helpful indicators that consistency as between accounts given by particular sources, plus a reliable track-record on the part of the source(s) in question would likely rate highly for the Committee in its assessment of reliability and well-foundedness, even at the initiation stage.[42]

[5.08] Likewise, it is not possible to know exactly what standard is applied by the Committee at this stage in interpreting whether the information received indicates that torture is being 'systematically practised'. Again, as we shall see, the Committee has clearly articulated the criteria which it applies in deciding whether torture has been

---

[34] Rule 81(1) provides that the CAT may ascertain, through the Secretary General, the reliability of the information and/or the sources of such information brought to its attention under art 20 or obtain additional relevant information substantiating the facts of the situation.
[35] CAT Summary Account of Inquiry on Egypt, UN Doc A/51/44, paras 180–222.
[36] CAT Summary Account of Inquiry on Egypt, UN Doc A/51/44, para 182.
[37] CAT Summary Account of Inquiry on Egypt, UN Doc A/51/44, para 182.
[38] CAT Summary Account of Inquiry on Egypt, UN Doc A/51/44, para 183.
[39] CAT Summary Account of Inquiry on Egypt, UN Doc A/51/44, para 188–195.
[40] CAT Summary Account of Inquiry on Egypt, UN Doc A/51/44, para 219.
[41] CAT Summary Account of Inquiry on Egypt, UN Doc A/51/44, para 219.
[42] It is possible that the Committee does not apply anything close to such an exacting standard at the initiation stage.

systematically practised in a particular State at the conclusion of the inquiry process.[43] At this stage of the process, it is likely that the Committee focuses on whether the information received is well-founded and reliable, and concerns practices that appear to be widespread, leaving the substantive assessment as to whether the practices in question are 'systematic' to a later stage of the proceedings.

[5.09] If the Committee does take the view that the information in question appears to be reliable and well-founded, it shall then invite the State concerned, through the Secretary General, to cooperate in its examination of the information and to submit observations with regard to that information.[44] The Committee shall indicate the time limit for the submission of those observations 'with a view to avoiding undue delay in its proceedings'.[45] Typically, the Committee has given the State three to four months to comply with this request and States have generally been cooperative in this respect.[46] In reviewing all of the information received, the Committee is bound to take into account any observations made to it by the State concerned, as well as any other relevant information.[47] It may again seek additional information from the State, governmental or non-governmental organisations, individuals, or answers to questions relating to the information under examination.[48] The Committee has a wide discretion to decide the form and manner by which such additional information may be obtained.[49] If the Committee decides, on the basis of the information received, that an inquiry is warranted, it will proceed to designate one or more of its members to conduct the inquiry and to report to it within a specified time limit.[50]

---

[43] See para **5.14** below.
[44] UNCAT, art 20(1) and CAT Rules of Procedure, r 82(1).
[45] CAT Rules of Procedure, r 82(2).
[46] A notable exception was the government of Turkey which refused to cooperate with the Committee's initial request for observations by stating that it considered the Committee's actions '... to exceed the powers conferred on it under the Convention': UN Doc CAT/A/48/44/Add 1, paras 6 and 7. A new government, appointed during the inquiry process, subsequently agreed to the Committee's request to visit the State territory as part of its investigations: see below. Brazil also failed to furnish the Committee with any observations, as requested, on the initial allegations made against it by NGOs in pursuance of an art 20 inquiry: CAT Report on Brazil, UN Doc CAT/C/39/2, para 5.
[47] CAT Rules of Procedure, r 82(3).
[48] CAT Rules of Procedure, r 82(4). Rule 83 specifically provides that the Committee may at this stage or indeed at any time obtain, through the Secretary General, any relevant documentation from United Nations bodies or specialised agencies that may assist it in the examination of the information received under UNCAT, art 20.
[49] CAT Rules of Procedure, r 82(5). The practice of the Committee at this stage has often been to designate two to three of its members to analyse the information received and to advise the plenary Committee on how best to proceed. This occurred in the cases of Turkey, Egypt, Peru and Mexico.
[50] UNCAT, art 20(2) and CAT Rules of Procedure, r 84(1).

The inquiry

[5.10] When the Committee decides to embark on an inquiry, it has a wide discretion in regard to the form and procedure of that inquiry.[51] The Committee's rules stipulate that the members of the inquiry team shall determine their own methods of work in conformity with the Convention and the rules themselves.[52] The Convention is not prescriptive in this regard, stipulating only that the conduct of the inquiry must remain at all times confidential[53] and that the Committee must seek the cooperation of the State party concerned.[54] To this end, the Committee may request the State party to designate a representative to meet with the inquiry team; to provide the team with any information that they, or the State party, may consider useful in ascertaining the relevant facts; and to indicate any other form of cooperation that the State may wish to extend to the Committee or the inquiry team to facilitate the conduct of the inquiry.[55] Of the States which have thus far been subject to the inquiry procedure, most have generally been cooperative with the Committee in these various respects.[56]

[5.11] By far the most intrusive aspect of the inquiry process is the possibility, provided for in the Convention, of the inquiry team visiting the territory of the State in question.[57] Such a visiting mission can only happen with the imprimatur of the State concerned. To make it happen, therefore, the Committee must firstly request permission from the State to make a visit, informing it of its wishes in regard to the timing of the mission, as well as the facilities required to carry out the task.[58] Again, as a general rule, States have been surprisingly willing to accede to requests for visiting missions. In a number of cases

---

[51] CAT Rules of Procedure, r 82(2).
[52] CAT Rules of Procedure, r 82(3).
[53] UNCAT, art 20(5).
[54] UNCAT, art 20(3).
[55] CAT Rules of Procedure, r 85.
[56] The government of Brazil appears to have been completely unresponsive, however, during this phase to the Committee's requests for cooperation. This was subsequently explained on the basis of ongoing governmental change in the federal and State levels at the time in question (2002–2003): Report on Brazil, UN Doc CAT/C/39/2, para 210.
[57] UNCAT, art 20(3).
[58] CAT Rules of Procedure, r 86. In its report on Mexico, the Committee sets forth the general conditions and principles which were agreed in advance with the State party as regards the conduct of the visit. These included the stipulation that the inquiry team should have '... access to any place where persons might be deprived of their liberty; guaranteed access in all such places to all premises, not just cells; access to any written document that members might feel it useful to consult, including registers of detainees; possibility of private conversations with anybody, including detainees and officials of detention centres, whom the members might wish to interview; possibility of returning to places of detention that had already been visited': UN Doc CAT/C/75, para 20. In its report on Brazil, it would appear that the conditions which the Committee insisted on were even more stringent than the above. They included the further stipulation of freedom of movement in the whole country and facilitation of transport in restricted areas; assurances by the government that no retaliatory measures would be taken in regard to interviewees or their families; and appropriate security arrangements, without restricting freedom of movement: UN Doc A/63/44, paras 18–19.

(notably Brazil,[59] Mexico[60] and Sri Lanka[61]), the State has requested a postponement of the visit on logistical grounds, while in the case of Egypt, the government appears to have attempted to stall completely any such visit to its territory.[62] However, while permission must be granted to conduct an on-site investigation, any attempt to frustrate that intention in the manner adopted by the Egyptian government does not appear to be of benefit to the State. In that instance, as we have seen, the Committee proceeded to adopt very hard-hitting conclusions regarding the systematic practice of torture in Egypt on the basis of the information supplied to it from other sources.[63]

[5.12] Visiting missions generally take place over a two-week period. The Committee's rules expressly provide that in addition to the staff and facilities provided by the Secretary General, the inquiry team may also invite persons with special competence in the medical field or in the treatment of prisoners, as well as interpreters, to provide assistance at all stages of the inquiry, including the visiting mission.[64] The rules also provide for the possibility of conducting hearings in connection with the inquiry,[65] the conditions and guarantees for which shall be established in cooperation with the State concerned.[66] In the event of a hearing, the inquiry team shall request the State party to ensure that no obstacles are placed in the way of witnesses and other individuals who are willing to meet with the team and that no retaliatory measures are taken against them or their families.[67] So far, the Committee has not conducted formal hearings, preferring instead to adopt a more informal approach of conducting interviews with a wide range of persons during its visiting missions. Such persons have typically included government officials, members of the legislature and the judiciary, medical experts, law enforcement personnel, detainees and alleged victims of torture or ill-treatment, relatives, NHRIs, NGOs and other relevant associations. In each of the missions so far undertaken, inquiry teams have inspected and met with detainees in a variety of places of detention,[68] including prisons, pre-trial detention centres, juvenile detention centres[69]

---

[59] CAT Summary Report on Brazil, UN Doc CAT/C/39/2, para 7.
[60] CAT Summary Report on Mexico, UN Doc CAT/C/75, para 14.
[61] CAT Summary Account of Inquiry on Sri Lanka, UN Doc A/57/44, para 128.
[62] CAT Summary Account of Inquiry on Egypt, UN Doc A/51/44, paras 188–195.
[63] As Nowak and McArthur have noted: 'The denial of a fact-finding mission to its territory, as in the case of Egypt, does not shield the respective government from any finding of systematic torture, and may even nurture the suspicion that the government wishes to hide such practice': Nowak and McArthur, *The United Nations Convention Against Torture: A Commentary* (OUP, 2008), p 694.
[64] CAT Rules of Procedure, r 88(1). In the case of Brazil, two inquiry teams were in fact constituted, involving Committee members, members of the secretariat of the Committee and interpreters.
[65] CAT Rules of Procedure, r 87(1).
[66] CAT Rules of Procedure, r 87(2).
[67] CAT Rules of Procedure, r 87(2).
[68] In its report on Brazil, the Committee indicated that while it had received allegations of ill-treatment in psychiatric detention centres, it had declined to visit these during its mission on account of the fact that it did not have appropriate medical expertise for such assessment: CAT Report on Brazil, UN Doc CAT/C/39/2, para 193.
[69] Visits to juvenile detention centres were first made by the Committee during its mission to Brazil: CAT Report on Brazil, UN Doc CAT/C/39/2, paras 84–88.

and police stations to interview detainees in conditions of complete confidentiality. There is no limitation on the type of institution that can be visited, provided of course that cooperation from the State is forthcoming and resources allow. In regard to the latter issue, it is alarming to note that while allegations of ill-treatment of detainees were made in respect of psychiatric detention centres in Brazil, the inquiry team did not visit them because they did not have the necessary medical expertise for the purpose.[70] In respect of the issue of cooperation, however, the Committee has generally been very complimentary to States in terms of their apparent willingness to facilitate the operation of its on-site visits to date.[71]

Decision and report

[5.13] Once the visiting mission has been completed, the inquiry team draws up its report and transmits it to the plenary Committee for its consideration. Article 20(4) of the Convention provides that after examining the findings of the members designated to conduct the inquiry, 'the Committee shall transmit these findings to the State party concerned together with any comments or suggestions which seem appropriate in view of the situation'.[72] Obviously, this stage of the procedure involves the Committee in deciding whether to endorse the report of the inquiry team both as regards its findings and recommendations.

[5.14] In regard to the findings, the key question for the Committee will be whether torture has been systematically practised in the State concerned. In this respect, the Committee has consistently used the same standard for determining the existence of a 'systematic practice' of torture. This was first elaborated by it in its report on Turkey in 1993 in which it stated its view that torture is practised systematically when:

> '... it is apparent that the torture cases reported have not occurred fortuitously in a particular place or a particular time, but are seen to be habitual, widespread and deliberate in at least a considerable part of the territory of the country in question. Torture may in fact be of a systematic character without resulting from the direct intention of the Government. It may be the consequence of factors which the Government has difficulty in controlling, and its existence may indicate a discrepancy between policy as determined by the central Government and its implementation by the local administration. Inadequate legislation

---

[70] CAT Report on Brazil, UN Doc CAT/C/39/2, para 193.

[71] See, for example, in regard to Mexico, where the Committee specifically commented that the high degree of cooperation and facilitation by the State enabled the inquiry team to visit certain places of detention with as little as one or two hours notice: CAT Report on Mexico, UN Doc CAT/C/75, para 21. In the case of Brazil, which vehemently disputed the findings of the Committee in its art 20 report, the Committee still noted the full cooperation and support which it had received from the government of Brazil during its visit: CAT Report on Brazil, UN Doc CAT/C/39/2, para 19. While generally very pleased with the degree of assistance and cooperation given to it by the federal and republican authorities in Serbia and Montenegro during its on-site visit, the Committee did bemoan the failure to make arrangements necessary to interview pre-trial detainees which caused a certain degree of delay in its work programme: CAT Summary Account of Inquiry on Serbia and Montenegro, UN Doc A/59/44, para 160.

[72] See also CAT Rules of Procedure, r 89(1).

which in practice allows room for the use of torture may also add to the systematic nature of this practice'.[73]

[5.15] This is undoubtedly a broad interpretation. It represents a considerable softening of the definition of torture in art 1 of the Convention itself. The latter provision clearly stipulates that for ill-treatment to be designated as 'torture', it must involve not only severe pain or suffering which is intentionally inflicted for a particular stated purpose, but also be done 'by or at the instigation of or with the consent or acquiescence of a public official or other person acting in an official capacity'. Thus, while art 1 places considerable emphasis on the question of intention, the interpretation articulated by the Committee in regard to its art 20 inquiries moves away from this absolutist position by stating that torture can be systematic even where it is not the result of a deliberate, intentional policy on the part of the government in question. Theoretically, this definition could be applied to situations where widespread torture is perpetrated by non-state agents whom the government has difficulty in controlling.[74] The expansive interpretation of the term 'systematic practice' has not been lost on all States which have so far been subject to the procedure. In its reply to the Committee's report on Brazil, the Brazilian government rejected the Committee's interpretation on the basis that it seemed to 'diverge from the common meaning of the expression and thus from the general rule of interpretation of treaties ...'[75]

[5.16] It is also interesting to note that the Committee has not adopted a technical approach in assessing whether a systematic practice of torture has occurred. In other words, it tends not to analyse forensically whether particular treatment or conditions in a State amount to 'torture' as opposed to 'inhuman' or 'degrading' treatment, as is the practice of the European Court of Human Rights, for example, in interpreting art 3 of the European Convention on Human Rights.[76] Nowak and McArthur sum up the *modus operandi* of the Committee in identifying a systematic practice of torture precisely:

> 'If it is apparent from information provided by reliable sources that torture is widespread, and if at least some of these cases are corroborated during the fact-finding mission by testimonies from victims, witnesses and/or government officials, first hand-impressions of particularly harsh prison conditions, an analysis of inadequate legislation and other means of taking evidence such as forensic examinations, the Committee may find a systematic practice of torture by government acquiescence or lack of control'.[77]

---

[73] CAT Summary Account of Inquiry on Turkey, UN Doc A/48/44/Add 1, para 39.
[74] In its report on Sri Lanka, for example, while it stopped short of finding that torture had been systematically practised in that country, the Committee noted that it was frequently resorted to by paramilitaries who are not fully under the control of the civilian or military authorities: CAT Summary Account of Inquiry on Sri Lanka, UN Doc A/57/44, paras 175–176.
[75] CAT Report on Brazil, UN Doc CAT/C/39/2, paras 229–241.
[76] Evans, 'Getting to Grips with Torture' (2002) 51 ICLQ 365–383.
[77] Nowak and McArthur, *The United Nations Convention Against Torture: A Commentary* (OUP, 2008), p 694.

Thus far, the Committee has found that torture has been systematically practised in six of the seven countries that have been subject to the procedure.[78] Most typically, it has been inflicted against detainees in the context of counter-terrorist measures, as well as in the investigation of ordinary crimes. Deplorable conditions of detention have also been found, either explicitly[79] or implicitly,[80] to amount to torture. In reaching its conclusions, the Committee also pays particular attention to whether the legal system and/or legislation in a State facilitates the practice of torture and to whether a culture of impunity generally prevails. Accordingly, many of its usually detailed recommendations are directed towards addressing the latter deficiencies as a means to eliminating the practice of torture.[81]

[5.17] Once the Committee has transmitted its views to the State concerned, the latter shall be invited to inform the Committee within a reasonable time of the action it intends to take concerning the Committee's conclusions.[82] All of the States thus far examined under the procedure have responded to the Committee's inquiry report and recommendations in a timely manner. The opportunity to gauge a government's reaction to the Committee's findings depends on the final phase of the process which is dealt with in art 20(5) of the Convention. It provides for the possibility of the Committee producing a summary account of the result of the inquiry in its annual report *after* the proceedings of the inquiry have been completed. This may be done after consultation with the State concerned.[83] In other words, it is at this stage that the rule of confidentiality which hangs over the procedure while it is operative can be dispensed with.

[5.18] The practice that has emerged from the seven inquiries so far concluded reveals a number of interesting aspects to this crucial phase of the process. Firstly, States have generally acceded to the requests made by the Committee to produce a summary account of the inquiry proceedings. Even in the cases of Turkey and Egypt, where the

---

[78] Sri Lanka is the only State which has thus far escaped the designation. The conclusions of the Committee in that case are somewhat dubious. It found that while the number of instances of torture were 'high' and 'disturbing', its practice was not 'systematic'. The Committee also took into consideration the fact that the government and the security forces began implementing most of the Committee's recommendations in reaching its conclusions: CAT Summary Account of Inquiry on Sri Lanka, UN Doc A/57/44, paras 177, 181 and 183.

[79] CAT Summary Account of Inquiry on Peru, UN Doc A/56/44, para 186.

[80] CAT Report on Brazil, UN Doc CAT/C/39/2, paras 178 and 188. Although it is interesting to note that this aspect of the Committee's report was also vehemently opposed by the Brazilian government in its reply to the Committee's report: paras 242–252.

[81] In the case of Serbia and Montenegro, the Committee found that while torture had been systematically practised prior to October 2000, the incidence of torture had dropped considerably afterwards and was no longer systematic. The Committee still went on to issue a broad sweep of recommendations aimed at eliminating isolated instances of torture: CAT Summary Account of Inquiry on Serbia and Montenegro, UN Doc A/59/44, paras 212–213.

[82] CAT Rules of Procedure, r 89(2).

[83] See also CAT Rules of Procedure, r 90.

governments vehemently objected to publication,[84] the Committee still proceeded to produce a summary account of those inquiries in its annual report. This reveals that the Committee interprets the phrase 'consultation' in art 20(5) as meaning just that, and as not requiring it to obtain a government's consent before issuing a summary report. It also discloses the importance that the Committee places on publication as a means of drawing attention to a systematic practice of torture and of putting pressure on a recalcitrant State to rectify the situation.[85]

[5.19] In contrast to the cases of Egypt and Turkey, the governments of Mexico and Brazil each agreed to the full publication of the inquiry report in their respective cases, together with publication of their replies thereon.[86] Thus, even though the Convention itself only speaks to publication of a 'summary account' of the proceedings, the Committee has gone a step further in these two cases, with the consent of the States concerned. This effort to increase the level of transparency built into the procedure is to be welcomed on a number of grounds. First, it obviously allows for a more detailed account of what is happening in a particular State to reach the public domain. Second, it shines a clearer light on the manner in which the Committee itself operates the inquiry procedure, particularly as regards its visiting missions. Obviously, however, the advantage of transparency cuts both ways. Publication of a full report, together with the State's replies, affords the State the opportunity not only to explain its position, but also, crucially, to maintain control on the way that position is articulated publicly. The Brazilian government, for example, took the opportunity of full publication to lambaste the Committee for what it clearly considered to be an over-broad interpretation of its mandate under art 20.[87]

[5.20] Publication, even in summary form, is clearly a useful way of obtaining information on the outcome and operation of the inquiry procedure and the attitude of the State in question to its application in its particular case. Some States have cooperated with the procedure, but have robustly rejected certain or all of the Committee's conclusions.[88] Others appear to have broadly welcomed the Committee's

---

[84] The reasons for the objection in the case of Turkey are not recorded, though it is clear from the summary produced that the State completely rejected the Committee's findings: CAT Summary Account of Inquiry on Turkey, UN Doc A/48/44/Add, 1, para 20. The objection in the case of Egypt was made on national security grounds: CAT Summary Account of Inquiry on Egypt, UN Doc A/51/44, para 199.

[85] In both instances, the Committee makes the point that publication is necessary to ensure full respect for the provisions of the Convention in the respective States parties: CAT Summary Account of Inquiry on Turkey, UN Doc A/48/44/Add, 1, para 21; and CAT Summary Account of Inquiry on Egypt, UN Doc A/51/44, para 200.

[86] CAT Article 20 Report on Mexico, UN Doc CAT/C/75 and CAT Article 20 Report on Brazil, UN Doc CAT/C/39/2.

[87] CAT Report on Brazil, UN Doc CAT/C/39/2, paras 229–252.

[88] In addition to the cases of Egypt, Turkey and Brazil, the government of Peru did not agree that torture was systematically practised in its territory: CAT Summary Account of Inquiry on Peru, UN Doc A/56/44, para 189.

recommendations.[89] Indeed, as Nowak and McArthur point out, in the case of Sri Lanka, the government's willingness to embrace the Committee's recommendations appears to have operated so favourably as to have counted as a factor in the Committee's decision to conclude that torture was not being systematically practised in its territory.[90]

[5.21] Before leaving this issue, it is interesting to note that in the case of Peru, the Committee purposefully delayed publishing the summary account of the procedure for approximately 18 months, apparently as a means of continuing a confidential dialogue with the government on means to improve the situation operating in that State.[91] This would appear to be a strategic choice being made by the Committee that confidentiality, as opposed to publication, might provide a better context for inducing progress on the part of the State in question.

Conclusion

[5.22] In reviewing the effectiveness of the art 20 procedure, it is important to remind oneself that its insertion in the Convention to begin with nearly proved to be a deal-breaker, such was the resistance on the part of certain States to the notion of on-site inspections by an international supervisory body on their territories. As matters have panned out, the up-take on the procedure has generally improved with States that initially opted-out of the procedure, later relinquishing their initial reservations. Moreover, as we have seen, in the seven States known to have been subject to the procedure, most have been entirely cooperative with the process. The outcome of each case has seen the Committee draw up a detailed series of recommendations for each State on how to eradicate the practice of torture in its territory and how to improve conditions for the future.

[5.23] On the negative side, the usefulness of the procedure can be queried on a number of grounds. To begin with, there is an element of 'closing the door after the horse has bolted' effect attaching to the operation of the procedure generally. Delays and hold-ups in its progress and application in individual cases are sometimes quite breathtaking. For example, as regards the inquiry into Serbia and Montenegro, the Committee decided to postpone its examination of whether or not to conduct an inquiry 'owing to the political situation in the country at that time'.[92] Thus, despite having been appraised of allegations relating to the systematic use of torture within the territory of Serbia and Montenegro in December 1997, the Committee did not in fact establish a confidential inquiry into those allegations until November 2000. It took a further one and a half years before an inquiry team visited the territory in July 2002. By the Committee's own admission, the characteristics and frequency of the practice of torture which had

---

[89] See the replies of the government of Mexico, UN Doc CAT/C/75, para 227; and Serbia and Montenegro, CAT Summary Account of Inquiry on Serbia and Montenegro, UN Doc A/59/44, para 215.

[90] CAT Summary Account of Inquiry on Sri Lanka, UN Doc A/57/44, para 183. Nowak and McArthur also reach this conclusion: *The United Nations Convention Against Torture: A Commentary* (OUP, 2008), p 695.

[91] CAT Summary Account of Inquiry on Peru, UN Doc A/56/44, para 145.

[92] CAT Summary Account of Inquiry on Serbia and Montenegro, UN Doc A/59/44, para 156.

grounded the original allegations had completely changed following the fall of the Milosevic regime.[93] It found that torture was no longer systematic under the new regime, but that isolated cases of torture still occurred, particularly in police stations. In fairness, the Committee concluded that a certain culture of impunity continued to prevail in regard to the practice of torture and accordingly it went on to make a number of useful recommendations in that respect.[94]

[5.24] In the case of Peru, the procedure was first applied to the State in April 1995 and concluded over four years later in May 1999. Again, by the time the Committee had visited the State, it was fortunately able to conclude that the number of cases of torture in regard to persons had decreased in 1997 to 1998, especially as regards persons detained in connection with terrorist offences.[95]

[5.25] Likewise, the time-lag between the first contact by an NGO with the Committee regarding the application of the procedure and the ultimate publication of the concluded inquiry is usually astonishingly lengthy. On average, it has taken between four and seven years between activation and publication, which, by any stretch, is a worrying factor where allegations of systematic torture are involved.[96]

[5.26] Obviously, the Committee's part-time status and lack of capacity in terms of resources to carry out comprehensive inquiries compromises the effectiveness of the procedure. This is illustrated with spectacular effect in the case of its inquiry on Brazil in which the Committee explained its failure to follow-up allegations of ill-treatment in psychiatric detention centres on the basis that it did not have appropriate medical expertise for the purpose.[97] This is of considerable concern given the vulnerability of the category of persons in question. The Committee's incapacity to conduct a comprehensive inquiry under art 20 on resource grounds constitutes a significant weakness in the potential effectiveness of the procedure.

Optional Protocol to the Convention on the Elimination of Discrimination Against Women

[5.27] The Optional Protocol to the Convention on the Elimination of Discrimination Against Women (OP-CEDAW)[98] also makes provision for an inquiry procedure which was clearly inspired by the art 20 procedure in UNCAT. The rationale for including it in

---

[93] CAT Summary Account of Inquiry on Serbia and Montenegro, UN Doc A/59/44, paras 162 and 165.
[94] CAT Summary Account of Inquiry on Serbia and Montenegro, UN Doc A/59/44, para 213.
[95] CAT Summary Account of Inquiry on Peru, UN Doc A/56/44, para 160. The inquiry was by no means a waste of time, however, insofar as it did reveal that torture was being used systematically in Peru as a method of investigation, and particularly as regards persons detained for ordinary offences. Moreover, it was being used with the authorities' acquiescence, in a climate of impunity which was fortified by domestic legislation: see para 164.
[96] Seven years in the case of Serbia and Montenegro; six in the case of Peru; five years in the cases of Mexico, Egypt, and Brazil; and four years in the cases of Turkey and Sri Lanka.
[97] CAT Report on Brazil, UN Doc CAT/C/39/2, para 193.
[98] See generally, Ch 3, para **3.71** and see generally paras **3.64–3.72** – in relation to the CEDAW.

the text of the Protocol is clearly articulated by Byrnes and Connors in their seminal work on the draft text.[99] In their view, an inquiry procedure would augment a complaint procedure in circumstances where abuses are more systematic in nature and where individuals or groups are simply not able to avail of the latter.[100] A broader range of issues can also be tackled in an inquiry, which would also enable the Committee on the Elimination of Discrimination against Women (CEDAW Committee)[101] to make more focused recommendations where appropriate for structural change in an offending State.[102]

[5.28] Support for the insertion of such a procedure into the terms of the Protocol was by no means unanimous amongst States.[103] Indeed, according to one participant in the negotiations, the inclusion of an inquiry procedure proved to be one of the most sensitive for many States, given its obviously intrusive capacity in terms of State sovereignty.[104] The majority, however, favoured its inclusion on the basis that it would complement the individual complaint procedure (also being provided for in the Protocol) by making it possible for the CEDAW Committee to tackle systemic violations of women's human rights which could not properly be dealt with by means of an individual complaint procedure.[105]

[5.29] The aim of the procedure, as it was initially envisaged, was to enable the CEDAW Committee, on receipt of reliable information indicating a serious or systematic violation by a State party to the Convention, with the cooperation of that State, to conduct an inquiry into the matter. Indeed, the CEDAW Committee's original suggestion for an inquiry procedure was formulated in the following terms:

> 'If the Committee received reliable information indicating a serious or systematic violation by a State party of rights under the Convention or of a failure to give effect to its Convention obligations, the Committee should have the right to invite that State party to cooperate in examining the information and in submitting observations on it. After considering those

---

[99] Byrnes and Connors, 'Enforcing the Human Rights of Women: A Complaints Procedure for the Women's Convention?' (1995) 21 Brook J Int'l L 679.

[100] Byrnes and Connors, 'Enforcing the Human Rights of Women: A Complaints Procedure for the Women's Convention?' (1995) 21 Brook J Int'l L 679, pp 704–705.

[101] On the composition and mandate of CEDAW, see Ch 3, paras **3.70–3.72**.

[102] Byrnes and Connors, 'Enforcing the Human Rights of Women: A Complaints Procedure for the Women's Convention?' (1995) 21 Brook J Int'l L 679, pp 704–705.

[103] China, Cuba and Morocco, in particular, voiced objections to the inclusion of an inquiry procedure in the Protocol from the outset. Austria initially took the position that if a discussion on the inquiry procedure was going to delay the discussion on the Protocol, then it should be provided in a separate Protocol at later date. Additional Views of Governments, Inter-Governmental Organizations and Non-Governmental Organizations on an Optional Protocol to the Convention, Report of the Secretary General to the Commission on the Status of Women (18 February 1997): UN Doc E/CN6/1997/5, paras 191–193.

[104] Gómez Isa, 'The Optional Protocol For the Convention On the Elimination of All Forms of Discrimination Against Women: Strengthening The Protection Mechanisms of Women's Human Rights' (2003) 20 Ariz J Int'l & Comp L 291, p 316.

[105] Additional Views of Governments, IGOs and NGOs: UN Doc E/CN6/1997/5, paras 75–79.

observations and any other relevant information, the Committee should have the power to designate one or more of its members to conduct an inquiry and report urgently to the Committee'.[106]

The inquiry would be confidential[107] and might entail a visit to the territory of the State concerned, with its consent.[108] Having invited responses from the State at various junctures,[109] the Committee would ultimately be empowered to publish a report.[110]

[5.30] The final wording of arts 8–9 of the Protocol, containing the mandate for the CEDAW Committee to conduct inquiries, does not in fact stray very far from this original proposal. This specific mandate is supplemented by the Committee's Rules of Procedure[111] which flesh out in more detail the Committee's *modus operandi* for the conduct of an inquiry under the Protocol. The *quid pro quo* for the minority of States which opposed the establishment of such a procedure is that it should be optional.[112] Thus, art 10 of the Protocol contains an 'opt-out clause' allowing a State party to declare at the time of signature, ratification or accession to the Protocol that it does not recognise the competence of the CEDAW Committee to conduct inquiries pursuant to arts 8 and 9. It is worth noting also that even where a State party to the Protocol has not opted-out of the procedure, the CEDAW Committee's powers to conduct an inquiry would be similarly constrained if that State had entered a reservation as regards the operation of any relevant article(s) of the Convention.[113]

Preliminary Phase

[5.31] As regards initiation of the inquiry, art 8(1) of the Protocol provides that:

> 'If the Committee receives reliable information indicating grave or systematic violations by a State Party of the rights set forth in the Convention, the Committee shall invite that State Party to cooperate in the examination of the information and to this end to submit observations with regard to the information concerned'.

Thus, the threshold requirement for the initiation of an inquiry is that an inquiry can only be launched where the CEDAW Committee receives reliable information concerning 'grave or systematic violations' of the Convention. This formulation is

---

[106] See Element 17 of the CEDAW Committee's Suggestion No 7: Elements for an Optional Protocol to the Convention: Report of the Committee on the Elimination of All Forms of Discrimination Against Women (14th Session): UN Doc A/50/38, pp 2–5.

[107] Element 20, CEDAW Committee's Suggestion No 7.

[108] Element 18, CEDAW Committee's Suggestion No 7.

[109] Elements 19 and 21, CEDAW Committee's Suggestion No 7.

[110] Element 22, CEDAW Committee's Suggestion No 7.

[111] Rules of Procedure of the CEDAW Committee: UN Doc HRI/GEN/3/Rev 3, Rules 76–91.

[112] See Gómez Isa, 'The Optional Protocol For the Convention On the Elimination of All Forms of Discrimination Against Women: Strengthening The Protection Mechanisms of Women's Human Rights' (2003) 20 Ariz J Int'l & Comp L 291, pp 316–317.

[113] This is by no means a non-issue considering that States have traditionally entered more reservations to the Women's Convention than any other of the core human rights treaties: see Cook, 'Reservations to the Convention on the Elimination of All Forms of Discrimination against Women' (1989–1990) 30 Va. J. Int'l L. 643.

arguably less demanding than the standard required to trigger an inquiry under the UNCAT where reliable information of a 'systematic' practice is absolutely required.[114] It indicates that while something more than an individual complaint is envisaged here, there is still sufficient flexibility to allow the Committee to initiate an inquiry in circumstances where it receives an individual complaint which is indicative of an abuse occurring on a wider but not necessarily systematic scale.[115] Normally, such information will be conveyed to the Committee through the Secretary General who is required, by the Committee's rules to bring to its attention information that is submitted, or appears to be submitted, for the Committee's consideration under art 8(1) of the Protocol.[116]

[5.32] It is for the Committee to determine whether the information received contains 'reliable information' indicating grave or systematic breaches of the Convention.[117] As regards the meaning of 'reliable information', neither the Protocol nor the Committee's Rules of Procedure attempt to define the meaning of 'reliable information', nor to circumscribe the sources from which such information might emanate. The most probable source of information would be NGOs or groups of individuals, but other possible sources would include NHRIs, the specialised agencies of the United Nations and other governmental organisations. Moreover, there is nothing to stop the Committee initiating an inquiry of its own motion, based, for example, on information it receives from a State as part of the reporting procedure in art 18. In carrying out its assessment as to whether to initiate the inquiry based on the standard provided for in art 8, the Committee is free to ascertain the reliability of the information and/or its sources, through the Secretary General, and to obtain additional information substantiating the facts of the situation. It may also request a working group of its members to assist it in carrying out the task.[118]

[5.33] If the Committee is satisfied that the information received is reliable and indicates that the threshold has been satisfied, the Committee shall invite the State party concerned to submit observations to it with regard to that information within fixed time limits.[119] The Committee shall take into account those observations, as well as any other

---

[114] UNCAT, art 20(1), see para **5.05**.

[115] This point is made by Byrnes and Connors in their commentary on the original Maastricht draft for a Protocol to the Convention: Byrnes and Connors, 'Enforcing the Human Rights of Women: A Complaints Procedure for the Women's Convention?' (1995) 21 Brok J Int'l L 679, p 771. This interpretation is buttressed by the fact that during the negotiations on the draft text for inquiries in the Protocol, there was some discussion on whether the threshold requirement should only be met where the information contained reliable information concerning violations that were serious *and* systematic, as opposed to simply those which were either serious *or* systematic. In the finish, the lower threshold was adopted, presumably to allow for the above-mentioned contingency.

[116] CEDAW Committee's Rules of Procedure, r 77. Rule 78 provides that the Secretary General shall maintain a permanent register of information brought to the attention of the Committee in accordance with r 77 and shall make the information available to any member of the Committee upon request.

[117] CEDAW Committee's Rules of Procedure, r 82(1).

[118] CEDAW's Rules of Procedure, r 82(3).

[119] CEDAW's Rules of Procedure, r 83(1).

relevant information that may have been obtained from other sources.[120] In that regard, the Committee's rules allow it to obtain additional information from representatives of the State party concerned; governmental organisations; NGOs; and individuals.[121]

At this point, the Committee may decide to designate one or more of its members to conduct the inquiry and to report urgently to the Committee within a fixed time limit.[122]

The inquiry procedure

[5.34] Members of the inquiry team shall determine their own methods of work.[123] The inquiry shall be conducted confidentially and the cooperation of the State party shall be sought at all stages of the proceedings.[124] While certain delegations argued during the negotiations that the inquiry could only proceed if the State's cooperation was forthcoming,[125] the formulation chosen in art 8(2) of OP-CEDAW clearly indicates that while the State's participation is desirable and should be sought after, it is by no means mandatory. The State's consent is only necessary if the members of the inquiry team decide that a visit to its territory is warranted for the purposes of the inquiry. If this is the case, the Committee shall make such a request to the State party concerned through the Secretary General, and shall inform it of its wishes regarding the timing of the visit and the facilities that it requires for the purpose.[126] The Committee may also invite interpreters and/or persons with 'special competence in the fields covered by the Convention' to provide assistance at all stages of the inquiry.[127]

[5.35] With the State's consent, a visit to the State's territory may include hearings to enable the inquiry team to determine facts or issues relevant to the inquiry.[128] The inquiry team and the State party concerned shall establish the necessary conditions and guarantees concerning the hearing.[129] However, the rules do specify that persons appearing before the hearing shall make a solemn declaration as to the veracity of their testimony and the confidentiality of the procedure.[130] The Protocol and the rules in turn

---

[120] See OP-CEDAW, art 8(2) and CEDAW Committee's Rules of Procedure, r 83(2).
[121] CEDAW Committee's Rules of Procedure, r 83(3). Rule 83(4) goes on to specify that the Committee shall decide the form and manner in which such additional information shall be obtained. It may also, through the Secretary General, request any relevant documentation from the United Nations system (r 83(5)).
[122] OP-CEDAW, art 8(2) and the CEDAW Committee's Rules of Procedure, r 84(1).
[123] CEDAW Committee's Rules of Procedure, r 84(3).
[124] CEDAW Committee's Rules of Procedure, r 85(1).
[125] Additional Views of Governments, intergovernmental organisations and non-governmental organisations on an optional protocol to the Convention: UN Doc E/CN6/1997/5, paras 203 and 205 respectively.
[126] CEDAW Committee's Rules of Procedure, r 86(2) and (3). Staff and facilities may also be provided by the Secretary General, including during a visit to the state territory (r 88(1)).
[127] CEDAW Committee's Rules of Procedure, r 88(1).
[128] CEDAW Committee's Rules of Procedure, r 87(1).
[129] CEDAW Committee's Rules of Procedure, r 87(2).
[130] CEDAW Committee's Rules of Procedure, r 87(3).

anticipate and attempt, at least procedurally, to guard against the possible intimidation or ill-treatment of witnesses.[131]

[5.36] As regards the ultimate outcome of the procedure, the Protocol provides that once the full Committee has examined the report of the inquiry team, it shall transmit these findings to the State party concerned together with any comments and recommendations.[132] On receipt, the State party concerned must then submit its observations to the Committee within six months.[133] A follow-up mechanism is specifically provided for in art 9 of the Protocol whereby the Committee may, if necessary, at the end of the six-month period, invite the State to inform it of the measures taken in response to the inquiry.[134] It may also invite it to do the same as part of its reporting obligations pursuant to art 18 of the Convention.[135]

[5.37] It is important to emphasise that the requirement of confidentiality as regards the inquiry procedure must be respected at all stages of the inquiry process. Obviously, it is possible for news of an inquiry to leak out in circumstances where a visit is taking place to the territory of a State by an inquiry team. However, the CEDAW Committee, as well as all participants in the inquiry, would still be obliged to respect the confidentiality of the proceedings.[136] The only deviation from this basic requirement is provided for in art 12 of the OP-CEDAW which obliges the Committee to include a summary of its activities under the Protocol in its annual report pursuant to art 21 of the Convention. This means that the Committee must give information in its annual report about any on-going inquiry, as well as with regard to one that has concluded. As we shall see in the next section, it seems that the Committee is prepared to interpret the provision in art 12 liberally by making public its inquiry report in full and the State's response to same at the conclusion of the entire inquiry procedure.

---

[131] OP-CEDAW, art 11 enjoins States parties to take all appropriate steps to ensure that individuals under its jurisdiction are not subjected to ill-treatment or intimidation as a consequence of communicating with the Committee under the Protocol; and in regard to inquiries specifically, r 87(4) of the CEDAW Committee's Rules of Procedure places an onus on the Committee to inform the State party concerned that it shall take all appropriate steps to ensure that individuals are not ill-treated as a consequence of participating in any hearings conducted for the purposes of an inquiry. See also r 91 which provides that the Committee shall draw the State's attention to its obligation under art 11 of the Protocol and makes provision for the Committee to call the State to task if its receives reliable information that this obligation has been breached.

[132] OP-CEDAW, art 8(3) and the CEDAW Committee's Rules of Procedure, r 89(1).
[133] OP-CEDAW, art 8(4) and the CEDAW Committee's Rules of Procedure, r 89(2).
[134] OP-CEDAW, art 9(2) and the CEDAW Committee's Rules of Procedure, r 90(2).
[135] OP-CEDAW, art 9(1) and the CEDAW Committee's Rules of Procedure, r 90(1).
[136] Sullivan, 'The Optional Protocol to CEDAW and Its Applicability 'On the Ground' (Association of Women's Rights in Development, January 2004): http://secure1.awid.org/eng/Issues-and-Analysis/Library/The-Optional-Protocol-to-CEDAW-its-applicability-on-the-ground (last accessed May 2011).

The procedure in practice

[5.38] At the time of writing, the Committee has initiated only one inquiry under art 8 of the Protocol. This inquiry concerned allegations concerning the 'abduction, rape and murder of women in the Ciudad Juárez area of Chihuahua, Mexico'.[137] The request to initiate the inquiry was made in October 2002 by a combination of NGOs (Equality Now and Casa Amiga, located in New York and Ciudad Juárez, respectively).[138] It is interesting to note that the two organisations requested the Committee to conduct the inquiry under art 8 of the Protocol, following the Committee's examination of Mexico's fifth periodic report to the Committee in August 2002.[139] In its concluding comments on that report, the Committee had expressed particular concern at the incidents in Ciudad Juárez, the continuing disappearances and murders of women, the apparent lack of results of the investigations and the failure to identify and prosecute the perpetrators.[140] Two months later, the two organisations provided further specific information to the CEDAW Committee on the situation and requested the Committee to conduct an inquiry, using its powers under art 8.

[5.39] At its 28th session in January 2003, the CEDAW Committee requested two of its members to examine the information provided and other information available to the Committee.[141] In the light of their examination, the Committee concluded that the information submitted by Equality Now and Casa Amiga was reliable and that it reached

---

[137] These allegations included information 'in particular that, since 1993, more than 230 young women and girls ... had been killed in or near Ciudad Juárez'. The women and girls were mostly maquiladora workers. A maquiladora is a foreign-owned '... manufacturing plant that imports and assembles duty-free components for export'. Maquiladoras enjoy a privileged existence in Mexico under a dedicated program aimed at attracting foreign investment into the country, by offering numerous advantages to the companies involved, particularly that of cheap labour: Morales, Aguilera and Armstrong, 'An Overview of the Maquiladora Program' (1994): Report for the United States Department of Labour, Bureau of International Affairs, http://www.dol.gov/ilab/media/reports/nao/maquilad.htm(last accessed May 2011). See generally, Rodriguez, *The Daughters of Juárez: A True Story of Serial Murder South of the Border* (Atria Books, 2007).

[138] Equality Now is an international NGO in consultative status with ECOSOC (www.equalitynow.org) and Casa Amiga is a rape crisis centre in Ciudad Juárez (www.casa-amiga.org). The information was transmitted to the Committee by the Secretary General in pursuance of r 77 of the CEDAW Committee's Rules of Procedure.

[139] UN Doc CEDAW/C/MEX/5, (1 December 2000).

[140] Concluding Observations of CEDAW on Mexico's 5th periodic report: UN Doc A/57/38, para 440.

[141] This decision was taken pursuant to r 82 of the Rules of Procedure at the Committee's 28th Session. The members appointed were Ms Yolanda Ferrer Gómez and Ms Maria Regina Taveres da Silva. Further information assessed included the relevant conclusions of the other treaty bodies and the reports of the United Nations special rapporteurs on extra judicial, summary or arbitrary executions and on the independence of judges and lawyers. Report on Mexico produced by the Committee on the Elimination of Discrimination against Women under article 8 of the Optional Protocol to the Convention, and reply from the Government of Mexico: UN Doc CEDAW/C/2005/OP 8/Mexico, para 4.

the relevant threshold required by art 8(1) to trigger an inquiry. The Committee next invited the Mexican government to cooperate with it in the examination of the information and, to that end, to submit its observations to it by 15 May 2003.[142] The government cooperated with the inquiry from the outset. It submitted detailed observations on time, offered immediately to facilitate a visit by the Committee to the area concerned, and promised to implement any recommendations adopted by the Committee after an inquiry.[143] Following the submission and consideration by the Committee of additional information by the NGOs concerned,[144] the Committee decided to conduct a confidential inquiry.[145]

[5.40] In terms of the process, the same two Committee members were appointed to conduct the inquiry.[146] The government acceded to the Committee's request[147] to allow the inquiry team to visit the area from 18 to 26 October 2003.[148] During this visit, the inquiry team interviewed public authorities and officials, United Nations bodies, organisations of the victims' relatives, as well as representatives of civil society.[149] They also visited sites where numerous victims' bodies had been found, sites of the maquiladoras and the poorest areas of Ciudad Juárez.[150]

[5.41] After examining the findings of the inquiry team, the Committee adopted its final report on 23 January 2004. Following the procedure set out in the Protocol and the Committee's rules set forth above, the report was then sent confidentially to the Mexican government with a request that it submit observations within six months of receipt. This request having been duly complied with, the Committee formally concluded its inquiry into the matter at its 31st session in July 2004. During that session, it decided, in accordance with art 9(2) of the Protocol, to invite the State to submit to it, by 1 December 2004, a detailed report on the steps taken, measures implemented and results

---

[142] This request was made by way of a letter from the Chairperson of the Committee, sent by the Secretary General on the 30 January 2003. CEDAW Committee's Report on Mexico: UN Doc CEDAW/C/2005/OP 8/Mexico, para 4.
[143] CEDAW Committee's Report on Mexico, para 5.
[144] It should be noted that they were joined at this stage by the Mexican Committee for the Defence and Promotion of Human Rights, which had previously supplied information to the Committee prior to its examination of the Committee's fifth periodic report about the situation in Ciudad Juárez. CEDAW Committee's Report on Mexico, para 6.
[145] Pursuant to OP-CEDAW, art 8(2) and the CEDAW Committee's Rules of Procedure, r 84. CEDAW Report on Mexico, para 8.
[146] Again, this was done pursuant to OP-CEDAW, art 8(2) and the CEDAW Committee's Rules of Procedure, r 84(3). CEDAW Report on Mexico, para 8.
[147] This was made pursuant to OP-CEDAW, art 8(2) and the CEDAW Committee's Rules of Procedure, r 86. CEDAW Report on Mexico, para 8.
[148] Pursuant to the CEDAW Committee's Rules of Procedure, r 85(1), the Mexican government appointed a representative to meet with the inquiry team. The team was also assisted by two United Nations officials. CEDAW Report on Mexico, para 8.
[149] For a detailed description of the inquiry team's programme of work during the visit. See the CEDAW Committee's Report on Mexico, paras 9–21.
[150] CEDAW Committee's Report on Mexico, para 15.

achieved in relation to all of the recommendations made by the Committee in its earlier report. It also decided to make public at a later date its findings and recommendations in the original inquiry report.[151] As noted above, this decision to interpret art 12 of the Protocol flexibly, in such a way as to sanction the publication of the entire inquiry report, is an important one. It ensures maximum public scrutiny not only of the inquiry process itself, but also, very importantly, of the nature of the abuses under investigation and the State's responses thereto.

[5.42] On 27 January 2005, the Committee finally released the report, together with the government's observations thereon. The report documents the facts that the '... city's erratic growth, together with a combination of social, economic and criminal factors, have resulted in a complex situation characterised by the rupture of the social fabric'.[152] The Committee concluded that violence against women is regarded as a 'normal' phenomenon within the context of systematic and generalised gender-based discrimination;[153] and that a culture of impunity has also taken hold which 'facilitates and encourages terrible violations of human rights'.[154] In the result, there have been widespread kidnappings, disappearances, rapes, mutilations and murders.[155] The Committee concluded further that the authorities have not only failed to deal with the structural problems in society which led to this abuse,[156] but also the policies adopted and the measures taken since 1993 in the areas of prevention, investigation, punishment of crimes of violence against women have been ineffective and have fostered a climate of impunity and lack of confidence in the justice system.[157] The Committee was especially critical of the patently indifferent attitude shown by the local and municipal police to the murders and the families of the disappeared.[158] It explicitly referred to multiple allegations of complicity and fabrication of cases against alleged perpetrators on the part of those authorities.[159] It expressed grave concern at the 'inefficiency, negligence, and tolerance shown by the authorities charged with investigating the crimes'[160] and at the complete lack of due diligence shown by the State and municipal authorities in cases involving disappeared women.[161] Notwithstanding the greater political will shown, in particular, by the federal agencies to tackle discrimination and violence against women, the Committee concluded that there have been serious lapses in the Mexican government's fulfilment of its responsibilities under the Convention,

---

[151] This chronology of events is detailed in the CEDAW Committee's Annual Report (2004): UN Doc 59/38, Part II, Chapter V(B), paras 388–408.
[152] CEDAW Committee's Report on Mexico, para 24.
[153] CEDAW Committee's Report on Mexico, para 24.
[154] CEDAW Committee's Report on Mexico, para 26.
[155] CEDAW Committee's Report on Mexico, para 26. This is documented in detail in Part IV of the Report.
[156] CEDAW Committee's Report on Mexico, para 34.
[157] CEDAW Committee's Report on Mexico, para 55.
[158] CEDAW Committee's Report on Mexico, paras 75–76.
[159] CEDAW Committee's Report on Mexico, para 87.
[160] CEDAW Committee's Report on Mexico, para 273.
[161] CEDAW Committee's Report on Mexico, para 275.

especially as regards arts 2,[162] 5,[163] 6[164] and 15[165] of the Convention.[166] The report lays out a very detailed and obviously useful series of general recommendations aimed at eliminating discrimination against women and establishing gender equality in society.[167] The report also includes specific recommendations on measures that should be taken concerning the investigation of the crimes in question and the punishment of the perpetrators;[168] the need to investigate thoroughly and punish the negligence and complicity of the public authorities in the disappearances and murders:[169] and on preventing violence, guaranteeing security and promoting and protecting the human rights of women.[170]

[5.43] In its observations to the Committee, the government immediately acknowledged that the murders of women in Ciudad Juárez are a 'grave attack on the human rights of women' and that it is committed 'to bringing all efforts to bear to resolve them and to eradicate their causes'.[171] It proceeded then mainly to set forth in detail the progress which it believes it has so far made in responding to the situation and by documenting various actions taken by the State governor, as well as the municipal and federal government.[172] However, as Sokhi-Bulley has noted already, the 'tone of the

---

[162] CEDAW, art 2 sets forth specific obligations on States to condemn discrimination against women in all its forms and to pursue by all appropriate means and without delay a policy of eliminating discrimination against women.

[163] In this respect, the Committee specifically drew attention to CEDAW, art 5(a) which requires States to take all appropriate measures to modify the social patterns of conduct of men and women, with a view to achieving the elimination of prejudices and customary and all other practices which are based on the idea of the inferiority or the superiority of either of the sexes on stereotyped roles for men and women. It found that this duty had not been duly fulfilled and that even the campaigns aimed at preventing violence against women actually perpetuated cultural stereotypes. CEDAW Committee's Report on Mexico, paras 56 and 57.

[164] CEDAW, art 6 obliges States to take all appropriate measures, including legislation, to suppress all forms of traffic in women and exploitation of prostitution of women. CEDAW Committee's Report on Mexico, para 58.

[165] In regard to CEDAW, art 15, the Report specifically referred to para 1, which states that 'States Parties shall accord to women equality with men before the law' in all aspects of life; and para 4 which provides for the free movement of persons, holding that neither of these rights are provided for in Ciudad Juáerz where '... a climate of fear and danger prevents many women, especially young women and women from lower social classes, from freely living normal lives': CEDAW Committee's Report on Mexico, paras 58 and 59.

[166] CEDAW Committee's Report on Mexico, paras 48–60.

[167] CEDAW Committee's Report on Mexico, paras 263–270.

[168] CEDAW Committee's Report on Mexico, paras 271–286.

[169] CEDAW Committee's Report on Mexico, para 274.

[170] CEDAW Committee's Report on Mexico, paras 287–294.

[171] CEDAW Committee's Report on Mexico, Pt 2, Observations by the State party – Mexico, Introduction.

[172] These include, most notably, the establishment of the Chihuahua women's Institute (ICHIMU) by the State Governor and the Coordination and Liaison Sub-commission for the Prevention and Eradication of Violence Against Women in Ciudad Juárez by the Federal Government.

government's reply is one of helplessness and inevitability'.[173] Typical of this is the statement at the end of its observations that in Mexico '...there are social situations, stereotypes, attitudes, values and age-old cultural traditions that have been preserved throughout our history and restrict women's development potential, but which cannot be changed in an instant'.[174] It also states that the problems in Ciudad Juárez were compounded by a lack of human and financial resources to address it in a timely and effective manner.[175] Despite these weak assertions, the government's willingness to engage with the inquiry process and to reiterate its commitment to resolving the situation is at least encouraging.

Follow-up action

[5.44] Since the publication of the inquiry report and the government's response in January 2005, the CEDAW Committee has continued to apply pressure on the Mexican government in respect of the situation in Ciudad Juárez. At the same session during which it released its report, it also requested the Mexican government to submit additional information on follow-up measures adopted pursuant to the Committee's report by 1 May 2005. It also invited the NGOs that had submitted the information which led to the inquiry to submit their views and evaluation of the State's response by the same date. Having considered all of the latter information, the Committee decided at its 33rd session, in July 2005, to invite the Mexican government to provide further details of measures taken in response to the Committee's findings, comments and recommendations in its sixth periodic report to the Committee which was due to be submitted the following November.[176] The government complied with this request, submitting further information regarding, inter alia, the creation of new mechanisms and organisations to help deal with the situation.[177] The Committee's concluding comments on the State's report, released in August 2006, unfortunately assert that the efforts made thus far by the government are insufficient to successfully complete investigations, prosecute and punish offenders and to provide access to justice, protection and compensation to victims and their families.[178] Moreover, the Committee expressed particular concern that the efforts so far made have failed to prevent further crimes from

---

[173] Sokhi-Bulley, 'The Optional Protocol to CEDAW: First Steps' (2006) 6 HRLR 143, p 155.
[174] CEDAW Committee's Report on Mexico, p 93.
[175] CEDAW Committee's Report on Mexico, p 93.
[176] Report of the Committee on the Elimination of Discrimination against Women, 33rd Session: UN Doc A/60/38, paras 412 and 413. As noted above, specific provision is made for this action on the part of the Committee in OP-CEDAW, art 9(1) and in the CEDAW Committee's Rules of Procedure, r 90(1).
[177] These include the establishment in November 2005 of a Special Attorney's Office to monitor investigations into femicide in Mexico; centres providing services and shelters for women victims of violence; as well as a Media Monitoring Unit to provide a mechanism for denouncing sexist messages transmitted by the media: Sixth Periodic Report submitted by Mexico to CEDAW, 23 January 2006, UN Doc CEDAW/C/MEX/6, pp 145–148.
[178] Concluding Comments of the Committee on the Elimination of All Forms of Discrimination against Women: Mexico (25 August 2006) UN Doc CEDAW/C/MEX/CO/6, para 16.

being committed.[179] Hence, it reiterated the recommendations made in its inquiry and urged the government to strengthen its efforts to implement them fully.[180] In this regard, the Committee requested the State to establish concrete monitoring mechanisms which would enable it '...to systematically assess its progress in the implementation of the recommendations and in particular, to progress in efforts aimed at the prevention of such crimes'.[181]

Conclusion

[5.45] Theoretically speaking, the inquiry procedure established by the Protocol is a useful implementation tool for enforcing women's rights. It fulfils its intended function of shining light on situations of grave or systematic abuse of women's rights in situations throughout the world. Some commentators have doubted its potential efficacy on the basis of the opt-out clause in art 10;[182] however, that possibility has hardly been a huge factor in weighing against the operation of the procedure, given that only four of the 102 States parties to the Protocol have availed of it.[183] Rather, the unfortunate deficiency of the procedure is again a practical one: the inquiry procedure has not been fulfilling its true potential because the CEDAW Committee simply does not have the resources to initiate it very often. More than 10 years after entry into force of the Protocol, it has only been used on one occasion.

[5.46] The potential for use by NGOs and NHRIs of the opportunity presented by art 8 of the Protocol to submit information to the CEDAW Committee for the purposes of conducting an in-depth inquiry into a situation of grave or systematic abuse of women's rights is amply evidenced by the Mexican example. In many ways, the Committee's handling of the inquiry appears to be exemplary. Within a relatively short space of time, it appears to have responded to the allegations, and acted decisively in producing a stinging rebuke on the authorities' handling of the situation, while at the same time offering concrete recommendations for change. Moreover, it has kept the pressure on the Mexican government in relation to the Ciudad Juárez murders at various junctures since then.

---

[179] CEDAW Committee's Concluding Comments on Mexico: UN Doc CEDAW/C/MEX/CO/6, para 16.
[180] CEDAW Committee's Concluding Comments on Mexico: UN Doc CEDAW/C/MEX/CO/6, para 17.
[181] CEDAW Committee's Concluding Comments on Mexico: UN Doc CEDAW/C/MEX/CO/6, para 17. Mexico was due to report formally to the Committee under the art 18 periodic reporting procedure in 2010.
[182] Sokhi-Bulley, 'The Optional Protocol to CEDAW: First Steps' (2006) 6 HRLR 143, p 145. This potential limitation is also noted by Tang, 'Internationalizing Women's Struggle against Discrimination: The UN Women's Convention and the Optional Protocol' (2004) 34 British Journal of Social Work 1173, p 1182.
[183] Source: http://treaties.un.org/Pages/ViewDetails.aspx?src=TREATY&mtdsg_no=IV-8-b&chapter=4&lang=en (last accessed May 2011). The four States in question are Bangladesh, Belize, Colombia and Cuba (last accessed May 2011).

[5.47] The CEDAW Committee is by no means the only international body to have shone a spotlight on the situation in the area. The Inter-American Commission on Human Rights has also launched its own investigations,[184] as have high-profile NGOs like Amnesty International. Despite all this, it is a devastating fact that the situation in the area appears to have worsened, rather than improved, with Amnesty International reporting an increase in the numbers of women murdered in Ciudad Juárez in its 2010 Annual Report on Mexico.[185]

[5.48] Instead of leaping to a trite conclusion that this fact demonstrates the ineffectiveness of the inquiry procedure *per se*, perhaps a more realistic assessment is that no matter how sophisticated the process, or the diligence with which it is implemented, an international human rights procedure cannot be expected to produce immediate results in a context such as that which is operating in Ciudad Juarez. Where the disjuncture between respect for basic human rights seeps down into the very fabric of a society, backed up by an attitude of total indifference, complicity and virtual inertia on the part of the various State authorities, it is difficult to see how an international human rights body can have a truly significant impact. While it is true that the sanctions and penalties for non-compliance in the Protocol are simply not strong enough,[186] this is hardly the fault of the CEDAW Committee, but rather that of the States which drafted the instrument in the first place. The most that can be hoped for, therefore, is that the Committee, in conjunction with other bodies, continues to apply pressure on the Mexican government to implement its recommendations; and that crucially, the government begins to take those recommendations seriously.

Optional Protocol to the Convention on the Rights of Persons with Disabilities

[5.49] Articles 6 to 8 of the OP-CRPD,[187] as eventually adopted,[188] make provision for the possibility of the Committee on the Rights of Persons with Disabilities (CRPD

---

[184] See the Report of the Special Rapporteur on the Rights of Women of the Inter-American Commission on Human Rights, 'The Situation of the Rights of Women in the Ciudad Juarez, Mexico: The Right to be Free from Violence and Discrimination' (7 March 2003) OEA/Ser L/V/II 117: http://cidh.oas.org/annualrep/2002eng/chap.vi.juarez.htm (last accessed May 2011).

[185] The report states that at least 35 women were reportedly abducted in 2009 and their whereabouts remained unknown at the end of the year: Amnesty International, *Amnesty International Report 2010 – Mexico* (28 May 2010), available at: http://www.unhcr.org/refworld/docid/4c03a814c.html (accessed May 2011). The anomaly between the number of investigations conducted on Ciudad Juárez and the absence of results is also highlighted by Rodriguez, *The Daughters of Juárez: A True Story of Serial Murder South of the Border (Atria Books,* 2007), p 293.

[186] '... the OP is 'inadequate' as a remedy for what some see as the ineffectiveness and failings of CEDAW – for instance the absence of compelling sanctions and penalties for non-compliance with its obligations and the outcome of its procedure': Sokhi-Bulley, 'The Optional Protocol to CEDAW: First Steps'(2006) 6 HRLR 143, p 158.

[187] On the Convention on the Rights of Persons with Disabilities, the OP-CRPD and the Committee on the Rights of Persons with Disabilities generally, see Ch 3, paras **3.102–3.115**.

[188] The facilitator's draft text was adopted at the end of the first sitting of the eighth session of the Ad Hoc Committee, subject to a technical review by a drafting group. (contd.../)

Committee) conducting confidential inquiries.[189] Clearly modelled on arts 8–10 of the Optional Protocol to the Women's Convention, the procedure applies to any State that has ratified the Protocol, provided that the State has not taken advantage of the 'opt-out clause' in art 8 thereof.[190] The latter provision allows for any State party to the Protocol to declare at the time of signature, ratification or accession to the Protocol that it does not recognise the competence of the CRPD Committee to conduct inquiries pursuant to arts 6 and 7 of the text. Even where a State party has not availed of the opt-out clause, there is further potential for constraints on the Committee's powers in relation to inquiries where it has entered a reservation in respect of any relevant article(s) of the Convention.[191]

[5.50] Like the OP-CEDAW, art 6 of the OP-CRPD employs a less demanding standard than UNCAT[192] by providing that an inquiry may be triggered on receipt by the CRPD Committee of 'reliable information' indicating 'grave or systematic' violations by a State party to the Protocol of the rights set forth in the Convention, in which case the State party concerned shall be invited to cooperate in the process.[193] The Committee's Rules of Procedure require the Secretary General to bring information that is or appears to have been submitted to the UN for the Committee's consideration under art 6.[194] Interestingly, the rules provide for the possibility of the Committee itself compiling such information as is available to it, *on its own initiative*, for the purposes of considering whether to launch an inquiry under art 6.[195] This provision makes explicit a prospect that is at best implicit in the other procedures, namely, that of a treaty body being pro-active in considering the possibility of an inquiry based on information which it has gathered

---

[188] (\...contd) The final proposed text was eventually adopted by a second sitting of the eighth session of the Ad Hoc Committee, before being referred to the GA for adoption. On the drafting history of the Protocol, see Kayess and French, 'Out of the Darkness into Light? Introducing the Convention on the Rights of Persons with Disabilities' (2008) Hum Rts Law Rev 1 and see generally: http://www.un.org/esa/socdev/enable/rights/ahc8.htm (last accessed May 2011).

[189] See generally Stein and Lord, 'Monitoring the Convention on the Rights of Persons with Disabilities: Innovations, Lost Opportunities, and Future Potential' Human Rights Quarterly, Vol. 31, 2010. Available at http://ssrn.com/abstract=1533482 at pp 27–28 (last accessed May 2011).

[190] One of the 61 States parties to the Protocol has availed of this opt-out clause, namely, the Syrian Arab Republic.

[191] A significant number of reservations to the substantive provisions of the Convention have already been entered by several contracting states: see http://www.un.org/disabilities/default.asp?id=475 (last accessed May 2011).

[192] UNCAT, art 20(1) and see para **5.05**.

[193] Stein and Lord suggest as potential examples for inquiries'… the institutionalization of persons with disabilities, or the systematic exclusion of disabled children from schools': Stein and Lord, 'Monitoring the Convention on the Rights of Persons with Disabilities: Innovations, Lost Opportunities, and Future Potential' at 27.

[194] Rules of Procedure of the Committee on the Rights of Persons with Disabilities, r 78(1): UN Doc CRPD/C/4/2.

[195] CRPD Committee's Rules of Procedure, r 79.

together itself. Regardless of the conduit of the information, once it has been gathered, the Committee must next ascertain the reliability of the information concerned and/or the sources of that information[196] and decide whether it satisfies the threshold test to proceed to an inquiry.[197] It may also decide to request a working group to assist it in making its assessment.[198]

[5.51] If the Committee is satisfied that the information it has received or has compiled on its own initiative meets the threshold of 'grave or systematic' violations of the rights set forth in the Convention, the Committee shall invite the State party concerned to submit observations with regard to that information within fixed time limits.[199] The Committee shall then take into account the observations that are submitted by the State party concerned, as well as any other relevant information.[200] Additional information may be obtained from a wide range of actors including (a) representatives of the State party concerned; (b) regional integration organisations; (c) governmental organisations; (d) NHRIs; (e) NGOs; and (f) individuals, including experts.[201] The Committee may also request any relevant information or documentation from the UN system.[202]

[5.52] Having taken into account all of the information and observations submitted, the CRPD may decide to designate one or more of its members to conduct the inquiry and to report urgently to the Committee within a fixed time limit.[203] The Committee's Rules of Procedure in regard to the conduct of an inquiry follow the same pattern as those of CAT and the CEDAW Committee. Thus, any such inquiry must be conducted confidentially and in accordance with the modalities determined by the Committee.[204] The cooperation of the State concerned must be sought at all stages of the inquiry, including its consent to a visit, where the making of a visit is deemed necessary.[205] If this is the case, the Committee shall make such a request to the State party concerned through the Secretary General, and shall inform it of its wishes regarding the timing of the visit and the facilities that it requires for the purpose.[206] The Committee may also invite interpreters and/or persons with 'special competence in the fields covered by the Convention' to provide assistance at all stages of the inquiry.[207]

[5.53] Any such visit may include hearings to enable the designated members of the Committee to determine facts or issues of relevance to the inquiry.[208] The inquiry team

---

[196] CRPD Committee's Rules of Procedure, r 82(1).
[197] CRPD Committee's Rules of Procedure, r 82(2).
[198] CRPD Committee's Rules of Procedure, r 82(3).
[199] OP-CRPD, art 6(1) and CRPD Committee's Rules of Procedure, r 83(1).
[200] CRPD Committee's Rules of Procedure, r 83(2).
[201] CRPD, Rules of Procedure, r 83(3).
[202] CRPD, Rules of Procedure, r 83(5).
[203] OP-CRPD, art 6(2) and CRPD Committee's Rules of Procedure, r 84(1).
[204] OP-CRPD, art 6(5) and CRPD Committee's Rules of Procedure, r 84(2).
[205] OP-CRPD, art 6(2) and CRPD Committee's Rules of Procedure, rr 85(1) and 86.
[206] CRPD Committee's Rules of Procedure, r 86(3).
[207] CRPD Committee's Rules of Procedure, r 88.
[208] CRPD Committee's Rules of Procedure, r 87(1).

and the State party concerned shall establish the necessary conditions and guarantees concerning the hearing.[209] Persons appearing before the hearing shall make a solemn declaration as to the veracity of their testimony and the confidentiality of the procedure.[210] The rules also require the State party to take all appropriate measures to protect witnesses from possible intimidation or ill-treatment.[211]

[5.54] In terms of the output of the procedure, the Protocol provides that once the full Committee has examined the report of the inquiry team, it shall transmit these findings to the State party concerned together with any comments and recommendations.[212] On receipt, the State party concerned must then submit its observations to the Committee within six months.[213] A follow-up mechanism is built in to the terms of art 7(2) of the Protocol whereby the Committee may, if necessary, at the end of the six-month period, invite the State to inform it of the measures taken in response to the inquiry.[214] It may also invite it to do the same as part of its reporting obligations pursuant to art 35 of the Convention.[215] It is important to stress that all of the documents, proceedings and meetings of the Committee relating to an inquiry are confidential save for these provisions relating to follow-up in art 7 of the Protocol.[216]

[5.55] Thus, the procedure outlined above is practically identical to that which obtains under the OP-CEDAW. As such, it includes the less demanding threshold for instigation provided in the OP-CEDAW (as opposed to that which obtains under UNCAT) and also provides for an integrated follow-up mechanism.[217] As Stein and Lord have stressed, the deployment of these follow-up procedures will be key to the success of any inquiry.[218] On the other hand, it is noteworthy that while art 12 of the OP-CEDAW explicitly provides that CEDAW shall include in its annual report under art 21 of the Convention a summary of its activities under the Protocol, there is no such

---

[209] CRPD Committee's Rules of Procedure, r 87(2).
[210] CRPD Committee's Rules of Procedure, r 87(3).
[211] CRPD Committee's Rules of Procedure, r 87(4).
[212] OP-CRPD, art 6(3) and CRPD Committee's Rules of Procedure, r 89(1).
[213] OP-CRPD, art 6(4) and CRPD Committee's Rules of Procedure, r 89(2).
[214] See also CRPD Committee's Rules of Procedure, r 90(2).
[215] OP-CRPD, art 7(1) and CRPD Committee's Rules of Procedure, r 90(1).
[216] OP-CRPD, art 6(5) and CRPD Committee's Rules of Procedure, rr 80 and 81.
[217] In this respect, it is interesting that the inquiry mechanism adopted in the OP-CRPD and fleshed out by the CRPD' Committee's Rules of Procedure contains all of the elements advocated by the OHCHR in the expert paper submitted by that office to the Seventh Session of the Ad Hoc Committee which was responsible for drafting the terms of the Protocol. Expert paper on existing monitoring mechanisms and possible innovations in monitoring mechanism for a comprehensive and integral international convention on the protection and promotion of the rights and dignity of person with disabilities: UN Doc A/AC 265/2006/CRP 4, paras 49–50.
[218] Stein and Lord, 'Monitoring the Convention on the Rights of Persons with Disabilities: Innovations, Lost Opportunities, and Future Potential' at 28.

corresponding provision in the Optional Protocol to the Disability Convention.[219] This omission is significant insofar as the CEDAW Committee, as we have seen, has interpreted art 12 of the Protocol as allowing it to publish its inquiry reports. It is likely that the CRPD Committee will consider itself free to adopt a similar interpretation of art 39 of the Disability Convention in relation to the publication of inquiry reports.[220] The latter provides that the Committee shall report every two years to the General Assembly and to ECOSOC 'on its activities' and may 'make suggestions and recommendations based on the examination of reports and information received from the States Parties'. However, even if this is the case, it is unfortunate that a potential two-year lag in publication will inevitably lessen the impact of public exposure, particularly where serious violations are at stake.

International Convention for the Protection of All Persons from Enforced Disappearance

[5.56] While negotiations on the appropriate form of the monitoring body for the International Convention for the Protection of All Persons from Enforced Disappearances (ICPED) may have been contentious,[221] the inclusion of an inquiry procedure as a means of implementing it was on the drafting table from the outset. The first draft of the Convention contained detailed provision for an inquiry procedure which was clearly based on the formula previously adopted in art 20 of the Convention Against Torture.[222] The independent expert appointed by the Commission on Human Rights to examine the need for a legally binding instrument on the subject also concluded that any future binding instrument would have to incorporate an inquiry procedure with visits to the State territory, including, possibly, preventative ones.[223] Perhaps based on the latter consideration, the working group, which progressed the drafting of the instrument, initially considered making provision for 'fact-finding missions' by the monitoring body, to any territory under the jurisdiction of a State party if it considered that such a

---

[219] The International Disability Caucus, which was an umbrella group for disabled peoples' organisations, and actively involved in the drafting of the Convention had advocated the inclusion of a specific provision analogous to art 12 in the Disability Convention: http://www.un.org/esa/socdev/enable/rights/ahcstata34es.htm (last accessed May 2011).

[220] A linkage between the Committee's annual report and the inquiry procedure appears to have been contemplated by the special rapporteur on disability in her report on the question of monitoring to the Ad Hoc Committee which drafted the draft text of the Convention Report by the United Nations Special Rapporteur on Disability on the Question of Monitoring; available at: http://www.un.org/esa/socdev/enable/rights/ahc8documents.htm (last accessed May 2011).

[221] See Ch 3, para **3.119**.

[222] See art 28 of the Draft International Convention on the Protection of All Persons from Forced Disappearance: UN Doc E/CN.4/Sub.2/1998/19, Annex, elaborated by elaborated by the working group on the administration of justice of the former Sub-Commission on Human Rights.

[223] Report Submitted by Mr Manfred Nowak, independent expert charged with examining the existing international criminal and human rights framework for the protection of person from enforced or involuntary disappearances pursuant to paragraph 11 of Commission resolution 2001/46: UN Doc E/CN4/2002/71, para 101.

visit was necessary 'for the discharge of its mandate'.[224] Such missions could therefore be activated in a variety of circumstances, including in respect of widespread disappearances or in the case of the disappearance of a particular named person.[225] In this respect, a linkage was thus established during the drafting between the provision on 'fact-finding' and a separate 'urgent procedure' whereby requests could be made to the monitoring body to seek and find any person alleged to have disappeared within the jurisdiction of one of the contracting States.[226] While some delegations favoured limiting the visiting mechanism to situations in which breaches of the instrument were 'massive or systematic', others opposed such a narrow formulation, emphasising the potentially 'preventative' function of the visiting mechanism and the fact that it complemented the urgent procedure.[227] A compromise formula was eventually agreed to in the resulting art 33 of Convention, which contains an interesting variation on the usual format for the inquiry procedures that have been analysed above.

[5.57] Firstly, art 33 provides for the possibility of a 'visit' to a State party to the Convention being triggered where the Committee receives reliable information indicating that the State in question is 'seriously violating' the provisions of the Convention. This threshold is akin to that provided for in art 8 of the OP-CEDAW and art 6 OP-CRPD which each speak of 'grave or systematic violations'. As such, art 33 ICPED is arguably less demanding than the expression 'systematic' practice provided for in art 20(1) of UNCAT, since 'seriously violating' the Convention does not necessarily equate with a 'systematic' practice. Accordingly, such a visit could still conceivably occur, following a request made under the 'urgent procedure' provided for in art 30 of the Convention, or even as a response to an individual complaint under art 31.

[5.58] Rather than adopt the language of 'inquiry', art 33 provides that once such information is received, the Committee on Enforced Disappearances (CED)[228] may, after consultation with the State party concerned, request one or more of its members to undertake a 'visit' to the State and to report back to it without delay.[229] The State will be informed in writing of the intention to make the visit, its purpose and the composition of the delegation concerned.[230] If the State party agrees to the visit, the Committee and the State shall work together to define the modalities of the visit and the State shall provide the Committee with all the facilities necessary for its successful completion.[231] Following the visit, the Committee shall communicate its observations and

---

[224] UN Doc E/CN4/2006/57, para 47 and see preceding discussion of earlier drafts at UN Doc E/CN4/2005/66, paras 125–133.

[225] The sub-commission draft had also provided for the initiation of an inquiry pursuant to information gleaned from an individual complaint about an enforced disappearance: UN Doc E/CN4/Sub2/1998/19; see ICPED, art 30(4).

[226] UN Doc E/CN4/2006/57, para 49.

[227] UN Doc E/CN4/2006/57, para 49.

[228] As to the mandate and composition of the CED, see Ch 3, paras **3.119–3.122**.

[229] ICPED, art 33(1).

[230] ICPED, art 33(2).

[231] ICPED, art 33(4).

recommendations to the State concerned.[232] While there is no formal 'opt-out' clause for this procedure such as that which is applicable in regard to other UN inquiry procedures,[233] the State still retains the right simply to refuse a visit; and, even if initially agreed to, upon a 'substantiated request' by the State party, the Committee may decide to postpone or cancel a visit.[234]

[5.59] Nonetheless, any attempt by a State to frustrate the Committee's efforts to conduct an on-site visit may be countered by two further interesting aspects of the new Convention. First, art 26(9) contains a unique provision whereby States are obliged to cooperate with the Committee and assist its members in the fulfilment of their mandate, to the extent of the Committee's functions that the State has accepted. As McCrory has noted, a refusal by a State to comply with a request for an on-site visit could potentially be regarded as a violation by that State of its obligations under art 26(9).[235] Second, art 34 explicitly empowers the Committee to urgently bring to the attention of the General Assembly information regarding the possibility of widespread or systematic disappearances in the territory of any State party to the Convention. This may be done where the Committee receives information which appears to contain well-founded indications that enforced disappearance is being practised on a widespread or systematic basis in the territory of the State party concerned. Prior to notifying the General Assembly of the matter, the Committee is obliged to seek all relevant information from the State on the situation. Thus, in a situation where a State simply refuses to consent to an on-site inspection, the Committee's hands are by no means tied, at least where allegations of 'systematic' disappearances are concerned. The possibility of the Committee taking the matter before the General Assembly may, of itself, induce a State to cooperate with the Committee in regard to a request under art 33.

[5.60] Finally, before leaving this inquiry procedure, it may be noted that in contrast to the inquiry procedures provided for in the UNCAT,[236] OP-CEDAW[237] and OP-CRPD,[238] art 33 of ICPED does not stipulate that the proceedings must be confidential. A discussion on confidentiality during the drafting produced divergent views, with several delegations taking the view that confidentiality rules amounted to a 'step backwards', while others asked that such rules should be retained.[239] Much will depend on the attitude of the Committee on Enforced Disappearances to this issue, since it is open to it to specify conditions of confidentiality in its Rules of Procedure or to agree to such conditions with the State concerned as part of the modalities of a specific visit under the terms of art 33(4) of ICPED. It is equally open to the Committee, however, to take the

---

[232] ICPED, art 33(5). Interestingly, there is no explicit reference to 'confidentiality' in this regard.
[233] See UNCAT, art 28(1); OP-CEDAW, art 10(1) and OP-ICRPD, art 8.
[234] ICPED, art 33(2).
[235] McCrory, 'The International Convention for the Protection of all Persons from Enforced Disappearances' (2007) 7 HRLR 545, p 564.
[236] UNCAT, art 20(5).
[237] OP-CEDAW, art 8(5).
[238] OP-CRPD, art 6(5).
[239] UN Doc E/CN4/2005/66, paras 143–144.

view that confidentiality is not a pre-requisite of the procedure and that any endeavour on the part of a State to insist on it might trigger the application of art 34 of ICPED.

Optional Protocol to the International Covenant on Economic, Social and Cultural Rights

[5.61] The most recent inquiry procedure to be adopted by the United Nations is that which has been incorporated into the Optional Protocol to the International Covenant on Economic, Social and Cultural Rights (OP-ICESCR).[240] The driving force behind the establishment of this instrument was undoubtedly that of achieving parity of esteem between civil and political rights on the one hand and economic, social and cultural rights on the other.[241] This was to be done principally by establishing an individual complaint mechanism for alleged breaches of economic, social and cultural rights which would mirror the mechanism previously established for civil and political rights in the OP-ICCPR.[242] The suggestion of including an inquiry mechanism also into the terms of the OP-ICESCR surfaced at an early juncture in the negotiations of the open-ended working group established to draft the instrument.[243] That suggestion gathered sufficient momentum to be incorporated into a paper drafted by the chairperson of the working group which initially set out the various 'elements' which might be included in any Optional Protocol to the ICESCR.[244] Initial support for such a procedure was based on the fact that it would be an important means of addressing situations where individual

---

[240] Article 11, OP-ICESCR. As to the OP-ICESCR generally, see Ch 3, para **3.51**.

[241] See further below, Ch 13, para **13.01**.

[242] Indeed, the original initiatives of the Commission on Human Rights in 2002 in regard to the possibility of establishing an Optional Protocol to the ICESCR seem to have been entirely focused on a complaint mechanism, with no mention being made of an inquiry mechanism. These initiatives included the appointment of an independent expert with a mandate to examine the question of a draft Optional Protocol, focusing exclusively on issues of justiciability of economic, social and cultural rights and the benefits and practicalities of establishing such an instrument. This initiative was followed by the creation of an open-ended working group in 2003 with a mandate of '... considering options regarding the elaboration of an optional protocol to the International Covenant on Economic, Social and Cultural Rights': CHR Res 2002/24, para 9(f), http://www2.ohchr.org/english/issues/escr/intro.htm (last accessed May 2011).

[243] While the working group was originally established by the Commission on Human Rights in 2002 to consider options regarding an Optional Protocol, its mandate was extended by the Human Rights Council in 2006 with the specific task of elaborating the text of the instrument: Human Rights Council Res 1/3, Open-Ended Working Group on OP-ICESCR (29 June 2006), para 2. There was some discussion of the issue at the first session of the working group, based on a presentation given by the secretariat on the process leading up to the adoption of the OP-CEDAW which also included an inquiry procedure: UN Doc E/CN4/2004/44, para 52. At the second session, a former member of CEDAW, Goran Melander, encouraged the working group to consider the inclusion of an inquiry procedure in its consideration of an OP-ICESCR: UN Doc E/CN4/2005/52, para 39.

[244] At the second session, the working group had invited its chairperson, Catarina de Albuquerque, to draft such a paper with elements for an optional protocol in order to facilitate a more focused discussion at the third session of the working group. (contd.../)

complaints would not adequately address the gravity or systematic nature of a violation.[245] The fact that the Committee on Economic, Social and Cultural Rights (CESCR)[246] had already undertaken country visits was noted, as well as the fact that an inquiry procedure would enable the Committee to take preventive measures.[247] Some negative views were expressed, on the other hand, regarding the inclusion of an inquiry procedure, with concerns being raised about the criteria to be used for defining 'gross and systematic violations', the provenance of information that might be used, as well as the role of such a procedure vis-à-vis other human rights mechanisms.[248] On the strength of that discussion, nonetheless, provision was made in the first draft of the OP-ICESCR for an inquiry procedure.[249] Despite opposition from Australia, China, India, Russian and the United States, amongst others,[250] the procedure was retained through the drafting process until its ultimate adoption in December 2008.[251]

[5.62] Modelled closely on the agreed language of previous inquiry mechanisms, the text contains few surprises. Resembling the text of the OP-CEDAW and the OP-CRPD most closely, it provides for the inquiry procedure to be triggered in circumstances where the Committee receives 'reliable information'[252] indicating 'grave or

---

[244] (\...contd) The subject of inquiry procedures was one of the elements which the chairperson was requested to include in her paper: UN Doc E/CN4/2005/52, para 109 and see sub-para (h). The chairperson duly presented her 'Elements Paper' which incorporated information relating to the provision of inquiry procedures in other United Nations human rights treaties: UN Doc E/CN4/2006/WG23/2, paras 27–30.

[245] Azerbaijan, Finland, Mexico and Portugal all spoke in support of including an inquiry procedure. Report of the Open-ended Working Group regarding the elaboration of an optional protocol to the International Covenant on Economic, Social and Cultural Rights on its third session: UN Doc E/CN4/2006/47, para 70. Several NGOs, including Amnesty International and the International Commission of Jurists also spoke in favour of an inquiry procedure: para 74.

[246] As to the mandate and composition of the CESCR, see Ch 3, paras **3.49–3.52**.

[247] Report of the Open-ended Working Group regarding the elaboration of an optional protocol to the International Covenant on Economic, Social and Cultural Rights on its third session: UN Doc E/CN4/2006/47, para 70.

[248] Report of the Open-ended Working Group regarding the elaboration of an optional protocol to the International Covenant on Economic, Social and Cultural Rights on its third session: UN Doc E/CN4/2006/47, para 73.

[249] UN Doc A/HRC/6/WG4/2, arts 10–11.

[250] See Report of the Open-ended Working Group on an optional protocol to the International Covenant on Economic, Social and Cultural Rights on its fourth session: UN Doc A/HRC/6/8, paras 111–118.

[251] See the revised drafts (UN Doc A/HRC/8/WG4/2 and UN Doc A/HRC/8/WG4/3) considered by the working group at its fifth and final session: UN Doc A/HRC/8/7, paras 96–102.

[252] Mr Riedel, the Member of the CESCR who participated in the discussions of the working group on the draft OP-ICESCR, pointed out that the Committee would determine whether information was 'reliable' on the same basis as it did under its reporting procedure. Report of the Open-ended Working Group on an optional protocol to the International Covenant on Economic, Social and Cultural Rights on its third session: UN Doc E/CN4/2006/47, para 75.

systematic'[253] violations by a State party of *any* of the economic, social and cultural rights set forth in the Covenant.[254] The Committee shall invite the State party to cooperate in the examination of the information and to submit observations.[255] Taking account of those observations and any other reliable information available to it, the Committee may then decide to designate one or more members to conduct an inquiry.[256] The inquiry may include a visit to the State's territory where warranted and with the consent of the State concerned.[257] The Protocol specifically provides that the inquiry will be conducted confidentially and the cooperation of the State party shall be sought at all stages of the proceedings.[258] After examining the findings of the inquiry team, the Committee shall transmit these findings, together with any comments and recommendations, to the State party concerned.[259] The State party shall revert to the Committee with its observations within six months.[260] A follow-up procedure is provided for in art 12 of OP-ICESCR whereby the CESCR may, if necessary, at the end of the six month period invite the State to inform it of the measures taken in response to the inquiry.[261] It may also invite it to do so in the context of the reporting procedure in arts 16 and 17 of the ICESCR.[262]

[5.63] As with other inquiry procedures, publication of the results of an inquiry is ensured by the discretion vested in the CESCR to decide, after consultations with the State party concerned, whether to include a 'summary account' of the result of the proceedings in its annual report.[263] In marked contrast, however, to the other procedures, rather than allowing State parties to 'opt-out' of the procedure, the inquiry procedure under the OP-ICESCR manifests instead as an 'opt-in' provision. Under the terms of art 11(1), any State party to the Protocol may decide to 'opt-in' to the terms of the procedure at any stage. This formula was introduced and adopted in the final session of the working group, partly in order to achieve a degree of technical symmetry with the inter-State complaint procedure provided for in art 10 of the Protocol and partly as a

---

[253] It is interesting to note that Brazil pointed to the need for clear 'human rights indicators' to identify situations of grave and systematic violations which would justify an inquiry. Report of the Open-ended Working Group on an optional protocol to the International Covenant on Economic, Social and Cultural Rights on its fourth session: UN Doc A/HRC/6/8, para 115.

[254] OP-ICESCR, art 11(2). Courtis and Sepúlveda argue that extra-territorial obligations could conceivably form the subject of an inquiry under art 11, since the text of art 11(2) does not contain a jurisdiction clause: 'Are Extra-Territorial Obligations Reviewable under the Optional Protocol to the ICESCR?', (2009) 27 Nordic Journal of Human Rights pp 54–63, pp 61–62.

[255] OP-ICESCR, art 11(2).
[256] OP-ICESCR, art 11(3).
[257] OP-ICESCR, art 11(3).
[258] OP-ICESCR, art 11(4).
[259] OP-ICESCR, art 11(5).
[260] OP-ICESCR, art 11(6).
[261] OP-ICESCR, art 12(1).
[262] OP-ICESCR, art 12(2).
[263] OP-ICESCR, art 11(7). Provision for the annual report is made in art 15 of the Protocol.

means of underscoring the optional nature of the procedure.[264] Whatever the reason, it is likely that the change will affect the practical impact of the procedure, since it now requires the '... positive support by States in order to be of any use'.[265]

[5.64] From the above, it can be seen that the procedure provided for in the OP-ICESCR does not mark a progression in the development of the 'inquiry' procedure as an implementation technique. Indeed, perhaps the most significant, if not ironic, element about it is the fact that it was included at all, given that no inquiry mechanism exists for civil and political rights in the terms of the OP-ICCPR.[266] In short, the exercise of achieving parity with the OP-ICCPR ended up, at least theoretically, garnering greater protection for economic, social and cultural rights in terms of implementation mechanisms. As with the provisions in the OP-CRPD and the ICED, it remains to be seen whether its addition as an implementation mechanism will have a significant bearing on the enjoyment of the rights in practice.

Optional Protocol to the United Nations Convention on the Rights of the Child

[5.65] Finally, in terms of inquiry mechanisms, it seems certain that such a procedure will soon be adopted in regard to the Convention on the Rights of the Child (CRC).[267] As discussed further in Ch 15, a working group of the States parties to that instrument was established by the Human Rights Council in 2009 to explore the possibility of elaborating a complaint procedure in a Protocol to the Convention.[268] Even though the resolution establishing the working group only made reference to the possibility of establishing a complaint procedure, the question of whether an inquiry procedure should also be incorporated into such a Protocol was floated at the first session of the working group in December 2009.[269] Following that discussion and inspired by the inclusion of inquiry procedures in similar instruments, the chairperson of the working group made provision for an inquiry mechanism in the text of his initial draft Protocol on a complaint procedure for the CRC.[270] Borrowing substantially from the agreed language

---

[264] Report of the Open-ended Working Group on an optional protocol to the International Covenant on Economic, Social and Cultural Rights on its fifth session: UN Doc A/HRC/8/7, paras 101 and 179.

[265] Mahon, 'Progress at the Front: the draft Optional Protocol to the International Covenant on Economic, Social and Cultural Rights' (2008) H.R. L. Rev. 617 at 641.

[266] This fact was noted by the United States (which opposed the inclusion of an inquiry procedure) during the negotiations on the Protocol. Report of the Open-ended Working Group on an optional protocol to the International Covenant on Economic, Social and Cultural Rights on its fourth session: UN Doc A/HRC/6/8, para 112.

[267] As to the CRC generally and the composition and mandate of the Committee on the Rights of the Child which monitors its implementation, see Ch 3, paras **3.89–3.91**.

[268] Resolution 11/1 of 17 June 2009: UN Doc A/HRC/11/L3.

[269] Report of the open-ended working group to explore the possibility of elaborating an optional protocol to the Convention on the Rights of the Child to provide a communications procedure: UN Doc A/HRC/13/43 (21 January 2010), paras 22 and 47.

[270] See arts 10 and 11 of the Proposal for a draft optional protocol prepared by Chairperson-Rapporteur of the Open-ended Working Group on an optional protocol to the Convention on the Rights of the Child to provide a communications procedure: (contd.../)

of previous instruments, the chairperson's proposal provided for the Committee on the Rights of the Child (CRC Committee) to initiate an inquiry when it receives 'reliable information' indicating 'grave or systematic' violations by a State party of the rights set forth in the Convention or either of its two substantive Protocols to which the State is party, namely, the Optional Protocol to the Convention on the Sale of Children, Child Prostitution and Child Pornography (OPSC) and the Optional Protocol to the Convention on the Involvement of Children in Armed Conflict (OPAC).[271] The draft proposal was revised and finally adopted by the working group in February 2011 following debates over the course of two sessions,[272] before being finally adopted by the Human Rights Council in June 2011.[273]

[5.66] As regards the actual conduct of an inquiry, the proposed procedure is practically identical to that contained in art 8 of the OP-CEDAW and art 6 of the OP-CRPD. Thus, it provides that on receipt of such information, the CRC Committee shall invite the State party concerned to cooperate in the examination of the information in question and to submit observations 'without delay' with regard to the information concerned.[274] Having taken into account any observations that may have been submitted by the State party concerned, as well as any other reliable information available to it, the Committee could then designate one or more of its members to conduct an inquiry and to report urgently to the Committee. Where warranted and with the consent of the State party involved, the inquiry could include a visit to the territory of that State.[275] As with previous procedures, any such inquiry would be confidential and the cooperation of the State sought at all stages of the proceedings.[276] After examining the findings of the inquiry, the CRC Committee will be required to transmit these findings, 'without delay', together with any comments and recommendations.[277] The State party would then submit its observations to the Committee 'as soon as possible and within six months'.[278] After these proceedings are completed, the Committee may decide, after consultation with the State party concerned, to publish a summary account of the results of the proceedings in

---

[270] (\...contd) UN Doc A/HRC/WG7/2/2 (1 September 2010). See in particular the explanatory memorandum, paras 30 and 31.
[271] See above, Ch 3, para **3.81**.
[272] See Revised Proposal for a draft optional protocol prepared by the Chairperson-Rapporteur of the Open-ended Working Group on an optional protocol to the Convention on the Rights of the Child to provide a communications procedure: UN Doc A/HRC/WG7/2/4 (13 January 2011); and the final text adopted in February 2011: Draft optional protocol to the Convention on the Rights of the Child: UN Doc A/HRC/17/36.
[273] The Human Rights Council adopted the draft Protocol in June 2011 (UN Doc A/HRC/17/L.8) and it is anticipated that the draft Protocol will be adopted by the General Assembly in December 2011: http://www.crin.org/NGOGroup/childrightsissues/ComplaintsMechanism/ (last accessed June 2011).
[274] Article 13(1), Draft optional protocol to the Convention on the Rights of the Child: UN Doc A/HRC/17/L.8.
[275] Article 13(2), Draft optional protocol to the Convention on the Rights of the Child.
[276] Article 13(3), Draft optional protocol to the Convention on the Rights of the Child.
[277] Article 13(4), Draft optional protocol to the Convention on the Rights of the Child.
[278] Article 13(5), Draft optional protocol to the Convention on the Rights of the Child.

its biannual report to the General Assembly.[279] A follow-up mechanism is also contemplated whereby the Committee may, if necessary, at the end of the six-month period within which the State must submit its observations to the Committee, invite the State to inform it of the measures taken in response to the inquiry.[280] It may also invite it to do the same as part of its reporting obligations under art 44 of the CRC and, where relevant, art 12 of OPSC and/or art 8 of OPAC.[281] Finally, as with the corresponding provisions of the OP-CEDAW, the OP-CRPD and UNCAT, the proposed procedure is optional in that States parties to the Protocol may 'opt-out' of the inquiry mechanism by making a specific declaration in that respect.[282]

[5.67] It is interesting to note that during the debates on the draft Protocol which took place in the working group on the draft Protocol at its second session in December 2010 and later in February 2011, a number of issues were raised. Some States queried whether it might be appropriate to define more clearly the meaning of 'reliable information' in the text.[283] This suggestion was greeted with caution by the OHCHR which advised that it would be 'unwise to limit the scope of reliable information for initiating inquiry procedures given their high threshold and rare use'.[284] Had such a suggestion been adopted, it might have had implications for the other inquiry procedures outlined above.

[5.68] Other more progressive suggestions did not find favour. These included the submission by the CRC Committee itself that the threshold for initiating inquiries in this context should not be restricted to grave or systematic breaches of the Convention. Rather it proposed that the procedure should be capable of being initiated in the case of any 'repeated or recurrent violations'.[285] Likewise, the Chairperson of the working

---

[279] Article 13(6), Draft optional protocol to the Convention on the Rights of the Child.
[280] Article 14(1), Draft optional protocol to the Convention on the Rights of the Child.
[281] Article 14(2), Draft optional protocol to the Convention on the Rights of the Child.
[282] Article 13(7), Draft optional protocol to the Convention on the Rights of the Child: UN Doc A/HRC/17/36. By the terms of art 13(8), such declaration could be withdrawn at a later stage.
[283] Pakistan and Egypt queried what types of information might be considered 'reliable' enough to trigger an inquiry. Iran believed that acceptable sources should be specified and Brazil agreed that the definition of 'reliable information' should be more precise: CRIN Daily Summary, 8 December 2010 (arts 10, 11 and 14), http://www.crin.org/resources/infodetail.asp?id=23700 (last accessed May 2011).
[284] CRIN Daily Summary, 8 December 2010 (arts 10, 11 and 14), http://www.crin.org/resources/infodetail.asp?id=23700 (last accessed May 2011). Slovenia also expressed misgivings about limiting the scope of reliable information by listing acceptable sources.
[285] CRIN Daily Summary, 8 December 2010 (arts 10, 11 and 14), http://www.crin.org/resources/infodetail.asp?id=23700 (last accessed May 2011). In its written comments submitted on the chairperson's proposal, the CRC Committee explained that the use of the phrase 'systematic' suggests the existence of a deliberate policy of the State aimed at violating children's rights. It also suggested that the CRC Committee could develop rules, defining criteria on 'grave and repeated violations'. Comments by the CRC Committee on the original proposal issued by the Chairperson in October 2010: UN Doc A/HRC/WG7/2/3 (October 2010), para 21, http://www2.ohchr.org/english/bodies/hrcouncil/OEWG/2ndsession.htm (last accessed May 2011).

group's initial attempts to insert shorter time-limit for States to respond to an inquiry to ensure a 'rapid procedure in the best interests of children' [286] were jettisoned during the drafting, [287] much to the strenuous resistance of NGOs and independent experts. [288] Equally contentious was the issue of whether States should be entitled to 'opt-out' of the procedure. NGOs and the CRC Committee suggested that this possibility be deleted from the provision on inquiries,[289] advocating instead the example of art 33(1) of the Convention for the Protection of All Persons from Enforced Disappearances which does not allow for opt-ins[290] or opt-outs but which still requires the consent of the States concerned before organising country visits.[291] While some participants in the working group were receptive to this idea,[292] many other States welcomed the possibility of

---

[286] Draft protocol on a communications procedure for the CRC, Explanatory memorandum, para 31.

[287] France, Poland, New Zealand, Iran, Thailand, Egypt, Japan, Australia, Brazil, Canada and Algeria all advocated the extension of the time-limit proposed by the Chairperson: CRIN Daily Summary, 8 December 2010 (arts 10, 11 and 14), http://www.crin.org/resources/infodetail.asp?id=23700 (last accessed May 2011).

[288] Comments to this effect were made by the NGO Campaign for a CRC Complaints Mechanism, the Committee on the Rights of the Child and independent expert, Peter Newell who apparently noted the '... contradiction between asking the Committee to initiate inquiries without delay and yet granting States more time to respond': CRIN Daily Summary, 8 December 2010 (arts 10, 11 and 14), http://www.crin.org/resources/infodetail.asp?id=23700 (last accessed May 2011).

[289] CRIN Daily Summary, 8 December 2010 (arts 10, 11 and 14), http://www.crin.org/resources/infodetail.asp?id=23700 (last accessed May 2011). This position was supported by independent expert, Peter Newell. In its written submission, the CRC Committee encouraged removing the opt-out clause in order to ensure that it could '... provide the same protection to all children, irrespective of the country under whose jurisdiction they find themselves': CRC Committee's Comments, UN Doc A/HRC/WG7/2/3, para 22.

[290] A small group of States at the second drafting session, led by Egypt, advocated the insertion of an 'opt-in' clause: CRIN Daily Summary, 14 February 2011 (Part III. Inquiry Procedure/Part IV Final Provisions): http://crin.org/resources/infodetail.asp?id=24105 (last accessed May 2011).

[291] See the Joint NGO Submission to the Open-ended Working Group on an Optional Protocol to the Convention on the Rights of the Child to provide a communications procedure, which was submitted by the NGO Group for the CRC in advance of the second session in October 2010, p 10: http://www2.ohchr.org/english/bodies/hrcouncil/OEWG/2ndsession.htm (last accessed May 2011).

[292] Liechtenstein, France and possibly Sweden believed that the procedure was too important to allow States parties to opt-out. Slovenia agreed but would consider requiring the consent of the State party before arranging a country visit: CRIN Daily Summary, 8 December 2010 (arts 10, 11 and 14), http://www.crin.org/resources/infodetail.asp?id=23700 (last accessed May 2011).

opting-out.[293] In the result, the draft procedure that has emerged is substantially the same as the other inquiry procedures previously provided for in UN treaties with no demonstrable concessions being made to the particular vulnerabilities of children.

---

[293] Germany, the United Kingdom, Brazil, Canada, China, the Russian Federation and Algeria: CRIN Daily Summary, 8 December 2010 (arts 10, 11 and 14), http://www.crin.org/resources/infodetail.asp?id=23700. At the meeting in February 2011, Azerbaijan argued on behalf of a group of States that an opt-out clause would '...allow for greater flexibility and wider ratification': CRIN Daily Summary, 14 February 2011 (Part III. Inquiry Procedure/Part IV Final Provisions), http://crin.org/resources/infodetail.asp?id=24105 (last accessed May 2011).

Chapter 6

Preventive Mechanisms

INTRODUCTION

[6.01] The *raison d'être* of the inquiry procedures developed by the United Nations discussed in Chapter 5 was clearly to arm certain treaty bodies with a specific means of identifying and addressing grave or systematic human rights violations. The objective of these procedures ultimately is to engage with governments which have already indulged in, permitted or inherited such a practice in the hope of pressurising or assisting them to eliminate it. The development of inquiry procedures marked a major departure from existing human rights treaty-based procedures by enabling treaty bodies to engage in fact-finding expeditions to a State's territory with its consent.

[6.02] We turn now to examine a new breed of investigative mechanism that has recently emerged in the family of human rights treaties promulgated by the UN. Rather than focusing on the investigation of human rights violations *after* they have already occurred, this new type of mechanism is forward-looking, and *preventive* in nature. By means also of fact-finding, these mechanisms are aimed at diagnosing problems before they reach crisis stage and at assisting States in improving the situation of persons who are the subjects of the particular treaty in question. This Chapter examines the essential character of this type of procedure, beginning with its original incarnation in an Optional Protocol to the Torture Convention.

OPTIONAL PROTOCOL TO THE CONVENTION AGAINST TORTURE, AND OTHER FORMS OF CRUEL, INHUMAN AND DEGRADING TREATMENT OR PUNISHMENT 2002[1]

[6.03] Long before negotiations on the UNCAT had begun, the Swiss Committee Against Torture[2] had been pioneering the idea that the best way to combat the practice of torture was by means of an international *preventive* mechanism, with authority to make regular inspections of places where people are deprived of their liberty with a view to

---

[1] The following section is an updated version of Egan, 'The Optional Protocol to the UN Convention Against Torture: Paying the Price for Prevention' (2009) Irish Jurist 182.
[2] The idea of a preventive mechanism is attributed to the Swiss banker, Jean-Jaques Gautier, who, following his retirement, established the Swiss Committee Against Torture (now renamed as the Association for the Prevention of Torture (APT)) with the aim of campaigning for the eradiation of torture worldwide. See *Optional Protocol to the United Nations Convention Against Torture and Other Cruel, Inhuman or Degrading Treatment or Punishment: A Manual for Prevention* (Inter-American Institute for Human Rights and Association for the Prevention of Torture, 2005), pp 38–39.

making appropriate recommendations. This idea garnered support in certain quarters and was eventually taken up by the government of Costa Rica during the negotiations on the Torture Convention. In April 1980, it tabled a draft Optional Protocol to the Convention, the text of which essentially proposed the establishment of an international committee, which would be authorised to make periodic, unannounced visits to all of the States parties, to inspect places of detention of all kinds under their jurisdiction, and to report with recommendations to each government. Recognising that such a radical proposal was unlikely to be accepted in the prevailing international climate,[3] Costa Rica suggested that its draft Protocol should be considered once the Convention itself had been adopted.[4]

[6.04] Nonetheless, while the idea for a preventive visiting mechanism was temporarily shelved at the international level at that time, it was soon to be embraced in Europe.[5] In 1983, the Parliamentary Assembly of the Council of Europe adopted a recommendation which called on the Council of Ministers to adopt a draft Convention which echoed the basic elements of the Costa Rican draft Protocol.[6] The Assembly was clearly persuaded that while the time may not have been politically ripe for such a dynamic approach to torture prevention internationally, conditions in Europe were less 'sensitive', and hence governments might be more receptive to blazing the trail with such an initiative.[7] This, in

---

[3] The strategy not to propose that the preventive approach be adopted in the text of the Torture Convention itself is attributed to Niall McDermot, the former Secretary General of the International Commission of Jurists: *Optional Protocol to the United Nations Convention Against Torture and Other Cruel, Inhuman or Degrading Treatment or Punishment: A Manual for Prevention* (Inter-American Institute for Human Rights and Association for the Prevention of Torture, 2005), p 39.

[4] UN Doc E/CN4/1409, 10 April 1980.

[5] See generally, Evans and Morgan, *Preventing Torture: A Study of the European Convention for the Prevention of Torture and Inhuman or Degrading Treatment or Punishment* (OUP, 1998), pp 112–117.

[6] Indeed, the text of the draft Convention proposed by the Parliamentary Assembly had been drafted by the SCAT and the International Commission of Jurists (ICJ): Evans and Morgan, *Preventing Torture: A Study of the European Convention for the Prevention of Torture and Inhuman or Degrading Treatment or Punishment* (OUP, 1998), p 114.

[7] As part of a consultation process that led to the Assembly recommendation, the ICJ and the Swiss Committee Against Torture had responded that such an initiative '…could serve to establish the viability and value of the system in what is perhaps the least sensitive region of the world. Europe would once again lead the way, as it did with the ECHR': Letter of 23 April 1992 from the Secretary General of the ICJ, Niall McDermot, to the clerk of the Parliamentary Assembly, quoted in Evans and Morgan, *Preventing Torture: A Study of the European Convention for the Prevention of Torture and Inhuman or Degrading Treatment or Punishment* (OUP, 1998), p 114. On the drafting history of the Convention, see also Cassese, 'A New Approach to Human Rights: The European Convention for the Prevention of Torture' (1989) 83 AJIL 128, pp 130–133, who also makes the point that the drafters of the Convention were completely aware that the European Model could serve as a 'prototype for testing the validity and practicality of the system at the regional before it came to be implemented at the more difficult universal level pursuant to Costa Rica's draft Optional Protocol' (p 133).

effect, is exactly what happened, with the subsequent negotiation and drafting by European States of the European Convention for the Prevention of Torture and Inhuman or Degrading Treatment or Punishment 1987.[8] Together with the European Convention on Human Rights (ECHR), this instrument has since become one of the great success stories of the Council of Europe's human rights endeavours. Variously described as a 'model text'[9] and a 'courageous attempt at a novel approach to human rights',[10] the Convention presented a paradigmatic shift in the landscape of human rights monitoring by changing the focus from *reactive* scrutiny to a *preventive* approach. It did this by establishing a body of independent experts drawn from the Contracting States, to be known as the European Committee for the Prevention of Torture and Inhuman or Degrading Treatment (CPT).[11] Each of the States parties is obliged to permit the CPT to make regular, periodic and ad hoc[12] visits to any place within its jurisdiction where persons are deprived of their liberty by a public authority.[13] The role of the CPT is to examine the treatment of persons in detention with a view to strengthening their protection from torture, inhuman or degrading treatment or punishment.[14] While the CPT is obliged to notify each State of its intention to carry out a visit to its territory, it is not obliged to specify the period between notification and the actual visit.[15] During a visit to a State party, members of the CPT[16] have unrestricted access to any place of detention within the jurisdiction, and are entitled to interview detainees in private and communicate freely with anyone who can provide information.[17] After each visit, the CPT draws up a confidential report on the facts found during the visit, together with a

---

[8] The Convention (ECPT) was adopted by the Council of Europe on 26 November 1987 and entered into force on 1 February 1989: ETS No 126, http://www.cpt.coe.int/en/documents/ecpt.htm (last accessed May 2011). It currently enjoys a 100% participation ratio in that all 47 member States of the Council of Europe have ratified it. Article 18(2) of the Convention, as amended by Protocol 1, provides that the Committee of Ministers may invite non-member States of the Council of Europe to accede to the Convention.

[9] Evans and Morgan, *Preventing Torture: A Study of the European Convention for the Prevention of Torture and Inhuman or Degrading Treatment or Punishment* (OUP, 1998), p 382.

[10] Cassese, 'A New Approach to Human Rights: The European Convention for the Prevention of Torture' (1989) 83 AJIL 128, p 153.

[11] See ECPT, arts 4–6 for the composition, method of election and procedure of the Committee.

[12] The current working schedule of the CPT allows for a periodic visit to each State party approximately every five years. The CPT may organise ad hoc visits at any time where it appears that such a visit is required in the circumstances: ECPT, art 7(1).

[13] ECPT, art 2.

[14] ECPT, art 1.

[15] A government may only object to the time or place of a visit on grounds of national defence, public safety, serious disorder, the medical condition of a person or on the basis that an urgent interrogation relating to a serious crime is in progress. In such cases the State must immediately take steps to enable the Committee to visit as soon as possible: ECPT, art 9.

[16] Visits are conducted by 'delegations' of the CPT which usually involve at least two members of the Committee, members of the Committee's secretariat, and where necessary, designated experts and interpreters: ECPT, art 7(2).

[17] ECPT, art 8.

detailed series of recommendations addressed to the State party.[18] If the State fails to cooperate or refuses to improve the situation in the light of the recommendations, the CPT may proceed to make a public statement on the matter.[19] Alternatively, the Convention also provides for the possibility of the CPT publishing its report, together with the comments of the relevant State party, whenever it is requested to do so by the State in question[20]. This is the preferred route taken by most of the contracting States since the visiting programme of the CPT first became operable. Indeed, since 1989, when the Convention entered into force, the CPT has conducted 300 visits to the territories of the States parties (180 periodic visits plus 120 ad hoc visits) and has issued over 250 reports.[21] While the work of the CPT is pressurised and inevitably subject to constant critique, in general terms, the Convention has fulfilled the basic expectation of its drafters by demonstrating that prevention constitutes the best means of tackling the problem of torture and ill-treatment.[22]

[6.05] By the early 1990s, over a decade after the submission of the Costa Rican draft Protocol, the situation appeared to be significantly more conducive for consideration of an international visiting mechanism aimed at preventing torture.[23] For one thing, the United Nations Convention against Torture (UNCAT) was already in force and the CAT was fully operative; a regional visiting mechanism had been successfully established in Europe by dint of the European Convention for the Prevention of Torture (ECPT); and the political tensions of the Cold War era, which had made a similar system completely untenable at the international level, had substantially diminished. Prompted once again by the campaigning efforts of the APT and the ICJ, Costa Rica submitted an updated

---

[18] ECPT, art 10(1).

[19] This may be done only after the State party has had an opportunity to make known its views and provided that two-thirds of the members agree: ECPT, art 10(2).

[20] ECPT, art 11.

[21] Source: http://www.cpt.coe.int/en/about.htm (last accessed May 2011).

[22] Meanwhile, efforts to devise a similar regional instrument under the auspices of the Organisation of American States (OAS) proved far less fruitful. The Inter-American Convention to Prevent and Punish Torture 1985 contains a much weaker control mechanism whereby States parties are simply obliged to report to the Inter-American Commission on Human Rights (an autonomous organ of the OAS) on legislative, administrative and other measures which they have adopted in their jurisdictions to implement the Convention: OAS Treaty Series No 67, http://www.oas.org (last accessed May 2011). The Convention entered into force on 28 February 1987 and has been ratified by 17 States. Subsequent attempts on the part of NGOs to garner support among member States of the OAS for a system of unannounced visits similar to the European model were wholly unsuccessful, largely for financial reasons: See generally, *Optional Protocol to the United Nations Convention Against Torture and Other Cruel, Inhuman or Degrading Treatment or Punishment: A Manual for Prevention* (Inter-American Institute for Human Rights and Association for the Prevention of Torture, 2005), p 41.

[23] On the development of the OPCAT, see generally Evans and Haenni Dale, 'Preventing Torture? The Development of the Optional Protocol to the UN Convention Against Torture' (2004) 4 HRL Rev 19; Nowak and McArthur, *The United Nations Convention Against Torture: A Commentary* (OUP, 2008), pp 879ff.

draft Optional Protocol to the United Nations Commission on Human Rights in January 1991.[24] Taking into account developments in the emergent international architecture for the eradication of torture,[25] the new draft focused entirely on filling the gap in preventive techniques by proposing a system of visits to places of detention by a dedicated international supervisory body.[26] The Commission on Human Rights responded accordingly by appointing an open-ended working group to agree a definitive draft text of an optional protocol, to be submitted to the General Assembly for its approval.[27]

[6.06] However, the negotiations that proceeded on the draft Protocol soon became fraught with difficulty, as positions became polarised between States on a number of issues. These included, in particular, financial concerns over the cost of creating yet another mechanism to combat torture; the possibility of making reservations to the text; and the scope of the powers to be granted to an international supervisory committee.[28] The latter issue proved to be particularly contentious, with opinions being sharply divided on whether a State's prior consent would be necessary before the committee could embark on a visiting mission to its territory, as well as whether it should be given unrestricted access to *any* 'place of detention', once there. The turning point in the virtually dead-locked discussions on these points occurred finally in 2001 when the government of Mexico proposed including the notion of a 'national preventive mechanism' into the structure of the Protocol.[29] The idea here was that the Protocol would oblige States to set up national mechanisms for torture prevention in their jurisdictions, which would operate simultaneously with the international mechanism. This idea received broad support and was eventually incorporated in the final draft text proposed by the chairperson–rapporteur of the working group in 2002.[30] This text

---

[24] Introductory Memorandum to the Draft Optional Protocol to the Convention Against Torture Proposed by Costa Rica, Commission on Human Rights, 47th session: UN Doc E/CN4/1991/66, 22 January 1991.

[25] By this stage, the Commission on Human Rights had also appointed a Special Rapporteur on Questions Relating to Torture: See Ch 2, para **2.16** and Ch 4, para **4.42**.

[26] See Introductory Memorandum to the Draft Optional Protocol to the Convention Against Torture Proposed by Costa Rica: UN Doc E/CN4/1991/66, pp 3–7.

[27] CHR Resolution 1992/43, 3 March 1992. The impetus for drafting the Protocol was bolstered in 1993 by the World Conference on Human Rights, which called for the adoption of an optional protocol to the Torture Convention, establishing a preventive system of regular visits to places of detention: See Vienna Declaration and Programme of Action, 12 July 1993, UN Doc A/CONF157/23, para 61. The position of the World Conference on Human Rights in this respect is reproduced in the Preamble to the Optional Protocol that eventually emerged from the negotiations.

[28] See Evans and Haenni Dale, 'Preventing Torture? The Development of the Optional Protocol to the UN Convention Against Torture' (2004) 4 HRL Rev 19, pp 31–37; and *Optional Protocol to the United Nations Convention Against Torture and Other Cruel, Inhuman or Degrading Treatment or Punishment: A Manual for Prevention* (Inter-American Institute for Human Rights and Association for the Prevention of Torture, 2005), pp 44–48.

[29] Nowak and McArthur, *The United Nations Convention Against Torture: A Commentary* (OUP, 2008), pp 1067–1068 and see UN Doc E/CN4/2001/WG11/CRP1.

[30] Nowak and McArthur, *The United Nations Convention Against Torture: A Commentary* (OUP, 2008), p 1068 and see UN Doc E/CN4/2002/WG11/CRP1.

proposed the establishment of a 'two-pillar' control mechanism for torture prevention, involving an international visiting mechanism (to be known as the Subcommittee on Prevention of Torture, Inhuman and Degrading Treatment or Punishment (SPT)) as well as a 'national preventive mechanism' in each State party to the Protocol. States parties would thus be obliged to permit regular visits to places of detention by both the international and the national mechanisms. The aim of the Protocol and of the bodies established under it would be to create an effective system of preventive visits that would assist States in eliminating ill-treatment and in improving conditions for detainees, as opposed to sanctioning them for ill-treatment that has already taken place. Following its tense passage through the working group as well as the hierarchy of United Nations human rights bodies,[31] the draft text was eventually adopted as the Optional Protocol to the Convention against Torture and Other Cruel, Inhuman and Degrading Treatment or Punishment (OPCAT) by the General Assembly on 18 December 2002.[32] There are currently 59 States parties to the Protocol and 68 signatories thereto.[33] The following section describes the form and scope of the Protocol, analysing its strengths and weaknesses as an instrument for the protection of persons deprived of their liberty.

The Protocol: Machinery, Scope and Obligations

[6.07] In its final form, the Protocol provides for a system of regular visits to the territories of the contracting States by an 'interlocking network of mechanisms'[34] at the

---

[31] See APT Manual, *Optional Protocol to the United Nations Convention Against Torture and Other Cruel, Inhuman or Degrading Treatment or Punishment: A Manual for Prevention* (Inter-American Institute for Human Rights and Association for the Prevention of Torture, 2005), pp 50–59.

[32] GA Res 39/46, Annex, 39 UN GAOR Supp (No 51), p 197, UN Doc A/39/51 (1984); 1465 UNTS 85. In addition to sources cited in paras **6.05–6.06**, see generally Casale, 'A System of Preventive Oversight' (2009) 1 Essex Human Rts Rev 9; Tayler, 'What is the Added Value of Prevention?' (2009) 1 Essex Human Rts Rev 22; Olivier and Narvaez, 'OPCAT Challenges and the Way Forwards: The Ratification and Implementation of the Optional Protocol to the UN Convention Against Torture' (2009) 1 Essex Hum Rts Rev 39; Harding and Morgan, 'OPCAT in the Asia-Pacific and Australasia' (2009) 1 Essex Hum Rts Rev 99; Hallo de Wolf, 'Visits to Less Traditional Places of Detention: Challenges Under the OPCAT' (2009) 1 Essex Hum Rts Rev 73; and Rehman, *International Human Rights Law* (Pearson, 2010) pp 847–850. Further useful information can be obtained from the website of the OPCAT Project at the School of Law, Bristol University: http://www.bris.ac.uk/law/research/centres-themes/opcat/index.html (last accessed May 2011); and from the website of the Association for the Prevention of Torture: http://www.apt.ch/ (last accessed May 2011).

[33] Source: http://treaties.un.org/Pages/Treaties.aspx?id=4&subid=A&lang=en (last accessed May 2011). It should be noted that by virtue of OPCAT, art 27(1), the Protocol is only open to signature by States which have already ratified the UNCAT. As Harding and Morgan have noted, a significant proportion of Latin American and European States have ratified the Protocol, and while a growing number of African states have also ratified, the take-up rate in the Asia-Pacific region is notably low: Harding and Morgan, 'OPCAT in the Asia-Pacific and Australasia' (2009) 1 Essex Hum Rts Rev 99.

[34] Second Annual Report of the SPT (February 2008 to March 2009): UN Doc CAT/C/42/2, 7 April 2009, para 6.

national and international level.[35] It does this by establishing, on the one hand, an international body, the SPT, and on the other, by obliging States to 'set up, designate or maintain' at the domestic level one or several bodies to be known as a 'national preventive mechanism' (NPM). The net obligation on the States parties is to allow visits by these latter two mechanisms 'to any place under its jurisdiction and control where persons are or may be deprived of their liberty…with a view to strengthening, if necessary, the protection of these persons against torture and other cruel, inhuman or degrading treatment or punishment'.[36] As we shall see, the SPT and the NPMs are intended to cooperate with each other in the performance of their respective mandates. This 'twin-pillar' approach, involving an international visiting body, supplemented by a national visiting mechanism, constitutes the unique feature of the Protocol, setting it apart not only from other United Nations human rights bodies, but also the CPT, which essentially operates in isolation.

[6.08] Under art 4(1) of the Protocol, each State party must allow regular visits by both the SPT and its NPM to any place of detention under its jurisdiction and control where persons are detained by a public authority or with its consent or acquiescence. According to art 4(2), a 'deprivation of liberty' means any form of detention or imprisonment or the placement of a person in a public or private custodial setting, which that person is not permitted to leave at will, by order of any judicial, administrative or other authority.[37] The more expansive language of para 1 can be interpreted to mean that places of detention for the purposes of the Protocol not only include detention facilities maintained or controlled by the State apparatus, but also private custodial settings where persons are detained by non-State agents, either with the consent or acquiescence of the State.[38] Thus, a place of detention would clearly include not just prisons, police stations, military barracks, and immigration detention centres but also places like psychiatric institutions, private hospitals or nursing homes, refugee camps[39] and other places of detention which a government may have contracted out to a private company. The use of the phrase 'under its jurisdiction and control' in para 1 must also be interpreted expansively to include places of detention under the effective *de facto* control of a State party, whether such control is being exercised within or outside its national territory.[40]

---

[35] OPCAT, art 1 defines the objective of the Protocol as establishing '…a system of regular visits undertaken by independent international and national bodies to places where people are deprived of their liberty in order to prevent torture and other cruel, inhuman or degrading treatment or punishment'.

[36] OPCAT, art 4(1).

[37] As to the interpretation of OPCAT, art 4, see generally Hallo de Wolf, 'Visits to Less Traditional Places of Detention: Challenges Under the OPCAT' (2009) 1 Essex Hum Rts Rev 73, pp 81–85.

[38] Nowak and McArthur, *The United Nations Convention Against Torture: A Commentary* (OUP, 2008), pp 931–932.

[39] See generally Edwards, 'The Optional Protocol to the Convention Against Torture and the Detention of Refugees' (2008) 57 ICLQ 789, pp 797–800.

[40] Nowak and McArthur give as useful examples here places of detention in Northern Cyprus, which is occupied by Turkey, (contd.../)

The SPT

[6.09] Article 2 of the Protocol provides for the creation of the SPT as the international component of the visiting system established by the Protocol. Initially, the Committee comprised 10 nationals of the States parties, but that number increased to 25 in October 2010, following the 50th ratification of the Protocol in September 2009.[41] It is important to note straight away the status of the Subcommittee as a treaty organ specifically created by States parties to the Protocol. Its designation as a 'Subcommittee' originates from the Costa Rican draft Protocol which had proposed that the SPT be established by, and be subsidiary to the CAT.[42] The framers of the draft Protocol believed that while the Subcommittee should operate independently in carrying out a confidential visiting programme,[43] it should be linked to the CAT in a number of ways, including the possibility of making its confidential reports and recommendations available to the latter body.[44] However, early in the drafting process, a consensus emerged amongst States that while some institutional linkage should remain between the two bodies, the character and integrity of the SPT as an essentially *advisory* body designed to cooperate with States through a confidential visiting programme, would be better preserved by a clear separation of functions from the CAT. In other words, the preventive role assigned to the SPT might be compromised by association with a body engaged in quasi-judicial functions in the same field.[45] In the result, while the SPT is still technically subsidiary to

---

[40] (\...contd) or the detention facilities at Guantanamo Bay, Iraq and Afghanistan, with respect to which the Turkish and US authorities would be obliged to allow visits by the SPT and NPMs, if they were party to the Protocol: *The United Nations Convention Against Torture: A Commentary* (OUP, 2008), pp 932–933. See also Edwards, 'The Optional Protocol to the Convention Against Torture and the Detention of Refugees' (2008) 57 ICLQ 789, pp 800–803.

[41] OPCAT, art 5(1).

[42] Introductory Memorandum to the Draft Optional Protocol to the Convention Against Torture Proposed by Costa Rica, art 2.

[43] The framers of the Costa Rican draft recognised immediately that there was a need to clearly separate the preventive function of the Subcommittee from the more adversarial functions already allocated to CAT under the UNCAT: 'The creation of a Subcommittee allows for a clear separation of the activity of preventive visits from the exercise of control by the Committee against Torture as embodied in Articles 19–22 of the Convention against Torture. As the purpose of the optional protocol is not to condemn States but to have them co-operate in order to improve, if necessary, the situation of persons deprived of their liberty, it is hardly conceivable that the Committee against Torture could carry out this preventive task aimed at building up a relationship of trust if, at the same time, it has for instance, to handle communications from other States or individuals according to articles 21 and 22 of the Convention': Introductory Memorandum to the Draft Optional Protocol to the Convention Against Torture Proposed by Costa Rica, para 8(b) of the Explanatory Memorandum.

[44] The proliferation of treaty bodies generally, as well as the need to preserve coherence in the functions already assigned to CAT were cited as reasons for not assigning the new preventive function to CAT directly: paras 6–10.

[45] Delegates were concerned that if confidential information concerning country visits were to be reported to the CAT, such information could ultimately be disclosed publicly by means of the State reporting, individual complaint or inquiry procedures under the UNCAT: Nowak and McArthur, *The United Nations Convention Against Torture: A Commentary* (OUP, 2008), pp 912–914 and 1060–1062.

the CAT,[46] it is directly elected by the States parties to the Protocol, and operates almost completely independently of the latter body, save for the limited circumstances provided for in art 16, which are outlined further below.

[6.10] The composition, method of election and terms of office of SPT members is dealt with in further detail in arts 5–8 of the Protocol. Members are elected by States parties to the OPCAT by secret ballot[47] from a list of two nominees supplied by each State party,[48] with consideration being given to equitable geographical distribution,[49] different forms of civilisation and legal systems and gender-balance.[50] Membership of the Subcommittee is part-time and unremunerated. Members are elected for four-year terms, with the possibility of re-election.[51] Members are required to serve in their individual capacity, independently, impartially and efficiently.[52] They shall be of high moral character and have proven 'professional experience in the field of the administration of justice, in particular criminal law, prison or police administration, or in the various fields relevant to the treatment of persons deprived of their liberty'.[53] To date, the SPT has so far been composed predominantly of lawyers – a factor that has obvious repercussions on the character of the body and potentially its capacity to fulfil its mandate effectively.[54] Problems have also emerged as regards equitable geographical distribution and gender balance.[55] While some strides have been made since the expansion of the SPT's membership to redress these imbalances,[56] it is vital, as the SPT itself has noted, that this be done in order for the SPT to gain greater legitimacy and acceptance.[57]

[6.11] The unique mandate of the SPT is set forth in art 11 of the Protocol. It comprises three essential elements:

---

[46] By virtue of OPCAT, art 16(3), the SPT is obliged to present a public annual report on its activities to the CAT.
[47] OPCAT, art 7(1)(c).
[48] OPCAT, art 6(1).
[49] OPCAT, art 5(3).
[50] OPCAT, art 5(4).
[51] OPCAT, art 9.
[52] OPCAT, art 5(6). It is interesting to note the insertion for the first time into this standard clause the requirement that members be available to serve the Subcommittee 'efficiently'.
[53] OPCAT, art 5(2).
[54] Details of each of the members of the SPT are accessible on the SPT's website: http://www2.ohchr.org/english/bodies/cat/opcat/membership.htm (last accessed May 2011). See also Hallo de Wolf, 'Visits to Less Traditional Places of Detention: Challenges Under the OPCAT' (2009) 1 Essex Hum Rts Rev 73, pp 88–89.
[55] At one stage, the membership of the Subcommittee was composed entirely of men and there were no members from Africa or Asia: SPT Third Annual Report, UN Doc CAT/C/44/2, 25 March 2010, para 5.
[56] There are now seven women on the Subcommittee, two members from Africa and three from Asia. Western Europe and Latin America still appear to be over represented on the SPT.
[57] SPT Third Annual Report, UN Doc CAT/C/44/2, 25 March 2010, para 6.

(a) To visit places where people are or may be deprived of their liberty;
(b) In regard to the national preventive mechanisms (NPMs):
   (i) to advise and assist States parties, when necessary in their establishment;
   (ii) to maintain direct contact with NPMs and offer them training and technical assistance; advise and assist NPMs in evaluating the needs and necessary means to improve safeguards against ill-treatment; and make necessary recommendations and observations to States parties with a view to strengthening the capacity and mandate of NPMs;
(c) To cooperate with relevant United Nations bodies as well as with international regional bodies for the prevention of ill-treatment.[58]

From its inception, the SPT has considered these three elements of its mandate to be essential for the prevention of torture, inhuman or degrading treatment or punishment.[59]

[6.12] It is important to note here that the SPT is required to carry out its work 'within the framework of the Charter of the United Nations' and shall be guided by the purposes and principles of that instrument, as well as the 'norms of the United Nations concerning the treatment of people deprived of their liberty'.[60] This provision appears to act both as a break and an accelerator for the Subcommittee in the fulfilment of its mandate. The reference to the framework of the Charter constitutes the break in that it was apparently inserted to remind the members of the Subcommittee that they should tread carefully in carrying out their work, bearing continually in mind the principles of sovereign equality, territorial integrity and non-intervention set forth in art 2(1), (4) and (7) of the Charter respectively.[61] On the other hand, the requirement to be guided by the 'norms' of the United Nations concerning persons deprived of their liberty acts as an accelerator for the Subcommittee, since it enables it to sweep with a very broad brush in conducting its visits and in making recommendations. The term 'norms' clearly extends beyond the narrow confines of UNCAT and allows the Committee to refer to all UN instruments regarding the treatment of persons deprived of their liberty, regardless of whether they are legally binding or not. Thus, in addition to the relevant articles of the ICCPR and UNCAT, a range of instruments has been identified by Nowak and McArthur as constituting reference points for the SPT. These include, but are not be limited to:[62]

---

[58] This paraphrasing of art 11 is taken from the SPT's First Annual Report: UN Doc CAT/C/40/2, 14 May 2008, para 7.
[59] SPT's First Annual Report UN Doc CAT/C/40/2, para 8.
[60] OPCAT, art 2(2).
[61] 'The drafters wished to express the principle that the SPT, in conducting visits to the territory of the States parties, shall avoid any behaviour which might be interpreted as violating the sovereignty, equality and territorial integrity of any State. In other words, the Subcommittee shall act in a spirit of cooperation rather than confrontation and respect the customs, traditions, religious and similar rules of the respective countries': Nowak and McArthur, *The United Nations Convention Against Torture: A Commentary* (OUP, 2008), p 916.
[62] See generally, Nowak and McArthur, *The United Nations Convention Against Torture: A Commentary* (OUP, 2008), pp 916–917; (contd.../)

- Standard Minimum Rules for the Treatment of Prisoners;[63]
- Declaration on the Protection of All Persons from Being Subjected to Torture and Other Cruel, Inhuman or Degrading Treatment or Punishment;[64]
- Code of Conduct for Law Enforcement Officials;[65]
- Principles of Medical Ethics relevant to the Role of Health Personnel particularly Physicians, in the Protection of Prisoners and Detainees against Torture and other Cruel and Inhuman, Degrading Treatment or Punishment;[66]
- Standard Minimum Rules for the Administration of Juvenile Justice ('The Beijing Rules');[67]
- Body of Principles for the Protection of All Persons under Any Form of Detention or Imprisonment;[68]
- Basic Rules for the Treatment of Prisoners;[69]
- Rules for the Protection of Juveniles Deprived of their Liberty;[70]
- Basic Principles on the Use of Force and Firearms by Law Enforcement Officials;[71]
- Principles for the Protection of Persons with Mental Illness and the Improvement of Mental Health Care;[72]
- Principles on the Effective Investigation and Documentation of Torture and Other Cruel, Inhuman and Degrading Treatment or Punishment ('The Istanbul Protocol');[73]

---

[62] (\...contd) and *Optional Protocol to the United Nations Convention Against Torture and Other Cruel, Inhuman or Degrading Treatment or Punishment: A Manual for Prevention* (Inter-American Institute for Human Rights and Association for the Prevention of Torture, 2005), pp 71–72.

[63] ECOSOC Res 663c (XXIV), 31 July 1957 (amended in 1977: ECOSOC Res 2076 (LXII), 13 May 1977).

[64] GA Res 3452 (XXX), 9 December 1979.

[65] GA Res 34/69, 17 December 1979.

[66] GA Res 37/194 of 18 December 1982.

[67] GA Res 40/33, 29 November 1985.

[68] GA Res 34/173, 9 December 1988.

[69] GA Res 45/111, 14 December 1990.

[70] GA Res 45/113, 14 December 1990.

[71] Eighth UN Congress on the Prevention of Crime and treatment of Offenders, 27 August to 7 September 1990: http://www.osce.org/documents/odihr/2004/09/3660_en.pdf (last accessed May 2011).

[72] GA Res 46/119, 17 December 1991.

[73] GA Res 55/89, 4 December 2000. In its Second Annual Report, the SPT highlighted the validity and usefulness of the Istanbul Protocol as an instrument of soft law, advising States that they should '…promote, disseminate and implement it as a legal instrument to document torture cases of people deprived of their liberty through medical and psychological reports drafted under adequate technical standards'. See para 24 and the SPT's analysis of the Protocol at Annex VII of the Report: UN Doc CAT/C/42 2.

The Protocol also directs the SPT to be guided in its work by the principles of 'confidentiality, impartiality, non-selectivity, universality and objectivity'.[74] The importance of preserving confidentiality as regards certain information arising from its unique mandate has been highlighted by the SPT on a number of occasions since its inception.[75]

Visits

[6.13] The Protocol confers extensive powers on the SPT in regard to its visiting function, as well as imposing correspondingly far-reaching obligations on the contracting States. Specifically, each State party is obliged to allow visits by the SPT to any place under its jurisdiction and control where persons are or may be deprived of their liberty.[76]

[6.14] Obviously, the effectiveness of the visiting function depends hugely on the SPT's ability (a) to travel to the territory of the State in the first place (or 'conduct a mission'); and (b) once there, to make *unannounced* visits to places of detention. On the first point, there seems to be no doubt but that ratification of the Protocol carries with it the automatic obligation, by virtue of art 4, to allow missions by the SPT to its territory. This does not necessarily mean that the SPT may literally descend on a State's territory without a moment's notice, as to do so would likely jeopardise the effectiveness of the visit. Accordingly, art 13(2) provides that the Subcommittee shall notify the States parties of its programme of visits so that they may, without delay, 'make the necessary practical arrangements for the visits to be conducted'.[77] Thus, the Subcommittee will notify each State in advance of the intended dates of a mission to its territory, together with information on the personnel involved in its visiting delegation.

[6.15] On the question of the ability of the SPT to conduct unannounced visits to places of detention in the process of a mission, Evans and Haani-Dale have hinted that the wording of the Protocol is ambiguous, in that the text 'neither prohibits nor authorises

---

[74] OPCAT, art 2(3). In its most recent annual report, the SPT has set forth a series of further key principles which it believes should guide it in its approach to its preventive mandate under the OPCAT: Fourth Annual Report of the Subcommittee on Prevention of Torture and Other Cruel, Inhuman or Degrading Treatment or Punishment, UN Doc CAT/C/46/2 (3 February 2011), para 107.

[75] SPT First Annual Report, pp 64–65; and SPT Second Annual Report, p 81. In its most recent annual report, the SPT has stated that in its view 'Confidentiality lies at the heart of the philosophy underlying the Protocol', enabling as it does the development of a constructive dialogue and relationship of mutual respect between the SPT and the States parties to the Protocol. As is discussed further below, however, the SPT has also encouraged States to dispense with confidentiality by authorising publication of the SPT reports and recommendations: SPT Fourth Annual Report, paras 46–48.

[76] OPCAT, arts 4 and 12.

[77] See also ECPT, art 8(1) which also provides for States to be notified in advance of the CPT's intention to visit its territory.

such [unannounced] visits...'.[78] However, based on a combination of arts 4(1), 12(a)[79] and 14(1) of the Protocol, as well as the overall objective expressed in art 1 of preventing torture, the prevailing view at this stage would appear to be that the SPT has the right to make unannounced visits to places of detention during a mission to a State party.[80] The SPT has certainly adopted this interpretation and so far has met with no contradiction.[81] States parties may only object to a visit of the SPT on 'urgent and compelling grounds of national defence, public safety, natural disaster or serious disorder in the place to be visited' that temporarily prevent the carrying out of the visit. Moreover, the existence of a declared state of emergency shall not be invoked as a reason to object to a visit.[82]

[6.16] The Protocol requires the SPT to establish a 'programme of regular visits' to the States parties.[83] Following the practice of the CPT, the Protocol specifically provides that the first programme of regular visits shall be determined by lot.[84] Thereafter, the SPT was free to determine its own means of selecting countries and it has decided to do so by means of a 'reasoned process', with reference to the principles of confidentiality, impartiality, non-selectivity, universality and objectivity set forth in art 2 of the Protocol.[85] Among the factors to be taken into account in considering the choice of countries to be visited are: the date of ratification/development of NPMs; geographic distribution; size and complexity of the State; regional preventive monitoring; and urgent issues reported.[86] In addition to its regular visits, the SPT is empowered to make 'follow-up' visits to a State, if it considers that appropriate.[87]

---

[78] Evans and Haenni Dale, 'Preventing Torture? The Development of the Optional Protocol to the UN Convention Against Torture' (2004) 4 HRL Rev 19, p 47. Similar doubts as regards the ability of the SPT to conduct ad hoc visits have been expressed by Rodley, 'Reflections on Working for the Prevention of Torture' (2009) 1 Essex Hum Rts Rev 15, p 20.

[79] This provision obliges states to '...receive the SPT on their territory and grant it access to the places of detention as defined in Article 4 of the Protocol'.

[80] Nowak and McArthur, *The United Nations Convention Against Torture: A Commentary* (OUP, 2008), pp 933–944; and *Optional Protocol to the United Nations Convention Against Torture and Other Cruel, Inhuman or Degrading Treatment or Punishment: A Manual for Prevention* (Inter-American Institute for Human Rights and Association for the Prevention of Torture, 2005), pp 75–76.

[81] SPT Second Annual Report, para 22.

[82] OPCAT, art 14(2). This provision mirrors ECPT, art 9.

[83] OPCAT, art 13(1).

[84] OPCAT, art 13(1).

[85] SPT First Annual Report, para 14. Mauritius, Maldives and Sweden were the first countries drawn by lot.

[86] SPT First Annual Report, para 14. Using this process, the SPT has thus far conducted visits to Benin, Mexico, Paraguay, Honduras, Cambodia, Lebanon, Bolivia and Liberia: http://www2.ohchr.org/english/bodies/cat/opcat/spt_visits.htm (last accessed May 2011). In the course of 2011, it plans to conduct visits to Brazil, Mali and Ukraine: SPT Fourth Annual Report, para 111.

[87] OPCAT, art 13(4). The first such follow-up visit by the SPT was to Paraguay in September 2010.

[6.17] In planning each visit, the SPT will request information from each State party to be visited about the legislation and institutional features of the system related to deprivation of liberty, as well as statistical and other relevant information regarding their operation in practice.[88] Ideally, the NPMs should also provide information to the SPT regarding their composition, mandate, monitoring activities and recommendations to government to date in relation to persons deprived of their liberty in the State in question.[89] APT has aptly characterised the interconnected relationship between the states parties, the SPT and the NPMs as a 'triangular' one.[90] But the relationship is by no means a closed one. There is in fact huge scope for NGOs and civil society to make their own contribution to the process by providing additional, and possibly less self-serving, information to the SPT in advance of its visit on the situation of persons deprived of their liberty in their jurisdiction.[91]

[6.18] As regards the practical operation of the visits, these may be conducted by at least two members of the Subcommittee, who may be accompanied, if necessary, by experts of 'demonstrated professional experience and knowledge in the fields covered by the Protocol'.[92] While the possibility of including experts was contentious during the drafting stage, it was eventually agreed that some provision should be made for their inclusion, if necessary.[93] The compromise reached was that their selection should be controlled by the compilation of a roster prepared on the basis of names proposed by the States parties, the OHCHR and the United Nations Centre for International Crime Prevention.[94] Perhaps predictably, this procedure has proved to be somewhat unsatisfactory in practice. Indeed, in the period covered in the Annual Report for 2009–2010, it was not possible for delegations of the SPT to be accompanied by a single expert on any of its country visits, owing to budgetary constraints.[95] Thus, notwithstanding the increased size of the SPT itself, the possibility of providing the

---

[88] SPT Second Annual Report, para 19.

[89] APT Briefing Note 2: Role of Civil Society in Preparation of SPT Visits, http://www.apt.ch/index.php?option=com_k2&view=item&id=692%3Athe-un-subcommittee-on-prevention-of-torture-spt&Itemid=269&lang=en, p 1 (last accessed May 2011).

[90] APT Briefing Note 2: Role of Civil Society in Preparation of SPT Visits, p 1.

[91] APT Briefing Note 2: Role of Civil Society in Preparation of SPT Visits, p 1.

[92] OPCAT, art 13(3).

[93] Nowak and McArthur, *The United Nations Convention Against Torture: A Commentary* (OUP, 2008), pp 1029–1030.

[94] Nowak and McArthur, *The United Nations Convention Against Torture: A Commentary* (OUP, 2008), pp 1029–1030. States parties are entitled to propose no more than five experts. The State party is entitled to oppose the inclusion of a specific expert on the visit, whereupon the Subcommittee shall propose another expert.

[95] SPT Third Annual Report, para 34. The Fourth Annual Report does not specifically allude to the issue of experts. It emphasises, hover, the urgent need for an increase in administrative assistance for the SPT to fulfil its mandate: 'The Subcommittee believes that an expansion in the size of its secretariat is an essential prerequisite for the further expansion of its work, and that a failure to do so would frustrate the object and purpose of the second sentence of Article 5, paragraph 1', SPT Fourth Annual Report, para 109.

multidisciplinary expertise that is clearly necessary to complement its membership has not materialised.[96]

[6.19] For the purposes of a visit, art 14 provides that the States parties shall grant to the SPT unrestricted access to all information concerning the number of persons deprived of their liberty;[97] and on the treatment of those persons as well as their conditions of detention.[98] As well as granting unrestricted access to the SPT to places of detention of their choosing,[99] the States parties must grant it the opportunity to conduct private interviews with detainees without witnesses, either personally or through a translator, as well as with any other person whom the Subcommittee believes may supply relevant information.[100] A specific provision is included in the Protocol to the effect that persons who communicate with the Subcommittee cannot be subjected to any form of sanction as a result.[101] In addition to visiting places of detention and interviewing detainees during a mission, the SPT will also take time to meet with senior officials of the ministries responsible for law enforcement and detention of any kind within the meaning provided for in the Protocol. It will also meet with the relevant NPM, if it is already set up, as well as NHRIs and NGOs, and any other persons who may have information of relevance to its mandate.[102] It will meet further with officials in the relevant ministries and bodies at the conclusion of its visit, to identify issues raised and situations which may require immediate action, and generally to give the authorities an opportunity to respond accordingly.

[6.20] Once the visit has been concluded, the Protocol provides for the SPT to draw up a report, in which it shall communicate its recommendations and observations

---

[96] 'Notwithstanding the extensive experience and the commitment of the current members, the SPT is thus not in a position to deploy multidisciplinary teams without additional experts': 'Providing the Subcommittee of Torture with Experts', APT Position Paper, May 2007, p 2: http://www.apt.ch/index.php?option=com_k2&view=item&id=692%3Athe-un-subcommittee-on-prevention-of-torture-spt&Itemid=269&lang=en (last accessed May 2011).

[97] See also OPCAT, art 12(b) which obliges States to provide all relevant information that the SPT may request to evaluate the needs and measures that should be adopted to strengthen the protection of persons deprived of their liberty against torture and other cruel, inhuman or degrading treatment or punishment.

[98] OPCAT, art 14(1)(b).

[99] OPCAT, arts 14(1)(c) and (e).

[100] OPCAT, art 14(1)(d). In its most recent annual report, the SPT has noted that it is still having practical difficulties in conducting its visits, including having access to registers and interviewing witnesses in private. These difficulties have been ameliorated where a member of the Committee has been able to go to a country in advance of a visit for informal briefings – a practice which the SPT would like to undertake prior to each of its visits, if possible: SPT Fourth Annual Report, paras 50–51.

[101] OPCAT, art 15.

[102] See the 'Outline of a Regular SPT Visit' prepared by the SPT, available at: http://www2.ohchr.org/english/bodies/cat/opcat/outline.htm (last accessed May 2011).

confidentially to the State party, and, if relevant, to the NPM.[103] The State, in turn, is obliged to examine the recommendations and to enter into dialogue with the SPT on possible measures of implementation.[104]

[6.21] The SPT's report shall remain confidential except in three sets of circumstances:

(i) The SPT shall publish the report, together with any comments of the State party concerned, if requested to do so by that State party.

This provision in art 16(2) reflects the importance of the principle of confidentiality in building a culture of trust as between the SPT and the States parties. Save for the exceptional circumstances outlined below, States are assured that they keep control of whether the information gleaned by the SPT during one of its visits enters the public domain. On the other hand, the benefits of allowing publication are clearly stated by the SPT:

> 'Publication of an SPT visit report and the response from the authorities concerned is a sign of the commitment of the State party to the objectives of the OPCAT. It enables civil society to consider the issues addressed in the report and to work with the authorities on implementation of the recommendations to improve the protection of peoples deprived of their liberty'.[105]

Article 11(2) of the ECPT incorporates a corresponding provision whereby the CPT will only publish its reports if requested to do so by the relevant State party. As matters have panned out, the States parties to that Convention have routinely requested the CPT to publish its reports, and publication is now the rule, rather than the exception.[106] It is too early to judge whether a similar pattern will emerge under the OPCAT, though the SPT believes that there is a 'welcome trend towards publication'.[107]

[6.22]

(ii) The SPT may publish the report in whole or in part, if the State party makes part of the report public.[108]

---

[103] OPCAT, art 16(1). Before this is issued, the State party will have been given a further opportunity to provide information regarding developments that have taken place since the SPT's visit. See 'Outline of a Regular SPT Visit' prepared by the SPT: http://www2.ohchr.org/english/bodies/cat/opcat/outline.htm (last accessed May 2011).

[104] OPCAT, art 12(d).

[105] SPT Second Annual Report, para 29. The SPT has reiterated this point in its most recent report: SPT Fourth Annual Report, para 47.

[106] As mentioned *supra* at para **6.04**, the CPT has published 250 reports.

[107] SPT Fourth Annual Report, para 58. Six of the eleven States visited have opted for publication (Honduras, the Maldives, Paraguay, Benin, Mexico and Sweden). This is indeed a promising trend since three of the other reports have only recently been sent (Cambodia, Lebanon and Bolivia), while a fourth has not yet been transmitted to the State party (Liberia). The Maldives thus appears to be the only State which has thus far opted not to authorise publication: http://www2.ohchr.org/english/bodies/cat/opcat/spt_visits.htm (last accessed May 2011).

[108] OPCAT, art 16(2). In either of the two circumstances outlined in art 16(2), no personal data shall be published without the consent of the person concerned.

The second clause of art 16(2) was inserted to guard against States selectively publishing passages of an SPT report in order to create a positive impression of that State's practices in regard to detention. It enables the SPT to dispense with the principle of confidentiality and to publish the full report or omitted passages in order to present a more truthful account.

[6.23]

(iii) If the State party refuses to cooperate with the SPT,[109] or to take steps to improve the situation in the light of its recommendations, the SPT may request the Committee Against Torture to make a public statement on the matter or to publish the report of the SPT.[110] This may be done by a majority vote and only after the State party has had an opportunity to make its views known to the CAT.

This provision is analogous to art 10(2) of the ECPT[111] and was inserted in the Protocol to act as a sanction against non-cooperative States. It indicates that the principle of confidentiality underpinning the work of the SPT is '…a means to an end and not an end in itself'.[112] The making of a public statement or publication of a report should only occur in the most exceptional of circumstances against governments that are completely uncooperative, obstructive and who refuse to take on board the recommendations of the Subcommittee, in violation of their obligations under the Protocol.[113] It should be noted that the final say on this matter was entrusted to the CAT, rather than the SPT, presumably as a means of distancing the SPT from the making of such a confrontational decision.[114]

[6.24] Finally, it should be noted that the SPT is obliged to publish a public annual report on its activities to the CAT.[115] This requirement is another manifestation of the linkage which States wished to retain between the SPT and the CAT in the text of the Protocol.[116] The principle of confidentiality is necessarily respected in the obligation to make such 'public annual reports' since the Protocol forbids the SPT from publishing its reports on missions to the States parties, save for the specific circumstances provided

---

[109] In this respect, the Protocol specifically refers to the State's obligations in OPCAT, arts 12 and 14.

[110] OPCAT, art 16(4).

[111] However, it is interesting that CAT may make this decision by a simple majority vote. Under the corresponding ECPT, art 10(2), the CPT may only issue a public statement in similar circumstances where two-thirds of its membership agrees.

[112] This aphorism was used by the representatives of Amnesty International and El Salvador during negotiations on this provision in the working group established to draft the Protocol: UN Doc E/CN4/1996/28, para 64.

[113] In particular, OPCAT, arts 2(4), 12, 14 and/or 15: Nowak and McArthur, *The United Nations Convention Against Torture: A Commentary* (OUP, 2008), p 1063.

[114] This suggestion was made by representative of Australia during the drafting process: UN Doc E/CN4/1996/28, para 40.

[115] OPCAT, art 16(3).

[116] See para **6.09** above.

for in art 16(2) and (4). Thus, as regards the Subcommittee's visiting function, the annual report only includes general information on the countries visited, and the methods adopted by the Subcommittee in carrying out these visits.

National Preventive Mechanisms (NPMs)

[6.25] Article 3 of the Protocol provides for the establishment or designation in each State party of an NPM.[117] It obliges them to 'set up, designate or maintain at the domestic level one or several visiting bodies for the prevention of torture and other cruel, inhuman or degrading treatment or punishment'. NPMs are the national equivalent of the SPT in the Protocol's implementation structure. As well as permitting visits from the SPT, each State party must allow regular visits by its NPM to any place of detention in its jurisdiction where persons are detained by a public authority or with its consent or acquiescence[118].

[6.26] Article 3 is, in effect, a manifestation in the Protocol of the principle of subsidiarity in international human rights law, namely, that the national authorities have the primary responsibility for implementing human rights law, while international bodies are only intended to play a subsidiary role.[119] If properly established and resourced, NPMs could alleviate the inefficiencies that would inevitably have occurred in the SPT's visiting programme in the event of substantial ratifications of the Protocol.[120] Thus, as noted above, the creation of this extra layer of prevention in art 3 constitutes the unique feature of the Protocol and potentially its most valuable aspect.

[6.27] The particular characteristics and means of establishing an NPM are elaborated upon in Part IV of the Protocol. As regards NPM's characteristics, art 18(4) provides that States parties should give due consideration to the Paris Principles in establishing national preventive mechanisms.[121] The latter principles set forth the appropriate standards for the establishment of properly functioning national human rights institutions. They indicate, inter alia, that a national human rights institution should have:

- a broad-based mandate, which is clearly defined in a constitutional or legislative text, specifying its composition and sphere of competence;
- independence from government;

---

[117] See also OPCAT, art 17.

[118] OPCAT, art 4(1).

[119] Nowak and McArthur, *The United Nations Convention Against Torture: A Commentary* (OUP, 2008), p 923. See above, Ch 1, para **1.14**.

[120] Nowak and McArthur, *The United Nations Convention Against Torture: A Commentary* (OUP, 2008), p 923.

[121] See UN Doc GA Res 48/134, 20 December 1993. The distinction between accreditation as a national human rights institution and its suitability as an NPM is discussed in a policy paper by the OPCAT Research Team at Bristol University: 'The Relationship Between Accreditation by the International Coordinating Committee of National Human Rights Institutions and the Optional Protocol to the UN Convention Against Torture' (November 2008): http://www.bris.ac.uk/law/research/centres-themes/opcat/opcatdocs/iccaccreditationandnpms.pdf (last accessed May 2011).

- pluralist representation;
- an adequate infrastructure that is suited to the smooth conduct of its activities, including adequate funding and sufficient resources.

Together with further guidelines which the SPT itself has produced,[122] these principles, provide an important source of guidance for States in regard to the establishment or designation of NPMs. The reference to them in para (4) is supplemented by the other elements of art 18 which oblige States to guarantee the *functional independence* of NPMs as well as the independence of their personnel;[123] to take the necessary measures to ensure that experts on the NPMs have the 'required capabilities and professional knowledge', as well as striving for a gender balance and adequate representation of ethnic and minority groups;[124] and lastly to make available the necessary resources for the functioning of the NPMs.[125]

[6.28] As regards the process of establishing NPMs, art 17 repeats the point made in art 3 that States may 'maintain, designate or establish' one or several independent NPMs for the prevention of torture at the domestic level. This means that States are faced with a choice as to whether one or more bodies should be created or whether an existing body or bodies should be invested with the status of an NPM and mandated to carry out the necessary functions.[126] Specific advantages and disadvantages are associated with the establishment of a new body versus the designation of an existing body or bodies, and with the use of a single unified mechanism for the whole country or several mechanisms for different types of places of detention.[127] The clear trend which has emerged thus far appears to be that of designating existing bodies as NPMs (frequently NHRIs or

---

[122] The SPT has recently published revised guidelines concerning the process of establishing, as well as the key features, of NPMs which elaborate on and augment the basic requirements of the Protocol: SPT Guidelines on National Preventive Mechanisms, UN Doc CAT/OP/12/5, reproduced in SPT Fourth Annual Report, paras 63–102. These revised guidelines elaborate on the preliminary guidelines set forth in the SPT's First Annual Report, para 28. See the commentary of the Research Team on the OPCAT, established at the University of Bristol, School of Law on the preliminary guidelines: http://www.bris.ac.uk/law/research/centres-themes/opcat/opcatdocs/bristolcommentsonsptnpmguidelines.pdf (last accessed May 2011). See also Amnesty International's 10 Guiding Principles for the Establishment of National Preventive Mechanisms: AI Index IOR/51/009/2007. See also Olivier and Narvaez, 'OPCAT Challenges and the Way Forwards: The Ratification and Implementation of the Optional Protocol to the UN Convention Against Torture' (2009) 1 Essex Hum Rts Rev 39, pp 45–53.

[123] OPCAT, art 18(1).
[124] OPCAT, art 18(2).
[125] OPCAT, art 18(3).
[126] See the SPT's Guidelines on National Preventative Mechanisms, U.N. Doc.CAT/OP/12/5, reproduced in SPT Fourth Annual Report, paras 63–102.
[127] See further *Guide to Establishment and Designation of National Preventive Mechanisms* (APT, 2006): available at http://www.apt.ch (last accessed May 2011); and Murray, 'National Preventive Mechanisms Under the Optional Protocol to the Torture Convention: One Size Does Not Fit All' (2008) 26(4) Neth Q Hum Rts 485–516.

ombuds-institutions)[128] and tailoring their mandates to satisfy the functions of an NPM.[129] The main danger that may arise where this option is exercised is that existing bodies are simply 'designated' by law, without any meaningful effort being made to adapt their mandates appropriately or to provide them with the necessary resources to fulfil their functions under the Protocol.[130] The SPT itself has made it clear that it does not have a preferred model for an NPM, but rather will look at NPMs from a 'functional perspective', recognising that 'just because one model works well in one country does not mean it will work well in another'.[131]

[6.29] In any case, the obligation to maintain or designate an NPM must be done at the latest one year after the entry into force of the Protocol or of its ratification or accession.[132] However, a temporary opt-out clause is provided for in art 24 of the Protocol, allowing States to postpone their obligations in this respect (as well as with respect to the SPT) for a maximum of three years, which period may be extended for a further two years by the CAT, following consultation with the SPT.[133] The SPT has

---

[128] As to the different challenges faced in designating NHRIs as opposed to ombuds-institutions, see: Steinerte and Murray, 'Same But Different: National Human Rights Commissions and Ombudsman Institutions as National Preventive Mechanisms under the Optional Protocol to the UN Convention Against Torture' (2009) 1 Essex Hum Rts Rev 54.

[129] See APT Report on Country Status: Ratification and Implementation: http://www.apt.ch/index.php?option=com_k2&view=item&layout=item&id=678&Itemid=253&lang=en (last accessed May 2011). Occasionally, States have designated NHRIs or an ombudsman in combination with other bodies, including NGOs (as is the case in the Republic of Moldova and Slovenia). One interesting example of this approach is the one adopted in New Zealand. New Zealand has opted to fulfil its obligations under the OPCAT in respect of NPMs by designating a mosaic of existing visiting mechanisms which will include an Ombudsman, the Police Complaints Authority, and the Children's Commissioner. The New Zealand Human Rights Commission has been designated as the central NPM and will coordinate the activities of the other NPMs and liaise with the SPT. Under this model, the other NPMs will advise the Commission and provide appropriate information when requested on the outcome of their inspections. In carrying out its functions the Commission must consult and liaise with the NPMs, review the reports prepared by them, and coordinate the submission of those reports to the SPT. Flowing from these tasks, the Commission is also responsible for making recommendations to government on any matter relating to the prevention of torture and other cruel, inhuman or degrading treatment or punishment in places of detention in New Zealand: see Crimes of Torture Act 1989 (as amended), pp 26–32. On the other hand, one less impressive example of implementation is that of the United Kingdom where 18 existing oversight bodies were designated as the UK NPM without any changes to their mandates or powers. The Inspectorate for Prisons will assume the NPM coordination role for these 18 bodies.

[130] See the problems identified to this effect by the SPT in respect of the establishment of NPMs in the Maldives (UN Doc CAT/OP/MDV/1, paras 65–70) and Sweden (UN Doc CAT/OP/SWE/1, paras 19–40).

[131] SPT Fourth Annual Report, para 62.

[132] OPCAT, art 17.

[133] A discrepancy in the various texts of the Protocol has necessitated a correction procedure to be taken in respect of art 24. (contd.../)

expressed serious concern at the lack of progress to date in the designation and indeed maintenance of NPMs in many of the States parties to the Protocol and with their levels of official engagement on this most crucial aspect of the Protocol.[134] Data collected by the SPT as of February 2011 indicated that only 27 of the 57 States parties to the Protocol had officially designated NPMs.[135] Taking account of the provisions of art 24, 20 States parties are in breach of their obligations to establish or designate a national preventive mechanism.[136] Moreover, in those States which have moved to establish their NPMs, gaps have been identified as regards '...the necessary legislative foundation and the practical provision, including human and budgetary resources to enable NPMs to work effectively'.[137]

[6.30] The mandate of NPMs, together with the obligations of States parties in respect of them, is set forth in Part IV of the Protocol. States parties are obliged to grant NPMs 'at a minimum', the power to:

(i) Regularly examine the treatment of persons deprived of their liberty, including the power to conduct visits to places of detention in their jurisdiction under similar conditions to those which apply to the SPT;[138]

(ii) Make recommendations to the authorities with the aim of improving the treatment and conditions of persons deprived of their liberty;[139]

(iii) Submit proposals and observations concerning existing or draft legislation.[140]

NPMs have the right to have contacts with the SPT, to send it information and to meet with it.[141] The State is obliged to examine the recommendations of the NPM and to enter into a dialogue with it on possible implementation measures.[142] Under art 23, the States parties must undertake to publish and disseminate the annual report of the national preventive mechanism.

---

[133] (\...contd) As the Third Annual Report of the SPT explains, whereas the Arabic, Chinese, English and French texts of art 24 each provided that the opt-out clause could be exercised 'upon ratification', the Russian and Spanish versions provided that such could be done 'once ratified'. Accordingly, a procedure has been applied whereby the latter versions of art 24 were brought into line with the former in April 2010 with retroactive effect: SPT Third Annual Report, para 48.

[134] SPT Second Annual Report, paras 33–39; SPT Third Annual Report, paras 37–53; and SPT Fourth Annual Report, para 23.

[135] SPT Fourth Annual Report, para 20.

[136] SPT Fourth Annual Report, para 23.

[137] SPT Second Annual Report, para 35. While the Third Annual Report is less critical of States parties on this point, a similar conclusion can be drawn from the 'issues' which it raises in relation to the establishment of NPMs: paras 49–53. The Fourth Annual Report refers to the importance of establishing an 'Optional Protocol-compliant' NPM as a vital component of the preventive system created by the Protocol: Fourth Annual Report, para 60.

[138] OPCAT, arts 19(a) and 20.

[139] OPCAT, art 19(b).

[140] OPCAT, art 19(c).

[141] OPCAT, art 20(f).

[142] OPCAT, art 22.

[6.31] A number of interesting issues arise in regard to the mandate of NPMs, which is much vaguer in many respects than that of its counterpart, the SPT. First, the Protocol stipulates the need for NPMs to 'regularly' examine the treatment of detainees, and there can be little doubt but that a regime of frequent visits on the part of NPMs is the only guaranteed means of ensuring a meaningful fulfilment of their mandate.[143] While the Protocol does not itself specify a timetable for NPMs in regard to their visiting functions, it is clear that NPMs will need to differentiate as between different types of detention facilities with respect to the frequency of their visits.[144] The lack of specificity in the Protocol as regards a visiting programme leaves room for the NPMs to conduct periodic as well as follow-up visits, as is explicitly provided for in the case of the SPT.[145]

[6.32] Unlike the provisions of the Protocol which elaborate on States' obligations in regard to the SPT, the Protocol does not specify the right of NPMs to 'unrestricted' access to places of detention or to relevant information.[146] On the other hand, nor does the Protocol stipulate exceptional grounds on which a State can object to a visit by an NPM, as is the case in regard to visits by the SPT.[147] This certainly leaves room for varying interpretations on the question of whether governments might be able to object to a visit by an NPM on urgent and compelling grounds.[148] As regards the question of whether visits by an NPM may be unannounced, again the Protocol is silent on this point. However, as with the provisions in regard to visits by the SPT, a purposive interpretation of arts 4(1), 20 and 1 of the Protocol would appear to be that NPMs may make unannounced visits on a similar basis to the SPT.[149]

---

[143] Long, 'Mandate and Methodology of the Preventive Mechanisms under the Optional Protocol to the UN Convention Against Torture' in *Optional Protocol to the United Nations Convention Against Torture and Other Cruel, Inhuman or Degrading Treatment or Punishment: A Manual for Prevention* (Inter-American Institute for Human Rights and Association for the Prevention of Torture, 2005), p 121.

[144] Thus, for example, pre-trial detention centres will need to be visited more frequently than prisons, given the more limited opportunities for contact with the outside world afforded to detainees in such facilities. In its most recent report, the SPT has identified the overuse and 'misuse' of pre-trial detention as a '... general problem that needs to be tackled as a matter of priority': Fourth Annual Report, para 52.

[145] OPCAT, arts 13(1) and (4).

[146] Compare OPCAT, arts 14(c) and 20(c).

[147] OPCAT, art 14(2).

[148] Nowak and McArthur, *The United Nations Convention Against Torture: A Commentary* (OUP, 2008), pp 1090–1091, who conclude that it might not be unreasonable for a government to refuse a visit in the case of a prison riot, but certainly not in the case of a natural disaster or for public safety reasons.

[149] 'While the Optional Protocol does not expressly provide for the national preventive mechanisms to have access to any place of detention at any time, in order for these mechanisms to effectively prevent torture, in addition to planned regular visits, the national preventive mechanisms should be able to react to any special event and carry out ad hoc visits': *Optional Protocol to the United Nations Convention Against Torture and Other Cruel, Inhuman or Degrading Treatment or Punishment: A Manual for Prevention* (Inter-American Institute for Human Rights and Association for the Prevention of Torture, 2005), p 136. (contd.../)

[6.33] While the Protocol is explicit as regards the obligation on the SPT to issue a confidential report to each State party on each of its missions,[150] the provisions in regard to reporting by NPMs are surprisingly imprecise. The Protocol simply provides that NPMs must be given the power 'to make recommendations to the relevant authorities'[151] which the latter are required to examine.[152] Unlike the unequivocal obligations on the SPT in regard to confidentiality, NPMs are not required to keep their recommendations confidential,[153] presumably on the basis that critique by a national body will have less damaging implications for a government than one provided by an international body. Also of relevance here is the obligation in art 23 of the Protocol on NPMs to publish an annual report which the States parties are required to publish and disseminate. Certainly, the ability of the NPMs to publish their reports and recommendations gives rise to an extremely valuable opportunity for such bodies to raise awareness on conditions of persons deprived of their liberty on the national stage.

[6.34] Finally, one uncertainty arising from the text in regard to the international and national framework of prevention is the question of whether NPMs are accountable to the SPT. On this point, it may be noted that the SPT is specifically mandated to maintain direct, and if necessary, confidential contact with NPMs, and to offer them training, advice and technical assistance,[154] while art 16(1) also obliges it to communicate its mission reports confidentially to the State party, and 'if relevant' to the NPM. On the other hand, while NPMs have the right 'to have contacts' with the Subcommittee,[155] there is no mention of an obligation on NPMs to 'report' to the SPT or even to inform it about its visits to places of detention. The emphasis in the Protocol, therefore, appears to be firmly on facilitating cooperation between NPMs and the SPT, rather than on making the former, strictly speaking, accountable to the latter. While the SPT is clearly very conscious that its mandate in regard to supporting and advising NPMs is of the utmost importance,[156] it has expressed regret at its inability to devote as much attention as it would like to the process of their establishment.[157]

---

[149] (\...contd) These views are expressed even more firmly by APT in, 'Visiting Places of Detention at the National Level: Recommendations of the European Committee for the Prevention of Torture Considered in the Light of the OPCAT', p 6: 'The criteria of unannounced visit is not expressly mentioned in the OPCAT. The APT however considers that the possibility of NPMs to carry out unannounced visits is fundamental for visits to really have a preventive effect'.

[150] OPCAT, art 16.
[151] OPCAT, art 19(b).
[152] OPCAT, art 22.
[153] Confidential information collected by NPMs shall be privileged and no personal data shall be published without the consent of the persons concerned: OPCAT, art 23.
[154] OPCAT, art 11(1)(b)(ii).
[155] OPCAT, art 20(f). Article 12(c) also obligates States to 'encourage and facilitate contacts' between the SPT and NPMs.
[156] SPT Second Annual Report, para 39.
[157] SPT Fourth Annual Report, para 44. The Subcommittee is now inclined to a model for it to follow in this respect whereby it would seek to visit a State as soon as possible following ratification in order to offer advice and assistance regarding the establishment of its NPM.

Prospects

[6.35] There can be little doubt but that at an abstract level, the preventive scheme established by the Protocol appears to 'open the prospect of a new era in the work of torture prevention'.[158] The in-built complementarity of these two mechanisms, working together, to monitor and inspect places of detention seems to be an ideal theoretical solution for the prevention of torture. Moreover, the creation of a preventive body at the international level could never have seriously hoped to replicate the practical experience of the CPT, given the potentially greater number of States parties involved. Even the CPT, with its 47 states parties, is straining at the seams to fulfil its workload. Therefore, the innovative move to establish national preventive mechanisms was well-placed to remedy the inevitable burden that would be placed on an international inspection body if it had been forced to go it alone.

[6.36] That the SPT could add real value to the realm of torture prevention generally is amply demonstrated by the reports which have been published of its visits to date. Each provides an interesting and contrasting perspective on how this body can add value across a wide spectrum of laws, policy and practice in different states on the issue of detention. In the course of its visits to Honduras,[159] Mexico[160] and Paraguay,[161] for example, the SPT collected harrowing evidence of very extreme and systematic methods of torture and ill-treatment by police in those countries.[162] Deficiencies in the legal and institutional framework for the prevention of torture,[163] overcrowding and the generally deplorable conditions in which persons are deprived of their liberty in police stations

---

[158] Evans and Haenni Dale, 'Preventing Torture? The Development of the Optional Protocol to the UN Convention Against Torture' (2004) 4 Hum Rts L Rev 19, p 55.

[159] SPT Report on Honduras: UN Doc CAT/OP/HND/1 (10 February 2010). The visit to Honduras took place during a time of intense social and political upheaval in the State, following the events of 28 June 2009, when President Manuel Zelaya was effectively removed to Costa Rica by the army and ousted from office. The SPT was conducting its visit to the country in September 2009 when President Zelaya returned to the country. It witnessed acts of violence that took place during demonstrations at that time and had difficulty leaving the country: see paras 18–23.

[160] SPT Report on Mexico: UN Doc CAT/OP/MEX/1 (31 May 2010).

[161] SPT Report on Paraguay: UN Doc CAT/OP/PRY/1 (7 June 2010).

[162] SPT Report on Honduras: UN Doc CAT/OP/HND/1 (10 February 2010), paras 26–74. SPT Report on Mexico: UN Doc CAT/OP/MEX/1 (31 May 2010), paras 224–225 and 235. As well as reporting on torture and ill-treatment by the police, the SPT Report on Paraguay also reveals patterns of systematic torture and episodes of sexual violence in the country's prisons: UN Doc CAT/OP/PRY/1 (7 June 2010), paras 134–143 and paras 211–214. The SPT's report on its follow-up visit to Paraguay a year later showed little evidence of improvement: UN Doc CAT/OP/PRY/2, paras. 40 – 67.

[163] SPT Report on Honduras: UN Doc CAT/OP/HND/1 (10 February 2010), paras 75–138; SPT Report on Mexico: UN Doc CAT/OP/MEX/1 (31 May 2010), paras 34–82; and SPT Report on Paraguay: UN Doc CAT/OP/PRY/1 (7 June 2010), paras 21–55.

and prisons were also identified.[164] Though far less shocking in substance, the report on the Maldives reveals that despite a programme of criminal law reform currently in train in that jurisdiction, serious problems exist with respect to the detention of persons in police custody, particularly in relation to their treatment, procedural rights and police methods of investigation.[165] The Subcommittee's forthright conclusions and constructive recommendations in each of these reports testify to the obvious merit of such an expert body operating at the universal level since, without its input, it is unlikely that the situation of persons deprived of their liberty would receive such intense and hands-on scrutiny from an international monitoring body.[166] At the opposite end of the spectrum, the Swedish report discloses a generally human-rights compliant system of detention in police facilities and remand prisons. As a consequence, the SPT recommendations are aimed largely at fine-tuning existing policies and practices already in place.[167] The report highlights the mutually reinforcing value of prevention as well as benchmarking that may take place in the course of a visit to a country, whereby the SPT can spot potential glitches in an otherwise compliant system of detention, while simultaneously taking account of what can be achieved in terms of good practice, and most importantly, *how* it can be achieved. In each report, the SPT identified significant problems with the

---

[164] SPT Report on Honduras: UN Doc CAT/OP/HND/1 (10 February 2010), paras 165–179, 198–232; SPT Report on Paraguay: UN Doc CAT/OP/PRY/1 (7 June 2010), paras 110–129 and paras 147–193; and SPT Report on Mexico: UN Doc CAT/OP/MEX/1 (31 May 2010), paras 111–113, 176–178 and 186.

[165] SPT Report on the Maldives: UN Doc CAT/OP/MDV/1, 26 February 2009, paras 73–133. The SPT, for example, noted the fact that under the law in force it is possible for a court to convict a person on the basis of a confession alone and that several detainees interviewed by the delegation alleged that the police still resorted to physical force and ill-treatment in order to obtain confessions (paras 89 and 90).

[166] Paraguay has not reported to the Committee against Torture under the UNCAT, art 18 periodic reporting procedure since 2000; Honduras recently reported in 2009, but its initial report had been overdue for ten-years (see concluding observations of CAT: UN Doc CAT/C/HND/CO/1); and the initial report under art 18 from the Maldives has been overdue since 2005: Treaty Bodies Database, http://tb.ohchr.org/default.aspx. That the SPT has achieved a significant level of constructive engagement with the government of Paraguay is evidenced in the replies which it received from the government: UN Doc CAT/OP/PRY/1/Add 1 (10 June 2010).

[167] SPT Report on Sweden: UN Doc CAT/OP/SWE/1 (10 September 2008). The replies of the Swedish government to the SPT's recommendations are published in UN Doc CAT/OP/SWE/1/Add 1 (30 January 2009). The fact that Sweden is also party to the ECPT presents an interesting opportunity for analysing the potential complementarity of the two visiting mechanisms in regard to States parties to both instruments. The CPT undertook its fourth periodic visit to Sweden in June 2009: http://www.cpt.coe.int/en/states/swe.htm (last accessed May 2011). Certain of these observations in regard to safeguards against ill-treatment and restrictions applied to remand prisoners appear to reinforce the observations made by the SPT in its report. On the relationship between the OPCAT and the CPT, see the policy paper by the OPCAT Research Team at Bristol University, 'Relationship Between the Optional Protocol to the UN Convention against Torture (OPCAT) and Other International and Regional Visiting Mechanisms' (August 2009): http://www.bris.ac.uk/law/research/centres-themes/opcat/opcatdocs/relationshipopcatandothervisitingmechanisms.pdf (last accessed May 2011).

designation of the NPM, in the process demonstrating the importance of international scrutiny of the manner in which States propose to fulfil their obligations in this regard.[168]

[6.37] On a practical level, however, the outlook for meaningful implementation of the Protocol for the foreseeable future is discouraging. In each of its annual reports, the SPT has referred to significant budgetary constraints which it has encountered since its inception in fulfilling its mandate. Despite the fact that the Protocol itself mandates the United Nations to equip the SPT with the necessary funding to fulfil its functions,[169] a failure to do so has had an impact not only on the quantity of country visits,[170] but also on the quality of those visits. This is manifest from the SPT's own admission that there are insufficient funds to allow the Subcommittee to utilise outside expertise[171] which it so obviously needs in conducting its visits. Lack of funding has also given rise to problems in regard to the institutional development of the SPT[172] as well as to its capacity to work directly with States in the establishment of their NPMs and with the NPMs themselves.[173] The latter deficit is particularly regrettable in view of the important part which such bodies have to play in the preventive strategy designed by the Protocol and the halting progress so far made in their establishment. It seems, therefore, that while the framework for torture prevention established by the Protocol is an undeniably positive development, it cannot realistically be expected to fulfil its true potential in the future without a sustained increase in UN funding.[174]

---

[168] On the appropriate role of the SPT in this regard, see 'The Relationship Between Accreditation by the International Coordinating Committee of National Human Rights Institutions and the Optional Protocol to the UN Convention Against Torture' (OPCAT Research Team at Bristol University), p 7ff.

[169] OPCAT, art 25 specifically states that the 'expenditure incurred by the Subcommittee on Prevention in the implementation of the present Protocol shall be borne by the United Nations' and that the Secretary General shall provide the necessary staff and facilities for the effective performance of the SPT's functions.

[170] Since its inception four years ago, the SPT has conducted only 11 country visits. Yet, by its own projection, the SPT would need to carry out 10 to 12 visits *per year* if it is to be in a position to visit each country every four to five years. The truncated programme of visits to date is directly a result of budgetary constraints: Third Annual Report, para 21.

[171] This issue was emphasised in the SPT's Third Annual Report, para 34.

[172] In the eight visits carried out up until 2010, the SPT had worked with a total of 14 different staff members: SPT Third Annual Report, paras 75–76. No details are provided in this regard in the Fourth Annual Report, save to state that '...the existing secretariat is already struggling to cope with its demanding workload and it is simply not possible for it to service the increased level of activity which the expansion of the Subcommittee is intended to bring': SPT Fourth Annual Report, para 109.

[173] SPT Third Annual Report, para 41; SPT Fourth Annual Report, para 44.

[174] This fact has been emphasised in each of the SPT's Annual Reports to date: First Annual Report, UN Doc CAT/C/40/2, 14 May 2008, para 68; Second Annual Report, UN Doc CAT/C/42/2, 7 April 2009, paras 75–76; (contd.../)

UNITED NATIONS CONVENTION ON THE RIGHTS OF PERSONS WITH DISABILITIES (2006)

[6.38] Despite the difficulties that have been encountered in the implementation of the OPCAT, it did serve, to some extent, as a precedent in the framing of the implementation provisions in the Convention on the Rights of Persons with Disabilities (CRPD).[175] While the latter Convention does not confer a 'visiting' function on the Committee on the Rights of Persons with Disabilities (CRPD Committee), its provisions in the realm of national implementation and monitoring are reminiscent of the 'preventive' aspect inherent in the establishment of NPMs by the OPCAT. By virtue of art 33(1) of the CRPD, States parties are obliged to designate one or more 'focal points' within government for matters relating to the implementation of the Convention; and 'due consideration' must be given to the establishment or designation of a coordination mechanism within government to facilitate related action in different sectors and at different levels. Article 33(2) of the Convention further obliges the States parties to '...maintain, strengthen, designate or establish within the State party, a framework, including one or more independent mechanisms, as appropriate, to promote, protect and monitor implementation' of the Convention. Civil society, and in particular, persons with disabilities and their representative organisations shall be involved and participate fully in the monitoring process.[176] However, aside from the prescription that the Paris Principles be taken into account in the establishment or designation of the national monitoring mechanism, art 33 provides no further detail on the appropriate shape and character, functions or powers of such mechanism(s). Neither does the Convention elaborate on the corresponding duties owed by the State which would be necessary for such mechanisms to fulfil their functions, nor the time-frame within which such a mechanism should be established.[177] In short, nothing like the detail provided for as regards NPMs in the OPCAT is provided for in the CRPD.

[6.39] A close inspection of the drafting history of this article of the Convention reveals that States deliberately eschewed the possibility of framing measures regarding national monitoring in more prescriptive terms. The idea of including a monitoring mechanism had been put on the table at the outset by the working group of the ad hoc committee

---

[174] (\...contd) Third Annual Report, para 86; and SPT Fourth Annual Report, para 42. The financial difficulties encountered by the SPT in operating its mandate have also been highlighted by its former chairperson, Silvia Casale, 'A System of Preventive Oversight' (2009) 1 Essex Human Rts Rev 9, pp 13–14.

[175] See the daily summary of discussion at the seventh session of the ad hoc committee which drafted the Disability Convention produced by Rehabilitation International, available at: http://www.un.org/esa/socdev/enable/rights/ahc7sum27jan.htm (last accessed May 2011).

[176] OP-CRPD, art 33(3).

[177] Schulze speculates that the time-frame could perhaps be interpreted as being two years following the entry into force of the Convention for each state party, based on the reporting requirement in OP-CRPD, art 35(1): Schulze, 'Effective Exercise of the Rights of Persons with Disabilities: National Monitoring Mechanisms' in Benedek, Gregory, Kozma, Nowak, Strohal, Theurmann (eds), *Global Standards – Local Action: 15 Years Vienna World Conference on Human Rights* (Intersentia, 2009), p 224.

which produced the initial draft text, where it was strongly favoured by NGOs and NHRIs and broadly supported by States involved in the negotiations.[178] NHRIs and NGOs later proposed draft texts on monitoring which envisaged the establishment of national monitoring bodies with detailed functions and powers which would be linked to an international monitoring body.[179] An expert paper submitted to the seventh session of the ad hoc committee by the OHCHR also recommended that the CRPD should include provisions which built on the OPCAT.[180] When the negotiations on implementation measures generally began in earnest at the seventh session of the ad hoc committee, the chair introduced a similarly comprehensive 'discussion text' which included provision for a national monitoring mechanism which was directly based on the NPM provisions of the OPCAT.[181] This text also set forth details relating to the establishment of such a mechanism, its precise character and role, associated rights regarding access to information, confidentiality of information and specifically its right to have contact with an international monitoring body.[182] The notion of including such a detailed mechanism into the body of the Convention, however, was overwhelmingly resisted by a majority of States at that stage of the negotiations.[183] The view was taken that although the level of specificity in the chair's text might be possible in an Optional Protocol, the approach

---

[178] Report of the Working Group of the Ad Hoc Committee on a Comprehensive and Integral International Convention on the Protection and Promotion of the Rights and Dignity of Persons with Disabilities: UN Doc A/AC265/2004/WG1, art 25. This draft text was drawn from a more detailed provision on national implementation and monitoring which had been proposed in the 'Bangkok Draft' developed earlier in 2003 by a sub-group of the ad hoc committee (see art 34): www.un.org/esa/socdev/enable/rights/bangkokdraft.htm. See also, Schulze, 'Effective Exercise of the Rights of Persons with Disabilities: National Monitoring Mechanisms' in Benedek et al (eds), *Global Standards – Local Action: 15 Years Vienna World Conference on Human Rights* (Intersentia, 2009), pp 221–222.

[179] Draft Text on Monitoring Presented by National Human Rights Institutions to the 6th Session of the Ad Hoc Committee (10 August 2005): http://www.un.org/esa/socdev/enable/rights/documents/ahc6nhrida25.doc; and International disability Caucus (IDC) Draft on Article 33 and 34 International and National Monitoring and Other Aspects of Implementation (February 1, 2006): www.ableinfo.co.kr/upload/libFile/Nega_treatyFile_131.doc (last accessed May 2011).

[180] Expert paper on existing monitoring mechanisms, possible relevant improvements and possible innovations in monitoring mechanisms for a comprehensive and integral international convention on the protection and promotion of the rights and dignity of persons with disabilities: UN Doc A/AC265/2006/CRP4, para 77 (and see generally paras 73–77).

[181] Discussion Text Proposed by the Chair On Monitoring: www.un.org/esa/socdev/enable/rights/ahc7discussmonit.htm, (last accessed May 2011).

[182] Discussion Text Proposed by the Chair On Monitoring: www.un.org/esa/socdev/enable/rights/ahc7discussmonit.htm (last accessed May 2011), arts 52–53.

[183] Draft summary of discussion at the seventh session 27 January 2006, vol 8, no 10: The International Service for Human Rights and the International Disability Caucus, Amnesty International and NHRIs each expressed strong support for robust monitoring provisions, as did the governments of Mexico and Jamaica.

taken to the issue of torture might necessarily differ to one regarding disability.[184] The need for flexibility and discretion in the framing of a national monitoring mechanism was stressed, so that States could develop their own.[185] Finally, the backdrop of on-going debate around UN treaty body reform seems also to have influenced the negotiations regarding national implementation and monitoring.[186] In that context, certain States had already expressed resistance towards creating a new international monitoring mechanism. Given the linkage which had been stressed by a number of delegations between national and international monitoring mechanisms, this issue may have encouraged a 'spirit of consensus' in the negotiations, even around provisions relating to national monitoring.[187] It may also explain why the suggestion of linking the national monitoring mechanism with the international one was ultimately dropped.

[6.40] In the result, the lack of specificity in the text of the Convention as regards the form, functions and powers of a national monitoring mechanism in art 33(2) is likely to produce mixed results across the contracting States to the Convention. On a positive note, there is definitely great potential in the provisions which did emerge, if properly implemented, for meaningful exchanges to take place between government, civil society and the independent mechanism(s) on issues that may arise regarding a State's implementation of the Convention.[188] While the linkage between national monitoring and international monitoring is less emphatic than it is in the OPCAT, there is still an opportunity for limited input by the CRPD Committee on the process in individual States through the periodic reporting procedure provided for in arts 35 and 36 of the Convention. Moreover, as Schulze notes, art 16 of the Convention contains a 'hidden monitoring provision'[189] which adds a further layer of protection to the architecture of monitoring generally in the Convention. Article 16(3) provides that:

---

[184] See, for example, the contributions to the discussion made by Australia, Serbia and Montenegro, Austria on behalf of the EU and Indonesia: Draft summary of discussion at the seventh session 27 January 2006.
[185] See, for example, the contributions of Japan, Canada, China and Yemen: Draft summary of discussion at the seventh session 27 January 2006.
[186] See Schulze, 'Effective Exercise of the Rights of Persons with Disabilities: National Monitoring Mechanisms' in Benedek et al (eds), *Global Standards – Local Action: 15 Years Vienna World Conference on Human Rights* (Intersentia, 2009), p 222; and de Búrca, 'The EU in the Negotiation of the UN Disability Convention' (2010) ELR 174, p 185.
[187] Schulze, 'Effective Exercise of the Rights of Persons with Disabilities: National Monitoring Mechanisms' in Benedek et al (eds), *Global Standards – Local Action: 15 Years Vienna World Conference on Human Rights* (Intersentia, 2009), p 222.
[188] 'The real key to implementation in all contexts…is the degree to which civil society-government is fostered and engaged to identify substantive areas of concern and remedial proposals. The Convention promotes such inter-active domestic dialogues by requiring one or more focal points (and a framework) for matters relating to the implementation of the Convention': Melish, 'The UN Disability Convention: Historic Process, Strong Prospects, and Why the U.S. Should Ratify', http://ssrn.com/abstract=997141 (last accessed May 2011), p 11.
[189] Schulze, 'Effective Exercise of the Rights of Persons with Disabilities: National Monitoring Mechanisms' in Benedek et al (eds), *Global Standards – Local Action: 15 Years Vienna World Conference on Human Rights* (Intersentia, 2009), p 225.

'In order to prevent the occurrence of all forms of exploitation, violence and abuse, States Parties shall ensure that all facilities and programmes designed to serve persons with disabilities are effectively monitored by independent authorities'.

As she points out, the fact that this provision is not linked to the national monitoring mechanism in art 33(2) gives rise to numerous possibilities, including that role being performed by the NPM established under art 17 of the OPCAT for States which have also ratified that instrument.[190]

---

[190] Schulze, 'Effective Exercise of the Rights of Persons with Disabilities: National Monitoring Mechanisms' in Benedek et al (eds), *Global Standards – Local Action: 15 Years Vienna World Conference on Human Rights* (Intersentia, 2009), p 225. It should be noted, however, that such linkage could only occur in cases where the persons concerned are 'deprived of their liberty' within the meaning of OPCAT, art 1.

Part III:
Individual Complaint Procedures

Chapter 7

Optional Protocol to the International Covenant on Civil and Political Rights

INTRODUCTION

[7.01] Individual complaint procedures are probably the most familiar human rights implementation technique to have been developed by the United Nations to date. These are mechanisms by which individuals may bring complaints[1] or send a petition to particular treaty bodies regarding perceived breaches of their rights under the treaties in question. Each of these treaty bodies in turn has jurisdiction to assess whether there has been a breach of the impugned right or rights and to 'forward its views' to the State concerned. Unlike the periodic reporting procedures examined in Ch 4, these mechanisms are optional in nature insofar as the States parties may decide whether to accept the authority of the treaty body in question to receive and consider complaints from individuals within their jurisdiction concerning an alleged breach of their rights under the treaty concerned. Byrnes has identified the following objectives as inherent in an effective individual complaint procedure: (i) providing an effective and timely remedy for the victim; (ii) bringing about changes in the law and practice which will benefit the victim as well as other similarly situated persons; and (iii) providing guidance to the States parties on the meaning of the rights enshrined in the respective treaty, through the elaboration of jurisprudence.[2] Beyond these core values, Alston has noted the fact that such procedures tend to disclose problems and difficulties experienced first-hand by individuals that may not necessarily be noted, discussed and finessed in the context of periodic reporting procedures.[3] Moreover, the very existence of such a procedure at the international level can motivate governments to make domestic remedies available.[4] In short, an effective individual complaint procedure can be a valuable implementation technique.

---

[1] While in reality the matters raised are 'complaints', they are formally dubbed less confrontationally as 'communications' in the actual texts of the treaties.
[2] Byrnes, 'An Effective Individual Complaint Mechanism in the Context of International Human Rights Law' in Bayefsky, The UN Human Rights Treaty System in the 21st Century (Kluwer Law: London, 2000) p 139 at pp 141–142.
[3] Alston, 'Establishing a Right to Petition under the Covenant on Economic, Social and Cultural Rights' Vol. 4/2 Collected Courses of the Academy of European Law (1995) at 107, extract reproduced in Steiner, Alston and Goodman, International Human Rights in Context: Law, Politics and Morals (3rd ed, OUP, 2008), pp 363–364.
[4] Alston, 'Establishing a Right to Petition under the Covenant on Economic, Social and Cultural Rights' Vol. 4/2 Collected Courses of the Academy of European Law (1995) at 107, extract reproduced in Steiner, Alston and Goodman, International Human Rights in Context: Law, Politics and Morals (3rd ed, OUP, 2008), pp 363–364.

[7.02] Optional complaint procedures are currently operative in regard to the following United Nations human rights treaties: the International Covenant on Civil and Political Rights (ICCPR); the International Convention on the Elimination of All Forms of Racial Discrimination; the Convention against Torture and Other Cruel, Inhuman or Degrading Treatment or Punishment; the Convention on the Elimination of All Forms of Discrimination Against Women; and the Convention on the Protection and Promotion of the Rights and Dignity of Persons with Disabilities. Individual complaint mechanisms have also been developed under the International Convention on the Protection of the Rights of All Migrant Workers and their Families and the International Convention for the Protection of all Persons from Enforced Disappearance, and, most recently, under the International Covenant on Economic, Social and Cultural Rights (ICESCR), though none of these is yet operative. Each of these mechanisms (whether operative or dormant) is examined in this section of the book. The final chapter examines developments in relation to a complaint procedure for the Convention on the Rights of the Child, recently adopted by the Human Rights Council.

OPTIONAL PROTOCOL TO THE INTERNATIONAL COVENANT ON CIVIL AND POLITICAL RIGHTS[5]

[7.03] As noted in Ch 3, the drafting of the International Bill of Rights was a long, drawn out process, giving rise to complex political negotiations on a whole range of human rights issues. Amongst the most crucial of these was the question of implementation. Aside from the minority view that no measures of implementation whatsoever should be provided for in either of the Covenants,[6] initial views regarding

---

[5] See generally, Tyagi, *The Human Rights Committee* (Cambridge University Press, 2011), pp 386–630; McGoldrick, *The Human Rights Committee: Its Role in the Development of the International Covenant on Civil and Political Rights* (OUP, 1991); Opsahl, 'The Human Rights Committee' in Alston (ed), *The United Nations and Human Rights* (OUP, 1992), pp 369–443; Nowak, *UN Covenant on Civil and Political Rights: CCPR Commentary* (N.P. Engel, 1993), pp 647–712; O'Flaherty and Heffernan, *International Covenant on Civil and Political Rights: International Human Rights Law in Ireland* (Brehon Publishing, 1995); Kretzmer, 'Commentary on Complaint Processes by Human Rights Committee and Torture Committee Members: (a) The Human Rights Committee' in Bayefsky (ed), *The UN Human Rights Treaty System in the 21st Century* (Kluwer Law, 2000), pp 163–166; Ghandi, 'The Human Rights Committee and the Right of Individual Communication' (1986) 57 BYIL 201; and Davidson, 'The Procedure and Practice of the Human Rights Committee Under the Optional Protocol to the International Covenant on Civil and Political Rights' (1991) 4 Canterbury Law Review 337–355.

[6] A minority of States took the view that there should be no measures of implementation at all in either of the two Covenants, on the basis that their inclusion would be contrary to the principle of 'domestic jurisdiction' in art 2(7) of the United Nations Charter and would undermine the sovereignty and independence of States. The prevailing view, however, appears to have been that implementation was 'at the heart of the Covenants' and that the latter would have little practical value without measures to give effect to them: see Annotations on the Text of the Draft International Covenants on Human Rights: UN Doc A/2929 (1 July 1955), Ch II, paras 31 and 37 respectively.

implementation of civil and political rights ranged along a broad spectrum. The most progressive view expressed was that such violations should be resolved by an international court of human rights to which individuals, States and NGOs should have access. A second view was that violations should be settled by diplomatic negotiations between the States concerned and only submitted to ad hoc fact-finding committees in the event of failure. A third view favoured the establishment of a permanent, independent body, with fact-finding and conciliation powers, to consider complaints either from States only, or from individuals and NGOs as well as States.[7]

[7.04] Having reached agreement that implementation of the ICCPR necessitated the establishment of a permanent body, to be known as the 'Human Rights Committee',[8] the debate on implementation of the Covenant was focused on whether the right to take proceedings before the Committee should be confined to the States parties or whether the Committee should have jurisdiction to act on its own initiative or to receive petitions from individuals, groups of individuals and NGOs.[9] Those States which opposed the concept of a right of individual petition argued that such a procedure would offend the essential basis of international law which was 'inter-State law', founded on the premise that States were the true subjects of that law. Moreover, it was argued that the substance of the rights provided for in the Covenant could be adequately protected by means of an inter-State complaint mechanism. Since the notion of international responsibility for the protection of human rights was a relatively recent phenomenon, it would be 'unwise' to allow other means of initiating proceedings for fear that this would prove to be unacceptable to many countries.[10] On the opposite side of the debate, these views were countered on the basis that international law was not so restrictive; and that since signing the Charter, member States had recognised the enhanced role of the individual on the international stage.[11] Accordingly, the problem of implementation had to be seen from the point of view of the individual whose rights were being guaranteed.[12] Complaints from States only would not guarantee the effective enforcement of the Covenant, particularly since political considerations would inevitably influence the

---

[7] See Annotations on the Text of the Draft International Covenants on Human Rights: UN Doc A/2929 (1 July 1955), Ch II, para 25.

[8] Annotations on the Text of the Draft International Covenants on Human Rights: UN Doc A/2929 (1 July 1955), Ch II, para 26.

[9] Annotations on the Text of the Draft International Covenants on Human Rights: UN Doc A/2929 (1 July 1955), Ch II, para 59.

[10] Annotations on the Text of the Draft International Covenants on Human Rights: UN Doc A/2929 (1 July 1955), Ch II, para 63 and ff.

[11] Annotations on the Text of the Draft International Covenants on Human Rights: UN Doc A/2929 (1 July 1955), Ch II, paras 67 and 68.

[12] Annotations on the Text of the Draft International Covenants on Human Rights: UN Doc A/2929 (1 July 1955), Ch II, para In this regard, the view was expressed further that '...a covenant which recognized that the rights contained therein derived from the inherent dignity of the human person must give the individual human being the basic right to protest when his dignity was impaired': Ch II, para 73.

decision to initiate or not to initiate such proceedings.[13] A special appeal was made to allow NGOs having consultative status with ECOSOC the right of petition. NGOs had played an invaluable role in the promotion of human rights, both nationally and internationally. In situations where individuals were unable to lodge petitions personally, or through another State for fear of being charged with treason, NGOs could do so on their behalf, without fear or favour.[14]

[7.05] Despite this wide-ranging theoretical discussion, the Commission failed to reach agreement on the inclusion of a complaint procedure for individuals or for NGOs in the Covenant. While the possibility of including such a procedure in a separate protocol was apparently considered,[15] a draft protocol submitted by the United States of America and subsequently withdrawn, was not discussed in any detail.[16] The notion of a complaint procedure specifically for individuals was subsequently revived and apparently rehashed, however, during the debate on the draft covenant in the third committee of the General Assembly. This discussion yielded more favourable results, with views being expressed to the effect that the inclusion of such a right of petition in the European Convention on Human Rights as well as in the ICERD[17] had transformed the status of the individual in international law.[18] This argument, coupled with the suggestion that inclusion of a right of petition in the Covenant could be done on an optional basis, eventually prevailed.[19] The mechanism chosen was by means of an optional protocol annexed to the draft covenant. Thus, after two decades of discussion, the final text of the ICCPR, which was now supplemented by an Optional Protocol (OP-ICCPR) providing for the right of petition, was finally adopted and opened for signature and ratification by the General Assembly in 1966.[20] The OP-ICCPR would eventually enter into force in

---

[13] Annotations on the Text of the Draft International Covenants on Human Rights: UN Doc A/2929 (1 July 1955), Ch II, para 71.

[14] Annotations on the Text of the Draft International Covenants on Human Rights: UN Doc A/2929 (1 July 1955), Ch II, para 73. In their observations and suggestions to the Commission on the draft covenants, NGOs emphasised the importance of granting capacity to individuals and NGOs to submit petitions under the Covenant, arguing, *inter alia*, that the support of public opinion would be greatly diminished if such a possibility were omitted. Draft International Covenants on Human Rights and Measures of Implementation: Observations and Suggestions by Non-Governmental Organizations (Memorandum by the Secretary General): UN Doc E/CN 4/660 (9 April 1952), paras 50–64.

[15] Annotations on the Text of the Draft International Covenants on Human Rights: UN Doc A/2929 (1 July 1955), Ch II, paras 81 and 82.

[16] Annotations on the Text of the Draft International Covenants on Human Rights: UN Doc A/2929 (1 July 1955), Ch II, para 83.

[17] See Ch 8, para **8.01**.

[18] See UN Doc A/6546, cited in McGoldrick, *The Human Rights Committee: Its Role in the Development of the International Covenant on civil and Political Rights* (OUP, 1991), p 123, note 17.

[19] McGoldrick, *The Human Rights Committee: Its Role in the Development of the International Covenant on civil and Political Rights* (OUP, 1991), p 123, note 17.

[20] GA Res 2200 A (XXI), 21 UN GAOR (1496th meeting) para 60, p 6.

1976, after the requisite number of ratifications.[21] Since described as a 'giant leap for mankind', and the most 'visible and effective'[22] of all the complaints procedures administered by the UN treaty bodies, the OP-ICCPR has been ratified by 113 of the 167 States parties to the ICCPR.[23] The next section outlines the procedure for initiating a petition under the Protocol, followed by an outline of some of the key decisions made by the Human Rights Committee (CCPR) in implementing it. The final section offers an appraisal of the efficacy of the OP-ICCPR in practice.

PROCEDURE[24]

[7.06] While the Protocol is technically a separate treaty to the ICCPR, a State may only become party to it when it is already party to the Covenant.[25] On becoming party to the Protocol, the State recognises the competence of the Human Rights Committee (CCPR), 'to *receive and consider* communications from individuals subject to its jurisdiction who claim to be victims of violations by that State party of any of the rights set forth in the Covenant'.[26] A 'communication'[27] should contain essential information relating to the author as well as information relating to the nature of the complaint, identifying which articles of the Covenant have been breached. It should be sent initially to the

---

[21] Ireland ratified the Optional Protocol on 8 December 1989, the same date as it ratified the International Covenants: see Power and Quinn, 'Ireland's Accession to the United Nations Human Rights Covenants' (1989) 7 ILT 36.

[22] Schmidt, 'Individual Human Rights Complaints Procedures Based on United Nations Treaties and the Need for Reform' (1992) 41 ICLQ 645, p 646.

[23] See:http://treaties.un.org/Pages/ViewDetails.aspx?src=TREATY&mtdsg_no=IV-5&chapter=4&lang=en (last accessed May 2011).

[24] As to the procedure of the Human Rights Committee in operating the Optional Protocol to the ICCPR, see generally: Bayefsky, *How to Complain to the UN Human Rights Treaty System* (Transnational Publishers, 2002), pp 58–66; Nowak, *UN Covenant on Civil and Political Rights: CCPR Commentary* (N.P. Engel, 1993), pp 647–712; O'Flaherty, *Human Rights and the UN: Practice Before the Treaty Bodies* (Kluwer Law International, 2002), pp 40–45; and Vandenhole, *The Procedures Before the UN Human Rights Treaty Bodies: Divergence or Convergence?* (Intersentia, 2004), pp 196–241.

[25] OP-ICCPR, art 1.

[26] OP-ICCPR, art 1 (emphasis added). It follows that the CCPR will not consider communications which concern a State that is not party to the Protocol: r 84(3), Rules of Procedure of the Human Rights Committee: UN Doc CCPR/C/3/Rev 9 (13 January 2011).

[27] The use of the term 'petition' during early discussions on the draft Protocol was subsequently substituted by the word 'communication', though this was not intended to have any substantive consequences: McGoldrick, *The Human Rights Committee: Its Role in the Development of the International Covenant on civil and Political Rights* (OUP, 1991), p 125. The CCPR itself uses the term 'communication' as provided for in art 1 of the Protocol, instead of such terms as 'complaint' or 'petition'. Nonetheless, somewhat confusingly, as the CCPR has itself pointed out, the term 'petition' is adopted in the administrative structure of the OHCHR where communications under the Optional Protocol are initially handled by a section known as the 'Petitions Team': CCPR General Comment No 33 on *The Obligations of States Parties under the Optional Protocol to the International Covenant on Civil and Political Rights* (5 November 2008) UN Doc CCPR/C/GC/33, para 6.

Office of the High Commissioner for Human Rights (OHCHR), where it will be screened by a member of the petitions team, before being sent to the CCPR's Special Rapporteur on New Communications.[28] The special rapporteur is a member of the CCPR whose task is to scrutinise communications to ensure that they contain all the necessary information, before deciding whether to register the complaint. The special rapporteur also has a role to play in regard to cases which appear to raise special circumstances of urgency falling within the parameters of r 92 of the Committee's Rules of Procedure. In such cases where immediate action is required to 'avoid irreparable damage to the victim of the alleged violation' (such as the implementation of the death penalty or deportation), the special rapporteur will request the State party to take such interim measures as may be desirable in the circumstances.[29] The CCPR has adopted the position that failure by a State to implement such interim or provisional measures as are indicated by the Committee in a particular case is incompatible with the obligation to respect the procedure of individual petition established under the Protocol.[30]

[7.07] The pre-registration phase is often extremely time-consuming and resource-intensive.[31] During this phase, the complainant may be asked for further information or observations relevant to the questions of admissibility and merits of the complaint. The special rapporteur will not register a case if it is patently clear that it fails to disclose an issue under the Covenant.[32] If the communication clearly fails to meet the admissibility criteria in the Covenant, the special rapporteur may decide to register it but send it to the plenary Committee directly for a decision without requesting comments from the State party. In all other cases, if a communication is registered, it passes to an individual member of the CCPR, who will act as a designated rapporteur for the case during the next phase of examination before the Working Group on Communications, and beyond

---

[28] CCPR Rules of Procedure, r 95(3) provides for the possibility of the Committee designating special rapporteurs from among its members to assist it in handling communications under the Protocol: Rules of Procedure of the Human Rights Committee (13 January 2011): UN Doc CCPR/C/3/Rev 9. The position of Special Rapporteur on Communications was created in 1989 to assist the Committee and the UN Secretariat to handle communications in the preliminary stages.

[29] In doing this, r 92 clearly states that the State party shall be informed that such expression of its views on interim measures does not imply a determination on the merits of the communication.

[30] CCPR General Comment No 33, para 19. In *Piandiong et al v The Philippines* Communication No 869/1999 (2000), the Committee effectively held that a State which deliberately flouts a request for interim measures commits 'grave breaches of its obligations under the Protocol' (para 8).

[31] See the analysis by Bayefsky in her seminal report on *The UN Treaty System: Universality at the Crossroads* (Transnational Publishers, 2001), pp 28–30.

[32] A negative decision on registration is not necessarily fatal as the author may still insist that the communication is registered, in which case it will normally be sent by the special rapporteur directly to the plenary CCPR with a recommendation that it be declared inadmissible. Faced with such a scenario, the CCPR will in turn usually accept the advice of the special rapporteur: Bayefsky, *How to Complain to the UN Human Rights Treaty System* (Transnational Publishers, 2002), p 64.

before the plenary Committee.[33] The Working Group on Communications is composed of at least five members of the CCPR who meet together for one week prior to each session of the CCPR. The working group has a role to play in making decisions or recommendations to the Committee on admissibility, as well as 'laying the groundwork' for the Committee's decisions on the merits.[34]

[7.08] The respondent State will normally be asked to make submissions on both the admissibility and merits of a communication that has been registered in respect of it, unless the Committee, the working group or the special rapporteur has decided, because of the exceptional nature of the case, to request a written reply that relates *only* to the admissibility of the case.[35] The rules of procedure also allow for a State which has been asked to plead on admissibility and merits, to object to admissibility and to apply in writing within two months, for separate consideration of admissibility.[36] While this does not technically absolve the State of the obligation to provide submissions on the merits within the stipulated six-month time-frame, the CCPR, a working group or the special rapporteur may decide to extend the time for submissions on the merits until a decision has been taken on the question of admissibility.[37] This course of action is useful in order to avoid unnecessary pleadings on the merits. The Rules of Procedure allow the Committee, the working group or the special rapporteur to request additional information relevant to admissibility or the merits, with the possibility for each party to be given an opportunity to comment on each other's submissions within fixed time-limits.[38] This process of exchange may be repeated until the CCPR believes it has enough information to determine the case.

[7.09] The role of the designated rapporteur initially is to study the communication in all its aspects and provide the working group (and the plenary Committee at a later stage) with a draft decision on the case, with respect to either admissibility alone (in the exceptional circumstances described above) or admissibility and the merits. Having discussed the matter and reviewed the recommendation of the designated rapporteur, the working group makes an initial evaluation on admissibility of the complaint.[39] It may declare the communication to be admissible unanimously.[40] In such cases, the State party will be informed of the decision and if it has not already done so, will be requested to

---

[33] Rule 95(1) of the CCPR's Rules of Procedure provides for the establishment of one or more working groups to make recommendations to the plenary Committee on admissibility.
[34] Nowak, *UN Covenant on Civil and Political Rights: CCPR Commentary* (Engel, 1993), p 544, cited in Vandenhole, *The Procedures before the UN Human Rights Treaty Bodies* (Intersentia, 2004), p 201.
[35] CCPR's Rules of Procedure, r 97(2).
[36] CCPR's Rules of Procedure, r 97(3).
[37] CCPR's Rules of Procedure, r 97(3).
[38] CCPR's Rules of Procedure, r 97(4).
[39] CCPR's Rules of Procedure, r 96.
[40] CCPR's Rules of Procedure, r 93(2) stipulates that complaints may only be deemed admissible unanimously provided that the working group is composed of five members and all the members so decide.

make submissions to the plenary Committee on the merits of the case.[41] The author will be given an opportunity to respond within fixed time-limits.[42] In 2005, the Committee introduced a new rule of procedure which provides that where the working group of at least five members unanimously takes the view that a communication is *inadmissible*, it will transmit that decision to the plenary Committee, which may confirm it *without formal discussion*.[43] However, if any Committee member requests a plenary discussion, the plenary will examine the communication and take a decision. This rule of procedure expedites the process of decision making in regard to cases which are obviously inadmissible in the view of the working group.

[7.10] In situations where a case has been referred to the plenary Committee by the working group for a decision on admissibility and/or the merits, it falls to the Committee to decide the case. It should be noted that a decision taken previously that a case is admissible can be altered at this phase of the proceedings.[44] Where the plenary Committee decides that a case is inadmissible, written reasons are provided to the author, thus putting an end to the case.[45] Otherwise, it will issue its decision on admissibility and merits jointly.[46] Before making a determination, the Committee may take on board the recommendation of the Working Group on Communications[47] but ultimately the final decision rests with the Committee.

[7.11] An obvious lacuna in the complaint procedure is that the Human Rights Committee does not conduct oral hearings to assist it in fulfilling its functions under the OP-ICCPR. The Protocol itself makes no provision for the conduct of oral hearings, providing instead that communications under the Protocol shall be considered by the Committee 'in the light of all *written* information made available to it by the individual and by the State Party'.[48] While it is arguable that the initiation of oral hearings would be incompatible with this provision,[49] the prevailing view appears to be that the wording of the Protocol does not necessarily preclude the holding of oral hearings and that the CCPR could make provision for the possibility of oral hearings to be conducted with the

---

[41] CCPR's Rules of Procedure, r 99(1) and (2).
[42] CCPR's Rules of Procedure, r 99 (3). It should be noted that upon consideration of such a case at the merits stage, the plenary Committee may again review the decision on admissibility in light of any explanations submitted by the State: Committee's Rules of Procedure, r 99(4).
[43] CCPR's Rules of Procedure, r 93(3).
[44] CCPR's Rules of Procedure, r 99(4).
[45] CCPR's Rules of Procedure, r 98. A decision that a communication is inadmissible for reasons referred to in OP-ICCPR, art 5(2) may be reviewed at a later date by the Committee following a written request from an individual.
[46] CCPR's Rules of Procedure, r 100.
[47] CCPR's Rules of Procedure, r 100.
[48] OP-ICCPR, art 5(1).
[49] Tomuschat refers to the 'shaky legal foundations' of art 5(1) as presenting an obstacle to oral hearings: Tomuschat, 'Human Rights Committee' in *Max Planck Encyclopaedia of Public International Law* (OUP, 2009): www.mpepil.com, p 32.

consent of the State party concerned.[50] There can be little doubt but that, in principle, oral hearings would enhance decision-making in particular cases since oral testimony can certainly provide speedy clarification of facts or arguments which may be difficult to decipher from the written pleadings. On the other hand, in the absence of a fundamental restructuring of the Committee's work under the Protocol,[51] the provision of oral hearings may add more problems than it would solve. In particular, it would likely exacerbate the backlog in the Committee's caseload and lead to inequality of bargaining power as between complainants in circumstances where certain respondent States simply refused to consent to a hearing.[52] Precisely the same issues arise in regard to the possibility of enhancing the Committee's fact-finding capabilities under the Protocol. Such an extension of the Committee's practice is not necessarily foreclosed by the terms of the Protocol, and would no doubt assist its deliberations in contentious cases.[53] However, while proposals in that direction may have been plausible a decade ago, they would appear to be completely unfeasible at the moment in the absence of a massive extension of budgetary resources to the Committee.

[7.12] It is also important to note that consideration of communications under the Protocol is entirely confidential, as regards the involvement of the special rapporteur, the working group, and the work of the plenary Committee. Article 5(3) of the OP-ICCPR itself provides that the CCPR shall hold 'closed meetings' when examining communications under the Protocol. This provision is bolstered by the CCPR's Rules of Procedure which underscore the principle that oral deliberations and summary records of these meetings shall remain confidential.[54] Moreover, all working documents issued for the Committee, the working group and the special rapporteur, shall remain confidential, unless the Committee decides otherwise.[55] At the same time, authors of communications and respondent States are not generally precluded from making public any submissions or information bearing on the proceedings, unless the Committee has requested the parties to maintain confidentiality.[56]

[7.13] Having reached a determination on the merits, the CCPR's only formal obligation at that stage under the Protocol is that it must 'forward its views' to the State party

---

[50] McGoldrick, *The Human Rights Committee: Its Role in the Development of the International Covenant on Civil and Political Rights* (OUP, 1991), pp 143–145; Schmidt, 'Individual Human Rights Complaints Procedures Based on United Nations Treaties and the Need for Reform' (1992) 41 ICLQ 645, p 653; and Opsahl, 'The Human Rights Committee' in Alston (ed), *The United Nations and Human Rights* (OUP, 1992), p 427.

[51] McGoldrick, *The Human Rights Committee: Its Role in the Development of the International Covenant on Civil and Political Rights* (OUP, 1991), p 145.

[52] Kretzmer, 'Commentary on Complaint Processes by Human Rights Committee and Torture Committee Members: (a) The Human Rights Committee' in Bayefsky (ed), *The UN Human Rights Treaty System in the 21st Century* (Kluwer Law, 2000), p 165.

[53] McGoldrick, *The Human Rights Committee: Its Role in the Development of the International Covenant on Civil and Political Rights* (OUP, 1991), p 145.

[54] CCPR's Rules of Procedure, r 102(1).

[55] CCPR's Rules of Procedure, r 102(2).

[56] CCPR's Rules of Procedure, r 102(3).

concerned and to the individual.[57] The CCPR tries to reach its views by consensus, although members are free to append to any views their individual opinions (either concurring or dissenting).[58] While the CCPR is constrained by the Protocol to conduct its proceedings in 'closed meetings', the text is silent as regards the publication of the Committee's views. From the outset, the Committee took the decision to publish its views, thus creating 'a bold and important precedent'[59] which has considerably enhanced the importance of the Protocol as a vehicle for the implementation of human rights.

[7.14] The CCPR's views normally provide detailed legal reasoning. Where the Committee reaches the conclusion that the Covenant has been violated, it usually includes its views on what action(s) should be taken to remedy the breach. The Committee's recommendations in these circumstances will usually be of a general nature, taking into account the importance of allowing States a certain measure of discretion as regards implementation within its own legal or administrative system. Recommendations may in some instances be quite specific such as, for example, the amendment of legislation,[60] provision of compensation,[61] commutation of a death sentence[62] and even the release of the author from custody.[63] The Committee will usually request the State to inform it within 90 days of the remedy that it has taken to rectify the situation.

[7.15] As to the legal status of the views, technically they are not legally binding on the State party concerned. This limitation to the individual complaint procedure is in marked contrast, for example, to the judgments of the European Court of Human Rights in interpreting the substantive guarantees of the European Convention on Human Rights which are binding on the State(s) concerned.[64] Strictly speaking, the fact that the 'views' are non-binding necessarily reduces their impact and lessens the chances of their being adopted by certain States to whom they are addressed. On the other hand, the more forceful position, which has been espoused by commentators on the Protocol, as well as the Committee itself, is that the CPPR's views are 'authoritative'[65] determinations, which

---

[57] OP-ICCPR, art 5(4).
[58] CCPR's Rules of Procedure, r 104.
[59] Opsahl, 'The Human Rights Committee' in Alston (ed), *The United Nations and Human Rights: A Critical Appraisal* (Clarendon Press, 1992), p 421.
[60] *Toonen v Australia*, Communication No 488/1992, para 10.
[61] *Jung et al v Republic of Korea*, Communication Nos 1593–1603/2007, para 9.
[62] *Persaud v Guyana*, Communication No 812/1998, para 9.
[63] *Kelly v Jamaica*, Communication No 253/1987, para 7, recommending the release of the applicant who was sentenced to death after a trial which failed to respect the guarantees in the Covenant, in circumstances where no further appeal was available under national law.
[64] ECHR, art 46. The 'views' of the CCPR under the Protocol are analogous to the 'opinions' on the merits of cases rendered by the former European Commission on Human Rights under the petition procedure which prevailed prior to the adoption by the Contracting States to the Convention of Protocol No 11 in 1998.
[65] CCPR General Comment No 33, para 13.

appear to all intents and purposes as written judicial opinions.[66] The Committee has consistently striven to invest its views with greater legal authority, arguing that the obligation on States parties in art 2(3) of the ICCPR to provide an effective remedy to authors of complaints, combined with the duty to act in good faith, both in respect of participation in the procedures under the Protocol and in relation to the ICCPR itself, enhances the character and the importance of the Committee's 'views', and, by implication, the duty of States to abide by them.[67] Beyond their legal status, of course, the views of the CCPR are public documents, and, as such, have the potential to attract adverse publicity for a State in the event that it is found to be in violation of the Covenant. There is certainly evidence to suggest that many States do take the views of the CCPR seriously and have moved to implement those views in their domestic jurisdictions.[68] Others choose, for reasons of domestic political or economic expediency usually, to ignore its views and non-compliance remains a persistent problem for the Committee.[69]

[7.16] Conscious of this difficulty, and the fact that it was rarely informed of action being taken by respondent States to comply with its views, the CCPR decided in 1990 to establish a procedure for monitoring the implementation of its views under art 5(4) of the Protocol.[70] Accordingly, it created the mandate of the Special Rapporteur for follow-

---

[66] 'While the function of the Human Rights Committee in considering individual communications is not, as such, that of a judicial body, the views issued by the Committee under the Optional Protocol exhibit some important characteristics of a judicial decision. They are arrived at in a judicial spirit, including the impartiality and independence of Committee members, the considered interpretation of the language of the Covenant, and the determinative character of the decisions': CCPR General Comment No 33, para 11. See McGoldrick, *The Human Rights Committee: Its Role in the Development of the International Covenant on civil and Political Rights* (OUP, 1991), p 151. See also Tomuschat, 'Evolving Procedural Rules: The United Nations Human Rights Committee's First Two Years of Dealing with Individual Communications' (1980) 1 HRLJ 249, p 255.

[67] CCPR General Comment No 33, paras 13–15 and 20. See also Joseph et al, who characterise the CCPR as '... the pre-eminent interpreter of the ICCPR which is itself legally binding' and whose decisions are '... therefore strong indicators of legal obligations, so rejection of those decisions is good evidence of a State's bad faith attitude towards its ICCPR obligations': Joseph, Schultz and Castan, *The International Covenant on Civil and Political Rights: Cases, Materials and Commentary* (2nd ed, OUP, 2004),p 24.

[68] The Committee provides a summary in each of its annual reports of the results of its activities under the Optional Protocol in the period under consideration, including the remedies called for by the Committee and provided by States parties following a finding of violation(s). See, for example, its most recent annual report for 2007/2008, paras 168 to 194.

[69] In each of its annual reports, the Committee always draws attention to the problem of non-compliance with the views of the Committee under the Protocol. See most recently, CCPR Annual Report 2010, UN Doc. A/65/40 (Vol 1), p iii. See also para 18 of CCPR General Comment No 33, in which the CCPR acknowledges problems of non-compliance.

[70] CCPR Annual Report 1990, UN Doc A/45/40, Vol 2, Annex XI.

up on Views.[71] The rapporteur is a member of the Committee, with a two-year renewable term, whose role is to ascertain the measures taken by the States parties to give effect to the Committee's views.[72] This role is to be fulfilled in a variety of ways, but essentially involves the rapporteur in communicating with the victims and with respondent States parties, to elicit information on what action(s), if any, has been taken on foot of the Committee's views, and to report with recommendations to the Committee.[73] Where information is received from a State party, this is normally transmitted to the author who is given two months to respond. Summaries of the State's comments and the author's response are presented by the rapporteur in the form of interim reports, and discussed in public session by the Committee. If no response is received, the rapporteur sends reminders to the State party at regular intervals, and will ultimately seek meetings with its representatives to obtain a response. A summary of the rapporteur's activities is published in the CCPR's annual reports to the General Assembly. Thus, even though there is no supervisory body charged with the task of implementing the Committee's views (as is the case in regard to judgments of the European Court of Human Rights), failure to implement the Committee's views, in whole or in part, becomes a matter of public record,[74] with all the negative publicity that such a scenario may potentially attract.[75]

ADMISSIBILITY CRITERIA

[7.17] Much of the CCPR's work is taken up with making decisions on the admissibility of individual communications. Rule 96 of the CCPR's Rules of Procedure elucidates the admissibility criteria for individual communications which are otherwise variously 'scattered throughout the Protocol'.[76] While they resemble the admissibility criteria for

---

[71] Prior to the creation of the mandate of the special rapporteur, the Committee had sought to obtain information regarding implementation of its views from States parties by means of *notes verbales* or by raising decided cases with the relevant States during the examination of their periodic reports under art 40 ICCPR. However, these methods had proved unsatisfactory as very often the Committee had no information on implementation and it had received numerous letters from victims indicating that no action had been taken following the delivery of the Committee's views: CCPR Annual Report 1990, Vol 1, para 633.

[72] CCPR's Rules of Procedure, r 101. The terms 'Special Rapporteur for the Follow-Up *on* Views' and 'Special Rapporteur for the Follow-Up *of* Views' appear to be used interchangeably. The former designation was certainly adopted in 1997 when provision was formally made for the rapporteur's role in the Committee's Rules of Procedure: UN Doc CCPR/C/3/Rev 5, r 95. Following subsequent amendment of the Rules, the operative Rule in regard to the Special Rapporteur is now r 101. Reference is made to the role of the special rapporteur by the Committee in General Comment No 33, para 16.

[73] The detailed mandate of the special rapporteur is set forth in Annex X1 of the CCPR's Annual Report (1990): UN Doc A/45/40. See also CCPR's Rules of Procedure, r 101.

[74] This point is emphasised by the CCPR itself in General Comment No 33, para 17.

[75] Joseph et al, *The International Covenant on Civil and Political Rights* (2nd ed, OUP, 1994), p 25.

[76] Tomuschat, 'Human Rights Committee' in *Max Planck Encyclopaedia of Public International Law* (OUP, 2009), para 13.

individual applications provided for in art 35 of the European Convention on Human Rights, the CCPR's track record in terms of positive decisions on admissibility is much more favourable than that of the European Court of Human Rights.[77] The following paragraphs set forth the grounds on which a communication under the Protocol may be found to be inadmissible, based on the provisions of the OP-ICCPR and interpretive decisions of the Committee.

Anonymous, abusive or incompatible communications

[7.18] Article 3 of the Protocol provides that the CCPR shall consider inadmissible any communication which is anonymous, abusive or incompatible with the provisions of the Covenant.

(a) *Anonymity*: The CCPR does not accept anonymous communications. Thus, where an author refuses to disclose his or her identity, the communication will be deemed inadmissible. It is possible for the author to request the Committee not to disclose his or her identity in its final decision or views when the case is published and such requests are normally respected by the Committee.

(b) *Abusive Communications*: In extraordinary cases, the CCPR may deem a complaint inadmissible for being 'abusive' under art 3 of the Protocol. This condition is designed to enable the CCPR, like other treaty bodies which operate complaint procedures, to deem a communication inadmissible where it is 'frivolous, vexatious or constitutes an otherwise inappropriate usage of the procedure provided for in the Protocol'.[78] This has happened, for example, in regard to cases where the author persists in submitting communications in respect of acts or facts which have already been deemed inadmissible under the Protocol.[79]

[7.19] Unlike the European Convention on Human Rights[80] or the United Nations Convention on the Elimination of All Forms of Racial Discrimination,[81] the OP-ICCPR does not contain any fixed time limits for the submission of communications. However,

---

[77] Between 1977, when the CCPR started its work under the Protocol, and the date of its last annual report in July 2010, 1960 communications have been registered for consideration. Of that number, 557 were declared inadmissible, 274 were discontinued or withdrawn, and 398 were not yet concluded. Final views have been adopted in 731 cases: CCPR Annual Report 2010, para 81. This record compares very favourably, for example, with the experience of applicants under the individual petition procedure under the European Convention on Human Rights in respect of which it has been estimated that the European Court of Human Rights declares over 90% of registered cases inadmissible: Caflisch, 'The Reform of the European Court of Human Rights: Protocol No 14' (2006) HRL Rev 403, p 405.

[78] See OHCHR note on procedure for complaints by individuals under the human rights treaties: http://www2.ohchr.org/english/bodies/petitions/individual.htm (last accessed May 2011).

[79] See, for example, recently the case of *Conde v Spain*, Application No 1527/2006.

[80] ECHR, art 35(1).

[81] United Nations Convention on the Elimination of All Forms of Racial Discrimination, art 14(5).

the issue of how to treat communications which are submitted after considerable delay has been a source of protracted debate on the part of Committee members.[82] For many years, the CCPR proceeded on the basis that in exceptional circumstances, 'undue delay' could constitute an 'abuse of the right of submission',[83] but was reluctant to set down fixed time limits for what will constitute an 'undue delay', preferring instead to make its decisions on this matter on a case-by-case basis.[84] However, at its 100th session, in 2010, the CCPR amended its Rules of Procedure to provide that a complaint may constitute an abuse of submission when it is submitted '... after five years from the exhaustion of domestic remedies by the author ... or, where applicable, after three years from the conclusion of another procedure of international investigation or settlement, unless there are reasons justifying the delay taking into account all of the circumstances of the communication'.[85] The new rule is likely to act as a useful guideline for the Committee, while at the same time preserving sufficient flexibility for it to admit delayed applications in exceptional circumstances.[86]

Incompatible communications

[7.20] A communication may be deemed incompatible under the Protocol on each of the following four grounds.[87]

Incompatible ratione temporis

[7.21] A communication may be incompatible *ratione temporis* (by reason of time) where it is brought by an individual against a State party to the Covenant in respect of

---

[82] See the account of the CCPR's internal discussion on this matter by the International Service for Human Rights (ISHR), Treaty Body Monitor: Human Rights Committee, 95th Session, Discussion on Methods of Work, 16 March to 3 April 2009: http://www.ishr.ch/treaty-body-monitor/hrc#95 (last accessed May 2011).

[83] See, for example, *Gobin v Mauritius*, Application No 787/97, in which a majority of the Committee held the application to be inadmissible as an abuse of the right of submission in circumstances where the alleged violation had taken place five years prior to the submission of the communication, and where no 'convincing explanations' had been given for the delay.

[84] The reluctance was well expressed by Mr Rodley at the Committee's 95th Session when he warned that the Committee should 'think twice' before taking any action that might appear 'cavalier'; and that it should have regard to the political implications if it were to 'arbitrarily introduce time limits': See Discussion on Methods of Work at the CCPR's 95th Session, ISHR, Treaty Body Monitor, p 7.

[85] CCPR's Rules of Procedure, r 96(c). Note that the rule in its amended form will only apply to complaints received by the Committee after 1 January 2012.

[86] See for example, the CCPR's decision in *Brychta v Czech Republic*, Communication No 1618/2007 in which the Committee deemed an application admissible in circumstances where the author had waited almost nine years since the final decision taken by the former European Commission on Human Rights in his case and more than ten and a half years since the last domestic decision. In reaching its decision, the CCPR took account of the fact that the applicant had approached the Committee two years after the negative decision of the Commission but had not received an answer; and that it had taken until 2004 before he was informed by the European Court of Human Rights that the Commission's decision was final.

[87] See CCPR's Rules of Procedure, r 96(d).

acts or facts which pre-date the entry into force of the Protocol for the respondent State.[88] This ground of inadmissibility derives from the well-settled principle of international law that the terms of a treaty should not be applied retrospectively.[89] However, the CCPR has recognised the concept of 'continuing violations' whereby a communication based on acts or facts which occurred prior to entry into force of the Protocol, may be accepted where the effects of the measure(s) is continuing post-ratification. In such circumstances, the 'continuing effects' of the original violation may be deemed to be violations themselves. This occurred in the case of *Lovelace v Canada*, where the author complained about the loss of her status as a Maliseet Indian under the Indian Act then in force in Canada, following her marriage to a non-Indian, six years prior to the entry into force of the ICCPR and the Protocol for Canada.[90] The CCPR declared that the loss by the author of her status under the Act took place at a time when Canada was not even party to the Covenant, and hence could not be examined pursuant to the Protocol. However, the essence of her claim concerned the 'continuing effects' of the application of the Indian Act, in particular, her inability to reside on an Indian reserve. As these effects persisted after entry into force of the Covenant and Protocol, that aspect of her communication was admissible under the Protocol.[91] In *Simunek v the Czech Republic*, the CCPR went on to define a 'continuing violation' as '...an affirmation, after the entry into force of the Optional Protocol, by act or clear implication, of the previous violations of the State party'.[92]

[7.22] The question of what constitutes a 'continuing violation', however, is notoriously difficult to pin down,[93] as is evidenced in a number of cases concerning the application of amnesty laws to executions and disappearances occurring prior to entry into force of the Covenant or Protocol for the State concerned.[94] In *Carlos Acua Inostroza et al v Chile*, the authors' representatives complained about the failure of the respondent State

---

[88] See, for example, *Tim Anderson v Australia*, Communication No 1367/2005, para 7.3.
[89] As Vaji has explained, 'The aim of the *ratione temporis* principle in international law is not only to avoid the revival of old disputes between States, but also to preclude the submission to international courts of facts and situations dating from a period when the State whose action is impugned was not in a position to foresee the legal proceedings to which these facts and situations might give rise': Vaji, 'Before...And After: Ratione Temporis Jurisdiction of the (New) European Court of Human Rights and the *Blei* Case' in Caflisch et al (eds), *Liber Amicorum Luzius Wildhaber: Human Rights – Strasbourg Views* (Engel, 2007), p 486.
[90] *Lovelace v Canada*, Communication No R 6/24.
[91] *Lovelace v Canada*, Communication No R 6/24, para 7.3.
[92] *Simunek v the Czech Republic*, Communication No 516/1992, para 4.5.
[93] See Loucaides, 'The Concept of 'Continuing Violations' of Human Rights' in *The European Convention on Human Rights: Collected Essays* (Martinus Nijhoff, 2007), pp 17–23. The International Law Commission has articulated helpful standards in regard to the concept of 'continuing violations' and the case law of the European Court of Human Rights could provide useful guidance for the Committee in this regard: see generally, Van Pachtenbeke and Haeck, 'From De Becker to Varnava: The State of Continuing Violations in the Strasbourg Case Law' (2010) 1 EHRLR 47–58.
[94] See, for example, *SE v Argentina*, Communication No 275/1988.

to investigate their apparent disappearances and execution which had occurred in 1973 at the hands of the Pinochet regime.[95] A decision of the Supreme Court in 1995, upholding the application of the amnesty laws to the facts, had effectively ruled out an investigation into their deaths. The CCPR decided that the communication was inadmissible *ratione temporis* because the acts giving rise to the claims related to the deaths of persons occurring prior to the entry into force of the Covenant.[96] Ms Christine Chanet gave an interesting dissent, in which she took the view that the right to recognition as a person before the law in art 16 of the Covenant has effects beyond a person's death, especially where his or her absence is shrouded in uncertainty. In that sense, she took the view that the judicial decision of the Supreme Court foreclosing an investigation related to a continuing situation which, as it had not permanently ended, had long term consequences.

Incompatible ratione personae

[7.23] A communication may be deemed incompatible *ratione personae* by reason of the State being complained about; and the person making the complaint.

Incompatibility vis-à-vis the State

The CCPR is only competent to examine communications submitted to it against a State that is party to the OP-ICCPR. Thus, a State party that has not ratified or acceded to the terms of the Protocol, or one that has validly denounced, suspended or withdrawn from the ICCPR or the Protocol itself, cannot be subject to proceedings under the Protocol. The State is responsible under art 2 of the ICCPR for all acts of the legislature, executive, judiciary, and all other public and governmental bodies (national, regional or local) which violate the list of rights enshrined therein.[97] Thus, while actions that are carried out by private parties do not *prima facie* give rise to grounds for a communication under the Protocol, the CCPR has clarified that States can be responsible for a violation of the ICCPR where they have failed to protect individuals from the activities of private parties in violation of the Covenant.[98] Indeed, the ICCPR specifically envisages such positive obligations on the part of the States parties to protect individuals from the activities of private parties or entities in arts 7, 17 and 26.[99]

Incompatibility vis-à-vis the individual

[7.24] Complaints may also be declared incompatible *ratione personae* where the CCPR is of the opinion that the author is not an 'individual' or 'victim' of a violation within the meaning of art 1 of the Protocol. Article 1 provides that States parties recognise the competence of the CCPR to receive and consider communications from '*individuals* subject to its jurisdiction who claim to be *victims* of a violation by that State Party of any

---

[95] *SE v Argentina*, Communication No 717/1996, declared inadmissible on 23 July 1999.
[96] *Carlos Acua Inostroza et al v Chile*, Communication No 717/1996, para 6.4.
[97] CCPR General Comment No 31, Nature of the General Legal Obligation Imposed on States Parties to the Covenant, UN Doc. CCPR/C/21/Rev 1/Add 13, para 4.
[98] CCPR General Comment No 31, para 8. Such a development has also taken hold in respect of the ECHR in the wake of the decisions by the European Court of Human Rights in *Costello-Roberts v United Kingdom* (1994) 19 EHRR 112 and *A v UK* (1999) 27 EHRR 611.
[99] CCPR General Comment No 31, para 8.

of the rights set forth in the Covenant' (emphasis added). Thus, *locus standi* under the Protocol is limited to 'individuals', in contrast with the right of individual petition in the European Convention on Human Rights which extends also to NGOs.[100] In practice, the CCPR has consistently refused to entertain communications from NGOs or associations in their own right. Accordingly, organisations which have been the subject of a violation are only able to submit communications to the CCPR through an individual who has the necessary standing to make the complaint, even if the complaint relates to a group such as the right to freedom of association.[101] In such a scenario, individual members of an association may bring proceedings *qua* individuals,[102] as there is nothing to prevent large numbers of individuals from bringing a joint communication under the Protocol.[103]

[7.25] In its Rules of Procedure, the CCPR has tempered the apparently absolutist phraseology of the Protocol by specifying that while communications should normally be submitted by the individual personally or by that individual's representative, a communication may be submitted *on behalf* of an alleged victim when it appears that the individual in question is unable to submit the communication personally.[104] Communications will be accepted from representatives in circumstances where there is clear evidence that the author has authorised the representative to act on his or her behalf; otherwise the communication will be deemed inadmissible.[105] Communications

---

[100] ECHR, art 34.

[101] See *JRT and the WG Party of Canada v Canada*, Communication No 104/1991, para 8 in which the CCPR held the complaint to be inadmissible insofar as it concerned the WG party because it was an association and not an individual. As an individual, on the other hand, JRT had the necessary standing to make the complaint, though it was found to be inadmissible on other grounds.

[102] If, however, domestic proceedings in regard to the communication were launched in the name of the association, subsequent communications by individual members of that association under the Protocol may fall foul of this particular hurdle of admissibility. Thus, in *Beydon* and 19 other members of the association, *DIH Mouvement de Protestation Civique v France*, Communication No 1400/2005, para 4.3, the CCPR noted that it was not the authors but an association with legal personality under French law that was party to the domestic proceedings raised in the case. Hence, the authors were deemed not to be victims within the meaning of art 1 of the Protocol.

[103] A complaint by 6588 citizens in regard to a claimed breach of the right to life in art 6 of the Covenant was not necessarily inadmissible by reason of the large number of complainants involved in the case of *EW et al v The Netherlands*, Communication No 429/1990, para 6.3.

[104] CCPR's Rules of Procedure, r 96(b).

[105] See *Zvozskov et al v Belarus*, Communication No 1039/2001, para 6.3, where the CCPR considered that the author had standing to act on behalf of himself and on behalf of 23 individuals in respect of whom he had provided letters, authorising him to act on their behalf. The complaint was deemed inadmissible, however, in respect of 10 other individuals whom he had named in the complaint but in respect of whom there was no material indicating that they had authorised him to act on their behalf. Similarly, in *Korneenko et al v Belarus*, Communication No 1274/2004, para 6.3, Mr Korneenko's complaint was deemed admissible in regard to himself, but not with respect to 105 individuals whom he had claimed to represent but with respect to whom there was no proof whatsoever of their consent to allow him to act on their behalf in regard to the proceedings before the CCPR.

may also be deemed admissible in circumstances where they are submitted on behalf of individuals who are allegedly being held incommunicado in detention or who may have disappeared[106] or where a violation of the right to life is alleged. In these sorts of cases, where it is simply not possible for the victim personally to submit or otherwise authorise the communication, the Committee will allow another person to act on his or her behalf, provided there is a sufficiently strong personal link between that person and the victim.[107] Finally, it is possible for parents to act as representatives for their children and for heirs of a deceased person to do so in circumstances where the communication had been initiated under the Protocol prior to the death.[108]

[7.26] It is important to note in this context the fact that art 2(1) of the ICCPR itself obliges the States parties to respect and ensure the rights enshrined in the Covenant to all individuals within its territory and subject to its jurisdiction. Thus, States are liable under the Covenant for breaches thereof in respect of *all* individual victims within their territory,[109] regardless of citizenship.[110] This point is also reflected in the terms of art 1 of the OP-ICCPR which essentially confers the right of individual petition on 'individuals subject to a State party's jurisdiction'.

The victim requirement

[7.27] Communications may also be incompatible and hence inadmissible under art 1 of the OP-ICCPR where the author is found not to be a 'victim' within the meaning of art 1 of the Protocol. In order to be a victim, or to have the necessary standing to make the complaint, a person must be able to show that she or he is actually affected by the alleged breach. If the impugned law or practice has not already been applied to the detriment of the individual, she or he must show that the risk of being affected is more than a theoretical possibility and that breach of the right is imminent.[111] As the CCPR stated in the case of *Aumeeruddy-Cziffra v Mauritius*, '…it is a matter of degree how concretely this requirement should be taken'. However, no individual can in the abstract,

---

[106] See, for example, the case of *Laureano v Peru*, Communication No 540/1993 where the communication was submitted by a grandfather on behalf of his 16 year old granddaughter, whom he claimed had disappeared as a result of action taken by the Peruvian armed forces.

[107] A close family tie (including aunts, uncles, cousins, nephews and nieces) will normally be sufficient to establish this connection: Joseph et al, *The International Covenant on Civil and Political Rights* (2nd edn, OUP, 1994), p 73. If the victim is living, he or she must confirm his or her intention to pursue the complaint once he or she is in a position to do so; otherwise it will be deemed inadmissible.

[108] This, for example, occurred without any difficulty in *Croes v The Netherlands*, Communication No 164/84, para 1.

[109] As regards the territorial reach of the ICCPR, see below para **7.28–7.31** on inadmissibility *ratione loci*.

[110] See General Comment No 15 (1986), paras 1 and 2 and General Comment No 31 (2004), which also provides that '…the enjoyment of Covenant rights is not limited to citizens of State Parties but must also be available to all individuals, regardless of nationality or statelessness, such as asylum seekers, refugees, migrant workers and other persons, who may find themselves in the territory or subject to the jurisdiction of the State Party': para 10.

[111] In *EW et al v The Netherlands*, Communication No 429/1990, para 6.4, (contd.../)

by way of an *actio popularis*, challenge a law or practice claimed to be contrary to the Covenant'.[112] This interpretation of the Protocol rules out the possibility of complaints being lodged in the public interest. However, there are circumstances in which the Committee will accept that an individual is a victim for the purposes of art 1, even in the absence of specific measures of implementation against him or her personally. The classic illustrative example of such a situation is the case of *Toonen v Australia* which concerned legislation criminalising homosexual activities in Tasmania.[113] While the legislation in question had not actually been applied to the author and had not been enforced by the authorities in Tasmania for many years, the CCPR considered that he was still a 'victim' for the purposes of art 1. The Committee's decision was based on the view that the author had made reasonable efforts to demonstrate that the *threat* of enforcement, as well as the pervasive impact of the provisions on administrative practice and public opinion had affected him and continued to affect him personally.[114]

Inadmissible ratione loci

[7.28] As noted already, the alleged violation must have been submitted by 'individuals subject to the jurisdiction' of the State party to the Protocol.[115] Having regard to the further stipulation in art 2(1) of the Covenant that State responsibility under the ICCPR is limited to 'persons subject to a State's jurisdiction and within its territory', the CCPR has interpreted art 1 as being clearly applicable to individuals subject to its jurisdiction *at the time of the alleged violation of the Covenant*, irrespective of their nationality. Thus, there is no bar to an individual making a complaint to the CCPR under the Protocol where he or she has left the territory of a State party in which the alleged violation has taken place.[116]

[7.29] A respondent State can be held responsible for an extra-territorial violation of the Covenant, '…if it is a link in the causal chain that would make possible violations in another jurisdiction'.[117] Thus, as the CCPR opined in *Kindler v Canada*, '… if a State party takes a decision relating to a person within its jurisdiction, and the necessary and foreseeable consequence is that that person's rights under the Covenant will be violated in another jurisdiction, the State party itself may be in violation of the Covenant'.[118] Accordingly, a State party would itself be in violation of the Covenant if it deported,

---

[111] (\…contd) the CCPR held that the preparations for deployment and continuing deployment of nuclear missiles did not at the relevant period in time place the authors in a position where their right to life was violated or under imminent prospect of violationOn that ground, therefore, they could not claim to be victims of a violation.

[112] *Aumeeruddy-Cziffra v Mauritius*, Communication No 35/1978, para 9.2.

[113] *Toonen v Australia*, Communication No 488/1992.

[114] *Toonen v Australia*, Communication No 488/1992, para 5.1.

[115] See OP-ICCPR, art 1.

[116] This point was decided in a series of cases against Uruguay in the 1970s. See, for example, *Estrella v Uruguay*, Communication No 74/1980, para 4.1 and *Massiotti and Baritussio v Uruguay*, Communication No R 6/25, paras 7.1–7.2.

[117] *Munaf v Romania*, Communication No1539/2006, para. 14.2.

[118] *Kindler v Canada*, Communication No 470/91, para 6.2.

extradited, expelled or in any other way removed or facilitated the transportation[119] of a person to another State in circumstances in which it was foreseeable that torture or cruel, inhuman or degrading treatment or punishment or a breach of the right to life[120] would take place.[121]

[7.30] A State party can also be held responsible for the acts of its organs committed outside its territory. In *López Burgos v Uruguay*, the applicant complained, *inter alia*, about the kidnapping of her husband in Argentina by members of the Uruguayan security and intelligence forces, aided by Argentinean para-military groups.[122] In considering the admissibility of the complaint, the CCPR opined that:

Article 2(1) of the Covenant places an obligation upon a State party to respect and to ensure rights 'to all individuals within its territory and subject to its jurisdiction', but it does not imply that the State Party concerned cannot be held accountable for violations of rights under the Covenant which its agents commit upon the territory of another State, whether with the acquiescence of the Government of that State or in opposition to it.[123]

And further, that: 'it would be unconscionable to interpret the responsibility under art 2 of the Covenant as to permit a State party to perpetrate violations of the Covenant on the territory of another State, which violations it could not permit on its own territory'.[124] The CCPR's interpretation of the ICCPR in this respect has been broadly endorsed by the International Court of Justice.[125]

---

[119] In *Alzery v Sweden*, Communication No 1416/2005, paras 11.5–11.6, the CCPR found that the author's expulsion to Egypt violated ICCPR, art 7 in that it exposed him to a real risk of torture or other ill-treatment in Egypt. There was also a violation of art 7 by reason of the ill-treatment inflicted on him by foreign officials of another State on Swedish territory in implementing the expulsion. Since these actions took place within the jurisdiction of the respondent State, with the acquiescence of its officials, they were accordingly imputable to Sweden.

[120] *Ng v Canada*, Communication No 469/1991 and *Judge v Canada*, Communication No 829/1998.

[121] See CCPR General Comment No 31: '... the article 2 obligation requiring that States Parties respect and ensure the Covenant rights for all persons in their territory and all persons under their control entails an obligation not to extradite, deport, expel or otherwise remove a person from their territory, where there are substantial grounds for believing that there is a real risk of irreparable harm, such as that contemplated by articles 6 and 7 of the Covenant' (para 12).

[122] *López Burgos v Uruguay*, Communication No 52/1979.

[123] *López Burgos v Uruguay*, Communication No 52/1979, para 12.3.

[124] *López Burgos v Uruguay*, Communication No 52/1979, para 12.3. See also, General Comment No 31, para 10, which provides that the requirement in art 2(1) means '... that a State party must respect and ensure the rights laid down in the Covenant to anyone within the power or effective control of that State Party, even if not situated within the territory of the State Party'.

[125] Advisory Opinion on Legal Consequences on the Construction of a Wall in the Occupied Palestinian Territory (9 July 2004) 43 International Legal Materials 1009 (2004), in which the court held that the ICCPR applied to the conduct of Israel in the Occupied Territories. See generally, Cerone, 'The Application of Regional Human Rights Law Beyond Regional Frontiers: The Inter-American Commission on Human Rights and US Activities in Iraq' (25 October 2005): http//:www.ASIL.org/insights051025.cfm (last accessed May 2011).

[7.31] The principle of State responsibility under art 2(1) of the ICCPR has since been refined by the CCPR to mean that States must respect and ensure the rights laid down in the Covenant to anyone

... within the power or effective control of the forces of a State party acting outside its territory, regardless of the circumstances in which such power or effective control was obtained, such as forces constituting a national contingent of a State Party assigned to an international peace-keeping or peace-enforcement operation.[126]

This means that individuals may validly submit communications under the Protocol in respect of the actions of a contracting State's armed forces while stationed abroad.[127]

Inadmissible ratione materiae

[7.32] A complaint will be inadmissible *ratione materiae* (by reason of subject-matter) where the author invokes a right that is not protected under the Covenant. This occurred, for example, in *KJL v Finland*,[128] where the complaint related to the right to property which is not guaranteed under the Covenant.[129] However, as has been noted already above, a claim that on the face of it does not violate a right protected by the Covenant *might* be examinable on its merits on closer inspection. Thus, *Kindler v Canada* effectively raised the principle of *non-refoulement* which is not explicitly protected in the text of the Covenant, but which was ultimately considered by the CCPR in relation to the facts of the author's claim.[130]

[7.33] Communications may also be considered incompatible *ratione materiae* where the complaint concerns a provision of the Covenant which is subject to a valid reservation on the part of the respondent State.[131] However, the CCPR has taken the view that it is competent to rule on the permissibility of reservations made with respect to the

---

[126] CCPR General Comment No 31, para 10.

[127] See also the case of *Munaf v Romania* where an alleged failure on the part of the Romanian embassy in Iraq to take action to avert a real risk of extra-territorial violations of the Covenant was deemed admissible but rejected on the merits: Communication No1539/206. The CCPR has yet to develop its jurisprudence on the extraterritorial application of the ICCPR. See further, McGoldrick, 'Extraterritorial Application of the International Covenant on Civil and Political Rights' and Scheinin, 'Extraterritorial Effect of the International Covenant on Civil and Political Rights' in Coomans and Kamminga (eds), *Extraterritorial Application Of Human Rights Treaties* (Intersentia, 2004), pp 41 and 73 respectively. See also, King, 'The Extraterritorial Human Rights Obligations of States' (2009) Hum Rts L Rev 521.

[128] *KJL v Finland* Communication No 544/1993 (1994) 1 IHRR 74, para 4.2.

[129] While not guaranteed by the Covenant, property rights have been considered by the CCPR in the context of the right to non-discrimination in Article 26 of the ICCPR. See, for example, Simunek et al v Czech Republic, Communication No 516/1992.

[130] Communication No 470/91, para 14.2, see para **7.29**. See also *Ng v Canada*, Communication No 469/1991, paras 6.1 and 16.4.

[131] See CCPR General Comment No 24 of the CCPR on Issues relating to reservations made upon ratification or accession to the Covenant or the Optional Protocols thereto, or in relation to declarations under article 41 of the Covenant: UN Doc CCPR/C/21/Rev1/Add 6. See Joseph et al, *The International Covenant on Civil and Political Rights* (2nd ed, OUP, 1994), pp 25.02–25.37.

ICCPR and the OP-ICCPR;[132] and that the consequence of an impermissible reservation is that it is severable, leaving the State bound by the treaty without the benefit of the reservation.[133] This interpretation has proven to be controversial.[134] In *Kennedy v Trinidad and Tobago*, the CCPR applied this approach to a reservation that had been entered by the respondent State in 1998, purporting to eliminate the competence of the CCPR to receive and consider communications relating to prisoners on death row.[135] In its admissibility decision, the Committee held that the reservation was incompatible with the object and purpose of the OP-ICCPR and that accordingly the Committee was not precluded from considering the communication.[136] It went on to find that the State had violated a number of aspects of the Covenant in the author's case, including in relation to the imposition of the death penalty itself as well as with respect to the conditions of his detention.[137] Three months later, the government of Trinidad and Tobago denounced the First Optional Protocol, thus eliminating the possibility of any individual complaints being lodged against that State in respect of acts taking place within its jurisdiction that might be in violation of the Covenant.[138]

Unsubstantiated claims

[7.34] The Protocol does not contain a 'manifestly ill-founded' criterion of inadmissibility such as that which is contained in the European Convention on Human Rights.[139] Nonetheless, the CCPR has derived a similar criterion in practice from the terms of art 2 of the Protocol, which provides that 'individuals who *claim* that any of their rights enumerated in the Covenant have been violated and who have exhausted all available domestic remedies may submit a written communication to the Committee for consideration'. The Committee takes the view that a 'claim' for the purposes of art 2 '... is not just an allegation, but an allegation supported by substantiating material'.[140] Thus, where the author fails to substantiate a claim, the CCPR will deem the communication inadmissible.[141] Cases in which the author asks the CCPR to re-evaluate issues of fact

---

[132] CCPR General Comment No 24, para 18 and paras 13 and 14.
[133] CCPR General Comment No 24, para 18.
[134] See Joseph et al, *The International Covenant on Civil and Political Rights* (2nd ed, OUP, 1994), paras 25.02–25.37.
[135] *Kennedy v Trinidad and Tobago*, Communication No 845/1999, para 4.1.
[136] *Kennedy v Trinidad and Tobago*, Communication No 845/1999, para 6.
[137] *Kennedy v Trinidad and Tobago*, Communication No 845/1999, see paras 7.3 and 7.8.
[138] See McGrory, 'Reservations of Virtue: Lessons of Trinidad and Tobago's Reservation to the First Optional Protocol' (2001) 23 HRQ 769.
[139] See ECHR, art 35(3).
[140] CCPR Annual Report 2010, para 98.
[141] Rules of Procedure, r 96(b). See, for example, *Stolyar v the Russian Federation*, Communication No 996/2001, declared inadmissible on 31 October 2006 in which the CCPR held that the author had failed to substantiate his claim of a violation under art 7 of the Covenant sufficiently for the purposes of admissibility, noting in particular the absence of a detailed description of the acts of ill-treatment that the author was allegedly subjected to by police, and the absence of medical evidence or information as to whether the author or counsel had complained about that ill-treatment. See also, *Fernandes et al v The Netherlands*, Communication No 1513/2006, decision adopted on 22 July 2008, para 6.3.

and evidence that have already been decided by domestic courts will generally be treated as an instance of 'lack of substantiation' and hence inadmissible under art 2. This is because the Committee has repeatedly stated that it is not appropriate for it to substitute its own views for the judgment of domestic courts on the evaluation of the facts and evidence in a case, unless it considers the latter evaluation to be manifestly arbitrary or as amounting to a denial of justice.[142] Thus, a reasonable conclusion reached by a jury or a court on a matter, based on all the available evidence, will not be considered as manifestly arbitrary or to amount to a denial of justice.[143]

Competing international procedures

[7.35] Article 5(2)(a) of the Protocol requires the CCPR to ascertain that the same matter (ie, the same individual's case)[144] is not being examined simultaneously under another procedure of international investigation or settlement.[145] The term 'another international procedure' appears to mean individual complaint procedures operated by other United Nations treaty bodies,[146] or regional human rights bodies implementing the European Convention on Human Rights, the Inter-American Convention on Human Rights and the African Charter.[147] It does not refer to more broadly based 'inquiries' or investigative mechanisms such as those considered in Ch 5; or an investigation of a particular form of abuse in a number of States such as that which may be conducted by one of the human rights special procedures.[148]

[7.36] Since art 5(2)(a) is specifically concerned with *simultaneous* proceedings, it does not preclude an individual from submitting a communication to the CCPR after it has *already* been submitted to and considered by another international body,[149] regardless of whether the latter body has deemed the case inadmissible or has pronounced on the

---

[142] *Errol Simms v Jamaica*, Communication No 541/1993, para 6.2.

[143] See, for example, *Weerasinghe v Sri Lanka*, Communication No 1031/2001, para 6.2; and *Stow and Modou Gai v Portugal*, Communication No 1496/2006, para 6.5.

[144] OP-ICCPR, art 5(2)(a) will not be relevant, for example, if the same legal issue(s), or matters arising from the same legal incident, are being raised by different individuals in another forum. See *Fanali v Italy*, Communication No 75/1980, para 7.2.

[145] See also CCPR's Rules of Procedure, r 96(e). See generally Nowak, *UN Covenant on Civil and Political Rights: CCPR Commentary* (NP Engel, 1993), p 695–702.

[146] See generally, Schmidt, 'Individual human rights complaints procedures based on United Nations treaties and the need for Reform' (1992) ICLQ 645, pp 653–654.

[147] As to the latter procedures, see Ch 1, paras **1.25–1.26**.

[148] *Baboeram et al v Suriname*, Communication No 146/1983 and 148–154/1983, para 9.1. As Ghandi has stated, this interpretation is 'obviously desirable if the whole procedure is not to be thwarted or rendered illusory at the slightest semblance of any other international body being involved in the general situation in relation to which a particular breach or breaches of the Covenant are alleged by an individual with respect to himself': Ghandi, 'The Human Rights Committee and the Right of Individual Communication' (1986) 57 BYIL 201, p 229.

[149] See, for example, *Stow and Modou Gai v Portugal*, Communication No 1496/2006, para 6.2 in which the CCPR refused to find the complaint inadmissible purely on the ground that it had already been considered by the European Court of Human Rights.

merits of the case.[150] Indeed, it should be noted that if the communication is deemed inadmissible by the CCPR on this ground because of simultaneous proceedings, the possibility exists for the Committee to review that decision at a later date in exceptional circumstances where, in the meantime, the matter has been settled before the international body in question.[151]

[7.37] To circumvent this apparent loophole in the OP-ICCPR, many European States have entered reservations to the Protocol, declining competence to the CCPR in regard to communications which have already been the subject of another international procedure. With their eyes no doubt focused principally on the possibility of competing proceedings under the ECHR, the trend of entering such reservations by European States is clearly aimed at preventing individuals from the practice of so-called 'forum-shopping', whereby a decision by one international body may be effectively appealed to another.[152] Such a possibility is largely sealed off now by the taking out of such a reservation since art 35(1)(b) of the ECHR clearly provides that a complaint to the latter Court is inadmissible if, *inter alia,* it has *already* been submitted to another procedure of international investigation or settlement.[153] Nonetheless, it should be noted that the CCPR takes the view that reservations to art 5(2)(a) of the Protocol which purport to constrain the competence of the Committee 'if the same matter is being examined or has already been considered under another procedure of international investigation or settlement' will not render a communication inadmissible if the latter decision pertains only to an issue of procedure.[154] An 'examination' for the purposes of such reservations requires that the concrete case has previously undergone a certain consideration on the merits, which can in some cases happen during the course of the European Court's

---

[150] See *Wright v Jamaica*, Communication No 349/1989. Likewise, OP-ICCPR, art 5(2)(a) will not preclude the CCPR from examining a communication which has already been submitted to but been withdrawn from another procedure or international investigation or settlement, since the substance is no longer under active consideration in the other body at the time of the Committee's decision on admissibility: *Ramirez v Uruguay*, Communication No R 1/4, UN Doc Supp No 40 (A/35/40) at 121 (1980), para 9.

[151] CCPR'S Rules of Procedure, r 98(2).

[152] In *Coeriel & Aurik v The Netherlands*, Communication No 453/1991, para 10.5, for example, where no such reservation had been made to the terms of ICCPR, art 5(2)(a), the CCPR found that there had been a violation of the authors' right to privacy under ICCPR, art 17, arising out of the respondent State's refusal to allow them to change their surnames for religious reasons.The former European Commission of Human Rights had previously considered the claimed violation of ECHR, arts 9 and 14 arising out of the same facts to be manifestly ill-founded (para 2.4); and see (1994) 15 HRLJ 448.

[153] See *Calcerrada Fornieles and Cabeza Mato v Spain* (Application 17512/90), decision of the European Commission of Human Rights in rejecting an application by the applicants which had already been submitted to the CCPR: Vol 55–56 D & R, 214.

[154] Thus, for example, in *Vincent v France*, Communication No 1505/2006, paras 7.2 and 7.3, the author's complaint regarding a breach of ECHR, art 14 was not found to be inadmissible merely on the ground that the issue had already been examined by the European Court of Human Rights. (contd.../)

evaluation of admissibility.[155] Individuals wishing to complain about a breach of their human rights in European States which are parties to the ECHR, as well as the OP-ICCPR (modified by such a reservation), will need to choose their forum very carefully, paying close attention to the rights that may be subject to complaint under both conventions[156] and the manner in which each is interpreted by the CCPR and the European Court respectively.[157]

Exhaustion of domestic remedies

[7.38] Article 5(2)(b) of the Protocol provides that the CCPR shall not consider any communication unless it has ascertained that the author has exhausted all available domestic remedies.[158] This provision gives effect to the general procedural rule of international law that all domestic remedies must have been resolved before a State presents a claim against another State before an international tribunal. The rationale for the rule is that putative victims should in the first instance seek redress from the domestic authorities, who must be given an opportunity to afford redress for the alleged wrong before the Committee is seised of the matter.[159] In other words, a State should not be accused under international law if it can remedy the situation.

[7.39] This condition of admissibility is by no means absolute. The Protocol itself provides for an exception where the application of the remedies is unreasonably

---

[154] (contd.../) The CCPR found that the State's reservation did not operate to invalidate the proceedings because the decision of the European Court had been a procedural one, namely, that the author had failed to exhaust his domestic remedies. The CCPR went on, however, to decide that the complaint was inadmissible under the Covenant for failure to exhaust domestic remedies under ICCPR, art 5(2)(b). See also *Bertelli Gálvez v Spain*, Communication No 1389/2005, para 4.3 and *Wdowiak v Poland*, Communication No 1446/2006, para 6.2.

[155] *Schmidl v Germany*, Communication No 1516/2006, para 4.5 in which the CCPR found the State's reservation under ICCPR, art 5(2)(a) applicable on the basis that the European Court of Human Rights had previously 'examined' the matter in the context of its decision of inadmissibility. Specifically, the Committee noted that the European Court's decision made it clear that it had examined the facts of the case, and having done so, had concluded that the facts 'do not disclose any appearance of a violation of the rights and freedoms set out in the Convention'.

[156] Certain rights in the ICCPR which may be the subject of a complaint under the OP-ICCPR are not explicitly protected under the ECHR, for example, the right of access to one's minority culture (art 27) and the prohibition on incitement to racial hatred (art 20).

[157] The scope of the particular rights in each instrument may differ. For example, the equality provision in ECHR, art 14 is narrow in scope, whereas the provision in ICCPR, art 26 is much broader. This substantive difference, however, is not relevant in respect of States which have ratified ECHR, Protocol 12, which implements a free-standing non-discrimination principle, similar to that provided for in ICCPR, art 26.

[158] For a detailed exposition of this requirement, see generally, McGoldrick, *The Human Rights Committee: Its Role in the Development of the International Covenant on Civil and Political Rights* (OUP, 1991), pp 187–197; and Joseph, *The International Covenant on Civil and Political Rights* (2nd ed, OUP, 1994), pp 103–138.

[159] A similar rationale was articulated by the European Court of Human Rights in interpreting ECHR, art 35(1) in *Akdivar v Turkey* (1997) 23 EHRR 143, para 65.

prolonged,[160] and the CCPR has consistently maintained that this rule of inadmissibility only applies to the extent that such remedies are available and effective.[161] Thus, the author is required only to have raised the substance[162] of his or her Covenant right in domestic proceedings which offer a reasonable prospect of success in providing redress for the alleged wrong.[163] The State, on the other hand,[164] is required to give details of any remedies which it maintains were available to the author, together with evidence that there was a reasonable prospect that such remedies would be effective.[165] In circumstances where the State fails to produce information to refute a credible account by the author that domestic remedies have been satisfied, the CCPR considers that it is not precluded from examining the claim by art 5(2)(b).[166]

[7.40] The question of which remedies are contemplated is one for national law. 'Domestic remedies' implies judicial remedies (including constitutional proceedings where appropriate),[167] but it also includes administrative remedies[168] and in general terms any other legally binding procedures that can substantially affect the decision on its merits.[169] While *ex post facto* remedies are normally considered sufficient, there may be

---

[160] Complainants cannot, however, rely on this exception where such delay is either attributable to the author or results from the complexities of the case: *HS v France*, Communication No 184/84, para 9.4; and *Fillastre and Bizoarn v Bolivia*, Communication No 336/88, para 5.2.

[161] CCPR Annual Report 2010, para 110. A remedy that is unduly prolonged may also be considered ineffective for the purposes of the domestic remedies rule: see *Ominayak et al v Canada*, Communication No 167/84, para.13.2.

[162] 'A complainant bringing the issues in question before the domestic courts need not use the precise language of the Covenant for legal remedies differ in their form from State to State. The question is rather whether the proceedings in their totality raised facts and issues presently before the Committee': *Kavanagh v Ireland*, Communication No 819/1998, UN Doc CCPR/C/71/D/819/1998, para 9.3.

[163] CCPR Annual Report 2010, para 110. See, for example, *Rodríguez Domínguez v Spain*, Communication No 1471/2006, para 6.3.

[164] As regards the burden of proof in regard to exhaustion, McGoldrick takes the view that while the initial burden of proof as to exhaustion rests with the author, this burden 'may not be very heavy'. Once it is satisfied, the burden of proof moves to the State Party: McGoldrick, *The Human Rights Committee: Its Role in the Development of the International Covenant on Civil and Political Rights* (OUP, 1991), p 189. Joseph et al suggest that the State Party bears a 'substantial burden' in proving the existence and efficacy of the relevant domestic remedies, but that the CCPR has not always been consistent on this issue: *The International Covenant on Civil and Political Rights* (2nd edn, OUP, 1994), pp 134–138.

[165] The State must specify which remedies were available to the author in the particular circumstances of his case: *Ramirez v Uruguay*, Communication No R 1/4, para 5.

[166] See, for example, *Kodirov v Uzbekistan*, Communication No 1284/2004, para 8.4.

[167] See, for example, *APA v Spain*, Communication No 433/1990, para 6.2; and *Bibaud v Canada*, Communication No 1747/2008, para 7.3.

[168] This point is made by the Committee, for example, in *Patino v Panama*, Communication No 437/90, para 5.2.

[169] See, for example, *C v Australia*, Communication No 900/99 in which the CCPR held that remedies before the Commonwealth Ombudsman and the Human Rights and Equality Opportunity Commission which (contd.../)

circumstances in which a complainant may only be expected to avail of injunctive relief, rather than being required to exhaust a remedy that could only be availed of following the destruction of his or her Covenant rights.[170]

[7.41] While the CCPR has shown some flexibility in the interpretation of this particular admissibility hurdle, complainants cannot afford to take a cavalier approach in respect of it. Financial considerations or mere doubt or a subjective belief as to the prospects of success, for example, will not absolve the author from pursuing a relevant remedy.[171] Remedies must also be pursued to their conclusion before the Committee can assess a claim. The latter principle is well illustrated by the outcome in *Ahmad and Abdol-Hamid v Denmark,* which concerned the publication of caricatures of Mohamed and Islam.[172] The authors claimed violations of the Covenant because they had been denied an effective remedy for incitement of hatred against Muslims, prohibited under art 20 of the Covenant. At the time that the case was being considered by the CCPR, a judgment of the domestic courts, which dealt at length with the criminal responsibility of the senior managers of the publishing newspaper in question, was under appeal. Since the authors were closely involved with these proceedings, the CCPR held that the complaint was inadmissible for failure to exhaust domestic remedies at the time of its consideration by the Committee.[173]

It should be noted that in common with the admissibility criterion relating to competing international procedures, the possibility exists for the Committee to review a decision of inadmissibility on the ground of failure to exhaust domestic remedies at the written request of an author.[174] Such an option may be exercised where the author subsequently satisfies the domestic remedies in question.[175]

SUBSTANTIVE VIEWS

Burden of proof

[7.42] A crucial dilemma faced by the CCPR at the outset of its work under the OP-ICCPR was how to deal with communications where a respondent State fails to engage

---

[169] (\...contd) were ostensibly available to the author but not pursued by him were ineffective for the purposes of ICCPR, art 5(2)(b) because they only had the status of recommendations and did not have binding effect.

[170] See, for example, *Ominayak et al v Canada*, Communication No 167/84, para 13.2.

[171] *PS v Denmark*, Communication No 397/90, para 5.4.

[172] *Ahmad and Abdol-Hamid v Denmark*, Communication No 1487/2006, declared inadmissible on 22 July 2008.

[173] *Ahmad and Abdol-Hamid v Denmark*, Communication No 1487/2006, para 6.2.

[174] CCPR Rules of Procedure, r 98(2).

[175] Nowak, *UN Covenant on Civil and Political Rights: CCPR Commentary* (Engel, 1993), citing a number of cases in which the Committee expressly referred to this rule when declaring a series of cases concerning the death penalty inadmissible in respect of Jamaica. In its decisions, the Committee expressly requested the respondent State to postpone imposition of the death penalty until the authors had had an opportunity to seek a review of the decisions of inadmissibility once they had exhausted the remedies in question: p 672. See, for example, *AS v Jamaica*, Communication No 231/1987.

with the process. In *Conteris v Uruguay*, for example, the author submitted detailed allegations about the horrific ill-treatment and detention incommunicado of her brother in various military establishments because of his previous connections to the opposition regime in Uruguay.[176] The complaint was submitted in 1983 and when it was transmitted to the government for observations on the merits, the latter responded that the complainant had been released from prison but gave no further explanation regarding the allegations made.[177] The Committee seized the opportunity to state its view that it is the State's duty under art 4(2) of the Protocol to investigate in good faith all alleged violations of the Covenant made against it and to provide the Committee with all information available to it. In cases where the author has submitted allegations to the Committee, which are supported by witness testimony, and where further clarification can only be supplied by the State party, '...the Committee may consider such allegations as substantiated in the absence of satisfactory evidence and explanations to the contrary submitted by the State party'.[178] Citing an identical decision of the Committee in *Bleir v Uruguay*,[179] McGoldrick has noted that this is a very positive interpretation of the Protocol as it ensures that the burden of proof in regard to complaints under the OP-ICCPR does not rest completely with the author.[180] The State has a clear obligation to investigate the allegations being made and any attempt to frustrate that process by a failure to supply the Committee with information will not be of benefit to the State.[181] The stance taken by the CCPR has since become so entrenched in the practice of the CCPR[182] as to be akin to a power to make 'default findings'.[183] While this may be a welcome development in the sense identified by McGoldrick, the depressing reality still exists that the views eventually arrived at are unlikely to be taken seriously by a

---

[176] *Conteris v Uruguay* Communication No 139/1983, adopted on 17 July 1985.

[177] *Conteris v Uruguay* Communication No 139/1983, para 6.2.

[178] *Conteris v Uruguay* Communication No 139/1983, para 7.2. On the facts, the CPPR went on to find that the treatment that had been meted out to Conteris involved multiple violations of the Covenant. These included violations of arts 7 and 10 (ill-treatment), art 9 (right to liberty and security) and art 14 (fair trial).

[179] *Bleir v Uruguay*, Communication No 30/1978, adopted on 29 March 1982.

[180] McGoldrick, *The Human Rights Committee: Its Role in the Development of the International Covenant on Civil and Political Rights* (OUP, 1991), p 149.

[181] This conclusion is echoed by the CCPR itself in its recent General Comment No 33 on the obligations of States under the Protocol where it specifically stated that by failing to respond to a communication or responding incompletely, a State '...puts itself at a disadvantage, because the Committee is then compelled to consider the communication in the absence of full information relating to the communication. In such circumstances, the Committee may conclude that the allegations contained in the communication are true, if they appear from all the circumstances to be substantiated': CCPR General Comment No 33, UN Doc CCPR/GC/33, para 10.

[182] See, for example, *Sathasivam et al v Sri Lanka*, in which the CCPR found the respondent State responsible for a breach of the right to life in circumstances where it had not provided any explanation for the death of the applicant in custody: *Sathasivam et al v Sri Lanka*, Communication No 1436/2005, para 6.4.

[183] Tomuschat, 'Human Rights Committee' in *Max Planck Encyclopaedia of Public International Law* (OUP, 2009), p 33.

government which has refused to engage with the process from the outset. Paradoxically, in cases where governments *do* provide detailed refutations of the allegations made by the author, the power of the CCPR to provide reasoned views is practically emasculated. Since there are no oral hearings by which a discrepancy in accounts can be teased out, the CCPR may find itself at a complete loss to unscramble the factual situation.[184]

Right to life

[7.43] In the early years, many of the complaints received by the CCPR related to blatant violations of the ICCPR concerning the rights to life (art 6), liberty (art 9) and freedom from torture and other ill-treatment (art 7). In regard to the right to life, the Committee has held that States have negative obligations not to kill[185] or to attempt[186] to kill people arbitrarily, and obligations to investigate and punish appropriately all killings carried out by agents of the state.[187] The obligation in art 6 further enjoins the Contracting States to ensure that the law strictly controls and limits the circumstances in which a person may be deprived of his life by the authorities.[188] Further positive duties to protect life include the duty to investigate the circumstances of suspicious deaths,[189] to prevent and investigate disappearances;[190] and to prevent, investigate and punish appropriately deprivations of life by the criminal acts of third parties.[191] States are also obliged by art 6 to reduce infant mortality and to increase the life expectancy of its population.[192] The CCPR has also found the imposition of the death penalty to violate the right to life in several circumstances.[193] Moreover, the removal by a contracting State that has

---

[184] On the particular challenges faced by the CCPR in terms of fact-finding under the OP-ICCPR, see Fitzpatrick, 'Human Rights Fact-Finding' in Bayefsky (ed), *The UN Human Rights Treaty System in the 21st Century* (Kluwer Law, 2000), pp 70–72.

[185] See CCPR General Comment No 6 on the Right to Life, UN Doc HRI/GEN/1/Rev 6 at 127, 30 April 1982, para 3.

[186] *Chongwe v Zambia*, Communication No 821/1998, para 5.2.

[187] *Baboeram et al v Suriname*, Communication No 146/1983 and 148–154/1983. In *Eshonov v Uzbekistan*, Communication No 1225/2003, the CCPR held that the failure by the State to exhume the body of the author's son in order to properly address the claim that the State was responsible for his killing constituted a violation of ICCPR, arts 6(1) and 7 (para 9.7).

[188] See, for example, *Suárez de Guerrero v Colombia*, Communication No R 11/45 (1979), para 13.1.

[189] See, for example, the case of *Hugo Dermit Barbato v Uruguay*, Communication No 84/81, para 11, concerning the failure to establish the facts of a suspicious death in custody.

[190] CCPR General Comment No 6, para 4. See *El Alwani v Libyan Arab Jamahiriya*, Communication No 1295/2004.

[191] CCPR General Comment No 6, para 3.

[192] CCPR General Comment No 6, para 5.

[193] *Uteev v Uzbekistan*, Communication No 1150/2003 (imposition of death sentence after an unfair trial violates ICCPR, art 6); *Persaud v Guyana*, Communication No 812/1998 (imposition of the death penalty without regard to the defendant's personal circumstances or the particular circumstances of the offence violates art 6); and *Chisanga v Zambia*, Communication No 1132/2002 (imposition of death penalty for aggravated robbery in which a firearm was used violated ICCPR, art 6 since the crime in question was not sufficiently 'serious' within the meaning of ICCPR, art 6(2)).

eliminated the death penalty of a person to a country in which there are substantial grounds for considering that there is a real risk of execution will violate art 6.[194]

Freedom from torture or ill-treatment

[7.44] The CCPR has all too frequently had occasion to find violations of the right to be free from torture and lesser forms of ill-treatment enshrined in art 7 of the ICCPR.[195] Unlike the European Court of Human Rights, which interprets and applies a similar provision in art 3 of the ECHR, the CCPR has not focused in its jurisprudence on defining the ingredients of the prohibited forms of ill-treatment prohibited by art 7,[196] preferring instead in most cases to identify whether a violation of art 7 of the ICCPR generally has taken place in a given case.[197] Article 10(1) of the ICCPR complements the prohibition of ill-treatment in respect of detainees by providing that: 'All persons deprived of their liberty shall be treated with humanity and with respect for the inherent dignity of the human person'.[198]

---

[194] *Judge v Canada*, Communication No 829/1998, UN Doc CPR/C/78/D/829/1998, para 10.4. See also, *Kwok v Australia*, Communication No 1442/2005.

[195] See generally, CCPR General Comment No 20, UN Doc HRI/GEN/1/Rev 1 at 30. Note that ICCPR, art 7 is supplemented by the requirement in art 10 of the Covenant that all persons deprived of their liberty shall be treated with humanity and with respect for the inherent dignity of the human person. See General Comment No 21 (10/04/1992). For a comprehensive analysis of the Committee's application of these articles, see Joseph et al, *The International Covenant on Civil and Political Rights* (2nd ed, OUP, 1994), pp 194–293.

[196] The Committee takes the view that it may not be necessary '...to draw up a list of prohibited acts or to establish sharp distinctions between the different kinds of punishment or treatment; the distinctions depend on the nature, purpose and severity of the treatment applied': General Comment No 20 (10/03/92) concerning Torture or Cruel, Inhuman or Degrading Treatment or Punishment, para 4.

[197] Joseph et al, *The International Covenant on Civil and Political Rights* (2nd edn, OUP, 1994), para 9.20.

[198] General Comment No 21 concerning humane treatment of persons deprived of their liberty UN Doc HRI/GEN/1/Rev 1 at 33, para 3. Joseph et al make the comment that '...the line between the two provisions has been blurred' by the CCPR: Joseph et al, *The International Covenant on Civil and Political Rights* (2nd edn, OUP, 1994), paras 9.138–9.144. It would seem that ICCPR, art 10(1) is mostly applied where the author complains about the *conditions* in which he or she is being detained, as opposed to more specific ill-treatment directed at him or her personally. Indeed, in some such cases, the CCPR has simply refrained from reaching a view as to whether there has been a breach of art 7 where it has already found a violation of ICCPR, art 10 to exist on the facts (see recently, *Mawamba v Zambia*, Communication No 1520/2006, para 6.4). But there have also been cases in which the CCPR has found a breach of ICCPR, art 7, as well as ICCPR, art 10, to exist where the conditions of detention are severe enough to reach the ICCPR, art 7 threshold, particularly where they result in negative effects on the health of the author. See recently, for example, *Marinich v Belarus*, Communication No 1502/2006, paras 10.2–10.3.

The CCPR has found a range of treatment to violate the absolute guarantee in art 7 which extends to acts of physical pain as well as mental suffering.[199] It has confirmed that art 7 not only involves negative obligations on States not to inflict torture or ill-treatment, but also involves obligations to ensure effective protection from ill-treatment (whether at the hands of State agents or third parties) through some machinery of control.[200] Those found guilty must be held responsible and victims must have access to effective remedies to obtain redress.[201] Failure to investigate allegations of torture or other ill-treatment promptly and impartially will entail a violation of art 7.[202]

The Committee has followed the example of the European Court of Human Rights in finding violations of art 7 to exist in circumstances were a person's expulsion or extradition raises a substantial risk of ill-treatment in the receiving State.[203] While the Committee's jurisprudence in respect of this aspect of art 7 is not perhaps as well developed as that of the European Court of Human Rights,[204] recently it has expanded its view to include a prohibition on *refoulement* in circumstances where the State is unable

---

[199] CCPR General Comment No 20, para 5. See the survey of cases set forth in Joseph et al, *The International Covenant on Civil and Political Rights* (2nd edn, OUP, 1994), paras 9.34–9.40. The CCPR's most recent annual report for 2010 includes cases in which the CCPR determined that violations of ICCPR, art 7 were established in respect of a wide variety of circumstances including beatings and electroshock treatment in custody (*Kirpo v Tajikistan*, Communication No 1401/2005); and incommunicado detention involving the complete isolation of a prisoner (*Kulov v Kyrgyztan*, Communication No 1369/2005). In *Kaba v Canada*, Communication No 1465/2006, para 10.1, it held that subjecting a woman to genital mutilation undoubtedly constitutes treatment prohibited by ICCPR, art 7. In *KNLH v Peru*, Communication No 1153/2003, in the absence of any information submitted by the respondent State on the case, the Committee held that the refusal of the medical authorities to terminate the pregnancy of a 17 year old girl who was carrying an anencephalic foetus, in circumstances where the continuation of the pregnancy entailed a risk to her life and exposed her to mental suffering after the birth constituted a violation of art 7 of the ICCPR (paras 6.2–6.3).

[200] General Comment No 20, para 1.

[201] In this respect, ICCPR, art 7 must be read in conjunction with the right to an effective remedy provided for in ICCPR, art 2(3): General Comment No 20, para 14.

[202] General Comment No 20, para 14. See, for example, *Kirpo v Tajikistan*, Communication No 1401/2005, para 6.3.

[203] In *Ng v Canada*, Communication No 469/1991 the CCPR held that extradition of the author to the USA where he faced death by gas asphyxiation was in violation of ICCPR, art 7. In *Alzery v Sweden*, Communication No 1416/2005, paras 11.3–11.5, the CCPR was confronted with a case which apparently involved rendition by CIA agents of the author from Sweden to Egypt with the consent of the Swedish government. Finding that Sweden had violated art 7 because of the circumstances of the author's expulsion, the Committee went on to hold that diplomatic assurances obtained by Sweden from the government of Egypt which contained no mechanism to monitor their enforcement were insufficient to eliminate the risk of ill-treatment to a level consistent with the requirements of ICCPR, art 7. It also found the State responsible for acquiescing to treatment in violation of art 7 by foreign agents of another State at the airport in Bromma, which included stripping the complainant naked, shackling and hooding him as well as forcibly drugging him *per rectum* for the purposes of rendition (paras 3.11 and 11.6).

[204] In *GT v Australia*, Communication No 706/1996, the CCPR considered whether the extradition of a person gave rise to a substantial risk of corporal punishment in the receiving State. (contd.../)

to protect an individual from a threat of ill-treatment by non-State actors.[205] The Committee's jurisprudence in regard to art 7 mirrors other novel interpretations by the European Court of art 3 of the ECHR. For example, the CCPR has held that where a person is injured while in custody, it is incumbent on the State party to provide a plausible explanation for the injuries and to produce evidence refuting the allegations of ill-treatment made by the author; otherwise, it will find in favour of the author.[206] Further, the infliction of extreme anguish on a person by failing to give information on the disappearance[207] or fate of a family member can also constitute inhuman treatment in violation of art 7.[208] Moreover, the imposition of a death sentence on an individual, after the conclusion of proceedings which fail to meet the requirements of the right to a fair trial provided for in art 14 of the ICCPR will of itself violate art 7.[209]

Right to liberty and security

[7.45] The right to liberty of the person provided for in art 9 of the ICCPR applies in principle to all deprivations of liberty, whether these occur in the criminal or civil context.[210] A deprivation of liberty will only be permissible under this provision if it is in 'accordance with procedures as are established by law',[211] ie, the detention must be in conformity with the procedural and substantive law of the State which authorises it.[212]

---

[204] (\...contd) It did not reach the issue of whether such a risk would entail a violation of ICCPR, art 7 since the risk in question was found not to exist on the facts. See also, *ARJ v Australia*, Communication No 692/1996.

[205] Thus, in *Kaba v Canada*, Communication No 1465/2000, para 10.2, the CCPR held that the deportation of a 15 year old to Guinea in circumstances where there were substantial grounds for believing that she faced a real risk of genital mutilation would constitute a violation of ICCPR, art 7.

[206] *Zheikov v Russian Federation*, Communication No 889/1999. This view was previously articulated by the European Court of Human Rights in *Tomasi v France* (1993) 15 EHRR 1.

[207] See, for example, *Benaziza v Algeria*, Communication No 1588/2007, para 9.6.

[208] *Ruzmetov v Uzbekistan*, Communication No 915/2000. See also *Bazarov v Uzbekistan*, Communication No 985/2001 and *Shukurova v Tajikistan*, Communication No 1044/2002. This conclusion is consistent with the case law of the European Court of Human Rights: see, for example, *Akkoc v Turkey* (2002) EHRR 1173.

[209] *Larrañaga v the Philippines*, Communication No 1421/2005, para 7.11, following the judgment of the European Court of Human Rights in *Öcalan v Turkey* (2005) 41 EHRR 985, paras 167–175. See recently, *Mwamba v Zambia*, Communication No 1520/2006, para 6.8. The *Larrañaga* case also confirms that the imposition of the death sentence in circumstances which cannot be justified under art 6 will automatically breach ICCPR, art 7 (para 7.11).

[210] See CCPR General Comment No 8 on the Right to liberty and security of persons, UN Doc HRI/GEN/1/Rev 1 at 8 (1994), and in particular para 1 in which the Committee opines that this right applies for example to cases of '…mental illness, vagrancy, drug addiction, educational purposes, immigration control etc'.

[211] ICCPR, art 9(1).

[212] The Committee has often encountered cases under this provision involving flagrant violations where persons have been detained for lengthy periods without charge in contravention of domestic law: *Titiahonjo v Cameroon*, Communication No 1186/2003, paras 6.5–6.6; and *El Hassy v Libyan Arab Jamahiriya*, Communication No 1422/2005, para 6.5.

Secondly, the detention must not be 'arbitrary', ie, the law itself and the manner in which it is implemented must be reasonable in the circumstances.[213] While most cases arising under art 9 concern persons in formal detention, art 9 also protects a discrete right to security of the person outside the context of formal detention. The latter aspect of the right obligates States not to ignore threats made to the personal security of non-detained persons in their jurisdiction.[214]

[7.46] Specific provisions relating to detention in the criminal law context are provided for in art 9(2) and (3). Article 9(2) provides for the right of any person who has been arrested to be informed at the time of the arrest of the reasons for the arrest and to be informed 'promptly' of any charges against him. While the term 'promptly' has not been defined,[215] this provision requires an arrested person to be '… informed sufficiently of the reasons for his arrest to enable him to take immediate steps to secure his release if he believes that the reasons given are invalid or unfounded'.[216] Article 9(3) requires that in criminal cases, any person arrested or detained must be brought 'promptly' before a judge or other officer authorised by law to exercise judicial power. The CCPR has taken the view that since the purpose of this provision is to bring the detention of a person charged with a criminal offence under judicial control, it is imperative that such power be exercised by an authority which is 'independent, objective and impartial' in relation to the issues being dealt with.[217] The meaning of 'promptly' in this section implies that delays must not exceed a 'few days'.[218] Incommunicado detention as such may violate

---

[213] As to the meaning of 'arbitrariness', see the views of the CCPR in the case of *Van Alphen v The Netherlands*, Communication No 305/88, para 5.8: '… 'arbitrariness' is not to be equated with 'against the law', but must be interpreted more broadly to include elements of inappropriateness, injustice and lack of predictability. This means that remand in custody pursuant to lawful arrest must not only be lawful but reasonable in all the circumstances. Further, remand in custody must be necessary in all the circumstances, for example, to prevent flight, interference with evidence or the recurrence of crime'. In *A v Australia*, Communication No 560/1993, para 9.2, the Committee stated that 'the element of proportionality becomes relevant' in assessing the necessity of the circumstances of a detention.

[214] See *Delgado-Páez v Colombia*, Communication No 195/1985, para 5.5 and *Chongwe v Zambia*, Communication No 821/198, para 5.3.

[215] In *Komarovski v Turkmenistan*, Communication No 1450/2006, para 7.3, the failure to inform the author of the reasons for his arrest until the third day of his detention was found to constitute a violation of ICCPR, art 9(2) (in the absence of any information from the respondent State).

[216] *Drescher Caldas v Uruguay*, Communication No 43/1979, para 13.2.

[217] In *Ruzmetov v Uzbekistan*, Communication No 915/2000, para 7.7, the Committee was not satisfied that the public prosecutor could be characterised as having '…the institutional objectivity and impartiality necessary to be considered as an 'officer authorised to exercise judicial power".

[218] CCPR General Comment No 8, para 2.

this provision.[219] Article 9(3) goes on to provide that persons who have been arrested under this provision shall be entitled to trial within a reasonable time[220] or to release pending trial. While release should be the norm, detention without bail may be justified '... to ensure the presence of the accused at the trial, avert interference with witnesses and other evidence, or the commission of other offences'.[221] Article 9(4) provides for the crucially important right of a detained person[222] to have his or her detention judicially reviewed before a court in order that that court may decide without delay on the lawfulness of the detention and to order release if the detention is not lawful.[223] Such review is not limited to a review of compliance with domestic law; it must be 'real and not merely formal' in that the court must be able to order release if the detention is incompatible with art 9(1) or the other provisions of the Covenant.[224] The question of whether review has been delayed beyond permissible limits is one to be decided on the facts of each case.[225] Finally, art 9(5) of the Covenant provides for an enforceable right to compensation in domestic law for persons who have been unlawfully deprived of their liberty, ie, where there has been a breach of any other aspect of art 9.[226]

---

[219] *Medjnoune v Algeria*, Communication No 1297/2004, para 8.7. See also *Boimurodov v Tajikistan*, Communication No 1042/2001, para 7.4, in which the detention incommunicado of the author for a period of 40 days was considered to be a breach of ICCPR, art 5(3).

[220] What constitutes a 'reasonable time' is a matter for assessment in each particular case: *Fillastre and Bizouarn v Bolivia*, Communication No 336/88, para 6.5. It should be noted here also that there is an overlap between this aspect of ICCPR, art 9(3) and ICCPR, art 14(3)(c). Whereas ICCPR, art 9(3) concerns the total length of *pre-trial* detention, ICCPR, art 14(3)(c) concerns the total length of time which it takes for a person's trial to take place (irrespective of whether that person is detained or not). In many cases, therefore, a person who has been kept in detention before and during his or her trial will complain about simultaneous breaches of ICCPR, art 9(3) and ICCPR, art 14(3)(c).

[221] *WBE v The Netherlands*, Communication No 423/90, para 6.3 and *Hill and Hill v Spain*, Communication No 526/93, para 12.3 in which the Committee held that the mere fact of being a foreigner does not of itself justify a refusal of bail.

[222] Responsibility for activating this right rests with the detained person and not with the State: *Stephens v Jamaica*, Communication No 373/89, para 9.7.

[223] See, for example, the case of *Komarovski v Turkmenistan*, Communication No 1450/2006, in which the CCPR had no difficulty in finding that there had been a breach of this provision in circumstances where the right was completely denied to the author for the entire duration of his five-month detention: para 7.4.

[224] *A v Australia*, Communication No 560/1993, para 9.5.

[225] Joseph et al are critical of the fact that the CCPR has occasionally sanctioned long delays in the implementation of this right, citing the views of the Committee in *Torres v Finland*, Communication No 291/1988 and *A v New Zealand*, Communication No 754/1997: Joseph et al, *The International Covenant on Civil and Political Rights* (2nd edn, OUP, 1994), pp 331–333.

[226] See, for example, *Bolaos v Ecuador*, Communication No 238/87, in which the Committee took the view that the respondent State was under an obligation pursuant to ICCPR, art 9(5) to pay the author compensation arising from his detention in violation of ICCPR, art 9(1) and (3).

Fair trial

[7.47] Article 14 of the Covenant provides in detail for the right to a fair hearing[227] and the CCPR's jurisprudence in respect of it is necessarily extensive.[228] Aimed as it is at ensuring the 'proper administration of justice',[229] art 14 is a multifaceted provision which delineates the minimum guarantees necessary to ensure a fair hearing in the civil and criminal law contexts. Article 14(1) contains an overarching guarantee[230] to equality before the courts and tribunals[231] and to a fair trial[232] by a competent,[233] independent[234] and impartial[235] tribunal established by law.[236] The media and the public may be excluded from the hearing only in the circumstances provided for in the third sentence.[237] The guarantee in art 14(1) applies to all stages of a criminal or civil law proceedings.[238]

[7.48] Paragraphs (2) to (7) go on to specify further rights necessary to secure a fair hearing in a criminal trial and appeal.[239] Article 14(2) spells out the presumption of

---

[227] CCPR General Comment No 32, Article 14: Right to equality before courts and tribunals (replacing General Comment No 13): UN Doc CCPR/C/GC/32. In addition to the specifics of ICCPR, art 14, particular note should be taken of the relationship between it and other provisions of the Covenant: paras 58–65.

[228] It is therefore not possible here to give a complete account of the CCPR's jurisprudence in this area. See further, Joseph et al, *The International Covenant on Civil and Political Rights* (2nd ed, OUP, 1994), pp 388–461; McGoldrick, *The Human Rights Committee: Its Role in the Development of the International Covenant on Civil and Political Rights* (OUP, 1991), p 413–439; and Nowak, *UN Covenant on Civil and Political Rights: CCPR Commentary* (NP Engel, 1993), pp 233–273.

[229] CCPR General Comment No 32, para 2.

[230] The 'over-arching' aspect of the guarantee to a 'fair hearing' is particularly true in regard to ICCPR, art 14(3) which sets forth the minimum guarantees that must be provided for in criminal proceedings. See further para **7.49**.

[231] The right to equality before courts and tribunals guarantees equal access to courts and tribunals and equality of arms during proceedings: CCPR General Comment No 32, paras 7–14.

[232] The notion of a 'fair trial' includes '…the guarantee of a fair and public hearing': General Comment No 32 and case law cited there, paras 25–28.

[233] CCPR General Comment No 32, para 18.

[234] CCPR General Comment No 32, paras 19–20.

[235] The concept of 'impartiality' has subjective and objective elements: see, *Jenny v Austria*, Communication No 1437/2005, paras 9.3–9.5.

[236] CCPR General Comment No 32, paras 18 and 22–24.

[237] CCPR General Comment No 32, para 29.

[238] As to the concept of a 'criminal charge' and 'civil proceedings', see General Comment No 32, paras 15–17 and case law cited there.

[239] It is interesting to note that ICCPR, art 14 (5) to (7) stole a march on the ECHR in respect of the right of appeal in criminal matters, compensation for a miscarriage of justice and the rule against double jeopardy in criminal proceedings respectively. The latter guarantees were not initially included in the terms of the fair trial provision of the ECHR (art 6), but rather were made the subject of separate provision later in the ECHR, Seventh Protocol in 1984 (ETS No 117). In regard to ICCPR, art 14(5) to (7), see further paras **7.51–7.53**.

innocence, which in the view of the Committee is 'fundamental to the protection of human rights'.[240] By reason of this principle, the burden of proof in a criminal trial is placed firmly on the prosecution to prove the charge beyond a reasonable doubt and the accused must be given the benefit of the doubt.[241] The 'presumption of innocence' further implies a duty on all public authorities to refrain from prejudging the outcome of a criminal trial, by, for example, making public statements attributing guilt to an accused person.[242] A similar duty is incumbent on the media to avoid news coverage which undermines the presumption of innocence.[243]

[7.49] Article 14(3) specifies certain 'minimum guarantees' required to ensure a fair hearing in a criminal trial. These include the right to be informed promptly and in detail in a language which one understands, the nature and cause of the charge in question;[244] the right to have adequate time and facilities for the preparation of one's defence and to communicate with counsel of one's choosing;[245] the right to be tried without undue delay;[246] the right to be present during the hearing[247] and to be able to defend oneself in

---

[240] CCPR General Comment No 32, para 30.
[241] See, for example, *Ashurov v Tajikistan*, Communication No 1348/2005, para.6.7.
[242] See, for example, *Karimov and Nursatov v Tajikistan*, Communication No 1108/2002 and 1121/2002, para 7.4.
[243] See, for example, *Mwamba v Zambia*, Communication No 1520/2006, para 6.5.
[244] ICCPR, art 14(3)(a). See CCPR General Comment No 32, para 31. Note, in particular, the distinction between this guarantee and that which is provided in ICCPR, art 9(2) which requires a person to be informed of the reason for his or her arrest, prior to the issue of a criminal charge: See para **7.45**.
[245] ICCPR, art 14(3)(b). See CCPR General Comment No 32, paras 32–34. See, for example, *Lyashkevich v Uzbekistan*, Communication No 1552/2007, para 9.4.
[246] ICCPR, art 14(3)(c). This right covers the period of time between the bringing of formal charges against an accused and the rendering of the final appeal judgment. It is '…not only designed to avoid keeping persons too long in a state of uncertainty about their fate…but also to serve the interests of justice': *Lumanog and Santos v the Philippines*, Communication No 1466/2006, para 8.4. The Committee assesses whether the trial has taken place within a 'reasonable time', having regard, to the circumstances of the case, taking into account mainly its '…complexity, the conduct of the accused and the manner in which the matter was dealt with by the administrative and judicial authorities': General Comment No 32, para 35. See, for example, the disposal of the claim made that a trial was unreasonably prolonged in *Morael v France*, Communication No 207/86, para 9.4. Where bail is denied, the case must be tried as expeditiously as possible: *Sextus v Trinidad and Tobago*, Communication No 818/1998, para 7.2. The CCPR has emphasised the importance of this guarantee on several occasions in the context of cases involving capital punishment: see, for example, *Lumanog and Santos v The Philippines*, Communication No 1466/2006, para 8.5.
[247] ICCPR, art 14(3)(d). See General Comment No 32, para 36. Trials *in absentia* may be permissible in the interests of the proper administration of justice, provided that the '… necessary steps are taken to summon accused persons in a timely manner and to inform them beforehand about the date and place of their trial and to request their attendance': *Mbenge v Zaire*, Communication No 16/1977, para 14.1.

person[248] or with legal assistance, and if necessary with legal aid;[249] the right to examine and to cross-examine witnesses and to obtain the attendance of and examination of witnesses on an equal basis to the prosecution;[250] the right to an interpreter;[251] and the right not to be compelled to testify against oneself or to confess guilt.[252] In many cases, the CCPR does not necessarily examine whether particular aspects of art 14(3) have been breached, preferring instead to determine that the right to a fair hearing 'as a whole' in art 14(1) has been violated.[253]

[7.50] Article 14(4) contains special protection for juvenile persons, requiring as it does that their age should be taken into account in trial proceedings. So too should the desirability of promoting their rehabilitation.[254]

[7.51] Article 14(5) provides for the right to an appeal in a criminal trial.[255] The latter right imposes on the States parties an obligation '…substantially to review, both on the basis of the sufficiency of the evidence and of the law, the conviction and sentence, such that the procedure allows for due consideration of the nature of the case'.[256]

---

[248] ICCPR, art 14(3)(d). See General Comment No 32, para 37. On the right to defend oneself in person, see *Correia de Matos v Portugal*, Communication No 1123/2002, paras 7.2–7.5.

[249] ICCPR, art 14(3)(d). CCPR General Comment No 32, para 38. In particular, it should be noted that it is '… incumbent upon the State party to ensure that legal representation provided by the State guarantees effective representation': *Borisenko v Hungary*, Communication No 852/1999, para 7.5.

[250] ICCPR, art 14(3)(e). CCPR General Comment No 32, para 39.

[251] ICCPR, art 14(3)(f). CCPR General Comment No 32, para 40. This right is not absolute insofar as it need only be provided where the accused or the defence witnesses have difficulty in understanding or expressing themselves in the language adopted by the court for the proceedings in question: See *Guesdon v France*, Communication No 219/86, para 10.2.

[252] ICCPR, art 14(3)(g). This guarantee is often referred to as the privilege against self-incrimination. The burden of proof that a confession was made without duress is on the prosecution: *Ruzmetov v Uzbekistan*, Communication No 915/2000, para 7.3. An obligation exists on States parties to take account of claims made by an accused that statements made during pre-trial detention were made under duress, regardless of whether the confession is subsequently relied upon: *Kouidis v Greece*, Communication No 1070/2002, para 7.5.

[253] See for example, *Carranza Alegre v Peru*, Communication No 1126/2002, para 7.5.

[254] For the special protections that must, in the view of the CCPR, be afforded to juveniles over and above the guarantees specified in art 14, see General Comment No 32, paras 42 44. See further *Sharifova et al v Tajikistan*, Communication Nos 1209/2003, 1231/2003 and 1241/2004, para 6.6.

[255] See further, CCPR General Comment No 32, paras 45–51. In regard to the right to have one's conviction and sentence reviewed by a higher tribunal, ICCPR, art 14(5) is the *lex specialis* in relation to ICCPR, art 2(3): General Comment No 32, para 58.

[256] *Aliboeva v Tajikistan*, Communication No 985/2001, para 6.5. See also *Oliveró Capellades v Spain*, Communication No 1211/2003, para 7, in which the CCPR effectively held that the trial of an individual in exceptional cases in a higher court (in this case, the Supreme Court) could not extinguish his or her right to review of the conviction and sentence imposed by that court.

[7.52] Article 14(6) provides for the right to compensation in the case of a miscarriage of justice.[257]

[7.53] Finally, art 14(7) provides for the rule against double jeopardy, thus guaranteeing a substantive freedom to '...remain free from being tried or punished again for an offence for which an individual has already been finally acquitted or convicted'.[258]

Privacy, family, home and correspondence

[7.54] Article 17(1) prohibits 'arbitrary or unlawful interference' with a person's 'privacy, family,[259] home[260] or correspondence',[261] as well as unlawful attacks on a person's honour and reputation.[262] It gives rise to both positive obligations on States to adopt legislative and other measures to protect individuals from interferences by State

---

[257] CCPR General Comment No 32, para 52. Possible exceptions to the applicability of the guarantee are indicated in General Comment No 32, para 53. In *Dumont v Canada*, Communication No 1467/2006, paras 23.3–23.6, the CCPR found a violation of ICCPR, art 14(6) in conjunction with art 2(3) by reason of the failure of the State to provide an effective remedy to the author to establish his factual innocence so that he might claim the compensation he was entitled to under ICCPR, art 14(6).

[258] CCPR General Comment No 32, para 3 and see in particular paras 54–57. The prejudicial effect on a fair trial of being tried a second time, in combination with other charges, for an offence of which one has already been convicted are explored in *Babkin v Russian Federation*, Communication No 1310/2004, para 13.6.

[259] The term 'family' is to be given a broad interpretation to include all those comprising the family as understood in the society of the State party concerned: General Comment No 16 on the right to respect of privacy, family, home and correspondence, and protection of honour and reputation, UN Doc HRI/GEN/1/Rev 1 at 21, para 5. In *Tcholatch v Canada*, Communication No 1052/2002, para 8.2, the CCPR held that the term 'family' '...refers not solely to the family home during marriage or cohabitation, but also to the relations in general between parents and a child...Where there are biological ties, there is a strong presumption that a 'family' exists and only in exceptional circumstances will such relationship not be protected by article 17'. ICCPR, arts 23 and 24 give further expression to the particular rights in respect of protection of the family and children respectively. See further, CCPR General Comment No 19 on Protection of the family, the right to marriage and equality of the spouses, UN Doc HRI/GEN/1/Rev 1 at 28.

[260] 'Home' is understood to mean '...the place where a person resides or carries out his usual occupation': General Comment No 16, para 5.

[261] General Comment No 16 (written in 1988) indicates that correspondence clearly includes postal communications as well as '...telephonic, telegraphic and other forms of communication': para 8. The compatibility of interferences with prisoners' correspondence was considered by the CCPR in the case of *Pinkney v Canada*, Communication No 27/1978.

[262] See General Comment No 16, para 11. Note that there has been some doubt as regards the scope of the right to protection from attacks on one's honour and reputation, specifically as regards whether it only extends to attacks which are 'unlawful' under domestic law. Authority for the latter proposition is unfortunately to be found in the decision of the CCPR in *IP v Finland*, Communication No 450/91. In that case, a complaint about disclosure of information on the author's tax status as amounting to an attack on his honour and reputation was found to be inadmissible on the basis that there was lawful authority for the disclosure, without any further inquiry into whether such disclosure was nevertheless arbitrary. (contd.../)

authorities or from private parties,[263] and negative obligations not to engage in such interferences directly.[264] In its jurisprudence under art 17, the CCPR has adopted a similar approach to that of the European Court of Human Rights in regard to the vexed issue of defining the concept of privacy.[265] In that respect, it has avoided an all-encompassing definition of the concept, preferring instead to identify particular interests of the individual which attract the protection of art 17.[266]

[7.55] Nonetheless, the CCPR has had to clarify the meaning of 'arbitrary or unlawful interference' with privacy rights. In this respect, the term 'unlawful' means that 'no interference can take place except in cases envisaged by the law...which itself must comply with the provisions, aims and objectives of the Convention'.[267] In order to be 'lawful' the law must be sufficiently precise and accessible and must convey in sufficient detail the scope of any discretion conferred thereunder. An interference that is 'lawful' may be nonetheless 'arbitrary', where it is not in accordance with the

---

[262] (\...contd) Joseph et al have predicted that the CCPR's more progressive interpretation of the meaning of the term 'unlawful' in the context of ICCPR, art 9(4) might herald further potential evolution of its jurisprudence in the context of protection of honour and reputation under ICCPR, art 17: Joseph et al, *The International Covenant on Civil and Political Rights* (2nd edn, OUP, 1994), p 494. Subsequent cases bear this prediction out. See, for example, *MG v Germany*, Communication No 1482/2006, para.10.2, in which the issuance of a lawful court order on the applicant to undergo a medical examination, on the basis of the case file and without having seen or heard her in person, amounted to a disproportionate interference with her privacy and her honour and reputation, which was 'arbitrary' and in violation of ICCPR, art 17. Even more dramatically, in *Nabil Sayadi and Patricia Vinck v Belgium*, a majority of the CCPR held Belgium reponsible, *inter alia,* for violating the authors' honor and reputation contrary to art 17 because it had provided information to the UN Sanctions Committee (prior to the conclusion of a domestic criminal investigation) which had led to the authors names appearing on publicly accessible UN, European Union and State party sanctions lists concerning restrictive measures taken against persons associated with Osama Bin Laden, Al-Quaida and the Taliban. The argument made by Belgium that its actions were based on the need to comply with a Security Council Resolution adopted under Chapter VII of the UN Charter led a number of Members to dissent from the majority's views: Communication No 1472/2006, para 10.13.

[263] CCPR General Comment No 16, paras 1 and 2.

[264] CCPR General Comment No 16, para 9.

[265] On the jurisprudence of the European Court of Human Rights in interpreting ECHR, art 8 as regards the right to private life, see generally, Moreham, 'The Right to Respect for Private Life in the European Convention on Human Rights: A Re-examination' (2008) EHRLR 44; Marshall, 'A Right to Personal Autonomy at the European Court of Human Rights' (2008) EHRLR 337; and Liddy, 'Article 8: The Pace of Change' (2000) 51 NILQ 397.

[266] The Committee considers that the notion of privacy '....refers to the sphere of a person's life in which he or she can freely express his or her identity, be it by entering into relationships with others or alone': *Coeriel and Aurik v The Netherlands*, Communication No 453/91, para 10.2. Aspects of privacy identified by the CCPR to date include sexual privacy (*Toonen v Australia*, Communication No 488/92) as well personal and identity information (*Coeriel and Aurik v The Netherlands*, para 10.2) (General Comment 16, para 10).

[267] CCPR General Comment No 16, para 3.

provisions, aims and objectives of the Covenant and is not, in any event, 'reasonable' in the particular circumstances.[268] In *Toonen v Australia*,[269] in assessing whether a law which criminalised homosexual activity between consenting male adults was an 'arbitrary' interference with privacy rights, the CCPR looked to whether the provisions met the test of 'reasonableness', ie, whether they were proportionate to the end sought and necessary in the circumstances. In the CCPR's view, the law failed this test, given that it was unique in Australia and could not be said to be 'necessary' given the fact that it had never been enforced.[270] While art 17 does not enumerate particular grounds on which restrictions may be limited (as is the case in regard to other analogous guarantees in the Covenant), this has not led to any particular difficulties in practice as the aim on which the restriction is based will undoubtedly be factored into the consideration of whether it meets the test of 'reasonableness'.

[7.56] In general terms, the jurisprudence of the CCPR in regard to art 17 is not yet as developed as that of the European Court of Human Rights in interpreting art 8 of the European Convention on Human Rights. The latter Court has been forced to tease out a myriad of controversial issues in terms of the scope of privacy rights including, for example, euthanasia,[271] transsexualism,[272] and reproduction.[273]

Freedom of thought, conscience and religion

[7.57] Article 18 of the ICCPR protects the right to freedom of thought, conscience and religion (which in the view of the CCPR includes freedom to hold beliefs).[274] Each of

---

[268] CCPR General Comment No 16, para 4.
[269] *Toonen v Australia* (1994) 1(3) IHRR 99.
[270] The CCPR does not, however, consider that the refusal of a State to provide for marriage between homosexual couples to be a violation of, *inter alia*, arts 17 and 23 of the ICCPR: *Joslin v New Zealand*, Communication No 902/1999, para 8.3.
[271] *Pretty v United Kingdom* (2002) 35 EHRR 1.
[272] *Goodwin (Christine) v United Kingdom* (2002) 35 EHRR 447. While the CCPR has not ruled on a complaint involving a transsexual under the Protocol, it has nonetheless made it clear in the context of the Covenant's reporting obligations that States parties are required to recognise the right of transsexuals to a change of gender by permitting the issuance of new birth certificates: see Concluding Observations of the CCPR on Ireland's third periodic report: UN Doc CCPR/C/IRL/CO/3, para 8.
[273] *Evans v United Kingdom* (2008) 46 EHRR 34. As regards the issue of abortion, note that in *KNLH v Peru*, Communication No1153/2003, the CCPR held that the refusal of the medical authorities to terminate the author's pregnancy in circumstances where a termination on grounds of a risk to life was authorised by domestic law constituted a violation of art 17 of the ICCPR (para 6.4). The European Court has reached a similar, if somewhat more nuanced, conclusion in the recent case of *A, B & C v Ireland*. It held that the State was responsible for a violation of the right to private life in ECHR, art 8 by reason of its failure to put in place a legislative or regulatory regime providing an accessible and effective procedure by which a woman with cancer could have established whether she qualified for a lawful abortion in Ireland in accordance with relevant provision of the Constitution, as interpreted by the Supreme Court: Application no. 25579/05, para 267.
[274] CCPR General Comment No 22, UN Doc HRI/GEN/1/Rev 1 at 35, para 1. See generally Joseph et al, *The International Covenant on Civil and Political Rights* (2nd edn, OUP, 1994), pp 501–516.

these aspects of art 18 is protected equally under the terms of the article, the fundamental nature of which is underscored by the fact that it cannot be made the subject of a derogation under art 4(2) of the Covenant. The CCPR has adopted a broad interpretation of the term 'religion' in art 18, taking the view that it includes theistic, non-theistic and atheistic beliefs.[275] It is not limited to '...traditional religions or to religions and beliefs with institutional characteristics or practices analogous to those of traditional religions'.[276]

[7.58] Article 18 makes a distinction between freedom of thought, conscience and religion or belief and freedom to *manifest* religion or belief.[277] While limitations may be imposed on freedom to manifest religion or belief,[278] the CCPR has unambiguously stated that the terms of art 18 do not permit any limitations whatsoever on freedom of thought and conscience or on the freedom to have or adopt a religion or belief of one's choice.[279] This stricture is consistent with the terms of art 18(2) which provides that 'no one shall be subject to coercion which would impair his freedom to have or adopt a religion or belief of his choice', either directly or indirectly.[280]

[7.59] The right to manifest one's religion does not, in the CCPR's view, imply the right to refuse all obligations imposed by law, but it does provide a 'certain protection against being forced to act against genuinely held religious beliefs'. Restrictions against the manifestation of religion or belief may only be imposed where they are 'prescribed by law' and 'necessary'[281] to protect 'public safety, order, health or morals or the

---

[275] CCPR General Comment No 22, para 2.
[276] CCPR General Comment No 22, para 2. Thus, the CCPR recently considered on its merits the complaint about freedom to manifest religion made by a Rastafarian against South Africa by reason of the failure of domestic law to allow Rastafarians to use cannabis. In its decision, the CCPR implicitly considered Rastafarianism to constitute a religion for the purposes of ICCPR, art 18. The fact that the latter movement promotes the spiritual use of cannabis did not detract from its status as a religion; however, a general prohibition on the use of such substances which has the effect of compromising an adherent's manifestation of that belief can be justified under ICCPR, art 18(3): see *Prince v South Africa*, Communication No 1474/2006, paras 7.2–7.3.
[277] On the indicia of 'manifestation' of belief, see General Comment No 22, para 4.
[278] See ICCPR, art 18(3).
[279] This position obtains also in respect of the right of everyone to hold opinions without interference which is protected by ICCPR, art 19(1): CCPR General Comment No 22, para 3.
[280] An example of a form of indirect coercion which the CCPR deems to be contrary to ICCPR, art 18(2) is the Constitutional requirement in Ireland for the President and members of the judiciary to take a religious oath before assuming office: Concluding Observations on Ireland's first periodic report, UN Doc CCPR/C/79/Add 21, 3 August 1993, para 15; concluding observations on Ireland's second periodic report, UN Doc A/55/40, 24 July 2000, paras 422–451, para 29(b); and concluding observations on Ireland's third periodic report, UN Doc CCPR/C/IRL/CO/3, 30 July 2008, para 21.
[281] To be necessary, restrictions must be 'directly related and proportionate to the specific need on which they are predicated': CCPR General Comment No 22, para 8.

fundamental rights and freedoms of others'.[282] The issue of manifestation of religion or belief has been raised before the CCPR in regard to two cases involving restrictions imposed by States on the wearing of religious dress. In *Karnel Singh Bhinder v Canada*, the CCPR found that a requirement imposed on the author, a Sikh, to wear safety headgear at work, pursuant to federal law, was a justifiable restriction on his right to manifest his religion.[283] Unfortunately, as Joseph, Schultz and Castan point out, the CCPR declined to specify on which ground the restriction was justified, effectively ignoring the author's specific argument that the restriction in question was not necessary to protect '*public* safety', since any safety risk ensuing from his refusal to wear safety headgear was confined to himself.[284] In *Raihon Hudoyberganova v Uzbekistan*, the CCPR decided that the suspension of a female Muslim student from university for wearing a headscarf was a violation of art 18(2).[285] The fact that no justification was advanced by the State for the *prima facie* interference with the author's freedom to manifest her religion left the Committee with little choice but to find a violation.[286]

[7.60] By contrast, the CCPR has rendered a detailed decision in which it has recognised that art 18(1) includes a right to conscientious objection to military service.[287] In *Yoon and Choi v The Republic of Korea*,[288] the authors complained that art 18 had been breached by reason of the respondent State's failure to put in place an alternative to compulsory military service for conscientious objectors like himself in circumstances

---

[282] ICCPR, art 18(3). Note that the aim of protecting 'national security', which is specified as a permissible ground for restricting other rights in the ICCPR, is not included here. Strictly speaking, therefore, restrictions on such a ground cannot be allowed under ICCPR, art 18(3): General Comment No 22, para 8. However, as Joseph et al note, most restrictions aimed at protecting national security would probably be simultaneously aimed at protecting public order and hence justifiable on the latter ground: Joseph et al, *The International Covenant on Civil and Political Rights* (2nd ed, OUP, 1994), p 508.

[283] *Karnel Singh Bhinder v Canada*, Communication No 208/1986, para 6.2.

[284] *Karnel Singh Bhinder v Canada*, Communication No 208/1986, para 3. Joseph et al, *The International Covenant on Civil and Political Rights* (2nd ed, OUP, 1994), p 509.

[285] *Raihon Hudoyberganova v Uzbekistan*, Communication No 931/2000, para 6.2.

[286] The obscurity of the facts and the potential issues raised by this case led one member of the Committee, Professor Ruth Wedgwood, to offer the dissenting view that there was not an adequate basis on which to find a violation in the case. It would have been interesting to test the CCPR's reasoning in the event that any such justification had been raised. Compare, for example, the judgment of the European Court of Human Rights in the case of *Leyla Sahin v Turkey* (2007) 44 EHRR 5, discussed in Lewis, 'What Not to Wear: Religious Rights, the European Court and the Margin of Appreciation' (2007) 56(2) ICLQ 395–414.

[287] Previous case law had not extended this far: see *LTK v Finland*, Communication No 185/84, para 5.2. It will be interesting to see whether the decision to overrule previous case law in regard to conscientious objection to military service will have ramifications in regard to other instances of conscientious objection, such as the withholding of taxes on the same grounds. See, for example, *JP v Canada*, Communication 446/91, para 4.2, in which the CCPR held that the refusal to pay taxes on grounds of conscientious objection falls outside the scope of ICCPR, art 18.

[288] *Yoon and Choi v The Republic of Korea*, Communication No 1321–1322/2004.

where their refusal to perform military service had resulted in prosecution and imprisonment. In analysing the claim, the CCPR held that refusal for conscientious reasons to be drafted for compulsory military service may be considered as a direct expression of religious beliefs.[289] In assessing whether the failure of the State to provide an alternative to compulsory military service, under pain of criminal prosecution and imprisonment, breached art 18, the CCPR noted that there was no procedure for recognition of conscientious objection to military service under national law. The absence of such a procedure contrasted with that of other States parties which had introduced alternatives to active service in cases of conscientious objection. Moreover, the State party had failed to show any special disadvantage that it would suffer if the rights of the authors under art 18 were fully respected. Respect on the part of the State for conscientious objection, in the view of the CCPR, was itself an important factor in ensuring cohesive and stable pluralism in society.[290] Accordingly, the CCPR held that the restrictions could not be justified as being necessary, within the meaning of art 18(3) of the Covenant.[291] In this respect, it is interesting to note that the CCPR's case law on conscientious objection has been in the vanguard compared to that of the European Court of Human Rights which has only recently ruled that the equivalent guarantee of freedom of religion in art 9 of the ECHR guarantees a right to refuse to perform military service on such grounds.[292]

[7.61] Finally, art 18(4) contains a positive obligation on States parties to respect the liberty of parents and guardians to ensure the religious and moral education of their children in conformity with their own convictions. In this respect, the CCPR takes the view that this article permits public school instruction in subjects such as the general history of religions and ethics, so long as it is given in a neutral and objective way.[293] Public education that includes instruction in a particular religion or belief is inconsistent with art 18(4), unless provision is made for non-discriminatory exemptions or alternatives that would accommodate the wishes of parents or guardians.[294] It would seem that contracting States are also under an obligation to ensure greater access to non-

---

[289] *Yoon and Choi v The Republic of Korea*, Communication No 1321–1322/2004, para 8.3.

[290] *Yoon and Choi v The Republic of Korea*, Communication No 1321–1322/2004, para 8.10. The decision in *Yoon and Choi v The Republic of Korea* was subsequently affirmed by the Committee in the more recent case of *Jung et al v The Republic of Korea*, Communication No 1593–1603/2007.

[291] *Yoon and Choi v The Republic of Korea*, Communication No 1321–1322/2004, paras 8.3–8.4. These views have been repeated by the Committee in the cases of *Jung et al v The Republic of Korea*, Communication No 1593–1603/2007.

[292] See *Bayatyan v Armenia*, Application 23459/03, Judgment of the Grand Chamber of the European Court of Human Rights (7/7/2011). In deciding to reverse its previous caselaw on this issue and to recognise that conscientious objection falls within the guarantee in art 9, the Court explicitly referred to the recognition by the CCPR of the right of conscientious objection, art 18 ICCPR both in its caselaw under the OP-ICCPR and in General Comment No 22 (see para 105 of the Court's judgment).

[293] CCPR General Comment No 22, para 6. See also *Hartikainen v Finland*, Communication No 40/1978, para 10.4

[294] CCPR General Comment No 22, para 6.

denominational schools where a disproportionate number of private schools in a State adopts a particular religious curriculum.[295]

Freedom of expression

[7.62] Article 19 of the Covenant provides for the right to hold opinions without interference and the right to freedom of expression. While the former right can never be the subject of an exception or restriction,[296] freedom of expression can be restricted in accordance with the strict criteria set forth in art 19(3), examined below.

[7.63] The right to freedom of expression includes the right to 'impart information and ideas of all kinds' and to seek and receive them 'regardless of frontiers'.[297] Article 19 does not distinguish between the various *forms* of expression which deserve protection. As the Human Rights Committee has made clear:

> Article 19(2) must be interpreted as encompassing every form of subjective ideas and opinions capable of transmission to others, which are compatible with Article 20 of the covenant, of news and information, of commercial expression and advertising,[298] of works of art etc; it should not be confined to means of political,[299] cultural or artistic expression.[300]

Moreover, the *means* by which a form of expression is communicated is given explicit protection under art 19(1), whether it be communicated 'orally, in writing or in print, in the form of art, or through any other media' of choice.[301]

---

[295] In circumstances where the vast majority of Ireland's primary schools are privately run denominational schools that have adopted a religious integrated curriculum based on the Roman Catholic faith, the State has come under increasing pressure from the CCPR to increase its efforts to ensure greater access to non-denominational primary education in all regions of the State: Concluding Observations on Ireland's third periodic report, General Comment No 22, para 22.

[296] CCPR General Comment No 10: Freedom of Expression (Article 19): 29 June 1983, para 1.

[297] ICCPR, art 19(2). In its latest Draft General Comment No 34 on Freedom of Expression, the Human Rights Committee has emphasised the essential role of a 'free, uncensored and unhindered' press or other media in ensuring the enjoyment of both freedom of opinion and expression and the enjoyment of other Covenant Rights: UN Doc CCPR/C/GC/34/CRP6, para 12 and see further paras 41–47. Note also the view of the CCPR that ICCPR, art 19(2) includes a general right of access to information held by public bodies: Draft General Comment No 34, paras 17–18.

[298] *Ballantyne v Canada*, Communication Nos 359/1989 and 385/1989, para 11.3.

[299] Freedom of political speech is regarded by the CCPR as the 'essence' of a 'free and democratic society': *Aduayom Diasso and Dobou v Togo*, Communication Nos 422/1990, 423/1990 and 424/1990, para 7.4. Moreover, freedom to criticise the actions of public figures, in the context of a public debate in a democratic society, is given special protection under ICCPR, art 19: *Bodroži v Serbia and Montenegro*, Communication No 1180/2003, para 7.2. See further General Comment No 25 on the importance of freedom of expression for the conduct of public affairs and the exercise of the right to vote, UN Doc CCPR/C/21/Rev 1/Add.7 – an issue which is reinforced in Draft General Comment No 34, para 19.

[300] See, for example, *Hak-Chul Sin v Republic of Korea*, Communication No 926/2000, para 7.2.

[301] In *Kivenmaa v Finland*, Communication No 412/1990, views adopted on 31 March 1994, para 9.3, for example, the Committee held that the holding up of a banner containing the expression of a political opinion, was clearly protected by ICCPR, art 19. (contd.../)

[7.64] The Covenant expressly recognises that the right to freedom of expression carries with it special 'duties and responsibilities', which may lead to the imposition of certain restrictions in the interests of other persons or to the community as a whole.[302] In this respect, art 19(3) provides that the right may be restricted, provided that such restriction is 'provided by law' and 'necessary' to respect the rights[303] or reputations of others,[304] to protect national security,[305] public order,[306] public health or morals.[307]

---

[301] (\...contd) The CCPR's Draft General Comment No 35 clearly contemplates the operation of websites, blogs or any other internet-based, electronic or other such dissemination system as a *means* of expression for the purposes of ICCPR, art 19: CCPR Draft General Comment No 35, paras 45–46.

[302] The particular nature of those duties and responsibilities can have a bearing on the outcome of a case, depending on the context. In *Ross v Canada*, Communication No 736/1997, para 11.6, for example, the special duties and responsibilities of the author, a school teacher, in the school system were taken into account by the Committee in its finding that his removal from a teaching position for the expression of discriminatory views was necessary to protect the rights and freedom of Jewish school children to have a school system free of bias, prejudice and intolerance.

[303] The term 'rights' includes '...human rights as recognised in the Covenant and more generally in international human rights law': CCPR Draft General Comment No 35, para 29. Restrictions aimed at protecting the 'rights' of others may relate to the interests of other persons or to the community as a whole: see the decision of the CCPR in the case of *Faurisson v France*, Communication No 550/1993, views adopted on 2 January 1993, para 9.6, in which the Committee found that censorship of the author for denying the existence of the Holocaust was permissible under the terms of ICCPR, art 19(3)(a). The Committee considered that the restriction (in this case the imposition of a fine) served 'the respect of the Jewish community to live free from fear of an atmosphere of anti-Semitism'. As to the compatibility of blasphemy laws and 'memory-laws' generally (such as the one at issue in *Faurisson*) with the right to freedom of expression, see CCPR Draft General Comment No 35, paras 50–51.

[304] The CCPR takes the view that the limits of acceptable criticism of persons in the public domain are wider in the interests of public debate in a democratic society than for ordinary citizens: *Bodroži v Serbia and Montenegro*, Communication No 1180/2003, para 7.2. See further CCPR Draft General Comment No 35, para 40. As to the compatibility of defamation laws with the right to freedom of expression, see further CCPR Draft General Comment No 35, para 49.

[305] The CCPR has urged that: 'Extreme care must be taken to ensure that treason law and similar provisions relating to national security...are crafted and applied in a manner that conforms to paragraph 3': CCPR Draft General Comment No 35, para 31. See, for example, the case of *Kim v Republic of Korea*, Communication No 574/1994, paras 12.4–12.5, in which the CCPR found that the necessity for prosecuting the author for publishing material in contravention of the National Security Law in that case had not been established by the State.

[306] The CCPR recognises that it may be permissible in certain circumstances to regulate speech making in a particular public place or to put in place laws which guard against contempt of court: CCPR Draft General Comment No 35, para 32. The proportionality of measures aimed at protecting public order was at issue in the case *Gauthier v Canada*, Communication No 633/1995, views adopted on 5th May 1999.

[307] The CCPR has recognised that the content of the term 'public morals' '...may differ widely from society to society – there is no universally applicable common standard': (contd.../)

The phrase 'provided by law' means that there must be a sufficient legal basis or 'framework'[308] for the restriction in domestic law;[309] while the term 'necessity' requires the restriction in question to be proportionate to one of the aims set forth in para 3.[310] Where the method of censorship is so extreme as to involve arbitrary arrest, torture and threats to life, however, the Committee will not be prepared to enter into a determination of whether such measures meet the 'necessity' test in art 19(3).[311]

Any propaganda for war or expression which advocates national, racial or religious hatred is specifically prohibited by the terms of art 20 of the Covenant.[312]

Equality and non-discrimination

[7.65] The concepts of equality and non-discrimination infuse the entire text of the ICCPR.[313] Article 2(1) specifically provides for the general obligation of States to respect and ensure to all persons within their territories and subject to their jurisdiction the rights recognised in the Covenant without distinction of *any* kind such as race,

---

[307] (...contd) CCPR Draft General Comment No 35, para 33. See also *Hertzberg v Finland*, Communication No 61/1979, views adopted on 2 April 1992. This decision is most notable by reason of the CCPR's reference to the existence of a certain 'margin of discretion' on the part of the national authorities in assessing whether the censorship of programmes involving the authors was necessary for the protection of public morals (see para 10.3). It is, in fact, an isolated occasion in which the CCPR has explicitly referred to this concept, as compared with the European Court of Human Rights which routinely draws on the concept of a 'margin of appreciation' in interpreting articles of the ECHR. In its most recent draft General Comment, the CCPR has firmly stated that the scope of the right to freedom of expression is not to be assessed by reference to a 'margin of appreciation': Draft General Comment No 35, para 37.

[308] *Ross v Canada*, Communication No 736/1997, para 11.3.

[309] Draft General Comment No 35 specifies that 'law' in this regard 'may include statutory law [and, where appropriate, case-law]. It may include the law of parliamentary privilege and the law of contempt of court': para 25. In line with the jurisprudence of the European Court of Human Rights in interpreting a similar phrase in ECHR, art 10, the CCPR takes the view that for a norm to be characterised as 'law', it '...must be formulated with sufficient precision to enable an individual to regulate his or her conduct accordingly and it must be made public': CCPR Draft General Comment No 35, para 26.

[310] As to the principle of proportionality, see CCPR Draft General Comment No 35, paras 35–37. In *Coleman v Australia*, Communication No 1157/2003, para 7.3, for example, the CCPR found that the prosecution, conviction and penalty imposed on the author by the State party for making a public address at a shopping mall to be simply 'disproportionate' in the circumstances and hence an unjustifiable restriction of his right to freedom of expression which was incompatible with ICCPR, art 19(3).

[311] *Afuson v Cameroon*, Communication No 1353/2005, para 6.4.

[312] CCPR General Comment No 11: Prohibition for propaganda for war and inciting national, racial or religious hatred, UN Doc HRI/GEN/1/Rev 1 at 12 and CCPR Draft General Comment No 35, paras 52–54.

[313] The extent to which the principles of non-discrimination and equality are reflected in the ICCPR is highlighted in CCPR General Comment No 18 on Non-Discrimination, UN Doc HRI/GEN/1/Rev 1 at 26.

colour, sex, language, religion, political or other opinion, national or social origin, property, birth or other status; while art 26 not only entitles all persons to equality before the law and equal protection of the law but also prohibits any discrimination under the law, as well as guaranteeing all persons equal and effective protection against discrimination on any ground such as those outlined above. Explicit reference is also made to the general principles of equality and non-discrimination in arts 3,[314] 4,[315] 14,[316] 20,[317] 23,[318] 24[319] and 25[320] of the Covenant. It is hardly surprising that so many articles of the Covenant make reference to non-discrimination since there can be little doubt but that 'discrimination is at the root of virtually all human rights abuses'.[321]

[7.66] The jurisprudence of the CCPR in regard to these various provisions is simply too vast to attempt a comprehensive account in this context. Much of the case law revolves around interpretation of the guarantee in art 26.[322] In this respect, the CCPR has clarified that art 26 '…does not merely duplicate the guarantee already provided for in art 2 but provides in itself an autonomous right'.[323] Unlike art 2, its scope is not limited to the rights and obligations provided for in the Covenant; rather, art 26 prohibits discrimination in fact or in law in any field regulated and protected by public authorities.[324] Accordingly, art 26 sweeps with a very broad brush insofar as *any*

---

[314] ICCPR, art 3 obliges the States parties to undertake to ensure the equal right of men and women to the enjoyment of all civil and political rights set forth in the Covenant. See generally, CCPR General Comment No 28 on the equality of rights between men and women: UN Doc CCPR/C/GC/32.

[315] ICCPR, art 4(1) provides that measures of derogation otherwise authorised by the terms of that article shall not involve discrimination solely on the ground of race, colour, sex, language, religion or social origin.

[316] ICCPR, art 14(1) provides for equality of all persons before the courts and tribunals.

[317] ICCPR, art 20(2) provides that any advocacy of national or religious hatred that constitutes incitement of discrimination, hostility or violence shall be prohibited by law.

[318] ICCPR, art 23(4) provides for the equality of rights and responsibilities of spouses as to marriage, during marriage and at its dissolution.

[319] ICCPR, art 24(1) provides that every child shall have, without any discrimination as to race, colour, sex, language, religion, national or social origin, property or birth, the right to such measures of protection as are required by his status as a minor, on the part of his family, society and the State.

[320] ICCPR, art 25 provides for the right and opportunity of every citizen, without discrimination on any of the grounds mentioned in ICCPR, art 2 and without unreasonable restriction to take part in the conduct of public affairs, to vote and to be elected at periodic elections, and to have access, on general terms of equality, to the public service of his country.

[321] Joseph et al, *The International Covenant on Civil and Political Rights* (2nd edn, OUP, 1994), p 680.

[322] See generally, Edelenbos, 'The Human Rights Committee's Jurisprudence under Article 26 of the ICCPR: The Hidden Revolution' in Alfredsson et al (eds), *International Human Rights Monitoring Mechanisms* (2nd edn, Martinus Nijhoff, 2009), p 77.

[323] CCPR General Comment No 18, para 12.

[324] See CCPR General Comment No 18 on Non-Discrimination, para 12.

legislation[325] or administrative practice[326] adopted by a State party must comply with its requirements. This interpretation of art 26 as an independent, free-standing right may be contrasted with the ancillary non-discrimination principle provided for in art 14 of the European Convention on Human Rights.[327]

[7.67] The CCPR has interpreted 'discrimination' for the purposes of art 26 as meaning:

'...any distinction, restriction or preference which is based on any ground such as race, colour, language, religion, political or other opinion, national or social origin, property, birth of other status, and which has the purpose or effect of nullifying or impairing the recognition, enjoyment or exercise by all persons, on an equal footing, of all rights and freedoms'.[328]

This definition embraces both direct discrimination and indirect discrimination, where the effect of an impugned measure, discriminates against a person, albeit unintentionally.[329] The main controlling principle implemented by the Committee in its jurisprudence under the Protocol in respect of art 26 is that distinctions made between comparable partie[330] must be justified on reasonable and objective grounds, in pursuit of an aim that is legitimate under the Covenant.[331]

---

[325] In *Broeks v The Netherlands*, Communication No 172/1984, paras 12.3 and 12.4, the CCPR clarified that ICCPR, art 26 extends to legislation governing rights not otherwise covered by the Covenant, including in the realm of social security which was at issue in that case. See also *Zwaan de Vries v Netherlands*, Communication No 182/1984.

[326] See, for example, *Lecraft v Spain*, Communication No 1493/2006, UN Doc CCPR/C/96/D/1493/2006 in which the CCPR held that ICCPR, art 26, in conjunction with ICCPR, art 2(3) had been violated by reason of police identity checks, as applied to the author, which were motivated by race or ethnicity.

[327] Note that ECHR, Protocol 12 introduces a free-standing prohibition of discrimination similar to that which is provided for in ICCPR, art 26. However, only 18 of the 47 Contracting States to the ECHR have ratified Protocol 12: http://conventions.coe.int/(last accessed May 2011).

[328] CCPR General Comment No 18, para 7.

[329] *Althammer v Austria*, Communication No 998/2001, para 10.2. In *Simunek et al v Czech Republic*, Communication No 516/1992, para 11.7, the CCPR explained that: 'A politically motivated differentiation is unlikely to be compatible with ICCPR, art 26. But an act which is not politically motivated may still contravene ICCPR, art 26 if its effects are discriminatory'.

[330] A claim to discrimination is established where there has been differential treatment of similarly situated persons without reasonable or objective justification. A failure to provide sufficient information to the CCPR that one has been treated differently to persons in 'comparable' cases may result in the communication being deemed inadmissible under ICCPR, art 2: see *Tiyagarajah v Sri Lanka*, Communication No 1523/2006, para 5.3. On the other hand, in order to refute the claim, the State must establish either that no such differential treatment has occurred (eg, that the author is differently situated to the persons with whom he or she compares him or herself) or that reasonable and objective criteria exist for distinguishing his or her claim. See, for example, *Joseph et al v Sri Lanka*, Communication No 18/11/2005, para 7.4.

[331] General Comment No 18, para 13. See also *Broeks v The Netherlands*, Communication No 172/1984, para 13: 'The right to equality before the law and to equal protection of the law without any discrimination does not make all differences of treatment discriminatory. A differentiation based on reasonable and objective criteria does not amount to prohibited discrimination within the meaning of Article 26'.

[7.68] The case of *Kavanagh v Ireland*,[332] demonstrated the 'revolutionary character'[333] of the more frequently litigated arm of art 26 regarding the right to 'equal protection of the law'.[334] In that case, the author sought to argue, *inter alia*, that his trial before the Special Criminal Court for involvement in a bank raid and kidnapping violated the right to fair trial guaranteed by art 14 of the Covenant and was discriminatory contrary to art 26. The Special Criminal Court is a non-jury, three-judge court which was established by emergency legislation for the purposes of trying offences in cases where it may be determined that the ordinary courts are inadequate to secure the effective administration of justice and public order in the State. The court has jurisdiction to try persons for certain scheduled and non-scheduled offences in circumstances where the Director of Public Prosecutions thinks it is proper that a person be tried before that court rather than before the ordinary courts. The CCPR did not find that the author's trial before the court breached art 14 of the Covenant on the basis that a trial before courts other than ordinary courts is not necessarily *per se* a violation of the right to a fair hearing under art 14. [335] However, the Committee did find that there had been a violation of art 26. In this respect, the Committee accepted in principle the author's claim that he had been seriously disadvantaged as compared to other persons accused of similar crimes who were tried before the ordinary courts, since they were in a position to avail themselves of a wider range of possible safeguards.[336] As such, the author had been deprived of certain procedures under domestic law, distinguishing him from others charged with similar offences. The State had failed to provide objective and reasonable grounds for such a distinction in treatment.[337] The inherent weakness of the OP-ICCPR as an implementation technique is illustrated by the fact that notwithstanding the CCPR's views, the State has taken no positive steps to satisfy the concerns raised by the Committee,[338] opting instead to retain the existence[339] and indeed, extend the capacity of the Special Criminal Court.[340]

---

[332] *Kavanagh v Ireland*, Communication No 819/1998, views adopted on 4 April 2001: UN Doc CCPR/C/71/D/819/1998.

[333] Edelenbos, 'The Human Rights Committee's Jurisprudence under Article 26 of the ICCPR: The Hidden Revolution' in Alfredsson et al (eds), *International Human Rights Monitoring Mechanisms* (2nd edn, Martinus Nijhoff, 2009), p 77.

[334] As Joseph et al note, this aspect of ICCPR, art 26 is more frequently raised in communications under the Protocol than the more broadly based principle of 'equality before the law': Joseph et al, *The International Covenant on Civil and Political Rights* (2nd ed, OUP, 1994), p 745.

[335] *Kavanagh v Ireland*, Communication No 819/1998, para 10.1.

[336] *Kavanagh v Ireland*, Communication No 819/1998, paras 4.1 and 10.2.

[337] *Kavanagh v Ireland*, Communication No 819/1998, para 10.3.

[338] See the recommendations made by an independent committee established by the government in May 1999 to review the operation of the Special Criminal Court: Third periodic report by Ireland on the measures adopted to give effect to the ICCPR, 4 September 2007, UN Doc CCPR/C/IRL/3, paras 357–359.

[339] Third periodic report by Ireland on the measures adopted to give effect to the ICCPR, paras 369–381.

[340] Particular provisions of the recently enacted Criminal Justice (Amendment) Act 2009 extend the remit of the Special Criminal Court to deal with certain organised crime offences: http://www.oir.ie/viewdoc.asp?DocID=12287&&CatID=59 (last accessed May 2011).

[7.69] In the more controversial case of *O'Neill and Quinn v Ireland*,[341] the authors claimed that they had been discriminated against in violation of art 26 by reason of the State's refusal to grant them early release from prison in accordance with legislation implementing provisions of the Belfast/Good Friday Agreement.[342] Specifically, they argued that they qualified for early release from prison under the terms of the statutory scheme, invoking for comparative purposes the situation of others prisoners in similar circumstances who had been released. The CCPR took the view that since the statutory scheme in question was enacted pursuant to the Belfast Good Friday agreement, it could not examine the case outside its political context.[343] In the course of its opinion, it noted that the early release scheme did not create an entitlement to early release, but was rather a discretionary scheme under which the relevant authorities could decide in individual cases whether the person(s) concerned should benefit from the scheme.[344] The Committee took account of the fact that the government had justified the authors' exclusion from the scheme because of the circumstances of the incident in question which resulted in their convictions (which included the manslaughter of a police officer in the course of an attempted armed robbery), its timing in the context of a cease-fire, its brutality and the need to ensure public support for the Belfast/Good Friday Agreement.[345] In a rare deployment of the 'margin of appreciation' type reasoning so frequently resorted to by the European Court of Human Rights, the CCPR considered that it was not in a position to substitute its own views for the respondent State's assessment of the facts, especially with regard to a decision that was made nearly 10 years ago, in a political context, and leading up to a peace agreement.[346] In the result, a majority found that the situation complained about did not disclose arbitrariness and that the authors' rights under art 26 to equality before the law and to equal protection of the law had not been violated.[347] While the decision affirms that even discretionary decisions of the executive may be reviewed for their compatibility with art 26,[348] the decision is certainly open to criticism for endorsing the State's prioritisation of political

---

[341] *O'Neill and Quinn v Ireland*, Communication No 1314/2004, views adopted on 24 July 2006, UN Doc CCPR/C/87/D/1314/2004. See Joseph, 'Human Rights Committee: Recent Jurisprudence' (2007) HRL Rev 567, pp 567–575.

[342] The prisoner release scheme provided for in the Belfast/Good Friday Agreement was implemented in the Republic of Ireland by means of the Criminal Justice (Release of Prisoners) Act 1998. On the Agreement generally see: http://cain.ulst.ac.uk/events/peace/docs/agreement.htm (last accessed May 2011).

[343] *O'Neill and Quinn v Ireland*, Communication No 1314/2004, para 8.4.

[344] *O'Neill and Quinn v Ireland*, Communication No 1314/2004, paras 2.7 and 8.2.

[345] *O'Neill and Quinn v Ireland*, Communication No 1314/2004, para 8.4.

[346] *O'Neill and Quinn v Ireland*, Communication No 1314/2004, para 8.4.

[347] Mr Solari-Yrigoyen dissented on the basis that the State had failed to provide a fair and reasonable justification for excluding the authors from the scheme. In his view, the state's decision was based on political and other considerations which are unacceptable under the Covenant. Similar dissenting views were given by Mr Lallah and Ms Chanet.

[348] Edelenbos, 'The Human Rights Committee's Jurisprudence under Article 26 of the ICCPR: The Hidden Revolution' in Alfredsson et al (eds), *International Human Rights Monitoring Mechanisms* (2nd edn, Martinus Nijhoff, 2009), p 81.

necessity at the expense of human rights.[349] On the other hand, it may be argued that as long as its usage is strictly controlled, the allocation of a 'margin of appreciation' to decisions restricting rights for public interest reasons is appropriate, especially in a case such as this where the decision was partly aimed at ensuring continued public support for an agreement underpinning the entire Northern Ireland peace process.

Right to an effective remedy

[7.70] Article 2(3) of the ICCPR obliges each State party to ensure an effective remedy to any person whose rights or freedoms have been breached.[350] The CCPR has elevated this provision into a substantive right in certain circumstances when it is raised in conjunction with another right. In the case of *Rodriguez v Uruguay*, for example, the Committee found a violation of art 7 of the ICCPR, in conjunction with art 2(3)(a),[351] arising out of the application of an amnesty law to a complaint made by the author regarding severe torture inflicted on him by the secret police in Uruguay in 1983.[352] The CCPR held that amnesties for gross violations of human rights and legislation such as that which was in issue in this case are incompatible with the obligations of States parties under the Covenant.[353] The adoption of such a law effectively excludes the possibility of investigation into past human rights abuses and thereby prevents a State party from discharging its responsibility to provide effective remedies to the victims of such abuses.[354] The CCPR expressed concern that the adoption of such a law contributes to an atmosphere of impunity which may undermine the democratic order and lead to further violations.[355] The author was entitled under art 2(3)(a) to an effective remedy involving an official investigation to identify the perpetrators and to assist him in seeking civil redress.[356]

[7.71] It would seem, however, that this provision does not constitute a free-standing right to have the views of the CCPR implemented in one's own particular case, or in regard to others. In *Kavanagh v Ireland*[357] the author complained that the State had

---

[349] Joseph, 'Human Rights Committee: Recent Jurisprudence' (2007) HRL Rev 567, pp 574–575.
[350] CCPR General Comment No 31: The Nature of the General Legal Obligations Imposed on States Parties to the Covenant, 29 March 2004, UN Doc CCPR/C/21/Rev1/Add13, paras 15 and 16.
[351] ICCPR, art 2(3)(a) states the general obligation on States to ensure an effective remedy, while ICCPR, art 2(3)(b) spells out the requirement to ensure that individuals shall have their rights to such remedies determined by a competent authority (judicial, administrative, legislative or otherwise) and to develop the possibilities of a judicial remedy. ICCPR, art 2(3)(c) requires States to ensure the enforcement of such remedies when granted.
[352] *Rodriguez v Uruguay*, Communication No 322/1988, views adopted on 19 July 1994.
[353] *Rodriguez v Uruguay*, Communication No 322/1988, para 12.4.
[354] *Rodriguez v Uruguay*, Communication No 322/1988, para 12.4.
[355] *Rodriguez v Uruguay*, Communication No 322/1988, para 12.4.
[356] See also, *Massiotti and Baritussio v Uruguay*, Communication No 25/1978, in which a violation of ICCPR, art 9(4) in conjunction with ICCPR, art 2(3) was found to exist in Baritussio's case because there was no competent court to which she could have appealed during her arbitrary detention (para 13).
[357] *Kavanagh v Ireland*, Communication No 1114/2002.

violated art 2(3)(a) of the Covenant by reason of its failure to provide him with an effective remedy pursuant to an earlier decision of the Committee that the State had violated art 26 of the Covenant in his case.[358] The CCPR found the author's fresh complaint to be inadmissible on the ground that it was not based on any new factual developments, and hence did not stretch beyond that which the Committee had already decided in regard to his previous communication.[359] Moreover, his claim that the State party continued to commit the same violation in respect of art 26 as regards other individuals, despite the views of the CCPR in his case, was deemed inadmissible as an *actio popularis*.[360] The case demonstrates further the limits of the individual complaint mechanism provided for in the OP-ICCPR in ensuring adequate remedial action on the part of respondent States, even in cases where the CCPR has found a violation of the Covenant to exist on the facts.

The relationship between art 2(3) and art 14 of the Covenant is important insofar as the right to an effective remedy must be respected whenever any guarantee provided for in art 14 is violated.[361]

Minority rights

[7.72] Article 27 of the ICCPR guarantees rights to ethnic, religious or linguistic minorities within the States parties to the ICCPR to enjoy their minority culture, to profess and practise their own religion, or to use their own language. These rights are supplementary to the other rights in the Covenant enjoyed by individual members of minority groups generally.[362] Article 27 should not be confused with the right to self-determination which is provided to peoples under art 1 of the ICCPR and which cannot, as such, be invoked by an individual in proceedings under the Protocol.[363] Likewise, art 27 is distinct from the various duties imposed on States parties in regard to equal treatment and non-discrimination provided for in arts 2 and 26 of the Covenant.[364]

[7.73] According to the CCPR, the terms used in art 27 indicate that the persons who are meant to be protected under its rubric are 'those who belong to a group and who share in common a culture, a religion and/or a language', regardless of citizenship.[365] What constitutes a 'minority', and whether a person belongs to such group, for the purposes of art 27, falls to be decided on a case-by-case basis by the Committee which decides these matters autonomously, ie, independently of national law.[366] In a somewhat controversial decision in *Ballantyne et al v Canada*, the Committee took the view that in a federal

---

[358] *Kavanagh v Ireland*, Communication No 819/1998, See **7.68**.
[359] *Kavanagh v Ireland*, Communication No 1114/2002, para 4.2.
[360] *Kavanagh v Ireland*, Communication No 1114/2002, para 4.3.
[361] CCPR General Comment No 32, para 58.
[362] CCPR General Comment No 23: The rights of minorities (Art 27): (08/04/94) UN Doc CCPR/C/21/Rev1/Add5, para 1.
[363] CCPR General Comment No 23, paras 3.1 and 4. See also *Lubicon Lake Band v Canada*, Communication No 167/1984, para 13.3.
[364] CCPR General Comment No 23, para 4.
[365] CCPR General Comment No 23, para 5.1.
[366] *Lovelace v Canada*, Communication No R 6/24, p 17. (contd.../)

State, the protection of art 27 is only applicable to groups which constitute a minority in the State as a whole.[367] This qualification applies even, as in this case, where the group concerned constitutes a minority within a particular province and as such is subject to provincial laws which allegedly violate the terms of art 27. The authors in that case were English speakers from the pre-dominantly French-speaking province of Quebec who complained about a provincial law which prohibited them from advertising in English. The Committee held that since English speakers were not a minority in Canada as a whole, they did not constitute a linguistic 'minority' for the purposes of art 27.[368] While indigenous peoples have a distinct status under other international instruments, they are considered to constitute a 'minority' by the Committee for the purposes of art 27.[369] Most cases decided by the Committee in regard to art 27 concern indigenous peoples and specifically their access to land resources or fishing rights.[370]

[7.74] As regards the scope of art 27, the Committee has decided that although it is expressed in negative terms, the article obliges States to take positive measures of protection, whether through their legislative, judicial or administrative authorities, against acts of the State party itself that might violate the right, but also against the acts of third parties. Such measures should extend to protecting '...the identity of a minority and the rights of its members to enjoy and develop their culture and language and to practise their religion in community with other members of the group'.[371] In practice, it seems that the Committee applies a proportionality test in deciding whether minority rights under art 27 can be limited by domestic laws or practices which are usually implemented for the purposes of economic development.[372] Where the measures taken interfere with culturally significant economic activities of a minority or indigenous community, the CCPR will also take into account whether the minorities affected have been included in the decision-making process that led to the interference in question.[373]

---

[366] (\...contd) In that case, the Committee decided that the author belonged to the Maliseet Indian ethnic minority, and hence was entitled to claim the protection of ICCPR, art 27, even though she had lost her status as an Indian under domestic law. As the Committee noted: 'Protection under the Indian Act and protection under ICCPR, art 27 therefore have to be distinguished' (para 14).

[367] *Ballantyne et al v Canada*, Communications Nos 359/1989 and 385/1989, para 11.2

[368] *Ballantyne et al v Canada*, Communications Nos 359/1989 and 385/1989, para 11.2. As Joseph et al note, while this decision certainly compromises the position of groups in similar situations, other rights may still be applicable to vindicate their claim under the Protocol, such as the rights to equal treatment, non-discrimination and political participation, and the right to freedom of expression which was successfully pleaded on the facts in *Ballantyne*: Joseph et al, *The International Covenant on Civil and Political Rights* (2nd edn, OUP, 1994), p 755.

[369] CCPR General Comment No 23, paras 3.2 and 7.

[370] See, for example, Lubicon Lake Band v Canada, Communication No 167/1984 and Mahuika v New Zealand, Communication No 547/1993.

[371] CCPR General Comment No 23, para 6.2. See generally, Joseph et al, *The International Covenant on Civil and Political Rights* (2nd edn, OUP, 1994), pp 768–793.

[372] *Länsman v Finland*, Communication No 511/92; and *Äärelä Näkkäläjärvi v Finland*, Communication No 779/97.

[373] See *Poma Poma v Peru*, Communication No 1457/2006, para. 7.6.

APPRAISAL

[7.75] The above analysis has demonstrated that the Human Rights Committee has been instrumental in breathing life into the 'rather barebones procedure'[374] provided for in the Optional Protocol to the ICCPR. It has produced an impressive volume of views on practically every aspect of the Covenant. As to the quality of those views, there can be little doubt but that the preference for consensual decision-making has resulted over the years in some tersely stated decisions on the merits which fail to elaborate the legal reasoning by which the Committee has arrived at its position on a given issue.[375] To the extent that this continues to happen, it diminishes the prospects of those views having widespread influence in domestic courts, especially in States where the ICCPR is as yet unincorporated. At the same time, there has been a discernible improvement on this front in recent years,[376] especially with the systematic input of the petitions unit in the process.

[7.76] However, the genesis of the OP-ICCPR as a product of political compromise considerably weakened its structure from the outset as an implementation technique.[377] The fact that communications are examined in closed meetings, on the basis of written information only, by a Committee empowered merely to 'forward its views' to an offending State, in the absence of a legal or political mechanism for enforcement, is hardly a recipe for success if the aim of the procedure is assumed to be that of achieving individuated justice. While the latter goal is not necessarily clear from the text of the OP-ICCPR, it would certainly appear to be the goal which the CCPR increasingly sees itself as fulfilling in respect of the Protocol.[378] The challenge for the Committee is that while it does function in formalistic terms as an adjudicatory body analogous to a court, it is simply not equipped, either legally or politically with the back-up to achieve compliance to an extent comparable with national courts or even the European Court of Human Rights. The Committee's own data on follow-up has been described in a recent study as 'grim', with an estimate of compliance with its views running at just above 12 percent.[379]

---

[374] Steiner, Alston and Goodman, *International Human Rights Law in Context: Law, Politics and Morals* (3rd edn, OUP, 2008), p 892.

[375] Joseph et al, *The International Covenant on Civil and Political Rights* (2nd ed, OUP, 1994), pp 50–51.

[376] Joseph et al acknowledge this fact and point to 'outstanding' examples of views on the merits in the realm of Holocaust denial as well as death penalty cases: Joseph et al, *The International Covenant on Civil and Political Rights* (2nd ed, OUP, 1994), pp 50–51.

[377] As Opsahl has noted, a consequence of this compromise was that '...many specific issues were left unresolved, perhaps intentionally. As a result the subsequent evolution of the arrangements has had to be shaped by a continuing give-and-take within the Committee over many years': Opsahl, 'The Human Rights Committee' in Alston (ed), *The United Nations and Human Rights* (OUP, 1992), p 372.

[378] As is evidenced by the tone of paras 11 and 13 of CCPR General Comment No 33 which depicts the Committee's 'views' as being analogous to judicial opinions and as having an 'authoritative' and 'determinative' character: see generally para **7.15**.

[379] Open Society Justice Initiative, *From Judgment to Justice: Implementing International and Regional Human Rights Decisions'* (Open Society Foundations, 2011), pp 118–119.

[7.77] Even if the goal of individuated justice is assumed to be theoretically compelling and cognisable from the text of the Protocol, it is to be doubted whether it is practically attainable. The Committee's caseload had more than doubled between the years of 2000 and 2007.[380] Notwithstanding this increase in communications, the work of the Committee is still relatively unknown amongst the general population in many countries. And while this is an issue which the CCPR is constantly striving to address in terms of media strategy,[381] greater inroads in terms of publicity runs the risk of swamping the Committee with a completely unmanageable caseload. As Kretzmer has noted, '...even if the legal basis were to be strengthened (for example, by expressly stating that the Committee's views are binding), it is unlikely that the United Nations, will commit significantly greater resources to the communications system'.[382]

[7.78] Various proposals for improving the output of the CCPR under the OP-ICCPR may be considered. Steiner has convincingly argued that the long-term effectiveness of the CCPR in implementing the Protocol could be greatly enhanced if it were to move towards exercising a discretionary jurisdiction.[383] As well as involving amendment of the Protocol, this would necessitate the Committee fundamentally re-conceptualising its role in regard to communications from that of dispensing with individuated justice to that of 'expounding' the rights provided for in the Covenant. By deepening its analysis of norms in the Covenant through a more focused selection of issues, the Committee could in effect fulfil a constitutional role, hitherto not really entertained by it.[384] If such an approach were to accommodate the obvious concerns regarding egregious human rights violations,[385] it could increase the Committee's impact on the normative development of human rights most crucially at the domestic level. Notwithstanding the

---

[380] In 2000, the Committee had 182 cases pending as of 31 December. That figure had increased to 455 by 31 December 2007: CCPR Annual Report, 2007/2008, UN Doc A/63/40 (Vol 1), p 97.

[381] Human Rights Committee, 'A Strategic Approach to Public Relations, Including Relations with the Media' (23 October 2008) UN Doc CCPR/C/94/CRP2/Rev 1.

[382] 'Commentary on Complaint Processes by Human Rights Committee and Torture Committee Members: (a) The Human Rights Committee' in Bayefsky (ed), *The UN Human Rights Treaty System in the 21st Century* (Kluwer Law, 2000), p 164.

[383] Steiner, 'Individual Claims in a World of Massive Violations: What Role for the Human Rights Committee?' in Alston and Crawford (eds), *The Future of UN Human Rights Treaty Monitoring* (CUP, 2000), pp 45–48.

[384] As Steiner has argued, the Committee has never really identified the purpose served by the Protocol: Steiner, 'Individual Claims in a World of Massive Violations: What Role for the Human Rights Committee?' in Alston and Crawford (eds), *The Future of UN Human Rights Treaty Monitoring* (CUP, 2000), p 17.

[385] To become a reality, Steiner argues that the OP-ICCPR would need to be amended, with specific provision made for the methodology by which particular communications would be selected for review. He suggests that such a methodology could include the proviso that any cases involving the death penalty or allegations of torture be reviewed on a mandatory basis: Steiner, 'Individual Claims in a World of Massive Violations: What Role for the Human Rights Committee?' in Alston and Crawford (eds), *The Future of UN Human Rights Treaty Monitoring* (CUP, 2000), p 48.

undoubted merits of this proposal, it has thus far received very little attention and is unlikely to do so in the immediate future. Indeed, a similar proposal failed to gain traction in the context of reform of the European Court of Human Rights[386] chiefly on the basis that the goal of individuated justice is simply too important to sacrifice in order to secure the long-term security of that institution.[387] Accordingly, attention must be fixed on continued efforts in the realm of follow-up as well as on discrete procedural reform, such as setting time limits on the submission of individual communications. Further reforms could also be generated through the process of reform of the treaty system generally, considered further in Chapter 16.

---

[386] This proposal is propounded in detail by Greer, *The European Convention on Human Rights: Achievements, Problems and Prospects* (CUP, 2006).

[387] See the Report of the Group of Wise Persons to the Committee of Ministers (CM (2006) 203, 15 November 2006)) in which the idea of giving the court a discretionary power to decide whether or not to take up cases for examination was described as being '...alien to the philosophy of the European human rights protection system' (para 42): https://wcd.coe.int/wcd/ViewDoc.jsp?id=1063779&Site=CM (last accessed May 2011). See further NGO Comments on the Group of Wise Person's Interim Report (AI Index: IOR 61/019/2006, para 12): http://www.londonmet.ac.uk/research-units/hrsj/affiliated-centres/ehrac/activities-general/long-term-effectiveness-of-the-european-court.cfm (last accessed May 2011).

Chapter 8

Article 14 of the International Convention on the Elimination of All Forms of Racial Discrimination

INTRODUCTION

[8.01] In contrast to the lengthy discussions that took place in various organs of the United Nations on the inclusion of implementation procedures in the body of draft Covenant on Civil and Political Rights, debate on the insertion of such measures in the International Convention on the Elimination of All Forms of Racial Discrimination (ICERD) appears not to have been quite so protracted. In point of fact, debate on the matter never really got off the ground until the draft Convention on the Elimination of All Forms of Racial Discrimination was submitted by the Commission on Human Rights to the Third Committee of the General Assembly.[1] Until that stage, proposals concerning a reporting procedure and an inter-State complaint mechanism had been floated, but not substantively discussed in any detail by the Sub-Commission or Commission on Human Rights due to time constraints.[2] During the debate in the Third Committee, however, a number of States jointly submitted a draft text for an optional, individual complaint procedure to be included in the body of the Convention.[3] While some objections were inevitably voiced in some quarters to the inclusion of such a procedure,[4] the proposal encountered surprisingly little resistance in principle.[5] The debate on the matter was undoubtedly influenced by the fact that the notion of including an individual petition procedure was already under consideration in regard to the draft Covenant on Civil and Political Rights.[6] The resulting text of art 14 of ICERD ultimately pre-dated the adoption of the first Optional Protocol to the International Covenant on Civil and Political Rights (OP-ICCPR) as the earliest incarnation of an individual complaint procedure in the history of United Nations human rights treaties.

---

[1] In debating the text of the draft Convention, the Commission simply ran out of time on the question of measures of implementation and decided instead to refer the matter of implementation to the Third Committee. See the discussion of delegates of the Commission on Human Rights at its 20th session: Commission on Human Rights, Summary Record of the 810th Meeting, UN Doc E/CN4/SR810 (15 May 1964).

[2] Report of the 16th session of the Sub-Commission on Prevention of Discrimination and Protection of Minorities to the Commission on Human Rights: UN Doc E/CN4/873, paras 120–122.

[3] Argentina, Chile, Colombia, Costa Rica, Ecuador, Ghana, Guatemala, Mauritania, Panama, Peru and Philippines: Revised text of Article XIII of the articles relating to measure of implementation to be added to the provisions of the draft International Convention on the Elimination of All Forms of Racial Discrimination, UN Doc A/C3/L 1308 (29 November 1965).

[8.02] As finally drafted, the text of art 14(1) of ICERD provides each State party with the option of declaring at any time that it recognises the competence of the Committee on the Elimination of Racial Discrimination (CERD)[7] to receive and consider communications concerning violations by that State party of any of the rights set forth in the Convention.[8] As Partsch has observed, a number of elements of the complaint procedure provided for in art 14 are distinguishable from the procedure under the OP-ICCPR.[9] First, unlike the OP-ICCPR, communications under art 14 may be submitted from 'groups of individuals', as well as 'individuals'. Second, whereas the Human Rights Committee (CCPR) is expressly forbidden from examining communications which are already being examined under another procedure of international investigation or settlement, no such stricture is to be found in the text of art 14 of ICERD. However, while this limitation is not explicit in the text, many States, including Ireland, have guarded against the possibility of so-called 'forum shopping' by entering interpretive declarations to the terms of art 14 when accepting the jurisdiction of CERD to receive communications under that article.[10] These declarations generally provide that

[4] Mr Ouedraogo (representative of Upper Volta) abstained from voting on the right of petition 'in the interests both of the Convention and of the prospective petitioners themselves'. He argued that if the article were accepted '...the proposed committee might be swamped by thousands of petitions which it would be unable to handle effectively, with resulting damage to its own prestige and to that of the United Nations'. He also cited the 'danger of jeopardising the impartiality of the committee's work', the lack of coercive powers and the dangers of breaches of confidentiality and reprisals against petitioners as reasons for his abstention: UN Doc A/C3/SR 1363, para 13.

[5] Indeed, some delegations did not believe that the draft text went far enough: Ms Tabara (representative of Lebanon) believed that in operating the procedure, CERD would be little more than a 'post-office'; while Mr Hedström (representative of Sweden) considered that the draft text '...did not provide a right of petition worthy of the name': UN Doc A/C3.SR 1362, paras 5 and 10 respectively. The text which was to form the body of art 14 was adopted by 66 votes to none with 19 abstentions: Report of the 20th session of the Third Committee of the General Assembly, UN Doc A/6181 (18 December 1965), para 153(e).

[6] This point was made by the representative of the Philippines, Mr Garcia, who spearheaded the introduction of measures of implementation in the Convention, arguing that without them, the Convention would remain a 'dead letter': UN GA, Report of the 1344th Meeting of the Third Committee, UN Doc A/C3/SR 1344, paras 24–27.

[7] As to the ICERD generally and the composition and functions of CERD, see Ch 3, paras **3.53–3.63**.

[8] Note that the wording of art 14(1) does not confine the application of the procedure to particular rights in the Convention, but rather applies to 'any of the rights set forth in this Convention'. As CERD made clear in the case of *The Jewish Community of Oslo v Norway*, Communication No 30/2003, UN Doc A/60/18, p 154, para 10.6, the procedure in art 14 is not simply applicable to the rights contained in art 5 (as had been claimed by the respondent State in that case).

[9] Partsch, 'The Racial Discrimination Committee' in Alston (ed), *The United Nations and Human Rights: A Critical Appraisal* (OUP, 1992), p 363.

[10] In addition to Ireland, the governments of Andorra, Austria, Denmark, Finland, Germany, Iceland, Italy, Liechtenstein, Malta, Norway, Portugal, Slovenia, Sweden, Switzerland and Macedonia have also entered such declarations.

the State in question accepts the competence of CERD to consider communications emanating from its jurisdiction provided that the Committee has ascertained that the same matter has not been, and is not being, examined under another procedure of international investigation or settlement.[11]

[8.03] A unique feature of art 14(2) of ICERD is that it provides for the possibility of States, which agree to be bound by the terms of the international complaint mechanism in art 14, to establish a similar mechanism at the domestic level. Specifically, it provides that that any such State '*may* establish or indicate a body within its national legal order' which shall be competent to receive and consider petitions from individuals and groups of individuals within its jurisdiction who claim to be victims of a violation of any of the rights set forth in the Convention. This provision was apparently inserted as a compromise for States which had advocated the establishment of national mechanisms only during the drafting process, as opposed to an international body for the consideration of individual complaints.[12] Certain requirements regarding the operation of such a national procedure are laid down in art 14(4).[13] Article 14(5) stipulates that where attempts to secure a remedy from the national body have failed, the petitioner shall have the right to communicate the complaint in question to CERD. As Meron has noted, despite the use of the word 'may' in art 14(2), CERD initially interpreted the Convention as *requiring* the establishment of such bodies on the basis that a failure to do so would make the international procedure inoperable.[14] Given the tentative language used, this stringent interpretation was unwarranted and indeed untenable.[15] CERD

---

[11] The full text of all such reservations, including that entered by Ireland, can be accessed at: http://treaties.un.org/Pages/ViewDetails.aspx?src=TREATY&mtdsg_no=IV-2&chapter=4&lang=en (last accessed May 2011).

[12] The right to petition a national authority, as opposed to an international body, was initially proposed by the government of Saudi Arabia (UN Doc A/C3/L1297): See Schwelb, 'The International Convention on the Elimination of all Forms of Racial Discrimination' (1966) 15 ICLQ 996, p 1048.

[13] ICERD, art 14(4) essentially requires that a register of petitions shall be kept by the national body in question and that certified copies of the register shall be filed annually through appropriate channels to the Secretary General of the United Nations, which copies shall not be publicly accessible.

[14] Meron, 'The Meaning and Reach of the International Convention on the Elimination of All Forms of Racial Discrimination' (1985) 79 AJIL 283, pp 313–314. This interpretation was made known in the context of the Committee's observations on the State report submitted by Uruguay. In response to a comment made by a representative of the Uruguayan government that designation of such a national body was optional, the Committee observed that '…while it was true that the word 'may' was used in that paragraph, it was the 'establishment' or 'indication' of that body that was optional, and not its existence; otherwise, the procedure prescribed in paragraphs 4 and 5 of art 14 of the Convention could not be put into operation': CERD Annual Report 1977, UN Doc A/32/18, cited in Meron, p 314.

[15] As Meron points out, 'Some countries may feel that the complexity of such complaints necessitates the involvement of various organs, depending upon the subject (eg housing or employment) or the various competent levels of government…': Meron, 'The Meaning and Reach of the International Convention on the Elimination of All Forms of Racial Discrimination' (1985) 79 AJIL 283, p 314. (contd.../)

ultimately abandoned this view, requiring instead that a petitioner[16] must have satisfied all available domestic remedies, 'including, *when applicable*, those mentioned in paragraph 2 of Article 14'.[17] Accordingly, it is clear that the establishment of national procedures is entirely optional and is not a necessary pre-requisite for the operation of the international complaint mechanism.

[8.04] Another aspect of art 14 which is unique compared to other individual complaint mechanisms is the stipulation in art 14(6)(a) that the identity of the petitioner(s) shall not be revealed to the State party without his or her express consent. Although this provision is no doubt well-intentioned, it could potentially render the procedure unworkable were the petitioner ever to withhold consent.[18] As Schwelb has pointed out, it would seem practically impossible for a State to answer a charge under art 14 if it does not know the identity of the petitioner in question.[19] For this reason, individuals who submit communications under art 14 (or indeed under any of the UN individual complaint mechanisms) inevitably run the gauntlet of State reprisal. In actual fact, this provision does not appear to have posed any particular problems in practice insofar as complainants have always been willing to reveal their identity.

[8.05] Finally, it may be noted that art 14(7)(b) of the Convention empowers CERD to forward its 'suggestions and recommendations'[20] to the respondent State and to the petitioner after its consideration of the communication in question. CERD has used this formulation to great effect in making very specific recommendations to respondent States in respect of cases where a violation of the Convention has been established. The Committee has also drawn on its mandate in this respect to furnish 'suggestions and recommendations' to States, even in cases where a violation has *not* been established. Nothing in ICERD precludes this approach, though the value of such recommendations is clearly diminished in such circumstances.

---

[15] (\...contd) At the time of their ratification/accession to the Convention, the following States specifically designated national bodies pursuant to art 14(2): Argentina, Belgium, Liechtenstein, Luxembourg, Montenegro, Portugal, Romania, Serbia and South Africa.

[16] Note that art 14 expressly uses the term 'petitioner' which term is in turn used by CERD.

[17] CERD Rules of Procedure, r 91(e): UN Doc HRI/GEN/3/Rev3, p 57.

[18] This point was raised by the representative of Iraq during the drafting of the provision who explained that in his delegation's opinion '…no State could accept a petition lodged against it if it did not know the identity of the author. In such cases it could not be sure that the petition came from one of its nationals and not from an alien. It would have no means of knowing whether a particular person had been harmed by the violation of one of his rights. It would have no means of verifying that the petitioner had first applied to the national courts': UN GA, Report of the 1357th Meeting of the Third Committee, UN Doc A/C3/SR.1357 (29 November 1965), para 45.

[19] Schwelb, 'The International Convention on the Elimination of all Forms of Racial Discrimination' (1966) 15 ICLQ 996, p 1044.

[20] This formulation can be contrasted with the subsequent usage in individual complaint procedures, such as the OP-ICCPR, of 'views'.

PROCEDURE

[8.06] The procedure by which communications under art 14 are considered by CERD may be deduced primarily from the Committee's Rules of Procedure,[21] read in conjunction with the terse text of the article itself. Communications from individuals or groups of individuals may firstly be directed in writing to the petitions unit at the Office of the High Commissioner for Human Rights (OHCHR). In some cases, where the intention of the petitioner is unclear, the petitions team may request further particulars from the author of a communication and/or clarification as to whether he or she definitely wishes to have the communication submitted to CERD.[22] If there is any doubt as to the wish of the author, CERD shall be seised of the communication.[23] Once satisfied that it has adequate information to register the case, a member of the petitions team will summarise the communication, and forward it to the Committee at its next available session.[24]

[8.07] CERD has made provision in its Rules of Procedure for the appointment of a special rapporteur from amongst its ranks, as well as a five-member working group to assist it in the handling of new communications.[25] However, while a working group has never been appointed (due to the low volume of new communications), one member of the Committee acts as a rapporteur for each complaint. He or she works closely with the petitions unit and ultimately makes recommendations to the plenary Committee on the admissibility and merits of each case.

[8.08] Once the case has been registered, the communication is transmitted to the respondent State which has three months to respond to the communication.[26] It is also possible for the Committee to decide that a communication is inadmissible *before* transmitting it to a State party for submissions or to decide, with the consent of both parties, to deal with question of admissibility and the merits jointly.[27] Decisions on admissibility and the merits of every complaint are made by the CERD in plenary sessions and are normally reached by consensus. In the event of serious disagreement, the Rules of Procedure do provide that decisions may be made by a majority of members 'present and voting'.[28] If a communication is deemed to be inadmissible, such decision will be communicated to the author and the respondent State.[29]

---

[21] Rules of Procedure of the Committee on the Elimination of Racial Discrimination: UN Doc HRI/GEN/3/Rev3, pp 57–92.
[22] CERD Rules of Procedure, r 83(2).
[23] CERD Rules of Procedure, r 83(2).
[24] CERD Rules of Procedure, r 85(1).
[25] CERD Rules of Procedure, r 87.
[26] ICERD, art 14(6)(b).
[27] CERD Rules of Procedure, r 94(7). In such cases, the State will normally be given three months to make submissions on admissibility and the merits and the author will be given two months to respond.
[28] CERD Rules of Procedure, r 50.
[29] CERD Rules of Procedure, r 93(1). (\...contd)

[8.09] The rules of procedure indicate that during the course of its consideration of a case, where the urgency of the situation so requires, the Committee may formally inform the respondent State of its views as to the desirability of taking interim measures to avoid irreparable damage to the petitioner. The Rules stipulate that should it make such views known to a respondent State, the Committee should inform the State party that its views on the matter should not be interpreted as pre-judging a final opinion on the merits or its eventual suggestions and recommendation.[30]

[8.10] If the decision on admissibility has been taken separately and the complaint has been deemed admissible, the decision will be transmitted to the author and the State party[31] and the respondent State will once again be given a deadline of some three months to submit observations on the merits of the claim.[32] In this respect, the Committee may indicate, if it deems it necessary, the precise type of information which it wishes to receive from the respondent State. The respondent State's submissions on the merits will then be transmitted to the author of the communication, who will in turn be given a deadline (usually of three months) to reply.[33] It should be noted that a decision of admissibility is not necessarily absolutely cast in stone as it is still possible for the Committee to revoke a decision of admissibility in the light of any explanations or statements submitted by the respondent State.[34] Before considering revocation, however, the Committee is required to transmit any such submissions to the author so that she or he might submit additional information or observations of their own on the points raised by the State.[35]

[8.11] The procedure followed by CERD during its consideration of communications under art 14 is entirely confidential.[36] As compared with the practice of the other treaty bodies, provision is uniquely made in CERD's Rules of Procedure for the Committee to invite the author or his/her representative and the State party's representative to furnish information orally to the Committee or to answer any questions on the merits of the communication.[37] Depending on how it is exercised, this provision could provide the basis for integrating an oral hearing (albeit in closed session) into the Committee's consideration at the merits phase. No question arises as regards the mandate of the Committee to introduce such a process as art 14 of the Convention simply provides that communications be considered in the light of 'all information' made available to it by

---

[29] (\...contd) A decision taken by CERD that a communication is inadmissible may be reviewed at a later date at the written request of a petitioner. The request must contain documentary evidence to the effect that the reasons why the communication was found to be inadmissible are no longer applicable: CERD Rules of Procedure, r 93(2).
[30] CERD Rules of Procedure, r 94(3).
[31] CERD Rules of Procedure, r 94(1).
[32] CERD Rules of Procedure, r 94(2).
[33] CERD Rules of Procedure, r 94(4).
[34] CERD Rules of Procedure, r 94(6).
[35] CERD Rules of Procedure, r 94(6).
[36] ICERD, art 14(6)(a) and CERD Rules of Procedure, r 88.
[37] CERD Rules of Procedure, r 94(5).

the State party and the petitioner.[38] This language is more flexible than that of the OP-ICCPR, which stipulates that communications shall be considered on the basis of 'all *written* information'[39] and in respect of which limited debate has ensued as regards the legitimacy of potential oral hearings.[40] In any event, however, this power has never been exercised by CERD. The Committee, or a working group set up by it, may also obtain any documentation that may assist in the disposal of a case from United Nations bodies or the specialised agencies.[41]

[8.12] Having considered all of the information that has been submitted to it on the merits, the Committee will issue an 'opinion' on whether the Convention has been violated.[42] An opinion of CERD has the equivalent status as the 'views' of the CCPR and the other treaty bodies which consider communications under individual complaint machinery, ie, it is a non-binding opinion on the merits. As noted above, art 14(7)(b) of ICERD empowers CERD to 'forward its suggestions and recommendations', if any, to the State party concerned and the petitioner. The Committee has interpreted this provision expansively such that it regularly furnishes States with recommendations and suggestions, even in circumstances where it has not actually found as a fact that the Convention has been violated. Again, all views are arrived at by consensus-decision making, though individual members are entitled to append individual opinions to the Committee's general opinion.[43] This is an exceptional occurrence and, as is outlined further below, the priority of reaching decisions by consensus has arguably diminished the quality of the Committee's decisions in particular cases.

[8.13] Once CERD has transmitted its opinion to the parties, the State is invited to inform the Committee 'in due course' of the action that it has taken on the suggestions and recommendations made to it.[44] In this respect, a follow-up procedure in respect of the Committee's opinions was adopted in 2005 which is reflected in r 95(6) and (7) of its Rules of Procedure. According to this procedure, a member of the Committee now acts as a rapporteur for follow-up to opinions with the role of ascertaining what measures have been taken by respondent States in response to the Committee's suggestions and recommendations.[45] The rapporteur may establish such contacts and take such follow-up action as is appropriate to discharge properly his or her mandate; and is required to make such recommendations for further follow-up action by the Committee as may be necessary. He or she must report to the Committee on follow-up activities, which

---

[38] ICERD, art 14(7)(a).
[39] OP-ICCPR, art 5(1).
[40] See Ch 7, para **7.11**.
[41] CERD Rules of Procedure, r 95(2)
[42] CERD Rules of Procedure, r 95(3).
[43] CERD Rules of Procedure, r 95(4).
[44] CERD Rules of Procedure, r 95(5).
[45] CERD Rules of Procedure, r 95(6) and (7), adopted by CERD on 15 August 2005: http://www2.ohchr.org/english/bodies/cerd/docs/newruleprocedure-august05.pdf (last accessed May 2011).

activities are ultimately reflected in detail in the annual reports of the Committee.[46] A summary of all the communications examined by the Committee in any given year, as well as a summary of the explanations and statements of the States parties concerned and the Committee's recommendations and suggestions are also included in each of its annual reports to the General Assembly.[47]

ADMISSIBILITY

[8.14] The admissibility criteria for individual communications are set forth in art 14(6) and (7) and fleshed out in further detail in r 91 of CERD's Rules of Procedure. The criteria are in most respects identical to the ones previously considered under the OP-ICCPR. Certain important differences obtain, however, which can affect the decision to submit a communication under the procedure. First, as has been noted above, in contrast to other complaint procedures, communications under art 14 are not necessarily inadmissible if the author has already submitted the complaint (either simultaneously or in the past) to another international procedure of investigation or settlement. Notwithstanding this lack of constraint, prospective petitioners would need to check carefully whether the respondent State in question has entered any interpretive declaration upon ratification forestalling consideration of communications by CERD which are being considered or have already been considered by another international body.

[8.15] A second point of difference in terms of admissibility requirements is that CERD applies a time-limit for accepting communications under art 14. Specifically, it will only accept communications (save in exceptional circumstances) that have been submitted within six months from the date of exhaustion of the last applicable domestic remedy.[48] This time-limit is obliquely referred to in art 14(5) of the Convention as being applicable in circumstances where a petitioner has failed to obtain satisfaction from a national complaints mechanism which has been established under the terms set forth in art 14(2). In the event of such a negative decision, the petitioner *must* apply to CERD within six months of such a negative decision. The Committee, however, has chosen, *via* its Rules of Procedure, to make that time-limit applicable in principle as regards *all* communications, not just those for which a national procedure has been established in the jurisdiction pursuant to art 14(2).[49]

---

[46] CERD Rules of Procedure, r 95(7): see, for example, the information on follow-up included in the CERD's most recent annual report for 2010: UN Doc A/65/18, pp 131–132.
[47] ICERD, art 14(8) and CERD Rules of Procedure, r 96.
[48] CERD Rules of Procedure, r 91(f).
[49] CERD Rules of Procedure, r 91(f). See *FA v Norway*, Communication No 18/2000, in which a complaint about discriminatory practices by housing agencies was deemed inadmissible by the Committee because it was submitted outside the six-month time limit specified in the CERD Rules of Procedure, r 91(f), paras 6.3 and 6.4. An argument by the author's counsel to the effect that appreciation of the time-limit was outside the legal expertise of the NGO which channelled the author's complaint (para 5.1) appears to have been implicitly rejected by CERD.

As with the other procedures, communications will be deemed inadmissible where they are submitted anonymously,[50] are abusive,[51] are insufficiently substantiated[52] or are otherwise incompatible with the provisions of ICERD.[53] The ground of incompatibility is examined specifically in the following section.

Incompatible communications

[8.16] As with the practice of the CCPR in examining the admissibility of communications under the OP-ICCPR, communications under art 14 may be deemed inadmissible for being 'incompatible' with the provisions of ICERD by CERD on a number of grounds. They may be deemed incompatible *ratione temporis* where they relate to acts or facts which took place prior to a declaration by the State party under art 14(1) accepting the right of individual petition. In *Dragan Durmic v Serbia and Montenegro,* for example, the petitioner attempted to argue that a declaration accepting the competence of the Committee to examine communications regarding potential violation(s) of the Convention had no temporal implications.[54] Specifically, he argued that art 14 is simply a jurisdictional clause which merely signified another means by which a State's implementation of the Convention can be monitored by CERD. Accordingly, he argued that art 14 contained no express temporal limitation which would prevent the Committee from examining petitions on the basis that the facts took place prior to the date of deposit of a declaration.[55] The case concerned the failure of the authorities to investigate properly and prosecute an alleged incident of racial discrimination involving a private club and a member of the Roma minority which had occurred prior to the declaration under art 14 being made by the respondent State. Acknowledging that the specific incident in question had taken place prior to the making of the declaration under art 14, the Committee held that what was at issue in this specific case was the failure by the authorities to investigate and prosecute the incident in accordance with the guarantee of an effective remedy in art 6 of the Convention.[56] It noted that such shortcomings were 'ongoing' and had continued since the date of the incident itself and after the State's declaration under art 14. The Committee's reasoning therefore implicitly refutes the author's suggestion that the making of a declaration under art 14 has no temporal implications as regards the admissibility of communications. Rather, it appears that the entry of a declaration under art 14, as opposed to ratification of the Convention, is the crucial point of reference in assessing whether a communication is inadmissible *ratione temporis*. As with the other treaty bodies, the Committee's application of the concept of 'continuing violation' to the facts

---

[50] ICERD, art 14(6) and CERD Rules of Procedure, r 91(a).
[51] CERD Rules of Procedure, r 91(d).
[52] *KRC v Denmark*, Communication No 23/2002, para 6.2; and *CP and his son MP v Denmark*, Communication No 5/1994, para 6.3.
[53] CERD Rules of Procedure, r 91(c).
[54] *Dragan Durmic v Serbia and Montenegro*, Communication No 29/2003, para 3.1.
[55] *Dragan Durmic v Serbia and Montenegro*, Communication No 29/2003, para 3.1.
[56] *Dragan Durmic v Serbia and Montenegro*, Communication No 29/2003, para 6.4.

of this case indicates that it will take a flexible attitude to the question of incompatibility on this ground.[57]

[8.17] The ground of incompatibility *ratione materiae* has rarely been invoked but was raised successfully in *AWRAP v Denmark*.[58] In that case, the petitioner complained about breaches of ICERD arising out of allegedly racist statements made by a politician concerning persons of Muslim or Arab background. While recognising the 'importance of the interface between race and religion' and that incidents of 'double discrimination' on grounds of race and religion may exist, the Committee did not believe that this was such a case.[59] Rather, it found that the petition related exclusively to discrimination based on religious grounds and that Islam is not a religion practised solely by a particular group which could otherwise be identified by its 'race, colour, descent, or national or ethnic origin'.[60] Accordingly, it found the communication to be inadmissible *ratione materiae* under art 14(1) of the Convention.[61] In reaching its decision on admissibility in this case, the Committee drew on its earlier decision on the merits in *Quereshi v Denmark*[62] in which a similar complaint about the statements made by a Danish politician in respect of 'foreigners' was at issue. Rather than finding the complaint to be inadmissible *ratione materiae* in that case, the Committee found no violation of the Convention on the merits for similar reasons, ie, an offensive statement about 'foreigners' generally does not amount to racial discrimination.[63]

[8.18] A significant number of admissibility decisions under art 14 have concerned the question of whether the author is a 'victim' of a violation by the respondent State of any of the rights in ICERD.[64] In order to qualify as a victim, petitioners must demonstrate that they have actually been disadvantaged by the measures in question, or that such measures have the potential to produce discriminatory effects in the future.[65] As has been noted above, art 14(1) does envisage the possibility of communications from individuals and 'groups of individuals'. While communications should normally be

---

[57] As to the concept of a 'continuing violation', see the views of the CCPR, Ch 7, para **7.21–7.22**.
[58] *AWRAP v Denmark*, Communication No 37/2006.
[59] *AWRAP v Denmark*, Communication No 37/2006, para 6.3.
[60] *AWRAP v Denmark*, Communication No 37/2006, para 6.3.
[61] *AWRAP v Denmark*, Communication No 37/2006, para 6.4.
[62] *Quereshi v Denmark*, Communication No 33/2003.
[63] '…a general reference to foreigners does not at present single out a group of persons, contrary to article 1 of the Convention, on the basis of a specific race, ethnicity, colour, descent or national or ethnic origin': *Quereshi v Denmark*, Communication No 33/2003, para 7.3. Even though the complaints in both cases were unsuccessful for the reasons outlined, the Committee nonetheless expressed serious concern about the offensive nature of the statements made in both cases.
[64] As to the distinction between establishing whether the author is a 'victim' for the purposes of ICERD and establishing whether there has been a *violation* of the Convention, see *DF v Australia*, Communication No 39/2006, para 6.3.
[65] The notion of a 'potential victim' is implicitly recognised in the recent case of *Hermansen et al v Denmark*, Communication No 44/2009, para 6.2 and see further para **8.20**.

submitted by individuals themselves, or by relatives or designated representatives, the Committee will, in exceptional cases, consider a communication submitted on behalf of an alleged victim when it appears that the victim is unable to submit the communication personally and the author of the communication justifies acting on the victim's behalf.[66]

[8.19] As regards complaints which emanate from 'groups of individuals', the fact that the petitioner is a legal entity will not necessarily be an impediment to admissibility on this ground, since CERD will take into account the nature of the particular organisation's activities and the groups of individuals that it represents. [67] As the Committee has made clear in *The Documentation and Advisory Centre on Racial Discrimination v Denmark*, it does not exclude the possibility of a group of persons representing the interests of a racial or ethnic group, provided that it is able to prove that there is a sufficient nexus between the group and the alleged violation in question, ie, that the group itself has been an alleged victim of a violation or that one of its members has been a victim, and if it is able at the same time to provide due authorisation to this effect.[68] It is certainly not required that each member of the group be an individual victim of an alleged violation, as to give art 14 that interpretation would be to 'render meaningless' the reference to 'groups of individuals'.[69]

[8.20] Even though in general terms an *actio popularis* will be deemed inadmissible *ratione personae* under art 14 where the purported victims fail to show the necessary linkage to the alleged violation in question,[70] the Committee has followed the lead of the CCPR in recognising victim status where there is a *risk* of a violation of the Convention in the future arising from a measure imputable to the State. In *The Jewish Community of Oslo et al v Norway*,[71] the petitioners complained about a decision of the Norwegian Supreme Court which had overturned the conviction of an individual for hate speech disseminated at a march of a group called 'Bootboys' in their area. They claimed that the Supreme Court's conclusion that penalising approval of Nazism is incompatible with freedom of speech left them bereft of protection against the dissemination of anti-Semitic and racist propaganda and incitement to racial discrimination contrary to arts 4 and 6 of the Convention.[72] Even though the petitioners were not present at the march in question, nor were they 'personally targeted by the remarks',[73] the Committee explicitly

---

[66] See CERD Rules of Procedure, r 91(b).
[67] *Zentralrat Deutscher Sinti und Roma et al v Germany*, Communication No 38/2006, para 7.2.
[68] *The Documentation and Advisory Centre on Racial Discrimination v Denmark*, Communication No 28/2003, para 6.4. In this case, in the absence of any identifiable victims personally affected by an allegedly discriminatory job advertisement whom the author would be authorised to represent, the Committee concluded that it had failed to substantiate that it constituted or represented a group of individuals claiming to be a victim of a violation by Denmark of particular articles of the Convention: para 6.7.
[69] *The Jewish Community of Oslo et al v Norway*, Communication No 30/2003, para 7.4.
[70] *The Documentation and Advisory Centre on Racial Discrimination v Denmark*, Communication No 28/2003, para 6.6.
[71] *The Jewish Community of Oslo et al v Norway*, Communication No 30/2003.
[72] *The Jewish Community of Oslo et al v Norway*, Communication No 30/2003, para 3.1.
[73] This was the argument of the respondent State party: *The Jewish Community of Oslo et al v Norway*, Communication No 30/2003, para 4.5.

adopted the approach of the CCPR and the European Court of Human Rights in finding that the petitioners had established that they belong to a category of 'potential victims' which might be adversely affected by the result and implications of Supreme Court's decision.[74]

Exhaustion of domestic remedies

[8.21] Article 14(7)(a) of the Convention[75] provides for the well-established domestic remedies rule whereby a petitioner must have exhausted all available domestic remedies before claiming a breach of any of the rights in the ICERD, except where the application of the remedies is 'unreasonably prolonged'.[76] As a general rule, domestic remedies must be exhausted by petitioners themselves and not by other organisations and individuals.[77] This requirement may be waived, however, where the putative remedy is not available or accessible to the author. Thus, in *The Jewish Community of Oslo et al v Norway*, where the complaint involved the effect which a decision of the Supreme Court potentially had on the petitioners generally in terms of exposing them to racial hatred, the fact that they had not personally made a complaint to the police about the conduct which led to the decision in question did not count against them. In the Committee's view, the fact that the petitioners had no possibility of altering criminal proceedings which had already been launched or the decision ultimately reached in respect of such proceedings was sufficient to satisfy the domestic remedies rule.[78]

[8.22] As with the jurisprudence of the other treaty bodies, a petitioner under art 14 is only required to exhaust such remedies as are effective in the circumstances of the particular case.[79] This might require an assessment by the Committee of the relevant remedies available in national law which may be contentious in certain cases.[80] Ignorance on the part of an author or his/her legal representative of the potential remedies available is not an excuse for lack of exhaustion.[81] As a general rule, a belief that resort to a particular remedy might incur costs will not suffice as an excuse for lack

---

[74] *The Jewish Community of Oslo et al v Norway*, Communication No 30/2003, para 7.3. A similar approach was taken by the Committee in *Murat Er v Denmark*, Communication No 40/2007; see, in particular, para 6.3.

[75] See also Rules of Procedure, r 91(e).

[76] As to whether the pursuit of a remedy would be 'unreasonably prolonged', the Committee has been known to take a generous approach to this exception: see *ZUBS v Australia*, Communication No 6/1995, CERD Decision 26 August 1999, UN Doc A/54/18, p 93 where it considered that the fact that domestic proceedings in the author's case had already taken two years justified the conclusion that a further appeal would be 'unreasonably prolonged' within the meaning of ICERD, art 14(7)(a); para 6.4.

[77] *POEM and FASM v Denmark*, Communication 22/2002, para 6.3.

[78] *The Jewish Community of Oslo et al v Norway*, Communication No 30/2003, para 7.2.

[79] *Anna Koptova v Slovak Republic*, Communication No 013/1998, para 6.4.

[80] See, for example, *Lacko v Slovakia*, Communication No 11/1998; and *LR v Slovak Republic*, Communication No 31/2003.

[81] *CP and his son MP v Denmark*, Communication No 5/199, para 6.2. Similarly, a failure on the part of judicial authorities to inform a person of potential remedies will not exempt him/her from the rule of exhaustion: *Barbaro v Australia*, Communication No 7/1995, para 10.4.

of exhaustion,[82] although there is some suggestion in the Committee's case law that an exception might be made where a petitioner provides sufficient information to the effect that the expenses involved would amount to a 'grave impediment'.[83] Likewise, mere doubt as to the possible outcome of a particular remedy will not absolve the petitioner from pursuing it.[84] Some variation in approach can be detected, however, on this latter point in the jurisprudence. An extremely lenient approach appears to have been adopted, for example, in *The Jewish Community of Oslo v Denmark*, where the respondent State had argued that the authors could have pursued defamation proceedings as a means of exhausting domestic remedies.[85] The Committee concluded that in view of the author's contention that the application of defamation laws to racist speech was 'unresolved' in Norwegian law, it was not in a position to conclude that such proceedings constituted a useful and effective domestic remedy.[86] Such flexibility can be contrasted with the rigorous application of the rule of exhaustion in *Nikolas Regerat v France*.[87] That case concerned a complaint about the imposition of higher postal fees for correspondence addressed in the Basque language. The petitioners had been denied legal aid to appeal a previous negative ruling of the Court of Cassation in their case on the basis that there was no serious argument for quashing the contested decision.[88] CERD nonetheless ruled that the denial of the request for legal aid did not in any way bind the Court of Cassation and that the petitioners' reservations as to the effectiveness of their appeal in such circumstances did not exempt them from personally pursuing the remedy in question.[89]

OPINIONS

[8.23] CERD takes a judicial approach to its consideration of complaints under art 14.[90] However, although the procedure provided for in art 14 has been in force since 1982, very few complaints have been considered on their merits. Indeed, as of November 2010, the Committee had adopted final opinions on the merits in only 28 cases, of which

---

[82] *DS v Sweden*, Communication No 9/1997, para 6.3.
[83] *DS v Sweden*, Communication No 9/1997, para 6.3.
[84] *Sarwar Seliman Mostafa v Denmark*, Communication No 19/2000, para 7.4; and *Ahmad Najaati Sadic v Denmark*, Communication No 25/2002, paras 6.3–6.5.
[85] *The Jewish Community of Oslo et al v Norway*, Communication No 30/2003, para 4.4 and 6.4.
[86] *The Jewish Community of Oslo et al v Norway*, Communication No 30/2003, para 7.2.
[87] *Nikolas Regerat v France*, Communication No 24/2002.
[88] *Nikolas Regerat v France*, Communication No 24/2002, para 2.8.
[89] *Nikolas Regerat v France*, Communication No 24/2002, para 6.3. See also *Barbaro v Australia*, Communication No 7/1995, in which the Committee held that the existence of a previous judgment of the Supreme Court of South Australia on issues similar to those of the author's case did not absolve him from seeking a remedy from that court. In reaching this decision, the Committee took into account that the previous decision in question was a majority and not a unanimous judgment: para 10.5.
[90] Banton, 'Decision-Taking in the Committee on the Elimination of Racial Discrimination' in Alston and Crawford, *The Future of UN Human Rights Treaty Monitoring* (Cambridge, 2000), p 55.

11 resulted in a finding of a violation of the Convention on the facts.[91] Not surprisingly, therefore, the jurisprudence built up under art 14 relates only to a discrete number of issues examined further below. Accordingly, a fuller knowledge of CERD's interpretation of the Convention must be gleaned from the detailed General Recommendations and reports of thematic discussions which the Committee has generated over the years since its establishment, as well as its concluding observations under the reporting procedures.[92]

[8.24] Article 1(1) of ICERD provides that the term 'racial discrimination' means any distinction, exclusion, restriction or preference based on race, colour, descent, or national or ethnic origin which has the 'purpose or effect' of nullifying or impairing the recognition, enjoyment or exercise, on an equal footing, of human rights and fundamental freedoms in the political, economic, social, cultural or any other field of public life.[93] In *LR v Slovak Republic*,[94] the Committee affirmed that this definition applies not just to direct forms of discrimination, but also to indirect forms of discrimination, ie, to measures that '… are not discriminatory at face value but are discriminatory in fact and effect'.[95] In assessing such indirect discrimination, the Committee will take full account of the particular context and circumstances of the Communication in question since indirect discrimination can only be demonstrated circumstantially.[96] A differentiation of treatment will not constitute discrimination if the criteria for such differentiation, judged against the objectives and purposes of the Convention, are legitimate or fall within the scope of art 1(4) of the Convention. The Committee applied this reasoning to the facts of *Sefic v Denmark* in finding that there had been no violation of the Convention in that case.[97] In its view, the State was not liable for its refusal to take action against an insurance company which had refused to insure the author on the basis that he could not speak Danish. In the Committee's view,

---

[91] CERD Annual Report 2010, UN Doc A/65/18, para 71.
[92] For an analysis of CERD's output in each of these respects, see Vandenhole, *Non-Discrimination and Equality in the View of the UN Human Rights Treaty Bodies* (Intersentia, 2005).
[93] In General Recommendation No 14, the Committee had already highlighted the comprehensive nature of the definition of discrimination in art 1(1) by stating that the fact that a distinction is contrary to the Convention if it has either the purpose or the effect of impairing particular rights and freedoms was confirmed by the obligation placed upon States parties by art 2, para 1(c), to nullify any law or practice which has the effect of creating or perpetuating racial discrimination: UN Doc A/48/18, http://www.unhchr.ch/tbs/doc.nsf/%28Symbol%29/d7bd5d2bf71258aac12563ee004b639e?Opendocument (last accessed May 2011).
[94] *LR v Slovak Republic*, Communication No 31/2003.
[95] *LR v Slovak Republic*, Communication No 31/2003, para 10.4. This approach is consistent with that of the CCPR in interpreting ICCPR, art 26: see Ch 7, para **7.67**.
[96] *LR v Slovak Republic*, Communication No 31/2003.
LR v Slovak Republic, Communication No 31/2003, para 10.4.
[97] *Sefic v Denmark*, Communication No 32/2003.

reasonable and objective grounds for the language requirement had been proffered by the company[98] which did not warrant further investigation by the State.[99]

[8.25] In considering whether an act or omission constitutes 'racial discrimination', the Committee is mindful that the ICERD is a 'living instrument' which must be interpreted and applied taking into account the circumstances of contemporary society.[100] In *Stephen Hagan v Australia*, the Committee recommended that the State party secure the removal of a public sign at a sporting fixture which it considered to be racially offensive.[101] While the sign may not have been considered offensive at the time that it had been erected in 1960, the Committee stated that it had a duty to recall the increased sensitivities that obtain in respect of the use of certain words in the present day.[102] Thus, acts which may not have been considered discriminatory in the past, may with the passage of time take on the mantle of discrimination. The corollary of this principle also appears to be true. In *Kamal Quereshi v Denmark*, the Committee took the view that regardless of what may have been the position in the State party in the past, a general reference to 'foreigners' does not at present single out a group of persons, contrary to art 1 of the Convention, on the basis of a specific race, ethnicity, colour, descent or national or ethnic origin.[103]

[8.26] Article 1(2) excludes the application of ICERD in regard to distinctions, exclusions, restrictions or preferences made by a State party as between citizens and non-citizens. This exclusion was included in order to allow the States parties to distinguish between citizens and non-citizens for the purposes of general immigration law and citizenship law. In *Enkelaar v France,* a complaint about discrimination in regard to access to the French Bar by a Senegalese lawyer failed where the refusal of admission was based on the fact that the author was not of French nationality as required by French law.[104] As such, the complaint related to a right which existed for French nationals only, which of itself does not raise an issue under the Convention on account of the terms of art 1(2). It did not concern a right that existed in principle (for non-citizens) and which had been denied to the petitioner contrary to art 1(1).[105] However, art 1(2)

---

[98] These included the need to be able to communicate with customers, their lack of resources in terms of employing persons speaking different languages and the fact that the company operated mainly through telephone contact: *Sefic v Denmark*, Communication No 32/2003, para 72.

[99] *Sefic v Denmark*, Communication No 32/2003, para 7.2.

[100] *Stephen Hagan v Australia*, Communication No 26/2002, para 7.2.

[101] *Sefic v Denmark*, Communication No 32/2003, para 7.2.
Stephen Hagan v Australia, Communication No 26/2002, para 8.

[102] *Stephen Hagan v Australia*, Communication No 26/2002, paras 7.2–7.3.

[103] *Kamal Quereshi v Denmark*, Communication No 33/2003, para 7.3.

[104] *Enkelaar v France*, Communication No 2/1989.

[105] *Enkelaar v France*, Communication No 2/1989, para 6.6. A similar conclusion was reached in cases against Australia concerning requirements for the registration of doctors trained overseas and in respect of access to social security benefits and education. See *BMS v Australia*, Communication No 8/1996, CERD Decision 12 March 1999, UN Doc a/54/18, p 80; *DF v Australia*, Communication No 39/2006; and *DR v Australia*, Communication No 42/2008.

does not permit States to discriminate against non-citizens lawfully working in a State on account of their race, colour, descent, or national or ethnic origin. Thus, a violation was established, for example, in the case of a Turkish national, lawfully working in the Netherlands, whose employment was terminated by her employer when she became pregnant.[106] The employer's decision, which was confirmed by a domestic court, was expressly based on a perceived difference in absenteeism owing to childbirth and illness between foreign women and Dutch women.[107] In such circumstances, the Committee concluded that the petitioner's right to work under art 5(e)(i) of the Convention had not been adequately protected.[108] The Committee's General Recommendation on discrimination against non-citizens indicates the limits of permissible restrictions of the rights of non-citizens under the Convention.[109]

[8.27] Article 2 of the Convention sets out the general obligations of States parties in regard to racial discrimination. These include both negative obligations (not to engage directly in discrimination[110] or defend, sponsor or support it)[111] and positive obligations (to amend, rescind or nullify legislation which creates or perpetuates discrimination,[112] to prohibit it by all appropriate means[113] and to encourage the elimination of barriers between races and discourage anything which tends to racial division).[114] The Committee takes a substantive as opposed to formalistic approach to the obligations of State parties under the Convention. Thus, the mere enactment of a law making racial discrimination an offence cannot be regarded as representing full compliance with the obligations of States under the Convention.[115] Likewise, the obligation not to engage directly in discrimination is not limited to the 'final step' in the implementation of a particular right, but also applies to the 'preliminary decision-making elements directly connected to that implementation'.[116]

---

[106] *Yilmaz-Dogan v The Netherlands*, Communication No 1/1984.

[107] *Yilmaz-Dogan v The Netherlands*, Communication No 1/1984, para 2.2.

[108] *Yilmaz-Dogan v The Netherlands*, Communication No 1/1984, para 9.3.

[109] CERD General Recommendation No 30 (2004), UN Doc CERD/C/64/Misc 11/rev 3: Vandenhole reads this recommendation as implying that apart from the right to participate in elections, to vote and to stand for elections – differentiation between citizens and non-citizens is no longer permissible: Vandenhole, *Non-Discrimination and Equality in the View of the UN Human Rights Bodies* (Intersentia, 2005), p 91.

[110] ICERD, art 2(1)(a).

[111] ICERD, art 2(1)(b).

[112] ICERD, art 2(1)(c).

[113] ICERD, art 2(1)(d).

[114] ICERD, art 2(1)(e). Article 2(1)(e) specifically obliges State parties to encourage where appropriate, multi-racial organisations and movements and other means of eliminating barriers between races.

[115] *LK v The Netherlands*, Communication No 4/1991, para 6.4.

[116] This principle was clearly articulated by the Committee in *LR et al v Slovakia*, Communication No 31/2003, paras 10.7–10.9, which concerned a resolution taken by a municipal council to rescind an earlier resolution to construct low-cost housing for Roma inhabitants of a particular town in the municipality. (contd.../)

[8.28] Article 4 of the ICERD requires States parties to adopt immediate and positive measures to eradicate incitement to racial hatred. This provision has been regarded from the outset by CERD as being 'central to the struggle against racial discrimination'.[117] It includes the duty to declare punishable by law 'dissemination of ideas based on racial superiority or hatred, incitement to racial discrimination', as well as '...the provision of any assistance to racist activities, including the financing thereof';[118] to declare illegal and prohibit racist organisations;[119] and not to permit public authorities or institutions to promote or incite racial discrimination.[120] Article 4 implicitly acknowledges the fact that its terms inevitably compromise other rights (most obviously the right to freedom of expression and association) by providing that the adoption of measures by States parties to comply with art 4 must be done with 'due regard' to the principles embodied in the Universal Declaration of Human Rights (UDHR) and the rights expressly set forth in art 5 of ICERD. In its case law under art 14, the Committee has had to consider whether statements at the heart of particular complaints fall within the various categories of art 4 or are protected by the latter 'due regard' clause.

In *The Jewish Community of Oslo v Norway*,[121] for example, the Committee was confronted with a ruling of the Supreme Court of Norway which had overturned the conviction of a Nazi sympathiser for making anti-Semitic statements at a march near Oslo. As well as making references to Adolf Hitler and Rudolph Hess and calling for a '... Norway built on National Socialism', the speaker had stated that his 'people and country are being plundered and destroyed by Jews'.[122] In overturning his subsequent conviction under the Norwegian Penal Code for racial hatred, a majority of the Supreme Court had concluded that '... penalizing approval of Nazism would involve prohibiting Nazi organisations, which it considered would be incompatible with the right to freedom of speech'.[123] Moreover, it took the view that while the speech contained offensive and derogatory remarks, no actual threats were made.[124] The petitioners had complained to

---

[116] (\...contd) The decision to rescind had apparently been taken on foot of a petition signed by a substantial number of residents of the town which had objected to the council's plan on the basis that it would lead to 'an influx of inadaptable citizens of Gypsy origin'. The Committee held that '...the council resolutions in question, taking initially an important policy and practical step towards realization of the right to housing, followed by its revocation and replacement with a weaker measure', taken together amounted to the impairment of the right to recognition or exercise on an equal basis of the right to housing protected in art 5(e)(iii) of the Convention. Accordingly, the Committee found that the State was in breach of its obligations under art 2(1)(a) not to engage in racial discrimination, as well as its obligation to guarantee the right of everyone to equality before the law in the enjoyment of the right to housing, contrary to art 5(e)(iii) of the Convention.

[117] See generally, CERD General Recommendation No 15 on Article 4, UN Doc A/48/18.

[118] ICERD, art 4(a).

[119] ICERD, art 4(b).

[120] ICERD, art 4(c).

[121] Communication No 30/2003 and see para **8.22**.

[122] *The Jewish Community of Oslo et al v Norway*, Communication No 30/2003, para 2.1.

[123] *The Jewish Community of Oslo et al v Norway*, Communication No 30/2003, para 2.7.

[124] *The Jewish Community of Oslo et al v Norway*, Communication No 30/2003, para 2.7.

CERD under art 14 that the ruling of the Supreme Court left them bereft of protection from dissemination of ideas of racial discrimination and hatred as well as incitement to such acts; and that they were not afforded a remedy against such conduct as required by the Convention.[125] In its decision, the Committee considered whether the statements at issue fell within the categories of impugned speech provided for in art 4 or were protected by the 'due regard' clause. The Committee held emphatically that the statements contained ideas based on racial superiority or hatred and must at least be taken to constitute racial discrimination if not violence.[126] In considering whether they were protected by the 'due regard' clause in art 4, the Committee expressed the view that the principle of freedom of speech '... has been afforded a lower level of protection in cases of racist and hate speech dealt with by other international bodies' and recalled its previously expressed view that the prohibition of such ideas is compatible with the right to freedom of expression and opinion.[127] As the statements in question were of such an 'exceptionally/manifestly offensive character', the Committee held that they were not protected by the 'due regard' clause and that accordingly, the acquittal of the individual in question by the Supreme Court gave rise to a violation of art 4 and the right to a remedy provided for in art 6 of the Convention.[128]

[8.29] Although some complaints have concerned allegations of discrimination in regard to civil and political rights,[129] most concern alleged failures on the part of respondent States to prohibit and eliminate racial discrimination in the enjoyment of economic, social and cultural rights contrary to art 5(e) of the Convention, particularly the rights to work,[130] education[131] and housing.[132] The Committee has stated that the rights provided for in art 5(e) are of a 'programmatic character' and are subject to progressive implementation. It is not within the Committee's mandate to see that such rights are established within a State; but rather to monitor whether, once established, they are implemented on an equal basis.[133] Many complaints also concern the right of access on an equal basis to places or services for use by the general public provided for in art 5(f)[134] – a provision which, like art 5(e), brings into play the responsibility of

---

[125] *The Jewish Community of Oslo et al v Norway*, Communication No 30/2003, para 3.1.
[126] *The Jewish Community of Oslo et al v Norway*, Communication No 30/2003, para 10.4.
[127] *The Jewish Community of Oslo et al v Norway*, Communication No 30/2003, para 10.5. See General Recommendation No 15, para 4.
[128] *The Jewish Community of Oslo et al v Norway*, Communication No 30/2003, para 10.5. In relation to the right to a remedy in ICERD, art 6, see paras **8.30–8.32** below.
[129] See ICERD, art 5(a)–(d). A notable example is *Narrainen v Norway*, Communication No 3/1991, UN Doc A/49, p 128 (1994), which concerned a complaint about alleged discrimination in respect of the right to equal treatment before the tribunals and all other organs administering justice provided for in ICERD, art 5(a).
[130] *Yilmaz-Dogan v The Netherlands*, Communication No 1/1984.
[131] See, for example, *Murat Er v Denmark*, Communication No 40/257.
[132] *LK v The Netherlands*, Communication No 4/1991.
[133] *Enkelaar v France*, Communication No 2/1989, para 6.4.
[134] See, for example, *MB v Denmark*, Communication No 20/2000; *Dragan Durmic v Serbia and Montenegro*, Communication No 29/2003; and *BJ v Denmark*, Communication No 17/1999.

States parties in respect of discriminatory acts by non-State actors.[135] In virtually all of these cases, the specific grounds raised are the failure by the respondent State in question to prohibit and bring to an end such discrimination, contrary to art 2(1)(d) and/or a failure properly to secure effective protection and remedies against it, contrary to art 6.

[8.30] The Committee's case law in respect of art 6 is well-developed, stressing as it does the importance of effective remedies for victims of racial discrimination. It is not necessary for a petitioner to establish a violation of one of the other articles of ICERD in order to be able to rely on art 6. Indeed, CERD has found that violations of art 6 have occurred without making any finding about a violation of one of the substantive articles in a number of cases.[136] In *Dragan Durmic v Serbia and Montenegro*, the Committee explained its reasoning on this point.[137] In its view, the provision in art 6 obliges the States parties to provide an adequate remedy to a person who presents an 'arguable' claim of racial discrimination, by conducting a prompt, thorough and effective investigation into allegations of racial discrimination; as well as providing for the determination of this right through national tribunals and other institutions.[138] Otherwise, the guarantee itself would be void since the failure to carry out a thorough investigation or reach a determination in a given case may deprive the petitioner of an opportunity of establishing whether a substantive violation had in fact taken place.[139] The question of whether an adequate remedy has been provided in each case must be decided on its own facts,[140] but the overarching principle ensures that any attempt on the

---

[135] See Boyle and Baldaccini, 'A Critical Evaluation of International Human Rights Approaches to Racism' in Fredman (ed), *Discrimination and Human Rights* (OUP, 2001), pp 159–160.

[136] See, for example, *Habassi v Denmark*, Communication No 10/1997 and *Kashif Ahmad v Denmark*, Communication No 16/1999.

[137] *Dragan Durmic v Serbia and Montenegro*, Communication No 29/2003.

[138] *Dragan Durmic v Serbia and Montenegro*, Communication No 29/2003, para 9.6.

[139] In *Dragan Durmic v Serbia and Montenegro*, Communication No 29/2003, the failure of the police to carry out any thorough investigation into a complaint that the petitioner had been denied access to a discotheque in Belgrade on racial grounds, the failure of the public prosecutor to reach any conclusion on the matter and the failure of the Court of Serbia and Montenegro to set a date for the consideration of the case six years after the incident meant that the petitioner was unable to establish whether a substantive violation had taken place on the facts: para 9.5. Similar conclusions were reached in *Ahmad v Denmark*, Communication No 16/1999, para 6.4.

[140] See, for example, the rather surprising decision of *Miroslav Lacko v Slovakia*, Communication No 11/1998, para 10, in which the Committee held that the imposition of a criminal sanction on the perpetrator of an act of racial discrimination during the course of the procedure was sufficient for the Committee to absolve the respondent State of liability under art 6, even though the penalty had been imposed a long time after the events in question. Likewise, note the failure of the Committee to make a decision on whether art 6 had been violated in the case of *Anna Koptova v Slovak Republic*, Communication No 13/1998, para 10.2 apparently on the basis that discriminatory resolutions at issue in the case, which had been taken by two town councils in the Slovak Republic aimed at restricting the right of freedom of movement of Roma, were rescinded following the submission of the communication in the case.

part of a State party to the Convention to evade responsibility under it by failing to respond to a claim of discrimination will be futile.[141]

[8.31] As to the *nature* of the remedies that must be available, ICERD is not prescriptive as regards whether a criminal remedy is required in all cases of racial discrimination, save in respect of art 4 which requires criminalisation of hate speech and organisations which promote and incite racial hatred.[142] As Boyle and Baldaccini have noted, most claims of racial discrimination concern the denial of economic and social rights, for which civil law remedies may often be preferable to the institution of criminal proceedings.[143] In the Committee's view, the imposition of a criminal sanction alone on the perpetrator may not always suffice for the purposes of art 6 as regards any act of racial discrimination.[144] In *BJ v Denmark,* the Committee highlighted the fact that:

> 'Being refused access to a place of service intended for the use of the general public solely on the ground of a person's national or ethnic background is a humiliating experience which…may merit economic compensation and cannot always be adequately repaired or satisfied by merely imposing a criminal sanction on the perpetrator'.[145]

Thus, regardless of the particular act of racial discrimination at issue, the right of a victim to seek just and adequate reparation for any damage suffered must be respected in every case, '….including those cases where no bodily harm has been inflicted but where the victim has suffered humiliation, defamation or other attack against his/her reputation and self-esteem'.[146]

[8.32] Where criminal remedies are at issue, the Committee takes the view that the Convention imposes particular requirements on prosecutors in making decisions whether to prosecute alleged perpetrators of racial discrimination. In the early case of *Yilmaz-Dogan v The Netherlands,* the Committee acknowledged that the operation of the 'expediency principle' in certain jurisdictions (whereby an element of discretion is

---

[141] In some cases, the failure to conduct an effective investigation may not only constitute a violation of ICERD, art 6; CERD has found that it may contribute to a finding that a substantive violation has occurred in respect of ICERD, arts 2(1)(d) and 4. See *Adan v Denmark*, Communication 43/2008, para 7.7.

[142] In *Mohammed Hassan Gelle v Denmark*, Communication No 34/2004, para 7.3, the Committee emphasised that criminalisation requires not only the paper enactment of criminal laws and other legal provisions prohibiting racial discrimination but also the effective implementation of such laws by the competent national tribunals and other State institutions. See also *Ahmed Farah Jama v Denmark*, Communication No 41/2008, para 7.3.

[143] 'Alternative civil justice models may prevent the need to bring cases of discrimination to court and are often more effective than criminal prosecution in combating prejudice, promoting understanding and tolerance, and in protecting victims from retaliation': Boyle and Baldaccini, 'A Critical Evaluation of International Human Rights Approaches to Racism' in Fredman (ed), *Discrimination and Human Rights* (OUP, 2001), p 164.

[144] General Recommendation No 26 on Article 6, UN Doc A/55/18: http://www.unhchr.ch/tbs/doc.nsf/%28Symbol%29/c11647a2f7823d62802568bd0055ac51?Opendocument (last accessed May 2011).

[145] *BJ v Denmark*, Communication No 17/1999, para 6.3.

[146] *BJ v Denmark*, Communication No 17/1999, para 6.2.

vested in decision makers whether to prosecute criminal offences at an early stage of the criminal justice process)[147] is governed by considerations of public policy.[148] Nevertheless, it pointed out that in cases of alleged racial discrimination, the latter principle must be applied in the light of the guarantees laid down in the Convention.[149] In subsequent cases, the Committee has applied this reasoning rigorously, especially in cases involving threats of racial violence. Thus, in *LK v The Netherlands,* the inadequate response of the police and the prosecutorial authorities to an on-the-street incident involving public incitement of racial hatred was found by the Committee to constitute a violation of art 6 of the Convention.[150] In the light of its finding, the Committee recommended that the State party review its policy and procedures concerning the decision to prosecute in cases of alleged racial discrimination in the light of its obligations under ICERD.[151]

Finally, regarding the extent of available remedies, the Committee has concluded that the terms of art 6 do not impose on States parties the duty to institute a mechanism of sequential remedies, up to and including the Supreme Court level, in cases of alleged racial discrimination.[152]

APPRAISAL

[8.33] Article 14 was the first individual complaint mechanism and as such was the blue-print for all the mechanisms that followed.[153] During the drafting of this 'vital measure of implementation', the hope was expressed that if it was accepted by a number of States '… a body of experience would be built up which was bound to create confidence and win over new adherents'.[154] Unfortunately, it would appear that this hope has not substantially materialised. Only 54 of the 174 States parties to ICERD have accepted CERD's competence to receive communications under art 14, a fact which CERD itself recognises has resulted in the individual complaint procedure being

---

[147] See generally, Fionda, *Public Prosecutors and Discretion: A Comparative Study* (OUP, 1995), pp 8–10.
[148] *Yilmaz-Dogan v The Netherlands*, Communication No 1/1984, para 9.4.
[149] *Yilmaz-Dogan v The Netherlands*, Communication No 1/1984, para 9.4.
[150] *LK v The Netherlands*, Communication No 4/1991, para 6.7.
[151] *LK v The Netherlands*, Communication No 4/1991, para 6.8.
[152] *Yilmaz-Dogan v The Netherlands*, Communication No 1/1984, para 9.4. In *Kamal Quereshi v Denmark*, Communication No 27/2002, para 7.5, the Committee raised the possibility that art 6 requires the possibility of judicial review of a decision not to bring a criminal prosecution in a particular case, but did not make a decision on that point on the basis that Danish law already provided for such a possibility.
[153] During the debates on measures of implementation for the Convention in the Third Committee of the General Assembly, one speaker commented that: '…in considering the implementation of the Convention, the Committee was in fact blazing a trail and paving the way for similar measures in instruments of a like nature': Statement of Mr Garcia (representative of the Philippines), UN GA, 1344th Meeting of the Third Committee (16 November 1965), UN Doc A/C3/SR1344, para 30.
[154] Statement of Mr MacDonald (representative of Canada), UN GA, 1357th Meeting of the Third Committee (29 November 1965) UN Doc A/C3/SR1357, para 11.

'underutilized'.[155] This slender participation ratio is reflected in the meagre amount of communications received and processed to date as compared with the other individual complaint procedures currently in operation.[156] Van Boven has speculated that the reason why so few States have agreed to the procedure might be because many of them still consider ICERD to be a foreign policy document;[157] while the reason for so few communications might be attributed to a lack of general knowledge in the public mind of its very existence.[158] Data in respect of States' actual implementation of CERD's views is similarly disconcerting. Of the 11 cases in which the Committee had actually sought a response from States in respect of recommendations made under the complaint procedure, only four were deemed to be 'satisfactory'.[159] While it is important to remember that the petition procedure is but one aspect of the Committee's work under ICERD, clearly the potential for art 14 remains largely untapped. The key to improving this state of affairs may lie in increased publicity campaigns by NGOs and NHRIs about the procedure, as well as by CERD itself.[160] In the meantime, one positive aspect of CERD's modest case load is that petitions are processed relatively quickly under art 14[161] as compared, for example, with the operation of the OP-ICCPR.[162]

---

[155] See the letter of transmittal written by the current chairperson of CERD to the Secretary General of the UN: CERD Annual Report 2010, p 1.

[156] See above, para **8.23**.

[157] There is reason to believe, however, that this attitude may be changing, having regard to the observation made by the International Service for Human Rights that officials representing States parties at the 77th Session of CERD in August 2010 were predominantly from the relevant line ministries, rather than foreign affairs ministries: (2010) 3 Human Rights Monitor Quarterly 12.

[158] Van Boven, 'The Petition System under the International Convention on the Elimination of All Forms of Racial Discrimination: A Sobering Balance Sheet' in Frowein and Wolfrum (eds), *Max Planck Yearbook of United Nations Law* (Kluwer Law International, 2000), pp 284–285. See more recently by the same author, 'The Petition System under ICERD: An Unfulfilled Promise' in Alfredsson et al (eds), *International Human Rights Monitoring Mechanisms* (2nd edn, Martinus Nijhoff, 2009), pp 89–90.

[159] CERD Annual Report 2010, paras 68–71 and see accompanying table. 6 responses were 'ongoing' while the remaining one was simply recorded as 'received'.

[160] Van Boven, 'The Petition System under the International Convention on the Elimination of All Forms of Racial Discrimination: A Sobering Balance Sheet' in Frowein and Wolfrum (eds), *Max Planck Yearbook of United Nations Law* (Kluwer Law International, 2000), pp 285–286. For an example of a practical attempt to raise awareness about the ICERD (including the operation of the reporting and petition procedures), see 'A User's Guide to the International Convention on the Elimination of Racial Discrimination (Joint Committee of the Irish Human Rights Commission and the Northern Ireland Human Rights Commission, 2003: http://www.ihrc.ie/publications/list/a-users-guide-to-the-international-convention-on-t/ (last accessed May 2011) (last accessed May 2011).

[161] See, for example, the relatively speedy disposal of the cases in *Adan v Denmark*, Communication 43/2008 (two years for a decision on admissibility and merits) and *Hermansen et al v Denmark*, Communication No. 44/2009,(18 months for a decision on admissibility): CERD Annual Report 2010, pp 142 and 151 respectively.

[162] See Ch 7, para **7.77**.

Chapter 9

Article 22 of the United Nations Convention against Torture and Other Cruel, Inhuman or Degrading Treatment or Punishment

INTRODUCTION

[9.01] The insertion of an individual complaint procedure into the text of the United Nations Convention against Torture and Other Cruel, Inhuman or Degrading Treatment or Punishment (UNCAT)[1] was relatively non-contentious. In fact, during the drafting of UNCAT, the most divisive issues arising in regard to implementation were two-fold: one concerned proposals to include a mandatory inquiry procedure in the text; and the second concerned the idea of giving its monitoring body, the Committee Against Torture (CAT),[2] an explicit mandate to make 'comments' and 'suggestions' when considering States' reports, as opposed to simply issuing 'general comments'.[3] While there was no precedent for either of these latter proposals in the text of other human rights instruments, the Rubicon had already been crossed in respect of an optional complaint procedure regarding torture since the OP-ICCPR already gave rise to such a possibility given the terms of art 7 of the parent instrument.[4] Thus, debate on the text of what became art 22 of UNCAT was mostly uncontroversial, save for the question of which body should have responsibility for its implementation.[5] In this respect, the original draft text had proposed that this responsibility could be devolved to the Human Rights Committee (CCPR) which could consider such complaints in accordance with the procedure which it already followed under the OP-ICCPR.[6] However, misgivings were soon raised about the 'iniquity' of such a scheme, whereby complaints made against States that had voluntarily assumed obligations under UNCAT could potentially be

---

[1] See Ch 3, paras **3.73–3.77**.
[2] See Ch 3, paras **3.78–3.80**.
[3] This point is clear from a review of the summary record of the 40th session of the Commission on Human Rights at which the output of the open-ended working group of the Commission, which had drafted the draft text of the Convention, was discussed: UN Doc E/CN4/1984/SR33.
[4] This fact was explicitly recognised by the delegate of Spain at the first stage of deliberations on the draft text of art 22: UN Doc E/CN4/1314, para 110.
[5] On the *travaux préparatoires* of art 22, see Nowak and McArthur, *The United Nations Convention Against Torture: A Commentary* (OUP, 2008), pp 723–726.
[6] Nowak and McArthur, *The United Nations Convention Against Torture: A Commentary* (OUP, 2008), pp 723–726.

decided by individuals whose nominating States had not assumed the same obligations.[7] The text was subsequently revised so as to vest authority to consider individual communications in the newly established Committee against Torture.[8] The re-drafted text was ultimately agreed upon as the final wording of art 22 of the Convention.

[9.02] With some slight variation, art 22 is essentially a replica of the text of the complaint procedure in the OP-ICCPR.[9] Thus, it provides for the possibility of States parties to UNCAT making an optional declaration at any time to recognise the competence of the CAT to receive and consider communications 'by or on behalf of individuals subject to its jurisdiction who claim to be a victim of a violation of the provisions of the Convention'.[10] As such, it sits alongside a multiplicity of different complaint procedures (including the OP-ICCPR) which can potentially be invoked to remedy this most grave of human rights violations.[11] The procedure entered into force on 26 June 1987.[12] Less than half of the States parties to the Convention have made declarations under art 22 agreeing to be bound by the complaint procedure.[13]

---

[7] See the contribution made by the delegate of Austria during the discussion of the draft text by the Commission on Human Rights: Commission on Human Rights, 35th session, (19 December 1978) UN Doc E/CN4/1314, para 109. See also Ingelse, *The UN Committee Against Torture: An Assessment* (Kluwer Law International, 2001), p 76.

[8] Commission on Human Rights, 38th Session (31 December 1981): UN Doc E/CN4/1493; Nowak and McArthur, *The United Nations Convention Against Torture: A Commentary* (OUP, 2008), pp 724–725.

[9] Burgers and Danelius affirm that the text is mostly 'borrowed' from the OP-ICCPR: Burgers and Danelius, The United Nations Convention against Torture: A Handbook on the Convention against Torture and Other Cruel, Inhuman, or Degrading Treatment or Punishment, (Martinus Nijhoff, 1988), p 166.

[10] Thus, pursuant to UNCAT, art 22(1), States parties must opt-in to the procedure. Pursuant to art 22(8), they can withdraw declarations made under art 22(1) at any time by notifying the United Nations Secretary General. Such notification shall take effect the day after it has been made. Any such withdrawal shall not, however, prejudice CAT's consideration of any complaint which has already been transmitted to it under that article. See also CAT's Rules of Procedure, r 96(2): UN Doc CAT/C/3/Rev5 (21 February 2011). In contrast to the experience under the OP-ICCPR (which has been denounced by Jamaica, Trinidad and Tobago and Guyana respectively), only one State (Ukraine) has made use of this facility under UNCAT.

[11] In addition to the OP-ICCPR, for example, ECHR, art 3 can be invoked in regard to individual complaints concerning torture, inhuman and degrading treatment or punishment under that Convention's mandatory complaint procedure (art 34). Individual complaints about torture, cruel, inhuman and degrading treatment or punishment may also be made under the complaint procedure provided for under the American Convention on Human Rights (art 44).

[12] Following the requisite five declarations made by five States parties in accordance with the terms of art 22(8).

[13] 77 out of 147 States parties have made declarations under art 22(1): http://treaties.un.org/Pages/Treaties.aspx?id=4&subid=A&lang=en (last accessed May 2011). This low participation ratio bears out the pessimism expressed by the representative of Bangladesh during the drafting of the Convention as regards the number of States which would be willing to make the necessary declarations under art 22: (contd.../)

PROCEDURE

[9.03] The procedure for processing individual complaints under art 22 is largely imitative of the procedure in OP-ICCPR.[14] It is essentially a confidential procedure which is based on the written submissions of the parties.[15] As with the latter procedure and those of the other treaty bodies, the bare structure provided for in the text of art 22 itself is supplemented by the Committee's Rules of Procedure.[16] Under those rules, communications received under art 22 are officially designated as 'complaints'. A complaint under art 22 should be sent in writing to the petitions unit at the Office of the High Commissioner for Human Rights (OHCHR), where it will be screened prior to registration.[17] As has been noted, there is a certain degree of overlap between the provisions of UNCAT and art 7 of the ICCPR and it will be for the complainant in the first place to specify which procedure he or she wishes to access. In circumstances where the complainant fails to specify which treaty body should be seised of the complaint, the petitions unit will seek clarification from the complainant on this matter.[18] Where clarification is not forthcoming, and in circumstances where the complaint is exclusively concerned with torture or ill-treatment, the CAT shall automatically take responsibility for the complaint.[19] However, where additional elements are raised (such as deprivation of liberty or abuse of the right to a fair trial), a decision will usually be made in favour of referral to the CCPR. At this initial pre-registration phase, the complainant may also be requested to clarify particular issues of relevance to the complaint that may be unclear on the face of the original communication.[20] While time limits may be imposed for the provision of such

---

[13] (\...contd) Commission on Human Rights, 40th Session, Summary of the 33rd Meeting: UN Doc E/CN4/1984/SR33 at para 32. The representative of Amnesty International (Mr Hammarberg), who participated in the debate, also expressed regret regarding the optional nature of the mechanism, which in his view resulted in a danger that CAT '...would be precluded from action when and where the need was most acute': para 50.

[14] Ingelse, *The UN Committee Against Torture: An Assessment* (Kluwer Law International, 2001), pp 176–193; and Vandenhole, *The Procedures Before the UN Human Rights Treaty Bodies: Divergence or Convergence?* (Intersentia, 2004), pp 255–270.

[15] UNCAT, art 22(6) and Rules of Procedure of the Committee Against Torture, r 107(1): UN Doc CAT/C/3/Rev 5 (21 February 2011).

[16] CAT's Rules of Procedure Rules of Procedure of the Committee Against Torture: UN Doc CAT/C/3/Rev 5 (21 February 2011).

[17] Even a vague letter to the CAT will be treated as a complaint for the purposes of art 22: see, for example, *VL v Switzerland*, Communication No 262/2005, para 8.1.

[18] CAT Rules of Procedure, r 103(2).

[19] CAT's Rules of Procedure, r 103(2). See also Ingelse, *The UN Committee Against Torture: An Assessment* (Kluwer Law International, 2001), pp 177–178.

[20] These may include, in particular, the name or address of the complainant, his or her age or occupation; evidence of identity; the name of the respondent State; the object of the complaint; the relevant provisions of the Convention; the facts of the complaint; details of the steps taken to exhaust domestic remedies; and whether the same matter is being examined under another procedure of international investigation or settlement: CAT's Rules of Procedure, r 105(1).

information,[21] there may in practice be several exchanges between the petitions unit and the complainant to clarify matters before the complaint is ready for registration. As a result of this process, time-limits are seldom enforced.[22]

[9.04] In 2002, the CAT decided to establish the position and designate one of its members as Special Rapporteur for New Complaints and Interim Measures.[23] The special rapporteur has a role to play in regard to interim measures of protection (discussed further below); deciding on registration; and drafting recommendations for the Committee's consideration of the admissibility of complaints.[24] Although technically new petitions may be registered by either the secretariat, the Committee or the rapporteur,[25] they are normally registered by the rapporteur acting on the advice of the petitions unit.[26] A complaint will not be registered where it concerns a State that has not made the declaration provided for in art 22(1), where it is anonymous,[27] or where it is not submitted by the alleged victim or by close relatives of the victim on his or behalf, or by a representative with appropriate authorisation.[28] Nowak and McArthur have estimated that less than half of the complaints that are sent to the Committee are registered, which record compares favourably to that of the Human Rights Committee in its consideration of complaints under the OP-ICCPR.[29]

Interim measures

[9.05] Technically, either the Committee, a working group of its members or the special rapporteur for new complaints and interim measures may at any time after the receipt of a complaint, request the respondent State to take such interim measures as may be deemed necessary to avoid irreparable damage to the victim or victims of the alleged violation.[30]

---

[21] CAT's Rules of Procedure, r 105(2).
[22] Nowak and McArthur, *The United Nations Convention Against Torture: A Commentary* (OUP, 2008), p 731.
[23] Annual Report of CAT (2002): UN Doc A/57/44, para 203.
[24] The mandate of the rapporteur is detailed in CAT's Annual Report 2002, Annex VIII: UN Doc A/57/44.
[25] CAT's Rules of Procedure, r 104(1).
[26] Nowak and McArthur, *The United Nations Convention Against Torture: A Commentary* (OUP, 2008), p 731.
[27] CAT's Rules of Procedure, r 104(2). It is interesting to note that the submission of an anonymous complaint (mentioned in UNCAT, art 22(2) as a condition of admissibility) has been inserted into the rules as a bar on registration.
[28] CAT's Rules of Procedure, r 104(2)(c). It is possible that a complaint might survive registration in this respect but later be found to be inadmissible at the admissibility stage: *Faïsal Barakat and Family v Tunisia*, Communication No 14/1994, paras 4.2–4.5.
[29] Nowak and Mc Arthur, *The United Nations Convention Against Torture: A Commentary* (OUP, 2008), p 731.
[30] CAT's Rules of Procedure, r 114(1). On the evolution of the Committee's mandate in respect of interim measures, see Nowak and McArthur, *The United Nations Convention Against Torture: A Commentary* (OUP, 2008), pp 733–737.
[31] A decision to grant interim measures will be made on the basis of information contained in the complainant's submission: r 114(3). (contd.../)

Such a request is normally made, however, by the special rapporteur.[31] A decision to request interim measures, however, does not imply a determination of the admissibility or merits of the complaint.[32] Moreover, a request made by the CAT for interim measures may subsequently be withdrawn at a later stage (usually by a decision of the special rapporteur)[33] in circumstances where the respondent State presents convincing arguments as to why the request should be lifted.[34]

[9.06] Described by Ingelse as 'an important Committee tool',[35] provision to seek interim measures has assumed particular importance in the work of the Committee in relation to complaints regarding breaches of art 3 of the Convention. In its 2008 Annual Report, the Committee specifically noted States' concern about the high volume of requests being made to it in cases alleging breaches of art 3, which were insufficiently supported by the necessary factual elements.[36] Such concern appears to have been reflected, unfortunately, in the decisions taken by certain States in particular cases to ignore requests for interim measures and to deport the individuals concerned to receiving States before the Committee has had an opportunity to assess the merits of the claim. The CAT initially met such negative practices by expressing deep concern at the failure of the State to accede to its request for interim measures.[37] More recently, the CAT has followed the lead of the Human Rights Committee (CCPR) by declaring that failure to abide by a request for interim measures constitutes a breach by the respondent State of its obligations in respect of art 22 of the Convention.[38] Most requests for measures of protection are complied with by respondent States.[39]

---

[31] (\...contd) See also the working methods and the formal and substantive criteria applied by the rapporteur in granting or rejecting requests for interim measures outlined in the CAT's Annual Report (2010): UN Doc A/65/44, paras 93–96.

[32] CAT's Rules of Procedure, r 114(2).

[33] Although the Rules of Procedure provide that decisions on withdrawal may be made by the rapporteur, a working group of the Committee or the plenary Committee, in practice this function is fulfilled by the special rapporteur. Note the misgivings of Committee member, Mr Mariño Menéndez, on the advisability of assigning such an important power to the rapporteur, acting alone: UN Doc CAT/C/SR527, para 25.

[34] CAT's Rules of Procedure, r 114(7) and (8).

[35] Ingelse, *The UN Committee Against Torture: An Assessment* (Kluwer Law International, 2001), p 179.

[36] UN Doc A/63/44, para 80.

[37] See, for example, *TPS v Canada*, Communication No 99/1997, para 15.6.

[38] See, for example, *Elif Pelit v Azerbaijan*, Communication No 281/2005, para 10.2. See the forthright views expressed by CAT on this issue in the later case of *Adel Tebourski v France*, Communication No 300/2006, paras 8.2–9. Note that in *Nadeeem Ahmed Dar v Norway*, Communication No 249/2004, para 16.4. CAT took the view that the respondent State had remedied its breach of art 22 in regard to a request for interim measures by facilitating the safe return of the complainant and offering him a residence permit for three years prior to the Committee's decision on the merits

[39] Nowak and McArthur, *The United Nations Convention Against Torture: A Commentary* (OUP, 2008), p 737.

Consideration of Admissibility and the Merits

[9.07] Once registered, a member of the petitions unit will prepare a brief summary of the complaint and circulate it to all members of the Committee.[40] The material submitted by the complainant will be sent to the respondent State with a request for a written reply to be submitted within six months.[41] Such reply will normally be sought in relation to compliance with the admissibility of the complaint and the merits, though exceptionally a written reply may be requested on admissibility alone.[42] If the request relates to admissibility and the merits, the State party may reply in writing within two months for the complaint to be rejected as inadmissible, setting out the grounds for inadmissibility.[43] The Committee or the special rapporteur may or may not agree to consider admissibility separately from the merits.[44] If a decision is taken on admissibility separately, the Committee will fix the deadline for submissions on the merits on a case-by-case basis.[45] In either eventuality, the State and the complainant may be requested to supply additional information, clarifications or observations on admissibility or merits to assist the Committee in its consideration of the complaint,[46] subject to specific time limits.[47] If such time limits are ignored, the Committee may proceed to consider the admissibility and/or the merits of the complaint in the light of the available information.[48] Both the State party and the complainant will be given an opportunity to comment on submissions received by the other party, which must again be forwarded within a specific time-frame.[49]

[9.08] The CAT's Rules of Procedure make reference to the possibility of the rapporteur, the Committee itself or a working group of the Committee having authority to take action in respect of art 22 at various stages of the procedure. In this respect, it should be noted that the Committee had previously established a pre-sessional working group of three to five members in 2002 to assist it in its work in respect of art 22 complaints,[50] but

---

[40] CAT's Rules of Procedure, r 106.
[41] UNCAT, art 22(3) and CAT's Rules of Procedure, r 115(1). Note that pursuant to r 115(8), a complaint may not be declared admissible unless the respondent State has received its text and has been given an opportunity to furnish information or observations as provided in para 1.
[42] CAT's Rules of Procedure, r 115(2). Note that pursuant to r 118(3), the Committee shall not decide on the merits of any complaint unless it has first considered the applicability of all of the admissibility grounds in UNCAT, art 22.
[43] CAT's Rules of Procedure, r 115(3).
[44] CAT's Rules of Procedure, r 115(3) and see also r 117(1)–(3).
[45] CAT's Rules of Procedure, r 115(4).
[46] CAT's Rules of Procedure, r 115(5).
[47] CAT's Rules of Procedure, r 115(6).
[48] CAT's Rules of Procedure, r 115(7). See, for example, *EJVM v Sweden*, Communication No 213/2002, para 7.2, in which the Committee declined to consider submissions made by the complainant after the end of the relevant deadline.
[49] CAT's Rules of Procedure, r 115(10).
[50] Annual Report of CAT (2002): UN Doc A/57/44, para 203. Authority to establish a working group is maintained in CAT's Rules of Procedure, r 112.

this working group has not been convened since 2005.[51] Thus, while the possibility always remains of a working group taking decisions on admissibility[52] and making recommendations on the merits,[53] at the present time such decisions are made by the plenary Committee. The CAT makes its decision on admissibility by a simple majority vote.[54] Decisions of inadmissibility are normally final, though provision is made in the rules for the CAT to review such decisions at a later date upon request from a member of the Committee or a written request by or on behalf of the individual concerned.[55] This occurs most typically in circumstances where the CAT decides that the complainant has failed to exhaust domestic remedies in accordance with the requirement in art 22(5)(b). Indeed, it is the CAT's usual practice now when declaring a case inadmissible on this ground to include a statement to the effect that its decision may be reviewed at a later stage at the request of the alleged victim;[56] and it has in fact reconsidered and deemed admissible cases found previously inadmissible for non-exhaustion of domestic remedies.[57] Provision is also made in the rules for the possibility of the CAT revoking its decision on admissibility in the light of the information or statements submitted by the respondent State, provided that the complainant has first been given an opportunity to respond.[58]

[9.09] As regards the final decision on the merits, in cases in which the Committee has decided to consider questions of admissibility and the merits at the same session, or in which a decision on the admissibility has already been taken and the parties have made their submissions on the merits, the Committee shall consider the complaint in the light of all of the information available to it.[59] In addition to the submissions of the parties, this may include information obtained from United Nations bodies, specialised agencies or other sources that may assist in the consideration of the complaint.[60] Where the State fails to provide additional information or clarifications, the practice of the CAT is similar to that of the CCPR whereby it will give 'due weight' to the complainant's allegations.[61] The Rules of Procedure allow for the possibility of quasi-oral hearings whereby the complainant and the State party concerned may be invited to be present at closed meetings of the Committee in order to provide further clarifications or to answer

---

[51] Nowak and McArthur, *The United Nations Convention Against Torture: A Commentary* (OUP, 2008), p 729.
[52] CAT's Rules of Procedure, r 111(2).
[53] CAT's Rules of Procedure, r 118(1).
[54] CAT's Rules of Procedure, r 111(1). In the event of a working group being established in the future to assist the Committee in its work under art 22, the working group would only be able to declare a complaint to be inadmissible by a unanimous vote or admissible by a majority vote: r 111(2).
[55] CAT's Rules of Procedure, r 116(2).
[56] See, for example, *ZT v Norway*, Communication No 127/1999, para 8(b).
[57] See, for example, *Henri Unai Parot v Spain*, Communication No 6/1990, paras 3.1–3.2.
[58] CAT's Rules of Procedure, r 117(5).
[59] CAT's Rules of Procedure, r 118 (1).
[60] CAT's Rules of Procedure, r 118(2).
[61] *Dragan Dimitrijevic v Serbia and Montenegro*, Communication No 207/2002, para 5.3.

questions on the merits of the complaint.[62] In practice, however, this option has never been exercised by the CAT to date.

[9.10] The CAT seeks to make its 'decisions'[63] on the merits by consensus, though provision is made for the possibility of members appending their individual opinions separately.[64] The Committee's decisions on the merits may also contain specific recommendations to States to remedy an identified breach of the Convention.[65] The final paragraph of each decision will then invite the State party to inform it of the action which it has taken to comply with the decision,[66] usually within a period of 90 days.

[9.11] As with all UN treaty complaint procedures, the legal status of the CAT's decisions on the merits raises interesting issues of interpretation. Despite the Committee's insistence that its findings on the merits be referred to as 'decisions', art 22 of the Convention itself directs the Committee to 'consider communications'[67] received from individuals and to 'forward its views' to the State party concerned and the individual.[68] This formulation certainly points to the conclusion that the Committee's decisions are not legally binding on respondent States. However, many commentators argue that such a blunt conclusion is not justified from the text and that, in fact, a more nuanced position is warranted from a purposive interpretation of the Convention as a whole.[69] Ingelse, for example, maintains that the fact that the CAT has authority to take decisions under art 22, together with the legal duty assumed on ratification to observe the obligations in the Convention, leads to the conclusion that a respondent State cannot simply ignore the views of the Committee when it has established a breach of the Convention under the procedure in respect of that State.[70] He argues further that the obligation in art 14 on States to grant a remedy to victims of torture provides a further basis for concluding that the decisions of the Committee are binding, when the Committee determines that a person within the respondent State's jurisdiction is a victim

---

[62] CAT's Rules of Procedure, r 117(4).
[63] CAT's Rules of Procedure, r 118(4) specifies that the Committee's findings on the merits shall be known as 'decisions'.
[64] CAT's Rules of Procedure, r 119. This happens extremely rarely.
[65] This may include the payment of compensation (where breaches of art 1, 14 or 16 are at issue) or to conduct an investigation, where arts 12 and/or 13 have been breached: see, for example, *Saadi Ali v Tunisia*, Communication No 291/2006, para 17 and *Besim Osmani v Republic of Serbia*, Communication No 261/2005, paras 10.8 and 12. Even in cases in which no breach has been identified (eg, where the complaint is deemed to be inadmissible), the Committee may express concern about a particular situation and make recommendations accordingly. See, for example, *OR, MM and M S v Argentina*, Communication Nos 1/1988, 2/1988 and 3/1988, paras 9 and 10.
[66] CAT's Rules of Procedure, r 118(5).
[67] UNCAT, art 22(4).
[68] UNCAT, art 22(7).
[69] Nowak and McArthur, *The United Nations Convention Against Torture: A Commentary* (OUP, 2008), pp 777–778.
[70] Ingelse, *The UN Committee Against Torture: An Assessment* (Kluwer Law International, 2001), p 196.

of a violation.[71] Thus far, the Committee has not taken a robust stance on this issue, comparable to that taken by the Human Rights Committee in regard to its views under the OP-ICCPR.[72] It has, however, moved to put in place a formalised follow-up procedure which infuses the decisions with what Nowak and McArthur have described as 'quasi-binding'[73] authority.

[9.12] Thus, in 2002, the CAT created the role of rapporteur for follow-up on decisions on complaints submitted under art 22.[74] The mandate of the rapporteur consists, *inter alia*, of liaising with the respondent State about measures taken to comply with the CAT's decisions on the merits and making recommendations to the plenary Committee regarding appropriate action in the event of non-implementation. [75] He or she must also prepare reports to the Committee on his or her activities.[76] The role of the rapporteur is further widely framed in the Committee's Rules of Procedure, whereby he or she is given authority 'to make such contacts and take such actions as appropriate for the due performance of the follow-up mandate and report accordingly to the Committee'.[77] He or she may make such recommendations for further action 'as may be necessary for follow-up';[78] 'regularly report to the Committee on follow-up activities';[79] and with the approval of the Committee 'engage in necessary visits to the State party concerned'.[80] The Committee includes the texts of its final decisions in its annual report,[81] together with detailed information on its follow-up activities.[82] In this respect, the Committee's follow-up activity exerts further pressure on the States parties to comply with its decisions.

ADMISSIBILITY

[9.13] The admissibility requirements for individual complaints under art 22 are to all intents and purposes identical to those provided for in the OP-ICCPR. Certain textual

---

[71] Ingelse, *The UN Committee Against Torture: An Assessment* (Kluwer Law International, 2001), p 196.
[72] See Ch 7, para **7.15**.
[73] Nowak and McArthur, *The United Nations Convention Against Torture: A Commentary* (OUP, 2008), p 777.
[74] CAT Annual Report (2002): UN Doc A/57/44, para 203. See also CAT's Rules of Procedure, r 120(1), enabling the CAT to designate one or more rapporteur(s) for follow-up on decisions adopted under art 22 of the Convention, for the purpose of ascertaining the measures taken by State parties to give effect to the Committee's findings.
[75] CAT Annual Report (2002), Annex IX.
[76] CAT Annual Report (2002), Annex IX.
[77] CAT's Rules of Procedure, r 120(2).
[78] CAT's Rules of Procedure, r 120(2).
[79] CAT's Rules of Procedure, r 120(3).
[80] CAT's Rules of Procedure, r 120(4).
[81] CAT's Rules of Procedure, r 121(2). It may also decide to include summaries of the complaints examined and if it considers appropriate, the texts of the explanations and statements of the States parties concerned and the Committee's evaluation thereof: CAT's Rules of Procedure, r 121(1).
[82] CAT's Rules of Procedure, r 121(3).

differences do arise, but as Byrnes has noted, these are of little practical importance.[83] The criteria are set out in the text of art 22, paras (1), (2) and (5) and are reproduced systematically in r 113 of the Rules of Procedure. Interestingly, the CAT revised the latter rule in 2002 so as to make certain of the admissibility requirements part of the registration process.[84] Thus, complaints that are submitted anonymously[85] or those made against States that have not entered a declaration accepting the procedure are filtered out at the registration phase of the procedure. Rule 113 also reflects further developments in the CAT's case law whereby it has expanded the bare text of the admissibility criteria in art 22 to include a time-limit in regard to the submission of complaints and a bar on complaints that are 'manifestly unfounded'. Each of these latter issues is considered further below.

Incompatible communications

[9.14] Article 22(2) provides that the CAT shall consider inadmissible any communication that is 'incompatible' with the provisions of the Convention.[86] As we have seen, a complaint may be incompatible for a variety of reasons, including the identity of the alleged victim or respondent State (*ratione personae*), on temporal grounds (*ratione temporis*), territorial grounds (*ratione loci*) and by reason of its subject matter (*ratione materiae*).[87]

Incompatibility ratione personae

[9.15] Article 22(1) stipulates that complaints can only be considered '*from or on behalf of individuals* subject to its jurisdiction who claim to be *victims* of a violation by that State party of the provisions of the Convention'. In common with the acquis of the other UN treaty bodies, a complainant must be able to demonstrate that he or she is personally affected by an alleged violation in order to have the necessary *locus standi* to make the complaint. This issue was central to the decision of the Committee in *Roitman Rosenmann v Spain* in which the author claimed to have been subjected to torture in Chile following the *coup d'état* in that State spear-headed by General Augusto

---

[83] Byrnes 'The Committee Against Torture' in Alston, *The United Nations and Human Rights: A Critical Appraisal* (OUP, 1992), p 536. Thus, for example, whereas the OP-ICCPR only provides for submission of a complaint by the alleged victim, art 22(1) allows for communications to be submitted 'by or on behalf' of an individual. Likewise, the Protocol provides only that domestic remedies must be exhausted, unless their application is 'unreasonably prolonged', whereas art 22(5)(b) contains a further exception in the case of remedies that are unlikely to bring 'effective relief'. As noted in Ch 7, however, the practice of the CCPR already covers these deficiencies in the text of the OP such as to make the textual variations inconsequential: Ch 7, paras **7.25** and **7.39**.

[84] Vandenhole, *The Procedures before the UN Human Rights Treaty Bodies* (Intersentia, 2004), p 259.

[85] UNCAT, art 22(2). Note that the important criterion here is simply that the Committee should know the complainant's identity. A complainant's identity may be kept confidential from the public at large in the publication of the Committee's decisions.

[86] See also CAT's Rules of Procedure, r 113(c).

[87] See generally in regard to the OP-ICCPR, Ch 7, paras **7.20–7.33**.

Pinochet.[88] The author complained about several alleged breaches of UNCAT by Spain by reason of its failure to follow-up and ensure the extradition of General Pinochet from the United Kingdom to its jurisdiction to face charges relating to torture. While the author had been a witness in domestic proceedings that had led to a request by Spain for the extradition of General Pinochet, he had not been involved as a party to those proceedings. This factor was a crucial one for the CAT in deciding that the complainant had failed to demonstrate that he was a victim of the alleged violation by *Spain* of the claimed obligation under the Convention to procure General Pinochet's extradition. The fact that he had not been a party to the proceedings meant that even if General Pinochet had been extradited, the complainant's situation would not have been materially altered (at least without further legal action on his part).[89]

[9.16] As with the OP-ICCPR, the text does not allude to the possibility of complaints being submitted by NGOs or 'groups of individuals', as is the case, for example under art 14(1) of ICERD. While it does not appear to be possible, therefore, for NGOs or other legal entities to submit complaints under art 22(1), a group of individuals can do so in practice, provided that each member of the group can be identified and can be shown to satisfy the victim requirement.[90] However, the text in turn deviates slightly from that of the OP-ICCPR by specifically providing for the possibility of complaints being made *on behalf of* victims.[91] In this regard, r 113(a) of the Rules of Procedure stipulates that in order to be admissible, such complaints must be submitted by relatives or designated representatives, or by others on behalf of the individual when it appears that the victim is unable personally to submit the complaint and when appropriate authorisation is submitted to the Committee. The reference to 'others' includes any person or organisation.[92] While the CAT has not formally specified what will suffice as proof of authorisation,[93] a written statement[94] or letter[95] from the alleged victim would appear to be sufficient in this regard. The requirement to show express authorisation is, however, a strict one with exemption only allowed where it is impossible in the circumstances. This point was spelt out in *PK et al v Spain*[96] in which the author (a

---

[88] *Roitman Rosenmann v Spain*, Communication No 176/2000.
[89] *Roitman Rosenmann v Spain*, Communication No 176/2000, para 6.4.
[90] Nowak and McArthur, *The United Nations Convention Against Torture: A Commentary* (OUP, 2008), p 744.
[91] However, note that the absence of explicit wording to this effect has been rectified by the practice of the CCPR in admitting complaints submitted on behalf of complainants under the OP-ICCPR procedure, subject to particular requirements: Ch 7, para **7.25**.
[92] See, for example, in *Mafhoud Brada v France*, Communication No 195/2002, para 7.2, the Committee considered that this admissibility condition was satisfied in respect of a claim submitted by an NGO on behalf of the complainant.
[93] As Nowak and McArthur point out, the complainant in *BM'B v Tunisia*, Communication No 14/1994 failed to provide sufficient proof, but there is no elucidation in the decision as to what constitutes 'sufficient proof': *The United Nations Convention Against Torture: A Commentary* (OUP, 2008), p 745.
[94] *Mafhoud Brada v France*, Communication No 195/2002, para 7.2.
[95] *Parot v Spain*, Communication No 6/1990, para 2.8.
[96] *PK et al v Spain*, Communication No 323/2007.

member of a Spanish NGO) had complained about the alleged torture and proposed expulsion by Spain of 23 Asian immigrants. At the time that the complaint was submitted, the alleged victims were in detention in the port of Nouadhibou, Mauritania, having been rescued from a cargo ship in international waters by a Spanish vessel. The author argued that they were unable to submit the complaint themselves because they were being detained, apparently without access to a lawyer and with no possibility of contacting their families.[97] When the immigrants were subsequently moved to Melilla in Spain, the author argued that he lacked the necessary financial resources to travel to interview them.[98] In assessing the question of admissibility on this ground, the CAT took note of the fact that the alleged victims had been interviewed by a number of relief agencies and had authorised domestic proceedings to be taken on their behalf by another Spanish NGO.[99] It could not, therefore, conclude that it would not have been possible *at any time* for the author to reach the alleged victims in order to obtain their consent to be represented before the Committee. Moreover, it took the view that the claimed lack of resources did not exempt the author from obtaining the consent of the alleged victims to act on their behalf.[100] It is possible to deduce from this decision that the only conceivable exception that might be entertained by the Committee from the requirement to submit tangible proof of authorisation might be in circumstances where an alleged victim has either disappeared or is proven to be detained incommunicado.

[9.17] Complaints may be deemed inadmissible *ratione personae* where the complainant is not 'subject' to the jurisdiction of the respondent State. The question of whether a potential victim is 'subject' to the jurisdiction of the respondent State appears to have led to some variation in the case law. Where a complaint against a respondent State concerns art 3 of UNCAT in circumstances where the complainant is clearly *legally present* in another State at the time of the CAT's consideration of the case, it seems that the complaint will be deemed inadmissible. In *HWA v Switzerland*,[101] the author had complained about a potential violation of art 3 of UNCAT by reason of the refusal by the Swiss authorities to grant him asylum. Having lodged his complaint, he subsequently moved to Ireland where he had since requested asylum and had been granted a residence permit. The Committee held that since he was 'legally present' in another State, art 3 of the Convention no longer applied since, by inference, the author was no longer 'subject to the jurisdiction' of Switzerland.[102] The decision marks a departure from the more benign approach taken by the CAT in the earlier case of *EA v Switzerland*,[103] where the fact that the author of a similar complaint had left the jurisdiction was not regarded as a bar to admissibility. At the time of the Committee's consideration of his case, the complainant was believed to be residing with relatives in

---

[97] He also noted that most of them had a 'low cultural level' and did not know their rights. *PK et al v Spain*, Communication No 323/2007, para 2.10.
[98] *PK et al v Spain*, Communication No 323/2007, para 7.3.
[99] *PK et al v Spain*, Communication No 323/2007, para 8.3.
[100] *PK et al v Spain*, Communication No 323/2007, para 8.3.
[101] *HWA v Switzerland*, Communication No 48/1996.
[102] *HWA v Switzerland*, Communication No 48/1996, para 4.3, UN Doc CAT/C/20/D/048/1996.
[103] *EA v Switzerland*, Communication No 28/1995.

Germany, although his status in the latter country is not mentioned in the decision. The CAT reasoned that since he had been within the jurisdiction of the respondent State at the time of the submission of the communication, and the complaint was properly registered, it did not need to examine the reasons why he had subsequently left or to consider his absence as a ground of inadmissibility.[104] It is possible that the CAT would still adopt this approach in cases where it is not possible to establish clearly that the complainant is legally present in another State as was undoubtedly the case in *HWA*.

[9.18] In *Suleymayne Guengueng et al v Senegal*, the respondent State sought to argue that the complainants were not 'subject' to its jurisdiction.[105] The complaint concerned the failure of Senegal to take appropriate measures to establish universal jurisdiction over offences of torture committed by the former President of Chad, Hissène Habré, in violation of art 5(2); or to prosecute or extradite him in conformity with art 7. Habré had been resident in Senegal since 1990. Proceedings brought by the authors in Senegal to have him tried as an accomplice to torture had been unsuccessful and the authorities in Senegal had so far refused to comply with an extradition request from Belgium to facilitate his prosecution in that State. Senegal contested the admissibility of the claim on the basis that the torture referred to by the complainants could be presumed to have occurred in Chad, by a Chadian, as a result of which the complainants were not 'subject to the jurisdiction of the State party' within the meaning of art 22(1) of the Convention.[106] The Committee clearly recognised that this argument was based on a misconstruction of the substance of the claim. Accordingly, it held that in order to establish whether a complainant is effectively subject to the jurisdiction of the State party against which the complaint has been made within the meaning of art 22, it must take into account a variety of factors that are not confined to the author's nationality. The alleged violations in this case concerned the refusal of the respondent State to prosecute Habré in *its* jurisdiction in compliance with its obligations under arts 5(2) and 7 of UNCAT. Bearing in mind that the authors had been the plaintiffs in the proceedings against Habré and had, as such, accepted Senegalese jurisdiction for that purpose, the Committee found that the complaint was not inadmissible on the grounds claimed.

Incompatibility ratione temporis

[9.19] The CAT has had very little opportunity to consider the question of incompatibility *ratione temporis*. In general terms, it is clear that complaints may only be made about acts or facts which took place after a declaration has been made under art 22(1).[107] Thus, it is not surprising that in the case of *OR, MM and MS v Argentina*,[108] the CAT ruled that a complaint about the application of amnesty laws which pre-dated Argentina's ratification of the UNCAT itself was inadmissible *ratione temporis*.[109] It

---

[104] *EA v Switzerland*, Communication No 28/1995, para 5.2.
[105] *Suleymayne Guengueng et al v Senegal*, Communication No 181/2001.
[106] *Suleymayne Guengueng et al v Senegal*, Communication No 181/2001, para 4.
[107] Vandenhole, *The Procedures Before the UN Human Rights Treaty Bodies* (Intersentia, 2004), p 260.
[108] *OR, MM and MS v Argentina*, Communication Nos 1/1988, 2/1988 and 3/1988.
[109] *OR, MM and MS v Argentina*, Communication Nos 1/1988, 2/1988 and 3/1988, para 7.2. and 8.

went on to hold that there could be no question either of finding a violation post-entry into force of the Convention with respect to the right to a remedy for torture in arts 13 and 14 thereof.[110]

[9.20] The scope of the latter articles only applied to events which had taken place post-ratification, and did not therefore cover the torture complained about in this case which had taken place 10 years previously.[111] The CAT's decision in this case is consistent with the approach taken by the CCPR in similar circumstances and with the general principle of international law that a convention is not applicable to acts or facts that pre-date its entry into force for the State concerned.[112] It is arguable, however, that a more flexible approach could have been taken by deciding that the circumstances constituted a 'continuing situation', capable of being considered on the merits under arts 13 and 14.[113]

[9.21] The concept of 'continuing violation', as has been noted, is well embedded in the jurisprudence of the CCPR in applying art 3 of the OP-ICCPR[114] and that of CERD in implementing art 14 of ICERD.[115] It was recognised by CAT in the case of *AA v Azerbaijan*,[116] which concerned numerous allegations of a violation of the UNCAT by a prisoner on death row. The events complained of occurred after Azerbaijan had ratified the Convention, but before it had entered a declaration in respect of art 22.[117] In considering the admissibility of the application, the Committee noted that it can examine alleged violations of the Convention which occurred before the State in question has entered a declaration in respect of art 22, provided that the *effects* of the violations continued after the declaration became effective.[118] Furthermore, it held that '...a continuing violation must be interpreted as an affirmation, after the formulation of the declaration, by act or by clear implication, of the previous violations of the State party'.[119] While the Committee thus endorsed the applicability of the 'continuing effect' concept in this case, it actually deemed the case inadmissible on the basis that the same complaint had already been examined by the European Court of Human Rights.[120] Its reasoning would also seem to indicate that this exception will only apply to acts or facts which post-date ratification of the *Convention*, but which might pre-date a subsequent

---

[110] *OR, MM and MS v Argentina*, Communication Nos 1/1988, 2/1988 and 3/1988, para 7.3.
[111] *OR, MM and MS v Argentina*, Communication Nos 1/1988, 2/1988 and 3/1988, para 7.4.
[112] See Ch 7, para **7.21–7.22**.
[113] While the CAT eschewed this approach, it did express the view that Argentina was 'morally bound to provide a remedy to victims of torture and to their dependants, notwithstanding the fact that the acts of torture occurred before the entry into force of the Convention, under the responsibility of a government which is not the present government of Argentina': *OR, MM and MS v Argentina*, Communication Nos 1/1988, 2/1988 and 3/1988, para 9.
[114] See Ch 7, paras **7.21–7.22**.
[115] See Ch 8, para **8.16**.
[116] *AA v Azerbaijan*, Communication No 247/2004.
[117] *AA v Azerbaijan*, Communication No 247/2004, para 5.1.
[118] *AA v Azerbaijan*, Communication No 247/2004, para 6.4.
[119] *AA v Azerbaijan*, Communication No 247/2004, para 6.4.
[120] *AA v Azerbaijan*, Communication No 247/2004, para 6.6.

declaration in respect of art 22. However, there is nothing to prevent the Committee taking an even more lenient approach on this point, as appears to have been taken by the CCPR in *Lovelace v Canada,* whereby the continuing effects doctrine can be applied to acts or facts which pre-date entry into force of the Convention itself.[121]

Incompatibility ratione loci

[9.22] Article 2(1) of UNCAT creates a clear obligation on the States parties to *prevent* torture 'in any territory under its jurisdiction', while art 22(1) provides that the CAT has competence to deal with complaints from individuals 'within its jurisdiction'. Thus, complaints concerning a failure to comply with the preventative obligation outside its 'jurisdiction' will be inadmissible *ratione loci*. The recent decision of the Committee in *PK et al v Spain* makes clear that the Committee's conception of 'jurisdiction' is not confined to the national territory, but also applies to areas in respect of which it exercises *de facto* control.[122] In that case, the alleged victims had been rescued from a cargo ship, which had capsized in international waters, by a Spanish vessel and brought to the shores of Mauritania. Following an agreement made between the Spanish and Mauritanian governments, the passengers of the cargo vessel were allowed to disembark in the port of Nouadhibou in Mauritania where they were identified by members of the Spanish national police force.[123] They were subsequently detained temporarily in Mauritania before being either voluntarily repatriated or transferred to Spain. The substance of the complaint concerned the conditions of detention of the alleged victims while in Mauritania and their potential expulsion to India in violation of art 3. Although they were being detained in Mauritania, the author maintained that the putative violations were imputable to Spain as the detainees were effectively under the control of the Spanish authorities. This argument was contested by Spain on the basis that the incidents in question had taken place outside its territory and that the action it had taken far exceeded its existing international obligations in the matter of assistance and rescue at sea.

In resolving this issue of admissibility, the Committee recalled its General Comment No 2 that '…the jurisdiction of a State party refers to any territory in which a State exercises, directly or indirectly, in whole or in part, *de facto* or *de jure* control over persons in detention'.[124] Moreover, this interpretation of the concept of jurisdiction is applicable in respect of all provisions of the Convention, including art 22.[125] Taking account of the fact that Spain had exercised control over the alleged victims from the time that the vessel had been rescued, through to the identification and repatriation procedure in Mauritania, the Committee held that it had exercised (through its

---

[121] See Ch 7, para **7.21**.

[122] *PK et al v Spain*, Communication No 323/2007. See para **9.16**. As Nowak and McArthur have noted in *The United Nations Convention Against Torture: A Commentary* (OUP, 2008), pp 750–751, it was already possible to deduce this point of view from the CAT's concluding observations on the periodic report of the USA in 2006: UN Doc CAT/C/USA/CO/2, paras 15–17.

[123] *PK et al v Spain*, Communication No 323/2007, para 2.4.

[124] *PK et al v Spain*, Communication No 323/2007, para 8.2.

[125] *PK et al v Spain*, Communication No 323/2007, para 8.2.

diplomatic agreement with Mauritania) *de facto* control over the alleged victims during their detention in the latter jurisdiction.[126] Accordingly, the complaint was not declared inadmissible *ratione loci* since the alleged victims were clearly shown to be subject to Spanish jurisdiction.

Finally, before leaving this issue, it should be noted that States parties to UNCAT can be held responsible for acts or omissions which produce effects outside the national territory, as exemplified by the prohibition on *refoulement* or extradition to torture in art 3;[127] as well as for failing, within its 'jurisdiction', to respond appropriately to acts of torture committed elsewhere.[128]

Incompatibility ratione materiae

[9.23] A complaint will be deemed inadmissible *ratione materiae* in circumstances where the subject matter of the complaint falls outside the scope of the substantive provisions of the Convention. This may occur in respect of a complaint about the imminent return of a putative victim to a State in which he or she fears ill-treatment as opposed to 'torture' in the receiving State. In this respect, the Committee has held that the scope of the *non-refoulement* obligation in art 3 of the Convention does not extend to situations of ill-treatment envisaged by art 16, rendering any such complaint inadmissible *ratione materiae*.[129] It is striking that the text of art 3 necessarily renders such complaints inadmissible when an equivalent complaint about a breach of art 7 of the ICCPR could be considered on its merits under the OP-ICCPR[130] and by the European Court of Human Rights in respect of art 3 of the ECHR.[131]

[9.24] The complaint in *Roitman Rosenmann v Spain* about the failure of the Spanish authorities to ensure the extradition of General Pinochet from the United Kingdom to Spain was also deemed to be inadmissible *ratione materiae*.[132] In reaching this

---

[126] *PK et al v Spain*, Communication No 323/2007, para 8.2.
[127] See paras **9.34–9.41**.
[128] See UNCAT, arts 5–9. See *Suleymayne Guengueng et al v Senegal*, Communication No 181/2001 and text accompanying para **9.18**.
[129] See, for example, *TM v Sweden*, Communication No 228/2003, para 6.2; and *MV v The Netherlands*, Communication No 201/2002, para 6.2. In the recent case of *LJR v Australia*, Communication No 316/2007, para 6.2, CAT deemed a complaint under UNCAT, art 3 inadmissible *ratione materiae* because it concerned a claimed risk of an unfair trial or the imposition of the death penalty arising from the extradition of the author to the USA for a capital crime. On this issue see further below para **9.44** in respect of the possibility recognised by CAT that the *act* of returning a person to a State could constitute, in certain circumstances a violation of UNCAT art 16.
[130] See Ch 7, para **7.44**.
[131] See generally, O'Boyle, 'Extradition and Expulsion Under the European Convention on Human Rights: Reflections on the Soering Case' in O'Reilly (ed), *Human Rights and Constitutional Law* (Roundhall Press, 1992), p 93; Lillich, 'The Soering Case' 85 AJIL 128; and Egan, 'Human Rights Considerations in Extradition and Expulsion Cases: The European Convention on Human Rights Revisited' (1998) 2 Contemporary Issues in Irish Law and Politics 188.
[132] *Roitman Rosenmann v Spain*, Communication No 176/2000, para 6.7.

conclusion, the CAT held that the obligations invoked by the complainant in arts 8 and 9 of UNCAT do not impose any obligation to seek an extradition, or to insist on its procurement in the event of a refusal.[133] Furthermore, the Committee interpreted the obligation on States parties in art 5(1)(c) to establish its jurisdiction over torture-related offences 'when the victim is a national of that State if that State considers it appropriate' as amounting to a discretionary faculty rather than a mandatory obligation to make, and insist upon, an extradition request.[134] In a rare exercise of the power to append an individual opinion to the Committee's decision,[135] Committee member Guibril Camara expressed the partially dissenting view that the CAT had unnecessarily overstepped its mandate in declaring the complaint inadmissible on this ground. The majority should have limited itself to declaring the complaint inadmissible on other grounds, rather than engaging in a complex jurisdictional argument on the scope of the relevant articles which would have been more appropriately considered at the merits phase had the complaint been deemed admissible.

Abusive and manifestly unfounded communications

[9.25] Article 22(2) of UNCAT requires the CAT to consider inadmissible any communication which it considers to be an abuse of the right of submission.[136] As noted previously, this criterion of admissibility is normally designed to weed out applications that are 'frivolous', 'vexatious' or which constitute 'an otherwise inappropriate usage' of the complaint procedure in question.[137] In *AM v France*, the CAT did not accept the challenge by the respondent State that the complaint was an abuse of the right of petition on the grounds that the documentary evidence produced by the complainant was forged.[138] It reasoned that once the complaint had been submitted to the Committee, it was for the Committee '...to evaluate the good faith of the complainant in his presentation of facts and evidence' and their relevance for the purposes of admissibility.[139] Thus far, the CAT has rarely had occasion to deem a communication inadmissible on this ground.[140] It has refused to deem a number of applications against Tunisia 'abusive' for being allegedly unsubstantiated on the basis that 'any report of

---

[133] *Roitman Rosenmann v Spain*, Communication No 176/2000, para 6.7.
[134] *Roitman Rosenmann v Spain*, Communication No 176/2000, para 6.7.
[135] CAT's Rules of Procedure, r 119.
[136] This requirement is replicated in CAT's Rules of Procedure, r 113(b).
[137] OHCR, '23 FAQ about Treaty Body Complaint Procedures': http://www2.ohchr.org/english/bodies/petitions/individual.htm (last accessed May 2011).
[138] *AM v France*, Communication No 302/2006, para 12.2.
[139] *AM v France*, Communication No 302/2006, para 12.2.
[140] In *PR v Spain*, Communication No 160/2000, the complainant had sought to argue that the fact that his allegations of ill-treatment by the police were dealt with in minor-offence proceedings in the domestic courts, rather than in ordinary criminal proceedings for more serious offences, constituted a violation of UNCAT, arts 12 and 13. The CAT held that the fact that the complainant had himself requested that his complaint be dealt with under the minor-offence procedure, and had not sought to replace that procedure, rendered his attempt to argue this point in proceedings under art 22 an abuse of the right of petition: see paras 6.2–7.

torture was a serious matter and that only through consideration of the merits could it be determined whether or not the allegations were defamatory'.[141]

[9.26] While a complaint may not be considered 'abusive' for being allegedly unsubstantiated, it may still be deemed 'manifestly ill-founded' on that basis. While there is no textual basis for finding an application to be inadmissible on this latter ground, the CAT has explicitly incorporated this criterion into its Rules of Procedure.[142] Thus, complaints have been deemed inadmissible where they lack the 'minimum substantiation' necessary to render them admissible under art 22 of the Convention[143] or where the complaint as formulated does not give rise to any 'arguable'[144] or 'prima facie'[145] claim under UNCAT. This occurs usually in circumstances where the complainant fails to provide any corroborative documentary or other pertinent evidence in support of his or her allegations.[146] Ingelse has argued that this practice is inappropriate on the basis that any inquiry into the '....manifest unfoundedness' of a complaint is part of the consideration of the merits of a complaint.[147] However, the development of this criterion is obviously a purely pragmatic response of the CAT to deal more expeditiously with the submission of unsubstantiated claims in the art 22 procedure.[148] The development is consistent with the practice of the CCPR in implementing the OP-ICCPR and, if managed carefully, is unlikely to produce substantially different results than if the complaint proceeded to a decision on the merits.

Competing International Procedures

[9.27] Article 22(5)(a) of UNCAT precludes the CAT from considering any complaint unless it has first ascertained that the same matter has not been, and is not currently being, examined under another procedure of international investigation or settlement.[149]

---

[141] *Thabti v Tunisia*, Communication No 187/2001, para 7.3. See also *Abdelli v Tunisia*, Communication No 188/2001, para 7.3 and *Ltaief v Tunisia*, Communication No 189/2001, para 7.3. See more recently, *Saadi Ali v Tunisia*, Communication No 291/2006, para 12.4.

[142] CAT's Rules of Procedure, r 113(b).

[143] See, for example, *BSS v Canada*, Communication No 183/2001, para 10.2.

[144] *RS v Denmark*, Communication No 225/2003, para 6.2.

[145] *SA v Sweden*, Communication No 243/2004, para 4.3 and *Chorlango v Sweden*, Communication No 218/2002, paras 5.3–5.4.

[146] Nowak and McArthur have distilled from the case law that complaints are deemed manifestly unfounded either where the applicant has failed to produce any evidence at all, or where evidence of past ill-treatment submitted does not substantiate all of the key allegations made or does not support a claimed fear of future ill-treatment: Nowak and McArthur, *The United Nations Convention Against Torture: A Commentary* (OUP, 2008), pp 748–749.

[147] Ingelse, *The UN Committee Against Torture: An Assessment* (Kluwer Law International, 2001), p 184.

[148] As Ingelse has noted, this criterion evolved in response to a deluge of complaints regarding a breach of art 3: Ingelse, *The UN Committee Against Torture: An Assessment* (Kluwer Law International, 2001), p 184.

[149] See also CAT's Rules of Procedure, r 113(d).

This provision differs from the corresponding provision of the OP-ICCPR[150] in that it applies not only to simultaneous proceedings, but also to proceedings that have *already* been concluded before another international procedure. Again, 'another international procedure' includes individual complaint proceedings before regional human rights bodies implementing the European Convention on Human Rights,[151] and the Inter-American Convention on Human Rights.[152] This ground of inadmissibility does not apply to more broadly based procedures such as those being conducted under the auspices of the Human Rights Council.[153] What constitutes the 'same matter' has been interpreted as relating '…to the same parties, the same facts, and the same substantive rights'.[154]

[9.28] The extent to which a complainant must have engaged with another procedure for art 22(5)(a) to be applied appears to have shifted over the years. In the early days, mere submission to another procedure appears to have been sufficient for the complaint to be deemed inadmissible on this ground.[155] More recently, the CAT has held that a complaint which had been registered by the European Court of Human Rights but not yet transmitted under that procedure to the respondent State could not be considered as 'being' or 'having been' considered under another procedure for the purposes of art 22(5)(a).[156] It remains unclear, but is likely that the CAT would stretch the point of engagement in prospective cases to mean that an 'examination' requires that the case must have at least undergone a certain consideration of its merits in the other

---

[150] UNCAT, art 5(2)(a). In regard to the OP-ICCPR on this issue, see Ch 7, para **7.35–7.37**.

[151] *AG v Sweden*, Communication No 140/1999.

[152] *X v Canada*, Communication No 26/1995.

[153] See above, Ch 2, paras **2.34–2.35**. This is the view expressed by O' Flaherty, *Human Rights and the UN: Practice Before the Treaty Bodies* (2nd edn, Kluwer Law International 2002), pp 142–143 in reference to similar procedures operated by the former United Nations Commission on Human Rights. Certainly, CAT has stated that '…a written opinion or advice given by a regional or international body on a matter of interpretation of international law in relation to a particular case does not imply that the matter has been subject to international investigation or settlement': *VXN and HN v Sweden*, Communication Nos 130/1999 and 131/1999, para 13.1. In that case, an evaluation by the UN High Commissioner for Refugees (UNHCR) as to whether the authors' expulsion to Vietnam would be compatible with the 1951 Refugee Convention did not raise an issue under art 22(5)(a) since '….neither the 1951 Refugee Convention nor the Statute of UNHCR provides for the establishment of a procedure of international investigation or settlement'. See further Burgers and Danelius, *Punishment* (Martinus Nijhoff, 1988), p 167; Nowak and McArthur, *The United Nations Convention Against Torture: A Commentary* (OUP, 2008), p 794.

[154] *AA v Azerbaijan*, Communication No 247/2004, para 6.8 and *ARA v Switzerland*, Communication No 305/2006, para 6.2. In regard to what constitutes the 'same matter', Ingelse takes the view that where '…the laws applicable to the two cases do not agree, then they can no longer be deemed to be the same case which has been or is being investigated under a different procedure of international investigation or settlement': *The UN Committee Against Torture: An Assessment* (Kluwer Law International, 2001), p 185.

[155] *X v Canada*, Communication No 26/1995, para 3.

[156] *Keremedchiev v Bulgaria*, Communication No 257/2004, para 6.1.

international forum, albeit during an evaluation of admissibility, as is the current practice of the CCPR.[157] Certainly, art 22(5)(a) will not be an obstacle to examination of a complaint where a complainant has already withdrawn the same complaint from another international body before it was examined by that body.[158]

[9.29] The CAT has never had occasion to consider whether submission to another treaty body would fall foul of the criterion in art 22(5)(a). As noted above, where a complainant fails to identify a particular complaint procedure in circumstances where the issue in question is amenable to resolution by a number of different treaty bodies, the petitions unit will normally make a legal evaluation as to the most appropriate procedure for resolution. Thus, where the complaint is principally about torture, it should normally be referred to CAT under art 22.[159] Notwithstanding the absence of a specific precedent on this matter, it is certain that an attempt to petition the CAT under art 22 in respect of an allegation of torture already submitted to the CCPR, for example, would be deemed inadmissible under art 22(5)(a).[160] Schmidt and Ingelse have each advocated that the decision on the appropriate forum in cases where competing competence arises should be made by a coordinating group of treaty body members, but this proposal has never been implemented.[161]

Exhaustion of Domestic Remedies

[9.30] Article 22(5)(b) of the UNCAT incorporates the domestic-remedies rule whereby the CAT must first ascertain whether the complainant has exhausted all available domestic remedies before it can consider the complaint on its merits. Under this rule, the complainant is required to exhaust only such remedies as are directly related to the claimed risk of torture under the Convention.[162] The burden rests on the complainant in the first instance to provide information to the Committee on the question of exhaustion.[163] If the State wishes to dispute the complainant's assertions, it must provide evidence refuting same;[164] otherwise, the CAT will generally find that the rule requiring exhaustion has been satisfied.[165] Often, the question of whether a remedy actually exists,

---

[157] On the practice of the CCPR, see Ch 7, para **7.36**. See the views of Nowak and McArthur as regards the correct interpretation of Article 22(5)(a) on this point: *The United Nations Convention Against Torture: A Commentary* (OUP, 2008), p 794–795.

[158] *JAGV v Sweden*, Communication No 215/2002, para 6.1.

[159] Schmidt, 'Individual human rights complaints procedures based on United Nations treaties and the need for reform' (1992) ICLQ 645, p 654.

[160] Nowak and McArthur, *The United Nations Convention Against Torture: A Commentary* (OUP, 2008), p 793–794.

[161] Schmidt, 'Individual human rights complaints procedures based on United Nations treaties and the need for reform' (1992) ICLQ 645, p 654 and Ingelse, *The UN Committee Against Torture: An Assessment* (Kluwer Law International, 2001), p 185.

[162] In respect of art 3 cases, see *AR v Sweden*, Communication No 170/2001, para 7.1.

[163] Nowak and McArthur, *The United Nations Convention Against Torture: A Commentary* (OUP, 2008), p 753.

[164] CAT's Rules of Procedure, r 115(9).

[165] See, for example, *Danilo Dimitrijevic v Serbia and Montenegro*, Communication No 172/2000, para 6.2.

or whether the complainant has exhausted it, is contentious and the CAT is clearly conscious of its own limitations in evaluating national procedural requirements in regard to particular remedies.[166] Thus, it would appear that the CAT will usually be satisfied that the complainant has exhausted all available domestic remedies, except where there has been a 'manifest failure' to comply with the requirements of art 22(5)(b).[167] As with the practice of the CCPR, CAT has recognised that only those remedies which can still substantially affect a decision on the merits must be exhausted for the rule of exhaustion to apply.[168]

[9.31] As with all individual complaint procedures, this procedural rule of admissibility will not apply where the application of the remedies concerned is 'unreasonably prolonged'.[169] This exception was successfully invoked by the complainant in *Halimi-Nedzibi v Austria*, in which the Committee held that the domestic-remedies rule did not preclude consideration on the merits in circumstances where there had been an unreasonable delay of almost three years in the conduct of an investigation into the author's allegation of torture.[170] In *VNIM v Canada*, the CAT waived the requirement of exhaustion, noting that domestic proceedings to stay deportation had already taken over four years. It considered that any further extension would in any case have been unreasonable.[171]

[9.32] Likewise, the rule of exhaustion does not apply if the available remedies are unlikely to bring 'effective relief' to the complainant.[172] To rely on this exception, complainants must provide concrete evidence of such ineffectiveness.[173] Mere doubt as to the effectiveness of a remedy will not suffice.[174] The CAT has been obviously reluctant to apply this exception in numerous cases as is evidenced by its decision in *MA v Canada*.[175] In that case, the Committee stated that it was not within the scope of its

---

[166] In *MAK v Germany*, Communication No 214/2002, para 7.1, it noted that as an international body which supervises States parties' compliance with the Convention, it is simply not in a position to pronounce itself on the specific procedural requirements governing the submission, in that instance, of a complaint to the German Constitutional Court.

[167] *MAK v Germany*, Communication No 214/2002, para 7.2.

[168] This was recently reflected in CAT's decision on admissibility in *Osmani v Republic of Serbia*, Communication No 261/2005, para 7.1 in which it stated that: '...having unsuccessfully exhausted one remedy one should not be required, for the purposes of the (sic) article 22, paragraph 5(b) of the Convention, to exhaust alternative legal avenues that would have been directed essentially to the same end and would in any case not have offered better chances of success'. See also para **9.32**.

[169] UNCAT, art 22(5)(b) and CAT's Rules of Procedure, r 113(e).

[170] *Halimi-Nedzibi v Austria*, Communication No 8/1991, para 6.2.

[171] *VNIM v Canada*, Communication No 119/1998, para 6.2.

[172] UNCAT, art 22(5)(b) and CAT's Rules of Procedure, r 113(e).

[173] See Nowak and McArthur, *The United Nations Convention Against Torture: A Commentary* (OUP, 2008), pp 759–765. See, for example, *LO v Canada*, Communication No 95/1997, para 6.5.

[174] *Jensen v Denmark*, Communication No 202/2002, para 6.3.

[175] *MA v Canada*, Communication No 22/1995.

competence '...to evaluate the prospects of success of domestic remedies, but only whether they are proper remedies for the determination of the author's claims'.[176] As Ingelse has noted, however, the Committee's 'reticence' in this regard is quite inappropriate given that such an evaluation is mandated by the text of the Convention.[177] Occasionally, the exceptions relating to delay and effectiveness are conflated, as occurred in a series of cases against Tunisia in which allegations made by the authors of egregious incidents of torture had been publicly reported to the judicial authorities in the presence of international observers eight years prior to the submission of the complaint.[178] The fact that these reports had apparently failed to provoke an investigation on the part of the respondent State prompted the CAT to decide that it was very unlikely that the complainants would have obtained satisfaction by exhausting domestic remedies.[179] In the context of art 3 cases, it seems that an appeal against deportation that does not have suspensive effect is not an 'effective' domestic remedy,[180] especially where the deportation in question is carried out immediately following notification thereof.[181]

[9.33] While some flexibility has been shown in the application of this rule to particular cases,[182] complainants will generally need to be well prepared to surmount this important procedural hurdle. Ignorance of the availability of particular remedies will not be sufficient to excuse the applicant from exhaustion,[183] though the CAT is obviously

---

[176] *MA v Canada*, Communication No 22/1995, para 4.
[177] Ingelse, *The UN Committee Against Torture: An Assessment* (Kluwer Law International, 2001), p 187.
[178] *Thabti v Tunisia*, Communication No 187/2001, para 7.2; *Abdelli v Tunisia*, Communication No 188/2001, para 7.2 and *Ltaief v Tunisia*, Communication No 189/2001, para 7.2.
[179] *Thabti v Tunisia*, Communication No 187/2001, para 7.2; *Abdelli v Tunisia*, Communication No 188/2001, para 7.2 and *Ltaief v Tunisia*, Communication No 189/2001, para 7.2. See also *Jovica Dimitrov v Serbia and Montenegro*, Communication No 171/2000, para 6.1; *Danilo Dimitrijevic v Serbia and Montenegro*, Communication No 172/2000, para 6.2; and *Dragan Dimitrijevic v Serbia and Montenegro*, Communication No 207/2002, para 5.2. In *Besim Osmani v Republic of Serbia*, Communication No 261/2005, para.7.1, the protracted failure (over the course of some three years) of the authorities to investigate *ex officio* the complainant's allegations of inhuman and degrading treatment and to identify police officers allegedly involved in a breach of art 16, rendered the application of a remedy effectively impossible. See also *Saadi Ali v Tunisia*, Communication No 291/2006, para 12.3.
[180] *Ahmad Dar v Norway*, Communication No 249/2004, paras 6.4–6.5.
[181] *Josu Arkauz Arana v France*, Communication No 63/1997, para 6.1; and *Díaz v France*, Communication No 194/2001, para 6.1.
[182] In *Parot v France*, Communication No 6/1990, para 6.1, for example, CAT did not find the complaint inadmissible on this ground by reason of the complainant's failure to formally comply with the procedural requirements of domestic law in regard to a complaint about torture or ill-treatment. The Committee considered that, even if his attempts to engage available domestic remedies did not comply with the procedural formalities prescribed by domestic law, '... they left no doubt as to Mr. Parot's wish to have the allegations investigated'.
[183] See, for example, *R v France*, Communication No 52/1996, paras 6.3 and 7.2, in which the Committee refused to accept the complainant's ignorance of an available judicial remedy in respect of his deportation as a reason sufficient to waive the application of the domestic remedies rule.

mindful of the need for complainants to have access to information on their availability.[184] Likewise, mental and emotional problems will not absolve a complainant from exhausting domestic remedies.[185] Errors made by a private lawyer cannot be attributed to a State party and hence will not suffice as a reason for failure to exhaust.[186] If a complainant seeks to argue that the cost of a remedy is prohibitive, it appears that he or she will need to adduce precise evidence on the matter of cost (including courts fees and the costs of legal representation), as well as evidence of efforts on his or her part to obtain legal aid for the purposes of exhausting the remedy.[187]

VIEWS[188]

[9.34] The lion's share of complaints submitted under art 22 of the Convention relate to art 3, the text of which provides that:

> (1) No State Party shall expel, return ('refouler') or extradite a person to another State where there are substantial grounds for believing that he would be in danger of being subjected to torture.
>
> (2) For the purposes of determining whether there are such grounds, the competent authorities shall take into account all relevant considerations including, where applicable, the existence in the State concerned of a consistent pattern of gross, flagrant or mass violations of human rights.

This provision is a manifestation of the preventative aspect of UNCAT which is more specifically reflected in the terms of art 2(1).[189] Whereas art 2(1) enjoins the States parties to take measures to prevent acts of torture in any territory under their own jurisdiction,[190] the intention behind art 3 was to create a pro-active obligation on States to prevent torture by refraining from the expulsion of such person to another State in which there might be a danger that he or she would be subjected to torture.[191]

---

[184] In *ZT v Norway*, Communication No 127/1999, the Committee had recommended the respondent State to undertake measures to ensure that asylum-seekers are informed about all domestic remedies available to them, particularly the remedy of judicial review and legal aid for its pursuit (para 7.4), reproduced in Communication 238/2003 at para 4.1.

[185] *AH v Sweden*, Communication No 250/2004, para 7.2.

[186] *RSAN v Canada*, Communication No 284/2006, para 6.4.

[187] *RSAN v Canada*, Communication No 284/2006, para 6.4.

[188] The following is a summary of the main body of views generated by CAT under art 22. For further detailed reading, see the in-depth analysis carried out of the substantive articles of UNCAT by Nowak and McArthur, *The United Nations Convention Against Torture: A Commentary* (OUP, 2008), pp 25–576.

[189] UNCAT, art 16 also requires States to prevent acts of 'cruel, inhuman or degrading treatment or punishment' in any territory under its jurisdiction.

[190] As to the nature of the obligation in art 2, see General Comment No 2, Implementation of article 2 by States Parties: UN Doc CAT/C/GC/2/CRP1/Rev 4 (2007).

[191] 'The idea behind it is that States Parties will not ignore an opportunity to prevent torture taking place elsewhere': Ingelse, *The UN Committee Against Torture: An Assessment* (Kluwer Law International, 2001), p 290.

[9.35] Article 3 is based, 'to some extent'[192] on art 33 of the Convention Relating to the Status of Refugees 1951 (CRSR).[193] It differs from art 33 of the CRSR in a number of important respects. First, whereas art 33 of the CRSR admits of exceptions to the principle of *non-refoulement* in particular circumstances,[194] art 3 of UNCAT is an absolute prohibition which admits of no exceptions in the text.[195] Second, the threshold requirement necessary to qualify for protection under art 33, namely, demonstrating a well-founded fear of 'being persecuted',[196] is not quite so demanding as substantiating a risk of 'torture' as is required by art 3 of UNCAT.[197] And finally, while a claim to protection under art 33 must be based on specified grounds (ie, race, religion, nationality, membership of a particular social group or political opinion), art 3 of UNCAT prohibits *refoulement* where a fear of 'torture', as defined by art 1 of the Convention,[198] is substantiated in a receiving State, regardless of the grounds on which

---

[192] Burgers and Danelius, *The United Nations Convention against Torture: A Handbook on the Convention against Torture and Other Cruel, Inhuman, or Degrading Treatment or Punishment* (Martinus Nijhoff, 1988), p 125.

[193] Adopted on 28 July 1951: General Assembly Resolution 429 (V) of 14 December 1950 and amended by the 1967 Protocol Relating to the Status of Refugees: http://www2.ohchr.org/english/law/refugees.htm (CRSR) (last accessed May 2011). Article 33(1) provides that: 'No Contracting State shall expel or return ('refouler') a refugee in any manner whatsoever to the frontiers of territories where his life or freedom would be threatened on account of his race, religion, nationality, membership of a particular social group or political opinion'.

[194] CRSR, art 33(2) provides that: 'The benefit of the present provision may not, however, be claimed by a refugee whom there are reasonable grounds for regarding as a danger to the security of the country in which he is, or who, having been convicted by a final judgement of a particularly serious crime, constitutes a danger to the community of that country'.

[195] This difference is honoured in the case law of CAT in its interpretation of art 3 in which the Committee has frequently stated that the activities of the complainant cannot be a material consideration when making a determination under UNCAT, art 3. Thus, even refugee claimants who have been excluded from refugee status in the Contracting State on account of their activities may still qualify for protection under UNCAT, art 3: *Gorki Ernesto Tapia Paez v Sweden*, Communication No 39/1996, para 14.5; *MBB v Sweden*, Communication No 104/1998, para 6.4.

[196] The principle of *non-refoulement* in Article 33, applies to persons who satisfy the definition of refugee set forth in art 1A(2) of the CRSR, as amended by its 1967 Protocol, ie, he or she must be a person who '...owing to well-founded fear of being persecuted for reasons of race, religion, nationality, membership of a particular social group or political opinion, is outside the country of his nationality and is unable or, owing to such fear, is unwilling to avail himself of the protection of that country; or who, not having a nationality and being outside the country of his former habitual residence as a result of such events, is unable or, owing to such fear, is unwilling to return to it'.

[197] As to what constitutes 'persecution' for the purposes of refugee status, see Hathaway, *The Law of Refugee Status* (Butterworths, 1991), pp 99–134. For up to date caselaw from a variety of national jurisdictions, see further http://www.refugeecaselaw.org/Home.aspx (last accessed May 2011).

[198] See below, paras **9.42 and 9.45** in regard to in regard to CAT's interpretation of art 1. A fear of prosecution, without more, will not be sufficient to ground a claim under art 3: *PQL v Canada*, Communication No 57/1996, para 10.4; *SSH v Switzerland*, Communication No 254/2004, para 6.8.

such fear is based. In this respect, art 3 of UNCAT was obviously 'inspired' by early case law of the European Commission on Human Rights in its interpretation of art 3 of the ECHR.[199] Whereas the latter article merely stipulates that 'No one shall be subjected to torture, inhuman or degrading treatment or punishment', the Commission and later the European Court of Human Rights has developed its meaning to include a prohibition on extradition or deportation to a State in which there are substantial grounds for believing that a real risk of treatment in violation of art 3 of the ECHR arises.[200] This dynamic interpretation is in turn potentially more expansive than art 3 of the UNCAT since it applies not only to 'torture' but also to 'inhuman and degrading treatment'. The Human Rights Committee, as noted above, has construed the content of art 7 of the ICCPR in a similar way, although its case law on this issue is, as yet, under-developed.[201]

[9.36] Given the sheer volume of complaints that have been made under art 22 of UNCAT in respect of art 3 of UNCAT, it is not surprising that the CAT has greatly refined its interpretation of this provision over the years. In this respect, its case law on art 3 augments the principles first articulated in General Comment No 1 adopted by the Committee in 1997.[202] As noted above, persons who complain about a violation[203] must first satisfy the admissibility criteria including the obligation to establish a 'prima facie'

---

[199] Burgers and Danelius, The United Nations Convention against Torture: A Handbook on the Convention against Torture and Other Cruel, Inhuman, or Degrading Treatment or Punishment, (Martinus Nijhoff, 1988), p 125.

[200] See generally, O'Boyle, 'Extradition and Expulsion Under the European Convention on Human Rights: Reflections on the Soering Case' in O'Reilly (ed), *Human Rights and Constitutional Law* (Roundhall Press, 1992), p 93; Lillich, 'The Soering Case' 85 AJIL 128; and Egan, 'Human Rights Considerations in Extradition and Expulsion Cases: The European Convention on Human Rights Revisited' (1998) 2 Contemporary Issues in Irish Law and Politics 188.

[201] See Ch 7, para **7.44**.

[202] CAT General Comment No 1: Implementation of art 3 of the Convention in the Context of art 22 (Refoulement and communications), UN Doc HRI/GEN/1/Rev 9 (Vol II), pp 374–376.

[203] The obligation in UNCAT, art 3 is necessarily forward-looking in nature as it obliges States not to return persons who can substantiate a risk of torture in the receiving State. Most cases therefore concern a prospective assessment of foreseeable risk, culminating potentially in a decision by CAT that the respondent State must 'refrain' from returning the person in question: see, for example, the first case decided by the Committee, *Mutumbo v Switzerland*, Communication No 13/1993, para 9.7. In cases where the individual has already been returned to the receiving State (sometimes contrary to interim measures requested by CAT), the decision by CAT will be as to whether the actual removal amounts to a breach of UNCAT, art 3: *Cecilia Rosana Núñez Chipana v Venezuela*, Communication No 110/1998, para 7. In *Agiza v Sweden*, Communication No 233/2003, para 13.2, CAT clarified that where removal has already occurred, CAT's assessment is to be made in the light of the information that was known, or ought to have been known, to the respondent State at the time of the removal; and that subsequent events are relevant '…to the assessment of the State party's authorities' knowledge, actual or constructive, at the time of removal'. This position marks an improvement on previous cases in which the assessment of whether a violation of UNCAT, art 3 had taken place was based entirely on the situation of the complainant *post*-return: *TPS v Canada*, Communication No 99/1997, para 15.4.

breach of the Convention.[204] As regards the standard of proof to be met by an complainant whose case proceeds to a review on the merits, the CAT has interpreted the phrase 'substantial grounds' in art 3 as meaning that the risk of torture must be assessed by the State party in question and the Committee itself '...on grounds that go beyond mere theory or suspicion' but which fall short of being 'highly probable'.[205] A complainant must make an arguable case that this standard has been met by providing sufficiently reliable factual evidence of the risk before the burden of proof will shift to the respondent State.[206] In making its decision as to whether the risk has been sufficiently substantiated, the CAT considers itself capable of making a fresh assessment of the facts and circumstances of each case, while at the same time giving considerable weight to the assessments made by the national authorities.[207] Like any supervisory organ involved in assessing asylum/deportation matters, however, it is open to the criticism of being excessively deferential to the national authorities, particularly where issues of credibility are raised.[208] Occasionally, moreover, the reasoning of the CAT is terse on the question of whether the claimed risk of torture has been substantiated, with negative conclusions being reached summarily to the effect that there is not enough evidence to support the claim.[209]

[9.37] The assessment of risk should include an evaluation of whether there exists a consistent pattern of gross, flagrant or mass violations of human rights in the third State as *per* the terms of art 2; and/or an assessment of the circumstances that are personal to the applicant which substantiate the claimed fear of exposure to torture.[210] In other words, the fact that a consistent pattern of gross violations exists in the receiving State will not automatically qualify the complainant for relief under art 3; likewise, the absence of such a pattern will not disqualify him or her. In either case, he or she must adduce evidence of the risk that is specific to him or her.[211]

---

[204] See above, para **9.25**; and CAT General Comment No 1, para.4.

[205] CAT General Comment No 1: Implementation of article 3 of the Convention in the context of article 22: UN Doc A/53/44, Annex IX, para 6.

[206] CAT General Comment No 1: Implementation of article 3 of the Convention in the context of article 22 UN, para 5. See, for example, *MAK v Germany*, Communication No 214/2002, para 13.5; *Chedi Ben Ahmed Karoui v Sweden*, Communication No 185/2001, para 10; and *SPA v Canada*, Communication No 282/2005, para 7.5.

[207] *AR v The Netherlands*, Communication No 203/2002, para 7.6 and *Mustafa Dadar v Canada*, Communication No 258/2004, para 8.8.

[208] See para **9.38**.

[209] See, for example, *SL v Sweden*, Communication No 150/1999, para 6.4 and *MRP v Switzerland*, Communication No 122/1998, para 6.5.

[210] *SL v Sweden*, Communication No 150/1999, para 6.3 and *MRP v Switzerland*, Communication No 122/1998, para 6.5.

[211] This point was first made by CAT in *Mutumbo v Switzerland*, Communication No 13/1993, para 9.3 and has been reiterated on several occasions since then. See, recently, *LJR v Australia*, Communication No 316/2007, para 7.5. This requirement to show a risk of being 'targeted' for 'torture' is questionable in cases where the complainant can show that he or she belongs to a particular group, members of which have been targeted in the midst of a civil war: (contd.../)

[9.38] The types of personal factors taken into account by the CAT include, for example, evidence of previous exposure to torture;[212] and whether the complainant has engaged in activities either within or outside the State concerned that would tend to make him or her vulnerable to the claimed risk of torture if returned.[213] The complainant's credibility is a factor that can tilt the balance in any evaluation of whether the risk of torture has been substantiated. Where the respondent State contests the credibility of any aspect of the complainant's case, the complainant must rebut, with convincing arguments, the State party's assertions.[214] The CAT has stated that complete accuracy is seldom to be expected from victims of torture,[215] especially where it can be demonstrated that the author suffers from PTSD.[216] The crucial issue for the Committee appears to be whether the presentation of facts by the complainant raises significant doubts as to the trustworthiness and general veracity of the claim.[217] Where sufficiently reliable

---

[211] (\...contd) see, for example, *SS and SA v The Netherlands*, Communication No 142/1999, para 6.7. In such cases, it may well be asked why the complainant must show evidence of a heightened risk if it can be shown that the generality of the group of which he or she is a member is subject to such risk. This is a vexed issue in the realm of refugee law generally: see generally, Hathaway, *The Law of Refugee Status* (1991), pp 90–97; Kälin, 'Refugees and Civil War: Only a Matter of Interpretation?' (1991) 3 Intl J Refugee Law 435; and Von Sternberg, 'The Plight of the Non-Combatant in Civil War and the New Criteria for Refugee Status' (1997) 9 Intl J Refugee Law 169.

[212] CAT General Comment No 1, para 8. When assessing past incidents of torture, the Committee takes into consideration whether the incidents in question were recent and whether they have been medically certified: *TA v Sweden*, Communication No 226/2003, para 7.3. It must also consider whether such incidents occurred in circumstances that are relevant to the prevailing political realities: *ACC v Sweden*, Communication No 227/2003, para 8.3 and *Ruben David v Sweden*, Communication No 220/2002, para 8.3. The failure of a complainant to present medical reports of past incidents of torture in national proceedings may provide sufficient grounds for CAT to reject them under the UNCAT, art 22 procedure: *ZK v Sweden*, Communication No 301/2006, para 8.4. However, a delay in submitting a medical report was deemed to be reasonable where the incidents in question involved rape: *VL v Switzerland*, Communication No 262/2005, para 8.8.

[213] See, for example, *Gamal El Rgeig v Switzerland*, Communication No 280/2005, para 7.4. The Committee has specifically recognised that publicity surrounding the making of an asylum claim in a contracting State can heighten the risk of torture in the receiving State: *Sadiq Shek Elmi v Australia*, Communication No 120/1998, para 6.8.

[214] *AM v France*, Communication No 302/2006, para 13.5 and *VL v Switzerland*, Communication No 262/2005, para 8.8.

[215] *Ismail Alan v Switzerland*, Communication No 21/1995, para 11.3.

[216] *Kaveh Yaragh Tala v Sweden*, Communication No 43/1996, para 10.3. The CAT has stated that this principle applies even where the inconsistencies in a complainant's account of events are of a material nature: *Halil Haydin v Sweden*, Communication No 101/1997, para 6.7. In some cases, however, the Committee has deferred to a negative evaluation of credibility by the national authorities, even where medical evidence supported the claim and where the complainant was suffering from PTSD: *MO v Denmark*, Communication No 209/2002, paras 6.4–6.6.

[217] *MO v Denmark*, Communication No 209/2002, paras 6.5–6.6.

information has been adduced, the benefit of the doubt should be given to the complainant.[218]

[9.39] As to the receiving State, the CAT usually takes on board in its assessment whether or not that State is party to UNCAT,[219] but the fact that it is a party is not, of itself, considered sufficient to avert the risk of torture.[220] Likewise, the procurement of diplomatic assurances from the receiving State as to the future treatment of an individual will not suffice to protect against a substantiated risk of torture.[221] In making its substantive assessment as to the risk of ill-treatment in that State, the CAT may have regard to evidence regarding the fate of similarly situated persons,[222] as well as to conditions prevailing there which may give rise to a heightened risk of torture.[223] The

---

[218] See, for example, *Chedi Ben Ahmed Karoui v Sweden*, Communication No 185/2001, para 10. See also the explanation given by former Committee member Bent Srensen that Committee members often have 'a deep knowledge of torture' which enable them to appreciate the reasons behind possible inconsistencies in testimony: Srensen, 'CAT and arts 20 and 22' in Alfredsson et al (eds), *International Human Rights Monitoring Mechanisms* (Leiden, 2009), p 106, citing CAT's decision in *Kisoki v Sweden*, Communication No 41/1996.

[219] In *Mutombu v Switzerland* Communication No 13/1993, para 9.6, the fact that the receiving State (Zaire) was *not* a party to the Convention was a factor which the Committee took into account in deciding in favour of the complainant.

[220] See, for example, *Ismail Alan v Switzerland*, Communication No 21/1995, para 11.5. On this point, compare CAT's decisions in *Attia v Sweden*, Communication No 1999/2002 and *Agiza v Sweden*, Communication No 233/2003. In *Attia's* case, the Committee found that a potential violation of UNCAT, art 3 did not exist in her case, based partly on the fact that the receiving State (Egypt) was party to UNCAT. Just over a year later, it held that there had been a violation of art 3 in her husband, *Agiza's* case, taking account *inter alia* of the fact that '...it was known, or should have been known, to the State party's authorities at the time of the complainant's removal that Egypt resorted to consistent and widespread use of torture against detainees, and that the risk of such treatment was particularly high in the case of detainees held for political and security reasons': para 13.4.

[221] See the landmark case of *Agiza v Sweden*, Communication No 233/2003, para 13.4 in which CAT noted that the assurances offered in that case provided no mechanism for their enforcement. In *Elif Pelit v Azerbaijan*, Communication No 281/2005, para 11, the failure of the respondent State to produce the diplomatic assurances which it relied upon so as to enable CAT to perform its own evaluation; and to detail with sufficient clarity the monitoring which it had undertaken post-expulsion and the steps taken to ensure that it was both in fact, and in the complainant's perception, 'objective, impartial and sufficiently trustworthy' were central factors in finding a violation of UNCAT, art 3. See also the conclusions and recommendations of CAT on the second periodic report of the United States of America: 18 May 2006, UN Doc CAT/C/USA/CO/2, para 16. The *Agiza* case brought to the fore the potential applicability of UNCAT, art 3 in the context of so-called 'extraordinary rendition': see generally, Joseph, 'Rendering Terrorists and the Convention Against Torture' (2005) 5 HRL Rev 339; and Weissbrodt and Bergquist, 'Extraordinary Rendition: A Human Rights Analysis' (2006) 19 Harv Hum Rts J 123.

[222] *Josu Arkauz Arana v France*, Communication No 63/1997, para 11.4.

[223] This may include, for example, evidence of prolonged incommunicado detention: *Josu Arkauz Arana v France*, Communication No 63/1997, para 11.4.

CAT will also consider whether the claimed risk applies to the entire territory of the receiving State (the so-called 'internal flight alternative')[224] and to whether there has been a change of circumstances in that State since the events which are claimed to give rise to a fear of torture.[225] Interestingly, the CAT has given art 3 of UNCAT a dynamic interpretation by taking into account the potential risk of *refoulement* by the receiving State to a third country in which the claimed fear of torture arises. Where such a risk of indirect *refoulement* exists, the contracting State is obliged to refrain from removal.[226] In this respect, therefore, the phrase 'another State' in art 3 of UNCAT refers not only to the State in which the individual concerned is being returned, but also 'any State to which the author may subsequently be expelled, returned or extradited'.[227]

[9.40] As to matters of scope, the CAT has held that the obligations in art 3 explicitly apply in respect of expulsion or return to face 'torture' as opposed to 'cruel, inhuman or degrading treatment or punishment'.[228] Another important issue is whether its terms apply in circumstances where the risk of 'torture' emanates from non-State actors. The text of art 1 exerts a constraining influence on the CAT's approach to this issue since it requires that torture must be 'inflicted by or at the instigation of or with the consent or acquiescence of a public official or other person acting in an official capacity'. This begs the question whether a risk of torture emanating from non-State actors *without* the consent or acquiescence of the State (eg, in circumstances where the State is simply

---

[224] This possibility was first raised indirectly in *Ismail Alan v Switzerland*, Communication No 21/1995, para 11.4, in which CAT's decision that the respondent State was obliged to refrain from forcibly returning the complainant to Turkey was partly based on the fact that it was not likely that a 'safe' area existed anywhere for him in Turkey. In subsequent cases, the fact that the complainant could locate to other parts of the receiving State other than his ordinary place of residence has thwarted the claim in respect of UNCAT, art 3: *BSS v Canada*, Communication No 183/2001, para 11.5; *HMHI v Australia*, Communication No 177/2001, para 6.6; and *SSS v Canada*, Communication No 245/2004, para 8.5. This factor also inhibited the complainant's case in *SS v The Netherlands*, Communication No 191/2001, para 6.4, in which the claimed fear of torture emanated from a non-governmental entity exercising quasi-governmental authority in part of the receiving state (Sri Lanka). The fact that the complainant could be returned to a part of Sri Lanka other than that over which the non-State actor exercised control resulted in a decision by CAT not to consider that aspect of his claim.

[225] CAT General Comment No 1, para 8(d).

[226] *Avedes Hamayak Korban v Sweden*, Communication No 88/1997, para 7. In this case, CAT held that Sweden had an obligation to refrain from forcibly returning the author to Jordan in view of the risk that he would run of being expelled from that country to Iraq where his fear of torture under UNCAT, art 3 was sufficiently substantiated. CAT also took into account in reaching its decision that while Jordan was a party to UNCAT, it had not made a declaration under UNCAT, art 22. This factor meant that the author would not have the possibility of submitting a new communication to CAT if he was threatened with deportation from Jordan to Iraq.

[227] General Comment No 1, para 2. See also *Avedes Hamayak Korban v Sweden*, Communication No 88/1997, para 7.

[228] *MV v The Netherlands*, Communication No 201/2002, para 6.2 and *TM v Sweden*, Communication No 228/2003, para 6.2. See further below, para **9.23** and **9.44**.

unable to protect the complainant) fall within the scope of art 3?[229] The CAT has recognised that a risk of torture which emanates from non-State actors exercising quasi-governmental authority over the territory to which the complainant could be returned could ground a claim under art 3 of UNCAT.[230] Otherwise, the Committee has taken the view that claims arising from a fear which emanates from a non-governmental entity (absent the necessary ingredients of governmental consent or acquiescence) fall outside the scope of art 3.[231] It should be noted that the text of art 7 of the ICCPR contains no such textual delimitation. While the Human Rights Committee has not had the opportunity to consider this issue, one could anticipate that it would be likely to follow the approach of the European Court of Human Rights in finding that a substantial risk of ill-treatment from non-State actors, which the receiving State is unable to avert, falls within the scope of the principle of *non-refoulement* inherent in art 7 of ICCPR.[232]

[9.41] Finally, it should be noted that in a very positive development, the CAT has read a procedural right to an effective remedy into the terms of art 3 of UNCAT. Specifically, such a remedy requires that contracting States must provide '…an opportunity for effective, independent and impartial review' of a decision to expel or remove, once a decision is made, where there is a plausible allegation that art 3 issues arise.[233]

---

[229] Under the CRSR, a person is entitled to refugee status, and hence to the benefit of UNCAT, art 33 where the well-founded fear of persecution emanates from non-State actors in circumstances where the respondent State is 'unable' or unwilling to offer protection: CRSR, art 1A(2). See *Handbook on Procedures and Criteria for Determining Refugee Status under the 1951 Convention and the 1967 Protocol Relating to the Status of Refugees* (UNHCR, 1992), para 65: http://www.unhcr.org/3d58e13b4.html (last accessed May 2011). The failure or absence of State protection from ill-treatment threatened by non-State actors has also been recognised by the European Court of Human Rights as giving rise in principle to a breach of ECHR, art 3: *Ahmed v Austria* (1997) 24 EHRR 278 and *HLR v France* (1998) 26 EHRR 29.

[230] The only case in which CAT has upheld a claim on this basis was in the context of Somalia in *Sadiq Shek Elmi v Australia*, Communication No 120/1998, para 6.5. However, note that in the subsequent decision of *HMHI v Australia*, Communication No 177/2001, para 6.4, CAT held that with the subsequent passage of time since its decision in *Elmi* whereby Somalia currently possessed State authority in the form of a transitional national government, the exceptional circumstances outlined in *Elmi* no longer applied, such that acts of non-State agents now fell outside the scope of UNCAT, art 3.

[231] *GRB v Sweden*, Communication No 83/1997, para 6.5. In *SV v Canada*, Communication No 49/1996, para 9.5, CAT had held that a claimed risk of torture at the hands of the LTTE in Sri Lanka fell outside the scope of UNCAT, art 3. See also *MPS v Australia*, Communication No 138/1999, para 7.4.

[232] Nowak and McArthur, *The United Nations Convention Against Torture: A Commentary* (OUP, 2008), p 195.

[233] *Agiza v Sweden*, Communication No 233/2003, para 13.7. The failure of the Swedish authorities, because of national security concerns, to provide any review of the government's decision to expel the complainant did not meet the procedural obligation. (contd.../)

Interpretation of the Concepts of 'Torture' and 'Cruel, Inhuman and Degrading Treatment or Punishment'

[9.42] Writing soon after the establishment of the CAT in 1987, Byrnes commented that an important part of the prospective work of the Committee would be to give substantive content to the concepts of torture, inhuman or degrading treatment or punishment as they appear in UNCAT.[234] In this respect, it should be recalled that the concept of 'torture' appears in art 1 of the Convention, while art 16 obliges the States parties to prevent acts of 'cruel, inhuman or degrading treatment or punishment'. Unlike the CCPR, which has had ample opportunity to classify a range of activities as amounting to violations of art 7 of the ICCPR,[235] the CAT has had remarkably little opportunity to conduct a similar analysis of arts 1 and 16 of the Convention in its jurisprudence under art 22.[236] This is not such a great drawback in respect of art 1, however, since the Convention itself defines the key ingredients of the offence of 'torture' as including any act by which 'severe' pain and suffering has been inflicted 'intentionally' and for a particular 'purpose' by or at the instigation of or with the consent or acquiescence of a public official or other person acting in an official capacity.[237] While this may have made the task of applying the text of art 1 of the Convention somewhat easier for the CAT than for other human rights bodies in applying similar normative guarantees in their parent

---

[233] (\...contd) In reaching this decision, CAT held that while some adjustments may be made to the particular *process* of review where national security concerns arise in a case, the mechanism chosen must still satisfy art 3 of UNCAT's requirements in regard to an effective, independent and impartial review. CAT's firm elucidation of this procedural right in art 3 in *Agiza* develops its previous decision in *Jose Arkauz Arana v France* in which the inability of a suspected terrorist to challenge his expulsion before a judicial authority was found to be relevant to a finding of a violation of art 3: *Josu Arkauz Arana v France*, Communication No 63/1997, paras 11.5 and 12.

[234] Byrnes 'The Committee Against Torture' in Alston, *The United Nations and Human Rights: A Critical Appraisal* (OUP, 1992), p 512.

[235] See Ch 7, para **7.44** above and the case law referred to by Rehman, *International Human Rights Law* (2nd edn, Pearson, 2010), p 816.

[236] Likewise, an obvious comparison can be made on this point with the output of the European Court of Human Rights, which has gradually refined its interpretation of each of those particular concepts as they appear in ECHR, art 3, which provides that: 'No one shall be subjected to torture or to inhuman or degrading treatment or punishment'. See generally, Harris, O'Boyle and Warbrick *Law of the European Convention on Human Rights* (2nd edn, OUP, 2010), pp 69–112.

[237] UNCAT, art 1 provides that: 'For the purposes of this Convention, the term 'torture' means any act by which severe pain or suffering, whether physical or mental, is intentionally inflicted on a person for such purposes as obtaining from him or a third person information or a confession, punishing him for an act he or a third person has committed or is suspected of having committed, or intimidating or coercing him or a third person, or for any reason based on discrimination of any kind, when such pain or suffering is inflicted by or at the instigation of or with the consent or acquiescence of a public official or other person acting in an official capacity. It does not include pain or suffering arising only from, inherent in or incidental to lawful sanctions'.

instruments,[238] certain difficulties of interpretation and application of the definition inevitably remain. For example, it has been queried whether a sadistic act of severe violence, not perpetrated for any particular purpose, might nonetheless be designated as 'torture' despite the wording of art 1.[239] Second, the fact that 'torture' for the purposes of the Convention must be inflicted *by* or at the instigation of public authorities, or with their consent or acquiescence, has also been a source of criticism on the basis that this potentially excludes the application of art 1 to acts committed by private parties without the consent or acquiescence of the State.[240] Finally, the text begs the question whether an omission, as opposed to an act, which results in severe consequences for the victim may ever constitute 'torture'.[241] Thus far, the instances considered to amount to violations of art 1 of UNCAT have all involved severe beatings, intentionally inflicted for particular purposes, in some instances rendering the victims temporarily unconscious.[242] In the context of art 3, the CAT has also held that repeated acts of rape by public officials constitute torture.[243]

[9.43] A similar dearth of case law obtains in respect of art 16 of UNCAT as regards the meaning of 'cruel, inhuman or degrading treatment or punishment'. The result of this shortfall in cases is potentially more acute in this instance since the latter concepts are not defined at all by the terms of the Convention itself. [244] As far as the substantive

---

[238] ICCPR, art 7 and ECHR, art 3, on the other hand, make no attempt to define the concept of 'torture', leaving the concept wide open for the Human Rights Committee and European Court of Human Rights respectively to interpret.

[239] This point is considered in the abstract by Burgers and Danelius who conclude that only in exceptional cases would it be possible to conclude that such an act, perpetrated by a public official for purely private reasons, was not torture: Burgers and Danelius, The United Nations Convention against Torture: A Handbook on the Convention against Torture and Other Cruel, Inhuman, or Degrading Treatment or Punishment, (Martinus Nijhoff, 1988), p 119.

[240] See Flinkerman and Henderson in Hanski and Suksi (eds), *An Introduction to the International Protection of Human Rights: A Textbook* (Abo Akademi University, 1999), p 137 and Rehman, *International Human Rights Law* (2nd edn, Pearson, 2010), p 814–815. See para **9.45**.

[241] Burgers and Danelius as well as Rehman argue that omissions, *if intentionally conducted*, eg, denial of food to prisoners, amounts to torture: Burgers and Danelius, The United Nations Convention against Torture: A Handbook on the Convention against Torture and Other Cruel, Inhuman, or Degrading Treatment or Punishment, (Martinus Nijhoff, 1988), p 118; and Rehman, *International Human Rights* Law (2nd edn, Pearson, 2010), p 813, respectively.

[242] See *Danilo Dimitrijevic v Serbia and Montenegro*, Communication No 172/2000; *Jovica Dimitrov v Serbia and Montenegro*, Communication No 171/2000; *Dragan Dimitrijevic v Serbia and Montenegro*, Communication No 207/2002; and *Saadi Ali v Tunisia*, Communication No 291/2006. See further, Joseph, 'Committee Against Torture: Recent Jurisprudence' (2006) HRL Rev 571.

[243] *CT and KM v Sweden*, Communication No 279/2005, para 7.5 and *VL v Switzerland*, Communication No 262/2005, para 8.10.

[244] Fortunately, the resulting interpretative gaps have been filled to a large extent by CAT's concluding observations in respect of States' reports as is evidenced by the survey conducted by Nowak and McArthur, *The United Nations Convention Against Torture: A Commentary* (OUP, 2008), pp 540–569.

concepts are concerned, the CAT has only really had occasion in its case law under art 22 to establish that burning and destruction of houses can be classified as acts constituting 'cruel, inhuman or degrading treatment or punishment'.[245] The fact that such acts may be carried out for reasons relating to racial prejudice is considered by the Committee to be an aggravating factor.[246]

[9.44] One glaring interpretive difficulty that remains contentious in respect of art 16 of UNCAT concerns the precise scope of the obligations assumed by States parties in respect of 'cruel, inhuman or degrading treatment or punishment'. Most of the obligations in UNCAT are expressly related to torture. Article 16, however, obliges States to 'prevent' ill-treatment and goes on to specify that 'in particular', the obligations in arts 10,[247] 11,[248] 12[249] and 13[250] shall apply 'with the substitution for references to torture of references to other forms of cruel, inhuman and degrading treatment or punishment'. This begs the question as to the legal significance of the words 'in particular' as they appear in art 16, and, hence, whether other articles (besides arts 10 to 13) of the Convention also apply in respect of acts involving 'cruel, inhuman or degrading treatment'. Academic commentary has mainly been positive on the potential applicability of other articles in the Convention to 'cruel, inhuman or

---

[245] *Hajrizi Dzemajl et al v Yugoslavia*, Communication No 161/2000, para 9.2.

[246] *Hajrizi Dzemajl et al v Yugoslavia,* Communication No 161/2000, para 9.2. Particularly strong statements to this effect were made in *Besim Osmani v Republic of Serbia*, Communication No 261/2005, para 10.4, for example, where the destruction of the complainant's home, in his presence, together with the infliction of a number of slaps to his person by the police was regarded as a violation of UNCAT, art 16. CAT stated that: '…the infliction of physical and mental suffering aggravated by the complainant's particular vulnerability, due to his Roma ethnic origin and unavoidable association with a minority historically subjected to discrimination and prejudice, reaches the threshold of cruel, inhuman or degrading treatment or punishment'.

[247] UNCAT, art 10 provides as follows: '(1) Each State Party shall ensure that education and information regarding the prohibition against torture are fully included in the training of law enforcement personnel, civil or military, medical personnel, public officials and other persons who may be involved in the custody, interrogation or treatment of any individual subjected to any form of arrest, detention or imprisonment; (2) Each State Party shall include this prohibition in the rules or instructions issued in regard to the duties and functions of any such person.'

[248] UNCAT, art 11 provides that: 'Each State Party shall keep under systematic review interrogation rules, instructions, methods and practices as well as arrangements for the custody and treatment of persons subjected to any form of arrest, detention or imprisonment in any territory under its jurisdiction, with a view to preventing any cases of torture.'

[249] UNCAT, art 12 provides that: 'Each State Party shall ensure that its competent authorities proceed to a prompt and impartial investigation, wherever there is reasonable ground to believe that an act of torture has been committed in any territory under its jurisdiction.'

[250] UNCAT, art 13 provides that: 'Each State Party shall ensure that any individual who alleges he has been subjected to torture in any territory under its jurisdiction has the right to complain to, and to have his case promptly and impartially examined by, its competent authorities. Steps shall be taken to ensure that the complainant and witnesses are protected against all ill-treatment or intimidation as a consequence of his complaint or any evidence given.'

degrading treatment or punishment.[251] By contrast, the CAT has bluntly taken the view that the obligations in art 3 (the principle of *non-refoulement*)[252] and art 14 only refer to torture and that neither article applies to ill-treatment falling below the threshold of torture.[253] The CAT's failure to consider the significance of the words 'in particular' in art 16 is regrettable. On a more positive, but perhaps 'confusing'[254] note, it has however read a right to fair and adequate compensation into the terms of art 16 itself by holding that the positive obligations that flow from the first sentence of art 16 of the Convention include an obligation to grant redress and to compensate the victims of an act in breach of that provision.[255] It has also recognised in principle, though not in practice, that the *act of returning* a person to a third State could itself constitute cruel, inhuman or degrading treatment within the meaning of art 16 in exceptional circumstances.[256] Nonetheless,

---

[251] Ingelse, for example, believes that the use of the words 'in particular' in UNCAT, art 16 indicates that the obligations that flow from other articles of the Convention are not excluded from being applicable to cruel, inhuman or degrading treatment or punishment: Ingelse, *The UN Committee Against Torture: An Assessment* (Kluwer Law International, 2001), p 248. Burgers and Danelius do not express a view, but simply note that during the drafting process, different views were expressed on the question of whether arts 3, 14 and 15 should apply to cruel, inhuman and degrading treatment and that in the end, it was decided not to refer to those provisions in the body of UNCAT, art 16: Burgers and Danelius, The United Nations Convention against Torture: A Handbook on the Convention against Torture and Other Cruel, Inhuman, or Degrading Treatment or Punishment, (Martinus Nijhoff, 1988), p 150.

[252] See para **9.23**.

[253] As regards UNCAT, art 3, see *MV v Switzerland*, Communication No 201/2002, para 6.2 and *TM v Sweden*, Communication No 228/2003, para 6.2. As regards UNCAT, art 14, see *Hajrizi Dezmajil et al v Yugoslavia*, Communication No n161/2000, para 9.6 and *Besim Osmani v Republic of Serbia*, Communication No 261/2005, para 10.8.

[254] Nowak and McArthur, *The United Nations Convention Against Torture: A Commentary* (OUP, 2008), p 571.

[255] *Hajrizi Dezmajil et al v Yugoslavia*, Communication No n161/2000, para 9.6 and *Besim Osmani v Republic of Serbia*, Communication No 261/2005, para 10.8.

[256] This possibility was recognised in *GRB v Sweden*, Communication No 83/1997, para 6.7, in which CAT considered whether the forced return of the complainant who was suffering from post-traumatic stress disorder of itself could constitute a breach of UNCAT, art 3. It held that the aggravation of her health would not amount to the type of 'cruel, inhuman or degrading' treatment envisaged by UNCAT, art 3. See also, *BSS v Canada*, Communication No 183/2001, para 10.2, in which the complaint made there that the decision to return the complainant to India would in itself constitute an act of cruel, inhuman or degrading treatment or punishment in contravention of art 16 failed because it lacked the minimum evidence necessary to render it admissible under UNCAT, art 22. In *TM v Sweden*, Communication No 228/2003, para 6.2, CAT held that the aggravation of a person's physical or mental health through deportation is '...generally insufficient, *in the absence of other factors,* to amount to degrading treatment in violation of UNCAT, art 16' (emphasis added). In the absence of such 'exceptional circumstances', the claim was found to be inadmissible. It may be noted here that in rejecting the complaint as inadmissible, CAT specifically noted that the complainant's counsel had failed to respond to the State party's argument that it had not been shown that the appropriate medical care was unavailable in the receiving State. (contd.../)

given the limitations in the caselaw, persons who fear return to a State because of a risk of ill-treatment falling below the threshold of torture, might be advised to direct their complaints, where possible, to the European Court of Human Rights[257] or to the Human Rights Committee.[258]

[9.45] Finally, it should be noted again that the text of both art 1 and art 16 of UNCAT limits the concepts of 'torture' and 'cruel, inhuman or degrading' treatment or punishment respectively to acts which have been committed by or at the instigation of or with the consent or acquiescence of a public official or other person acting in an official capacity. This means that the activities of non-State actors or private individuals may be covered by the provisions of UNCAT in circumstances where the State has instigated, consented or acquiesced in such activities[259] or where the actors in question are exercising quasi-governmental authority over the State in question.[260] However, as pointed out already in regard to the scope of art 3, the wording of arts 1 and 16 means that ill-treatment by private individuals or non-State actors whom the respondent State is simply *unable* to control necessarily falls outside the scope of the Convention.[261] Where such activity is at issue, and provided that it reaches the necessary threshold, resort to the

---

[256] (\...contd) This seems to suggest that a successful refutation of the State party's argument in that regard might have amounted to 'exceptional circumstances' necessary to substantiate the claim, at least for admissibility purposes. Just such an argument bolstered the case of *D v United Kingdom* (1997) 24 EHRR 423, paras 51–54, before the European Court of Human Rights in which the court held that the act of expelling the applicant in that case who was in the advanced stages of a terminal illness to another country where he would no longer have specialist treatment, medication or other support would *itself* be inhuman treatment in breach of ECHR, art 3.

[257] Ingelse, *The UN Committee Against Torture: An Assessment* (Kluwer Law International, 2001), p 312. Complaints under ECHR, art 3 in respect of treatment falling below the level of torture are nevertheless hard to establish: see Egan, 'Human Rights Considerations in Extradition and Expulsion Cases: The European Convention on Human Rights Revisited' (1998) 2 Contemporary Issues in Irish Law and Politics 188, pp 212–214.

[258] See Ch 7, para **7.44**.

[259] See *Dzemajl et al v Yugoslavia*, Communication 161/000, para 9.2 and *Besim Osmani v Republic of Serbia*, Communication 261/2005, para 10.5.

[260] This inference is drawn from case law in relation to UNCAT, art 3, cited above in para **9.40**.

[261] This is the clear view expressed by CAT in cases concerning UNCAT, art 3: see *GRB v Sweden*, Communication No 83/1997, para 6.5; *SV v Canada*, Communication No 49/1996, para 9.5; and *MPS v Australia*, Communication No 138/1999, para 7.4. In respect of UNCAT, art 16, it has interpreted the concept of acquiescence quite widely so as to hold States responsible for failing to react to cruel, inhuman or degrading treatment meted out by private parties: *Dzemajl et al v Yugoslavia*, Communication No 161/000, para 9.2 and *Besim Osmani v Republic of Serbia*, Communication No 261/2005, para 10.5. However, in each of those cases, the implication seems clear that the police would have been capable of protecting the victims had they sought to do so.

Human Rights Committee under art 7 of the ICCPR,[262] or indeed to the European Court of Human Rights (where appropriate),[263] would be advised.

Duty of Investigation

[9.46] The final element of UNCAT which has been the subject of a significant number of cases under art 22 concerns the duty of States to investigate allegations of torture or ill-treatment. In this respect, the Convention provides for important procedural safeguards in arts 12 and 13. Article 12 obliges States to conduct an investigation *ex officio* wherever there is reasonable ground to believe that such acts have been committed[264] regardless of the origin of the suspicion;[265] while art 13 provides for the right of an alleged victim of torture to complain to, and to have his or her case examined by the competent authorities.[266] Nagan and Atkins have appropriately observed that while these provisions may appear 'to call for a fox to investigate the chicken coop', they recognise the complexity of State structures whereby a multiplicity of actors have the capacity to regulate each other.[267] These provisions can be distinguished from the general obligations on States provided for in arts 4–9 to criminalise torture on their territory[268] and to bring individual perpetrators of torture to justice.[269]

---

[262] See CAT General Comment No 20 on ICCPR, art 7 in which the CCPR states that States parties should '...afford everyone protection through legislative and other measures as may be necessary against the acts prohibited by article 7, whether inflicted by people acting in their official capacity, outside their official capacity or in a private capacity': UN Doc HRI/GEN/1/Rev 9 (Vol 1), p 200, para 2.

[263] The European Court of Human Rights has long since recognised that a threat of ill-treatment from non-State actors whom the State is unable to control is sufficient to ground a claim under ECHR, art 3: *Ahmed v Austria* (1997) 24 EHRR 278; and *HLR v France* (1998) 26 EHRR 29.

[264] UNCAT, art 12 provides as follows: 'Each State party shall ensure that its competent authorities proceed to a prompt and impartial investigation, wherever there is reasonable ground to believe that an act of torture has been committed in any territory under its jurisdiction'.

[265] *Encarnación Blanco Abad v Spain*, Communication No 59/1996, para 8.2.

[266] UNCAT, art 13 provides as follows: 'Each State party shall ensure that any individual who alleges that he has been subjected to torture in any territory under its jurisdiction has the right to complain to, and to have his case promptly and impartially examined by, its competent authorities. Steps shall be taken to ensure that the complainant and witnesses are protected against all ill-treatment or intimidation as a consequence of his complaint or any evidence given'. It is not necessary for the victim to formally lodge such a complaint: *Henri Unai Parot v Spain*, Communication No 6/1990, para 10.4. It is simply required that he or she bring the facts in question to the attention of the State authorities who are obliged to consider this to be a 'tacit but unequivocal expression of the victim's wish that the facts should be promptly and impartially investigated': *Encarnación Blanco Abad v Spain*, Communication No 59/1996, para 8.6.

[267] Nagan and Atkins, 'The International Law of Torture: From Universal Proscription to Effective Application and Enforcement' (2001) 14 Harv Hum Rts J 87, p 101.

[268] As to the obligation to criminalise torture in UNCAT, art 4, see the decision of CAT in *Kepa Urra Guridi v Spain*, Communication No 212/2002.

[269] Violations of UNCAT, art 5(2) and art 7 regarding the obligations to criminalise torture, and prosecute or extradite alleged perpetrators of torture were established in *Suleymane Guengueng et al v Senegal*, Communication No 181/2001. (contd.../)

[9.47] Investigations under arts 12 and 13 must be conducted promptly[270] and impartially.[271] It is not necessary to establish that torture or ill-treatment has in fact taken place before claiming a breach of either provision.[272] Indeed, in many cases, the complainant's incapacity to establish that such treatment took place in fact provides the motivation and grounds for resort to art 12 and/or 13.[273] A criminal investigation under either article must seek both to determine the nature and the circumstances of the alleged acts and to establish the identity of any person who might have been involved therein.[274] A finding that the State has violated art 12 is almost invariably accompanied by a violation of art 13 where the CAT finds that the failure to conduct an adequate criminal investigation into the incident in question results in the inability of the complainant to institute civil proceedings against the alleged perpetrator.[275] A delay in conducting an investigation may also result in a finding of a violation of art 14 of the Convention in respect of a torture victim's right to redress and to fair and adequate compensation at the domestic level.[276]

---

[269] (\...contd) See above para **9.18**; and Joseph, 'Committee Against Torture: Recent Jurisprudence' (2006) HRL Rev 571, pp 575–577.

[270] Promptness is considered to be essential by CAT '…both to ensure that the victim cannot continue to be subjected to such acts and also because in general unless the methods employed have permanent or serious effects, the physical traces of torture, and especially of cruel, inhuman or degrading treatment, soon disappear': *Encarnación Blanco Abad v Spain*, Communication No 59/1996, para 8.2. The chronology of events outlined in that case whereby a delay of some 10 months ensued in investigating the allegations of torture was considered to be insufficiently prompt. In *Qani Halimi-Nedzibi v Austria*, Communication No 8/1991, para 13.5, CAT held that a delay of 15 months before the initiation of an investigation is unreasonable and contrary to UNCAT, art 12.

[271] See, for example, *Slobodan Nikoli and Ljiljana Nikoli v Serbia and Montenegro*, Communication No 174/2000, para 6.5, in which CAT concluded that an investigation into the death of the complainants' son was not impartial in circumstances where the deputy public prosecutor informed the couple that he would not be investigating the death, three days before the results of the autopsy, as he considered the death to be an accident. Note that a formal, judicial investigation is not necessary in order for an investigation to satisfy the requirement of 'impartiality' in regard to UNCAT, art 13: *RS v Austria*, Communication No 111/1998, para 9.2.

[272] Thus, even though CAT found that the allegations of torture were not sustained in *Qani Halimi-Nedzibi v Austria*, Communication No 8/1991, paras 13.4–13.5, having regard to the medical evidence submitted by the respondent State, it nevertheless went on to find a violation of UNCAT, art 12 because of the delay in investigating the allegations in question. See also *Radivoje Ristic v Yugoslavia*, Communication No 113/1998.

[273] See, for example, *Radivoje Ristic v Yugoslavia*, Communication No 113/1998, paras 3.1–3.2.

[274] *Encarnación Blanco Abad v Spain*, Communication No 59/1996, para 8.8.

[275] See for example, *Dragan Dimitrijevic v Serbia and Montenegro*, Communication No 207/2002, para 5.4; *Jovica Dimitrov v Serbia and Montenegro*, Communication No 171/2000, para 7.3; *Danilo Dimitrijevic v Serbia and Montenegro*, Communication No 172/2000, para 7.3; and *Besim Osmani v Republic of Serbia*, Communication No 261/2005, para 10.7.

[276] See, for example, *Dragan Dimitrijevic v Serbia and Montenegro*, Communication No 207/2002, para 5.5; *Jovica Dimitrov v Serbia and Montenegro*, Communication No 171/2000, para 7.2; (contd.../)

Appraisal

[9.48] The structure of the art 22 complaint procedure in UNCAT is almost identical to the procedure provided for in the OP-ICCPR.[277] One variation in the text of art 22 which might have had the capacity to alter the character of the procedure is the fact that it does not bind the CAT to an exclusively written procedure.[278] In practice, however, the CAT has never thus far availed of the option of conducting oral hearings under the art 22 procedure and it is unlikely that this possibility will be explored in the future, having regard in particular to the Committee's limited meeting time and resources.

[9.49] Despite the fact that less than half of the Contracting States to UNCAT have accepted the competence of the CAT to consider complaints under art 22, the CAT has built up an impressive body of jurisprudence under that provision. In evaluating this output, it should be recalled that the CAT's jurisdiction in respect of torture and ill-treatment overlaps with a number of other human rights bodies, including the Human Rights Committee and other regional bodies. Given this context, it is obviously desirable that the approach taken by all of these bodies is consistent, as far as possible, in order to avoid fragmentation of standards.[279] In this respect, however, the CAT has been hampered to some extent in its work under art 22 by the text of the Convention itself. In particular, the requirement that 'torture' as defined in art 1 must be carried out 'at the instigation of' or 'with the consent or acquiescence' of a public official has had repercussions, particularly with respect to the scope of the *non-refoulement* principle in art 3. Other human rights bodies, such as the Human Rights Committee and the European Court of Human Rights, are unconstrained by the language of their parent conventions in this respect and are free to accept complaints where the fear of torture emanates from private individuals over whom the respondent or receiving State (in the case of an art 3 application) has no effective control. It is difficult to see how the CAT could accommodate such an expansive interpretation of art 1 of UNCAT without in effect re-writing its terms.[280] Constrained by the language of art 3 in regard to the

---

[276] (\...contd) *Danilo Dimitrijevic v Serbia and Montenegro*, Communication No 172/2000, para 7.4; and *Saadi Ali v Tunisia*, Communication No 291/2006, para 15.8. However, note that the failure to conduct a prompt and adequate investigation may impact on the ability of the CAT to make a determination as to whether torture has in fact taken place and hence whether the right of access to compensation in art 14 UNCAT has been violated. In such a case, the Committee may request the State party to carry out an investigation as a matter of urgency: *Radivoje Ristic v Yugoslavia*, Communication No 113/1998, para 9.9.

[277] In this respect, one commentator has critiqued it from the outset as being subject to the '...defective genes and deficiencies that have crippled the effectiveness of the individual petitions in the Optional Protocol': Boulesbaa, *The UN Convention on Torture and the Prospects of Enforcement* (Kluwer, 1999), p 290.

[278] Technically, as Burgers and Danelius note, the CAT could involve witnesses and experts in its proceedings under UNCAT, art 22: *Punishment* (Martinus Nijhoff, 1988), p 167.

[279] Byrnes 'The Committee Against Torture' in Alston, *The United Nations and Human Rights: A Critical Appraisal* (OUP, 1992), p 540.

[280] Notwithstanding the clear language of UNCAT, art 1, Weissbrodt and Hörtreiter advocate that CAT should nonetheless adopt a broader approach: (contd.../)

principle of non-refoulement, the approach of the CAT in regard to this principle in respect of art 16 of the Convention has been conservative where the feared ill-treatment amounts at most to 'cruel, inhuman or degrading treatment or punishment'.[281] In other respects, however, the CAT's jurisprudence on art 3 is consistent with that of its counterparts, especially in regard to the extra procedural safeguard that has been identified in art 3 of UNCAT to the effect that asylum seekers must be given an independent review of any negative decision on their status.

[9.50] On the other hand, other articles of UNCAT have received surprisingly little attention in the art 22 procedure. Much of this shortfall can probably be attributed to the existence of competing procedures under the OP-ICCPR and the ECHR.[282] Complainants are likely to choose the more effective procedure under the ECHR (where applicable) or the more comprehensive procedure under the OP-ICCPR where the case concerns violations of human rights additional to allegations of ill-treatment. In many instances, the CAT has mitigated the deficiency by fleshing out the meaning of particular articles of the Convention in its concluding observations under the reporting procedure.

[9.51] In terms of implementation of the CAT's views, the picture is also reasonably encouraging, certainly in comparison with other UN individual complaint procedures. A recent study estimates that compliance rates with the views of the CAT can be gauged at almost 50 per cent.[283] Thus, while the procedure may not yet have developed into an effective tool of implementation as regards extreme cases of torture,[284] it has clearly become a significant mechanism of last resort in the arsenal of lawyers in participating States for stalling the deportation of failed asylum seekers.[285]

---

[280] (\...contd) Weissbrodt and Hörtreiter, 'The Principle of Non-Refoulement: art 3 of the Convention Against Torture and Other Cruel, Inhuman or Degrading Treatment or Punishment in Comparison with the Non-Refoulement Provisions of Other International Human Rights Treaties' (1999) 5 Buff Hum Rts L Rev 1, pp 51–52.

[281] See above, para **9.44**.

[282] Ingelse, *The UN Committee Against Torture: An Assessment* (Kluwer Law International, 2001), p 201.

[283] Open Society Justice Initiative, *From Judgment to Justice: Implementing International and Regional Human Rights Decisions* (Open Society Foundations, 2011), p 121.

[284] Boulesbaa is extremely critical in this regard, arguing that CAT '...lacks the teeth necessary for real enforcement of the Convention': *The UN Convention on Torture and the Prospects of Enforcement* (Kluwer, 1999), p 293.

[285] Peter Burns has also observed that '...those states that have been most liberal in receiving potential refugees and that have also demonstrated the highest commitment to the object and ideals of the torture Convention have borne the heaviest brunt, both economically and politically, of the committee applying Article 3 in response to a communication': *'The United Nations Committee Against Torture and its Role in Refugee Protection'* (2000) 15 Geo. Immigr LJ 403 at 407. On the other hand, following his own analysis of the CAT's case law under art 22, Doerfel's advice to lawyers is:'do not waste your efforts': see Doerfel, 'The Convention Against Torture and the Protection of Refugees' (2005) 24(2) Refugee Survey Quarterly 83 at p 92.

Chapter 10

Optional Protocol to the Convention on the Elimination of All Forms of Discrimination Against Women

INTRODUCTION

[10.01] In terms of implementation machinery, the Convention on the Elimination of All Forms of Discrimination Against Women (CEDAW) was for many years regarded as the poor relation in the family of international human rights instruments promulgated by the United Nations.[1] At the time that it was drafted, very little attention was apparently paid to the question of whether it should include an individual and inter-State complaint mechanism, let alone an inquiry procedure.[2] Rather, the focus for debate on implementation centred on whether there should in fact be a monitoring procedure in the first place; and if so, what body should carry out the task.[3] While the possibility of inserting an individual complaint procedure was raised by a few States at an early stage in the negotiations for the Convention,[4] the suggestion did not find its way into any concrete draft text. Support for such a procedure was not even forthcoming from the Commission for the Status of Women (CSW),[5] during its consideration of the matter. As Byrnes and Connors have noted, objections were largely raised in that forum on the basis that there was no real need for any adversarial procedure in the realm of women's rights.[6] Thus, the most significant implementation mechanism to be included in the

---

[1] As to the Convention generally, see Ch 3, paras **3.64–3.72**.
[2] Byrnes and Connors, 'Enforcing the Human Rights of Women: A Complaints Procedure for the Women's Convention?' (1995) 21 Brok J Int'l L 679, pp 684–685.
[3] Byrnes and Connors, 'Enforcing the Human Rights of Women: A Complaints Procedure for the Women's Convention?' (1995) 21 Brok J Int'l L 679, p 686. Given that the Commission on the Status of Women (CSW) was already in existence and had the power to investigate abuses of women's rights, certain States argued that a monitoring mechanism was not necessary; and even if it was, the CSW could be charged with the task.
[4] Notably Canada and Sweden. Consideration of Proposals Concerning a New Instrument or Instruments of International Law to Eliminate Discrimination Against Women, Working Paper by the Secretary General, CSW, 25th session, Agenda Item 4(b), paras 100–107: UN Doc E/CN6/573 (1973).
[5] See Ch 2, para **2.06**.
[6] The perceived need for such a procedure was apparently stronger in regard to racial discrimination and apartheid: Byrnes and Connors, 'Enforcing the Human Rights of Women: A Complaints Procedure for the Women's Convention?' (1995) 21 Brok J Int'l L 679, pp 685–688.

Convention when it was ultimately adopted was the reporting procedure contained in art 18.[7]

[10.02] Nonetheless, soon after its entry into force, momentum began to gather apace for more effective supervisory mechanisms to be incorporated into the Convention. From the early 1990s, demands were being made by feminist activists and academics for the integration of women's rights into mainstream UN human rights activities and also for the strengthening of the implementation machinery by the adoption of a complaint procedure.[8] The rationale advanced for such a procedure was based on the belief that it would place the Convention on an equal footing with other human rights treaties, facilitate stronger implementation and ultimately improve the enjoyment by women of the rights guaranteed in the Convention.[9] Great strides towards these goals were achieved when the 1993 Vienna Declaration and Programme for Action explicitly advocated gender mainstreaming in all United Nations human rights activities[10] and the adoption of new procedures 'to strengthen implementation of the commitment to women's equality and the human rights of women'.[11] In regard to the latter, the Conference specifically called upon the CSW and the Committee on the Elimination of All Forms of Discrimination (CEDAW Committee)[12] to 'quickly examine the possibility of introducing the right of petition through the preparation of an optional protocol to the Convention on the Elimination of All Forms of Discrimination Against Women'.[13] Taking a pro-active position,[14] the CEDAW Committee went on to adopt Suggestion No 7[15] which outlined in detail the Committee's views on the types of procedural mechanisms which should be incorporated into the Protocol. The text of Suggestion

---

[7] See Ch 4, paras **4.51–4.59**.

[8] Byrnes, 'Slow and Steady Wins the Race: The Development of an Optional Protocol to the Women's Convention' (1997) 91 Am Soc Int'l L Proc 383; and Byrnes and Connors, 'Enforcing the Human Rights of Women: A Complaints Procedure for the Women's Convention?' (1995) 21 Brok J Int'l L 679, pp 685–688.

[9] Byrnes and Connors, 'Enforcing the Human Rights of Women: A Complaints Procedure for the Women's Convention?' (1995) 21 Brok J Int'l L 679, pp 698–699.

[10] Vienna Declaration and Programme for Action (1993), UN Doc A/CONF.157/23, para 37. See generally, Sullivan, 'Women's Human Rights and the 1993 World Conference on Human Rights' (1994) 88 Am J Int'l L 152.

[11] Vienna Declaration and Programme for Action (1993), para 40.

[12] As to the composition and functions of the CEDAW Committee generally, see Ch 3, paras **3.70–3.72**.

[13] Vienna Declaration and Programme for Action (1993), para 40.

[14] It is notable that while the CEDAW Committee pursued the matter directly after Vienna, by recommending at its 13th session in 1994 that the CSW establish a group of independent experts to prepare a draft Protocol, the CSW effectively ignored this recommendation. See, Report of the Committee on the Elimination of All Forms of Discrimination Against Women (Thirteenth Session): UN Doc A/49/38 (SUPP), Suggestion 5, Ch 1, s B, p xvi.

[15] Report of the Committee on the Elimination of All Forms of Discrimination Against Women (14th Session): UN Doc A/50/38, Ch 1, s B, p 5.

No 7 later formed the basis for further discussion of a draft Protocol within the CSW.[16] The Commission appointed an open-ended working group for the elaboration of a draft Optional Protocol in 1996.[17] Following lengthy and protracted discussion by members of the working group and the CSW itself,[18] the Protocol was eventually opened for ratification in October 1999. The final text of the Protocol (OP-CEDAW) contains an individual complaint procedure (discussed further below); and an inquiry procedure.[19] The Protocol entered into force on 22 December 2000. At the time of writing, just over half of the States parties to the Convention have ratified the Protocol.[20]

[10.03] A number of interesting issues were raised during the drafting of the OP-CEDAW, some of which proved to be highly contentious. First was the question of *who* should have standing to submit a complaint under the Protocol. Initially, views ranged along a spectrum from those delegations who favoured standing for individuals only, others who envisaged standing for individuals and groups of individuals, while certain delegations argued further for the possibility of complaints being submitted by non-governmental organisations which did not represent specific individual women.[21] It was

---

[16] Suggestion No 7 is largely based on a draft Protocol which had earlier been produced by an independent group of experts convened by the International Human Rights Law Group and the Maastricht Centre for Human Rights in 1994. The latter initiative proved very influential in getting the negotiations for an Optional Protocol off the ground at a political level: Byrnes and Connors, 'Enforcing the Human Rights of Women: A Complaints Procedure for the Women's Convention?' (1995) 21 Brok J Int'l L 679, pp 693–694.

[17] By means of Resolution No 1995/29, ECOSOC had requested the Secretary General of the UN to compile a report based on views invited from governments, inter-governmental agencies and NGOs on a protocol, taking into account the elements mentioned in Suggestion No 7 for the benefit of the CSW. The CSW in turn was then directed to establish an open-ended working group to consider the report with a view to elaborating a draft text of a Protocol: 50th plenary meeting, UN Doc 1995/95, Res E/1995/29 (24 July 1995), paras 5–7. By a series of further decisions, the Council later renewed the mandate of the working group so that it could continue its work. Support for this process was also voiced at the World Conference on Women's Rights at Beijing later that year. The platform for action which emerged from that conference specifically advocated an Optional Protocol, which would include an individual petition procedure that would enter into force 'in the near future': Report of the Fourth World Conference on Women, Beijing Declaration, UN Doc A/Conf 177/20 (17 October 1995) Annex II, Platform for Action, para 230(k).

[18] For an account of the deliberations of the working group, see Gómez Isa, 'The Optional Protocol For the Convention On the Elimination of All Forms of Discrimination Against Women: Strengthening The Protection Mechanisms of Women's Human Rights' (2003) 20 Ariz J Int'l & Comp L 291, pp 306–309. See also the outline of the history of the drafting of the Optional Protocol set forth on the website of the United Nations Division for the Advancement of Women: http://www.un.org/womenwatch/daw/cedaw/protocol/history.htm (last accessed May 2011).

[19] See Ch 5, paras **5.27–5.48**.

[20] 102 out of 186: http://treaties.un.org/Pages/Treaties.aspx?id=4&subid=A&lang=en (last accessed May 2011).

[21] Elaboration of a Draft Optional Protocol to the to the Convention on the Elimination of All Forms of Discrimination Against Women: Chairperson's Summary: UN Doc E/CN6/1997/WG/L4, p 3, para 10 (24 March 1997).

argued that such a possibility was necessary in circumstances where women do not have the ability or resources to represent themselves[22] and because some women could place themselves at considerable risk by submitting petitions.[23] Despite obvious support for this view from non-governmental organisations[24] as well as in academic quarters,[25] the view that eventually held sway was that communications under the OP-CEDAW could be filed *on behalf of* individuals and groups of individuals claiming to be victims of a violation, provided that the victim's consent is explicitly obtained 'unless the author can justify acting on their behalf without such consent'.[26] The retention of an explicit requirement of consent impedes the possibility of NGOs freely pursuing public interest complaints under the Protocol, but leaves them free to represent victims provided they can bring themselves within the terms of the latter clause in art 2 of the OP-CEDAW.[27]

[10.04] A second issue raised during the drafting stage was that of the *scope* of the Protocol and specifically the question of which obligations should be justiciable under it.[28] In this regard, it will be recalled that the obligations in CEDAW itself are organised in terms of the classic dichotomy of civil and political rights and rights of an economic, social and cultural nature.[29] Accordingly, certain of the provisions are phrased in terms of 'immediate' obligation,[30] while others are progressive in nature, affording to States a certain 'margin of appreciation' as regards implementation.[31] At an early juncture,

---

[22] See the observations of the Group from Costa Rica and other NGOs in 'Additional Views of Governments, intergovernmental organizations and non-governmental organisations on an optional protocol to the Convention', Report of the Secretary General: UN Doc E/CN6/1997/5, para 98 (Additional Views).
[23] See the observations of the government of Chile in Additional Views: UN Doc E/CN6/1997/5, para 94.
[24] See the observations of Amnesty International, cited in Gómez Isa, 'The Optional Protocol For the Convention On the Elimination of All Forms of Discrimination Against Women: Strengthening The Protection Mechanisms of Women's Human Rights' (2003) 20 Ariz J Int'l & Comp L 291, pp 310–311.
[25] See the persuasive arguments advanced by Byrnes and Connors, 'Enforcing the Human Rights of Women: A Complaints Procedure for the Women's Convention?' (1995) 21 Brok J Int'l L 679, pp 748–754.
[26] OP-CEDAW, art 2.
[27] The CEDAW Committee has admitted communications filed by NGOs in a number of domestic violence cases where the victims are deceased: see paras **10.17**. Clearly there is some concern around this issue because as Gómez Isa points out, several countries have entered interpretive statements on ratifying the Protocol as to the precise meaning of art 2: Gómez Isa, 'The Optional Protocol For the Convention on the Elimination of All Forms of Discrimination Against Women: Strengthening the Protection of Women's Human Rights' (2003) 20 Ariz J Int'l & Comp L 291, pp 312–313.
[28] See Additional Views: UN Doc E/CN6/1997/5, paras 38–61.
[29] See Ch 3, paras **3.69**.
[30] See for example, CEDAW, arts 9(1)–(2), 15(1)–(4), 16(1)–(2) and 7.
[31] CEDAW, arts 6, 8, 12. As Byrnes and Connors note further the classification is not so simple as certain obligations such as those contained in arts 7 and 16 contain general obligations to take 'appropriate measures', while at the same time going on to 'require' further specific rights: Byrnes and Connors, 'Enforcing the Human Rights of Women: A Complaints Procedure for the Women's Convention?' (1995) 21 Brok J Int'l L 679, pp 729–732.

questions were accordingly raised as to whether all these obligations would be susceptible to interpretation and application under a communications procedure by an international monitoring body. This issue did not in itself prove to be fractious, as consensus was apparently reached at an early stage that the CEDAW Committee itself would be the appropriate body to determine the question of justiciability;[32] and that justiciability was 'more an issue of degree, given the particularities of a case, rather than of particular rights'.[33] Accordingly, the final text of the OP-CEDAW gives the CEDAW Committee jurisdiction to examine complaints relating to of any of the *rights* set forth in the Convention.[34] While a technical argument could be made that this is in fact a restrictive formulation which would allow the CEDAW Committee to examine only obligations of immediate effect,[35] the preferable view is that it enables the Committee to accept communications on every substantive provision of the Convention.[36] The breadth of that jurisdiction, nonetheless, is bound to give rise to 'considerable difficulties'[37] of interpretation.

[10.05] A third interesting feature of the OP-CEDAW, which generated much discussion at the drafting stage, is the fact that it prohibits States parties from entering reservations to its terms.[38] This explicit prohibition on reservations was apparently intended to counteract a negative trend of this nature which had occurred in respect of the OP-ICCPR which is silent on the question of reservations.[39] While it was predicted that the insertion of such a clear prohibition on reservations in the OP-CEDAW would have the disadvantageous effect of diminishing the participation ratio,[40] the motivations for non-ratification would seem to be so multifarious as to make such a prediction impossible to verify in practice.

[10.06] Finally, it may be noted that the OP-CEDAW also marked a departure from existing individual complaint procedures by explicitly vesting competence in the CEDAW Committee to request respondent States in appropriate cases to adopt interim measures in order to avoid irreparable damage to victim(s) of any alleged violation.[41]

---

[32] See Additional Views: UN Doc E/CN6/1997/5, para 40.
[33] See Additional Views: UN Doc E/CN6/1997/5, para 52.
[34] OP-CEDAW, art 1.
[35] Gomez-Isa, 'The Optional Protocol For the Convention on the Elimination of All Forms of Discrimination Against Women: Strengthening the Protection of Women's Rights' (2003) 20 Ariz J Int'l & Comp L 291, pp 313–314.
[36] For the avoidance of any doubt, a number of States parties to the Protocol have entered interpretive declarations to this effect: Gomez-Isa, 'The Optional Protocol For the Convention on the Elimination of All Forms of Discrimination Against Women: Strengthening the Protection of Women's Rights' (2003) 20 Ariz J Int'l & Comp L 291, p 314.
[37] Tomuschat, *Human Rights: Between Idealism and Realism* (OUP, 2008), p 173.
[38] OP-CEDAW, art 17. As noted earlier, the existence of multiple reservations to the substantive terms of the Women's Convention itself has been a striking phenomenon since its entry into force: see Ch 3, para **3.69**.
[39] See Ch 7, para **7.33** above.
[40] *Additional Views*, para 65.
[41] OP-CEDAW, art 5.

Procedure

[10.07] The procedure by which communications are processed under the OP-CEDAW is similar to that of other individual complaint procedures. The requirements of the Protocol in relation to procedure must be read in conjunction with the CEDAW Committee's Rules of Procedure which were elaborated soon after the entry into force of the Protocol in 2001.[42] The rules allow for the establishment by the Committee of rapporteurs and working groups to make recommendations to it in relation to its work under the Protocol.[43] Immediately after the entry into force of the Protocol, the Committee appointed a five-member working group on communications (WGC) to assist it in the task of making decisions under the Protocol.[44] Individual case rapporteurs are appointed by the Committee to assist in the initial screening of each case.

[10.08] Following the transfer of responsibility for the servicing of the Committee from the Division for the Advancement of Women to the Office of the High Commissioner for Human Rights (OHCHR) in 2008, communications under the OP-CEDAW are now channelled through the petitions unit of the OHCHR. At an early stage, the WGC developed a model form for submission of a communication under the Protocol[45] which is still in usage.[46] The form indicates the essential information that must be included for a communication to be successfully processed, including the standard requirements that it include the relevant facts, any supporting documentation and indicate which provisions of CEDAW have allegedly been violated. The petitions unit will initially screen complaints, in conjunction with the case rapporteur, to ensure that they contain the necessary information and that they comply with the Protocol's admissibility criteria.[47] To save time, the petitions unit will seek clarification from complainants in cases where the complaint is 'unclear, incomplete or unintelligible'.[48] Any clarification that is requested must be provided within a set time limit.[49] If the complainant fails to supply the necessary information, this may result in the communication not being registered. The decision on registration is taken by the WGC having regard to the report provided to it by the petitions team.

---

[42] Rules of Procedure of the CEDAW Committee: UN Doc HRI/GEN/3/Rev3, p 93
[43] Rules of Procedure of the CEDAW Committee, r 62.
[44] Provision is made for the adoption of a working group in Rules of Procedure of the CEDAW Committee, r 62(1). The working group was appointed at the Committee's 24th session in 2001: UN Doc A/56/38, Part 1, Para 366.
[45] This form was adopted by CEDAW at its 26th session in 2002: UN Doc A/57/38, Part 1, para 407.
[46] See 'Information Note on the Submission of Individual Complaints under the CEDAW Optional Protocol': www2.ohchr.org/english/bodies/cedaw/doc.(last accessed May 2011).
[47] See para **[10.16]–[10.25]** below.
[48] Statement of Mr Markus Schmidt (Chief Petitions Unit, OHCHR) CEDAW Summary Record of the 819th Meeting (21 January 2008): 20th February 2008, UN Doc CEDAW/C/SR819, para 25.
[49] See Rules of Procedure of the CEDAW Committee, r 58.

[10.09] Once registered, the communication will normally be transmitted to the State party for a written reply.[50] The State's reply must in turn be received within six months, and normally must relate to the admissibility of the communication and its merits, as well as to any remedy that may have been provided in the matter.[51] In exceptional cases, the rules allow for the WGC or the Committee to request written explanations only as regards admissibility, but in such cases the State is entitled nonetheless to furnish written explanations relating both to admissibility and to the merits in its reply.[52] If the Committee's request for a written reply relates to admissibility and merits, the State may request in writing within two months that the complaint be rejected as inadmissible, setting out the grounds for inadmissibility,[53] but any such request will not affect the period of six months given to the State party to submit its written explanations formally to the CEDAW Committee, unless an extension is deemed appropriate.[54]

[10.10] As with all of the other procedures, great emphasis is placed in this procedure on giving significant opportunities to both the complainant and the State to comment on each party's submissions. In this respect, the Committee's Rules of Procedure provide that the rapporteur, WGC or Committee may transmit to each party the submissions made by the other party and may either request additional submissions[55] or afford each party an opportunity to comment on the submissions received within fixed time limits.[56] It is important to note here that the CEDAW Committee or the WGC may also, at any time in the course of its consideration of a communication under the OP-CEDAW, obtain documentation from any other United Nations body or other bodies that may be of assistance to it in its disposal of the communication, provided that it affords each party an opportunity to comment on such documentation within fixed time limits.[57]

[10.11] As has been noted above, art 5 of the OP-CEDAW specifically gives authority to the Committee to request a State to take such interim measures as it may consider necessary to avoid irreparable damage to the victim(s) of the alleged violation(s), and the rules devolve authority to case rapporteurs and the WGC in this respect.[58] Such measures can be requested at any time after the receipt of a communication and before a determination on the merits has been reached.[59] A request for interim measures is not to be considered in any way determinative of the Committee's views on the merits of a complaint.[60]

---

[50] OP-CEDAW, art 6(1) and Rules of Procedure of the CEDAW Committee, r 69(1). Note that under art 6(1), it is possible for the CEDAW Committee to deem a communication inadmissible without reference to the State party.
[51] OP-CEDAW, art 6(2) and Rules of Procedure of the CEDAW Committee, r 69(3).
[52] Rules of Procedure of the CEDAW Committee, r 69(4).
[53] Rules of Procedure of the CEDAW Committee, r 69(5).
[54] Rules of Procedure of the CEDAW Committee, r 69(7).
[55] Rules of Procedure of the CEDAW Committee, r 69(8).
[56] Rules of Procedure of the CEDAW Committee, r 69(9).
[57] Rules of Procedure of the CEDAW Committee, r 72(2).
[58] Rules of Procedure of the CEDAW Committee, r 63.
[59] OP-CEDAW, art 5(1) and Rules of Procedure of the CEDAW Committee, r 63(1).
[60] OP-CEDAW, art 5(2) and Rules of Procedure of the CEDAW Committee, r 63(4).

[10.12] The main task of the WGC is to scrutinise the complaints in terms of admissibility and where it deems them to be admissible, to make recommendations to the Committee on the merits of a communication. The WGC may only decide that the communication is admissible by a unanimous vote.[61] Where the WGC has been unable to reach a unanimous decision that the communication is admissible, the plenary Committee must decide on the admissibility of the communication before reaching a view on the merits.[62] It may decide to render its decision on admissibility separately, or in conjunction with its opinion on the merits.[63] If the Committee decides that the complaint is admissible separately, that decision will be transmitted to the parties and the Committee may later decide to revoke its decision in the light of any explanations or statements submitted by the State party.[64] If the Committee decides that the case is inadmissible, the reasons for the decision will be communicated to the author and that will normally put an end to the case.[65] A decision of inadmissibility may, however, be reviewed upon the receipt of a written request from the author to the effect that the reasons for inadmissibility no longer apply.[66]

[10.13] Where the CEDAW Committee makes a decision on the merits (either in conjunction with its decision on admissibility or separately as the case may be), its views, together with any recommendation(s), shall be transmitted to the author and the state party concerned.[67] The CEDAW Committee reaches its decisions on admissibility and its views on the merits by a simple majority.[68] Individual members are entitled to append separate opinions (whether dissenting of concurring) to the majority opinion.[69]

[10.14] As with the previous procedures, there is no provision in the Protocol for oral hearings, and consideration of communications is conducted in closed session and entirely confidentially.[70] With respect to confidentiality, neither the author nor the State party are precluded from making public any submissions or information with respect to the proceedings,[71] unless specifically requested not to do so.[72] Decisions on admissibility

---

[61] Rules of Procedure of the CEDAW Committee, r 64(2).
[62] Rules of Procedure of the CEDAW Committee, r 72(4).
[63] Rules of Procedure of the CEDAW Committee, r 66.
[64] Rules of Procedure of the CEDAW Committee, r 71.
[65] Rules of Procedure of the CEDAW Committee, r 70(1).
[66] Rules of Procedure of the CEDAW Committee, r 70(2).
[67] OP-CEDAW, art 7(3) and Rules of Procedure of the CEDAW Committee, r 72(5).
[68] Rules of Procedure of the CEDAW Committee, rr 64(1) and 72(5).
[69] Rules of Procedure of the CEDAW Committee, rr 70(3) and 72(6). Note that in recent times, the Committee has been discussing its preferred *modus operandi* in regard to the formulation and format of individual opinions on Committee decisions: Summary record of the 819th meeting, UN Doc CEDAW/C/SR819.
[70] OP-CEDAW, art 7(2) and Rules of Procedure of the CEDAW Committee, rr 69(1) and 74.
[71] Rules of Procedure of the CEDAW Committee, r 74(7).
[72] Rules of Procedure of the CEDAW Committee, r 74(6).

and the views of the Committee are public documents,[73] though the Committee may decide not to reveal the identity of the author.[74]

[10.15] The views of the Committee are not technically binding on the State party. Indeed, OP-CEDAW makes this plain by providing that the State need only give 'due consideration' to the views of the Committee and its recommendations.[75] Nonetheless, the OP-CEDAW does explicitly provide for follow-up measures by requiring respondent States to provide a written response to the Committee on any views addressed to them within six months, which should include details of any action taken.[76] The Committee may continue to seek further information from respondent States in regard to possible follow-on action,[77] if needs be in the context of the art 18 reporting procedure.[78] The Committee includes information on its follow-up activities in its annual report under art 21 of the Convention.[79]

ADMISSIBILITY

[10.16] The admissibility criteria for complaints under the Protocol are contained in arts 2, 3 and 4. The thrust of these criteria are essentially the same as those provided for in the OP-ICCPR, though certain modifications may be noted in the text.

[10.17] Pursuant to art 2 of the OP-CEDAW, communications may be submitted by individuals or groups of individuals or on their behalf, provided that the making of the communication is with their consent or the author can justify acting on their behalf without their consent.[80] This opens the possibility of NGOs representing individual victims, albeit in limited circumstances. Communications were successfully made on the latter basis in the cases of *Goeckce v Austria*[81] and *Yildirim v Austria*[82] in respect of the deceased victims by domestic NGOs that protect and support women victims of gender-based violence.

[10.18] Complaints must not be anonymous,[83] abusive[84] or incompatible with the provisions of the CEDAW.[85] As explained in Chapter 7 in regard to the OP-ICCPR, the

---

[73] Rules of Procedure of the CEDAW Committee, r 74(8).
[74] Rules of Procedure of the CEDAW Committee, r 74(5).
[75] OP-CEDAW, art 7(4).
[76] OP-CEDAW, art 7(4). See also Rules of Procedure of the CEDAW Committee, r 73.
[77] Rules of Procedure of the CEDAW Committee, r 73(2).
[78] OP-CEDAW, art 7(5) and Rules of Procedure of the CEDAW Committee, r 73(3). As to the reporting procedure, see Ch 4, paras **4.51–4.59**.
[79] Rules of Procedure of the CEDAW Committee, r 73(7).
[80] OP-CEDAW, art 2 and Rules of Procedure of the CEDAW Committee, r 60.
[81] *Goeckce v Austria*, Communication No 5/2005.
[82] *Yildirim v Austria*, Communication No 6/2005.
[83] Article 3 OP-CEDAW and Rules of Procedure of the CEDAW Committee, r 56(3)(a). Note again that it is possible for the complainant's identity/name not be published: Rules of Procedure of the CEDAW Committee, rr 74(5) and (6).
[84] OP-CEDAW, art 4(2)(d).
[85] OP-CEDAW, art 4(2)(b).

concept of incompatibility implicitly embraces complaints that are incompatible *ratione personae, materiae, loci* and *temporis*.[86] In regard to incompatibility *ratione temporis*, the OP-CEDAW provides that a complaint will be inadmissible where the facts which are the subject of the communication occurred prior to the entry into force of the Protocol for the State party concerned.[87] The CEDAW Committee has considered objections raised by respondent States to a number of communications made under the OP-CEDAW on this ground. In considering these communications, the Committee has embraced the concept of 'continuing violations', made explicit in the text of art 4(2)(e) whereby a communication based on acts or facts which occurred prior to entry into force of the Protocol may still be admissible where the effects of the measure(s) continue post-ratification. However, its application of this concept has not always been consistent. In *AT v Hungary*, for example, which concerned a communication about on-going domestic violence, the Committee considered itself competent *ratione temporis* to consider the communication in its entirety, notwithstanding that many of the incidents of violence cited by the author took place prior to entry into force of the Protocol.[88] It did so, quite correctly, on the basis that the incidents cited formed an uninterrupted series of attacks, beginning in 1998 (before the Protocol entered into force) until after 2001 when it did enter into force, the nature of which was central to the allegation of culpable inaction on the part of the State party.[89]

[10.19] Other cases concern identifiable acts which do not form part of a series of on-going events such as those at issue in the domestic violence cases. In this context, a particularly flexible attitude is apparent in the Committee's decision in *AS v Hungary*,[90] which concerned an allegation of forced sterilisation. In that case, despite the government's objection that the surgery which gave rise to the author's complaint had taken place prior to entry into force of the OP-CEDAW, the Committee held that the 'continuous nature' of the effects of that surgery, particularly its irreversible character, justified the communication being deemed admissible *ratione temporis*.[91] This outcome can be contrasted with the CEDAW Committee's decision in *Muños-Vargas Y Sainz de Vicuña v Spain*,[92] which concerned a complaint about alleged discrimination in Spanish succession law in regard to titles of nobility. The author complained that the law in question, which had resulted in her brother being given preference to her in succeeding to their late father's title, constituted discrimination generally and specifically a violation of art 2(f) of the Convention.[93] The Committee held that the communication was inadmissible *ratione temporis* pursuant to art 4(2)(e) of the OP-CEDAW. It held that

---

[86] See Ch 7, paras **7.20–7.34**.
[87] OP-CEDAW, art 4(2)(e).
[88] *AT v Hungary*, Communication No 2/2003.
[89] *AT v Hungary*, Communication No 2/2003, para 8.5.
[90] *AS v Hungary*, Communication No 4/2004.
[91] *AS v Hungary*, Communication No 4/2004, para 10.4.
[92] *Muños-Vargas Y Sainz de Vicuña v Spain*, Communication No 7/2005.
[93] CEDAW, art 4(2)(f) obliges the States parties to take all appropriate measures, including legislation, to modify or abolish existing laws, regulations, customs and practices which constitute discrimination against women.

the relevant point in time in this case was the date on which the title in question was vested in the author's brother, which had taken place well before the Convention had been ratified by the State party and indeed before the Optional Protocol had even been adopted.[94] The Committee did not appear to answer the author's contention that the claim was admissible *ratione temporis* because an appeal in her case was still pending at the time that the OP-CEDAW entered into force for Spain.[95] It dismissed the contention that the discrimination that she suffered was of a continuous nature on the basis 'that the complaint occurred and was completed at the time of the issuance of the decree'.[96] It is difficult to resist the conclusion that the Committee's dismissal of the communication may have been influenced by the triviality of its substance (particularly in comparison with the egregious nature of the complaint in *AS*). However, it would be helpful if the CEDAW Committee were to articulate clear and discernible criteria as regards what constitutes a 'continuing violation',[97] as otherwise it leaves itself open to the charge of inconsistency.[98]

[10.20] Another ground of incompatibility arises where a complaint is inadmissible *ratione personae* in circumstances where the author is deemed not to be a 'victim' of a violation of the Convention.[99] This issue has been contentious in the context of communications regarding legislation governing family names in France. As a result of this legislation, the two unmarried authors in the case of *GD and SF v France* had been unable to change their official family name from their father's name which had been given to them at birth to that of their mothers.[100] Both women had lived with their mothers, having been abandoned by their fathers at an early age. They had each unofficially used their mother's names for most of their lives and had sought to formally change their names on the basis that their psychological, familial, social and administrative identity rested with their mothers. They claimed that the legislation in question governing family names contravened the principle of equality between parents and constituted a violation of art 16(1)(g) of the Convention.[101] A majority of the Committee found, however, that the women were not 'victims' of a violation of art 16(1)(g) on the basis that this article is aimed at enabling married women or those in similar relationships to keep their maiden name upon marriage and to transmit that name to their children. As the authors were neither married, nor living in *de facto*

---

[94] *Muños-Vargas Y Sainz de Vicuña v Spain*, Communication No 7/2005, para 11.5.
[95] *Muños-Vargas Y Sainz de Vicuña v Spain*, Communication No 7/2005, para 8.5.
[96] *Muños-Vargas Y Sainz de Vicuña v Spain*, Communication No 7/2005, para 11.5.
[97] As noted above, assistance can be drawn in this respect from the work of the International Law Commission or indeed the case law of the European Court of Human Rights: Ch 7, paras **7.22**.
[98] See Murdoch, 'Unfulfilled Expectations: the Optional Protocol to the Convention on the Elimination of All Forms of Discrimination Against Women' (2010) EHRLR 26, p 37.
[99] The victim requirement is deduced from OP-CEDAW, art 2 and Rules of Procedure of the CEDAW Committee, r 68(1).
[100] *GD and SF v France*, Communication No 12/2007.
[101] OP-CEDAW, art 16(1)(g) obliges the States parties to ensure 'The same personal rights as husband and wife, including the right to choose a family name, a profession and an occupation'.

relationships, they could not claim to be victims of a right whose beneficiaries were only married women.[102] A significant number of Committee members dissented from this view, holding that the facts gave rise to an act of discrimination relating to 'family relations' which was covered by art 16(1) chapeau,[103] as well as arts 2 and 5 of the Convention.[104] In their view, the authors were indirect victims of the discriminatory legislation in question which was 'based on a patriarchal view of fathers as heads of family imposed by the State party during their childhood'.[105]

[10.21] The cases regarding transmission of family names also gave rise to the first occasion on which the Committee was faced with a challenge to the admissibility of a complaint on the basis that the respondent State had entered a reservation to the relevant provision of the Convention. Specifically, France challenged the admissibility of the communications on the grounds that they were incompatible with art 16(1)(g) of the Convention in respect of which France had already entered a reservation. Such an argument raises in essence the question of whether a complaint is incompatible *ratione materiae* with the State's obligations under CEDAW. The issue of entering reservations to CEDAW is particularly contentious, since an overwhelming proportion of States parties have done so over the years in respect of some of its most fundamental provisions.[106] Accordingly, the question of whether the CEDAW Committee would follow the practice of the Human Rights Committee (CCPR) in considering itself competent to rule on the validity of reservations made to the substantive provisions of the Convention is of critical importance.[107] In the cases against France, the female authors had urged the Committee to disregard the State party's reservations to art 16(1)(g), particularly in the light of the Committee's stated views on the subject. In this respect, the authors highlighted the fact that in its concluding comments on the State's most recent periodic report, the Committee had in fact urged France to withdraw its reservation on the basis that reservations made to art 16 of the Convention are

---

[102] *GD and SF v France*, Communication No 12/2007, para 11.10. A similar conclusion was also reached in a subsequent challenge to the legislation as regards two of the authors (Ms Dayras and Ms Zeghouani) in the case of *Dayras et al v France*, Communication No 13/2007, para 10.7.

[103] The term 'chapeau' refers to the over-arching sentence of Article 16(1) that the 'States Parties shall take all appropriate measures to eliminate discrimination against women in all matters relating to marriage and family relations and in particular shall ensure, on a basis of equality of men and women....' the various sub-paras outlined thereafter.

[104] *GD and SF v France*, Communication No 12/2007, para 12.10.

[105] *GD and SF v France*, Communication No 12/2007, para 12.13.

[106] The CEDAW Committee itself has highlighted this problem on a number of occasions. See, in particular: UN Doc A/53/38/Rev 1, Part 2, Ch 1 (para 17).

[107] See the discussion of the CCPR'S practice in Ch 7, para **7.33**. The expectation that the CEDAW Committee would follow the CCPR's practice in this respect had been raised by Byrnes and Connors during the drafting of the Protocol: 'Enforcing the Human Rights of Women: A Complaints Procedure for the Women's Convention?' (1995) 21 Brok J Int'l L 679, pp 741–742.

incompatible with the Convention.[108] Notwithstanding that clear recommendation, in the case of *GD and SF v France*, the Committee held that it was not necessary to consider the issue on the basis that the authors were not the appropriate beneficiaries of the right in question.[109] While this is a tenable position, it is possible that the Committee was simply reluctant to grasp the nettle of ruling whether the reservation itself was incompatible with the Convention in contentious proceedings under the OP-CEDAW. Since the Committee clearly believed that art 16(1)(g) was the applicable provision in the case, it is arguable that it should have taken the opportunity to assert explicitly its competence to rule on the matter and its view as to the validity of the reservation in question.[110]

[10.22] Article 4(2)(a) of the OP-CEDAW also renders inadmissible complaints in which the 'same matter' has already been examined by the CEDAW Committee or under another procedure of international investigation or settlement. It also explicitly rules out complaints that are *simultaneously* being examined by another international complaint procedure.[111] An attempt by the Turkish government to rely on this ground of inadmissibility in *Kayhan v Turkey* was summarily refuted by the Committee on the basis that the author was a different individual to the person who had brought the complaint to the European Court of Human Rights to which the State party had referred.[112] In this case, the Committee was clearly adopting the rationale of the CCPR that the 'same matter' means a complaint made by the 'same individual' to another international body of investigation or settlement.[113] Murdoch is critical of the CEDAW Committee, however, for failing to lay down clear guidance as regards the criteria on which it is basing its decisions on this ground and for avoiding engagement at all in some cases with submissions by respondent States on this issue.[114]

[10.23] Article 4(2)(c) of the OP-CEDAW specifically provides that the CEDAW Committee shall declare a communication inadmissible where it is 'manifestly ill-

---

[108] *GD and SF v France*, Communication No 12/2007, para 5.1 and see Report of the Committee on the Elimination of All Forms of Discrimination Against Women: UN Doc A/58/38/SUPP, Part II, Ch IV, paras 251–252.

[109] *GD and SF v France*, Communication No 12/2007, para 11.10. In *Dayras et al v France*, Communication No 13/2007, it again side-stepped the issue by deciding the issue of admissibility on grounds of victim status and exhaustion of domestic remedies.

[110] This appears to have been the view of the dissenters in regard to the Committee's majority opinion: *GD and SF v France*, Communication No 12/2007, para 12.8.

[111] The text of the OP-CEDAW is thus more muscular than that of the OP-ICCPR which only renders inadmissible complaints which are simultaneously being examined by another international procedure: see in this respect Ch 7, paras **7.35–7.36**.

[112] *Kayhan v Turkey*, Communication No 8/2005, para 7.3.

[113] See Ch 7, para **7.35**.

[114] Murdoch, 'Unfulfilled Expectations: the Optional Protocol to the Convention on the Elimination of All Forms of Discrimination Against Women' (2010) EHRLR 26, pp 35–36, citing the cases of *Muños-Vargas Y Sainz de Vicuña v Spain*, Communication No 7/2005, paras 7.4 and 11.6; and *NSF v United Kingdom*, Communication No 10/2005, paras 4.3 and 7.4.

founded' or 'not sufficiently substantiated'. Thus far, the CEDAW Committee has not had occasion to deem a complaint inadmissible on either of these grounds. It is likely that a communication will be deemed 'manifestly ill-founded' where it does not disclose a *prima facie* violation of CEDAW (for example, where the facts do not disclose on their face any interference with a protected right or where interference is clearly justified).[115] It may be anticipated that the CEDAW Committee will follow the lead of the CCPR in terms of the criteria to be applied in deciding whether a claim lacks substantiation.[116]

[10.24] Individual complaints made under the OP-CEDAW must also satisfy the domestic remedies rule in art 4(1) whereby the CEDAW Committee shall not consider a communication '...unless it has considered that all domestic remedies have been exhausted unless the application of such remedies is unreasonably prolonged or unlikely to bring effective relief'. In *Kayhan v Turkey,* the CEDAW Committee first indicated its interpretation of the rule as requiring that an author must have raised in substance at the domestic level the claim that he or she wishes to bring before the Committee so as to enable the domestic authorities and or the courts to have an opportunity to deal with the claim.[117] However, as Murdoch has argued, the Committee's application of this criterion in the *Kayhan* case itself is surprisingly 'harsh'.[118] The author was a female Muslim who had claimed a violation of art 11 of the Convention because of her dismissal from her job as a civil servant for wearing a headscarf.[119] The Committee found the communication inadmissible for failure to exhaust domestic remedies because none of the appeals which the author had taken against the authorities in relation to her use of the headscarf had ever been specifically based on sex-discrimination, but rather on other grounds.[120] The severity of the decision is evident when one considers that the State itself had not raised this argument in its pleadings on admissibility; and that the pleadings explicitly referred to decisions of the Supreme Court and the Constitutional Court in Turkey which had held that the prohibition on using the headscarf did not constitute discrimination against women.[121]

---

[115] This is the criterion applied by the European Court of Human Rights in determining that a complaint under the ECHR is 'manifestly ill-founded' and hence inadmissible under art 35(3) thereof: See generally, *Practical Guide on Admissibility Criteria* (Council of Europe/European Court of Human Rights, 2010), pp 82–90.

[116] See Ch 7, para **7.34**.

[117] *Kayhan v Turkey*, Communication No 8/2005, para 7.7. See also, the decision of the CEDAW Committee in *Zhen Zhen Zheng v The Netherlands*, Communication No 15/2007, para 7.3.

[118] Murdoch, 'Unfulfilled Expectations: the Optional Protocol to the Convention on the Elimination of All Forms of Discrimination Against Women' (2010) EHRLR 26, p 35.

[119] CEDAW, art 11 obliges States parties to CEDAW to take all appropriate measures to eliminate discrimination against women in the field of employment.

[120] *Kayhan v Turkey*, Communication No 8/2005, para 7.6–7.7.

[121] This critique is made by Facio in 'The OP-CEDAW as a Mechanism for Implementing Women's Human Rights: An Analysis of the First Five Cases under the Communications Procedure of the OP-CEDAW' (International Asia Pacific Occasional Papers Series No 12), p 41: http://www.iwraw-ap.org/aboutus/pdf/OPS12_Final_for_publication_April_28.pdf (last accessed May 2011). (contd.../)

[10.25] Interestingly, Article 4 OP-CEDAW explicitly stipulates that exhaustion of this rule is not required where the application of the remedies is unreasonably prolonged '...or unlikely to bring effective relief'. In regard to the meaning of 'effective' relief, the CEDAW Committee has drawn on the views of the Human Rights Committee in holding that 'mere doubts about the effectiveness of the remedies do not absolve an individual from exhausting domestic remedies'.[122] The CEDAW Committee's interpretation of the phrase 'unreasonably prolonged', however, has been somewhat erratic. In *AT v Hungary*, for example, the Committee quite correctly deemed a delay of over three years from the filing of a charge in a domestic violence case to conviction as constituting an unreasonably prolonged delay for the purposes of art 4(1) of the Protocol.[123] On the other hand, in *B-J v Germany*, the Committee deemed an application inadmissible for non-exhaustion even though domestic proceedings had apparently been on-going for some five years in a complaint regarding the financial impact of an unwanted divorce on a woman who had spent her life working in the home in Germany.[124]

VIEWS

[10.26] Even though the OP-CEDAW has been in force for over 10 years, the dearth of views rendered by the CEDAW Committee under it is striking. Indeed, only six cases have been decided on their merits to date. Three of the latter have involved communications regarding the inadequacy of the legal and institutional framework in place to deal with domestic violence in the respondent States.[125] The central finding in each of these cases was that there had been a failure on the part of the States parties to exercise their obligations of 'due diligence' to prevent violence on the part of private actors and to provide effective legal and institutional remedies to female victims of such crimes. Nonetheless, as Murdoch has noted, despite the similarity in the factual circumstances which grounded the claims in all three cases, violations were established

---

[121] (\...contd) A similarly tough stance was taken in *Zhen Zhen Zheng v The Netherlands*, Communication No 15/2007, para 7.3, in which the claim was also deemed inadmissible because of the failure of the complainant to raise the substance of her complaint in domestic proceedings. Three members of the Committee dissented because they did not believe that any of the domestic remedies cited by the State could have provided effective relief for a victim of trafficking such as the author. The same critique is made of the Committee's case law on this issue by Murdoch, 'Unfulfilled Expectations: the Optional Protocol to the Convention on the Elimination of All Forms of Discrimination Against Women' (2010) EHRLR 26, para 35.

[122] *Zhen Zhen Zheng v The Netherlands*, Communication No 15/2007, para 7.3.

[123] *AT v Hungary*, Communication No 2/2003, para 8.4.

[124] *B-J v Germany*, Communication No 1/2003, para 8.7. Note the dissenting views of Committee members Krisztina Morvai and Meriem Belmihoub-Zerdani on this point. See also the critique offered by Facio, 'The OP-CEDAW as a Mechanism for Implementing Women's Human Rights: An Analysis of the First Five Cases under the Communications Procedure of the OP-CEDAW' (International Asia Pacific Occasional Papers Series No 12), pp 4–13.

[125] *AT v Hungary*, Communication No 2/2003; *Goeckce v Austria*, Communication No 5/2005; and *Yildirim v Austria*, Communication No 6/2005.

as between them on different provisions[126] of the Convention.[127] On a more positive note, the Committee's views in each case included wide-ranging recommendations regarding the measures necessary to prevent and protect women generally from domestic violence in their respective jurisdictions.

[10.27] The fourth case to have yielded a determination on the merits involved a complaint regarding the scheme for maternity leave benefits in the Netherlands.[128] A majority of the Committee decided that the scheme in question did not violate art 11(2)(b) of the Convention which obliges States parties to CEDAW to take appropriate measures to introduce maternity leave with pay or with comparable social benefits without loss of former employment, seniority or social allowances. In its view, the scheme allowed for separate rules for self-employed women that took account of fluctuating income and related contributions and as such fell within the State's margin of discretion under the Convention.[129]

[10.28] A fifth case to have resulted in a decision on the merits is that of *AS v Hungary* concerning forced sterilisation of the author without her knowledge or consent.[130] In this case, the CEDAW Committee found that the failure of the State party, through the hospital at issue, to provide appropriate information and advice to the author on the consequences of sterilisation and family planning, constituted a violation of her right to educational information contrary to art 10(h) of the Convention.[131] It had little difficulty

---

[126] In *AT v Hungary*, Communication No 2/2003, the Committee determined that there had been a violation of art 2(a)(b) and (e), as well as arts 5 and 16 of the Convention; whereas in *Goeckce v Austria*, Communication No 5/2005 and *Yildirim v Austria*, Communication No 6/2005, the Committee grounded the violations in art 2(a) and (c)–(f) '... as well as in Article 3 in conjunction with Article 1 of the Convention and general recommendation 19 and the corresponding rights of the deceased...to life and physical and mental integrity'.

[127] 'The vital importance of collegiate decision-making seems not to have been recognised. This does not strengthen faith in the quality of adjudication on the part of states parties who may wish to be assured that the Committee is determining like cases in a like manner': Murdoch, 'Unfulfilled Expectations: the Optional Protocol to the Convention on the Elimination of All Forms of Discrimination Against Women' (2010) EHRLR 26, pp 39–40.

[128] *Dung Thi Thuy Nguyen v The Netherlands*, Communication No 3/2004.

[129] *Dung Thi Thuy Nguyen v The Netherlands*, Communication No 3/2004, para 10.3. Three members of the Committee dissented from the majority in this case on the basis that while the legislation did not reveal a direct form of discrimination on grounds of sex, it could be deemed to constitute *indirect* sex-based discrimination. They reached this view on the basis that the combination of salaried employment and part-time employment to which the scheme was applicable, as exemplified by the author's case, arose mainly in regard to women in the Netherlands, since in general it is mainly women who work part-time as salaried employees in addition to working as family helpers in their husband's businesses. Since this working assumption (derived principally from the State's fourth periodic report which had yet to be discussed by the Committee) had not been substantiated on the facts of the case, the dissenting members went on to make some general recommendations to the State in respect of the operation of the scheme in question: paras 10.4–10.6.

[130] See para **[10.19]**.

[131] *AS v Hungary*, Communication No 4/2004, para 11.2.

in finding that the State had violated art 12 of the Convention by reason of its failure to ensure that the author had given her fully informed consent to be sterilised.[132] Drawing on its General Recommendation No 19 on violence against women, which deals specifically with the issue of compulsory sterilisation,[133] the Committee found a violation of art 16(1)(e) of the Convention which obliges States to ensure equal rights to women in matters of family planning.[134]

[10.29] The final case in which a determination on the merits has been reached is that of *Vertido v The Philippines* in which the author claimed a number of violations of CEDAW arising from the trial and subsequent judgment of a person acquitted of her rape.[135] In that case, the CEDAW Committee found a violation of the right to an effective remedy in art 2(c) of CEDAW by reason of an inordinate delay of some eight years in the trial proceedings.[136] Of much more significance, however, is the central finding in the case that the State was responsible for breaching the Convention in regard to the deployment of wrongful gender stereotyping by the trial judge in reaching her decision on acquittal.[137] While recognising clearly the limits of its institutional competence in terms of reviewing the decisions of domestic courts,[138] the Committee pointed to several particular examples of gender stereotypes and 'rape myths' which had clearly influenced the judge's thinking in the case.[139] Accordingly, it found that the State had failed to fulfil its obligations in respect of arts 2(f)[140] and 5(a),[141] which are specifically concerned with

---

[132] *AS v Hungary*, Communication No 4/2004, para 11.3. CEDAW, art 12(1) obliges States parties to take all appropriate measures to eliminate discrimination against women in the field of health care in order to ensure, on a basis of equality of men and women, access to health care services, including those related to family planning.

[133] UN Doc A/47/38 at 1, see in particular para 22.

[134] *AS v Hungary*, Communication No 4/2004, para 11.4. CEDAW, art 16(1)(e) obliges States parties to take all appropriate measures to eliminate discrimination against women in all matters relating to marriage and family relations and in particular to ensure on a basis of equality of men and women, *inter alia*, '(e) the same rights to decide freely and responsibly on the number and spacing of their children and to have access to the information, education and means to enable them to exercise these rights'.

[135] *Vertido v The Philippines*, Communication No 18/2008.

[136] *Vertido v The Philippines*, Communication No 18/2008, para 8.3 '...for a remedy to be effective, adjudication of a case involving rape and sexual offenses claims should be dealt with in a fair, impartial, timely and expeditious manner'.

[137] *Vertido v The Philippines*, Communication No 18/2008, para 8.8–8.9

[138] In this respect, the Committee emphasised that '...it does not replace the domestic authorities in the assessment of the facts, nor does it decide on the alleged perpetrator's criminal responsibility': *Vertido v The Philippines*, Communication No 18/2008.

[139] *Vertido v The Philippines*, Communication No 18/2008, paras 8.5–8.6.

[140] CEDAW, art 2(f) obliges the Contracting states to 'to take all appropriate measures, including legislation, to modify or abolish existing laws, regulations, customs and practices which constitute discrimination against women'.

[141] CEDAW, art 5(a) obliges the States parties to modify the social and cultural patterns of conduct of men and women, with a view to achieving the elimination of prejudices and customary and all other practices which are based on the idea of inferiority or the superiority of either of the sexes or on stereotyped roles for men and women'.

the elimination of measures involving gender stereotyping.[142] As well as recommending compensation for the author, the CEDAW Committee made detailed recommendations to the State on the law, policy and legal procedures in the State with respect to the trial of rape and sexual offences.[143] As with the cases on domestic violence, the CEDAW Committee's views in this case are perhaps the best demonstration of the potential value of the Protocol in highlighting with particular clarity systemic practices which lie at the heart of women's individual experience of discrimination.

APPRAISAL

[10.30] Expectations for the value of an Optional Protocol to the Women's Convention were high from the outset of its drafting. It was, for example, predicted that the elaboration of a Protocol could make a 'significant contribution to strengthening the Convention, as well as the Committee',[144] that it 'would provide guidance to States parties in their efforts to implement the Convention',[145] as well as an incentive for them to 'embark expeditiously on the establishment of domestic control mechanisms in order to avoid international oversight'.[146] While the possibility of overlap or duplication, particularly with the OP-ICCPR, was raised at an early stage in the drafting of the OP-CEDAW, the advantages of a separate procedure were generally considered to trump the disadvantages. Specifically, the prospect of a separate communications procedure would ensure a dedicated focus to gender issues, particularly in the area of social and economic rights. The procedure under the OP-ICCPR was simply not suitable having regard to the very broad remit of the CCPR and the fact that it only applied to individual communications, whereas many violations of women's rights consisted of systematic failures to implement the obligations in CEDAW.[147]

[10.31] In actual fact, the experience to date of the operation of the OP-CEDAW has prompted one commentator to question whether it has any 'add-on-value' to the panoply of human rights procedures already available to tackle discrimination against women.[148] Even though the OP-CEDAW has only been in force since 2000, the range of views rendered to date is surprisingly low, as is the profile of respondent States.[149] The real value of the mechanism in principle is demonstrated by the cases on domestic violence and the recent one on gender stereo-typing. In this respect, the CEDAW Committee has made powerful use of the text of the OP-CEDAW in making detailed policy

---

[142] See the critique by Cusack and Timmer of the decision of the Committee in 'Gender Stereotyping in Rape Cases: The CEDAW Committee's Decision in Vertido v The Philippines' (2011) HRL Rev 1.
[143] *Vertido v The Philippines*, Communication No 18/2008, paras 8.8–8.9.
[144] See Additional Views: UN Doc E/CN6/1997/5, para 14.
[145] See Additional Views: UN Doc E/CN6/1997/5, para 18.
[146] See Additional Views: UN Doc E/CN6/1997/5, para 19.
[147] See Additional Views: UN Doc E/CN6/1997/5, paras 27–37.
[148] Murdoch, 'Unfulfilled Expectations: the Optional Protocol to the Convention on the Elimination of All Forms of Discrimination Against Women' (2010) EHRLR 26, pp 40–46.
[149] Complaints have only been considered to date in regard to Germany, Hungary, the Netherlands, Austria, Spain, Turkey, the United Kingdom, France and the Philippines.

recommendations to States parties on how to eliminate systematic practices that lie at the heart of the individual complaints in those cases. The reasonably robust follow-up procedure specifically provided for in the Protocol has yielded some promising results in at least two of the latter cases.[150] Many challenges still exist, however, for the CEDAW Committee in harnessing the value of the OP-CEDAW – from publicising the instrument more effectively, engaging potential complainants and improving the quality of its decision making on admissibility.

---

[150] See Report of the Committee under the Optional Protocol on follow-up to views of the Committee on Individual Communications, in Annual Report of the CEDAW Committee, Annex VII, pp 104–118. See, in particular, the reports on *Goeckce v Austria*, Communication No 5/2005 and *Yildirim v Austria*, Communication No 6/2005.

Chapter 11

Optional Protocol to the Convention on the Rights of Persons with Disabilities

INTRODUCTION

[11.01] As noted earlier, on-going debate in the United Nations on the subject of treaty-body reform generally had an inevitable effect on the negotiations of the Convention on the Rights of Persons with Disabilities (CRPD), especially with regard to the subject of international monitoring.[1] Opposition was voiced in some quarters during the negotiations to the establishment of a new international monitoring body to monitor the CRPD in the midst of wider debate on treaty-body reform.[2] Even when agreement was reached not to procrastinate on this issue, further resistance emerged to the notion of including an individual complaint procedure in the body of the CRPD itself.[3] Accordingly, a compromise was reached that a complaint procedure should be provided for in a separate Optional Protocol which would be adopted simultaneously with the parent Convention. Thus, the Optional Protocol to the Convention on the Rights of

---

[1] See Ch 3, para **3.102–3.115**.

[2] See, for example, the contributions of Australia and the US at the sixth session of the working group of the ad hoc committee that drafted the text of the CRPD: Daily summary of discussion at the sixth session (11 August 2005), http://www.un.org/esa/socdev/enable/rights/ahc6sum11aug.htm (last accessed May 2011). See further, the remarks of the US during the seventh session: Daily summary of discussion at the seventh session (27 January 2006), http://www.un.org/esa/socdev/enable/rights/a hc7sum27jan.htm (last accessed May 2011). These concerns were apparently raised again during negotiations at the eighth session by Sudan, China, the Russian Federation and Australia. See Ad Hoc Committee on a Comprehensive and Integral International Convention on the Protection and Promotion of the Rights and Dignity of Persons with Disabilities (eighth session, New York, 14–25 August 2006), International Service for Human Rights: http://www.handicap-international.fr/kit-pedagogique/documents/ressourcesdocumentaires/redactionconv/ISHR/8thsession.pdfat (last accessed May 2011), p 15. See also, DPI Disability Convention Daily Update, 14 August 2006 (Day One): www.dpi.org/lang-en/resources/topics_detail.php?page=676 (last accessed May 2011).

[3] DPI Disability Convention Daily Update, 14 August 2006 (Day One): www.dpi.org/lang-en/resources/topics_detail.php?page=676 (last accessed May 2011). The OHCHR had by that stage submitted an expert paper for the consideration of the ad hoc committee which had advocated the inclusion of inquiry and communication procedures: Expert paper on existing monitoring mechanisms and possible innovations in monitoring mechanism for a comprehensive and integral international convention on the protection and promotion of the rights and dignity of person with disabilities, UN Doc A/AC265/2006/CRP4, paras 43–50 (OHCHR expert paper).

Persons with Disabilities (OP-CRPD) was adopted in December 2006 and entered into force in 2008.[4]

[11.02] Despite high hopes on the part of NHRIs and civil society, in particular, that the drafting process could result in innovative approaches to monitoring that might even serve as a template for wider reform,[5] the complaint procedure in the OP-CRPD is largely imitative of the text and practical operation of previous complaints procedures.[6] Thus, like the procedure in the ICERD and the OP-CEDAW, it provides for the possibility of complaints being submitted[7] to the CRPD Committee by 'or on behalf of individuals or groups of individuals' who claim to be victims of a violation of *any*[8] of the provisions of the CRPD in the jurisdiction of any of the States parties to the Protocol.[9] The OHCHR had advised the ad hoc committee which drafted the text of the OP-CRPD of the need for a broad approach to the question of standing under the Protocol, given the particular challenges that might confront individuals with disabilities in accessing the complaint procedure.[10] It may be noted, therefore, that the possibility of complaints being submitted 'on behalf' of individuals is not expressly qualified as it is in the OP-CEDAW by the necessity for representatives to show that the victim's consent was explicitly obtained or that he or she is justified in acting without such consent.[11]

[11.03] The OHCHR had also advised the drafters to consider the possibility of broadening representation of complaints even further by making provision for the

---

[4] The OP-CRPD has been ratified by 61 of the 101 States parties to the CRPD: United Nations Treaty Collection, http://treaties.un.org/Pages/Treaties.aspx?id=4&subid=A&lang=en (last accessed May 2011).

[5] See the contributions of NHRIs and NGOs at the sixth session of the working group of the ad hoc committee that drafted the text of the UN Convention: Daily summary of discussion at the sixth session (11 August 2005), http://www.un.org/esa/socdev/enable/rights/ahc6sum11aug.htm (last accessed May 2011).

[6] Bruce, 'Negotiating the Monitoring Mechanism for the Convention on the Rights of Persons with Disabilities: Two Steps Forward, One Step Back' in Alfredsson et al (eds), *International Human Rights Monitoring Mechanisms* (Martinus Nijhoff, 2009), p 142.

[7] In accordance with Rules of Procedure of the CRPD Committee, r 55(3), the CRPD may receive communications in alternative formats, such as Braille and other accessible formats specified in r 24: UN Doc CRPD/C/4/2 (13 August 2010).

[8] Thus, as with the OP-CEDAW, the question of justiciability seems not to have been contentious during the drafting of the Protocol, as a result of which a complaint may be made in respect of any provision in the Convention: see Ch 10, para **10.04**.

[9] OP-CRPD, art 1(1).

[10] OHCHR expert paper: UN Doc A/AC265/2006/CRP4, para 48.

[11] See OP-CEDAW, art 2. Interestingly, NHRIs and NGOs had advocated the insertion of an explicit qualification regarding consent: Draft Text on Monitoring Presented by National Human Rights Institutions to the 6th Session of the Ad Hoc Committee (10 August 2005), http://www.un.org/esa/socdev/enable/rights/documents/ahc6nhrida25.doc (last accessed May 2011); and International disability Caucus (IDC) Draft on Article 33 and 34 International and National Monitoring and Other Aspects of Implementation (1 February 2006): www.ableinfo.co.kr/upload/libFile/Nega_treatyFile_131.doc (last accessed May 2011). Nonetheless, the CRPD Committee has chosen not to include any such proviso in its Rules of Procedure: CRPD Committee's Rules of Procedure, r 69.

possibility of 'collective complaints' under the OP-CRPD, including ones being submitted by NGOs and NHRIs.[12] Collective complaints are currently possible in the context of the International Labour Organisation and the Council of Europe's, European Social Charter,[13] but heretofore, they had not been incorporated in any other UN human rights treaty. Collective complaints may be distinguished from individual complaints by the fact that they may be launched by international as well as national, representative organisations and there is usually no requirement to demonstrate victim status, domestic remedies or indeed any particular time limit.[14] While the ad hoc committee ultimately decided not to depart from the standard complaint procedure by including an explicit provision for collective complaints, the fact that complaints may still be lodged *on behalf of* 'groups of individuals', without any express requirement of consent, goes close to achieving that objective in practice.[15]

ADMISSIBILITY

[11.04] The admissibility criteria for communications under the OP-CRPD are essentially the same as those provided for in art 4 of the OP-CEDAW. Thus, the CRPD Committee shall consider a communication to be inadmissible when:

(a) The communication is anonymous;

(b) The communication constitutes an abuse of the right of submission[16] or is incompatible with the provisions of the Convention;[17]

---

[12] OHCHR expert paper: UN Doc A/AC265/2006/CRP4, para 48. An explicit proposal to this effect was also made by NHRIs in art 45 of their Draft Text on Monitoring presented at the 6th session of the ad hoc committee (10 August 2005): http://www.un.org/esa/socdev/enable/rights/ahc6nhri.htm (last accessed May 2011).

[13] See the collective complaints system currently operated by the ILO Freedom of Association Committee: http://www.ilo.org/global/standards/applying-and-promoting-international-labour-standards/committee-on-freedom-of-association/lang--en/index.htm (last accessed May 2011). As regards the Council of Europe's Protocol to the European Social Charter Providing for a System of Collective Complaints (1995), see: http://conventions.coe.int/treaty/en/treaties/html/158.htm (last accessed May 2011).

[14] See generally, Cullen, 'The Collective Complaints System of the European Social Charter: Interpretative Methods of the European Committee of Social Rights' (2009) 9(1) HRL Rev 61.

[15] Bruce, 'Negotiating the Monitoring Mechanism for the Convention on the Rights of Persons with Disabilities: Two Steps Forward, One Step Back' in Alfredsson et al (eds), *International Human Rights Monitoring Mechanisms* (Martinus Nijhoff, 2009), p 143. Indeed, Stein and Lord actually use the term 'collective complaints' in describing the powers of the Committee in respect of art 1(1) OP-CRPD: 'Monitoring the Convention on the Rights of Persons with Disabilities: Innovations, Lost Opportunities, and Future Potential' Human Rights Quarterly, Vol. 31, 2010. Available at http://ssrn.com/abstract=1533482 at 7 (last accessed May 2011).

[16] As to what constitutes an 'abuse of the right of submission', see Ch 7, paras **7.18** in terms of the practice of the CCPR under the OP-ICCPR.

[17] In the practice of the other treaty bodies, communications are deemed to be incompatible on four distinct grounds: see Ch 7, paras **7.20–7.33** in respect of the CCPR's assessment of incompatibility under OP-ICCPR, art 3.

(c) The same matter has already been examined by the Committee or has been or is being examined under another procedure of international investigation or settlement;[18]
(d) All available domestic remedies have not been exhausted, unless the application of those remedies is 'unreasonably prolonged or unlikely to bring effective relief';[19]
(e) It is manifestly ill-founded or not sufficiently substantiated;[20] or
(f) The facts that are the subject of the communication occurred prior to the entry into force of the present Protocol for the State party concerned unless those facts continued after that date.[21]

PROCEDURE

[11.05] The CRPD Committee's Rules of Procedure,[22] read in conjunction with the text of the OP-CRPD, indicate the procedure that will be followed for consideration of complaints under the Protocol. The rules provide for the Secretary General of the United Nations to bring to the attention of the CRPD Committee all communications which appear to be submitted for the consideration of that Committee.[23] As is the case in respect of each of the human rights treaties, the role of the Secretary General in respect of communications has in fact been devolved to the petitions unit of the OHCHR. Accordingly, the petitions unit will be responsible for the initial processing of the petition. This will include clarifying, if necessary, essential information which is necessary for the communication to be registered.[24] The rules envisage that the CRPD Committee will designate one of its members as special rapporteur on communications to assist in the procedure.[25] The rapporteur will have a role in regard to the registration of communications and interim measures and may play a role in the handling of complaints post-registration.[26] The Rules of Procedure also provide for the establishment of one or more working group(s).[27] If established, such a working group will play a role in making decisions on admissibility as well as making recommendations to the plenary Committee on the merits.[28]

---

[18] This provision, like OP-CEDAW, art 4(2)(a) rules out communications that are *simultaneously* under consideration in another international procedure, as well as those previously decided by such procedure or by the Committee itself.
[19] This provision replicates OP-CEDAW, art 4(1): see Ch 10, para **10.25**.
[20] A communication is normally deemed to be 'manifestly ill-founded' in circumstances where the facts do not disclose a *prima facie* violation of the Convention. As regards complaints that lack substantiation, the CRPD will likely follow the practice of the CCPR in deciding when a communication is lacking in substantiation: see above, Ch 7 respectively.
[21] This provision (like OP-CEDAW, art 4(2)(e)) codifies the practice of the CCPR and CERD in regard to the concept of 'continuing violations': see Ch 7, paras **7.21–7.22**.
[22] Rules of Procedure of the CRPD Committee: UN Doc CRPD/C/4/2 (13 August 2010).
[23] Rules of Procedure of the CRPD Committee, r 55(1).
[24] Rules of Procedure of the CRPD Committee, rr 55(2) and 57.
[25] Rules of Procedure of the CRPD Committee, r 63(1).
[26] See Rules of Procedure of the CRPD Committee, rr 64 and 70.
[27] Rules of Procedure of the CRPD Committee, r 63(1).
[28] Rules of Procedure of the CRPD Committee, r 63(i), r 65, r 73(3).

[11.06] In regard to interim measures, explicit provision is made in the OP-CRPD for the CRPD Committee to request a respondent State to take such measures as may be necessary to avoid irreparable damage to a complainant under the Protocol.[29] A request for such measures may be made to the State at any time after the receipt of a communication and before a determination on the merits has been reached.[30] If the CRPD Committee does make such a request, it will be without prejudice to its determination on either the admissibility of the merits of the communication.[31] The rapporteur may act on behalf of the CRPD Committee in making requests for interim measures.[32]

[11.07] Once the communication is registered, the Special Rapporteur shall bring it confidentially to the attention of the State party and shall request it to submit a written reply.[33] Within six months, the State is required to submit written explanations or statements that shall relate to the admissibility of the communication and its merits, and also details as to any remedy that may have been provided in respect of the matter.[34] Provision is made in the rules in exceptional cases for the possibility of submissions being made initially only on admissibility, either on the invitation of the CRPD Committee[35] or pursuant to a request by the respondent State.[36] In any event, the rapporteur, working group or the Committee may seek further submissions from the State or the author of the communication;[37] transmit to each party the submissions made by the other party; and afford each party an opportunity to comment on the submissions

---

[29] OP-CRPD, art 4(1).
[30] OP-CRPD, art 4(1) and Rules of Procedure of the CRPD Committee, r 64(1).
[31] OP-CRPD, art 4(2).
[32] Rules of Procedure of the CRPD Committee, r 64(2).
[33] OP-CRPD, art 3; Rules of Procedure of the CRPD Committee, r 70(1).
[34] OP-CRPD, art 3; Rules of Procedure of the CRPD Committee, r 70(3). If the State party disputes the author(s)' contention that domestic remedies have been exhausted, it must provide details of the remedies available which it believes have not been exhausted: Rules of Procedure of the CRPD Committee, r 70(6). If it disputes the legal capacity of the author(s) under art 12 of the Convention, it must give details of the laws and remedies available to the alleged victim in the circumstances of the case: Rules of Procedure of the CRPD Committee, r 70(7).
[35] Rules of Procedure of the CRPD Committee, r 70(4). If such a request is made by the Committee, the State is not thereby precluded, however, from submitting, within six months of the request, a written reply that relates both to admissibility and the merits.
[36] Rules of Procedure of the CRPD Committee, r 70(5). Such a request must be submitted within two months of the State receiving a request for information and statements pursuant to Rules of Procedure of the CRPD Committee, r 70(1). A decision on such request shall be made by the Committee, a working group or the special rapporteur on communications: Rules of Procedure of the CRPD Committee, r 70(8). Where such request is made, it shall not extend the period of six months given to the State to provide written explanations or statements on the merits, unless the Committee, a working group or the special rapporteur on new communications decides to extend the time for submission: Rules of Procedure of the CRPD Committee, r 70(9).
[37] Rules of Procedure of the CRPD Committee, r 70(10).

received within fixed time limits.[38] In addition, the CRPD Committee or working group may at any time during the consideration of a communication obtain documentation from any other United Nations body or other bodies that may be of assistance to it in its disposal of the communication, provided that it affords each party an opportunity to comment on such documentation within fixed time limits.[39]

[11.08] Once all the relevant information has been obtained from either side, the first task of the Committee (or the working group once established)[40] will be to decide whether the communication complies with the admissibility criteria in arts 1 and 2 of OP-CRPD.[41] It is to be noted that in making a decision on admissibility, the rules provide that the CRPD Committee shall apply the criteria in art 12 of the CRPD recognising the legal capacity of the author before the Committee, regardless of whether this capacity is recognised in the respondent State.[42] Should the CRPD establish a working group for the purposes of deciding on admissibility, the working group will only be able to decide that the complaint is admissible[43] or inadmissible by a unanimous vote.[44] In the latter scenario, the decision of inadmissibility will be transmitted to the plenary Committee which may confirm it without formal discussion.[45] Where the working group is unable to reach a unanimous decision on the question of admissibility, the full Committee must decide on the admissibility of the communication before reaching a view on the merits.[46] Where decisions on admissibility are made by the plenary Committee, such decisions will be taken by a simple majority vote.[47] It may decide to render its decision on admissibility separately,[48] or in conjunction with its opinion on the merits.[49] If the decision on admissibility is taken separately that the complaint is admissible, that decision will be transmitted to the parties[50] and the Committee may revoke the decision on admissibility at the merits stage in the light of any explanations or statements submitted by the State party.[51] If the Committee decides that the case is inadmissible, the reasons for the decision will be communicated to the author and that will normally put

---

[38] Rules of Procedure of the CRPD Committee, r 70(11).
[39] Rules of Procedure of the CRPD Committee, r 73(2).
[40] Rules of Procedure of the CRPD Committee, r 65(1).
[41] Rules of Procedure of the CRPD Committee, r 68(1).
[42] Rules of Procedure of the CRPD Committee, r 68(2).
[43] Rules of Procedure of the CRPD Committee, r 65(2).
[44] Rules of Procedure of the CRPD Committee, r 65(3).
[45] Rules of Procedure of the CRPD Committee, r 65(3). If, however, any Committee member requests a plenary discussion, the plenary will examine the communication and take a decision.
[46] Rules of Procedure of the CRPD Committee, r 73(4).
[47] Rules of Procedure of the CRPD Committee, r 65(1).
[48] Rules of Procedure of the CRPD Committee, r 72(1).
[49] Rules of Procedure of the CRPD Committee, r 73(1).
[50] Rules of Procedure of the CRPD Committee, r 72(1).
[51] Rules of Procedure of the CRPD Committee, r 72(3).

an end to the case.[52] A decision of inadmissibility may, however, be reviewed upon the receipt of a written request from the author to the effect that the reasons for inadmissibility no longer apply.[53]

[11.09] Where the Committee makes a decision on the merits, its views, together with any recommendation(s), shall be transmitted to the author and the State party concerned.[54] The rules provide that decisions on the merits shall be determined by a simple majority vote,[55] but the CRPD Committee will emulate the practice of the other treaty bodies by striving to reach its decisions by consensus.[56] Individual members are entitled to append separate opinions to the majority opinion (whether dissenting or concurring).[57]

[11.10] There is no provision in the OP-CRPD for oral hearings, and consideration of the communications must be conducted confidentially.[58] The requirement of confidentiality, however, shall not affect the right of either the author or the respondent State to make public any submissions or information with respect to the proceedings, unless specifically requested not to do so.[59] The ultimate decisions on admissibility and the views of the Committee are, of course, public documents, though the CRPD Committee may decide not to reveal the identity of the complainant in the body of these texts.[60]

[11.11] The OP-CRPD stipulates that after its examination of a communication, the CRPD Committee 'shall forward its suggestions and recommendations' to the respondent State and to the petitioner.[61] This is arguably even weaker language than the nomenclature of 'views' normally used to specify the output of the treaty bodies under their respective complaint procedures.[62] Neither does the OP-CRPD make specific provision for a follow-up mechanism such as that which is provided for in the OP-CEDAW,[63] despite suggestions being made for such provision during the negotiations on

---

[52] Rules of Procedure of the CRPD Committee, r 71(1). It should be noted that any member of the Committee who has participated in the decision regarding admissibility may request that a summary of his or her individual opinion be appended to the Committee's decision declaring the complaint inadmissible: Rules of Procedure of the CRPD Committee, r 71(3).
[53] Rules of Procedure of the CRPD Committee, r 71(2).
[54] Rules of Procedure of the CRPD Committee, r 73(5).
[55] Rules of Procedure of the CRPD Committee, r 73(5).
[56] Rules of Procedure of the CRPD Committee, r 34(1).
[57] Rules of Procedure of the CRPD Committee, r 73(6).
[58] OP-CRPD, art 5. Rules of Procedure of the CRPD Committee, r 76.
[59] Rules of Procedure of the CRPD Committee, r 76(4).
[60] Rules of Procedure of the CRPD Committee, r 76(6).
[61] OP-CRPD, art 5. The language is the same as that used in ICERD, art 14(7)(b).
[62] In its Rules of Procedure, the CRPD has nonetheless adopted the terminology of 'views': see Rules of Procedure of the CRPD Committee, r 73.
[63] OP-CEDAW, arts 7(4) and (5); see para **10.15** above.

the text.[64] While the CRPD Committee clearly intends to pursue a strategy in relation to follow-up[65] similar to that which has been applied in practice by the other treaty bodies, the absence of specific provision in the text is clearly regressive.

[11.12] Ironically, perhaps the most striking feature of the complaint procedure in the OP-CRPD as it was finally elaborated is its similarity to other individual complaint procedures. Indeed, despite the agenda of treaty body reform which overshadowed the negotiations and the numerous suggestions for piecemeal adaptation of the complaint procedure itself, it is essentially the same as its predecessors,[66] if not weaker, insofar as the failure to incorporate an explicit 'follow-up mechanism' is concerned. The reluctance to innovate, however, as regards the international procedure, is compensated for to some extent by the inclusion of more dynamic features in the realm of national monitoring insofar as this may lessen the need for resort to the communications procedure. Thus far, it seems that the CRPD Committee has decided to adopt the working methods of the other treaty bodies, but the fact that it has not yet had an opportunity to apply the procedure in practice makes a full assessment of its potential value in implementing the rights in the CRPD somewhat premature. The most optimistic outlook would be that, if drawn on strategically by civil society as a supplement to national monitoring, the procedure could provide a means of intensifying scrutiny of policy and practice in relation to the rights of persons with disabilities.

---

[64] See art 43(4) and (5) of the Draft Text on Monitoring Presented by National Human Rights Institutions to the 6th Session of the Ad Hoc Committee (10 August 2005): http://www.un.org/esa/socdev/enable/rights/documents/ahc6nhrida25.doc (last accessed May 2011). See also suggestions for follow-up included in the International Disability Caucus (IDC) Draft on Article 33 and 34 International and National Monitoring and Other Aspects of Implementation (1 February 2006): www.ableinfo.co.kr/upload/libFile/Nega_treatyFile_131.doc (last accessed May 2011).

[65] Rules of Procedure of the CRPD Committee, r 75 essentially reproduces the provisions of OP-CEDAW, art 7(4) and (5) by requiring States to submit a written response within six months of receipt of the Committee's 'views', which shall include information on any action taken in light of the views and recommendations of the Committee. It may also seek information at a later date from the State and request it to include such information in its reports under the art 35 reporting procedure. A special rapporteur or working group may be designated to liaise with the State party and the Committee in regard to follow-up. The CRPD Committee's activities in regard to follow-up shall be included in its biennial report under art 39 of the Convention.

[66] As Bruce has noted: 'As the negotiations on monitoring in the Ad Hoc Committee moved from a general discussion to concrete negotiations, thinking new turned into thinking safe, both as in securing at least the same quality of monitoring as earlier conventions and as in the reluctance of States to sign up for untested methods of international scrutiny': 'Negotiating the Monitoring Mechanism for the Convention on the Rights of Persons with Disabilities: Two Steps Forward, One Step Back' in Alfredsson et al (eds), *International Human Rights Monitoring Mechanisms* (Martinus Nijhoff, 2009), p 148. On this issue, Stein and Lord argue that many of the innovative ideas for monitoring proposed during the drafting negotiations might still be used to inform on-going discussion on treaty body reform: 'Monitoring the Convention on the Rights of Persons with Disabilities: Innovations, Lost Opportunities, and Future Potential' Human Rights Quarterly, Vol. 31, 2010. Available at SSRN: http://ssrn.com/abstract=1533482 (last accessed May 2011).

Chapter 12

International Convention on the Protection of the Rights of All Migrant Workers and their Families

COMPLAINT PROCEDURE

[12.01] An optional individual complaint procedure was included in the International Convention on the Protection of the Rights of All Migrant Workers and their Families (ICRMW)[1] at the eleventh hour of the drafting process.[2] The idea for such a procedure was introduced by the representative of the Netherlands during the negotiations on the draft Convention, over eight years after those negotiations had begun.[3] He proposed a procedure, based entirely on art 22 of UNCAT, as a 'logical' accompaniment to the inter-State complaint which had been under consideration from the outset.[4] During discussion, objections were raised to the addition of such a procedure on the basis that it would be unsuitable in the context of a convention which imposed such a large number of obligations, some of which were very detailed, in areas such as labour relations, employment, social security, residence and education.[5] In this respect, traditional

---

[1] As to the ICRMW generally, see above Ch 3, paras **3.92–3.101**.
[2] The ICRMW was drafted by the Working Group on the Drafting of an International Convention on the Protection of the Rights of All Migrant Workers and Their Families, which was open to all Member States of the UN and established under General Assembly Resolution No 34/172 of 17 December 1979. It held its first session from 8 October to 19 November 1980. See generally, Cholewinski, *Migrant Workers in International Human Rights Law* (Clarendon Press, 1997), pp 194–196. On the drafting process generally, see also Hune, 'Drafting an International Convention on the Protection of the Rights of all Migrant Workers and Their Families' (1987) 3 IMR, pp 570–615 and (1987) 21 IMR 123; and Lönnroth, 'The International Convention on the Rights of All Migrant Workers and Members of Their Families in the Context of International Migration Policies: An Analysis of Ten Years of Negotiation' (1991) 25 IMR 710.
[3] The proposal for an individual complaint procedure was introduced at the Working Group's eighth inter-sessional meeting (31 May to 9 June 1989): Report of the open-ended Working Group on the Drafting of an International Convention on the Protection of the Rights of All Migrant Workers and Their Families: UN Doc A/C3/44/1 (19 June 1989), para 82 (Working Group's June 1989 Report).
[4] Working Group's June 1989 Report: UN Doc A/C3/44/1, para 82.
[5] Statement of the representative of the Federal Republic of Germany, Working Group's June 1989 Report: UN Doc A/C3/44/1, para 85. The delegate raised this point a second time when the proposal for an individual complaint mechanism was discussed at the subsequent session of the Working Group in October 1989. See Report of the open-ended Working Group on the Drafting of an International Convention on the Protection of the Rights of All Migrant Workers and Their Families (17 October 1989): UN Doc A/C3/44/4, para 267 (Working Group's October 1989 Report). (contd.../)

concerns about the justiciability of the economic, social and cultural rights contained in the draft Convention perturbed even those delegations which supported a complaint procedure in principle.[6] Notwithstanding such concerns, the majority of delegations ultimately supported the Dutch proposal because of the importance of establishing a dual monitoring system for individual complaints as well as inter-State complaints[7] and because optional individual complaint mechanisms had already been included in a number of existing international instruments.[8]

[12.02] An optional complaint procedure is thus provided for in art 77 of the ICRMW which vests competence in the Committee on Migrant Workers (CMW)[9] to receive and consider individual complaints. At the time of writing, however, reluctance on the part of States generally (particularly in Europe) to ratify the ICRMW is amplified by a general unwillingness to accept the terms of the complaint procedure. Only 2 of the 44 States parties to the Convention have entered declarations accepting the procedure in art 77,[10] as a result of which it has not thus far entered into force.[11] Since the CMW has not drawn up any Rules of Procedure in respect of art 77, the only clues obtaining as to its likely operation are to be gleaned from the text itself. In this respect, it should be noted that art 77 is based largely on the text of art 22 of UNCAT, although one adjustment to that model text was proposed and accepted 'to accommodate some concerns raised during the discussion'.[12] Specifically, it was decided to make provision for complaints from or on behalf of individuals who claim that their 'individual rights' as established by

---

[5] (\...contd) This view was shared by the representatives of France and the United States of America: Working Group's October 1989 Report, paras 269 and 278. Cholewinski also notes that seven Mediterranean and Scandinavian States, known collectively as the MESCA grouping (Finland, Greece, Italy, Norway, Portugal, Spain and Sweden) had originally voiced their objections to an individual complaints procedure in an analytical paper submitted earlier in the negotiations: Cholewinski, *Migrant Workers in International Human Rights Law*, p 195, note 245. However, none of these countries formally opposed the inclusion of the procedure when it was eventually tabled, with the representatives of Finland, Greece and Sweden actually expressing their support for same. See Working Group's June 1989 Report: UN Doc A/C3/44/1, para 101 and Working Group's October 1989 Report: UN Doc A/C3/44/4, paras 270 and 273.

[6] See, for example, the statement of the representative of Canada, Working Group's October 1989 Report: UN Doc A/C3/44/4, para 271.

[7] Statement of the representative of Sweden, Working Group's June 1989 Report: UN Doc A/C3/44/1, para 92.

[8] Statement of the representative of Algeria, Working Group's October 1989 Report: UN Doc A/C3/44/4, para 270.

[9] See above, Ch 3, paras **3.100–3.101**.

[10] Guatemala and Mexico: United Nations Treaty Database, http://treaties.un.org/Pages/Treaties.aspx?id=4&subid=A&lang=en (last accessed May 2011).

[11] In order for art 77 to enter into force, 10 States parties must have made declarations under art 77(1), accepting the competence of the CMW to receive and consider complaints: ICRMW, art 77(8).

[12] This amendment was proposed by the Dutch delegate, Working Group's October 1989 Report: UN Doc A/C3/44/4, para 274.

the present Convention have been violated, as opposed to complaints about 'the provisions of the Convention' generally.[13] The question of the proper scope of complaints that may be made under art 77 has never, of course, been tested since the complaint procedure has not yet come into force. Even if it does, however, it is difficult to see how the wording eventually arrived at would in any way preclude complaints about a failure to vindicate rights of an economic, social and cultural nature provided for in the ICRMW.[14]

[12.03] In every other respect, art 77 virtually replicates art 22 of UNCAT in terms of admissibility criteria and general procedure. Thus, communications submitted under art 77 may not be anonymous, an abuse of the right of submission, or incompatible with the provisions of the ICRMW.[15] The CMW shall not consider a communication unless it has ascertained that the matter has not been and is not being examined under another procedure of international investigation or settlement.[16] Complainants must have exhausted all domestic remedies, unless the application of the latter is unreasonably prolonged or unlikely to bring effective relief.[17] Any communication that is made to the CMW will be forwarded to the participating State party which shall have six months to make written submissions to the CMW, clarifying the matter and the remedy, if any, taken by the State.[18] As with the complaint procedure under UNCAT, art 77(5) provides that the CMW shall consider communications 'in the light of all information made available to it' by or on behalf of the individual and the State Party concerned.[19] There is no stipulation that the proceedings must be based on 'written' information, as is the case with the OP-ICCPR.[20] This means that it would certainly be technically possible for the CMW to accommodate oral hearings in its complaint procedure, though the likelihood of this is remote, given the absence of any such practice on the part of the other treaty bodies. As with the other treaty body complaint procedures, the CMW is bound to consider communications under art 77 in closed meetings,[21] following which it should 'forward its views' to the individual and the respondent State.[22] Strictly speaking, there is no provision for 'interim measures' or a 'follow-up' procedure, but there would be no legal impediment to the CMW adopting either course of action in the event of art 77 being activated.

---

[13] In supporting the adoption of the article, the representative of Canada warned that it might give rise in the future '...to problems of interpretation for the Committee and result in the Committee being burdened with an overwhelming number of unsubstantiated, frivolous complaints', Working Group's October 1989 Report: UN Doc A/C3/44/4, para 284.
[14] This conclusion is fortified by the recent elaboration of OP-ICESCR: see generally Ch 13.
[15] ICRMW, art 77(2).
[16] ICRMW, art 77(3)(a).
[17] ICRMW, art 77(3)(b).
[18] ICRMW, art 77(4).
[19] This provision is identical to UNCAT, art 22(4).
[20] OP-ICCPR, art 5(1). A suggestion by the Japanese delegate during the debate on the terms of the complaint procedure that it should be based on written proceedings only was emphatically rejected by Canada, Sweden and the Netherlands: Working Group's October 1989 Report: UN Doc A/C3/44/4, para 279.
[21] ICRMW, art 77(6).
[22] ICRMW, art 77(7).

Chapter 13

Optional Protocol to the International Covenant on Economic, Social and Cultural Rights

INTRODUCTION

[13.01] The recent adoption of the Optional Protocol to the International Covenant on Economic, Social and Cultural Rights (OP-ICESCR) is the product of a sustained campaign, spearheaded initially by the Committee on Economic, Social and Cultural Rights (CESCR), to have an optional individual complaints mechanism grafted onto the ICESCR.[1] The *raison d'être* for that campaign centred primarily around a belief that the failure to provide for such a mechanism during the drafting of the two Covenants had resulted in an imbalance in the perceived validity and effectiveness of economic, social and cultural rights on the one hand and civil and political rights on the other. This imbalance had effectively conferred an inferior status on the ICESCR as compared with its counterparts in the treaty system.[2] The increasing emphasis placed by the United Nations on the doctrine of interdependence and indivisibility of human rights underpinned the campaign for an individual complaint mechanism, which gained traction after the submission by the CESCR of a statement and 'analytical paper' on the

---

[1] UN General Assembly, *Optional Protocol to the International Covenant on Economic, Social and Cultural Rights: resolution / adopted by the General Assembly*, 5 March 2009, Un Doc A/RES/63/117, available at: http://www2.ohchr.org/english/bodies/cescr/docs/A-RES-63-117.pdf (last accessed May 2011). On the ICESCGR, see generally Ch 3, paras **3.37–3.52**. On the history of the initiative to draft an OP-ICESCR, see generally, Dennis and Stewart, 'Justiciability of Economic, Social and Cultural Rights: Should there be an International Complaints Mechanism to Adjudicate the Rights to Food, Water, Housing, and Health?' (2004) 98 Am J Int'l L 450; Mahon, 'Progress at the Front: The Draft Optional Protocol to the International Covenant on Economic, Social and Cultural Rights' (2008) HRL Rev 617; Vandenbogaerde and Vandenhole, 'The Optional Protocol to the International Covenant on Economic, Social and Cultural Rights: An Ex Ante Assessment of its Effectiveness in Light of the Drafting Process' (2010) HRL Rev 207; Langford, 'Closing the Gap?' – An Introduction to the Optional Protocol to the International Covenant on Economic, Social and Cultural Rights' (2009) 27 Nordic Journal of Human Rights 1; de Albuquerque, Chronicle of an Announced Birth 'The Coming into Life of the Optional Protocol to the International Covenant on Economic, Social and Cultural Rights—The Missing Piece of the International Bill of Human Rights' (2010) 32 HRQ 144–178 and Arambulo, *Strengthening the Supervision of the International Covenant on Economic, Social and Cultural Rights: Theoretical and Procedural Aspects* (Intersentia, 1999).

[2] Analytical paper adopted by the Committee on Economic, Social and Cultural Rights at its seventh session, 11 December 1992 (CESCR Analytical Paper): UN Doc A/CONF157/PC/62/Add.5, para 2.

subject of an Optional Protocol to the World Conference on Human Rights in 1993.[3] The output of that Conference – the Vienna Declaration and Programme of Action – specifically encouraged the Commission on Human Rights (CHR), in cooperation with the CESCR, to '...continue the examination of optional protocols to the International Covenant on Civil and Political Rights'.[4] A draft protocol was first elaborated by the CESCR itself, which envisaged an optional, individual complaint mechanism, involving adjudication by the CESCR on the full range of economic, social and cultural rights provided for in the ICESCR.[5] The Committee's draft was gradually reviewed by States, non-governmental organisations[6] and finally by an independent expert appointed by the CHR and ECOSOC in 2001.[7] Having reviewed the likely benefits and practicality of such an instrument, the expert ultimately recommended the elaboration of a complaint mechanism and the establishment of an open-ended working group for this purpose.[8] A

---

[3] Analytical paper adopted by the Committee on Economic, Social and Cultural Rights at its seventh session, 11 December 1992: UN Doc A/CONF157/PC/62/Add.5. See, in particular, para 41.

[4] The Vienna Declaration and Programme of Action is the output of the World Conference on Human Rights which took place in 1993: UN Doc A/CONF157/23, para 75. The CESCR had advocated the adoption of a complaint mechanism to the ICESCR in the analytical paper which it submitted to the World Conference in 1993, fn 2.

[5] CESCR Draft Optional Protocol to the International Covenant on Economic, Social and Cultural Rights: Note by the Secretary General, 18 December 1996 (CESCR Draft Protocol): UN Doc E/CN4/1997/105.

[6] On the process by which these views was compiled, see Mahon, 'Progress at the Front: The Draft Optional Protocol to the International Covenant on Economic, Social and Cultural Rights' (2008) HRL Rev 617, pp 622–633. See, in particular, Report of the High Commissioner on Human Rights on the workshop on the justiciability of economic, social and cultural rights, with particular reference to the draft optional protocol to the International Covenant on Economic, Social and Cultural Rights (22 March 2001): UN Doc E/CN4/2001/62/Add2.

[7] The independent expert, Professor Hatem Kotrane, was appointed by the Commission on Human Rights initially in 2001 '...to examine the question of a draft optional protocol to the International Covenant on Economic, Social and Cultural Rights in the light, inter alia, of the report of the Committee to the Commission on a draft optional protocol for the consideration of communications in relation to the Covenant, inter alia, of the Committee's proposal': CHR Res 2001/30, para 8(c). His mandate was renewed again in 2002 by CHR Res 2002/24 in which he was requested to submit a report which would further address: (i) the question of the nature and scope of States parties' obligations under the Covenant; (ii) conceptual issues on the justiciability of economic, social and cultural rights, with particular reference to the experience gained in recent years from the application of universal, regional and national human rights instruments and mechanisms; and (iii) the question of the benefits and the practicability of a complaint mechanism under the Covenant and the issue of complementarity between different mechanisms (para 9(c)).

[8] The independent expert issued two reports on the subject to the Commission on Human Rights: see UN Doc E/CN4/2002/57 and UN Doc E/CN4/2003/53. Following the expert's first report, the CHR had already decided to establish an open-ended working group to consider 'options' for such a Protocol in 2002: CHR Res 2002/24, UN Doc E/CN4/RES/2002/24, para 9(f).

working group was convened in 2003 which reached agreement on the text of a draft Optional Protocol to the ICESCR over the course of some five sessions of negotiations.[9] Having been considered and approved by the Human Rights Council,[10] the final text of the OP-ICESCR was adopted by the General Assembly on 10 December 2008.[11] It was opened for signature in September 2009 and has been ratified, thus far, by 3 of the 160 States parties to the ICESCR.[12]

[13.02] A number of contentious issues emerged during the negotiations, some of which threatened to derail the process from the outset. Chief amongst these was the question of whether economic, social and cultural rights are justiciable such as to warrant a complaints procedure comparable to that which is provided for in other human rights treaties.[13] As Langford has noted, this is a debate which extends back to the drafting of the Covenants and which has traditionally provoked a range of responses, including outright opposition to a complaints mechanism based on substantive, procedural and sovereignty grounds.[14] In this respect, a number of arguments were raised in the early stages of the negotiations regarding the susceptibility of ESC rights to quasi-judicial adjudication given their vague and programmatic nature;[15] the legitimacy of international supervision of their implementation;[16] as well as the competence of the

---

[9] For a detailed analysis of the negotiations of the working group, see Mahon, 'Progress at the Front: The Draft Optional Protocol to the International Covenant on Economic, Social and Cultural Rights' (2008) HRL Rev 617, pp 621–628; and Vandenbogaerde and Vandenhole, 'The Optional Protocol to the International Covenant on Economic, Social and Cultural Rights: An Ex Ante Assessment of its Effectiveness in Light of the Drafting Process' (2010) HRL Rev 207, pp 209–230.

[10] Human Rights Council Res 8/12, 18 June 2008: UN Doc A/HRC/8/L2/Rev1/Corr1 Annex.

[11] General Assembly Res 63/117, 10 December 2008: UN Doc A/RES/63/117.

[12] United Nations Treaty Collection: http://treaties.un.org/Pages/Treaties.aspx?id=4&subid=A&lang=en (last accessed, May 2011). 36 States have signed the Protocol.

[13] The issue of justiciability is central to the analysis of the need for a complaints mechanism made by Dennis and Stewart in 'Justiciability of Economic, Social and Cultural Rights: Should there be an International Complaints Mechanism to Adjudicate the Rights to Food, Water, Housing, and Health?' (2004) 98 Am J Int'l L 450 and that of Arambulo, *Strengthening the Supervision of the International Covenant on Economic, Social and Cultural Rights: Theoretical and Procedural Aspects* (Intersentia, 1999).

[14] Langford breaks down the 'justiciability' debate into four discrete themes which, he argues, characterised objections made to the Protocol. These include objections based on the imprecise nature of the norms, the democratic illegitimacy of social rights adjudication, the institutional competence of the CESCR to adjudicate on such issues and lastly, the utilitarian benefits of such a procedure: Langford, 'Closing the Gap? – An Introduction to the Optional Protocol to the International Covenant on Economic, Social and Cultural Rights' (2009) 27 Nordic Journal of Human Rights 1, pp 2–18.

[15] Report of the open-ended working group to consider options regarding the elaboration of an optional protocol to the International Covenant on Economic, Social and Cultural Rights on its first session (15 March 2004): UN Doc E/CN4/2004/44, paras 58–59.

[16] 'A number of delegations expressed concerns that the Committee's views concerning States' social policies and resource allocations might unduly interfere with the policy-making powers of legislatures': UN Doc E/CN4/2004/44, para 61.

CESCR to perform the task.[17] Resource implications as well as doubts about the overall benefits of such a scheme were also raised in some quarters.[18] However, the contribution of many more open-minded States as well as that of a significant NGO lobby steered the negotiations forward into discussions by the end of the second session about how such concerns could be managed in the text of the Protocol.[19]

THE FRAMEWORK OF THE OP-ICESCR

[13.03] The central feature of the OP-ICESCR is the complaint mechanism which vests competence in the CESCR to 'receive and consider' communications[20] from 'individuals and groups of individuals' [21] who claim to be 'victims of a violation of *any* of the economic, social and cultural rights set forth in the ICESCR by a State party to the Protocol'.[22] Although the Committee's Rules of Procedure in respect of the operation of the OP-ICESCR remain to be elaborated, the text of the Protocol itself lays out the framework by which complaints will be processed under it. Thus, the CESCR must first consider whether a complaint made under the OP-ICESCR satisfies broad conditions of admissibility, before advancing to an assessment of its merits. States parties will be given six months to respond to complaints by submitting written explanations or

---

[17] 'It was argued that economic, social and cultural rights are complex and must be considered in light of the national context, the implementation and adjudication of these rights were best left to courts at the national level. As it was noted, it would be difficult for a Geneva-based treaty monitoring body to acquire a complete and adequate understanding of the local context': UN Doc E/CN4/2004/44, para 63.

[18] See, for example, the submission of the United States of America at the second session of the working group to the effect that an optional protocol would be 'ineffective and costly' and that the working group had not presented '…any arguments that an optional protocol would improve the rights of people living under a Government unwilling or unable to protect their rights'. Similar scepticism was expressed by the representatives of Australia, Canada, Japan and Poland: Report of the open-ended working group to consider options regarding the elaboration of an optional protocol to the International Covenant on Economic, Social and Cultural Rights on its second session' (10 February 2005), UN Doc E/CN4/2005/52, paras 103–104.

[19] See Vandenbogaerde and Vandenhole who argue further that a 'psychological turning point' was reached at the end of the second session when agreement was reached that the chairperson should draft a paper for consideration at the third session which would contain 'elements' that might be included in an Optional Protocol: Vandenbogaerde and Vandenhole, 'The Optional Protocol to the International Covenant on Economic, Social and Cultural Rights: An Ex Ante Assessment of its Effectiveness in Light of the Drafting Process' (2010) HRL Rev 207, note 1 at pp 209–214. For the 'elements' paper subsequently elaborated by the chairperson, Catarina de Albuquerque, see: 'Elements for an optional protocol to the International Covenant on Economic, Social and Cultural Rights': UN Doc E/CN4/2006/WG23/2 (Chairperson's elements paper).

[20] OP-ICESCR, art 1.

[21] Provision is also made for an optional inquiry procedure in OP-ICESCR, arts 11–12 (see Ch 5, paras **5.61–5.64**) and for an optional inter-State complaint mechanism in art 10.

[22] OP-ICESCR, art 2.

statements clarifying the matter and the remedy, if any, provided.[23] In making its assessment, the CESCR shall consider all of the documentation submitted to it (including that which has been supplied by the individual(s) and the respondent State)[24] provided that this documentation is transmitted to the parties concerned.[25] The reference to 'documentation' does not necessarily rule out oral hearings, but the possibility for these is not specified in the Protocol.[26] Before a determination on the merits is made, the CESCR may indicate to the State party concerned interim measures 'in exceptional circumstances' to avoid irreparable damage.[27] Unusually in terms of UN human rights treaties, the Protocol makes express provision for the 'friendly settlement' of the complaint.[28] The Committee is thus required to make itself available to the parties concerned with a view to reaching such a settlement 'on the basis of the respect for the obligations set forth in the Covenant'.[29] The Committee's deliberations on complaints

---

[23] OP-ICESCR, art 6(2). Note that the CESCR may consider a complaint inadmissible without reference to the State: OP-ICESCR, art 6(1).

[24] Relevant documentation includes also documentation emanating from other United Nations bodies, specialised agencies, funds, programmes and mechanisms and any other international organisations: OP-ICESCR, art 8(3).

[25] OP-ICESCR, art 8(1).

[26] The CCPR does not engage in oral hearings in circumstances where the OP-ICCPR specifies that consideration on the merits under that instrument shall be based on the 'written' proceedings. There is some debate, however, as to whether the wording of the OP-ICCPR thus precludes the CCPR from conducting oral hearings: see Ch 7, para [7.11]. It remains to be seen what approach is adopted by the CESCR to this issue, though the likelihood of oral hearing seems remote.

[27] OP-ICESCR, art 5. The reference to 'exceptional circumstances' marks a departure from the agreed language used in OP-CEDAW, art 5(1) and OP-ICRPD, art 4(1). As to the evolution of this provision, see Langford, 'Closing the Gap? – An Introduction to the Optional Protocol to the International Covenant on Economic, Social and Cultural Rights' (2009) 27 Nordic Journal of Human Rights 1, note 1, p 24. Vandenbogaerde and Vandenhole are critical of the wording on the basis that it might have a 'discouraging effect' on the CESCR in making requests for interim measures: Vandenbogaerde and Vandenhole, 'The Optional Protocol to the International Covenant on Economic, Social and Cultural Rights: An Ex Ante Assessment of its Effectiveness in Light of the Drafting Process' (2010) HRL Rev 207, p 236.

[28] OP-ICESCR, art 7. While express provision for friendly settlement is made in the ECHR (art 39) and the American Convention on Human Rights (art 48(f)), its inclusion in a UN treaty complaints procedure is unprecedented. The idea of including a provision for friendly settlements was originally mooted by the CESCR in its Analytical Paper on the basis that '...the nature of many of the issues likely to be raised in connection with the International Covenant on Economic, Social and Cultural Rights would seem to make it appropriate to place a particular emphasis upon the desirability of seeking a friendly settlement of complaints': CESCR Analytical Paper, para. 92. Provision for a friendly settlement was further mooted by the Chairperson in her 'elements paper' (paras 14–16) and in her original Draft Protocol (UN Doc A/HRC/6/WG.4/2, Article 7), the text of which is essentially reproduced in the final text of OP-ICESCR, art 7.

[29] OP-ICESCR, art 7(1). The CESCR will have to develop rules of procedure in regard to the provision on friendly settlement in the Protocol. Article 7(2) provides that an agreement on a friendly settlement closes consideration of the communication under the Protocol.

shall be in closed meetings, following which it shall transmit its 'views' and 'recommendations', if any, to the parties concerned.[30] Like the OP-CEDAW, the OP-ICESCR does provide specifically for a 'follow-up' procedure whereby the State is required to submit a written response to the CESCR within six months, providing information to it on any action taken in the light of the Committee's views and recommendations.[31] The CESCR may also invite the State to submit further information in its periodic reports to the Committee under arts 16 and 17 of the ICESCR.[32]

As may be deduced from the bare bones of the procedure outlined above, the OP-ICESCR does not depart radically from complaint procedures provided for in other UN human rights treaties. However, certain aspects merit particular attention in terms of the potential reach of the Protocol, as well as other new features which differentiate it from its counterparts.

The Scope of Potential Complaints (art 2)

[13.04] The question of which rights in the ICESCR should be subject to the complaints procedure goes to the heart of the issue of 'justiciability' which dominated debate on a potential protocol for decades. From the outset of its campaign to establish a Protocol, the CESCR had advocated a comprehensive approach to this issue, rather than a 'smorgasbord' or 'à la carte' approach, whereby States would be entitled to pick and choose which rights they would consider themselves bound by.[33] A third approach, advocated by the independent expert appointed by the Commission on Human Rights to report on the question of a Protocol, was that of limiting the procedure to 'situations revealing a species of gross, unmistakable violations of or failures to uphold any of the rights set forth in the Covenant'.[34] While the latter approach was not substantially considered by the working group that drafted the Protocol,[35] the merits and de-merits of the 'comprehensive' versus the 'à la carte' approaches were debated extensively throughout the negotiations.

[13.05] Several different variations of the 'à la carte' approach were canvassed. These included the 'opt-in' version analogous to the approach taken in the European Social Charter (Revised) whereby a contracting State would be allowed to limit the application

---

[30] OP-ICESCR, art 9(1).
[31] OP-ICESCR, art 9(2).
[32] OP-ICESCR, art 9(3). On the reporting procedure under the ICESCR, see Ch 4, paras. [4.17]–[4.23].
[33] See CESCR Analytical Paper, paras 68–79 and see also CESCR Draft Protocol, paras 24–28.
[34] First report of the independent expert, UN Doc E/CN4/2002/51, para 34 and again in his second report, UN Doc E/CN4/2003/53, para 66.
[35] At an early stage of the discussions in the working group, France, Greece and the Republic of Korea did make the suggestion that the scope of the complaints procedure should be limited to 'serious' violations of Covenant rights, but this option was not taken up in the text of the first draft of the Protocol. Draft Optional Protocol to the International Covenant on Economic, Social and Cultural Rights: Explanatory Memorandum: UN Doc A/HRC/6/WG.4/2 (23 April 2007), para 6 (prepared by the chairperson of the open-ended working group on an OP-ICESCR) (Chairperson's Draft Protocol).

of the complaint procedure to certain provisions of the Covenant.[36] Alternatively, an 'opt-out' version was mooted whereby States would be allowed to exclude the application of the complaint procedure from one or several provisions of the ICESCR.[37] Whereas the 'opt-in' version starts from the premise that a State will only be bound by a limited number of provisions, the 'opt-out' version assumes that the procedure will apply to the treaty in its entirety, subject to specified exceptions.[38] Regardless of the preferred version that might be adopted, it was clear that the 'à la carte' approach was perceived by many States as a compromise solution to the divisive issue of justiciability. By enabling States to tailor the extent of their obligations under the Protocol, the procedure as a whole might encourage a greater number of ratifications.[39] It would also allow States to limit the procedure to those rights for which domestic remedies already existed in their jurisdictions.[40] Notwithstanding these advantages, it was the comprehensive approach which proved most acceptable to the majority of States, apparently for the reasons that it deflected the negative implications of the 'à la carte approach'. In their view, the adoption of a 'pick and choose' catalogue of rights would contradict the 'interrelated, interdependent and indivisible' nature of all human rights and would lead to a hierarchy of economic, social and cultural rights;[41] diminish the opportunity for effective remedies on the part of victims, and run counter to existing complaint mechanisms, all of which adopted a comprehensive approach.[42]

[13.06] As to the comprehensive approach, a number of different formats were canvassed, including the idea of allowing a complainant to allege a violation of *any* of the provisions of the ICESCR, or in respect of any of Part III of the Covenant, read in conjunction with Parts I and II (which would rule out complaints about procedural violations in respect of Part IV).[43] A third, more 'limited' version was also mooted whereby complaints could be made in respect of Parts II and III only of the Covenant, thus ruling out the possibility of complaints in respect of the right to self-determination

---

[36] This approach may also be referred to as the 'opt-in' approach. It was referred to as the 'opt-in à la carte' approach in the Chairperson's elements paper, para 5(b) and earlier in the CESCR Draft Protocol, para 26.

[37] Chairperson's elements paper, para 5(c).

[38] Chairperson's elements paper, para 5(c).

[39] This view was expressed very clearly by Canada, Greece and the Russian Federation during the third session of the working group: Report of the Open-ended Working Group to consider options regarding the elaboration of an Optional Protocol to the International Covenant on Economic, Social and Cultural Rights on its third session': UN Doc E/CN4/2006/47, para 30 (Report of the 3rd Session).

[40] Report of the Open-ended Working Group on an Optional Protocol to the International Covenant on Economic, Social and Cultural Rights on its fourth session': UN Doc A/HRC/6/8 (Report of the 4th session).

[41] This view was articulated clearly by the Group of African States during the third session of the negotiations: Report of the 3rd session, para 27.

[42] See the submissions of the NGO coalition at the third session, para 33. See also the Report of the 4th session, para 33.

[43] Chairperson's elements paper, para 5(a).

in Part 1.[44] While the working group settled on the exclusion of the right to self determination in favour of what has been termed a 'limited comprehensive approach',[45] this issue was re-opened subsequently during informal negotiations at the Human Rights Council with the result that the wording was ultimately changed to accommodate complaints in respect of 'any of the economic, social and cultural rights set forth in the Covenant...'.[46] While the change ensured that the right to self-determination in art 1 was no longer explicitly excluded from the range of rights that could be made the subject of a complaint under the OP-ICESCR, it is by no means clear that complaints based directly on art 1 will be accepted by the CESCR. The Human Rights Committee has long since regarded the right to self-determination as being a right of 'peoples' which is not 'cognizable' as an individual right under the OP-ICCPR, preferring instead to consider such complaints under other articles of the Covenant.[47] While the CESCR is not bound by this approach, it is has effectively stated that it will follow it by subsuming claims based broadly on the right to self-determination 'only in so far as economic, social and cultural rights dimensions of that right are involved'.[48] The increasing emphasis placed by the treaty bodies towards the adoption of a cohesive approach in their jurisprudence would also make such an approach more likely. Accordingly, the change made on that matter at the final hour of the drafting process in respect of the scope of complaints may end up being more apparent than real. It remains to be seen, however, whether the comprehensive approach adopted will have ramifications in regard to the matter of ratifications.

[13.07] One further issue of note in regard to the scope of complaints is the fact that art 2 of the OP-ICESCR specifically provides that communications may only be submitted by or on behalf of individuals '...*under the jurisdiction of a State party*....claiming to be victims of a violation of any of the...rights *by that State party*' (emphasis added). Courtis and Sepúlveda have pointed out that this jurisdictional limitation in the text of the Protocol is not matched in the text of the ICESCR itself which obliges the States parties '...to take steps, individually *and through international assistance and cooperation, especially economic and technical*', to achieve progressively the realisation

---

[44] Chairperson's elements paper, para 5(e).
[45] See the debate of the working group at the fifth session: UN Doc A/HRC/8/7, paras 144–146; Mahon, 'Progress at the Front: the Draft Optional Protocol to the International Covenant on Economic, Social and Cultural Rights' (2008) HRL Rev 617, p 632.
[46] OP-ICESCR, art 2. For an account of this process see Mahon, 'Progress at the Front: The Draft Optional Protocol to the International Covenant on Economic, Social and Cultural Rights' (2008) HRL Rev 617, pp 632–633 and Vandenbogaerde and Vandenhole, 'The Optional Protocol to the International Covenant on Economic, Social and Cultural Rights: An Ex Ante Assessment of its Effectiveness in Light of the Drafting Process' (2010) HRL Rev 207, pp 221–223.
[47] General Comment No 23: The rights of minorities (Art 27): (08/04/94) UN Doc CCPR/C/21/Rev1/Add 5, paras 3.1. and 4. See also *Lubicon Lake Band v Canada*, Communication No 167/1984, para 13.3.
[48] See the CESCR Draft Protocol, para 25.

of the rights in the Covenant (emphasis added).[49] The absence of a jurisdiction clause in art 2(1) ICESCR, together with the reference to 'international cooperation and assistance',[50] has given rise to the view that the States parties have extra-territorial obligations under the Covenant.[51] While the precise scope of such obligations is by no means clear,[52] it seems apparent that creative arguments in this respect will be almost impossible to make under the OP-ICESCR on account of the jurisdiction clause in art 2, save perhaps for situations where a State is clearly exercising 'effective control' in another territory.[53] It certainly will not provide a means for persons outside a State party's jurisdiction to argue, for example, that the State has failed to fulfil its obligations to provide development aid, for example, or that the State has violated the terms of the Covenant through its trade policy.[54]

---

[49] Courtis and Sepúlveda, 'Are Extra-Territorial Obligations Reviewable under the Optional Protocol to the ICESCR?', (2009) 27 Nordic Journal of Human Rights pp 54–63, pp 56–57.

[50] There are other references to international cooperation in the text of the ICESCR (arts 11, 22 and 23) and in art 8 of the OP-ICESCR itself: see below, para. **13.19**.

[51] See generally Ssenyonjo, 'Reflections on State Obligations with Respect to Economic, Social and Cultural Rights in International Human Rights Law' (2011) Int'l Journal of Human Rts 969, pp 986–989; Skogly 'Extraterritoriality—Universal Human Rights without Universal Obligations?' Lancaster University eprints (10 March 2009); http://eprints.lancs.ac.uk/26177/1/Microsoft_Word_-_Monash_-_Extraterritoriality_-_Final_draft.pdf (last accessed May 2011); Vandenhole 'Third State Obligations under the ICESCR: A Case Study of EU Sugar Policy' (2007) 76 *Nordic Journal of International Law* 73–100; and Courtis and Sepúlveda, 'Are Extra-Territorial Obligations Reviewable under the Optional Protocol to the ICESCR?', (2009) 27 Nordic Journal of Human Rights pp 54–63, pp 55–56.

[52] Coomans 'The Extraterritorial Scope of the International Covenant on Economic, Social and Cultural Rights in the Work of the United Nations Committee on Economic, Social and Cultural Rights' (2011) 11 *Human Rights Law Review* 1–35.

[53] This is the view of Courtis and Sepúlveda, 'Are Extra-Territorial Obligations Reviewable under the Optional Protocol to the ICESCR?', (2009) 27 Nordic Journal of Human Rights pp 54–63, pp 57–58: '…under the Optional Protocol petitioners will bear the burden of proof in establishing that a violation occurring outside a State's territory occurs *de jure* within the State's jurisdiction' (p 58). On the case law of the Human Rights Committee in respect of extra-territorial obligations under the ICCPR, see Ch 7, paras **7.29–7.31**.

[54] Courtis and Sepúlveda argue that extra-territorial obligations could conceivably be raised under the inter-State complaint procedure provided for in art 10 OP-ICESCR or form the subject of an inquiry under art 11: 'Are Extra-Territorial Obligations Reviewable under the Optional Protocol to the ICESCR?', (2009) 27 Nordic Journal of Human Rights pp 54–63, pp 59–62. CESCR Member Mr Riedel also noted the difficulty of invoking an obligation to provide international assistance in an individual complaint procedure during the drafting of the OP-ICESR, though he did see a possibility for so doing under an inter-State procedure: Report of the 2nd session, para. 79. While noting the difficulties involved in establishing a causal link between a failure to provide international assistance and a violation in an individual complaint procedure, the representative of the ICJ considered that '… lack of international assistance could be a mitigating factor in assessing States' ability to guarantee the rights in the Covenant': Report of the 2nd session, para 80.

Assessment on the Merits (art 8(4))

[13.08] A central aspect of the justiciability debate outlined above was the question of what criteria should be adopted in assessing whether or not a State party to the Protocol had complied with its obligations to implement the rights in the ICESCR. Much of the objection raised in regard to a complaints procedure was based on the view that an international monitoring body would be ill-equipped and unsuitable to determine whether the measures taken by a State corresponded to the best use of available resources.[55] Such a scenario might lead to undue interference with national policy-making and be perceived as 'anti-democratic'.[56] Proponents of the OP-ICESCR, on the other hand, argued that resource allocation was often part and parcel of the legislative review function of national courts.[57] After protracted debate on the issue,[58] the inclusion of explicit assessment criteria in the text of the Protocol inevitably became the *quid pro quo* for the sceptical States in capitulating to demands for a comprehensive approach to the question of justiciability.[59] Proposals for such criteria initially included incorporation of a standard of 'reasonableness' whereby the CESCR would be directed to assess the reasonableness of the 'steps' taken by a respondent State in implementing art 2(1) of the ICESCR.[60] During the fourth session of the working group, further proposals were made to include reference also to a 'broad margin of appreciation of the State party to determine the optimum use of its resources' and to replace the test of 'reasonableness' with one of 'unreasonableness'.[61] While there was significant support for explicit inclusion of a 'margin of appreciation' concept in the final drafting session of the

---

[55] See the contribution, for example, of Canada, France, Germany and Senegal during the second session of the working group: Report of the 3rd session, para 91.

[56] See the contribution of Poland which raised the issue of whether decisions on national resource allocations '....were not better left to domestic courts than to an international body which was not subject to a national democratic process': Report of the 3rd session, para 92.

[57] Report of the 3rd session, para 94.

[58] For a detailed analysis of the progression of debate on this issue see Porter, 'The Reasonableness of Article 8(4) – Adjudicating Claims from the Margins' (2009) 27 Nordic Journal of Human Rights, pp 48–50; Vandenbogaerde and Vandenhole, 'The Optional Protocol to the International Covenant on Economic, Social and Cultural Rights: An Ex Ante Assessment of its Effectiveness in Light of the Drafting Process' (2010) HRL Rev 207, pp 223–226; and Mahon, 'Progress at the Front: The Draft Optional Protocol to the International Covenant on Economic, Social and Cultural Rights' (2008) HRL Rev 617, pp 636–637.

[59] As Vandenbogaerde and Vandenhole put it, '...the comprehensive package came at a price, as it was only accepted as part of a package deal. This deal included explicit assessment criteria for the Committee in the OP': Vandenbogaerde and Vandenhole, 'The Optional Protocol to the International Covenant on Economic, Social and Cultural Rights: An Ex Ante Assessment of its Effectiveness in Light of the Drafting Process' (2010) HRL Rev 207, p 223.

[60] Article 8(4) of the Chairperson's Draft Protocol. This was first discussed at the fourth session of the Working Group: Report of the 4th session, paras 94–104.

[61] These proposals were made initially by the United States: Report of the 4th session, para 95. They were incorporated into the revised draft Protocol discussed at the fifth working group session: UN Doc A/HRC/8/WG4/2/Corr 1 (16 January 2008), art 8(4).

working group,[62] neither of the latter proposals was ultimately carried.[63] Instead, States opted for a formula adapted from the *Grootboom*[64] decision of the South African Constitutional Court in applying the 'reasonableness' standard in the context of the right to housing in art 26 of the South African Bill of Rights.[65] As finally drafted, therefore, art 8(4) of the Protocol provides that:

> 'When examining communications under the present Protocol, the Committee shall consider the reasonableness of the steps taken by the State Party in accordance with Part II of the Covenant. In doing so, the Committee shall bear in mind that *the State Party may adopt a range of possible policy measures for the implementation of the rights set forth in the Covenant*' (emphasis added).

As Mahon notes, the criteria of 'reasonableness' was thus included and while a margin of appreciation is not explicit, the discretionary room for manoeuvre vested in States in regard to the choice and application of those measures was maintained by the wording of the final sentence.[66]

[13.09] Looking to the future,[67] perhaps the best indicator of the CESCR's likely approach to the interpretation of the 'reasonableness of the steps' taken by a State party in fulfilling its obligations under art 2(1) is contained in a statement which it adopted on

---

[62] Austria, Ireland, Japan, Poland and Venezuela supported the inclusion of a 'margin of appreciation' generally, while Canada, Denmark, Greece, the Netherlands, New Zealand, Norway, Sweden, Turkey and the United Kingdom supported adding the word 'broad' or 'wide' before the word 'margin': Report of the Open-ended Working group on an Optional Protocol to the International Covenant on Economic, Social and Cultural Rights on its fifth session: UN Doc A/HRC/8/7, p 91 (Report of the 5th session). Switzerland and Poland had earlier expressed approval of the 'broad margin of appreciation': Report of the 4th session, paras 97 and 98.

[63] Argentina, Bangladesh, Belgium, Chile, Costa Rica, Ecuador, Finland, France, Germany, India, Liechtenstein, Mexico, Portugal, the Russian Federation and Sri Lanka supported the deletion of the concept of the margin of appreciation: Report of the 5th session, para 91. The NGO coalition also opposed its inclusion: Report of the 4th session, para 95.

[64] *Government of the Republic of South Africa and Others v Grootboom and Others 2000* (11) BCLR 1169 (CC).

[65] Porter, 'The Reasonableness of Article 8(4) – Adjudicating Claims from the Margins' (2009) 27 Nordic Journal of Human Rights, pp 49–50. On the manner in which the South African experience of adjudicating socio-economic rights could inform the future practice of the CESCR under the Protocol, see generally, Landa, 'Taking Dignity Seriously – Judicial Reflections on the Optional Protocol to the ICESCR' (2009) 27 Nordic Journal of Human Rights, pp 29–38.

[66] Mahon, 'Progress at the Front: The Draft Optional Protocol to the International Covenant on Economic, Social and Cultural Rights' (2008) HRL Rev 617, p 638.

[67] For a detailed analysis of the potential application of art 8(4) OP-ICESCR, see Griffey, 'The 'Reasonableness' Test: Assessing violations of State Obligations under the Optional Protocol to the International Covenant on Economic, Social and Cultural Rights' (2011) HRL Rev 275.

this issue during the negotiations on the Protocol in May 2007.[68] In that statement, the Committee stated that in examining whether the measures taken by a State were 'adequate' and 'reasonable', it would take into account, *inter alia*, the following considerations:

(a) The extent to which the measures taken were deliberate, concrete and targeted towards the fulfilment of economic, social and cultural rights;
(b) Whether the State party exercised its discretion in a non-discriminatory and non-arbitrary manner;
(c) Whether the State party's decision (not) to allocate available resources was in accordance with international human rights standards;
(d) Where several policy options were available, whether the State party adopted the option that least restricts Covenant rights;
(e) The time frame in which the steps were taken;
(f) Whether the steps had taken into account the precarious situation of disadvantaged and marginalised individuals or groups and, whether they were non-discriminatory, and whether they prioritised grave situations or situations of risk.

In the same document, the CESCR readily embraced the notion of a 'margin of appreciation' by stating that it bears in mind at all times

> '...its own role as an international treaty body and the role of the State in formulating or adopting, funding and implementing laws and policies concerning economic, social and cultural rights. To this end, and in accordance with the practice of judicial and other quasi-judicial human rights treaty bodies, the Committee always respects the margin of appreciation of States to take steps and adopt measures most suited to their specific circumstances.'[69]

[13.10] Where a State fails to take steps or adopts retrogressive steps, the CESCR noted that the burden of proof would rest with that State to show that such a course of action was based on the most careful consideration, that it could be justified by reference to the totality of rights provided for in the Covenant and that full use had been made of available resources.[70] Should a State use 'resource constraints' as an explanation for any retrogressive steps, the Committee would consider such information on a country-by-country basis in the light of objective criteria.[71] Having carried out such an assessment,

---

[68] 'An Evaluation of the Obligations to Take Steps to the 'Maximum of Available Resources' under an Optional Protocol to the Covenant': UN Doc E/C12/2007/1 (21 September 2007).

[69] 'An Evaluation of the Obligations to Take Steps to the 'Maximum of Available Resources' under an Optional Protocol to the Covenant': UN Doc E/C12/2007/1 (21 September 2007), para 11

[70] 'An Evaluation of the Obligations to Take Steps to the 'Maximum of Available Resources' under an Optional Protocol to the Covenant': UN Doc E/C12/2007/1 (21 September 2007), para 9.

[71] These were specified as including: (a) the country's level of development; (b) the severity of the alleged breach, in particular whether the situation concerned the enjoyment of the minimum core content of the Covenant; (contd.../)

the CESCR envisaged that in the context of an Optional Protocol, it could make recommendations, *inter alia,* along the following lines: [72]

(a) Recommending remedial action, such as compensation, to the victim, as appropriate;

(b) Calling upon the State party to remedy the circumstances leading to a violation;[73]

(c) Suggesting, on a case-by-case basis, a range of measures to assist the State party in implementing the recommendations, with particular emphasis on low-cost measures. The State party would nonetheless still have the option of adopting its own alternative measures;

(d) Recommending a follow-up mechanism to ensure ongoing accountability of the State party; for example, by including a requirement that in its next periodic report the State party explain the steps taken to redress the violation.

Clearly, the scope of supervisory review outlined above is ambitious and if the CESCR is to remain faithful to its statement, it will need to adopt rules of procedure that will assist it in its endeavour. As Porter notes, these might include rules which are new to a treaty body and which will allow it '…to hear evidence of rights' claimants, access independent experts, or hear from NGO interveners'.[74] Ironically, the resource

---

[71] (\...contd) These were specified as including: (a) the country's level of development; (b) the severity of the alleged breach, in particular whether the situation concerned the enjoyment of the minimum core content of the Covenant; (c) the country's current economic situation, in particular whether the country was undergoing a period of economic recession; (d) the existence of other serious claims on the State party's limited resources; for example, resulting from a recent natural disaster or from recent internal or international armed conflict; (e) whether the State party had sought to identify low-cost options; and (f) whether the State party had sought cooperation and assistance or rejected offers of resources from the international community for the purposes of implementing the provisions of the Covenant without sufficient reason. 'An Evaluation of the Obligations to Take Steps to the 'Maximum of Available Resources' under an Optional Protocol to the Covenant': UN Doc E/C12/2007/1 (21 September 2007), para 10.

[72] 'An Evaluation of the Obligations to Take Steps to the 'Maximum of Available Resources' under an Optional Protocol to the Covenant': UN Doc E/C12/2007/1 (21 September 2007), para 13.

[73] In making such a call, the CESCR clarified that '… it might suggest goals and parameters to assist the State party in identifying appropriate measures. These parameters could include suggesting overall priorities to ensure that resource allocation conformed with the State party's obligations under the Covenant; provision for the disadvantaged and marginalized individuals and groups; protection against grave threats to the enjoyment of economic, social and cultural rights; and respect for non-discrimination in the adoption and implementation of measures'. 'An Evaluation of the Obligations to Take Steps to the 'Maximum of Available Resources' under an Optional Protocol to the Covenant': UN Doc E/C12/2007/1 (21 September 2007), at para 13(b).

[74] Porter, 'The Reasonableness of Article 8(4) – Adjudicating Claims from the Margins' (2009) 27 Nordic Journal of Human Rights, p 53.

constraints operating on the CESCR itself make the adoption of such procedures doubtful.

Admissibility Criteria (arts 2,3 and 4)

[13.11] The CESCR itself had anticipated from an early stage that if a comprehensive approach were to be adopted in regard to the range of rights that could be made subject to the complaint procedure, various procedural safeguards could be put in place to ensure that the procedure '...did not lead to the consideration of matters which do not belong in such setting'.[75] In this respect, it had in mind the domestic remedies rule, as well as the other admissibility criteria that apply to other complaints procedures.[76] In actual fact, the admissibility criteria in the OP-ICESCR which emerged from the drafting process incorporate most of the criteria provided for in the other treaty complaint procedures, with some new features.

[13.12] One major issue in regard to the admissibility of complaints concerned the question of who should have the necessary standing (*ratione personae*) to make a complaint under the OP-ICESCR. A number of options were presented to the working group in regard to this issue, including the possibility of complaints by 'individuals' only, 'individuals and groups of individuals' as well as the option of collective complaints being made by organisations as well as particular interest groups.[77] Collective complaints, but not individual ones, are currently possible under the Council of Europe's, European Social Charter.[78] However, despite debate on the subject during the drafting of the OP-CRPD, they have not been included in respect of any UN human rights treaty.[79] They may be differentiated from individual communications insofar as they may be launched by representative organisations[80] without a requirement to demonstrate victim status, domestic remedies or, indeed, any particular time-limit.[81] A significant level of resistance emerged to the notion of such a broad concept of complaint during the negotiations on the OP-ICESCR such that the possibility of their explicit inclusion was deleted from the draft Protocol.[82] Rather, the working group opted

---

[75] CESCR Analytical Paper, para 79.
[76] CESCR Analytical Paper, paras 80–81.
[77] Chairperson's Elements Paper, para 10 and see draft art 3 of the Chairperson's Draft Protocol.
[78] Additional Protocol to the European Social Charter Providing for a System of Collective Complaints (1995): http://conventions.coe.int/treaty/en/treaties/html/158.htm (last accessed May 2011). See generally, Churchill and Khaliq, 'The Collective Complaints System of the European Social Charter: An Effective Mechanism for Ensuring Compliance with Economic and Social Rights?' (2004) 15 European Journal of International Law, pp 417–456.
[79] See Ch 11, para **[11.03]**.
[80] See arts 1 and 2(1) of the Additional Protocol to the European Social Charter Providing for a System of Collective Complaints (1995) for the range of organisations entitled to take complaints under that instrument.
[81] See generally, Cullen, 'The Collective Complaints System of the European Social Charter: Interpretative Methods of the European Committee of Social Rights' (2009) 9(1) HRL Rev 61.
[82] Report of the 4th session, paras 47–56. This is certainly the type of potential collective complaints mechanism that was envisaged by the chairperson of the working group in her elements paper: Chairperson's elements paper, para 10.

for the formula adopted previously in the OP-CEDAW and art 14 of the ICERD which allows for complaints 'by or on behalf of individuals and groups of individuals'. In this respect, the formula goes further than the narrower wording of the OP-ICCPR which only allows for complaints by 'individuals'.[83] A proposal to include a specific provision allowing for complaints by NGOs 'with relevant expertise and interest' was rejected at the final session, apparently on the basis that it would have allowed for communications without identified victims and risked inviting 'a flood of communications'.[84] Clearly, it is open to the CESCR to consider 'NGOs' as a 'group of individuals'. However, the further stipulation that the individual or group of individuals must either be a 'victim' of a violation, or be acting 'with their consent unless the author can justify acting on their behalf without such consent' narrows the possibilities for a 'collective complaint' in the true sense of that concept.[85] Any NGO seeking, therefore, to make a complaint under the ICESCR would need to satisfy this requirement, with consent only likely to be dispensed with in extreme circumstances such as the death of the victim.[86]

[13.13] A related and novel proposal during the drafting process was to include an express provision granting *amicus* standing to NGOs and NHRIs or to allow them to make submissions with respect to a communication submitted under the Protocol.[87] However, concern was expressed by some delegations about this proposal on the basis that NGOs could already participate as third parties in the procedure and that such a provision would be unprecedented in a complaints procedure.[88] As a result, a provision on *amicus* submissions was not incorporated into the final draft.[89] As Mahon notes, however, it is entirely possible that the CESCR could include provision for such submissions in its Rules of Procedure in respect of the Protocol.[90]

---

[83] The CCPR has interpreted this aspect of the OP-ICCPR narrowly, only allowing for communications to be submitted by individual victims of violations: See Ch 7, para **7.24**.

[84] See Revised Draft Optional Protocol to the International Covenant on Economic, Social and Cultural Rights, UN Doc A/HRC/8/WG4/2, art 2, 1 ter (Revised Draft Optional Protocol); and Report of the 5th session, para 44. Ecuador, the Netherlands and the NGO coalition only preferred its retention.

[85] Indeed, China had sought clarification during the negotiations on what was the difference between communications submitted by groups of individuals and collective communications: Report of the 4th session, para 45.

[86] Consent has been dispensed with on that basis by the CEDAW Committee in interpreting a similar clause in the OP-CEDAW, art 2: see Ch 10, para **10.17**.

[87] See Revised Draft Optional Protocol, art 2, 1 bis. Further proposals were made during the fifth session of the working group to make specific reference to NHRIs and/or trade unions and employers' organisations: Report of the 5th session, para 43.

[88] Mahon, 'Progress at the Front: The Draft Optional Protocol to the International Covenant on Economic, Social and Cultural Rights' (2008) HRL Rev 617 at 635.

[89] Revised Draft Optional Protocol to the International Covenant on Economic, Social and Cultural Rights: UN Doc A/HRC/8/WG4/3 (25 March 2008).

[90] Mahon, 'Progress at the Front: The Draft Optional Protocol to the International Covenant on Economic, Social and Cultural Rights' (2008) HRL Rev 617 at 635. (contd.../)

[13.14] Article 3(1) of the OP-ICESCR provides for the domestic remedies rule, according to which complaints shall not be considered unless the CESCR has first ascertained that all available domestic remedies have been exhausted, unless the application of those remedies is unreasonably prolonged.[91] The inclusion of an express exception to the rule where the remedies are 'unlikely to bring effective relief' was dropped at the final session, in response to objections by Canada, the United States, China and the African Group, amongst others.[92] The deletion of what is in fact agreed language from a series of other complaints procedures[93] is somewhat surprising, but not necessarily significant since it will be open to the CESCR to incorporate such an exception into its interpretation of the domestic remedies rule, as is the practice of the CCPR in interpreting the latter rule as it appears in the OP-ICCPR.[94]

[13.15] In a bid to extend the logic and effect of the domestic remedies rule, the African Group, amongst others, urged the adoption of a further admissibility criterion requiring all complainants also to exhaust regional remedies before making a complaint under the OP-ICESCR.[95] What might have been dubbed a 'regional remedies rule' was rejected, however, on a variety of bases including the diversity of regional mechanisms available, none of which corresponded fully with the procedure under the OP-ICESCR.[96] It was pointed out that victims should be free to decide which procedure to use and that such a

---

[90] (\...contd) However, as Mahon and Langford each point out, difficulties may arise in this eventuality for potential *amici* in accessing the documentation submitted by the parties, which is not generally made publicly available: Mahon, The Draft Optional Protocol to the International Covenant on Economic, Social and Cultural Rights' (2008) HRL Rev 617 at 635; and Langford, 'Closing the Gap? – An Introduction to the Optional Protocol to the International Covenant on Economic, Social and Cultural Rights' (2009) 27 Nordic Journal of Human Rights 1 at 25.

[91] Article 3(1), OP-ICESCR.

[92] See Reports of the fourth and fifth sessions of the working group, paras 59 and 49 respectively.

[93] See UNCAT, art 22(5)(b); OP-CEDAW, art 4(1); OP-CRPD, art 2(d); and ICRMW, art 77(3)(b).

[94] See Ch 7, para **7.39**.

[95] Report of the 3rd session, para 52. This issue had been raised at the second session (UN Doc E/CN4/2005/52, para 92) and by the Chairperson's elements paper, para 8.

[96] These include the Additional Protocol to the European Social Charter Providing for a System of Collective Complaints, and, see generally, Churchill and Kaliq, 'The Collective Complaints System of the European Social Charter: An Effective Mechanism for Ensuring Compliance with Economic and Social Rights' (2004) 15 EJIL, pp 417–456; and Cullen, 'The Collective Complaints System of the European Social Charter: Interpretative Methods of the European Committee of Social Rights' (2009) 9(1) HRL Rev 61. Article 26 of the American Convention on Human Rights and its additional Protocol on Economic, Social and Cultural Rights, which are subject to a complaints procedure governed by arts 44 –51 and 61–69 of the Convention: OAS Treaty Series No 36; 1144 UNTS 123; 9 ILM 99 (1969) and OAS Treaty Series No 69; 28 ILM 156 (1989) respectively. See generally Craven, 'The Protection of Economic, Social and Cultural Rights under the Inter-American System of Human Rights' in Harris and Livingston (eds), *The Inter-American System of Human Rights* (Clarendon Press, 1998), pp 289–321; (contd.../)

rule would prevent complaints from reaching the international level and potentially introduce a hierarchy among regional and universal mechanisms.[97]

[13.16] As regards other admissibility criteria, Article 3 of the OP-ICESCR provides that the CESCR shall also consider a communication inadmissible when:

(a) It is not submitted within one year after the exhaustion of domestic remedies, except in cases where the author can demonstrate that it had not been possible to submit the communication within that time limit;[98]

(b) The facts that are the subject of the communication occurred prior to the entry into force of the Protocol for the State Party concerned unless those facts continued after that date;[99]

(c) The same matter has already been examined by the Committee or has been or is being examined under another procedure of international investigation or settlement;[100]

(d) The communication is incompatible with the provisions of the Covenant;[101]

(e) The communication is manifestly ill-founded, not sufficiently substantiated or exclusively based on reports disseminated by the mass media;[102]

(f) The communication is an abuse of the right to submit a communication;[103] or

(g) It is anonymous or not in writing.[104]

From the italicised text, it can be seen that a number of additions have been made to the standard admissibility criteria found in other UN treaty complaint procedures. The first of these is the inclusion of a time limit for the initiation of a complaint of one year from the date of exhaustion of the last domestic remedy.[105] Although time limits are a standard

---

[96] (\...contd) and the 'communications procedure' provided for in art 55 of the African Charter on Human and Peoples' Rights: OAU Doc CAB/LEG/67/3 rev 5; 1520 UNTS 217; 21 ILM 58 (1982). Further, see generally, Evans and Murray (eds), *The African Charter on Human and Peoples' Rights: The System in Practice 1986–2006* (2nd edn, CUP, 2008), pp 76–138.

[97] Report of the 3rd session, para 53. See also Report of the 4th session, para 62.

[98] OP-ICESCR, art 3(2)(a).

[99] OP-ICESCR, art 3(2)(b). This provision (like OP-CEDAW, art 4(2)(e) and OP-CRPD, art 2(f)) codifies the practice of the CCPR and CERD in regard to the concept of 'continuing violations'. See Ch 7, paras **7.21–7.22** and Ch 8, para **8.16** respectively.

[100] OP-ICESCR, art 3(2)(c).

[101] OP-ICESCR, art 3(2)(d).

[102] OP-ICESCR, art 3(2)(e). A communication is normally deemed to be 'manifestly ill-founded' in circumstances where the facts do not disclose a *prima facie* violation of the ICESCR. As regards complaints that lack substantiation, the CESCR will likely follow the practice of the CCPR in deciding when a communication is lacking in substantiation: see Ch 7, para **7.34**. As to the issue of communications based exclusively on reports disseminated by the mass media, see below, para **13.17**.

[103] OP-ICESCR, art 3(2)(f).

[104] OP-ICESCR, art 3(2)(g).

[105] OP-ICESCR, art 3(2)(a). Although a six-month limit was initially proposed, this was extended to one year during the final drafting session: Report of the 5th session, para 149.

feature of regional human rights complaints mechanisms,[106] the adoption of such a provision in a UN instrument is rare (the only other example being that which is contained in art 14(5) of ICERD).[107] There can be little doubt that such a provision will operate to weed out a significant number of complaints, particularly, as Langford notes, from States in which there is a paucity of domestic remedies.[108] In such circumstances, complainants and their lawyers are less likely to be aware of international remedies than their counterparts in States in which a culture of rights litigation prevails.[109] In this respect, it is questionable whether a fixed time limit is appropriate in the context of a complaint procedure which is likely to be less visible than its regional counterparts.[110] Nonetheless, despite strenuous opposition from the NGO coalition, most delegations favoured the introduction of a fixed time limit for initiation of the procedure over a more flexible formulation such as submission 'within a reasonable period'.[111] As Langford notes further, the CESCR would probably permit cases of 'continuing violations' to fall outside this rule.[112]

[13.17] Article 3(2)(e) of the OP-ICESCR includes as a ground for rejecting a communication the fact that it is 'exclusively based on reports disseminated by the mass media'. This criterion contains echoes of the African Charter on Human and Peoples

---

[106] Both the European Convention on Human Rights and the American Convention on Human Rights operate a six month time limit (ECHR, arts 35(1) and ACHR, 46(1)(b), while the African Charter requires that communications must be submitted 'within a reasonable period from the time local remedies are exhausted or from the date the [African] Commission is seised of the matter' (art 56(6)). There is no time-limit for submission of a 'collective complaint' under the Additional Protocol to the European Social Charter Providing for a System of Collective Complaints.

[107] By virtue of ICERD, art 14(5), CERD applies a time-limit of six months to communications made under the article: see Ch 8, para **[8.15]**. The CCPR has recently adopted a new rule of procedure in respect of communications submitted after an undue delay (CCPR's Rules of Procedure, r 96(c)): Ch 7, para [7.19].

[108] Langford, 'Closing the Gap? – An Introduction to the Optional Protocol to the International Covenant on Economic, Social and Cultural Rights' (2009) 27 Nordic Journal of Human Rights 1, p 23.

[109] Langford, 'Closing the Gap? – An Introduction to the Optional Protocol to the International Covenant on Economic, Social and Cultural Rights' (2009) 27 Nordic Journal of Human Rights 1, p 23.

[110] The NGO Coalition opposed the introduction of a time limit on the basis that it would act as an 'unnecessary barrier to access to the procedure': Report of the 3rd session, para 61.

[111] Report of the 4th session, para 52.

[112] Langford, 'Closing the Gap? – An Introduction to the Optional Protocol to the International Covenant on Economic, Social and Cultural Rights' (2009) 27 Nordic Journal of Human Rights 1, p 23. As he observes, this exceptional rule tends to operate more favourably where cases concerning positive obligations are concerned as a 'failure to take action' can often 'continue' post ratification. The 'continuing violations' exception is normally raised (as is provided for explicitly in Article 3(2)(b) of the OP-ICESCR) in respect of acts or facts which predated the entry into force of a particular procedure for a State party, where the effects of such continue post-ratification: see above in regard to the OP-ICCPR, for example, Ch 7, paras **7.21–7.22**.

Rights which effectively prohibits communications which are based exclusively on 'news disseminated through the mass media'.[113] However, the latter instrument does not require that a person must establish victim status before bringing a complaint, thus engendering the possibility of complaints based on media reports.[114] Thus, its inclusion in the complaint procedure provided for under the OP-ICESCR is somewhat incongruous given the requirement that the complainant must be an individual or group of individuals capable of establishing victim status, or be acting on behalf of a victim with his or her consent save in exceptional circumstances. The only circumstance in which exclusion based on media reports might therefore be relevant would be as a trump to a complaint made on a person's behalf without their consent. For the most part, however, the direct linkage to victim status would appear to make the inclusion of this ground superfluous and it remains to be seen whether it will surface much in the jurisprudence of the CESCR in regard to admissibility.

[13.18] Finally, the CESCR may, if necessary, decline to consider a communication where it does not reveal that the author has suffered a clear disadvantage, unless the CESCR considers that the communication raises a serious issue of general importance.[115] This provision was in fact the brain child of the CESCR, dating back to the analytical paper which it submitted to the World Conference on Human Rights in 1993.[116] Taking particular account of the collective dimension of the remedies that would generally be sought, the CESCR advocated a more far-reaching criterion than simply requiring a complainant to be a 'victim'.[117] A requirement demanding that some detriment must have been suffered by the individual or group concerned would thus deter 'speculative' complaints.[118] Canada, New Zealand and the United Kingdom resurrected the idea at the final drafting session of the working group, and it found support on the basis that it would absolve the CESCR from having to deal with complaints of only minor importance.[119] One objection made to the proposal was that it would require the CESCR to undertake an examination of the merits at the admissibility stage and would imply that some violations could be considered insignificant which would be 'unacceptable'.[120] Similar concerns have been raised about the inclusion of an almost identical provision into the admissibility criteria of the European Convention on

---

[113] Article 56(4) of the *African Charter on Human and Peoples' Rights*.
[114] Evans and Murray, *The African Charter on Human and Peoples' Rights: The System in Practice 1986–2006* (2nd edn, CUP, 2008), p 110.
[115] OP-ICESCR, art 4.
[116] CESCR Analytical Paper, para 85.
[117] CESCR Analytical Paper, para 85.
[118] CESCR Analytical Paper, para 85.
[119] Report of the 5th session, para 59 and see further, para 155.
[120] Report of the 5th session, paras 59 and 156–157. China was concerned that the CESCR might end up applying a 'double-standard' when operating this criterion to the detriment of the uniform application of the Protocol: para 157. On the need to take a 'cautious approach' to the application of this criterion, see Scheinin and Langford, 'Evolution or Revolution? – Extrapolating from the Experience of the Human Rights Committee' (2009) 27 Nordic Journal of Human Rights 97, p 110.

Human Rights.[121] Thus far, the European Court of Human Rights has operated the provision sparingly to weed out cases which could not be deemed 'manifestly ill-founded' or abusive, but where the disadvantage suffered is so negligible as to make adjudication a waste of the court's resources.[122] It is to be hoped that the CESCR adopts a similar attitude in operating the new criterion in art 4.

International Cooperation and Assistance (art 14)

[13.19] As noted above, art 2(1) of the ICESCR obliges each State party to take steps '...*individually and through international assistance and cooperation*, especially economic and technical, to the maximum of its available resources ...' with a view to achieving progressively the rights in the ICESCR.[123] One of the dilemmas that emerged in the drafting of the OP-ICESCR concerned the question of how (if at all) this reference to 'international assistance and cooperation' should be incorporated in the complaint procedure.[124] Diametrically opposed views emerged during the negotiation process as to whether the reference in art 2(1) of the ICESCR imposed a legal obligation to provide assistance and if so, whether there was a corresponding right to receive it.[125] A compromise formula was eventually agreed to in the final drafting session which

---

[121] ECHR, art 35(3)(b), as amended by Protocol 14 provides that an individual application under ECHR, art 34 shall be deemed inadmissible where 'the applicant has not suffered a significant disadvantage, unless respect for human rights as defined in the Convention and the Protocols thereto requires an examination on the merits *and provided that no case may be rejected on this ground which has not been duly considered by a domestic tribunal*' (emphasis added). It may be noted that a significant difference between the two provisions is the absence of any qualification in art 4, OP-ICESCR that a case may not be rejected if it has not been duly heard by a domestic tribunal. In this respect, Article 35(3)(b) is in fact less stringent than art 4 OP-ICESCR.

[122] *Ionescu v Romania* (App No 36659/04), (01/06/2010); *Finger v Bulgaria* App No 37346/05 (10 May 2011, Fourth Section) and *Juhas uri v Serbia* App No 48155/06 (7 June 2011, Second Section).

[123] ICESCR, art 22 conferred a role on ECOSOC of bringing to the attention of other organs of the UN, their subsidiary organs and specialised agencies any matters arising out of State party reports under the Covenant to assist such bodies to decide on the advisability of international measures to implement the Covenant; while ICESCR, art 23 gives illustrative examples of the types of international cooperation measures which could be implemented for the achievement of the rights in the Covenant. As to the significance of ICESCR, art 22, see General Comment No 2 of the CESCR on international technical assistance measures: Un Doc HRI/GEN/1/Rev.6 at 11.

[124] Although the issue never came to a head in terms of whether individuals should to able to make complaints under the OP-ICESCR concerning a State party's failure to respect its obligations to provide international assistance or cooperation, this possibility would seem to be substantially ruled out by the jurisdiction clause in art 2 of the Protocol itself: see para **13.07**.

[125] See, for example, the exchange of views between States at the second session of the working group's deliberations: Report of the 2nd session, paras 76–78. For a detailed description of the debate on this issue, see Vandenbogaerde and Vandenhole, 'The Optional Protocol to the International Covenant on Economic, Social and Cultural Rights: An Ex Ante Assessment of its Effectiveness in Light of the Drafting Process' (2010) HRL Rev 207, pp 226–230 (contd....).

eschews the framing of the issue in terms of obligations or entitlements.[126] Rather, art 14 envisages firstly a central role for the CESCR to transmit to the UN specialised agencies, funds and programmes and other competent bodies,[127] with a State's consent, its views or recommendations concerning communications and inquiries that indicate a need for technical advice or assistance. The CESCR may also bring to the attention of such bodies any matter arising out of communications which may assist them in deciding on the advisability of international measures likely to contribute to assisting States in achieving progress in the implementation of the rights in the Covenant.[128] A trust fund is to be established, with a view to providing expert and technical assistance to States that are experiencing difficulties in implementing the rights on account of resource constraints.[129] While the establishment of such a fund does appear in the abstract to be a positive development, it remains to be seen how useful it will be in practice.[130] For one thing, contributions to the funds are not obligatory and for another, the idea of permitting access to it by victims was deliberately excluded by the drafters.[131]

Appraisal

[13.20] Speaking after its adoption by the Human Rights Council, the former High Commissioner for Human Rights, Louise Arbour, predicted that the OP-ICESCR could make '…a real difference in the lives of those who are often left to languish at the margins of society'.[132] Other forecasts for the Protocol are not quite so sanguine, with some complaining that political considerations and ideological differences have resulted

---

[125] (\...contd) The authors note that the debate on this issue took place against '…a long-standing, very often highly politicised and polarised discussion whether or not there is a legal obligation in the ICESCR to provide international assistance and cooperation, and in particular development aid' (p 227). See also Mahon, 'Progress at the Front: The Draft Optional Protocol to the International Covenant on Economic, Social and Cultural Rights' (2008) HRL Rev 617, pp 638–639.

[126] Vandenbogaerde and Vandenhole, 'The Optional Protocol to the International Covenant on Economic, Social and Cultural Rights: An Ex Ante Assessment of its Effectiveness in Light of the Drafting Process' (2010) HRL Rev 207, pp 226–230. The provisions of OP-ICESCR, art 14 are expressed to be 'without prejudice to the obligations of each State Party to fulfil its obligations under the Covenant'.

[127] These bodies would presumably include the Human Rights Council, as well as the other extant bodies referred to by the CESCR in its General Comment No 2 on international technical assistance measures, namely, the UNDP, UNICEF, the World Bank and IMF, the ILO, FAO, UNESCO and WHO: UN Doc E/1990/23, annex III at 86, para 2.

[128] OP-ICESCR, art 14(2).

[129] OP-ICESCR, art 14(3).

[130] Austria, Belgium, Germany and the United Kingdom questioned the practicality and effectiveness of the fund proposed in art 14 at the penultimate drafting session: Report of the 4th session, para 168.

[131] Mahon, 'Progress at the Front: The Draft Optional Protocol to the International Covenant on Economic, Social and Cultural Rights' (2008) HRL Rev 617, p 639.

[132] Arbour, 'Human Rights Made Whole' (2008, Project Syndicate): http://www.policyinnovations.org/ideas/commentary/data/000068/ (last accessed May 2011).

in 'weak' and 'retrogressive' provisions.[133] A middle-ground perspective estimates that while the instrument 'will not produce miracles for the world's deprived', it does give them 'a limited opportunity to hold their political leaders accountable for their actions (and inaction) relating to social, economic, and cultural rights'.[134]

[13.21] As with many of the other, as yet, dormant procedures, a rigorous appraisal of the effectiveness of the instrument will only be possible once there has been an opportunity to observe its operation in practice. In comparison with the OP-CRPD which was adopted only two years previously, the rate of ratification of the OP-ICESCR has been slow, with only three States having ratified it to date. Despite the compromises made during the negotiations, it seems likely that developed States will remain reticent about ratifying an instrument which they fear could have dramatic implications for budgetary and resource allocation and which could hold them to a higher standard than less developed States.[135]

[13.22] On the positive side, the adoption of the Protocol has, at the very least, gone some way to bridge the perceived gap in terms of the status of economic, social and cultural rights on the one hand, and civil and political rights on the other. The very fact that it contains an individual complaints procedure whereby individual victims can complain to an expert monitoring body about a breach of *any* of the rights in the Covenant is a positive development. Elaboration of a Protocol has in this sense undoubtedly reinforced the view that economic, social and cultural rights are justiciable and capable of judicial application (albeit in this case that the body in question is not 'judicial'). If it enters into force, the Protocol should also heighten awareness of the Covenant itself, as well as presenting a significant opportunity for the CESCR to flesh out the meaning of particular rights in the Covenant, over and above the opportunities currently derived from the reporting regime and General Comments.[136] If that opportunity is to be fully realised, much will depend on the competence of the CESCR and the resources allocated to it. The inclusion of the 'reasonableness' criterion, together

---

[133] Vandenbogaerde and Vandenhole, 'The Optional Protocol to the International Covenant on Economic, Social and Cultural Rights: An Ex Ante Assessment of its Effectiveness in Light of the Drafting Process' (2010) HRL Rev 207, p 237. They conclude that: 'Although the time seemed to be ripe for an optional protocol, the compromise that was eventually struck gives little cause for optimism for the victims of violations of ESC rights'.

[134] Simmons, 'Should States Ratify? – Process and Consequences of the Optional Protocol to the ICESCR' (2009) 27 Nordic Journal of Human Rights 64, p 65.

[135] Mahon, 'Progress at the Front: The Draft Optional Protocol to the International Covenant on Economic, Social and Cultural Rights' (2008) HRL Rev 617, p 644. For contrasting perspectives on the merits/demerits of ratification in relation to one such country, see the debate between the following two commentators: Evju, 'Should Norway Ratify the Optional Protocol to the ICESCR? – That is the Question' (2009) 27 Nordic Journal of Human Rights 82; and Lorange Backer, 'Ideals and Implementation – Ratifying Another Complaints Procedure' (2009) 27 Nordic Journal of Human Rights 91.

[136] 'Not only would it provide an additional means of supervision bringing extra force to bear on recalcitrant States, it would provide the Committee with the ability to develop the normative content of the rights in a specific and tangible manner': (contd..../)

with implicit acknowledgment of a 'margin of appreciation' in art 8(4) will clearly act as a break against over-zealous interpretation of the basic obligation in art 2(1) of the Covenant. On the other hand, adjudication of what is 'reasonable' in the circumstances of each particular State, on each set of particular facts, may still require expert input, oral hearings and significant fact-gathering – activities which will significantly stretch the resources and capacity of the CESCR in practice. In terms of procedure, the Protocol does not otherwise differ radically from other UN complaints procedures, aside from the inclusion of a 'friendly settlement' process, as well as some variation in terms of admissibility criteria.

---

[136] (\...contd) Craven, *The International Covenant on Economic, Social and Cultural Rights: A Perspective on its Development* (OUP, 1995), p 100. See also, Simmons, 'Should States Ratify? – Process and Consequences of the Optional Protocol to the ICESCR' (2009) 27 Nordic Journal of Human Rights 64, pp 66–72. As she notes, the requirement to exhaust domestic remedies may also influence the usage and development of domestic mechanisms to deal with violations of economic, social and cultural rights.

Chapter 14

International Convention for the Protection of all Persons from Enforced Disappearances

INTRODUCTION

[14.01] Although provision is ultimately made for an individual complaint mechanism in the International Convention for the Protection of all Persons from Enforced Disappearance (ICPED),[1] a certain scepticism on the part of members of the Commission on Human Rights (CHR) about its potential inclusion clearly pervaded the initial debates on the draft Convention.[2] While there was widespread agreement on the need for an emergency mechanism to allow for a monitoring body to 'seek and find a disappeared person',[3] some delegations questioned the value of the classic individual complaint procedure, emphasising that there was no need to duplicate procedures already in existence.[4] At the fourth session of the inter-sessional working group which drafted the ICPED, however, the chairperson of the CHR's working group which drafted the instrument introduced texts for an 'emergency procedure' as well as an optional, individual complaint procedure. Each of these received support from the majority of delegations and ultimately formed the basis of arts 30 and 31 of ICPED.[5]

THE URGENT PROCEDURE

[14.02] The inclusion of an 'emergency', 'tracing' or 'urgent' procedure as it has ultimately come to be known is provided for in art 30 of the Convention.[6] It is

---

[1] As to the ICPED generally, see above Ch 3, paras **3.116–3.121**.
[2] Report of the Inter-sessional Open-ended Working Group to Elaborate a Draft Legally Binding Normative Instrument for the Protection of All Persons from Enforced Disappearance: UN Doc E/CN4/2003/71, para 23.
[3] Report of the Inter-sessional Open-ended Working Group to Elaborate a Draft Legally Binding Normative Instrument for the Protection of All Persons from Enforced Disappearance: UN Doc E/CN4/2004/59, para.150.
[4] Report of the Inter-sessional Open-ended Working Group to Elaborate a Draft Legally Binding Normative Instrument for the Protection of All Persons from Enforced Disappearance: UN Doc E/CN4/2004/59, para 159.
[5] Report of the Inter-sessional Open-ended Working Group to Elaborate a Draft Legally Binding Normative Instrument for the Protection of All Persons from Enforced Disappearance: UN Doc E/CN4/2005/66, paras 125–130 and 136–137.
[6] In his seminal report on the pre-existing international framework for the protection of persons from enforced or involuntary disappearances to the Commission on Human Rights, Professor Manfred Nowak had concluded that a mechanism for tracing of disappeared persons should be added to the traditional monitoring procedures in any future instrument on enforced disappearances: UN Doc E/CN4/2002/71, para 101.

undoubtedly an innovative response to the need for increased measures of international protection necessary to combat the specific crime of enforced disappearance.[7] Described as being 'humanitarian' in nature[8] and as being a form of 'international *habeas corpus*',[9] it may be distinguished from the more traditional individual complaint procedure provided for in art 31 because its objective is 'to seek, find and afford immediate protection to the individual concerned, not to determine whether the State might be responsible for a violation of the provisions of the instrument'.[10] Additionally, most delegations during the negotiations conceptualised the procedure as being *preventive* in nature on the basis of its capacity '…not only to forestall enforced disappearances but also to put an end to any that had already occurred'.[11]

[14.03] As ultimately drafted, art 30(1) provides for the possibility of a request being submitted to the Committee on Enforced Disappearances (CED)[12] that a disappeared person should be sought and found, as a matter of urgency. Such a request may be submitted '…by relatives of the disappeared person or their representatives, their counsel or any person authorised by them, as well as any person having a legitimate interest'. The option of including non-governmental organisations explicitly in this list was not taken up during the negotiations[13] and it remains to be seen whether they would be deemed eligible to submit requests by the CED under the formula ultimately adopted.

[14.04] Certain admissibility criteria must be applied by the CED before it can take action in respect of the request.[14] It must first establish:

(a) That the request is not manifestly unfounded;
(b) That it is not an abuse of the right of submission;

---

[7] Andreu-Guzmán, 'The Draft International Convention on the Protection of All Persons from Forced Disappearance' (2001) 62–63 Review of the ICJ, p 17.
[8] This is the description given to the procedure by the Working Group on Enforced or Involuntary Disappearances in its comments on art 31 of the Sub-Commission's draft Convention, Question of enforced or involuntary disappearances: Note by the Secretariat: UN Doc E/CN4/2001/69, Annex II, p 29.
[9] Andreu-Guzmán, 'The Draft International Convention on the Protection of All Persons from Forced Disappearance' (2001) 62–63 Review of the ICJ, p 18.
[10] Report of the Inter-sessional Open-ended Working Group to Elaborate a Draft Legally Binding Normative Instrument for the Protection of All Persons from Enforced Disappearance: UN Doc E/CN4/2004/59, para 153
[11] UN Doc E/CN4/2005/66, para 126. Indeed, at an early stage in the negotiations, the suggestion was made that a preventive role should be explicitly assigned to the Committee in this provision, though this possibility appears to have been eschewed in favour of a more open-ended formula: UN Doc E/CN4/2004/59, para 151.
[12] As to the composition and functions generally of the CED, see Ch 3, paras **3.119–3.121**.
[13] UN Doc E/CN4/2004/59, para 150.
[14] ICPED, art 30(2).

(c) That the request has already been presented to the 'competent bodies' of the State party concerned;[15]

(d) That it is not incompatible with the provisions of the Convention; and finally

(e) That the same matter is not being examined under another procedure of international investigation or settlement of the same nature.[16]

On several occasions during the negotiations, the issue of whether domestic remedies should have been exhausted before the procedure in art 30 could be activated was raised.[17] However, that suggestion was ultimately resisted on the basis that such a requirement would be 'incompatible with the concept of urgency and was not necessary within a non-judicial procedure with essentially humanitarian aims'.[18] Accordingly, all that appears to be required under art 30(2)(c) is that the competent authorities must have been notified so as to allow the State to respond to a complaint under its domestic law.[19]

[14.05] Once satisfied in respect of each of these criteria, the CED shall request the State concerned to provide it with information on the situation of the person sought, within a time limit set by the Committee.[20] In the light of the information provided by the State, the Committee may transmit recommendations to the State, including a

---

[15] Note that ICPED further specifies '…such as those authorised to undertake investigations, where such a possibility exists': art 30(2)(c). This extra detail was included during the final stages of the drafting process so as to encompass national human rights institutions (NHRIs) which, it was noted, victims sometimes found it easier to contact: UN Doc E/CN4/2006/57, para 43.

[16] It seems unlikely that this stipulation would include action already taken on a case under the 'urgent procedure' currently being operated by the Working Group on Enforced and Involuntary Disappearances (WGEID). The WGEID is a five-member group of experts which has been given a 'special procedures' mandate by the Human Rights Council to assist the relatives of disappeared persons to ascertain the fate and whereabouts of their disappeared family members. It has developed its own particular procedures to fulfill that mandate which include an 'urgent appeal' procedure. During the drafting of ICPED, two representatives of the WGEID expressed the view personally during the negotiations that the mechanisms operated by it would be 'complementary' to the one in mind under the Convention which would be applicable only to contracting States and would be a 'hard-hitting, treaty-based emergency warning procedure setting deadlines and capable of leading, where appropriate with the State's consent, to an investigation mission': UN Doc E/CN4/2004/59. For the current working methods of the WGEID, including in respect of its urgent procedure, see Report of the Working Group on Enforced or Involuntary Disappearances (4 March 2010): UN Doc A/HRC/13/31 Annex 1, http://www2.ohchr.org/english/issues/disappear/docs/MOW2009.pdf (last accessed May 2011). Rather, ICPED, art 30(2)(e) would appear to contemplate the tracing procedure provided for in art XIV of the Inter-American Convention on Forced Disappearances of Persons 1994: Organization of American States, 9 June 1994, available at http://www.unhcr.org/refworld/docid/3ae6b38ef.html (last accessed May 2011).

[17] UN Doc E/CN4/2004/59, para 152; UN Doc E/CN4/2005/66, para 127; and UN Doc E/CN4/2006/57, para 41.

[18] UN Doc E/CN4/2006/57, para 41.

[19] UN Doc E/CN4/2006/57, para 41.

[20] ICPED, art 30(2).

request that the State take all 'necessary measures', including interim measures, 'to locate and protect' the person concerned in accordance with the Convention and to inform the Committee within a specified period of time of the measures taken, taking into account the urgency of the situation.[21] The person who submitted the urgent action request is at all times to be kept abreast of developments[22] and the CED is required to inform them of its recommendations and of the information provided by the State as it becomes available.[23] Once opened, a case will not be considered closed under the urgent procedure as long as the fate of the person sought remains unresolved.[24]

INDIVIDUAL COMPLAINT PROCEDURE

[14.06] Article 31 of the ICPED provides for an optional, individual complaint procedure of the 'classic' kind, typical of those in place in regard to the other UN human rights treaties. According to art 31(1), once a State party has accepted the competence of the CED to receive and consider communications, the Committee may consider communications from or on behalf of 'individuals' subject to that State's jurisdiction who claim to be a victim of a violation of 'any of the provisions of the Convention'. Two issues arise in respect of para 1 which remain to be clarified by the CED. First, whether the reference to 'individuals' only in art 31(1) will be interpreted in an expansive way so as to allow for submission by 'groups of individuals' and possibly NGOs.[25] The second matter that will require clarification is the scope of complaints that may be made under art 31(1) of the Convention.[26]

[14.07] The admissibility criteria for making an individual complaint under art 31 are virtually identical to those provided for in the OP-ICCPR. Thus, the CED shall consider a communication inadmissible where:

(a) The communication is anonymous;
(b) The communication constitutes an abuse of the right of submission or is incompatible with the provisions of the Convention;

---

[21] ICPED, art 30(3).
[22] ICPED, art 30(4).
[23] ICPED, art 30(3).
[24] ICPED, art 30(4).
[25] Submissions by NGOs were specifically envisaged during the drafting: UN Doc E/CN4/2006/57, para 53. See also the initial draft art 31 submitted by the Sub-Commission: UN Doc E/CN4/Sub2/1998/19, Annex, p 36 which very definitely would have allowed for an '*actio popularis*' type submission.
[26] Some doubt as to the scope of complaints that may be made under the procedure was expressed by the government of Sweden during the negotiations. It expressly reserved its position on this article on the basis that it was not clear which provisions of the instrument would be covered by the procedure: UN Doc E/CN4/2006/57, para 59.

(c) The same matter is being examined under another procedure of international investigation or settlement *of the same nature*[27] (emphasis added); or

(d) All effective[28] available domestic remedies have not been exhausted, except where the application of such remedies is unreasonably prolonged.

[14.08] If the communication satisfies these admissibility criteria to the satisfaction of the CED, it shall transmit the communication to the State party concerned with a request to provide observations and comments within a time limit set by the Committee.[29] Owing to the importance of interim measures in the context of enforced disappearances, the jurisdiction of the CED to transmit to the State party for its urgent consideration a request to take such measures is explicitly provided for in art 31(4) of ICPED.[30] A request for interim measures may be made at any time after receipt of the communication and before a determination on the merits has been made and does not *ipso facto* imply a determination on the admissibility or the merits of the communication.[31] As with all of the treaty complaint mechanisms, the CED shall hold closed meetings when examining complaints under art 31.[32] However, unlike its counterparts, the procedure has been tailored to allow for the CED to keep cases under its consideration, given the continuous nature of the crime of enforced disappearances.[33] Accordingly, art 31(5) provides that it shall inform the author of the responses provided by the State party concerned and will communicate its 'views' to the State party and the author at the point at which it decides 'to finalize the procedure'.

[14.09] The ICPED has only recently entered into force and the CED has only just been established.[34] Moreover, Art 35(1) of the Convention provides that the CED shall only have competence in respect of enforced disappearances which commenced after the

---

[27] Although the reasons as to why this phrase was deliberately inserted in this admissibility criterion are not recounted in the drafting history, it is likely that it was included to indicate that urgent procedures such as that provided for in ICPED, art 30 itself or the one operated by the WGEID would not be considered as 'another procedure of international investigation or settlement' for the purpose of ICPED, art 31(2)(c). See UN Doc E/CN4/2006/57, para 55. Moreover, it may be noted that many participants during the drafting of the emergency procedure specifically took the view that the two procedures were quite distinct and, further, the that the latter procedure should not be made subject to rules of litispendence: UN Doc E/CN4/2004/59, para 153.

[28] The Convention thus stipulates that which is regarded as implicit by the CCPR in respect of the similar criterion in OP-ICCPR, art 5(2)(b), namely, that the domestic remedies must be 'effective'.

[29] ICPED, art 31(3).

[30] UN Doc E/CN4/2006/57, para 57.

[31] ICPED, art 31(4).

[32] ICPED, art 31(5).

[33] UN Doc E/CN4/2006/57, para 58.

[34] The Convention entered into force on 23 December 2010 after the 20th ratification, in accordance with the provisions of art 39(1). The 10–member CED was elected on 31 May 2011: http://www.ohchr.org/EN/HRBodies/CED/Pages/Elections2011.aspx (last accessed May 2011).

entry into force of this Convention. It will take some time, therefore, before the value of these various mechanisms can be assessed.[35] In the meantime, it can at least be said that the decision to incorporate an urgent procedure in combination with an individual complaint procedure is a welcome step in providing appropriate avenues for victims and their families to highlight, establish accountability and potentially solve cases of enforced disappearances.

---

[35] The Convention itself contains an in-built mechanism for such an assessment to be made by the States parties by providing in art 27 that they must convene a conference between four and six years following the entry into force of the Convention 'to evaluate the functioning of the Committee' and to decide whether it is appropriate to transfer its functions to another body.

Chapter 15

Draft Optional Protocol to the Convention on the Rights of the Child

INTRODUCTION

[15.01] When the proposals for implementing the UN Convention on the Rights of the Child (CRC)[1] were first opened for discussion in 1986, the only method of implementation envisaged was a periodic reporting mechanism.[2] The idea of an individual complaint mechanism was not seriously entertained at any stage of the negotiations.[3] Even if it had, the fact that the drafting of the Convention was achieved on the basis of consensus would have made the adoption of such a mechanism unlikely as consensus-decision making clearly had the effect of making other contentious issues raised during the negotiations a non-starter.[4] It must be remembered also that at the time of the negotiations, individual complaint procedures had not been established in respect of every UN human rights treaty, so that the lacuna regarding one in the CRC was by no means exceptional. In recent years, however, the fact that such complaint mechanisms have been established in respect of all of the other core UN human rights treaties has meant that the momentum to establish one in respect of the CRC has been gathering pace rapidly. A coordinated campaign on the issue by NGOs worldwide,[5] supported by

---

[1] As to the CRC generally, see Ch 3, paras **3.81–3.91**.
[2] A draft Convention drawn up by Poland which formed the basis for the discussion within the Commission on Human Rights of a Convention on the Rights of the Child made reference only to a periodic reporting mechanism: Official Records of the Economic and Social Council (1978), Supplement No 4: UN Doc E/1978/34, Ch XXVI, s A, (arts XI and XII).
[3] As the current chairperson of the Committee on the Rights of the Child has noted, the proposal to include a complaint mechanism did not make much progress because '…at that time the international community was more focused on the definition of children's rights than on procedural matters'. Statement of Yanghee Lee, 'Report of the open-ended working group to explore the possibility of elaborating an optional protocol to the Convention on the Rights of the Child to provide a communications procedure': UN Doc A/HRC/13/43, para 26.
[4] See Cantwell, 'The Origins, Development and Significance of the United Nations Convention on the Rights of the Child' in Detrick (ed), *The United Nations Convention on the Rights of the Child: A Guide to the 'Travaux Préparatoires'* (Kluwer, 1992), p 22. McGoldrick has also argued that the inclusion of any such mechanism would have raised the 'difficult problem of determining whether the specific obligation alleged to have been violated was one of immediate or progressive obligation': McGoldrick, 'The United Nations Convention on the Rights of the Child' (1991) 5 Int'l J Law Soc and the Family 132–169, p 157.
[5] For information on this campaign, see NGO group for the CRC: http://www.crin.org/NGOGroup/childrightsissues/ComplaintsMechanism (last accessed May 2011) (contd.../)

the Committee on the Rights of the Child (CRC Committee),[6] undoubtedly contributed to the decision of the Human Rights Council in 2009 to establish an open-ended working group to explore the possibility of elaborating a complaints procedure in a Protocol to the Convention.[7]

[15.02] At its first session in December 2009, a majority of delegations which participated in the working group expressed the view that a communications procedure would constitute an additional tool to make further progress in the implementation of children's rights at national level.[8] If established, it would be part of a 'continuum of accountability mechanisms', beginning at the community level and comprising national and regional mechanisms.[9] Further reasons cited in favour of the proposal included the fact that the CRC was now the only major human rights treaty which did not have such a procedure. While children could make complaints under the other UN treaties, not all of the rights in the CRC were covered by those treaties.[10] In any case, it was pointed out that claims regarding children's rights should be assessed by the Committee on the Rights of the Child as it was the treaty body with the appropriate, multi-disciplinary expertise to deal with them.[11] A complaints procedure would assist in the development of the interpretation of the CRC's provisions, which in itself would be of assistance to national

---

[5] (\...contd) For information on this campaign, see NGO group for the CRC: http://www.crin.org/NGOGroup/childrightsissues/ComplaintsMechanism (last accessed May 2011) and the Child Rights Information Network: http://www.crin.org/law/CRC_complaints/ (last accessed May 2011).

[6] Statement by Yanghee Lee, chairperson of the CRC Committee to the 63rd session of the General Assembly, Third Committee, Item 60 (15 October 2008): www2.ohchr.org/english/bodies/crc/docs/Oral_statement_GA_63.doc.(Last accessed May 2011)

[7] Resolution No 11/1 of 17 June 2009: UN Doc A/HRC/11/L 3. No mention, however, is made of the campaign in the Human Rights Council's Resolution. Rather, the Council specifically refers to the almost universal ratification of the CRC, the fact that procedures allowing for individual communications have been established for other core international human rights instruments and views expressed by the CRC Committee to the General Assembly on the subject.

[8] Report of the open-ended working group to explore the possibility of elaborating an optional protocol to the Convention on the Rights of the Child to provide a communications procedure: UN Doc A/HRC/13/43 (21 January 2010), paras 19 and 29 (First Report of the working group). Some 37 delegations participated in the debate. Two NGOS, one of which represented a coalition of 11 organisations, and UNICEF also made statements. The contributions of various experts and NGOs are available at: http://www2.ohchr.org/english/bodies/hrcouncil/OEWG/1stsession.htm (last accessed May 2011).

[9] First Report of the working group, para 19. A specific topic addressed at the session was the current levels of efficiency in protecting children's rights at the national and regional levels: paras 41–59. According to one expert invited to contribute to the debate (Peter Newell), many States were still far from providing effective remedies for breaching children's rights. In his view, the process of elaborating, adopting and establishment of an optional protocol 'could intensify access to and better functioning of national mechanisms': paras 41–44.

[10] First Report of the working group, para 29

[11] First Report of the working group, paras 29 and 68(b). As to the composition and functions of the CRC Committee under the CRC, see Ch 3, paras **3.89–3.91**.

mechanisms and bodies operating in the field.[12] No arguments appear to have been raised *against* the elaboration of a new complaints procedure in principle, save for the *caveat* entered by some delegations that one should not be elaborated '…simply to replicate the procedures established under other treaties, but only after careful examination of its added value'.[13] Given the specific characteristics of the CRC, it was pointed out that 'new and differentiated' approaches must be considered and that existing procedures could not simply be reproduced.[14]

[15.03] Amongst the key issues identified during the session that would need to be addressed included the legal capacity of children; representation of children in a complaints procedure and the exercise of the child's right to be heard; how to ensure that complaints filed on behalf of children would be in the best interests of the child; the scope of an optional protocol (including the question of whether it should include an inquiry procedure); the possibility of submitting collective complaints; the implications of the procedure for the workload of the CRC Committee; as well as the resource constraints affecting the treaty body system generally.[15] In regard to the latter issues, the CRC Committee itself indicated that methods of work could be devised to examine communications (taking into account the experience gained by the other treaty bodies)[16] but that the budgetary implications of implementing such a procedure would need to be tabled to ensure additional resources necessary to allow the Committee to deal with complaints.[17]

[15.04] Having taken note of the working group's report of its first session, the Human Rights Council (HRC) decided in March 2010 to extend its mandate and requested the working group '…to elaborate an optional protocol to provide a communications procedure…'.[18] It further requested the chairperson of the working group to prepare a proposal for a draft optional protocol, based on the earlier debate, which should take into account the views of the CRC Committee, the UN special procedures and other experts.[19] Having engaged in informal consultations with States, as well as consultations with UN and civil society experts and members of the Committee, the chairperson prepared a proposal for a draft Optional Protocol together with a detailed explanatory memorandum on the text.[20] While clearly based on the agreed terms of previous

---

[12] First Report of the working group, para 19.
[13] First Report of the working group, para 20.
[14] First Report of the working group, para 20. In this respect, it may be noted that the unique nature of the rights of the child and those which were specific to the Convention (such as the right of the child to be heard in art 12) was a specific topic addressed in the session: paras 60–69.
[15] First Report of the working group, para 22.
[16] See generally First Report of the working group, paras 70–75.
[17] First Report of the working group, para 82.
[18] Resolution No 13/3: UN Doc A/HRC/13/L 5, paras 1–3.
[19] Resolution No 13/3, para 3.
[20] Proposal for a draft optional protocol prepared by Chairperson-Rapporteur of the Open-ended Working Group on an optional protocol to the Convention on the Rights of the Child to provide a communications procedure: UN Doc A/HRC/WG7/2/2 (1 September 2010) (Chairperson's Draft Protocol).

complaints mechanisms so as to ensure consistency and coherence,[21] the proposal also incorporated specific child-sensitive elements based on the discussions that had taken place at the first session. These included, *inter alia*, the specific reaffirmation of the 'best interests of the child' principle in the body of the draft Protocol,[22] inclusion of a collective complaints provision[23] and reduced time limits to ensure speedy consideration of complaints.[24] As envisaged by the HRC's resolution, this proposal served as the basis for the negotiations of the working group at its second session which took place over the course of two meetings in December 2010 and February 2011.[25] The final text of the draft Protocol that emerged from those meetings was adopted by consensus by the working group in February 2011.[26] This draft Protocol has since been adopted by the Human Rights Council in June 2011 and it is anticipated that the text will be endorsed and adopted without amendment by the General Assembly in December 2011.[27] The following section outlines the framework of this final draft Protocol. As will be seen, some of the more progressive elements envisaged in the chairperson's original draft text were ultimately jettisoned in favour of a text which makes few concessions to the specific needs of children.

THE FRAMEWORK OF THE DRAFT PROTOCOL

General provisions

[15.05] The first section of the final draft Protocol sets forth a series of general provisions regarding the operation of the complaint procedure. Of particular interest here are the terms of art 2, which include a requirement on the CRC Committee, in exercising the functions conferred on it by the Protocol to be:

> '... guided by the principle of the best interests of the child. It shall also have regard to the rights and views of the child, the views of the child being given due weight in accordance with the age and maturity of the child'.[28]

---

[21] See the letter from the chairperson, Mr Drahoslav Štefánek, addressed to members of the working group which is annexed to his proposal: Chairperson's Draft Protocol, pp 22–23.
[22] Article 1(2) of the Chairperson's Draft Protocol.
[23] Article 3, Chairperson's Draft Protocol.
[24] Chairperson's Draft Protocol, art 6(3) and art 9(1).
[25] Following the first meeting of the second session of the working group, the chairperson produced a 'Revised Draft Protocol' which served as a basis for the discussion at the second meeting of the second session in February 2011. Revised Proposal for a draft optional protocol prepared by the Chairperson-Rapporteur of the Open-ended Working Group on an optional protocol to the Convention on the Rights of the Child to provide a communications procedure: UN Doc A/HRC/WG7/2/4 (13 January 2011) (Revised Draft Protocol).
[26] Report of the Open-ended Working Group on an optional protocol to the Convention on the Rights of the Child to provide a communications procedure: UN Doc A/HRC/17/36, Annex, p 24 ('Second Report of the working group' and 'Final Draft Protocol', where applicable).
[27] See the resolution adopted by the HRC: UN Doc. A/HRC/17/L8 (9 June 2011). See also: http://www.crin.org/NGOGroup/childrightsissues/ComplaintsMechanism/(last accessed June 2011).
[28] Final Draft Protocol, art 2.

The chairperson's draft Protocol had initially made reference to the 'best interests' principle, by providing that the CRC Committee should exercise its functions in a manner that '... respects the rights of the child and ensures that the best interests of the child are a primary consideration in all actions concerning the child'.[29] The inclusion of the 'best interests' principle was intended to reflect the emphasis placed during the first session of the working group on the importance of reflecting the special status of the child and the rights of children in the text.[30] While this explicit reference to the principle was welcomed at the second session, concern was expressed by numerous State representatives,[31] NGOs[32] and the CRC Committee[33] that the chairperson's original draft had not gone far enough in reflecting the child's right to be heard in line with art 12(1) of the CRC itself. This concern was accommodated in the final draft text by the insertion of a reference to the 'views of the child' in the body of art 2. Article 3 of the final draft Protocol goes on to provide specifically that in adopting rules of procedure, the CRC Committee shall have regard, in particular, to art 2 '...in order to guarantee child-sensitive procedures'.[34]

[15.06] Anticipating possible negative consequences for complainants and others who participate in the procedure, art 4(1) of the final draft Protocol requires each State party to take all appropriate steps to ensure that such individuals are '...not subjected to any human rights violation, ill-treatment or intimidation as a consequence of communications or cooperation with the Committee pursuant to the present Protocol'.

---

[29] Chairperson's Draft Protocol, art 1(2).
[30] See 'explanatory memorandum', Chairperson's Draft Protocol, Pt 11, para 4.
[31] See the comments of Argentina, Australia, Austria, Switzerland and Peru in the summary of the discussions by the working group at its second meeting on arts 1 and 2 produced by the Child Rights Information Network: http://www.crin.org/resources/infodetail.asp?id=23653 (CRIN Daily Summary on arts 1 and 2, last accessed May 2011).
[32] See the Joint NGO Submission to the Open-ended Working Group on an Optional Protocol to the Convention on the Rights of the Child to provide a communications procedure, which was submitted by the NGO group for the CRC in advance of the second session in October 2010, p 3: http://www2.ohchr.org/english/bodies/hrcouncil/OEWG/2ndsession.htm (last accessed May 2011) (NGO Joint Submission, last accessed May 2011). A similar view was reiterated by the NGO Coalition for a CRC Complaints Mechanism, the International Commission of Jurists and the Norwegian Centre for Human Rights in statements made during the debate on arts 1 and 2 at the first meeting of the second session: CRIN Daily Summary on arts 1 and 2.
[33] See the comments by the CRC Committee on the original proposal issued by the chairperson in October 2010: UN Doc A/HRC/WG7/2/3 (October 2010) at para 9: http://www2.ohchr.org/english/bodies/hrcouncil/OEWG/2ndsession.htm (CRC Committee's Comments, last accessed May 2011). This view was reiterated by the vice-chair of the CRC Committee (Jean Zermatten) during the debates at the second session, who expressed the view that children were 'not visible enough' in the existing draft: CRIN Daily Summary on arts 1 and 2.
[34] Art 3(1), Final Draft Protocol. In this respect, the CRC Committee's vice-chair (Jean Zermatten) had reaffirmed during the second session that once the Protocol entered into force, the CRC Committee '...will draft more thorough working procedures which will address delegations' concerns about child sensitivity and seek to maximise opportunities for children to express themselves': CRIN Daily Summary on arts 1 and 2.

The reference to 'any human rights violation' expands on the scope of protective measures stipulated in the recently drafted OP-ICESCR and was inserted having regard to the heightened vulnerability of child complainants.[35] Article 4(2) provides further that the identity of any individual or group of individuals concerned shall not be revealed publicly without their express consent. This provision represents a compromise from the chairperson's original proposal that the author's identity not be revealed to the State party without his or her consent.[36] In the light of practical concerns on the part of States about their ability to respond effectively to complaints without knowing the alleged victim's identity,[37] it was agreed that confidentiality could still be maintained by not disclosing the victim's identity (or that of his or her representative where relevant) *to the public* without their consent.[38]

Complainants

[15.07] As regards eligibility to make a complaint, art 5(1) of the final draft Protocol provides for the possibility of communications being submitted by individuals or groups of individuals, within the jurisdiction of a State party, claiming to be victims of a violation by that State of any of the rights in the Convention or its two Protocols (ie, the Optional Protocol to the Convention on the Sale of Children, Child Prostitution and Child Pornography (OPSC) and the Optional Protocol To The Convention on the Involvement of Children in Armed Conflict (OPAC)).[39] Where a communication is

---

[35] This issue had been highlighted by the NGO group for the CRC in its joint submission in which it stressed the need for the instrument to be '…particularly attentive to the vulnerability of children as complainants'. In its view, the requirement only to prevent ill-treatment or intimidation (as was provided for in the original draft as well as in art 13 of OP-ICESCR) did not reflect the full range of negative measures to which child complainants could be subjected as a result of making a complaint under the Protocol. Accordingly, it recommended that the scope of protection measures be extended to prevent *any* retaliatory measures: NGO Joint Submission, para 11.

[36] Chairperson's Draft Protocol, art 6(2).

[37] With the support of the United Kingdom, Egypt, Argentina and China, Canada had argued at the second session that it would be important to know the identity of the victim in order to understand the circumstances of the alleged violation. The United States argued that it would be reasonable for States to know the identity of victims to ensure that concrete violations had taken place and effective remedies could be provided. Mexico also noted that the identity of the victim must be known in order to determine whether domestic remedies had been exhausted: Child Rights Information Network (CRIN), Daily Summary on arts 4, 5 and 6: http://www.crin.org/resources/infodetail.asp?id=23681 (last accessed May 2011). The CRC Committee had itself acknowledged that for the State party to take action on a complaint, the identity of the alleged victim could not be withheld: CRC Committee's Comments, para 18. NGOs also conceded the point during the debate. Compilation of joint oral statements delivered by the NGO group for the CRC on arts 4 to 6: http://www.crin.org/resources/infoDetail.asp?ID=23685&flag=news (last accessed May 2011).

[38] Note that the wording refers to all individuals 'concerned' so as to include representatives of children who have submitted a complaint on their behalf: Second Report of the working group, para 33.

[39] Final Draft Protocol, art 5(1). As to the OPSC and the OPAC, see, Ch 3, paras **3.81**.

submitted on behalf of an individual or group of individuals, this shall be with their consent, unless the author can justify acting on their behalf without such consent.[40] The issue of submission of complaints 'on behalf of children' proved to be particularly contentious during the second session of the working group's deliberations. As was pointed out during the debate, the need to make provision for indirect submission is particularly acute in the case of children as it is highly unlikely that they could submit complaints in most cases on their own.[41] While some delegations wished to restrict the categories of persons who could bring complaints on children's behalf, for example, to parents, legal guardians or relevant third parties, others warned against such a restrictive approach on the basis that it would not cover the case of children who did not have a legal guardian or situations where the parents themselves might be violating their children's rights.[42] In the end, the final wording agreed upon is sufficiently wide to embrace the submission of complaints by persons other than parents or legal guardians.[43] It was decided to insert a further safeguard against the risk of manipulation into the text of art 3(2) whereby the CRC Committee may decline to examine any communication which it considers not to be in the best interests of the child.[44]

[15.08] As we have seen, attempts to make provision for collective complaints in analogous UN treaty procedures have thus far foundered, notably in respect of the OP-CRPD[45] and the OP-ICESCR.[46] Following discussions on this issue during the first session of the working group on the CRC complaint procedure, the chairperson's original draft had provided for the possibility of such complaints. In general terms, he proposed that NHRIs, ombuds-institutions and NGOs in consultative status with ECOSOC should be entitled to make complaints in respect of 'grave or systematic violations' of any of the rights in the Convention and its two substantive Protocols.[47] During the initial debate on this in the second session of the working group, a number of

---

[40] Final Draft Protocol, art 5(2). The reference to 'individuals' as opposed to 'children' in art 5(1) was deliberately chosen for being more inclusive and so as to facilitate the making of complaints by victims who were children at the time of the violation(s) in question, but who had not exhausted domestic remedies before they reached the age of majority: Second Report of the working group, para 37.

[41] See the comments made by independent expert, Peter Newell: CRIN Daily Summary on arts 1 and 2.

[42] Second Report of the working group, para 39.

[43] The current wording would allow for third parties (such as social workers) to bring complaints in situations where a conflict of interest between parent(s) and the child existed. The latter point was made by the NGO group for the CRC during the debate: NGO Group for the CRC, Joint Statement on Articles 1 and 2 of the draft optional protocol: http://www.crin.org/resources/infoDetail.asp?ID=23683&flag=news (last accessed May 2011).

[44] Final Draft Protocol. See Second Report of the working group, para 41.

[45] Ch 11, para **11.03**.

[46] Ch 13, para **13.12**.

[47] See art 3(1) of the Chairperson's Draft Protocol. A further requirement under the Chairperson's draft art 3(1) was that the institutions in question should have particular competence in the rights covered by the CRC and its Protocols and have been approved by the CRC Committee for that purpose.

States voiced their concerns about the provision for collective complaints on a variety of grounds.[48] These included specific concerns that the submission of such abstract complaints might mislead the CRC Committee or 'sap' its limited resources[49] and undermine the integrity of the individual complaints procedure.[50] It was also argued that such complaints could be time-consuming without adding value;[51] and that they would, in any event, overlap with the inquiry procedure envisaged elsewhere in the draft Protocol.[52] Other States,[53] independent experts[54] (including the CRC Committee)[55] and civil society[56] spoke in favour of including collective complaints to cater for cases in which individual complaints would be impossible or impractical, for example, where the victims are unable to lodge complaints or cannot be identified.[57] Somewhat predictably, however, the momentum to maintain a provision for collective complaints (even on an optional basis) did not survive the final drafting stages, with 'numerous delegations' at

---

[48] Denmark, Greece and the Russian Federation each sought deletion of draft art 3 at this stage of the negotiations: http://www.crin.org/resources/infodetail.asp?id=23664 (CRIN Daily Summary on arts 3 and 12, (last accessed May 2011).

[49] Statement of the United Kingdom: CRIN Daily Summary on arts 3 and 12.

[50] United States, Australia and Mexico: CRIN Daily Summary on arts 3 and 12.

[51] New Zealand: CRIN Daily Summary on arts 3 and 12.

[52] Switzerland, Japan and Belgium: CRIN Daily Summary on arts 3 and 12. This point was made also by Brazil during discussions on the proposed inquiry procedure provided for in arts 10 and 11 of the draft Protocol: CRIN Daily Summary, 8 December 2010 (arts 10, 11 and 14): http://www.crin.org/resources/infodetail.asp?id=23700 (CRIN Daily Summary on arts 10, 11 and 14, (last accessed May 2011).

[53] Notably Liechtenstein, Uruguay, Slovenia, Brazil, Argentina: CRIN Daily Summary on arts 3 and 12.

[54] See the comments of independent expert Peter Newell: CRIN Daily Summary on arts 3 and 12; and again at the second meeting of the second session: CRIN Daily Summary (10 February 2011): http://crin.org/resources/infodetail.asp?id=24089 (last accessed May 2011). Mr Newell had also contributed a helpful briefing paper on the subject for the benefit of delegates at the second session of the working group: http://www.crin.org/resources/infoDetail.asp?ID=23491(last accessed May 2011).

[55] See the comments of the vice-chair of the CRC Committee, Jean Zermatten during the debate: CRIN Daily Summary on arts 3 and 12; and the previous submission of the CRC Committee on the issue: CRC Committee's Comments, paras 13–15.

[56] See the joint submission made by the NGO group for the CRC in advance of the second meeting of the working group in February 2011, pp 2–3: http://www.crin.org/docs/Joint_NGO_Submission_OP_CRC_OEWG_Feb2011.pdf (NGO Joint Submission, February 2011, (last accessed May 2011).

[57] The European Network of Ombudspersons for Children (ENOC) further submitted that such complaints add a 'valuable preventive element: the process does not have to wait until violations have occurred and victims have been identified and come forward...it could also avoid the need for the Committee to consider multiple similar communications on behalf of individual victims': Comments by ENOC on the proposal for a Draft Optional Protocol to the Convention on the Rights of the Child to provide a communications procedure (para 7): http://www2.ohchr.org/english/bodies/hrcouncil/OEWG/docs/ENOC_Comments_2ndSession.pdf (last accessed May 2011).

this stage reiterating the concerns raised earlier.[58] At the initiation of the chairperson, it was agreed to delete the article in its entirety as part of a final compromise text.[59]

Scope of the complaints mechanism

[15.09] Another contentious issue that provoked considerable debate during the drafting of the Protocol was the question of the scope of complaints that could be made under it. In this respect, the chairperson's initial draft Protocol extended the competence of the CRC Committee to complaints (either individual or collective) against a State party in respect of any of the rights in the Convention and its substantive Protocols, namely, the OPSC and the OPAC.[60] However, the original proposal allowed States to 'opt-out' at the time of ratification/accession to the possibility of complaints in respect of either of the two Protocols.[61] This formulation would enable States that are not party to the OPSC and the OPAC to ratify the Protocol on communications and opt-out of the procedure in respect of instruments which they had not actually ratified. A consequence of this approach, however, was that the 'opt-out' provision could also be invoked by States which *had* ratified one or both of the substantive Protocols. Not surprisingly, this formulation had proven unpopular with the CRC Committee and with NGOs because of its potential to lead to a differentiation in rights protection by States in respect of obligations already assumed by them in respect of children.[62] One means of resolving this dilemma suggested by NGOs would be to delete the opt-out clause entirely and insert a provision to the effect that a complaint may not be made against a State in respect of rights set forth in an instrument to which that State is not a party.[63] The issue remained contentious until the final drafting session, at which it was ultimately decided not to maintain the 'opt-out' provision.[64] Thus, the combination of art 5(1) and art 1(2) of the final draft Protocol (which expressly exclude the competence of the CRC Committee in respect of violations of rights set forth in an instrument to which the State is not party) means that a State which ratifies the Protocol, as currently drafted, will necessarily be accepting the competence of the CRC Committee to receive communications in respect of the CRC itself and either of the two Protocols to which it may be party.

---

[58] The provision for collective complaints was retained in art 7 of the Revised Draft Protocol after the first meeting of the second session (Revised Draft Protocol) but it was dropped from the Final Draft Protocol after the second meeting in February. See Second Report of the working group, para 48.
[59] See the Daily Summaries produced by CRIN for 15–17 February 2011: http://www.crin.org/resources/infodetail.asp?id=23908 (last accessed May 2011).
[60] Article 2(1) and 3(1) respectively of the Chairperson's Draft Protocol.
[61] Articles 2(3) and 3(2) respectively provided for the possibility of States withdrawing such a declaration at a later date: Chairperson's Draft Protocol.
[62] See NGO Joint Submission, para 3 and CRC Committee's Comments, para 10.
[63] NGO Joint Submission, para 3.
[64] See CRIN Daily Summary (16 February 2011): http://www.crin.org/resources/infodetail.asp?id=24181 (last accessed, May 2011).

Admissibility

[15.10] As regards the admissibility criteria for making individual complaints, art 7 of the final draft Protocol provides that the CRC Committee may deem a communication to be inadmissible when:

(a) The communication is anonymous;
(b) The communication is not in writing.
(c) The communication constitutes an abuse of the right of submission or is incompatible with the provisions of the Convention and/or the Optional Protocols thereto;
(d) The same matter has already been examined by the CRC Committee or has been or is being examined under another procedure of international investigation or settlement;
(e) All available domestic remedies have not been exhausted. This shall not be the rule where the application of the remedies is unreasonably prolonged or unlikely to bring effective relief;
(f) The communication is manifestly ill-founded or not sufficiently substantiated;
(g) The facts that are the subject of the communication occurred prior to the entry into force of the Protocol for the State party concerned, unless those facts continued after that date.
(h) The communication is not submitted within one year after the exhaustion of domestic remedies, except in cases where the author can demonstrate that it had not been possible to submit the communication within that time limit.

The ultimate failure of the working group to make concessions to the special position of children is perhaps most stark in the realm of admissibility. The chairperson's original draft was largely modelled on the agreed terms of the OP-CRPD, but it did incorporate a specific provision in respect of the domestic remedies rule which would have required the CRC Committee to apply the rule[65] in a child-sensitive way.[66] However, during the debate on his proposal in the second session of the working group, States decided to delete this provision on the basis that it departed from the wording used in other instruments.[67] Moreover, the working group went on to insert further restrictive criteria into the body of the final draft Protocol, derived largely from the additional criteria incorporated into the OP-ICESCR. These include the requirement in para (b) that the

---

[65] As to the operation of the 'domestic remedies rule' in the context of other complaint procedures, see, for example, the practice of the CCPR and CERD, Ch 7, paras **7.38–7.41** and Ch 8, paras **8.21–8.22** respectively.

[66] See art 4(d) of the Chairperson's Draft Protocol. The added wording would have required the CRC Committee to take into account the standpoint of the child when considering whether to waive the application of the domestic remedies rule on the commonly accepted ground of delay, by requiring it to '... interpret the application of the remedies in a manner sensitive to the impact that delays may cause to a child's well-being and development'.

[67] Second Report of the working group, para 56.

[68] The requirement that complaints be in writing is also included in the OP-CEDAW, art 3 and the OP-ICESCR, art 3(2)(g). (contd.../)

complaint be in writing;[68] and the imposition of a time limit in para (h) that the complaint must normally have been submitted within one year of the exhaustion of domestic remedies.[69] Despite vigorous opposition from NGOs and the CRC Committee that such requirements would particularly disadvantage children,[70] each was ultimately included in the text.[71] Serious consideration was also given to the possibility of adding a further criterion, ruling out communications were the author had not suffered a '... clear disadvantage, unless the Committee considers that the complaint raises a serious issue of general importance'.[72] While the latter proposal was eventually dropped, it is hard to reconcile the restrictive menu of admissibility criteria ultimately adopted in the final draft Protocol with the hortatory goals announced in the first session of making the procedure as 'child-friendly' as possible.

Interim measures

[15.11] Article 6 of the final draft Protocol makes explicit provision for the CRC Committee, at any time after the receipt of a complaint, to request that a State party take such interim measures as may be necessary to avoid irreparable damage to the victim(s) of alleged violations.[73] While this power has long since been regarded as implicit in the operation of early complaint procedures, and made explicit in later ones, it has increasingly become a source of tension vis-à-vis the treaty bodies and the contracting States. The tension is evident in the strident stance adopted on the matter by the Human Rights Committee (CCPR) in holding that a State which deliberately flouts a request for

---

[68] (\...contd) Its inclusion in the current draft Protocol was proposed by Poland, with the support of a number of delegations including Austria, the Russian Federation, Japan, Switzerland, New Zealand, Spain, Greece, China, Egypt, South Korea, Singapore and Sweden: CRIN Daily Summary of the working group's discussion on arts 4, 5 and 6 of the draft Protocol: http://www.crin.org/resources/infodetail.asp?id=23681 (CRIN Daily Summary on arts 4, 5 and 6, (last accessed May 2011).

[69] Support for a time limit was voiced at the outset by Denmark, Canada, France, Greece, the United Kingdom, South Korea, the Czech Republic, and Sweden (though the latter countries specified a six-month limit). Belgium suggested that a one-year time limit could be justified but that it should not begin to run until the child reached adulthood if the domestic legal system did not allow for children to file complaints: CRIN Daily Summary on arts 4, 5 and 6.

[70] The inclusion of the time limit was strongly resisted by NGOs and NHRIs, having regard to the 'particular status of children' and their lack of knowledge of the operation of international communications procedures: Second Report of the working group, para 52

[71] A proposal to supplement the requirement that complaints must be in writing by making allowance for the submission of further non-written materials was also deleted at a late stage in the drafting: See art 9(b) of the Revised Draft Protocol. However, it would seem open to the CRC Committee to receive such material as evidence in any case having regard to art 10(1) of the Final Draft Protocol which provides that the Committee shall consider communications received under the Protocol in the light of all 'documentation' submitted to it.

[72] This criterion was included in square brackets in art 10 of the Revised Draft Protocol which emerged from the negotiations at the first meeting of the second session. A similar criterion has recently been added to the framework of admissibility provided for in the ECHR and for the first time included in UN treaties in OP-ICESCR, art 4: see Ch 13, para **13.18**.

[73] Final Draft Protocol, art 6(1).

interim measures commits 'grave breaches' of its obligations under the OP-ICCPR[74] and that a failure by a State to implement such interim measures as are indicated by the CCPR in a particular case is incompatible with the obligation to respect the procedure of individual petition established under the Protocol.[75] In its most recent annual report, the Committee against Torture (CAT) acknowledged that complaints had been made by a number of States parties to UNCAT about the high volume of requests for interim measures being made by the CAT in respect of complaints alleging violations of the principle of *non-refoulement* in art 3 of the latter Convention.[76]

[15.12] In this context, it is hardly surprising, therefore that the NGO lobby and the CRC Committee [77] each advocated explicit recognition in the text of the mandatory nature of such measures.[78] This position was supported by Liechtenstein during the debate in the working group. Its delegate proposed that additional language be inserted, requiring States parties to take all appropriate steps to comply with such requests, leaving a certain 'margin of appreciation for acceptable responses'.[79] Mexico pressed further that interim measures should be taken by States parties as soon as complaints are received.[80] These suggestions were, however, given very short shrift by the majority of delegations. The United States, for example, advocated the very opposite approach, arguing that language should be added to the text to make it explicit that interim measures 'are not considered binding'.[81] Sweden suggested that the power to request interim measures should be removed entirely, or at least be limited only to situations where a complainant's life was at risk, while New Zealand believed that such measures should only be requested in 'exceptional circumstances'.[82] Accordingly, the suggestion for tougher wording was not taken up and it is likely that at some stage in the future, the CRC Committee will find itself (like some of its counterparts) in a 'stand-off' situation with non-compliant respondent States in the matter of interim measures.

PROCEDURE

Transmission of the communication

[15.13] As regards the processing of complaints, art 8 of the final draft Protocol provides that unless the CRC Committee considers a complaint inadmissible without

---

[74] *Piandiong et al v The Philippines*, Communication No 869/1999 (2000), para 5.2.
[75] CCPR General Comment No 33, UN Doc CCPR/C/GC/33, para 19.
[76] Annual Report of the United Nations Committee against Torture (2009–2010): UN Doc A/65/44, para 97.
[77] See CRC Committee's Comments, para 17.
[78] Joint NGO Submission, para 7.
[79] See CRIN Daily Summary on arts 4, 5 and 6.
[80] See CRIN Daily Summary on arts 4, 5 and 6.
[81] A similar position was adopted by China, Singapore and Australia though the latter did not see the need for adding additional language to the text in this respect: see CRIN Daily Summary on arts 4, 5 and 6.
[82] See CRIN Daily Summary on arts 4, 5 and 6. This view later received support from Ethiopia and other States: see further CRIN Daily Summary (Complaints Mechanism: Part II, Cont'd, 11 February 2011): http://www.crin.org/resources/infodetail.asp?id=23908 (last accessed May 2011). This is the formulation adopted in OP-ICESCR, art 5(1).

reference to the State party concerned, it shall bring the complaint confidentially to the attention of the State party.[83] The State party is then required to submit written explanations or statements, clarifying the matter and the remedy, if any, that may have been provided. In this regard, the State party must '...submit its response as soon as possible and within six months'.[84] Originally, the chairperson's draft Protocol had proposed a time-line of three months[85] for States to revert to the CRC Committee, taking into account the emphasis that had been placed on ensuring speedy processing of complaints concerning children at the working group's first session.[86] When this proposal was initially discussed, objections[87] raised to such a tight time frame resulted in a considerable relaxation of the text to a requirement that States should merely 'endeavour' to submit their responses as soon as possible within six months.[88] On review of the latter text, a compromise formula which now requires State parties to revert to the CRC Committee as soon as possible and within six months was eventually agreed to in the final text. Thus, notwithstanding the special context of children, the formula arrived at is essentially the same as that which is provided for in the other complaint procedures, and is even broader than the three-month time limit provided for in ICERD.[89]

Friendly settlement

[15.14] Following the lead taken by the drafters of the OP-ICESCR, art 9 of the draft Protocol makes provision for the CRC Committee to make available its offices to the parties concerned with a view to reaching a 'friendly settlement' of the matter on the basis of respect for the obligations set forth in the Convention and/or its substantive Protocols.[90] It may be expected that the CRC Committee will develop rules regarding the approval of such settlements in its Rules of Procedure, and in this respect, the overarching obligation on the Committee, stipulated in art 2, to be guided by the best interests of the child and to have regard to the rights and views of the child, will also have to be taken into account.

---

[83] Final Draft Protocol, art 8(1).
[84] Final Draft Protocol, art 8(2).
[85] The only other complaints procedure which provides for a three-month time limit in this respect is the ICERD, art 14(6)(b): see Ch 8, para **8.08**.
[86] Chairperson's Draft Protocol, art 6(3) and see para 21 of explanatory memorandum. This position was welcomed by civil society groups and the CRC Committee and also by certain States (notably the United Kingdom and Argentina) during the debate at the second session of the working group: See CRIN Daily Summary on arts 4, 5 and 6.
[87] Canada and the United States argued that a six-month limit would be more appropriate as a three-month limit would be very difficult to comply with for federal states in which the gathering of necessary facts and information can be more time-consuming. Thailand, the Czech Republic, Germany, Singapore, Belgium, Brazil, Egypt, New Zealand also supported extending the time limit to six months: See CRIN Daily Summary on arts 4, 5 and 6.
[88] Revised Draft Protocol, Article 11(2).
[89] ICERD, art 14(6)(b). This point was made by NGOs at the working group's second meeting, who '...recalled that a three month limit exists in the ICERD and saw no reason not to follow this precedent': Second Report of the working group, para 67.
[90] Final Draft Protocol, art 9(1).

[15.15] As is the case under art 7(2) of the OP-ICESCR, the chairperson had proposed in his original draft Protocol that an agreement on a friendly settlement would close consideration of a complaint under the Protocol.[91] However, the CRC Committee and the NGO group for the CRC had urged the inclusion of further safeguards in the text whereby the implementation of any settlement reached could be monitored by the Committee and the case re-opened or re-submitted in the event of non-implementation or unsatisfactory implementation of the settlement.[92] The value of a post-settlement monitoring mechanism was acknowledged by several States during the debate in the first meeting of the second session.[93] As a result, an extra sentence was added to the text on friendly settlements which specifically provided for the CRC Committee to follow-up on the implementation of any friendly settlement within 12 months of such settlement being reached.[94] While this was undoubtedly a progression in terms of the development of the friendly settlement procedure, it stopped short of explicitly empowering the Committee to re-open a case in the event of the settlement not being properly implemented.[95] Efforts to persuade the majority of States to agree to the re-opening of a settlement failed again at the final drafting session.[96] Instead, it was decided to revert to the original formula employed by the chairperson, whereby agreement on a settlement 'closes consideration of the case',[97] with the caveat that the CRC Committee may follow-up on the question of implementation in the context of the relevant reporting procedure.[98]

Consideration of the communication

[15.16] As with the other treaty body complaint procedures, consideration of communications under the Protocol will be entirely confidential. In this respect, art 10(2) of the final draft Protocol provides that the CRC Committee shall hold 'closed meetings' when examining communications under the Protocol. In making its assessment, the Committee is required to consider communications 'as quickly as

---

[91] Chairperson's draft Protocol, art 7(2).
[92] CRC Committee's Comments, para 19 and Joint NGO Submission, para 9.
[93] Positive views in this respect were expressed by France, Brazil, Slovenia, Sweden and Spain. CRIN daily Summary of the working group's discussion on arts 7, 8, 9 and 13 of the draft Protocol: http://www.crin.org/resources/infodetail.asp?id=23690 (CRIN Daily Summary on arts 7, 8, 9 and 13, (last accessed May 2011).
[94] Revised Draft Protocol, art 12(2).
[95] In this respect, note that under the ECHR, art 39 provides that a case may be struck from the list of the European Court of Human Rights following a friendly settlement of the matter. Article 39(4) mandates the Committee of Ministers of the Council of Europe to 'supervise the execution of the terms of the friendly settlement as set out in the decision of the Court', while art 37(2) empowers the court to restore any application to the list that has been previously struck off 'if it considers that the circumstances justify such a course'.
[96] Second Report of the working group, para 71. See further CRIN Daily Summary (Complaints Mechanism: Part II, Cont'd, 11 February 2011): http://www.crin.org/resources/infodetail.asp?id=23908 (last accessed May 2011).
[97] Final Draft Protocol, art 9(2).
[98] Final Draft Protocol, art 11(2).

possible', in the light of documentation submitted to it, provided that this documentation is transmitted to the parties concerned.[99] The Protocol also includes a provision requiring the Committee to expedite its consideration of communications with respect to which it has requested interim measures.[100]

[15.17] It may be noted that in directing the CRC Committee to consider complaints 'in light of all the documentation submitted to it', the text says nothing about the possibility of oral hearings. However, the Committee itself has stressed the need for it to be able to hear the views of any children when it examines complaints which have been submitted on their behalf. In its submissions to the working group, it urged that the draft text should indicate that '…when appropriate, the Committee will seek and invite the child or children to express their views (orally or in writing) in a manner compatible with the necessary celerity of the procedure and the spirit of the Convention'.[101] While the issue does not appear to have been pressed during the debate, Slovenia and Brazil did make the positive suggestion that the CRC Committee should incorporate child-sensitive and child-friendly provisions into its Rules of Procedure '…including a means to hear from children where appropriate'.[102] This suggestion is in line with the prevailing view that the failure to specifically allude to oral hearings in the texts of any of the UN treaty complaint procedures does not necessarily rule them out in principle. Accordingly, it should be open to the CRC Committee to make provision for oral hearings, especially in view of the stipulation in art 12 of the CRC of the child's right to be heard in any judicial or administrative proceedings affecting him or her. For resource reasons, however, the implementation of any such practice seems unlikely.

[15.18] A further blow to the hopes of achieving a child-centred Protocol was dealt in the final drafting session when assessment criteria for consideration of complaints regarding economic, social and cultural rights were incorporated into the text of art 10(4). Inspired, obviously, by the successful inclusion of such criteria into the terms of the OP-ICESR,[103] the United Kingdom argued that similar criteria should be introduced which would require the CRC Committee to consider the 'reasonableness of State actions and the variety of possible alternatives' where economic, social and cultural rights were at issue.[104] This suggestion was supported by New Zealand, Switzerland and Canada, with the United States and Algeria actually proposing that the 'reasonableness' standard of review should be incorporated as regards *all* complaints brought under the

---

[99] Final Draft Protocol, art 10(1). In this respect, it may be noted that a provision that had appeared during the drafting stage, specifying possible sources of other information was dropped from the text of the Revised Draft Protocol, art 13(3). However, it would seem that art 10(1) is thus widely drawn to include not only the parties' submissions but also any other documentation that may have been submitted to it by other bodies which appears to the CRC Committee to be relevant to the case.
[100] Final Draft Protocol, art 10(3).
[101] CRC Committee's Comments, para 20.
[102] CRIN Daily Summary on arts 7, 8, 9 and 13.
[103] OP-ICESCR, art 8(4) and see Ch 13, paras **13.08–13.09**.
[104] CRIN Daily Summary on arts 7, 8, 9 and 13.

Protocol.[105] NGOs and the CRC Committee had vigorously opposed this move on the basis that it would be difficult, impractical and unworkable to treat economic, social and cultural rights differently to civil and political rights as they appear in the CRC.[106] While the chair had apparently resisted the inclusion of such criteria in earlier drafts, the groundswell of support for such a provision during the final meeting resulted in its ultimate adoption in the text. There can be little doubt that its inclusion highlights the 'pandora's box' that was arguably opened by the inclusion of such criteria in the text of the OP-ICESCR.

[15.19] Once the Committee has reached a decision on the communication, its only formal obligation under the Protocol is that it must, without delay, 'transmit its views' to the State party concerned and to the complainant.[107] It is likely that the CRC Committee will follow the practice of the other treaty bodies in reaching its 'views'[108] on communications, ie, by means of consensus, with the proviso that members are free to append to any views their individual opinions (either concurring or dissenting). While the CRC Committee will be constrained by the Protocol to conduct its proceedings in 'closed meetings', the text actively requires the contracting States to 'make widely known' both the Protocol and the views and recommendations of the Committee, particularly in regard to matters involving the State party itself. This must be done by 'appropriate and active means and in accessible formats to adults and children, including those with disabilities'.[109]

Follow-up

[15.20] Like the OP-CEDAW and the OP-ICESCR, art 11 of the final draft Protocol provides specifically for a 'follow-up' procedure. As initially drafted, this procedure required the State party to give due consideration to the views of the CRC Committee, together with its recommendations, and submit a written response within three months.[110] Once again, in spite of vigorous objections from civil society and the CRC Committee itself regarding the importance of timely follow-up action in regard to children,[111] a suggestion to extend the time limit to six months for State responses was endorsed by the majority of States at the second session.[112] Before leaving this issue, it should also be noted that the Committee is empowered to invite the State to submit further information about any measures it has taken in response to its views or

---

[105] CRIN Daily Summary on arts 7, 8, 9 and 13.
[106] See the arguments made by the NGO Coalition for a CRC Complaints Mechanism, the ICJ, the vice-chair of the CRC Committee (Jean Zermatten) and Peter Newell (independent expert): CRIN Daily Summary on arts 7, 8, 9 and 13. See also Second Report of the working group, para. 75.
[107] Final Draft Protocol, art 10(5).
[108] On the legal status of treaty body views, see Ch 7, para **7.15** above in regard to the 'views' of the CCPR.
[109] Final Draft Protocol, art 17.
[110] Chairperson's Draft Protocol, art 9(1).
[111] CRIN Daily Summary on arts 7, 8, 9 and 13.
[112] Article 11(1) of the Final Draft Protocol specifically provides that the State party shall submit its response '…as soon as possible and within six months'. (contd.../)

recommendations, including, as deemed appropriate, in periodic reports to the Committee under the relevant provisions of the CRC (art 44), OPSC (art 12) and OPAC (art 8).[113]

INTERNATIONAL COOPERATION AND ASSISTANCE

[15.21] Article 15(1) of the final draft Protocol enables the CRC Committee to transmit to the UN specialised agencies, funds and programmes and other competent bodies, with a State's consent, its views or recommendations concerning communications and inquiries that indicate a need for technical advice or assistance. By virtue of art 15(2), the Committee may also bring to the attention of such bodies any matter arising from the communications which may assist them in deciding on the advisability of international measures likely to help States in implementing the rights in the CRC and/or the Optional Protocols thereto. These provisions are derived entirely from art 14(1) and (2) of the OP-ICESCR. As such, the latter instrument was the first complaint procedure to introduce a formal means by which a treaty body's views and recommendations could be used to alert other relevant UN bodies and agencies of the need for technical advice and assistance in particular States. The insertion of such a measure in the OP-ICESCR, however, was deemed necessary because of the ambiguous reference in art 2(1) of the parent instrument to the obligation on each State party to the ICESCR to take steps '… individually and through international assistance and cooperation, especially economic and technical, to the maximum of its available resources …' with a view to achieving progressively the rights in the Covenant. To give further expression to this obligation, the drafters of the OP-ICESCR also agreed to the establishment of a trust fund with a view to providing expert and technical assistance to States that are experiencing difficulties in implementing the rights in the ICESCR on account of resource constraints.[114] Although the idea of establishing a similar trust fund in the context of the CRC was discussed at the second session, it did not receive significant support.[115]

Appraisal

[15.22] The elaboration of the complaints procedure for the CRC and its substantive Protocols certainly completes the jigsaw in terms of enabling individual complaints to be made under each of the UN human rights treaties. While this was not the only motivation driving the campaign for such an instrument, it was certainly a dominant theme for those organisations which have lobbied intensively on the matter. Certainly, the rationale for having a complaints procedure for children to complain about breaches of the specific rights in the CRC is just as compelling as it is in respect of other categories of complainant. As outlined in the introduction to this chapter, positive

---

[112] (\...contd) An even weaker formulation that merely obliged States to 'endeavour' to submit its response 'as soon as possible within six months' was at one stage on the table, though this formulation (incorporated temporarily in art 14(1) of the Revised Draft Protocol) was strongly resisted by NGOs and experts: Second Report of the working group, para 78.

[113] Final Draft Protocol, art 11(2).

[114] OP-ICESCR, art 14(3). See Ch 13, para **13.19**.

[115] Second report of the working group, paras 90–91.

reasons for drafting the Protocol appear to have been thoroughly endorsed by the States which took part in the opening session of the working group in 2009. Delegates at that session also stressed the importance of ensuring that any such procedure should be 'child-friendly' and tailor-made in respect of the particular context at hand. Limited concessions to these goals have been made in the final text that has emerged from the negotiations of the working group and subsequently endorsed by the Human Rights Council. These include the addition of the 'best interests' principle as a guiding one for the CRC Committee in exercising its functions under the Protocol; and the expansion of the range of 'protective measures' that should be taken by States in respect of child-complainants. On the other hand, there are no meaningful allowances made for children in respect of the time limits provided for in the Protocol for responding to complaints or indeed in respect of the follow-up procedure; the admissibility criteria are in some respects more rigorous than other complaint mechanisms; and provision has been made to constrain the CRC Committee's assessment of communications where violations of economic, social and cultural rights are alleged. On top of all this, the compelling arguments made to introduce a system for collective complaints in the case of children were ultimately rejected by the drafters. In the result, the bare text that has emerged demonstrates very little context-specific, innovation from that of other UN treaty individual complaints procedures. Indeed, this point was poignantly made by the chairperson of the CRC Committee in her closing contribution to the proceedings when she said: 'I am afraid that we have affirmed that children are mini-humans with mini-rights and the current draft fits this idea of children'.[116] It may be expected, however, that the CRC Committee itself will certainly do its level best through its Rules of Procedure to develop the operation of the Protocol in a manner calculated to serve the best interests of children.

---

[116] CRIN Daily Summary: Complaints Mechanism: Chair's proposal largely accepted (16 February 2011), http://www.crin.org/resources/infodetail.asp?id=24181 (last accessed May 2011). The reference to 'mini-humans with mini-rights' is a quotation from a speech made by Maud de Boer Buquicchio, Deputy Secretary General of the Council of Europe: http://www.coe.int/t/dc/press/news/20061216_disc_sga_EN.asp (last accessed May 2011).

Part IV:
Proposals for Reform

Chapter 16

Reform of the UN Human Rights Treaty System

INTRODUCTION

[16.01] Despite the enormous contribution made by the treaty bodies since their establishment in monitoring States' implementation of human rights and in interpreting the treaties through the various procedures outlined above, chronic problems have accumulated over the years in the functioning of the treaty body system as a whole. The biggest difficulty, of course, is the fact that these are part-time and vastly under-resourced bodies, straining at the seams for decades to fulfil their mandates in a timely and comprehensive manner. Absent powers of compulsion, lacking in coordination, publicity and sometimes accurate information, the difficulties confronting the treaty bodies in fulfilling their functions have been mounting exponentially for decades.[1] Paradoxically, the stage is set for these difficulties to intensify, rather than improve, with the recent entry into force of ICPED, bringing to nine the number of core human rights treaties. In this context, it comes as no surprise that reform of the UN human rights treaty system has been a fairly constant theme on the agenda of the United Nations since the 1980s. This chapter traces the reform agenda as it has unfolded over the years, culminating in some tentative predictions regarding the outlook for the future.

REPORTS OF THE INDEPENDENT EXPERT 1989–1997

[16.02] Reform of the UN human rights treaty system has been on the agenda of the United Nations for at least two decades. Following Resolutions adopted by the General Assembly in 1988 and the former Commission on Human Rights in 1999,[2] the UN Secretary General appointed Professor Philip Alston as an independent expert to examine possible long-term approaches to enhancing the effective operation of existing and prospective treaty bodies established under United Nations instruments. Between 1989 and 1997, Professor Alston produced three substantial reports in fulfilment of his brief.[3] It is striking that many of the problems that he identified in his initial report in

---

[1] The Report of the Expert Workshop on Reform of United Nations Human Rights Treaty Monitoring Bodies (March 2006) succinctly identifies the current challenges facing the system (University of Nottingham, Human Rights Law Centre 2006): http://www.nottingham.ac.uk/shared/shared_hrlcprojects/Projects_Current_Projects_Nottingham_TB_Workshop_Report.pdf(last accessed May 2011), pp 4–6.

[2] GA Res 43/115 of 8 December 1988 and CHR Res 1989/47 of 6 March 1989.

[3] An initial report entitled 'Effective Implementation of International Instruments on Human Rights, Including Reporting Obligations under International Instruments on Human Rights': UN Doc A/44/668 (8 November 1989), (Initial Report). (contd.../)

1989 regarding the functioning of periodic reporting procedures still persist today. These include, *inter alia*, inadequate, unsatisfactory and non-submitted reports;[4] proliferation and overlapping of reporting requirements;[5] insufficient resources;[6] and insufficient meeting time and inadequate servicing for committee members.[7] In his initial and interim reports, the independent expert made a variety of recommendations for reform. These included, *inter alia*, the enhancement of the role of NGOs in reporting procedures;[8] the extension of committee meeting times;[9] advance preparation of lists of issues of concern to the committee prior to the constructive dialogue;[10] improving public access to information on the activities of the treaty bodies;[11] development of concerted practices and procedures by the committees to deal with persistent non-reporting States;[12] as well as various methods of reducing the overall burden of reporting requirements.[13]

[16.03] However, despite the fact that some improvements to the overall system of State reporting were initiated on foot of his recommendations, the independent expert had reached the conclusion in 1997 that the treaty monitoring system overall was 'unsustainable' and that significant reforms would need to be implemented for the overall regime to meet its objectives.[14] In his final report, Professor Alston set out a range of four options available to States in the medium-term for dealing with the crisis. The first option posed was that of simply ignoring it;[15] second was the adoption of modest reforms by the treaty bodies within their existing budgets (such as staffing the secretariat with interns and junior personnel, reducing the length of oral dialogues with states, and streamlining the procedure for assessing States' reports);[16] third was the provision of greatly enhanced budgetary resources to support and enhance the status quo. The first two options were dismissed by the independent expert as being

---

[3] (\...contd) Pursuant to the request of the General Assembly and the former Commission on Human Rights, Professor Alston updated this initial report and presented a further interim report to the General Assembly in 1993 which was made available at the World Conference on Human Rights in the same year. That report is entitled 'Interim Report on Updated Study by Mr. Philip Alston': UN Doc A/CONF157/PC/62/Add11/Rev 1, (22 April 1993), (Interim Report). The final report was completed and published in 1997 and is entitled: 'Final Report on Enhancing the Long-Term Effectiveness of the United Nations Treaty System': UN Doc E/CN 4/1997/74, (27 March 1997), (Final Report).

[4] Initial Report, para 35.
[5] Initial Report, paras 36–53.
[6] Initial Report, paras 55–64.
[7] Initial Report, paras 100–109.
[8] Initial Report, paras 119–122.
[9] Interim Report, paras 185–193.
[10] Initial Report, paras 100–113.
[11] Initial report, paras 132–136.
[12] Interim Report, paras 109–122.
[13] Interim Report, paras 164–182.
[14] Final Report, para 10.
[15] Interim Report, para 85.
[16] Interim Report, paras 86–87.

undesirable for obvious reasons; while the third was regarded as simply unrealistic. The fourth option posited in the report comprised many elements of qualitative change to the existing system.[17] These included the following:

(a) The preparation by States of a single consolidated report which could then be submitted in fulfilment of the requirements of *all* of the treaties to which States are parties;

(b) Elimination of comprehensive periodic reports and the substitution of reports based solely on the issues identified in advance by the committees as important for the particular State in question;

(c) Limiting the number of new treaty bodies;

(d) Simplification of the process of treaty amendment to ensure minor procedural change.

[16.04] As part of these latter recommendations, the independent expert harked back to a proposal previously made by him in his initial report regarding long-term reform of the entire treaty supervisory system,[18] namely, the possibility of consolidating the existing network of treaty bodies. While the precise modalities of such consolidation would need to be fleshed out, preferably by means of an expert study, the basic notion envisaged was that of an entirely new 'super-committee' or possibly two such committees, which would be responsible for supervising the implementation by States of all treaty obligations. This proposal was proffered at the time as 'food for thought' for the General Assembly and the former Commission on Human Rights;[19] not to be viewed as a 'radical or drastic' approach, but rather '…as a natural and eventually unavoidable response to a prolonged period of broadening and deepening of the treaty regime, which, perhaps by its very nature, has so far developed in a relatively uncoordinated or *ad hoc* fashion'.[20] The independent expert did note that '… the issues raised by the consolidation proposal will at some point warrant a sustained exchange of views in order that the advantages and disadvantages can be adequately articulated'.[21] As we shall see, in yet another clear example of the wheels of change grinding very slowly at the United Nations, it took another 15 years before such a dialogue was seriously entertained. Nonetheless, many of the reforms suggested by Alston have formed the basis of concrete improvements, if not outright solutions, to the reporting procedures.

[16.05] The proposals recommended by Professor Alston were reiterated and built-upon in subsequent academic literature.[22] Particular mention should be made in this regard of the study conducted by Professor Anne Bayefsky, published in 2001,[23] which was based

---

[17] Final Report, paras 89–101.
[18] Final Report, para 94 and Initial Report, Part VII, pp 67–69, paras 175–183.
[19] Final Report, para 176.
[20] Final Report, para 175.
[21] Initial Report, para 182.
[22] See the 'Survey and Analysis of Selected Previous Reform Proposals (1985–2005) annexed to the Report of the Expert Workshop on Reform of the UN Human Rights Treaty Monitoring Bodies (University of Nottingham, Human Rights Law Centre, 2006), Annex IV.
[23] Bayefsky, *The UN Human Rights System: Universality at the Crossroads* (Transnational Publishers, 2001).

in part on consultation with the treaty monitoring bodies themselves as well as a range of actors involved in the process, and a survey on the impact of the monitoring process at national levels.[24] The study concluded that a working group should be established to elaborate a new optional protocol to all of the UN human rights treaties, which would establish two consolidated treaty bodies.[25] These bodies would be designated by function: one for considering single consolidated State reports; the other for examining individual communications and conducting inquiries. Immediate steps to improve the functioning of the existing procedures were also recommended as regards, *inter alia*, consolidated reporting, concluding observations and follow-up.[26]

THE UNITED NATIONS: AN AGENDA FOR CHANGE

[16.06] As previously noted, it was not until the turn of the century that the United Nations organisation itself began to engage in a serious way with fundamental reform of the treaty monitoring system. In 2002, the former United Nations Secretary General identified reform of the treaty system as a key element in achieving an integrated human rights system (itself a fundamental precondition of the Millennium Declaration's goal of raising country level human rights capacity).[27] He called on the treaty bodies to consider crafting a more coordinated approach to their activities; standardising varied reporting requirements and allowing States to produce a single report, summarising their adherence to the full range of international human rights treaties to which they are party.[28] The report called on the High Commissioner for Human Rights to consult with the treaty bodies and make recommendations on 'new streamlined reporting procedures'.[29]

[16.07] On foot of the High Commissioner's subsequent consultation with the treaty bodies, a 'brainstorming meeting' was organised by the OHCHR and the Government of

---

[24] In an earlier report in 1996, prepared on behalf of the International Law Association, Professor Bayefsky described the enforcement regime associated with the UN treaties as being 'seriously flawed', with the reporting regime, in particular, being 'riddled with major deficiencies': International Law Association Report on the Treaty System (1996), available at: http//:www.bayefsky.com/reform/ila.php (last accessed May 2011).

[25] Bayefsky, *The UN Human Rights System: Universality at the Crossroads* (Transnational Publishers, 2001), p xvii. Similar arguments for consolidation of the treaty bodies are also made by Buergenthal, 'A Court and Two Consolidated Treaty Bodies' in Bayefsky (ed), *The UN Human Rights Treaty System in the 21st Century* (Kluwer Law, 2000), p 299; and by Clapham, in the same volume, 'Defining the Role of Non-Governmental Organizations with Regard to the UN Human Rights treaty Bodies', 183, at pp 192–194.

[26] Bayefsky, *The UN Human Rights System: Universality at the Crossroads* (Transnational Publishers, 2001), pp xv–xvii.

[27] UN GA Res 55/2: http://www.un.org/millennium/declaration/ares552e.htm (last accessed May 2011), part V.

[28] 'Strengthening of the United Nations: an agenda for further change': UN Doc A/57/387, (9 September 2002).

[29] This proposal was subsequently endorsed by the General Assembly: UN Doc A/Res/57/300 (7 February 2003), para 8; and the former Commission on Human Rights: CHR Res 2004/78 (21 April 2004), UN Doc E/CN4/2004/L11/Add7.

Liechtenstein at Malbun, Liechtenstein from 4 to 7 May 2003.[30] The meeting was attended by representatives of all of the treaty bodies and representatives of five State parties *per* regional group, United Nations entities and non-governmental organisations.[31] The meeting was significant for the agreement apparently reached between participants that treaty body reform should focus on practical and flexible measures. In particular, the participants agreed:[32]

(i) On the need for the development of harmonised reporting guidelines, which would be designed to assist States in fulfilling their reporting obligations both in form and in substance. The guidelines should relate to basic information which should be submitted by States in their reports in respect of each treaty which would include cross-cutting issues;

(ii) that the submission of a 'single report' summarising a State party's implementation of the full range of human rights provisions to which it was party was not desirable. In the view of the participants at the meeting, separate reports in regard to each treaty better enabled States to fulfil their reporting obligations under each treaty to which they are party;

(iii) that more detailed guidelines should be prepared on the specific information to be produced by States in an expanded core document;

(iv) that the notion of more focused periodic reports, in turn, required further exploration and definition;

(v) that the concept of 'thematic' or 'modular' reports required further clarification.[33]

(vi) that the treaty bodies should set their schedules for review of States parties' reports as far ahead as possible; and

(vii) that increased focus and efforts should be brought towards capacity building.

[16.08] Following the Secretary General's report in 2002 calling for greater coordination between the treaty bodies, inter-committee meetings of the treaty bodies (ICMs) have been convened whose specific focus has been that of harmonising the working methods and practices of the treaty bodies. Initially, these meetings took place biennially and were composed of the chairpersons plus two members from each of the treaty bodies, although recently it was decided to have one annual ICM as well as a thematic working group meeting between treaty body members on specific themes relating to

---

[30] The responses of the treaty bodies to the Commissioner's request for views, as expressed in letters from their respective chairpersons, formed the background document to the Malbun meeting: see UN Doc HRI/ICM/2003/3 and Add 1.

[31] A representative of one NHRI also attended.

[32] Report of a Brainstorming Meeting on Reform of the Human Rights Treaty Body System (Malbun, Liechtenstein, 4–7 May 2003): UN Doc HRI/ICM/2003/04 (10 June 2003), paras 10–93.

[33] Thematic reports are distinct from modular reports. Thematic reports are constructed along thematic lines and take into account areas common to a number of treaties: UN Doc HRI/ICM/2003/04 (10 June 2003), paras 50–51. 'A modular report is one consisting of a common document for all treaty bodies, to which specific reports under each treaty will be attached': UN Doc HRI/ICM/2003/04 (10 June 2003), para 49.

harmonisation and working methods.[34] Meetings of the chairpersons of the various treaty bodies had also been convened annually since 1995.[35] The report of the Malbun workshop was subsequently considered by a second ICM of the UN treaty bodies and by the 15th meeting of the chairpersons of those bodies, both of which took place in June, 2003.[36] The output of these two meetings certainly foreshadowed the attitude of the treaty bodies themselves to the best methods for future reform of periodic reporting procedures, in particular. In short, the notion of radical reform does not appear to have been seriously entertained at this juncture, with preference being given instead to greater emphasis on streamlining the current procedures through, *inter alia*, the expansion of the core document; treaty specific, targeted periodic reports; the development of harmonised reporting guidelines; strengthening the role of national human rights institutions in the procedures; and greater cross-referencing between the treaty bodies on concluding observations.[37]

[16.09] In March 2005, the Secretary General again alluded to the need for reform of treaty bodies in his report to the General Assembly in which he commented:

> '... the human rights treaty bodies ... need to be much more effective and more responsive to violations of the rights that they are mandated to uphold. The treaty body system remains little known; is compromised by the failure of many States to report on time if at all, as well as the duplication of reporting requirements; and is weakened further by poor implementation of recommendations'.[38]

These difficulties led the Secretary General to recommend specifically that harmonised guidelines on reporting to all treaty bodies should be finalised and implemented so that these bodies could function 'as a unified system'. The latter recommendation is to some extent ambiguous: it can be interpreted simply as a call for clearer, harmonised guidelines for States so that the overall *process* of reporting, as between the treaty bodies, will function more coherently; or, it could be interpreted as a call for a unified treaty body itself.

---

[34] This was decided at the 10th ICM in 2009: UN Doc A/65/190, para 40. Henceforth, each ICM shall consist of each of the chairpersons of the treaty bodies and one additional member of each treaty body. The first thematic working group established by the ICM was on the theme of follow-up of the human rights treaty bodies and was convened in January 2011. For an overview of ICMs, see generally: http://www2.ohchr.org/english/bodies/icm-mc/index.htm (last accessed May 2011).

[35] While meetings of the chairpersons had been convened sporadically since 1983, they have been convened annually on the recommendation of the chairpersons themselves since 1995: Effective implementation of international instruments on human rights, including reporting obligations under international instruments on human rights, UN Doc A/49/537, para 59. See also: http://www2.ohchr.org/english/bodies/icm-mc/index.htm (last accessed May 2011).

[36] The conclusions reached at both of these meetings are summarised in a note compiled by the OHCHR entitled: 'Effective Functioning of Human Rights Mechanisms Treaty Bodies': UN Doc E/CN4/2004/98 (11 February 2004).

[37] See 'Effective Functioning of Human Rights Mechanisms Treaty Bodies', paras 7 and 8.

[38] 'In Larger Freedom: towards development, security and human rights for all': UN Doc A/59/2005, 21 March 2005, para 147.

[16.10] The response from the then High Commissioner for Human Rights, Louise Arbour, to the Secretary General's recommendation incorporated both interpretations. In her subsequent plan of action on the future strategic direction of her office, published two months after the Secretary General's report,[39] Arbour advocated a twin-track approach to treaty body reform. Specifically, she stressed the need for greater country engagement between her office and States parties, increased resources and the need for the finalisation of harmonised reporting guidelines. In the longer term, however, the plan resurrected the kite flown by the independent expert over a decade previously, namely, that the route to fundamental reform and consolidation of the work of the treaty bodies was through the creation of a unified standing treaty body.[40] This proposal was subsequently presented in a 'Concept Paper' published by the OHCHR secretariat in March 2006.[41]

The following sections discuss the notion of a unified standing treaty body and how it would give effect, in particular, to fundamental reform of periodic reporting by States under the treaty system.

A unified standing treaty body

[16.11] The overarching objective of the Commissioner's proposal for a unified standing treaty body (USTB) was identified in the concept paper as being two-fold: first, '... to secure comprehensive and holistic implementation by States parties of the substantive legal obligations in the treaties which they have assumed voluntarily'; and second, '... to strengthen the level of protection provided to rights-holders at the national level through ensuring implementation by an authoritative, visible and effective system, which is easily accessible to rights-holders'.[42] The principles underlying the reform proposal were

---

[39] The plan of action was submitted in response to a specific request by the Secretary General for same which was referred to in his 'In Larger Freedom' report: UN Doc A/59/2005, 21 March 2005, at para 145. The plan is entitled 'The OHCHR Plan of Action: Protection and Empowerment': UN Doc A/59/2005/Add 3, 26 May 2005.

[40] It is interesting to note that warnings about the proliferation of treaty bodies generally had been issued right from the outset of their establishment. Buried within the drafting history of the International Convention for the Elimination of All Forms of Racial Discrimination, one finds the point made eloquently by Mr Mommersteeg of the Netherlands who wondered '...whether it was really desirable to establish several similar institutions each designed to ensure implementation of a separate international instrument. Was there not a danger, in view of the growing number of international instruments that that might lead to organizational complications, and would not it be preferable to considered the possibility of creating only one single machinery for the implementation of all the international instruments in the field of human rights, which raised the same problems of application?': UNGA, 'Report of the Third Committee, 1344th Meeting' (16 November 1965), para 62.

[41] 'Concept Paper on the High Commissioner's Proposal for a Unified Standing Treaty Body': UN Doc. HRI/MC/2006/2 [hereinafter Concept Paper for USTB].

[42] Concept Paper for USTB, para 6. This theme is reiterated in the paper a number of times, most notably at para 28: 'As States implement human rights obligations in an integrated rather than treaty-specific way, and individuals and groups do not enjoy their human rights or experience violations along treaty lines, a unified standing treaty body would provide a framework for a comprehensive, cross-cutting and holistic approach to implementation of the treaties'.

stated as being: first, that the human rights treaty system is essential in promoting and protecting human rights on the national and international level; second, that the achievements of the current system must be built upon; third, that the specificities of each treaty must be preserved with their focus on specific rights, while at the same time, the interdependence and indivisibility of the various treaty obligations must be highlighted; and fourth, while implementation must be strengthened, the substantive obligations must not be diminished or renegotiated.[43]

[16.12] Having set forth the myriad of challenges facing the current system,[44] many of which have been highlighted in the preceding chapters, the paper then outlined the ways and means by which a unified standing treaty body might be equipped to meet these challenges both in terms of periodic reporting and individual communications. Specifically, as regards reporting, the paper advocated that a USTB, composed of permanent and professional members,[45] would be capable of introducing both flexible and creative measures to encourage reporting.[46] By way of example, the paper suggested that a single cycle for reporting by each State, every three to five years, in respect of all of its treaty obligations, would provide both States parties and partners an 'opportunity to carry out in-depth, holistic, comprehensive and cross-cutting assessments and analysis of a State's human rights performance against all relevant obligations'.[47] It would also assist in identifying priorities for action, as well as 'mainstreaming of the rights of specific groups or issues in the interpretation and implementation of all human rights treaty obligations'.[48] The production of a single document at the end of the reporting process, identifying all concerns and recommendations, would also assist national stakeholders, such as NGOs and NHRIs, in integrating those concerns into their own work programmes.[49] Moreover, a USTB would ensure consistency in recommendations as well as in the interpretation of treaty provisions;[50] would give rise to a longer and more enhanced period of dialogue (possibly up to five days) with governments, and participation by civil society and other actors;[51] would give rise to stronger follow-up capacity;[52] would necessarily be more visible and accessible;[53] and would allow for even stronger links with other human rights bodies (such as the special

---

[43] Concept Paper for USTB, para 7.
[44] Concept Paper for USTB,, s II (C), paras 15–26.
[45] The issue of membership of the proposed body is addressed briefly at paras 61–63 of the concept paper. While the criteria for membership are not fleshed out, the paper stresses the importance of high calibre, independent expertise. It also highlights the need for such a permanent body to be sufficiently remunerated at a senior level to attract such candidates.
[46] Concept Paper for USTB, para 28.
[47] Concept Paper for USTB, para 28.
[48] Concept Paper for USTB, para 28.
[49] Concept Paper for USTB, para 29.
[50] Concept Paper for USTB, para 30.
[51] Concept Paper for USTB, para 31.
[52] Concept Paper for USTB, para 32.
[53] Concept Paper for USTB, paras 33 and 34.

procedures mechanisms or regional human rights systems) and political bodies (such as the Human Rights Council and the Security Council).[54]

[16.13] With regard to possible methods of State reporting, and regardless of the particular format by which a unified body might operate, the paper noted that a unified body could choose simply to adopt the approach of the current system and consider reports under each of the treaties to which a State is party. This could involve the submission by each State of an expanded core document, as well as treaty-specific reports in regard to each treaty to which it is party. Alternatively, the body might choose to adopt a practice whereby a State's responses to 'comprehensive and integrated lists of issues' relating to all of its treaty obligations would replace periodic reports. Numerous perceived advantages of the latter model are noted. In particular, that it would facilitate State reporting by eliminating backlogs, ensure up-to date information on implementation, enable pre-scheduling of reports according to a regular, agreed cycle and allow for proper budgeting and estimation of costs.[55]

[16.14] As regards the format in which such a body would operate, the concept paper was by no means comprehensive or prescriptive. Rather, it suggested that many different models for a USTB could be envisaged.[56] While the notion of a single body with no chambers is mentioned as one such possible option, the paper points out that it might potentially worsen the backlog and would pose difficulties for members in reaching consensus.[57] As against this, the paper points out that a chamber or working group system would certainly enable the body to take on a larger workload, and to develop stronger follow-up mechanisms and fresh approaches to monitoring implementation.[58] In this respect, a number of possible options are mooted, such as the establishment of chambers divided along functional lines (eg, reporting, petitions, inquiries and possibly follow-up).[59] While the paper notes that such a model would facilitate the development of specific expertise amongst the members along procedural lines, it also acknowledges the dangers of inconsistent interpretation of substantive treaty norms as between the various chambers.[60] Alternatively, chambers could be established, each of which would exercise all the monitoring functions of the various treaties. Interestingly, the concept paper points out the possible advantages of this model (namely, a balance of tasks and workload, as well as 'reciprocal enrichment' between the chambers), without noting any obvious disadvantages.[61]

---

[54] Concept Paper for USTB, para 36.
[55] Concept Paper for USTB, para 46.
[56] Concept Paper for USTB, para 39
[57] Concept Paper for USTB, para 40.
[58] Concept Paper for USTB, para 39.
[59] Conceivably, the work with respect to these functions could also be further divided along treaty, thematic or regional lines, or operating in parallel. Concept Paper for USTB, para 39; and see also para 42.
[60] Concept Paper for USTB, para 42.
[61] Concept Paper for USTB, para 42.

[16.15] Finally, the paper noted that chambers could also be established strictly along treaty lines,[62] thematic lines,[63] or regional lines.[64] While division along treaty lines may have the advantage of maintaining the specificity of each treaty and its membership, it is noted that it might not, for the same reasons, mark a significant advance on the status quo.[65] Division along thematic lines might reduce the risk of inconsistencies in the interpretation of overlapping provisions, but the paper points out that division by 'clusters of rights' would be difficult to organise and might lead to undue emphasis on certain rights at the expense of others.[66] As regards the division of chambers along regional lines, the paper notes that while such an arrangement might well strengthen relationships with regional systems, on the other hand, it would give rise to the risk of duplicating those systems and the emergence of regional as opposed to universal standards.[67]

[16.16] As regards subsequent reaction to the concept paper, academic commentary has been generally positive, at least with respect to the re-opening of debate on the matter. Johnstone, for example, while not necessarily endorsing the prospect of a unified standing treaty body, highlights its potential for improving the current system.[68] In particular, she notes, *inter alia*, that a unified body could reinforce the notion of the indivisibility of rights and promote a holistic approach to monitoring; that it would undoubtedly have a higher status and attract more publicity than the current treaty bodies; that it might facilitate mainstreaming of human rights through government departments; and that it would likely reduce costs and unnecessary repetition of information.[69] O'Flaherty and O'Brien share the view that the creation of a unified standing treaty body might well remedy many of the deficiencies of the current system as exposed over the years since the reform debate first began.[70] Whilst they appear to broadly welcome the concept paper's reinvigoration of the idea of a unified body, they make the point that the concept paper in many ways disappoints in failing to make a convincing, evidence-based argument in favour of unification.[71] In particular, they draw

---

[62] Concept Paper for USTB, para 43.
[63] Concept Paper for USTB, para 44.
[64] Concept Paper for USTB, para 45.
[65] Concept Paper for USTB, para 45.
[66] Concept Paper for USTB, para 44.
[67] Concept Paper for USTB, para 45.
[68] Johnstone, 'Cynical Savings or Reasonable Reform? Reflections on a Single Unified UN Human Rights Treaty Body' (2007) HRL Rev 173–200. At the other end of the spectrum, Hampson has characterised the concept paper as '... fundamentally flawed and irresponsible': Hampson, 'An Overview of the Reform of the UN Human Rights Machinery' (2007) HRL Rev 1, p 12.
[69] Johnstone, 'Cynical Savings or Reasonable Reform? Reflections on a Single Unified UN Human Rights Treaty Body' (2007) HRL Rev 173–200.
[70] O'Flaherty and O'Brien, 'Reform of the UN Human Rights treaty Monitoring Bodies: A Critique of the Concept Paper on the High Commissioner's Proposal for a Unified Standing Treaty Body' (2007) HRL Rev 141.
[71] O'Flaherty and O'Brien, 'Reform of the UN Human Rights treaty Monitoring Bodies: A Critique of the Concept Paper on the High Commissioner's Proposal for a Unified Standing Treaty Body' (2007) HRL Rev 141, p 144.

attention to the failure of the concept paper to back up its persistent claim that a unified system will not risk a loss of specificity in human rights protection.[72]

[16.17] An expert workshop convened by the Nottingham Human Rights Centre in 2006 to consider possible reform options reached similar conclusions regarding the potential advantages of a USTB in terms of '...enhanced coordination in information gathering and follow-up, more systematic prioritisation, and greater authority inside the UN system and beyond'.[73] Interestingly, the workshop explored other less extreme avenues of reform, such as the possibility of 'partial unification' by means of devolving particular functions of the treaty bodies (eg, adjudication of complaints or follow-up functions) to newly established structures.[74]

[16.18] The proposal to create a unified standing treaty body received short shrift, however, in most other quarters. This was made evident at a second 'brainstorming meeting' on the theme of treaty body reform, hosted again by the government of Liechtenstein, in July 2006.[75] This meeting, otherwise known as 'Malbun II', was attended by State representatives, members of the treaty bodies, NHRIs and NGOs. The record of the meeting indicated that the OHCHR's proposal to create such a body 'found very little support'.[76] While the concept paper was again welcomed as a valuable contribution to the debate, its overall conclusions were resisted on various grounds. These included the objections that the paper was unclear as to how a unified body would address the reporting burden on States as well as different ratification patterns; that the paper lacked in-depth analysis on the current challenges facing reform; and that more empirical information on how a unified body could meet those challenges was necessary before a leap could be taken in its direction.[77]

[16.19] Interestingly, and perhaps predictably given some of the vested interests at stake, the reaction to the OHCHR's proposal on the part of the treaty bodies has been mostly negative.[78] Again, resistance is based, *inter alia*, on the fear that the focus on specific issues which exists in the current system would be lost in a unified treaty body;[79] that the

---

[72] O'Flaherty and O'Brien, 'Reform of the UN Human Rights treaty Monitoring Bodies: A Critique of the Concept Paper on the High Commissioner's Proposal for a Unified Standing Treaty Body' (2007) HRLR 141, pp 165–172.

[73] Participation at the workshop included academics, treaty body members, State representatives, members of NGOs and key personnel at the OHCHR: Nottingham Report, p 7.

[74] Nottingham Report, pp 8–9. The workshop also considered more incremental means of reform, pp 10–13.

[75] Implementation of General Assembly Resolution 60/251 of 15 March 2006 Entitled 'Human Rights Council': UN Doc A/HRC/2/G/5, (25 September 2006).

[76] UN Doc A/HRC/2/G/5, (25 September 2006), para 12.

[77] UN Doc A/HRC/2/G/5, (25 September 2006), para 13.

[78] See the views of the treaty bodies as outlined in the Report of the Working Group on the Harmonization of Working Methods of Treaty Bodies: UN Doc HRI/MC/2007, 9 January 2007.

[79] UN Doc HRI/MC/2007, 9 January 2007. See also the Statement by CEDAW entitled 'Towards a Harmonized and Integrated Human Rights Treaty Body System': www.un.org/womenwatch/daw/cedaw/35sess.htm (last accessed May 2011); (contd.../)

creation of such a body would raise complex legal[80] and political problems, not easily solved in the short or medium term;[81] and that, fundamentally, there would be no guarantee that such a body would necessarily mark an improvement in human rights protection or provide a solution to the current challenges facing the treaty system.[82] CAT expressed the most openness to the proposal, while CERD proposed the establishment only of a single body to deal with individual complaints.[83] All of the treaty bodies, on the other hand, have expressed a strong preference for a more incremental approach to treaty reform, based on harmonisation and coordination, rather than fundamental structural reform.[84]

[16.20] Thus, despite the conviction and indeed assertiveness of the OHCHR's proposal, it would appear to have foundered for the moment and it seems clear that the possibility of a unified treaty body is unlikely to see the light of day, at least for a considerable time to come. Certainly, as we shall see, the current High Commissioner, Navanethem Pillay, has completely shelved the initiative and, in the absence of significant political support, it would seem foolhardy for the OHCHR to proceed further along this road. The risks of such a dramatic move are indeed high.[85] As Bowman has observed, the importance of governmental support for any such initiative is a key factor in any effort to achieve it and, as we have seen, support to date from that quarter has not been forthcoming.[86] Notwithstanding its failure to gain traction, its most enduring contribution will

---

[79] (\...contd) Schopp-Schilling, 'Treaty Body Reform; the Case of the Committee on the Elimination of Discrimination Against Women' (2007) HRL Rev 201, p 210; and the Statement by the CMW Concerning the Idea of Creating a Single Human Rights Treaty Body, Annual Report of the CMW (2007) UN Doc A/62/48, Annex IV.

[80] For an excellent analysis of the legal complexities posed in establishing a unified treaty body, see Bowman, 'Towards a Unified Treaty Body for Monitoring Compliance with UN Human Rights Conventions? Legal Mechanisms for Reform': (2007) HRL Rev 225–249.

[81] See, in particular, the views expressed by the CCPR in Report of the Working Group on the Harmonization of Working Methods of Treaty Bodies: UN Doc HRI/MC/2007, 9 January 2007, para 7.

[82] UN Doc HRI/MC/2007, 9 January 2007, paras 7 and 8.

[83] UN Doc HRI/MC/2007, 9 January 2007, paras 8 and 5 respectively.

[84] UN Doc HRI/MC/2007, 9 January 2007, para 11.

[85] As Johnstone notes, the ultimate risk being that States '...might take advantage of the confusion of transition to bring down the system...They may refuse to accept the authority of a single treaty body, refuse to submit and discuss reports and refuse to consider that body's pronouncements, as an excuse to escape the careful monitoring of their human rights progress, or lack thereof': Johnstone, 'Cynical Savings or Reasonable reform? Reflections on a Single Unified UN Human Rights Treaty Body' (2007) HRL Rev 173, p 193.

[86] 'A pessimist might well conclude that the exercise is, in fact, unlikely to be capable of achievement at all. In particular, the two key criteria that one would wish to see satisfied in this context – namely the utilization of legally unassailable methods and the speedy completion of the process – operate in direct opposition to one another, while the prevalence of institutionalized governmental inertia greatly adds to the difficulties in that regard': Bowman, 'Towards a Unified Treaty body for Monitoring Compliance with UN Human Rights Conventions? Legal Mechanisms for Treaty Reform' (2007) HRL Rev 225, p 249.

undoubtedly be that it has served to re-energise thinking about further reform of the UN treaty system.

[16.21] Besides the nuclear option of unification proposed in the concept paper, other far-reaching proposals have emerged over time, including, for example, the suggestion by Martin Scheinin that the CCPR and the CESCR should be fused into a single body (the Human Rights Committee) with responsibility for monitoring reports and complaints under the two Covenants.[87] Hampson, on the other hand, has suggested that the CCPR and the CESCR should be made into full-time bodies, with better resourcing of the remaining part-time treaty bodies.[88] Perhaps the most radical idea of all is that which has been systematically promoted by Manfred Nowak in recent years, ie, that of establishing a World Court of Human Rights which could ultimately replace the functions of the treaty bodies in regard to individual complaints and inquiries.[89] While each of these proposals has logically compelling elements, they have thus far failed to garner significant support in political quarters.[90] Thus, attention must turn to more incremental reform proposals currently in the pipeline.

Strengthening the treaty body system

[16.22] While debate on the merits of a unified standing treaty body was in train, the treaty bodies and the OHCHR had been working simultaneously on more incremental measures of reform. As mentioned in Ch 4, these have included most notably the development of new harmonised guidelines for the drafting of State reports under all of the human rights treaties;[91] and the development of a pioneering new method of

[87] Scheinin, 'The Proposed Optional Protocol to the Covenant on Economic, Social and Cultural Rights: A Blueprint for UN Human Rights Treaty Body Reform Without Amending the Existing Treaties' (2006) HRL Rev 131.

[88] Hampson, 'An overview of the reform of the UN human rights machinery' (2007) HRL Rev 1, p 12.

[89] Nowak, 'The Need for a World Court of Human Rights' (2007) HRL Rev 251 and 'Eight Reasons Why we Need a World Court of Human Rights' in Alfredsson et al (eds), *International Human Rights Monitoring Mechanisms* (2nd edn, Martinus Nijhoff, 2009), p 697. The idea of a world court of human rights was also floated tentatively but rejected as a realistic or indeed necessary option by Stefan Treschel (former President of the European Commission of Human Rights) in 'A World Court for Human Rights?' (2004) Nw U J Int'l Hum Rts 3.

[90] Indeed, it is difficult to see how Nowak's proposal, in particular, could command significant support in the foreseeable future, having regard to the reception given by States to the OHCHR concept paper. Many have remarked in this regard that a dominant reason for States' rejection of the proposal was because it contained the seeds of a world court of human rights which many were completely unprepared to accept. This observation is made by Michael O'Flaherty who concludes that although Nowak's proposal merits consideration, '…its presentation in the context of treaty body reform has introduced a perceived teleological element that greatly complicates discussions': O'Flaherty, 'Reform of the UN Human Rights Treaty Body System: Locating the Dublin Statement' (2010) HRL Rev 319, pp 325 and 327.

[91] Compilation of Guidelines on the Form and Content of Reports to be Submitted by States Parties to the International Human Rights Treaties: UN Doc HRI/GEN/2/Rev 4, 29 May 2008.

reporting by the CAT and the CCPR, known as 'lists of issues prior to reporting' (LOIPR). Through the vehicle of the ICM and the meetings of the chairpersons, a broad level of support was clearly discernible for further methods of harmonisation and coordination of the working methods of the treaty bodies.[92] A turning point occurred, however, in September 2009, when a year after her appointment, the current High Commissioner for Human Rights, Navanethem Pillay, invited States parties to human rights treaties as well as stakeholders '....to initiate a process of reflection on how to streamline and strengthen the treaty body system to achieve better coordination among those mechanisms, as well as in their interaction with Special Procedures and the UPR'.[93] The choice of words used for this invitation was significant, signalling as it did that the notion of a USTB was officially off the table and was being replaced by a far less threatening initiative, aimed at synchronising the working methods and processes of the existing mechanisms so as to make them function better as a coherent whole.

[16.23] The result of the High Commissioner's call has been the hosting of a series of meetings involving various actors in the treaty body system, organised by outside bodies and facilitated by the OHCHR. As the High Commissioner has further clarified, the aim of these events is to gather suggestions for how to 'bolster the treaty body system and make it more efficient and effective to improve the situation of human rights at the national level around the world'.[94] The following sections outline the main developments that have taken place since the reflection process initiated by the High Commissioner was initiated in September 2009.

The Dublin Statement on the Process of Strengthening of the United Nations Human Rights Treaty Body System

[16.24] The first manifestation of the new reform agenda was the elaboration of the Dublin Statement on the Process of Strengthening of the United Nations Human Rights Treaty Body System.[95] Drafted following a meeting in December 2009 by current and former treaty body members acting in a personal capacity,[96] the document has been aptly

---

[92] This willingness was clear even at the time that the proposal for the USTB was still under discussion: see Report of the Eighteenth Meeting of the Chairpersons of the Treaty Bodies: UN Doc A/61/385, 25 September 2006, paras 13–19. In his study in 2004, Vandenhole concluded that '...the open attitude of the Committees, the annual meetings of chairpersons of the Committees have given a strong impetus to convergence and harmonization. Reforms of the Secretariat have facilitated this...': Vandenhole, *The Procedures Before the UN Human Rights Treaty Bodies: Divergence or Convergence?* (Intersentia, 2004), p 314.

[93] Statement of Ms Navanethem Pillay, United Nations High Commissioner for Human Rights, at the 12th session of the Human Rights Council (14 September 2009):

[94] Speech of Ms Navanethem Pillay, UNHCHR at the 16th session of the Human Rights Council (7 March 2011), launching the Poznan Statement (see paras **16.30–16.32**): http://www2.ohchr.org/english/bodies/HRTD/docs/HCStatementTBStrengthening_070311.pdf (last accessed May 2011).

[95] The 'Dublin Statement': http://www2.ohchr.org/english/bodies/HRTD/docs/DublinStatement.pdf (last accessed May 2011). The statement is published also in (2010) Netherlands Human Rights Quarterly 116.

[96] As its title suggests, the meeting took place in Dublin, Ireland and was facilitated by the University of Nottingham Law Centre with financial support from the Irish Government.

described as a 'roadmap' for reform of the treaty system.[97] Recognising that the overarching purpose of reform must be that of enhanced protection of human rights on the ground, the Statement proceeds on the basis that reform is a multi-faceted and dynamic process, involving not only the treaty bodies themselves, but also reform at the domestic level by States, NGOs and NHRIs.[98] In addition to the latter entities, reform must include consultation with a range of other stakeholders such as rights-holders, human rights defenders, academics, the OHCHR, UN human rights special procedures and other UN actors.[99] In an obvious effort to assuage the fears raised by the USTB proposal concerning diminution of rights' protection for certain categories, the Statement affirms that reform should '...scrupulously avoid any initiatives that serve in purpose or effect to weaken or marginalise the protection of particular categories of human rights...'.[100] More specifically, the Dublin Statement emphasises the need for the treaty bodies to improve and to further harmonise their procedures and working methods, strengthen their systems for follow-up and facilitate more systematic involvement of UN and other actors at the country level.[101] It makes a wide range of recommendations to States to cooperate, facilitate and engage more fully with treaty body procedures, as well as ensuring compliance with recommendations at the domestic level.[102] NGOs and NHRIs are exhorted to step-up their respective levels of engagement with the treaty body system, including with regard to input in the procedures, publicity, follow-up and in monitoring implementation.[103] Finally, the Statement calls for greater resources from States to improve the functioning of the treaty system[104] as well as enhanced support and assistance from UN entities,[105] including the OHCHR.[106]

[16.25] While at first blush, the Dublin Statement is clearly less dynamic in its approach than the USTB, closer inspection reveals that it does contain real transformative potential for reform of the treaty body system. Its most obvious contribution is that it has re-oriented the reform agenda from one that was targeted almost exclusively at the functioning of the treaty bodies themselves, to one involving States (most crucially), as well as rights holders, NGOs and NHRIs. The Statement takes full account of the reality that the effectiveness of any international monitoring process can only really be measured by the experience of States parties in engaging with the reporting process[107]

---

[97] O'Flaherty, 'Reform of the UN Human Rights Treaty Body System: Locating the Dublin Statement' (2010) HRL Rev 319, p 328.
[98] Dublin Statement, para 11.
[99] Dublin Statement, para 6.
[100] Dublin Statement, para 10.
[101] Dublin Statement, para 17.
[102] Dublin Statement, para 18.
[103] Dublin Statement, paras 20 and 21.
[104] Dublin Statement, para 23.
[105] Dublin Statement, para 24.
[106] Dublin Statement, para 23.
[107] For an in-depth analysis of the experience of Timor-Leste against the background of potential reform of the treaty body system, see Devereux and Anderson, 'Reporting under International Human Rights Treaties: Perspectives from Timor Leste's Experience of the Reformed Process' (2008) HRL Rev 69.

and the *impact* which the process has on human rights policy or practice at the *domestic* level.[108] In this regard, a study by Heyns and Viljoen in 2001 revealed two key findings: First, that the treaty system has '... its greatest impact where treaty norms have been made part of domestic law more or less spontaneously (for example as part of constitutional and legislative reform) and not as a result of norm enforcement'.[109] Second, as far as international norm enforcement is concerned, 'its influence is very unevenly spread among countries that are part of the system'.[110] In regard to the latter point, the study further concluded that the various international enforcement mechanisms used by the treaty bodies '...appeared to have had very little demonstrable impact thus far'.[111] While one obvious response to this situation might be to focus on strengthening the monitoring mechanisms themselves, the authors of the study concluded that any such attempts '...must be supplemented by creative efforts to ensure that treaty norms are internalized in the domestic legal and cultural system and that they are enforced at that level'.[112] In short: 'The challenge is to harness the treaty system to domestic forces – 'domestic constituencies' – that will ensure its realization'.[113] It is this latter aspect of the Dublin Statement that is perhaps its greatest strength and has provided the momentum and direction for the evolving reform agenda.

Marrakech Statement on Strengthening the Relationship between NHRIs and the Human Rights Treaty Body System

[16.26] The next key input into the reform process is the Marrakech Statement on strengthening the relationship between NHRIs and the human rights treaty body system.[114] Organised also in response to the High Commissioner's call in 2009, this Statement was the product of a meeting in Marrakech, attended by representatives of NHRIs from all regional networks of such institutions at which treaty body members

---

[108] According to the OHCHR, the effectiveness of the treaty system must be assessed by the '...extent of national implementation of the recommendations resulting from constructive dialogue under reporting procedures', as well as on '...how successful the system has been in providing States with authoritative guidance on the meaning of the treaty provisions, preventing human rights violations, and ensuring prompt and effective action in cases where such violations occur.': OHCHR, Concept Paper for USTB, para 4. See also Heyns and Viljoen, 'The Impact of the United Nations Human Rights Treaties on the Domestic Level' (2001) 23 HRQ 483.

[109] Heyns and Viljoen, 'The Impact of the United Nations Human Rights Treaties on the Domestic Level' (2001) 23 HRQ 483, p 487.

[110] Heyns and Viljoen, 'The Impact of the United Nations Human Rights Treaties on the Domestic Level' (2001) 23 HRQ 483, pp 487–488.

[111] Heyns and Viljoen, 'The Impact of the United Nations Human Rights Treaties on the Domestic Level' (2001) 23 HRQ 483, p 488.

[112] Heyns and Viljoen, 'The Impact of the United Nations Human Rights Treaties on the Domestic Level' (2001) 23 HRQ 483, p 488.

[113] Heyns and Viljoen, 'The Impact of the United Nations Human Rights Treaties on the Domestic Level' (2001) 23 HRQ 483, p 488.

[114] The Marrakech Statement: http://www2.ohchr.org/english/bodies/HRTD/docs/ MarrakeshStatement_en.pdf (last accessed May 2011). On NHRIs, see Ch 4, para **4.05**.

and representatives of OHCHR also participated.[115] As the Dublin Statement had implicitly recognised, NHRIs can play a vital 'bridging' role[116] between the treaty body system and domestic implementation through their unique mandates to advise and monitor States' compliance with international human rights law. It is clear, as Murray has noted, that the extent to which these institutions can meaningfully engage in the treaty body procedures often depends on their mandates and their institutional competencies.[117] Where they are compliant with the Paris Principles[118] and well-resourced, they are well-placed to add value not just by feeding into those processes at the international level by the provision of shadow reports and oral interventions, but also at the crucial 'follow-up' stage.[119] Despite some variation in approach over the years, the treaty bodies themselves have begun to draw on the expertise of those institutions increasingly in the periodic reporting procedures.[120] The Marrakech meeting thus provided an important opportunity to elicit the perspectives of NHRIs on methods of enhancing the treaty body procedures and improving implementation of their outputs on the ground.

[16.27] In this respect, the Marrakech Statement affirms that the wide variety and diversity of existing practices among the treaty bodies has created difficulties for NHRIs in engaging with the treaty body system – a fact which is compounded by the entry into

---

[115] This meeting was organised by the Advisory Council on Human Rights of Morocco. The present author participated in the meeting in her capacity as a member of the Irish Human Rights Commission.

[116] Carver has noted that the extent to which this 'bridging' role routinely features in academic comment on NHRIs: Carver, 'A New Answer to an Old Question: National Human Rights Institutions and the Domestication of International Law' (2010) HRL Rev 1.

[117] In this respect, Murray has noted that 'Not all these institutions are credible, legitimate, or independent and many of them do not have the sufficient level of expertise with the UN system' and has '…cautioned against thinking that NHRIs and national bodies are the solution to the challenge of implementation in all cases': see 'Improving Implementation and Follow-Up: Treaty Bodies, Special Procedures, Universal Periodic Review', Report of Proceedings of a conference hosted by the Open Society Justice Initiative, the Brookings Institution's Foreign Policy program and UPR-Watch (November, 2010): http://www2.ohchr.org/english/bodics/HRTD/docs/ReportConference.pdf (last accessed May 2011).

[118] The Paris Principles set forth the proper role and functions of a national human rights institution, as well as stating the key attributes deemed necessary by the United Nations General Assembly for the proper functioning of such institutions.

[119] Conclusions of the International Roundtable on the Role of National Human Rights Institutions and Treaty Bodies: UN Doc HRI/MC/2007/3, 7 February 2007. This roundtable was attended by participants from NHRIs, treaty bodies and civil society and took place in Berlin, Germany on 23 and 24 November 2006 with an agenda to discuss the interaction between NHRIs and treaty bodies. See also the publication by the German Institute of Human Rights, *The Role of National Human Rights Institutions in the United Nations Treaty Body Process* (December 2007).

[120] See the survey by Carver, 'A New Answer to an Old Question: National Human Rights Institutions and the Domestication of International Law' (2010) HRL Rev 1, pp 19–25.

force and ratification of more instruments.[121] Two particular examples highlighted in the Statement are lack of meeting time and frequent lack of translation of documents.[122] Accordingly, the Statement asserts a 'compelling need' for greater harmonisation between the treaty bodies and offers a number of concrete suggestions to strengthen the treaty body system.[123] These include the need to enforce page limits on all treaty body documentation, including States' reports; further exploration of innovative working methods such as 'lists of issues prior to reporting'; the making of more focused, targeted and treaty-based recommendations; increased use of cross-referencing between each other's recommendations; increased development of general comments and, where appropriate, joint general comments; and the hosting of meetings in regional centres outside Geneva and New York.[124] In order to maximise the potential input of NHRIs into the treaty body procedures, the Statement advocates alignment of treaty body rules of procedure and working methods as regards their cooperation with NHRIs, including with respect to the format and timing of submission of written information and oral presentations.[125] It also exhorts the treaty bodies to encourage, systematise and harmonise participation by NHRIs in the follow-up activities of the treaty bodies in particular.[126]

[16.28] Other key elements of the Marrakech Statement include recommendations to States parties as well as commitments by NHRIs themselves in respect of the treaty body system. As regards the former, the Statement recommends that States should allocate further resources to NHRIs and the treaty body system;[127] implement a transparent and consultative process for nominating experts to the treaty bodies; and host a national consultation process during the preparation of their reports to the treaty bodies.[128] As regards their own commitments to the process, the Statement reiterates the obligations of NHRIs to keep under review States parties' implementation of their obligations under the treaties, to disseminate treaty body outputs and to maintain pressure on States to conform to the full spectrum of their treaty monitoring obligations.[129] NHRIs also commit to organising more training activities in respect of the treaty body system, to which end greater capacity building and assistance is requested from the OHCHR.[130]

[16.29] Interestingly, the Statement highlights the need to raise awareness of the individual complaint procedures – an issue that is often submerged in debate on treaty body reform. In particular, it encourages NHRIs to take a strategic approach in

---

[121] Marrakech Statement, paras 6 and 7.
[122] Marrakech Statement, para 7.
[123] Marrakech Statement, para 8.
[124] Marrakech Statement, para 16–18.
[125] Marrakech Statement, para 23.
[126] Marrakech Statement, para 23.
[127] Marrakech Statement, paras 12 and 19.
[128] Marrakech Statement, paras 20 and 21.
[129] Marrakech Statement, paras 24–26.
[130] Marrakech Statement, paras 28–30.

promoting cases that may build jurisprudence which can be used at the domestic level, as well as follow-up on the implementation of treaty body views.[131] As the relevant chapters of Part 3 of this book have indicated, the operative complaint procedures all share largely consistent procedures and admissibility criteria but there is significant variation between them in terms of participation by States, participation by individuals, the quality of the decision-making and the impact of those decisions on the ground. The Achilles heel of each of the UN complaint procedures is that the views rendered under them by the treaty bodies are not legally binding on the respondent States.[132] The status of the views, as such, has emboldened States over the years either to ignore them or even to challenge their substance.[133] For this reason, it is of crucial importance that the treaty bodies continue to focus on providing well reasoned and intellectually rigorous decisions – a goal that is not always helped by the continued emphasis on consensus-decision making. Where remedies are recommended, these should be clearly stated in the body of the particular decision. The emphasis that the treaty bodies themselves have placed in recent years on the issue of follow-up to the views rendered under the complaint procedures is crucial in tapping their full potential.[134] However, follow-up should not be confined to the treaty bodies, but should also be the subject of sustained attention on the part of NGOs, NHRIs as well as legal practitioners.[135] Thus, the specific commitment of NHRIs in the Marrakech Statement to follow-up on the implementation of treaty body views at the domestic level, to disseminate and use them in their human rights training programmes is to be particularly welcomed.

The Poznan Statement on the Reforms of the UN Human Rights Treaty Body System

[16.30] As part of the reflection process stimulated by the High Commissioner in September 2009, a further meeting of treaty body experts (including five chairpersons) was convened in Poznan in November 2010, at which members of NGOs and

---

[131] Marrakech Statement, para 27.
[132] Open Society Justice Initiative, *From Judgment to Justice: Implementing International and Regional Human Rights Decisions* (Open Society Foundation, 2011), p 125.
[133] See more recently, Open Society Justice Initiative, *From Judgment to Justice: Implementing International and Regional Human Rights Decisions* (Open Society Foundations, 2011), pp 123 and 131.
[134] See in this respect the improvements noted by Schmidt in respect of 'Follow-up Activities by UN Human Rights Treaty Bodies and Special Procedures Mechanisms of the Human Rights Council – Recent Developments' in Alfredsson et al (eds), *International Monitoring Mechanisms: Essays in Honour of Jacob Möller* (2nd edn, Martinus Nijhoff, 2009) pp 25–34. The issue of 'follow-up' was the subject of a dedicated Inter-Committee Meeting Working Group on Follow-Up of the treaty bodies in January 2011. See generally, First session of the Inter-Committee Meeting Working Group on Follow-up to Concluding Observations, Inquiries, Visits and Decisions (Geneva, 12–14 January 2011): http://www2.ohchr.org/english/bodies/icm-mc/WG_followup.htm (last accessed May 2011).
[135] See the recommendations in this respect made by the Open Society Justice Initiative, *From Judgment to Justice: Implementing International and Regional Human Rights Decisions* (Open Society Foundations, 2011), p 136.

representatives of the OHCHR acted as 'observers'.[136] The resulting product of that meeting – the Poznan Statement on the Reforms of the UN Human Rights Treaty Body System – builds on the Dublin and Marrakech Statements in a number of important ways.[137] Chief amongst these would appear to be the emphasis which the Poznan Statement places on the need for the treaty body system to move from a 'light' to an 'advanced' coordination and harmonisation mode.[138] To facilitate this, the Statement makes a crucial suggestion that the chairpersons of each the treaty bodies should be empowered to adopt measures on the working methods and procedures 'which are common across the treaty body system and have previously been discussed within each of the Committees'.[139] While this proposal may not appear far-reaching, if ultimately accepted, it could be a decisive means of coaxing the treaty bodies into viewing their respective mandates as *parts* of a comprehensive system which needs to function more effectively as a coherent whole. It is clear from the ICM meetings that the treaty bodies are willing to observe and learn from each other's working methods – a fact that should be recognised and facilitated further according to the Poznan Statement.[140] However, much of the difficulty with the harmonisation project thus far appears to be the tendency of each body to aim at improving the efficiency of its individual working procedures or to cleave to already established practices. The resulting variation, however, causes confusion and uncertainty for States as well as stakeholders in engaging with each of the respective treaty procedures. The devolution of such a restrained decision-making power to the chairpersons would certainly help to accelerate the harmonisation process and would be instrumental in strengthening the treaty body 'system' as a whole.

Turning to treaty body outputs, the Poznan Statement recognises that a fundamental means of enhancing their quality, as well as reputation and status at the national level is by ensuring the independence and expertise of the treaty body members. To this end, it recommends that the chairpersons entrust a working group to prepare guidelines on the eligibility and independence of experts, which may be adopted at an annual meeting of the chairpersons.[141]

---

[136] It would seem that NGO observers fully participated in the Poznan meeting, though they were not allowed to endorse the Statement: 'In practice we were allowed to participate fully but not to endorse the statement. Being able to engage in the meeting was probably one of the most useful opportunities to date, in addition to the submissions NGOs have been making and the statements at the Inter-Committee Meetings': Interview with treaty body expert Rachel Brett (Representative for Human Rights and Refugees, Quaker United Nations Office, Geneva) conducted by the International Service for Human Rights: (2011) 2 Human Rights Monitor 25.

[137] The Poznan Statement on the Reforms of the United Nations Human Rights Treaty Body System (28–29 September 2010): http://www2.ohchr.org/english/bodies/HRTD/docs/PoznanStatement.pdf (last accessed May 2011).

[138] Poznan Statement, para 16.

[139] Poznan Statement, para 17.

[140] Poznan Statement, para 18.

[141] Poznan Statement, para 19.

[16.31] In addition to these overarching recommendations, the Poznan Statement makes specific suggestions of ways to achieve a more streamlined approach to reporting procedures, such as the importance of page limits in State reports, updating of information in the common core document and the need for a coordinated approach to non-reporting States.[142] While it recognises that the adoption by some treaty bodies of the 'lists of issues prior to reporting' (LOIPR) approach could significantly improve the reporting procedure, the statement ultimately advocates a flexible approach that allows the treaty bodies to use LOIPR within a larger 'tool-box' of reporting options, under circumstances that so require.[143] It is submitted that this recommendation does not sit easily with the overall aim of harmonisation since the notion of a 'tool-box' of working methods in the realm of reporting is one of the precise problems which the reflection process was designed to address. Accepting that there are certainly legitimate concerns regarding the operation of the LOIPR approach,[144] it might be more prudent to monitor its implementation by the CCPR and CAT with a view to deciding whether it does, on balance, operate more effectively than the standard reporting approach. If this can be demonstrated, it is difficult to see why the adoption of such an approach would not be beneficial as regards each of the treaty bodies which operates a periodic reporting mechanism and how retention of the traditional method by particular bodies could be justified.

[16.32] As well as advocating the establishment of national frameworks for consultation during the reporting procedure, the Poznan Statement also emphasises the importance of such frameworks at the implementation stage. These should involve a broad range of actors, including governments, NHRIs, NGOs, academics and other parts of civil society, culminating potentially in the development of national action plans for coordinated implementation of treaty body recommendations.[145] It is significant that the Poznan Statement also voices support for the idea of regional meetings of the treaty bodies as a means of bringing their proceedings 'closer to the implementation level'.[146] The need for a more coordinated approach on the part of the treaty bodies themselves to the question of follow-up is also stressed,[147] together with a recommendation for improved cross-referencing as between treaty body outputs and the quality of concluding observations.[148]

---

[142] Poznan Statement, paras 11–13.
[143] Poznan Statement, para 9.
[144] These include the increased workload for the secretariats in compiling lists of issues, concerns around the comprehensiveness of the lists of issues; the opportunities for input from NHRIs and civil society; and the question of whether the procedure will move speedily enough. For a comprehensive overview of the LOIPR procedure, see Treaty bodies' lists of issues prior to reporting (targeted/focused reports): Overview of a new optional treaty-body reporting procedure: UN Doc HRI/ICM/2010/3 (19 May 2010).
[145] Poznan Statement, paras 13 and 14.
[146] Poznan Statement, paras 22.
[147] Poznan Statement, paras 25–28.
[148] Poznan Statement, paras 27 and 29.

Views of Non-Governmental Organisations on Reform of the Treaty Body System

[16.33] As has been made clear in other chapters of this book, the input of NGOs into the treaty body procedures is a vital ingredient in ensuring their effectiveness. The information that NGOs contribute to these procedures and the role that they play in monitoring compliance with treaty body recommendations makes their perspective on the functioning of the system an essential part in the current reflection process. To this end, a formal consultation with NGOs took place in Seoul, Korea in April 2011 as part of the reflection process at which 16 international and national NGOs with experience of the treaty body system attended. The consultation focused on the ways and means of strengthening the reporting procedure; enhancing the constructive dialogue in that procedure; and the question of follow-up and results for rights holders. A second consultation with NGOs is scheduled to take place in Pretoria, South Africa in July 2011. At the time of writing, the formal outcome document from the Seoul consultation has not been released. While the text is awaited, it is possible to glean the views of NGOs on the strengthening process from a number of other sources, including their regular submissions to ICMs and the meetings of the treaty body chairpersons.[149]

[16.34] Of particular note is the formal response issued by NGOs in November 2010 which builds on the body of submissions presented to ICMs over the years on the working methods of the treaty bodies.[150] The response offers the initial views of some 20 NGOs on the Dublin Statement specifically, as well as some proposals for strengthening the treaty bodies generally. In general terms, the response appears to implicitly endorse the 'roadmap' set forth in the Dublin Statement and particularly the core objective in the reform effort to strengthen 'the capacity of rights-holders to enjoy their human rights'.[151] In this respect, it identifies a number of overarching aims that should be incorporated in the process, such as increased accessibility, information, resources and institutional support for the work of the treaty bodies.[152]

[16.35] As regards the activities of the treaty bodies specifically, NGOs propose a review of the effectiveness of the common-core document which they maintain has produced an 'uneven' response from the States parties.[153] It also gives a 'cautious welcome' to the LOIPR method of State reporting, but does draw attention to the need for a qualitative assessment of that procedure as it has operated in practice before rolling

---

[149] NGO submissions to the 8th and 9th ICMs (and the 21st meeting of the chairpersons) can be accessed on the website of the International Service for Human Rights: http://www.ishr.ch/treaty-bodies-ngo-statements (last accessed May 2011). The submission to the 11th ICM meeting is available at: http://www2.ohchr.org/english/bodies/icm-mc/documents11.htm (last accessed May 2011).

[150] Dublin Statement on the Process of Strengthening the United Nations Human Rights Treaty Body System: Response by Non-Governmental Organizations (November 2010) (NGO Response to the Dublin Statement): http://www.bayefsky.com/getfile.php/id/486189700 (last accessed May 2011).

[151] NGO Response to the Dublin Statement, para 1.

[152] NGO Response to the Dublin Statement, paras 1–5

[153] NGO Response to the Dublin Statement, para 18.

it out to the other treaty bodies.[154] The response also highlights the need for a systematic response by the treaty bodies to address lack of State reporting; increased visibility and accessibility for the outputs of the individual complaints procedures; and the adoption of a consistent, transparent and consultative procedure for the drafting of general comments.[155] The need to enhance the visibility of the treaty bodies is also acknowledged, possibly through the hosting of regional meetings by the treaty bodies, particularly outside Europe and New York.[156]

[16.36] The response makes a number of more muscular recommendations which wholly support the emphasis in the current reform agenda on 'systematizing' the work of the treaty bodies. Most notably, NGOs endorse the idea of devolving decision-making capacity to the chairpersons 'and/or other relevant experts' in respect of working methods and procedures. This recommendation is based on the view expressed in the document that lack of decision-making capacity at ICM and chairpersons' meetings has to date made it '…very difficult to make progress, even in relation to fairly simple matters of working methods'.[157] The response also advocates consideration of a specific, inter-committee 'treaty body follow up mechanism' for all treaty bodies. This could take the form of a 'Treaty Body Follow Up Coordination Unit' or a senior level 'Treaty Body Follow Up Coordinator' post within the OHCHR. Finally, it should be noted that the response stresses the importance of enhancing the membership of the treaty bodies and encourages the chairpersons to prepare the guidelines proposed in the Poznan Statement.[158]

THE WAY FORWARD

[16.37] The reflection process initiated by the current High Commissioner is still ongoing, with further consultations planned for States, academics and UN entities.[159] A meeting in Dublin in Autumn 2011 will be convened to formally close the consultative phase. The process is set to culminate in a compilation of proposals by the High Commissioner which will be presented later in 2011. Given that a key constituency – namely the States parties – has yet to participate in the consultation process, it is too

---

[154] NGO Response to the Dublin Statement, para 19.
[155] NGO Response to the Dublin Statement, paras 20–22.
[156] NGO Response to the Dublin Statement, para 6.
[157] NGO Response to the Dublin Statement, paras 26 and 27.
[158] NGO Response to the Dublin Statement, para 17. This issue is clearly seen as a fundamental one in terms of treaty body reform by the NGO sector: 'The system of governments nominating and electing individuals to the treaty bodies as part of a bargaining process means focus on the quality of the individuals gets lost. Whatever results the reform has, if the way in which individuals become members remains the same, without any other safeguards, then the system is not really going to improve': Interview by ISHR with Rachel Brett, (2011) 2 Human Rights Monitor 25, p 26.
[159] The technical consultation for States is due to take place, in cooperation with treaty body chairs and the International Institute for the Rights of the Child in Sion, Switzerland on 12–13 May 2011; and a consultation for academics is being organised by the University of Teacher Education Lucerne (Switzerland), with the support of OHCHR in October, 2011.

early to predict the content of the outcome document. The picture that seems to be emerging thus far is that of widespread frustration on the part of stakeholders with the diverse working methods of the treaty bodies, which has made interaction with the procedures difficult to manage in practice. While very specific and valuable recommendations are embedded in the Marrakech and Poznan Statements to address this, a critical one, in this author's view, which appears to command significant support from consultees, is the need to devolve some element of decision-making power in procedural matters to the chairpersons of the treaty bodies in order to accelerate the process of harmonisation.

[16.38] Another clear trend emerging from the consultations is the focus on follow-up and enhancing the implementation phase of the process. In this respect, the notion of an inter-treaty body on follow-up (mooted by experts at the Nottingham workshop in 2006 and revived in the recent NGO submission on the Dublin Statement) is certainly worthy of further reflection. However, such a proposal may be ambitious, even at this stage, in light of the 'points of agreement' reached by a recent inter-committee working group on follow-up convened by the ICM. While the outcome paper from that meeting makes numerous recommendations to treaty bodies on ways to harmonise and enhance their methods of follow-up in respect of periodic reporting and individual communications, it stops short of making any suggestion for a coordinated mechanism in this respect.[160]

[16.39] At a substantive level, there can be no doubt that all of the recommendations made during the reflection process aimed at improving the quality of treaty body outputs are 'greater goods' upon which few reasonable people would differ. These include recommendations for increased cross-referencing between concluding observations and views, more focused recommendations and a call for guidelines on the appointment of experts to the treaty bodies so as to ensure the independence and expertise of their membership.

[16.40] Finally, it may be said that there is also a groundswell of support for meetings of the treaty bodies to take place outside Geneva and New York. This proposal would undoubtedly raise the visibility of the work of the treaty bodies and assist enormously in following through on an integrated approach to implementation.[161]

[16.41] One issue that has received limited attention in the reform discussion is the extent to which greater complementarity might be developed between the treaty body system and the universal periodic review (UPR) procedure being operated by the Human Rights Council. As mentioned in Chapter Two, a range of concerns has been raised since the initiation of the latter inter-governmental process that it might duplicate the work of

---

[160] Points of Agreement of the Inter-Committee Meeting Working Group on Follow-Up (12–14 January 2011): http://www2.ohchr.org/english/bodies/icm-mc/WG_followup.htm (last accessed May 2011).

[161] In this respect, it is to be noted that the chairpersons hosted their 22nd meeting in Brussels in July 2010 at which they met with representatives of institutions of the European Union and the Council of Europe. The chairpersons have decided to host a meeting every other year at the regional level: UN DocA/65/190, para 35.

the treaty bodies, or at the very least divert attention away from the more specific recommendations being made by those bodies. Other concerns include the extent to which resources devoted to UPR are detracting from the financial and human resources necessary to properly implement the work of the treaty bodies.[162] The recent response by NGOs to the *Dublin Statement* points out that it is important that '…synergies between the UPR and treaty bodies are maximized but not at the expense of States parties' legal obligations, or through undermining of treaty body recommendations or distortion of priorities'.[163] It would make sense, therefore, for more focus to be placed on the precise means of maximising synergies in the course of the reflection process.

[16.42] In conclusion, it remains to be seen whether any of the reform proposals currently under discussion will ever come to fruition, and, if so, whether they will yield positive results. The issue of resources crops up time and again in the discussions and will necessarily constrain overly-ambitious outcomes. Whatever emerges, it will clearly be much more modest than the 'root and branch' overhaul of the system that was mooted in the USTB proposal. Perhaps the most positive outcome of the more subtle reform agenda being advanced in the 'strengthening process' is that it has focused minds on the crucial role that is played by national bodies such as NHRIs and NGOs in the treaty body procedures as well as in the realm of monitoring implementation. Given the inherent limitations in the procedures themselves, mentioned at the outset of this book, it must be acknowledged that the treaty bodies, NHRIs and NGOs face a task of Sisyphean proportions in coaxing States to implement the treaty body recommendations. If the strengthening process serves to foster more sustained cooperation between these various actors in that common enterprise, that in itself will have served a useful purpose.

---

[162] *'Halfway to Where? The UPR in 2009'*: ISHR Human Rights Monitor 2009, *pp* 7–8: http://www.ishr.ch/index.php?option=com_content&task=view&id=112&Itemid=173 (last accessed May 2011).

[163] NGO response to the Dublin Statement, para. 28.

Index

All references are to *paragraph* numbers

Abolition of death penalty
  International Bill of Rights, and, 3.03
Abusive communications
  International Convention on the Elimination of All Forms of Racial Discrimination, 8.15
  International Convention on the Protection of All Persons from Enforced Disappearance, 14.07
  International Convention on the Protection of the Rights of All Migrant Workers and Members of Their Families, 12.03
  International Covenant on Civil and Political Rights, 7.18–7.19
  International Covenant on Economic Social and Cultural Rights, 13.16
  UN Convention against Torture and Other Cruel, Inhuman or Degrading Treatment or Punishment, 9.25–9.33
  UN Convention on the Elimination of All Forms of Discrimination against Women, 10.18
  UN Convention on the Rights of Persons with Disabilities, 11.04
  UN Convention on the Rights of the Child, 15.10
Academic writings and teachings
  source of international law, and, 1.12
Accession
  generally, 1.03
Actions of international bodies
  source of international law, and, 1.13
African Charter on Human and People's Rights 1981
  human rights law, and, 1.26
American Convention on Human Rights 1969
  human rights law, and, 1.26

American Declaration of Independence
  state sovereignty, and, 1.17
Anonymous communications
  International Convention on the Elimination of All Forms of Racial Discrimination, 8.15
  International Convention on the Protection of All Persons from Enforced Disappearance, 14.07
  International Convention on the Protection of the Rights of All Migrant Workers and Members of Their Families, 12.03
  International Covenant on Civil and Political Rights, 7.18–7.19
  International Covenant on Economic Social and Cultural Rights, 13.16
  UN Convention against Torture and Other Cruel, Inhuman or Degrading Treatment or Punishment, 9.13
  UN Convention on the Elimination of All Forms of Discrimination against Women, 10.18
  UN Convention on the Rights of Persons with Disabilities, 11.04
  UN Convention on the Rights of the Child, 15.10
Best interests principle
  UN Convention on the Rights of the Child, and, 3.82
Bilateral treaties
  generally, 1.03
Burden of proof
  International Covenant on Civil and Political Rights, and, 7.42
Children's Rights Convention
  abusive communications, 15.10
  admissibility criteria, 15.10
  anonymous communications, 15.10
  appraisal, 15.22

Children's Rights Convention (contd)
  background, 3.81
  'best interests' principle, 3.82
  'child', 3.82
  Committee, 3.89–3.91
  competing international procedures, 15.10
  complainants, 15.07–15.08
  complaints procedure
    abusive communications, 15.10
    admissibility criteria, 15.10
    anonymous communications, 15.10
    appraisal, 15.22
    competing international procedures, 15.10
    complainants, 15.07–15.08
    consideration of communication, 15.16–15.19
    exhaustion of domestic remedies, 15.10
    follow-up, 15.20
    framework, 15.05–15.12
    friendly settlement, 15.14–15.15
    general provisions, 15.05–15.06
    interim measures, 15.11–15.12
    international co-operation and assistance, 15.21
    introduction, 15.01–15.04
    manifestly ill-founded communications, 15.10
    procedure, 15.13–15.20
    scope of complaints mechanism, 15.09
    transmission of communication, 15.13
  consideration of communication, 15.16–15.19
  exhaustion of domestic remedies, 15.10
  follow-up, 15.20
  framework, 15.05–15.12
  friendly settlement, 15.14–15.15
  general provisions, 15.05–15.06
  interim measures, 15.11–15.12
  international co-operation and assistance, 15.21
  introduction, 3.81
  investigative procedures, 5.65–5.68
  manifestly ill-founded communications, 15.10
  periodic reporting procedures
    constructive dialogue, 4.48
    follow-up, 4.49–4.50
    formal examination of reports, 4.47–4.48
    generally, 4.45
    input from non-state actors, 4.47
    submission of reports, 4.46
  procedure, 15.13–15.20
  scope of complaints mechanism, 15.09
  state obligations, 3.82–3.88
  transmission of communication, 15.13

Commission on Human Rights
  generally, 2.10–2.20
  Sub-Commission, 2.21–2.25

Competing international procedures
  International Convention on the Protection of All Persons from Enforced Disappearance, 14.07
  International Covenant on Civil and Political Rights, 7.35–7.37
  International Covenant on Economic Social and Cultural Rights, 13.16
  UN Convention against Torture and Other Cruel, Inhuman or Degrading Treatment or Punishment, 9.27–9.29
  UN Convention on the Elimination of All Forms of Discrimination against Women, 10.22
  UN Convention on the Rights of Persons with Disabilities, 11.04
  UN Convention on the Rights of the Child, 15.10

Complaints procedures
  International Bill of Rights, and, 3.03

Complaints procedures (contd)
  International Convention on the Elimination of All Forms of Racial Discrimination
    abusive communications, 8.15
    admissibility criteria, 8.14–8.20
    anonymous communications, 8.15
    appraisal, 8.33
    exhaustion of domestic remedies, 8.21–8.22
    incompatible communications, 8.16–8.20
    introduction, 8.01–8.05
    opinions, 8.23–8.32
    procedure, 8.06–8.13
  International Convention on the Protection of All Persons from Enforced Disappearance
    abusive communications, 14.07
    admissibility criteria, 14.07
    anonymous communications, 14.07
    competing international procedures, 14.07
    exhaustion of domestic remedies, 14.07
    habeas corpus, and, 14.02
    general procedure, 14.06–14.09
    incompatible communications, 14.07
    introduction, 14.01
    urgent procedure, 14.02–14.05
  International Convention on the Protection of the Rights of All Migrant Workers and Members of Their Families, 12.01–12.03
  International Covenant on Civil and Political Rights
    abusive communications, 7.18–7.19
    admissibility criteria, 7.17–7.41
    anonymous communications, 7.18–7.19
    appraisal, 7.75–7.78
    burden of proof, 7.42
    competing international procedures, 7.35–7.37
    equality, 7.65–7.69
    exhaustion of domestic remedies, 7.37–7.41
    freedom from torture or ill-treatment, 7.42–7.44
    freedom of expression, 7.62–7.64
    freedom of thought, conscience and religion, 7.57–7.61
    generally, 7.03–7.05
    incompatible communications, 7.20–7.33
    minority rights, 7.72–7.74
    non-discrimination, 7.65–7.69
    procedure, 7.06–7.16
    right to effective remedy, 7.70–7.71
    right to fair trial, 7.47–7.53
    right to liberty, 7.45–7.46
    right to life, 7.42
    right to privacy, family, home and correspondence, 7.54–7.56
    substantive views, 7.42–7.74
  International Covenant on Economic Social and Cultural Rights
    admissibility criteria, 13.11–13.18
    appraisal, 13.20–13.22
    assessment on the merits, 13.08–13.10
    framework, 13.03–13.19
    international co-operation and assistance, 13.19
    introduction, 13.01–13.02
    scope of potential complaints, 13.04–13.06
  introduction, 7.01–7.02
  UN Convention against Torture and Other Cruel, Inhuman or Degrading Treatment or Punishment
    abusive applications, 9.25–9.33
    admissibility criteria, 9.13–9.24
    appraisal, 9.48–9.51
    competing international procedures, 9.27–9.29

Complaints procedures (contd)
   consideration of admissibility, 9.07–9.12
   'cruel, inhuman or degrading treatment or punishment', 9.43–9.45
   exhaustion of domestic remedies, 9.30–9.33
   incompatible communications, 9.14–9.24
   interim measures, 9.05–9.06
   introduction, 9.01–9.02
   investigation duty, 9.46–9.47
   manifestly unfounded applications, 9.25–9.33
   procedure, 9.03–9.04
   'torture', 9.42
   views, 9.34–9.41
  UN Convention on the Elimination of All Forms of Discrimination against Women
   abusive communications, 10.18
   admissibility criteria, 10.16–10.25
   anonymous communications, 10.18
   appraisal, 10.30–10.31
   competing international procedures, 10.22
   domestic violence, 10.19
   exhaustion of domestic remedies, 10.24–10.25
   incompatible communications, 10.18–10.22
   introduction, 10.01–10.06
   manifestly ill-founded communications, 10.23
   procedure, 10.07–10.15
   'same matter', 10.22
   transmission of family names, 10.21
   views, 10.26–10.29
  UN Convention on the Rights of Persons with Disabilities
   abusive communications, 11.04
   admissibility criteria, 11.04
   anonymous communications, 11.04
   competing international procedures, 11.04
   exhaustion of domestic remedies, 11.04
   incompatible communications, 11.04
   introduction, 11.01–11.03
   manifestly ill-founded communications, 11.04
   procedure, 11.05–11.12
   'same matter', 11.04
  UN Convention on the Rights of the Child
   abusive communications, 15.10
   admissibility criteria, 15.10
   anonymous communications, 15.10
   appraisal, 15.22
   competing international procedures, 15.10
   complainants, 15.07–15.08
   consideration of communication, 15.16–15.19
   exhaustion of domestic remedies, 15.10
   follow-up, 15.20
   framework, 15.05–15.12
   friendly settlement, 15.14–15.15
   general provisions, 15.05–15.06
   interim measures, 15.11–15.12
   international co-operation and assistance, 15.21
   introduction, 15.01–15.04
   manifestly ill-founded communications, 15.10
   procedure, 15.13–15.20
   scope of complaints mechanism, 15.09
   transmission of communication, 15.13

Constructive dialogue procedure
  International Convention on the Elimination of All Forms of Racial Discrimination, 4.26

Constructive dialogue procedure (contd)
   International Convention on the Protection of All Persons from Enforced Disappearance, 4.74
   International Convention on the Protection of the Rights of All Migrant Workers and Members of Their Families, 4.63
   International Covenant on Civil and Political Rights, 4.11
   International Covenant on Economic Social and Cultural Rights, 4.18–4.21
   UN Convention against Torture and Other Cruel, Inhuman or Degrading Treatment or Punishment, 4.41
   UN Convention on the Elimination of All Forms of Discrimination against Women, 4.55
   UN Convention on the Rights of Persons with Disabilities, 4.70
   UN Convention on the Rights of the Child, 4.48
Conventions
   generally, 1.03
Cruel, inhuman or degrading treatment or punishment
   International Covenant on Civil and Political Rights, 7.42–7.44
Cruel, Inhuman or Degrading Treatment or Punishment Convention
   abusive applications, 9.25–9.33
   admissibility criteria
      abusive applications, 9.25–9.33
      generally, 9.13
      incompatible communications, 9.14–9.24
   anonymous applications, 9.13
   appraisal, 9.48–9.51
   background, 3.73
   Committee against Torture, 3.78–3.80
   competing international procedures, 9.27–9.29
   complaints procedure
      abusive applications, 9.25–9.33
      admissibility criteria, 9.13–9.33
      appraisal, 9.48–9.51
      competing international procedures, 9.27–9.29
      consideration of admissibility, 9.07–9.12
      'cruel, inhuman or degrading treatment or punishment', 9.43–9.45
      exhaustion of domestic remedies, 9.30–9.33
      incompatible communications, 9.14–9.24
      interim measures, 9.05–9.06
      introduction, 9.01–9.02
      investigation duty, 9.46–9.47
      manifestly unfounded applications, 9.25–9.33
      procedure, 9.03–9.04
      'torture', 9.42
      views, 9.34–9.41
   consideration of admissibility, 9.07–9.12
   'cruel, inhuman or degrading treatment or punishment', 9.43–9.45
   exhaustion of domestic remedies, 9.30–9.33
   incompatible communications
      generally, 9.14–9.24
      ratione loci, 9.20
      ratione personae, 9.15–9.19
      ratione materiae, 9.23–9.24
      ratione temporis, 9.20–9.21
   interim measures, 9.05–9.06
   introduction, 3.73
   investigation duty, 9.46–9.47
   investigative procedures
      Article 20, 5.04
      conclusion, 5.22–5.26
      conduct of inquiry, 5.10–5.12
      decision, 5.06–5.09
      evaluation, 5.06–5.09
      generally, 5.04

Cruel, Inhuman or Degrading Treatment or Punishment Convention (contd)
  information gathering, 5.05
  introduction, 5.02–5.03
  report, 5.13–5.21
  manifestly unfounded applications, 9.25–9.33
  periodic reporting procedures
    constructive dialogue, 4.41
    follow-up, 4.43–4.44
    formal examination of reports, 4.40–4.41
    generally, 4.37–4.38
    input from non-state actors, 4.42
    submission of reports, 4.39
  preventive mechanisms
    generally, 6.03–6.06
    machinery, 6.07–6.08
    national preventive mechanisms, 6.25–6.34
    obligations, 6.07–6.08
    prospects, 6.35–6.37
    scope, 6.07–6.08
    Subcommittee, 6.09–6.12
    visits, 6.13–6.24
  procedure, 9.03–9.04
  state obligations, 3.74–3.77
  'torture', 3.74, 9.42
Customary international law
  source of international law, and, 1.07–1.08
Degrading Treatment or Punishment Convention
  abusive applications, 9.25–9.33
  admissibility criteria
    abusive applications, 9.25–9.33
    generally, 9.13
    incompatible communications, 9.14–9.24
  anonymous applications, 9.13
  appraisal, 9.48–9.51
  background, 3.73
  Committee against Torture, 3.78–3.80

competing international procedures, 9.27–9.29
complaints procedure
  abusive applications, 9.25–9.33
  admissibility criteria, 9.13–9.33
  appraisal, 9.48–9.51
  competing international procedures, 9.27–9.29
  consideration of admissibility, 9.07–9.12
  'cruel, inhuman or degrading treatment or punishment', 9.43–9.45
  exhaustion of domestic remedies, 9.30–9.33
  incompatible communications, 9.14–9.24
  interim measures, 9.05–9.06
  introduction, 9.01–9.02
  investigation duty, 9.46–9.47
  manifestly unfounded applications, 9.25–9.33
  procedure, 9.03–9.04
  'torture', 9.42
  views, 9.34–9.41
consideration of admissibility, 9.07–9.12
'cruel, inhuman or degrading treatment or punishment', 9.43–9.45
exhaustion of domestic remedies, 9.30–9.33
incompatible communications
  generally, 9.14–9.24
  ratione loci, 9.20
  ratione personae, 9.15–9.19
  ratione materiae, 9.23–9.24
  ratione temporis, 9.20–9.21
interim measures, 9.05–9.06
introduction, 3.73
investigation duty, 9.46–9.47
investigative procedures
  Article 20, 5.04
  conclusion, 5.22–5.26
  conduct of inquiry, 5.10–5.12
  decision, 5.06–5.09

Degrading Treatment or Punishment Convention (contd)
   evaluation, 5.06–5.09
   generally, 5.04
   information gathering, 5.05
   introduction, 5.02–5.03
   report, 5.13–5.21
   manifestly unfounded applications, 9.25–9.33
   periodic reporting procedures
     constructive dialogue, 4.41
     follow-up, 4.43–4.44
     formal examination of reports, 4.40–4.41
     generally, 4.37–4.38
     input from non-state actors, 4.42
     submission of reports, 4.39
   preventive mechanisms
     generally, 6.03–6.06
     machinery, 6.07–6.08
     national preventive mechanisms, 6.25–6.34
     obligations, 6.07–6.08
     prospects, 6.35–6.37
     scope, 6.07–6.08
     Subcommittee, 6.09–6.12
     visits, 6.13–6.24
   procedure, 9.03–9.04
   state obligations, 3.74–3.77
   'torture', 3.74, 9.42

Derogations
   generally, 1.05

Disabled Persons Convention
   background, 3.102
   Committee, 3.112–3.114
   introduction, 3.102–3.106
   investigative procedures, 5.49–5.55
   national implementation, 3.115
   periodic reporting procedures
     follow-up, 4.72
     formal examination of reports, 4.71–4.72
     generally, 4.68
     input from non-state actors, 4.71
     submission of reports, 4.69–4.70
   'persons with disabilities', 3.107
   preventive mechanisms, 6.38–6.40
   state obligations, 3.107–3.111

'Disappearance' Convention
   abusive communications, 14.07
   admissibility criteria, 14.07
   anonymous communications, 14.07
   background, 3.116
   Committee, 3.119–3.122
   competing international procedures, 14.07
   complaints procedures
     abusive communications, 14.07
     admissibility criteria, 14.07
     anonymous communications, 14.07
     competing international procedures, 14.07
     exhaustion of domestic remedies, 14.07
     habeas corpus, and, 14.02
     general procedure, 14.06–14.09
     incompatible communications, 14.07
     introduction, 14.01
     urgent procedure, 14.02–14.05
   'enforced disappearance', 3.118
   exhaustion of domestic remedies, 14.07
   habeas corpus, and, 14.02
   incompatible communications, 14.07
   introduction, 3.116–3.117
   investigative procedures, 5.56–5.60
   periodic reporting procedures, 4.73–4.74
   state obligations, 3.118
   urgent procedure, 14.02–14.05

Discrimination against Women Convention
   abusive communications, 10.18
   admissibility criteria
     abusive communications, 10.18
     anonymous communications, 10.18
     competing international procedures, 10.22
     domestic violence, 10.19

Discrimination against Women Convention (contd)
   exhaustion of domestic remedies, 10.24–10.25
   incompatible communications, 10.18–10.22
   introduction, 10.16
   manifestly ill-founded communications, 10.23
   'same matter', 10.22
   transmission of family names, 10.21
  anonymous communications, 10.18
  appraisal, 10.30–10.31
  background, 3.65
  Committee on the Elimination of Discrimination against Women, 3.70–3.72
  competing international procedures, 10.22
  complaints procedure
   abusive communications, 10.18
   admissibility criteria, 10.16–10.25
   anonymous communications, 10.18
   appraisal, 10.30–10.31
   competing international procedures, 10.22
   domestic violence, 10.19
   exhaustion of domestic remedies, 10.24–10.25
   incompatible communications, 10.18–10.22
   introduction, 10.01–10.06
   manifestly ill-founded communications, 10.23
   procedure, 10.07–10.15
   'same matter', 10.22
   transmission of family names, 10.21
   views, 10.26–10.29
  'discrimination against women', 3.66
  domestic violence, 10.19
  exhaustion of domestic remedies, 10.24–10.25
  incompatible communications, 10.18–10.22
  introduction, 3.64–3.65
  investigative procedures
   conclusion, 5.45–5.48
   follow-up action, 5.44
   generally, 5.27–5.30
   practice, 5.38–5.43
   preliminary phase, 5.31–5.33
   procedure, 5.34–5.37
  manifestly ill-founded communications, 10.23
  periodic reporting procedures
   constructive dialogue, 4.55
   follow-up, 4.58–4.59
   formal examination of reports, 4.53–4.55
   generally, 4.51
   input from non-state actors, 4.56–4.57
   submission of reports, 4.52
  procedure, 10.07–10.15
  'same matter', 10.22
  state obligations, 3.66–3.69
  transmission of family names, 10.21
  views, 10.26–10.29

Domestic remedies rule
  International Convention on the Elimination of All Forms of Racial Discrimination, 8.21–8.22
  International Convention on the Protection of All Persons from Enforced Disappearance, 14.07
  International Convention on the Protection of the Rights of All Migrant Workers and Members of Their Families, 12.03
  International Covenant on Civil and Political Rights, 7.38–7.41
  International Covenant on Economic Social and Cultural Rights, 13.14–13.15
  UN Convention against Torture and Other Cruel, Inhuman or Degrading Treatment or Punishment, 9.30–9.33

Domestic remedies rule (contd)
    UN Convention on the Elimination of All Forms of Discrimination against Women, 10.24–10.25
    UN Convention on the Rights of Persons with Disabilities, 11.04
    UN Convention on the Rights of the Child, 15.10

Domestic violence
    UN Convention on the Elimination of All Forms of Discrimination against Women, and, 10.19

Dualism
    domestic effect of treaties, and, 1.15

Dublin Statement
    proposals for reform, and, 16.24–16.25

Economic and Social Council
    generally, 2.06–2.09

Enforced Disappearance Convention
    abusive communications, 14.07
    admissibility criteria, 14.07
    anonymous communications, 14.07
    background, 3.116
    Committee, 3.119–3.122
    competing international procedures, 14.07
    complaints procedures
        abusive communications, 14.07
        admissibility criteria, 14.07
        anonymous communications, 14.07
        competing international procedures, 14.07
        exhaustion of domestic remedies, 14.07
        habeas corpus, and, 14.02
        general procedure, 14.06–14.09
        incompatible communications, 14.07
        introduction, 14.01
        urgent procedure, 14.02–14.05
    'enforced disappearance', 3.118
    exhaustion of domestic remedies, 14.07
    habeas corpus, and, 14.02
    incompatible communications, 14.07
    introduction, 3.116–3.117
    investigative procedures, 5.56–5.60
    periodic reporting procedures, 4.73–4.74
    state obligations, 3.118
    urgent procedure, 14.02–14.05

Equality
    International Covenant on Civil and Political Rights, and, 7.65–7.69

European Convention on Human Rights
    domestic effect of treaties, and, 1.16
    emergence of human rights law, and, 1.25

Exhaustion of domestic remedies
    International Convention on the Elimination of All Forms of Racial Discrimination, 8.21–8.22
    International Convention on the Protection of All Persons from Enforced Disappearance, 14.07
    International Convention on the Protection of the Rights of All Migrant Workers and Members of Their Families, 12.03
    International Covenant on Civil and Political Rights, 7.38–7.41
    International Covenant on Economic Social and Cultural Rights, 13.14–13.15
    UN Convention against Torture and Other Cruel, Inhuman or Degrading Treatment or Punishment, 9.30–9.33
    UN Convention on the Elimination of All Forms of Discrimination against Women, 10.24–10.25
    UN Convention on the Rights of Persons with Disabilities, 11.04
    UN Convention on the Rights of the Child, 15.10

Fair trial
    International Covenant on Civil and Political Rights, and, 7.47–7.53

Family
International Covenant on Civil and Political Rights, and, 7.54–7.56
Follow-up
International Convention on the Elimination of All Forms of Racial Discrimination
generally, 8.13
periodic reporting procedures, 4.31–4.32
International Convention on the Protection of All Persons from Enforced Disappearance, 4.74
International Convention on the Protection of the Rights of All Migrant Workers and Members of Their Families
generally, 12.03
periodic reporting procedures, 4.67
International Covenant on Civil and Political Rights
generally, 7.16
periodic reporting procedures, 4.13
International Covenant on Economic Social and Cultural Rights
generally, 13.03
periodic reporting procedures, 4.22–4.23
UN Convention against Torture and Other Cruel, Inhuman or Degrading Treatment or Punishment
generally, 9.11–9.12
periodic reporting procedures, 4.43–4.44
UN Convention on the Elimination of All Forms of Discrimination against Women
generally, 10.15
periodic reporting procedures, 4.58–4.59
UN Convention on the Rights of Persons with Disabilities
generally, 11.11–11.12
periodic reporting procedures, 4.72
UN Convention on the Rights of the Child
generally, 15.20
periodic reporting procedures, 4.49–4.50
Freedom from torture or ill-treatment
International Covenant on Civil and Political Rights, and, 7.42–7.44
Freedom of expression
International Covenant on Civil and Political Rights, and, 7.62–7.64
Freedom of thought, conscience and religion
International Covenant on Civil and Political Rights, and, 7.57–7.61
French Declaration of the Rights of Man
state sovereignty, and, 1.17
Friendly settlement
International Covenant on Economic Social and Cultural Rights, 13.03
UN Convention on the Rights of the Child, 15.14–15.15
General Assembly
generally, 2.02–2.05
General principles of law
source of international law, and, 1.10
Habeas corpus
International Convention on the Protection of All Persons from Enforced Disappearance, and, 14.02
Home
International Covenant on Civil and Political Rights, and, 7.54–7.56
Human rights
international law, 1.20–1.28
Human Rights Council
functions, 2.33–2.35
generally, 2.26–2.29
membership, 2.30–2.32
Incompatible communications
International Convention on the Elimination of All Forms of Racial Discrimination, 8.16–8.20

Incompatible communications (contd)
  International Convention on the Protection of All Persons from Enforced Disappearance, 14.07
  International Convention on the Protection of the Rights of All Migrant Workers and Members of Their Families, 12.03
  International Covenant on Civil and Political Rights
    introduction, 7.20
    ratione loci, 7.28–7.31
    ratione materiae, 7.32–7.33
    ratione personae, 7.23–7.27
    ratione temporis, 7.21–7.22
    victim requirement, 7.27
    vis-à-vis the individual, 7.24–7.27
    vis-à-vis the state, 7.23
  International Covenant on Economic Social and Cultural Rights, 13.16
  UN Convention against Torture and Other Cruel, Inhuman or Degrading Treatment or Punishment
    generally, 9.14–9.24
    ratione loci, 9.20
    ratione personae, 9.15–9.19
    ratione materiae, 9.23–9.24
    ratione temporis, 9.20–9.21
  UN Convention on the Elimination of All Forms of Discrimination against Women, 10.18–10.22
  UN Convention on the Rights of Persons with Disabilities, 11.0455

Independent Expert
  reports from 1989 to 1997, 16.02–16.05

Individual complaints procedures
  International Bill of Rights, and, 3.03
  International Convention on the Elimination of All Forms of Racial Discrimination
    abusive communications, 8.15
    admissibility criteria, 8.14–8.20
    anonymous communications, 8.15
    appraisal, 8.33

    exhaustion of domestic remedies, 8.21–8.22
    incompatible communications, 8.16–8.20
    introduction, 8.01–8.05
    opinions, 8.23–8.32
    procedure, 8.06–8.13
  International Convention on the Protection of All Persons from Enforced Disappearance
    abusive communications, 14.07
    admissibility criteria, 14.07
    anonymous communications, 14.07
    competing international procedures, 14.07
    exhaustion of domestic remedies, 14.07
    habeas corpus, and, 14.02
    general procedure, 14.06–14.09
    incompatible communications, 14.07
    introduction, 14.01
    urgent procedure, 14.02–14.05
  International Convention on the Protection of the Rights of All Migrant Workers and Members of Their Families, 12.01–12.03
  International Covenant on Civil and Political Rights
    abusive communications, 7.18–7.19
    admissibility criteria, 7.17–7.41
    anonymous communications, 7.18–7.19
    appraisal, 7.75–7.78
    burden of proof, 7.42
    competing international procedures, 7.35–7.37
    equality, 7.65–7.69
    exhaustion of domestic remedies, 7.38–7.41
    freedom from torture or ill-treatment, 7.42–7.44
    freedom of expression, 7.62–7.64

Individual complaints procedures (contd)
   freedom of thought, conscience and religion, 7.57–7.61
   generally, 7.03–7.05
   incompatible communications, 7.20–7.33
   minority rights, 7.72–7.74
   non-discrimination, 7.65–7.69
   procedure, 7.06–7.16
   right to effective remedy, 7.70–7.71
   right to fair trial, 7.47–7.53
   right to liberty, 7.45–7.46
   right to life, 7.42
   right to privacy, family, home and correspondence, 7.54–7.56
   substantive views, 7.42–7.74
  International Covenant on Economic Social and Cultural Rights
   admissibility criteria, 13.11–13.18
   appraisal, 13.20–13.22
   assessment on the merits, 13.08–13.10
   framework, 13.03–13.19
   international co-operation and assistance, 13.19
   introduction, 13.01–13.02
   scope of potential complaints, 13.04–13.06
  introduction, 7.01–7.02
  UN Convention against Torture and Other Cruel, Inhuman or Degrading Treatment or Punishment
   abusive applications, 9.25–9.33
   admissibility criteria, 9.13–9.24
   appraisal, 9.48–9.51
   competing international procedures, 9.27–9.29
   consideration of admissibility, 9.07–9.12
   'cruel, inhuman or degrading treatment or punishment', 9.43–9.45
   exhaustion of domestic remedies, 9.30–9.33
   incompatible communications, 9.14–9.24
   interim measures, 9.05–9.06
   introduction, 9.01–9.02
   investigation duty, 9.46–9.47
   manifestly unfounded applications, 9.25–9.33
   procedure, 9.03–9.04
   'torture', 9.42
   views, 9.34–9.41
  UN Convention on the Elimination of All Forms of Discrimination against Women
   abusive communications, 10.18
   admissibility criteria, 10.16–10.25
   anonymous communications, 10.18
   appraisal, 10.30–10.31
   competing international procedures, 10.22
   domestic violence, 10.19
   exhaustion of domestic remedies, 10.24–10.25
   incompatible communications, 10.18–10.22
   introduction, 10.01–10.06
   manifestly ill-founded communications, 10.23
   procedure, 10.07–10.15
   'same matter', 10.22
   transmission of family names, 10.21
   views, 10.26–10.29
  UN Convention on the Rights of Persons with Disabilities
   abusive communications, 11.04
   admissibility criteria, 11.04
   anonymous communications, 11.04
   competing international procedures, 11.04
   exhaustion of domestic remedies, 11.04
   incompatible communications, 11.04
   introduction, 11.01–11.03

Individual complaints procedures (contd)
   manifestly ill-founded communications, 11.04
   procedure, 11.05–11.12
   'same matter', 11.04
  UN Convention on the Rights of the Child
   abusive communications, 15.10
   admissibility criteria, 15.10
   anonymous communications, 15.10
   appraisal, 15.22
   competing international procedures, 15.10
   complainants, 15.07–15.08
   consideration of communication, 15.16–15.19
   exhaustion of domestic remedies, 15.10
   follow-up, 15.20
   framework, 15.05–15.12
   friendly settlement, 15.14–15.15
   general provisions, 15.05–15.06
   interim measures, 15.11–15.12
   international co-operation and assistance, 15.21
   introduction, 15.01–15.04
   manifestly ill-founded communications, 15.10
   procedure, 15.13–15.20
   scope of complaints mechanism, 15.09
   transmission of communication, 15.13

Inhuman or Degrading Treatment or Punishment Convention
  abusive applications, 9.25–9.33
  admissibility criteria
   abusive applications, 9.25–9.33
   generally, 9.13
   incompatible communications, 9.14–9.24
  anonymous applications, 9.13
  appraisal, 9.48–9.51
  background, 3.73
  Committee against Torture, 3.78–3.80
  competing international procedures, 9.27–9.29
  complaints procedure
   abusive applications, 9.25–9.33
   admissibility criteria, 9.13–9.33
   appraisal, 9.48–9.51
   competing international procedures, 9.27–9.29
   consideration of admissibility, 9.07–9.12
   'cruel, inhuman or degrading treatment or punishment', 9.43–9.45
   exhaustion of domestic remedies, 9.30–9.33
   incompatible communications, 9.14–9.24
   interim measures, 9.05–9.06
   introduction, 9.01–9.02
   investigation duty, 9.46–9.47
   manifestly unfounded applications, 9.25–9.33
   procedure, 9.03–9.04
   'torture', 9.42
   views, 9.34–9.41
  consideration of admissibility, 9.07–9.12
  'cruel, inhuman or degrading treatment or punishment', 9.43–9.45
  exhaustion of domestic remedies, 9.30–9.33
  incompatible communications
   generally, 9.14–9.24
   ratione loci, 9.20
   ratione personae, 9.15–9.19
   ratione materiae, 9.23–9.24
   ratione temporis, 9.20–9.21
  interim measures, 9.05–9.06
  introduction, 3.73
  investigation duty, 9.46–9.47
  investigative procedures
   Article 20, 5.04
   conclusion, 5.22–5.26

Inhuman or Degrading Treatment or Punishment Convention (contd)
   conduct of inquiry, 5.10–5.12
   decision, 5.06–5.09
   evaluation, 5.06–5.09
   generally, 5.04
   information gathering, 5.05
   introduction, 5.02–5.03
   report, 5.13–5.21
  manifestly unfounded applications, 9.25–9.33
  periodic reporting procedures
   constructive dialogue, 4.41
   follow-up, 4.43–4.44
   formal examination of reports, 4.40–4.41
   generally, 4.37–4.38
   input from non-state actors, 4.42
   submission of reports, 4.39
  preventive mechanisms
   generally, 6.03–6.06
   machinery, 6.07–6.08
   national preventive mechanisms, 6.25–6.34
   obligations, 6.07–6.08
   prospects, 6.35–6.37
   scope, 6.07–6.08
   Subcommittee, 6.09–6.12
   visits, 6.13–6.24
  procedure, 9.03–9.04
  state obligations, 3.74–3.77
  'torture', 3.74, 9.42

Inquiry procedures
  International Convention on the Protection of All Persons from Enforced Disappearance, 5.56–5.60
  International Covenant on Economic Social and Cultural Rights, 5.61–5.64
  introduction, 5.01
  UN Convention against Torture and Other Cruel, Inhuman or Degrading Treatment or Punishment
   Article 20, 5.04
   conclusion, 5.22–5.26
   conduct of inquiry, 5.10–5.12
   decision, 5.06–5.09
   evaluation, 5.06–5.09
   generally, 5.04
   information gathering, 5.05
   introduction, 5.02–5.03
   report, 5.13–5.21
  UN Convention on the Elimination of All Forms of Discrimination against Women
   conclusion, 5.45–5.48
   follow-up action, 5.44
   generally, 5.27–5.30
   practice, 5.38–5.43
   preliminary phase, 5.31–5.33
   procedure, 5.34–5.37
  UN Convention on the Rights of Persons with Disabilities, 5.49–5.55
  UN Convention on the Rights of the Child, 5.65–5.68

Interim measures
  International Convention on the Elimination of All Forms of Racial Discrimination, 8.09
  International Convention on the Protection of the Rights of All Migrant Workers and Members of Their Families, 12.03
  International Covenant on Civil and Political Rights, 7.06
  UN Convention against Torture and Other Cruel, Inhuman or Degrading Treatment or Punishment, 9.05–9.06
  UN Convention on the Elimination of All Forms of Discrimination against Women, 10.11
  UN Convention on the Rights of Persons with Disabilities, 11.06
  UN Convention on the Rights of the Child, 15.11–15.12

International Bill of Rights
  abolition of death penalty, 3.03
  complaints procedure, 3.03
  Declaration of Rights
   appraisal, 3.15–3.24

International Bill of Rights (contd)
    background, 3.02–3.03
    generally, 3.06–3.09
    juridical status, 3.10–3.14
    structure, 3.07
    substantive rights and freedoms, 3.07
  background, 3.02
  First Optional protocol, 3.03
  International Covenant on Civil and Political Rights
    background, 3.03
    generally, 3.25–3.26
    Human Rights Committee, 3.33–3.36
    nature and scope of obligations, 3.27–3.32
    structure, 3.26
    substantive rights, 3.26
  International Covenant on Economic Social and Cultural Rights
    background, 3.03
    Committee on Economic, Social and Cultural Rights, 3.49–3.52
    generally, 3.37–3.39
    nature and scope of obligations, 3.40–3.48
    structure, 3.37
    substantive rights, 3.37
  introduction, 3.06
  Second Optional Protocol, 3.03

International bodies
  source of international law, and, 1.13

International Convention on the Elimination of All Forms of Racial Discrimination
  abusive communications, 8.15
  admissibility criteria, 8.14–8.20
  anonymous communications, 8.15
  background, 3.53
  Committee on the Elimination of Racial Discrimination, 3.61–3.63
  complaints procedures
    abusive communications, 8.15
    admissibility criteria, 8.14–8.20
    anonymous communications, 8.15
    appraisal, 8.33
    exhaustion of domestic remedies, 8.21–8.22
    incompatible communications, 8.16–8.20
    introduction, 8.01–8.05
    opinions, 8.23–8.32
    procedure, 8.06–8.13
  exhaustion of domestic remedies, 8.21–8.22
  incompatible communications, 8.16–8.20
  introduction, 3.53
  opinions, 8.23–8.32
  periodic reporting procedures
    constructive dialogue, 4.26
    early warning procedure, 4.33–4.36
    follow-up, 4.31–4.32
    formal examination of reports, 4.26
    generally, 4.24–4.25
    input from non-state actors, 4.27–4.29
    recommendations, 4.30
    urgent action procedure, 4.33–4.36
  procedure, 8.06–8.13
  'racial discrimination', 3.54
  state obligations, 3.54–3.60

International Convention on the Protection of All Persons from Enforced Disappearance
  abusive communications, 14.07
  admissibility criteria, 14.07
  anonymous communications, 14.07
  background, 3.116
  Committee, 3.119–3.122
  competing international procedures, 14.07
  complaints procedures
    abusive communications, 14.07
    admissibility criteria, 14.07
    anonymous communications, 14.07
    competing international procedures, 14.07

International Convention on the Protection of All Persons from Enforced Disappearance (contd)
  exhaustion of domestic remedies, 14.07
  habeas corpus, and, 14.02
  general procedure, 14.06–14.09
  incompatible communications, 14.07
  introduction, 14.01
  urgent procedure, 14.02–14.05
  'enforced disappearance', 3.118
  exhaustion of domestic remedies, 14.07
  habeas corpus, and, 14.02
  incompatible communications, 14.07
  introduction, 3.116–3.117
  investigative procedures, 5.56–5.60
  periodic reporting procedures, 4.73–4.74
  state obligations, 3.118
  urgent procedure, 14.02–14.05
International Convention on the Protection of the Rights of All Migrant Workers and Members of Their Families
  background, 3.92
  Committee, 3.100–3.101
  complaints procedure, 12.01–12.03
  introduction, 3.92–3.93
  'members of the family', 3.95
  'migrant worker', 3.96
  periodic reporting procedures
    constructive dialogue, 4.63
    follow-up, 4.67
    formal examination of reports, 4.62–4.65
    generally, 4.60
    input from non-state actors, 4.66
    submission of reports, 4.61
  state obligations, 3.94–3.99
International co-operation and assistance
  International Covenant on Economic Social and Cultural Rights, 13.19
  UN Convention on the Rights of the Child, 15.21
International Covenant on Civil and Political Rights (ICCPR)
  abusive communications, 7.18–7.19
  admissibility criteria
    abusive communications, 7.18–7.19
    anonymous communications, 7.18–7.19
    competing international procedures, 7.35–7.37
    exhaustion of domestic remedies, 7.38–7.41
    incompatible communications, 7.20–7.33
    introduction, 7.17
    unsubstantiated claims, 7.33
  anonymous communications, 7.18–7.19
  appraisal, 7.75–7.78
  background, 3.03
  burden of proof, 7.42
  competing international procedures, 7.35–7.37
  equality, 7.65–7.69
  exhaustion of domestic remedies, 7.38–7.41
  freedom from torture or ill-treatment, 7.42–7.44
  freedom of expression, 7.62–7.64
  freedom of thought, conscience and religion, 7.57–7.61
  generally, 3.25–3.26
  Human Rights Committee, 3.33–3.36
  incompatible communications
    introduction, 7.20
    ratione loci, 7.28–7.31
    ratione materiae, 7.32–7.33
    ratione personae, 7.23–7.27
    ratione temporis, 7.21–7.22
    victim requirement, 7.27
    vis-à-vis the individual, 7.24–7.27
    vis-à-vis the state, 7.23
  individual complaints procedures

International Covenant on Civil and Political Rights (ICCPR) (contd)
   abusive communications, 7.18–7.19
   admissibility criteria, 7.17–7.41
   anonymous communications, 7.18–7.19
   appraisal, 7.75–7.78
   burden of proof, 7.42
   competing international procedures, 7.35–7.37
   equality, 7.65–7.69
   exhaustion of domestic remedies, 7.38–7.41
   freedom from torture or ill-treatment, 7.42–7.44
   freedom of expression, 7.62–7.64
   freedom of thought, conscience and religion, 7.57–7.61
   generally, 7.03–7.05
   incompatible communications, 7.20–7.33
   minority rights, 7.72–7.74
   non-discrimination, 7.65–7.69
   procedure, 7.06–7.16
   right to effective remedy, 7.70–7.71
   right to fair trial, 7.47–7.53
   right to liberty, 7.45–7.46
   right to life, 7.42
   right to privacy, family, home and correspondence, 7.54–7.56
   substantive views, 7.42–7.74
  minority rights, 7.72–7.74
  nature and scope of obligations, 3.27–3.32
  non-discrimination, 7.65–7.69
  periodic reporting procedures
   constructive dialogue, 4.11
   follow-up, 4.13
   formal examination of reports, 4.11–4.12
   generally, 4.07
   input from non-state actors, 4.14–4.16
   submission of reports, 4.08–4.10
  right to effective remedy, 7.70–7.71
  right to fair trial, 7.47–7.53
  right to liberty, 7.45–7.46
  right to life, 7.42
  right to privacy, family, home and correspondence, 7.54–7.56
  structure, 3.26
  substantive rights, 3.26
  unsubstantiated claims, 7.33

International Covenant on Economic Social and Cultural Rights (ICESCR)
  admissibility criteria, 13.11–13.18
  appraisal, 13.20–13.22
  assessment on the merits, 13.08–13.10
  background, 3.03
  Committee on Economic, Social and Cultural Rights, 3.49–3.52
  complaints procedure
   admissibility criteria, 13.11–13.18
   appraisal, 13.20–13.22
   assessment on the merits, 13.08–13.10
   framework, 13.03–13.19
   international co-operation and assistance, 13.19
   introduction, 13.01–13.02
   scope of potential complaints, 13.04–13.06
  framework, 13.03–13.19
  generally, 3.37–3.39
  international co-operation and assistance, 13.19
  investigative procedures, 5.61–5.64
  nature and scope of obligations, 3.40–3.48
  periodic reporting procedures
   constructive dialogue, 4.18–4.21
   follow-up, 4.22–4.23
   formal examination of reports, 4.19
   generally, 4.17–4.18
   input from non-state actors, 4.20–4.21
   submission of reports, 4.18

International Covenant on Economic Social and Cultural Rights (ICESCR) (contd)
  scope of potential complaints, 13.04–13.06
  structure, 3.37
  substantive rights, 3.37
International custom
  source of international law, and, 1.07–1.08
International human rights law
  generally, 1.20–1.28
International treaties
  domestic effect, 1.14–1.16
  source of international law, as, 1.03–1.05
  types, 1.03
Interpretative declarations
  generally, 1.04
Investigation duty
  UN Convention against Torture and Other Cruel, Inhuman or Degrading Treatment or Punishment, and, 9.46–9.47
Investigative procedures
  inquiry procedures
    International Convention on the Protection of All Persons from Enforced Disappearance, 5.56–5.60
    International Covenant on Economic Social and Cultural Rights, 5.61–5.64
    UN Convention against Torture and Other Cruel, Inhuman or Degrading Treatment or Punishment, 5.02–5.26
    UN Convention on the Elimination of All Forms of Discrimination against Women, 5.27–5.48
    UN Convention on the Rights of Persons with Disabilities, 5.49–5.55
    UN Convention on the Rights of the Child, 5.65–5.68
  introduction, 5.01

  preventive mechanisms
    generally, 6.01–6.02
    UN Convention against Torture and Other Cruel, Inhuman or Degrading Treatment or Punishment, 6.03–6.37
    UN Convention on the Rights of Persons with Disabilities, 6.38–6.40
Judicial decisions
  source of international law, and, 1.11
Jus cogens
  derogations, and, 1.05
  source of international law, and, 1.09
Liberty
  International Covenant on Civil and Political Rights, and, 7.45–7.46
Manifestly unfounded applications
  International Covenant on Civil and Political Rights, 7.33
  International Covenant on Economic Social and Cultural Rights, 13.16
  UN Convention against Torture and Other Cruel, Inhuman or Degrading Treatment or Punishment, 9.25–9.33
  UN Convention on the Elimination of All Forms of Discrimination against Women, 10.23
  UN Convention on the Rights of Persons with Disabilities, 11.04
  UN Convention on the Rights of the Child, 15.10
Marrakech Statement
  proposals for reform, and, 16.26–16.29
Migrant Workers Convention
  background, 3.92
  Committee, 3.100–3.101
  complaints procedure, 12.01–12.03
  introduction, 3.92–3.93
  'members of the family', 3.95
  'migrant worker', 3.96
  periodic reporting procedures
    constructive dialogue, 4.63
    follow-up, 4.67

Index

Migrant Workers Convention (contd)
    formal examination of reports, 4.62–4.65
    generally, 4.60
    input from non-state actors, 4.66
    submission of reports, 4.61
    state obligations, 3.94–3.99

Minorities Treaties of 1919
    human rights law, and, 1.20

Minority rights
    International Covenant on Civil and Political Rights, and, 7.72–7.74

Monism
    domestic effect of treaties, and, 1.15

Multilateral treaties
    generally, 1.03

Non-discrimination
    International Covenant on Civil and Political Rights, and, 7.65–7.69

OAS Charter System
    human rights law, and, 1.26

Office of the UN High Commissioner for Human Rights
    generally, 2.36–2.40

Periodic reporting procedures
    analysis, 4.75–4.84
    International Convention on the Elimination of All Forms of Racial Discrimination
        constructive dialogue, 4.26
        early warning procedure, 4.33–4.36
        follow-up, 4.31–4.32
        formal examination of reports, 4.26
        generally, 4.24–4.25
        input from non-state actors, 4.27–4.29
        recommendations, 4.30
        urgent action procedure, 4.33–4.36
    International Convention on the Protection of All Persons from Enforced Disappearance, 4.73–4.74
    International Convention on the Protection of the Rights of All Migrant Workers and Members of Their Families
        constructive dialogue, 4.63
        follow-up, 4.67
        formal examination of reports, 4.62–4.65
        generally, 4.60
        input from non-state actors, 4.66
        submission of reports, 4.61
    International Covenant on Civil and Political Rights
        constructive dialogue, 4.11
        follow-up, 4.13
        formal examination of reports, 4.11–4.12
        generally, 4.07
        input from non-state actors, 4.14–4.16
        submission of reports, 4.08–4.10
    International Covenant on Economic Social and Cultural Rights
        constructive dialogue, 4.18–4.21
        follow-up, 4.22–4.23
        formal examination of reports, 4.19
        generally, 4.17–4.18
        input from non-state actors, 4.20–4.21
        submission of reports, 4.18
    introduction, 4.01–4.06
    purpose, 4.75
    UN Convention against Torture and Other Cruel, Inhuman or Degrading Treatment or Punishment
        constructive dialogue, 4.41
        follow-up, 4.43–4.44
        formal examination of reports, 4.40–4.41
        generally, 4.37–4.38
        input from non-state actors, 4.42
        submission of reports, 4.39
    UN Convention on the Elimination of All Forms of Discrimination against Women
        constructive dialogue, 4.55
        follow-up, 4.58–4.59
        formal examination of reports, 4.53–4.55

Periodic reporting procedures (contd)
    generally, 4.51
    input from non-state actors, 4.56–4.57
    submission of reports, 4.52
    UN Convention on the Rights of Persons with Disabilities
        follow-up, 4.72
        formal examination of reports, 4.71–4.72
        generally, 4.68
        input from non-state actors, 4.71
        submission of reports, 4.69–4.70
    UN Convention on the Rights of the Child
        constructive dialogue, 4.48
        follow-up, 4.49–4.50
        formal examination of reports, 4.47–4.48
        generally, 4.45
        input from non-state actors, 4.47
        submission of reports, 4.46

Persons with Disabilities Convention
    background, 3.102
    Committee, 3.112–3.114
    introduction, 3.102–3.106
    investigative procedures, 5.49–5.55
    national implementation, 3.115
    periodic reporting procedures
        follow-up, 4.72
        formal examination of reports, 4.71–4.72
        generally, 4.68
        input from non-state actors, 4.71
        submission of reports, 4.69–4.70
    'persons with disabilities', 3.107
    preventive mechanisms, 6.38–6.40
    state obligations, 3.107–3.111

Poznan Statement
    proposals for reform, and, 16.30–16.32

Preventive mechanisms
    See also **Investigative procedures**
    generally, 6.01–6.02
    introduction, 5.01
    UN Convention against Torture and Other Cruel, Inhuman or Degrading Treatment or Punishment
        generally, 6.03–6.06
        machinery, 6.07–6.08
        national preventive mechanisms, 6.25–6.34
        obligations, 6.07–6.08
        prospects, 6.35–6.37
        scope, 6.07–6.08
        Subcommittee, 6.09–6.12
        visits, 6.13–6.24
    UN Convention on the Rights of Persons with Disabilities, 6.38–6.40

Principles of law
    source of international law, and, 1.10

Privacy
    International Covenant on Civil and Political Rights, 7.54–7.56

Proposals for reform
    introduction, 16.01
    reports of the Independent Expert 1989–1997, 16.02–16.05
    strengthening treaty body system
        Dublin Statement, 16.24–16.25
        generally, 16.22–16.23
        Marrakech Statement, 16.26–16.29
        Poznan Statement, 16.30–16.32
        Views of Non-Governmental Organisations, 16.33–16.36
    UN agenda for change, 16.06–16.10
    unified standing treaty body, 16.11–16.21
    way forward, 16.37–16.41

Protocols
    generally, 1.03

Racial Discrimination Convention
    abusive communications, 8.15
    admissibility criteria, 8.14–8.20
    anonymous communications, 8.15
    background, 3.53
    Committee on the Elimination of Racial Discrimination, 3.61–3.63
    complaints procedures
        abusive communications, 8.15

Racial Discrimination Convention (contd)
    admissibility criteria, 8.14–8.20
    anonymous communications, 8.15
    appraisal, 8.33
    exhaustion of domestic remedies, 8.21–8.22
    incompatible communications, 8.16–8.20
    introduction, 8.01–8.05
    opinions, 8.23–8.32
    procedure, 8.06–8.13
  exhaustion of domestic remedies, 8.21–8.22
  incompatible communications, 8.16–8.20
  introduction, 3.53
  opinions, 8.23–8.32
  periodic reporting procedures
    constructive dialogue, 4.26
    early warning procedure, 4.33–4.36
    follow-up, 4.31–4.32
    formal examination of reports, 4.26
    generally, 4.24–4.25
    input from non-state actors, 4.27–4.29
    recommendations, 4.30
    urgent action procedure, 4.33–4.36
  procedure, 8.06–8.13
  'racial discrimination', 3.54
  state obligations, 3.54–3.60

Ratification
  generally, 1.03

Reform proposals
  introduction, 16.01
  reports of the Independent Expert 1989–1997, 16.02–16.05
  strengthening treaty body system
    Dublin Statement, 16.24–16.25
    generally, 16.22–16.23
    Marrakech Statement, 16.26–16.29
    Poznan Statement, 16.30–16.32
    Views of Non-Governmental Organisations, 16.33–16.36
  UN agenda for change, 16.06–16.10
  unified standing treaty body, 16.11–16.21
  way forward, 16.37–16.41

Reservations
  generally, 1.04

Right to correspondence
  International Covenant on Civil and Political Rights, 7.54–7.56

Right to effective remedy
  International Covenant on Civil and Political Rights, 7.70–7.71

Right to fair trial
  International Covenant on Civil and Political Rights, 7.47–7.53

Right to family
  International Covenant on Civil and Political Rights, 7.54–7.56

Right to home
  International Covenant on Civil and Political Rights, 7.54–7.56

Right to liberty
  International Covenant on Civil and Political Rights, 7.45–7.46

Right to life
  International Covenant on Civil and Political Rights, 7.42

Right to privacy
  International Covenant on Civil and Political Rights, 7.54–7.56

Rights of the Child Convention
  background, 3.81
  'best interests' principle, 3.82
  'child', 3.82
  Committee, 3.89–3.91
  introduction, 3.81
  investigative procedures, 5.65–5.68
  periodic reporting procedures
    constructive dialogue, 4.48
    follow-up, 4.49–4.50
    formal examination of reports, 4.47–4.48
    generally, 4.45
    input from non-state actors, 4.47
    submission of reports, 4.46
  state obligations, 3.82–3.88

'Same matter'
  International Convention on the Protection of All Persons from Enforced Disappearance, 14.07
  International Covenant on Civil and Political Rights, 7.35–7.37
  International Covenant on Economic Social and Cultural Rights, 13.16
  UN Convention against Torture and Other Cruel, Inhuman or Degrading Treatment or Punishment, 9.27–9.29
  UN Convention on the Elimination of All Forms of Discrimination against Women, 10.22
  UN Convention on the Rights of Persons with Disabilities, 11.04
  UN Convention on the Rights of the Child, 15.10

Sources of international law
  academic writings and teachings, 1.12
  actions of international bodies, 1.13
  customary international law, 1.07–1.08
  general principles of law, 1.10
  generally, 1.06
  international custom, 1.07–1.08
  judicial decisions, 1.11
  jus cogens, 1.09
  other, 1.11–1.12
  principles of law, 1.10
  teachings, 1.12
  treaties, 1.03–1.05

State sovereignty principle
  generally, 1.17–1.19

Statute of the ICJ
  sources of international law, and, 1.13

Sub-Commission on the Promotion and Protection of Human Rights
  generally, 2.21–2.25

Teachings
  source of international law, and, 1.12

Torture
  International Covenant on Civil and Political Rights, and, 7.42–7.44

Torture Convention
  abusive applications, 9.25–9.33
  admissibility criteria
    abusive applications, 9.25–9.33
    generally, 9.13
    incompatible communications, 9.14–9.24
  anonymous applications, 9.13
  appraisal, 9.48–9.51
  background, 3.73
  Committee against Torture, 3.78–3.80
  competing international procedures, 9.27–9.29
  complaints procedure
    abusive applications, 9.25–9.33
    admissibility criteria, 9.13–9.33
    appraisal, 9.48–9.51
    competing international procedures, 9.27–9.29
    consideration of admissibility, 9.07–9.12
    'cruel, inhuman or degrading treatment or punishment', 9.43–9.45
    exhaustion of domestic remedies, 9.30–9.33
    incompatible communications, 9.14–9.24
    interim measures, 9.05–9.06
    introduction, 9.01–9.02
    investigation duty, 9.46–9.47
    manifestly unfounded applications, 9.25–9.33
    procedure, 9.03–9.04
    'torture', 9.42
    views, 9.34–9.41
  consideration of admissibility, 9.07–9.12
  'cruel, inhuman or degrading treatment or punishment', 9.43–9.45
  exhaustion of domestic remedies, 9.30–9.33
  incompatible communications
    generally, 9.14–9.24

Torture Convention (contd)
    ratione loci, 9.20
    ratione personae, 9.15–9.19
    ratione materiae, 9.23–9.24
    ratione temporis, 9.20–9.21
  interim measures, 9.05–9.06
  introduction, 3.73
  investigation duty, 9.46–9.47
  investigative procedures
    Article 20, 5.04
    conclusion, 5.22–5.26
    conduct of inquiry, 5.10–5.12
    decision, 5.06–5.09
    evaluation, 5.06–5.09
    generally, 5.04
    information gathering, 5.05
    introduction, 5.02–5.03
    report, 5.13–5.21
  manifestly unfounded applications, 9.25–9.33
  periodic reporting procedures
    constructive dialogue, 4.41
    follow-up, 4.43–4.44
    formal examination of reports, 4.40–4.41
    generally, 4.37–4.38
    input from non-state actors, 4.42
    submission of reports, 4.39
  preventive mechanisms
    generally, 6.03–6.06
    machinery, 6.07–6.08
    national preventive mechanisms, 6.25–6.34
    obligations, 6.07–6.08
    prospects, 6.35–6.37
    scope, 6.07–6.08
    Subcommittee, 6.09–6.12
    visits, 6.13–6.24
  procedure, 9.03–9.04
  state obligations, 3.74–3.77
  'torture', 3.74, 9.42

Transmission of family names
  UN Convention on the Elimination of All Forms of Discrimination against Women, and, 10.21

Treaties
  domestic effect, 1.14–1.16
  source of international law, as, 1.03–1.05
  types, 1.03

UN Charter (1945)
  human rights, and, 1.01

UN Convention against Torture and Other Cruel, Inhuman or Degrading Treatment or Punishment
  abusive applications, 9.25–9.33
  admissibility criteria
    abusive applications, 9.25–9.33
    generally, 9.13
    incompatible communications, 9.14–9.24
  anonymous applications, 9.13
  appraisal, 9.48–9.51
  background, 3.73
  Committee against Torture, 3.78–3.80
  competing international procedures, 9.27–9.29
  complaints procedure
    abusive applications, 9.25–9.33
    admissibility criteria, 9.13–9.33
    appraisal, 9.48–9.51
    competing international procedures, 9.27–9.29
    consideration of admissibility, 9.07–9.12
    'cruel, inhuman or degrading treatment or punishment', 9.43–9.45
    exhaustion of domestic remedies, 9.30–9.33
    incompatible communications, 9.14–9.24
    interim measures, 9.05–9.06
    introduction, 9.01–9.02
    investigation duty, 9.46–9.47
    manifestly unfounded applications, 9.25–9.33
    procedure, 9.03–9.04

UN Convention against Torture and Other Cruel, Inhuman or Degrading Treatment or Punishment (contd)
  'torture', 9.42
  views, 9.34–9.41
  consideration of admissibility, 9.07–9.12
  'cruel, inhuman or degrading treatment or punishment', 9.43–9.45
  exhaustion of domestic remedies, 9.30–9.33
  incompatible communications
    generally, 9.14–9.24
    ratione loci, 9.20
    ratione personae, 9.15–9.19
    ratione materiae, 9.23–9.24
    ratione temporis, 9.20–9.21
  interim measures, 9.05–9.06
  introduction, 3.73
  investigation duty, 9.46–9.47
  investigative procedures
    Article 20, 5.04
    conclusion, 5.22–5.26
    conduct of inquiry, 5.10–5.12
    decision, 5.06–5.09
    evaluation, 5.06–5.09
    generally, 5.04
    information gathering, 5.05
    introduction, 5.02–5.03
    report, 5.13–5.21
  manifestly unfounded applications, 9.25–9.33
  periodic reporting procedures
    constructive dialogue, 4.41
    follow-up, 4.43–4.44
    formal examination of reports, 4.40–4.41
    generally, 4.37–4.38
    input from non-state actors, 4.42
    submission of reports, 4.39
  preventive mechanisms
    generally, 6.03–6.06
    machinery, 6.07–6.08
    national preventive mechanisms, 6.25–6.34
    obligations, 6.07–6.08
    prospects, 6.35–6.37
    scope, 6.07–6.08
    Subcommittee, 6.09–6.12
    visits, 6.13–6.24
  procedure, 9.03–9.04
  state obligations, 3.74–3.77
  'torture', 3.74, 9.42

UN Convention on the Elimination of All Forms of Discrimination against Women
  abusive communications, 10.18
  admissibility criteria
    abusive communications, 10.18
    anonymous communications, 10.18
    domestic violence, 10.19
    exhaustion of domestic remedies, 10.24–10.25
    incompatible communications, 10.18–10.22
    introduction, 10.16
    manifestly ill-founded communications, 10.23
    'same matter', 10.22
    transmission of family names, 10.21
  anonymous communications, 10.18
  appraisal, 10.30–10.31
  background, 3.65
  Committee on the Elimination of Discrimination against Women, 3.70–3.72
  complaints procedure
    abusive communications, 10.18
    admissibility criteria, 10.16–10.25
    anonymous communications, 10.18
    appraisal, 10.30–10.31
    domestic violence, 10.19
    exhaustion of domestic remedies, 10.24–10.25
    incompatible communications, 10.18–10.22
    introduction, 10.01–10.06
    manifestly ill-founded communications, 10.23

UN Convention on the Elimination of All Forms of Discrimination against Women (contd)
   procedure, 10.07–10.15
   'same matter', 10.22
   transmission of family names, 10.21
   views, 10.26–10.29
  'discrimination against women', 3.66
  domestic violence, 10.19
  exhaustion of domestic remedies, 10.24–10.25
  incompatible communications, 10.18–10.22
  introduction, 3.64–3.65
  investigative procedures
   conclusion, 5.45–5.48
   follow-up action, 5.44
   generally, 5.27–5.30
   practice, 5.38–5.43
   preliminary phase, 5.31–5.33
   procedure, 5.34–5.37
  manifestly ill-founded communications, 10.23
  periodic reporting procedures
   constructive dialogue, 4.55
   follow-up, 4.58–4.59
   formal examination of reports, 4.53–4.55
   generally, 4.51
   input from non-state actors, 4.56–4.57
   submission of reports, 4.52
  procedure, 10.07–10.15
  'same matter', 10.22
  state obligations, 3.66–3.69
  transmission of family names, 10.21
  views, 10.26–10.29

UN Convention on the Rights of Persons with Disabilities
  abusive communications, 11.04
  admissibility criteria, 11.04
  anonymous communications, 11.04
  background, 3.102
  Committee, 3.112–3.114
  competing international procedures, 11.04
  complaints procedure
   abusive communications, 11.04
   admissibility criteria, 11.04
   anonymous communications, 11.04
   competing international procedures, 11.04
   exhaustion of domestic remedies, 11.04
   incompatible communications, 11.04
   introduction, 11.01–11.03
   manifestly ill-founded communications, 11.04
   procedure, 11.05–11.12
   'same matter', 11.04
  exhaustion of domestic remedies, 11.04
  incompatible communications, 11.04
  introduction, 3.102–3.106
  investigative procedures, 5.49–5.55
  manifestly ill-founded communications, 11.04
  national implementation, 3.115
  periodic reporting procedures
   follow-up, 4.72
   formal examination of reports, 4.71–4.72
   generally, 4.68
   input from non-state actors, 4.71
   submission of reports, 4.69–4.70
  'persons with disabilities', 3.107
  preventive mechanisms, 6.38–6.40
  'same matter', 11.04
  state obligations, 3.107–3.111

UN Convention on the Rights of the Child
  abusive communications, 15.10
  admissibility criteria, 15.10
  anonymous communications, 15.10
  appraisal, 15.22
  background, 3.81
  'best interests' principle, 3.82
  'child', 3.82

UN Convention on the Rights of the
   Child (contd)
  Committee, 3.89–3.91
  competing international procedures,
    15.10
  complainants, 15.07–15.08
  complaints procedure
    abusive communications, 15.10
    admissibility criteria, 15.10
    anonymous communications, 15.10
    appraisal, 15.22
    competing international procedures,
      15.10
    complainants, 15.07–15.08
    consideration of communication,
      15.16–15.19
    exhaustion of domestic remedies,
      15.10
    follow-up, 15.20
    framework, 15.05–15.12
    friendly settlement, 15.14–15.15
    general provisions, 15.05–15.06
    interim measures, 15.11–15.12
    international co-operation and
      assistance, 15.21
    introduction, 15.01–15.04
    manifestly ill-founded
      communications, 15.10
    procedure, 15.13–15.20
    scope of complaints mechanism,
      15.09
    transmission of communication,
      15.13
  consideration of communication,
    15.16–15.19
  exhaustion of domestic remedies,
    15.10
  follow-up, 15.20
  framework, 15.05–15.12
  friendly settlement, 15.14–15.15
  general provisions, 15.05–15.06
  interim measures, 15.11–15.12
  international co-operation and
    assistance, 15.21
  introduction, 3.81

investigative procedures, 5.65–5.68
manifestly ill-founded
  communications, 15.10
periodic reporting procedures
  constructive dialogue, 4.48
  follow-up, 4.49–4.50
  formal examination of reports,
    4.47–4.48
  generally, 4.45
  input from non-state actors, 4.47
  submission of reports, 4.46
procedure, 15.13–15.20
scope of complaints mechanism,
  15.09
state obligations, 3.82–3.88
transmission of communication,
  15.13
UN human rights treaties
  generally, 1.01–1.02
  International Bill of Rights
    abolition of death penalty, 3.03
    complaints procedure, 3.03
    Declaration of Rights, 3.06–3.24
    background, 3.02
    First Optional protocol, 3.03
    ICCPR, 3.25–3.36
    ICESPR, 3.37–3.52
    introduction, 3.06
    Second Optional Protocol, 3.03
  International Convention on the
    Elimination of All Forms of Racial
    Discrimination
    background, 3.53
    Committee on the Elimination of
      Racial Discrimination, 3.61–3.63
    introduction, 3.53
    'racial discrimination', 3.54
    state obligations, 3.54–3.60
  International Convention on the
    Protection of All Persons from
    Enforced Disappearance
    background, 3.116
    Committee, 3.119–3.122
    'enforced disappearance', 3.118
    introduction, 3.116–3.117

UN human rights treaties (contd)
    state obligations, 3.118
    International Convention on the Protection of the Rights of All Migrant Workers and Members of Their Families
        background, 3.92
        Committee, 3.100–3.101
        introduction, 3.92–3.93
        'members of the family', 3.95
        'migrant worker', 3.96
        state obligations, 3.94–3.99
    International Covenant on Civil and Political Rights
        background, 3.03
        generally, 3.25–3.26
        Human Rights Committee, 3.33–3.36
        nature and scope of obligations, 3.27–3.32
        structure, 3.26
        substantive rights, 3.26
    International Covenant on Economic Social and Cultural Rights
        background, 3.03
        Committee on Economic, Social and Cultural Rights, 3.49–3.52
        generally, 3.37–3.39
        nature and scope of obligations, 3.40–3.48
        structure, 3.37
        substantive rights, 3.37
    introduction, 3.01–3.05
    reform proposals
        Dublin Statement, 16.24–16.25
        introduction, 16.01
        Marrakech Statement, 16.26–16.29
        Poznan Statement, 16.30–16.32
        reports of the Independent Expert 1989–1997, 16.02–16.05
        strengthening treaty body system, 16.22–16.36
        UN agenda for change, 16.06–16.10
        unified standing treaty body, 16.11–16.21
        Views of Non-Governmental Organisations, 16.33–16.36
        way forward, 16.37–16.41
    UN Convention against Torture and Other Cruel, Inhuman or Degrading Treatment or Punishment
        background, 3.73
        Committee against Torture, 3.78–3.80
        introduction, 3.73
        state obligations, 3.74–3.77
        'torture', 3.74
    UN Convention on the Elimination of All Forms of Discrimination against Women
        background, 3.65
        Committee on the Elimination of Discrimination against Women, 3.70–3.72
        'discrimination against women', 3.66
        introduction, 3.64–3.65
        state obligations, 3.66–3.69
    UN Convention on the Rights of Persons with Disabilities
        background, 3.102
        Committee, 3.112–3.114
        introduction, 3.102–3.106
        national implementation, 3.115
        'persons with disabilities', 3.107
        state obligations, 3.107–3.111
    UN Convention on the Rights of the Child
        background, 3.81
        'best interests' principle, 3.82
        'child', 3.82
        Committee, 3.89–3.91
        introduction, 3.81
        state obligations, 3.82–3.88
    Universal Declaration of Human Rights
        appraisal, 3.15–3.24
        background, 3.02–3.03

UN human rights treaties (contd)
   generally, 3.06–3.09
   juridical status, 3.10–3.14
   structure, 3.07
   substantive rights and freedoms, 3.07

United Nations
  Commission on Human Rights
    generally, 2.10–2.20
    Sub-Commission, 2.21–2.25
  Economic and Social Council, 2.06–2.09
  General Assembly, 2.02–2.05
  Human Rights Council
    functions, 2.33–2.35
    generally, 2.26–2.29
    membership, 2.30–2.32
  introduction, 2.01
  Office of the UN High Commissioner for Human Rights, 2.36–2.40
  Sub-Commission on the Promotion and Protection of Human Rights, 2.21–2.25

Universal Declaration of Human Rights
  appraisal, 3.15–3.24
  background, 3.02–3.03
  generally, 3.06–3.09
  juridical status, 3.10–3.14
  structure, 3.07
  substantive rights and freedoms, 3.07

Unsubstantiated claims
  International Covenant on Civil and Political Rights, 7.33

  International Covenant on Economic Social and Cultural Rights, 13.16
  UN Convention against Torture and Other Cruel, Inhuman or Degrading Treatment or Punishment, 9.25–9.33
  UN Convention on the Elimination of All Forms of Discrimination against Women, 10.23
  UN Convention on the Rights of Persons with Disabilities, 11.04
  UN Convention on the Rights of the Child, 15.10

Urgent procedure
  International Convention on the Protection of All Persons from Enforced Disappearance, 14.02–14.05

Victim requirement
  International Convention on the Elimination of All Forms of Racial Discrimination, 8.18–8.20
  International Covenant on Civil and Political Rights, 7.24–7.27
  International Covenant on Economic Social and Cultural Rights, 13.03
  UN Convention against Torture and Other Cruel, Inhuman or Degrading Treatment or Punishment, 9.15–9.18
  UN Convention on the Elimination of All Forms of Discrimination against Women, 10.20
  UN Convention on the Rights of Persons with Disabilities, 11.03